SPORT IN SOCIETY

Issues and Controversies

SIXTH EDITION

Jay J. Coakley, Ph.D.
University of Colorado
Colorado Springs

Irwin McGraw-Hill

Boston, Massachusetts   Burr Ridge, Illinois   Dubuque, Iowa
Madison, Wisconsin   New York, New York   San Francisco, California   St. Louis, Missouri

WCB/McGraw-Hill
A Division of the McGraw-Hill Companies

SPORT IN SOCIETY
International Editions 1998

1 2 3 4 5 6 7 8 9 0 KKP PMP 9 8 7

Publisher: *Ed Bartell*
Sponsoring Editor: *Vicki Malinee*
Developmental Editor: *Jean Babrick*
Marketing Manager: *Pam Cooper*
Project Manager: *Marilyn Rothenberger*
Production Supervisor: *Laura Fuller*
Cover Designer: *Kay Fulton*
Cover Image: *Ernie Barnes, 1990. Collection of Whoopi Goldberg. Courtesy of The Company of Art, Los Angeles, CA.*
Photo Research Coordinator: *John Leland*
Art Editor: *Jodi Banowetz*
Compositor: *Interactive Composition Corporation*
Typeface: *Janson*

Library of Congress Cataloging-in-Publication Data

Coakley, Jay J.
    Sport in society: issues and controversies / Jay J. Coakley.–
6th ed.
        p.   cm.
    Includes index.
    ISBN 0-8151-2027-3
    1. Sports–Social aspects.   2. Sports–Psychological aspects.
I. Title.
GV706.5.C63   1997
306.4'83–dc21   97-17011
                                                                                    CIP

http://www.mhcollege.com

When ordering this title, use ISBN 0-07-115671-2

Printed in Singapore

SPORT IN SOCIETY

Issues and Controversies

Contents

Preface

PURPOSE OF THE TEXT

The sixth edition of *Sport in Society: Issues and Controversies* has a twofold purpose: *first*, it is designed to provide a sound introduction to the sociology of sport; and *second*, it is written to encourage students to ask questions and think critically about sports as parts of social life.

I have organized the chapters to focus on curiosity-arousing issues. These issues are discussed in terms of recent research and theory in the sociology of sport. Although the concepts and source materials are not taken exclusively from sociology, discussions throughout the book are grounded in a sociological approach. Therefore, the emphasis is clearly on sports and sport-related behaviors as they occur in social and cultural contexts.

FOR WHOM IS IT WRITTEN?

Sport in Society is written for those taking their first look at sports from a sociological perspective. The content of each chapter is presented so it can be understood by beginning college students in either physical education or sociology. The discussion of issues does not presume prior courses in social science or in-depth experiences in sports. However, I have tried to present materials in ways that push students to think more critically about sports and how sports are related to their social lives.

Although I intend this book as an introduction to the field, I have written it not so much to describe the issues in the sociology of sport as to involve the reader in the analyses those of us in the field have done. The emphasis is on how the concepts and theories of sociology enable us to dig into sports as parts of culture and see them as *more* than just reflections of the world in which we live.

Since the book is organized in terms of an "issues approach," the content of many chapters is useful for those concerned with sport policies and program administration. My emphasis through the book is on making sports more democratic and sport participation more accessible to all people.

CHANGES IN THE SIXTH EDITION

I have rewritten most sections of the sixth edition of *Sport in Society*. I have added updated material to all chapters, and reorganized chapters in response to new research findings and new theoretical developments in the field. Over 500 *new* references are cited in this edition; most of them highlight work published since the fifth edition went to press in 1993. This is three times the number of new references included in the fifth edition—an indication of the rapid expansion of research on sports and of the literature used by those of us in the field.

New Chapter on Socialization

One of the criticisms of past editions was the lack of a chapter devoted exclusively to socialization issues. Because recent qualitative research on socialization has provided new and insightful glimpses into the social worlds of sports and sport participation, the time was right for pulling this material together and discussing a wide range of issues key to the field. Chapter 4 focuses on what we know about becoming involved and staying involved in sports, about changing or ending active sport participation, and about the actual experience and consequences of being involved in sports. The chapter includes summaries of research dealing with socialization issues, and it highlights new approaches to socialization, including those dealing with the media and the production and reproduction of cultural ideology. I introduce the concepts of "power and performance sports" and "pleasure and participation sports" to help students understand the range of sport experiences in people's lives.

Revision Themes

This edition has a stronger emphasis on socialization themes than past editions do. But it also emphasizes the implications of what I would call the era of corporate sponsors in sports. The involvement of large corporations, including media companies, in sports has had a major impact on the presentation and use of sport-related images in society. We now see "Coca Cola-ized" versions of the Olympics, "Pepsi-ized" versions of the Super Bowl, "McDonald-ized" versions of intercollegiate sports, and "General Motor-ized" versions of anything men play and watch. We've been IOC'd, NFL'd, Super Bowl'd, World Cup'd, Final Four'd, World Series'd, and generally play-off'd to the point that it is hard to know where our own ideas about sports start and where the ideas of corporate sponsors and large sport organizations leave off. This edition is designed to provide students with a critically informed alternative view of sports, one they won't get on a Disney-owned network or cable channel.

New Materials

An expanded introductory chapter (chap. 1) includes new sections comparing the sociology and psychology of sport; discussing the relationship between sports and cultural ideology; and introducing the concepts of gender logic, race logic, class logic, and character logic to help students understand dominant ideology. There is a completely new approach to defining sports and a new section on "what gets to count as a sport in a culture."

This edition includes expanded coverage of critical theory and feminist theories (chap. 2), along with new examples of research guided by critical theories and interactionist theories. An updated table compares all the theoretical perspectives.

The chapter on youth sports (chap. 5) has been completely rewritten. There are new materials on privatization and the increased emphasis on the performance principle in youth sports, on families and parent-child relationships, and on gender and youth sport participation.

There is expanded coverage of deviance issues (chap. 6), including a new analysis of the connection between positive deviance and negative deviance in sports; the focus in this section is on binge drinking and sexual assault. There is a revised analysis of substance use in sports, with an emphasis on new "legal" substances, including DHEA, creatine monohydrate, and other substances now available in health food stores.

This volume provides expanded coverage of gender and aggression in sports (chap. 7), a section summarizing ethnographic research on boxing, and new material on pain and injury, and on violence and media coverage of sports.

I have expanded the chapter on gender (chap. 8) to incorporate the findings of new research on equity and gender relations, and included new material on changes in the dominant gender logic related to sports.

The chapter on race and ethnicity (chap. 9) includes new information on the concept of race and on how meanings associated with skin color impact sports and sport participation patterns. The chapter provides an updated analysis of racial ideology and sports, new information on ethnicity and sport participation, and new information on the use of Native American images in sports.

The chapter on social class and class relations (chap. 10) has been completely rewritten, with a new emphasis on inequality. I've included new materials on who has power in sports and how sports are used to transfer money from the public sector to the private sector of the economy. The chapter contains new analyses of the intersections of class, gender, and race/ethnicity in sports; new discussions of class segregation among sport fans in new luxury stadiums; updated information on social class and sport participation; and a new section on sport participation and social mobility.

I have completely rewritten the chapter on the economy (chap. 11). It contains new economic data, as well as new discussions of the consequences of commercialization, the use of sports by corporations, and the globalization of sports through the media. The chapter offers a new discussion of the reasons cities give public money to billionaires for new stadiums, new data on the legal status and incomes of athletes at all levels of participation in revenue-generating sports, and new tables on franchise values and revenue streams for team owners.

In the chapter on the media (chap. 12), I have included new information on the growth of media coverage, the media and globalization, and the use of media sports by transnational corporations. There is also a new analysis of media-driven forms of global sport celebrity.

The chapter on politics (chap. 13) has been rewritten to deal with the entry of major corporations into transnational relations. In this chapter, I present an analysis of the growth of media sports and the advertising needs of transnational corporations, along with new coverage of the Olympics as an international event, new coverage of the relationships between sports and national identities, and new material on politics in sports.

The chapter discussing education (chap. 14) contains updated NCAA information and new material on the experiences of intercollegiate athletes. There are new data on gender equity and on economic issues in intercollegiate sports.

The chapter on religion (chap. 15) includes updated information on how religious organizations use sports to promote religious beliefs, and how athletes use religion in their lives.

In the chapter on the future (chap. 16), you will find new material on alternative sports, and on athletes who resist organized, competitive, commercialized sports.

New boxed sections throughout the text discuss topics such as the following: sports as contested activities, the sport ethic in Nike ads, the new professional women's basketball leagues, and athletes as agents of change in society and in sports.

New Suggested Readings

Each chapter is followed by completely updated references to books and articles that provide analyses of topics raised in that chapter.

New Photographs and Cartoons

There are 88 new photos and 20 new cartoons in this edition. The use of photos, cartoons, tables, and figures has been carefully planned to visually break up the text and make reading more interesting for students (and instructors!). I've spent many weeks taking and selecting photos and reviewing cartoons directly related to the content of each chapter.

INSTRUCTOR'S MANUAL AND TEST BANK

An instructor's manual and test bank has been developed to assist those using *Sport in Society* in college courses. It includes the following:

Chapter outlines. These provide a quick overall view of the topics covered in each chapter. They are useful for organizing lectures, and they can be reproduced and given to students as study guides.

Test questions (multiple choice). These questions have been designed to test the students' awareness of central points made in each chapter. They focus on ideas rather than single, isolated facts. For the instructor with large classes, these questions are useful for chapter quizzes, midterm tests, or final examinations.

Discussion/essay questions. These questions can be used for tests or to generate classroom discussions. They are designed to encourage students to synthesize and apply materials in one or more of the sections in each chapter. None of the questions asks the students simply to list points or give definitions.

ACKNOWLEDGEMENTS

This book has evolved out of ideas coming from a variety of sources. I first must extend my thanks to the students in my sociology of sport courses. They have provided constructive critiques of my ideas and opened my eyes to new ways of looking at sports as social phenomena. Special thanks also go to the colleagues and friends who have influenced my thinking and provided valuable source materials over the past four years, especially Robert Hughes, Nancy Coakley, Peter Donnelly, and Bob Pearton. I thank also Jackie Beyer, for *New York Times* articles, Kimberly Gunn, for coverage and photos of the 1996 Atlanta Games, and Jean Babrick, for her critical comments on the revision manuscript.

My appreciation goes to the publisher's reviewers, whose suggestions were crucial in the planning and writing of this edition. They include the following:

Don E. Albrecht
    Texas A & M
Robert Curtin
    Northeastern University

Paul Dubois
    Bridgewater State College
Keith Harrison
    Washington State University
Victoria Paraschak
    University of Windsor
Jan Rintala
    Northern Illinois University
Michael Sachs
    Temple University
Franklin Ojeda Smith
    The Richard Stockton College
Lee Vandervelden
    University of Maryland

I selected some of the photographs in this edition from the files of the *Colorado Springs Gazette*. My thanks to sports editor Ralph Routon and the fine photographers who cover sports in this region. Other photos were provided by friends Tini Campbell, Dennis Coakley, and Danielle Hicks.

Jay Coakley

1

(Jay Coakley)

The Sociology of Sport
What is it and why study it?

A sport is defined, brought into being, by its rules. Sport is a method for administering play activity, a way to determine who should play and how they should play.

John Wilson, sociologist, Duke University (1994)

Sports is an element of American life so pervasive that virtually no individual is untouched by it . . . . [The] United States is a nation made up of sports fans . . . [and] sports participants.

Miller Lite Report on American Attitudes Toward Sports (1984)

Sport signifies a great deal about ourselves and about different ways of living and in so doing contributes to the ongoing production of social life itself.

Richard Gruneau, social scientist, University of British Columbia (1988)

The study of sport can take us to the very heart of critical issues in the study of culture and society.

Elliott Gorn, professor of American Studies, and Michael Oriard, professor of English (1995)

ABOUT THIS BOOK

Most of you reading this book have experienced sports personally, as athletes or spectators or both. You are probably familiar with the physical and emotional experiences of sport participation, and you may have extensive knowledge of the rules and regulations of certain sports. You probably know about the lives, on and off the field, of high-profile athletes in your school, community, or country. And you probably have followed certain sports by watching them in person and on television, reading about them in the print media or on Web pages, or even listening to discussions of them on talk radio. The purpose of this book is to take you beyond personal emotional experiences, and beyond statistics and personalities, to focus on what we might call the "deeper game" associated with sports, the game through which sports become an integral part of the social and cultural worlds in which we live.

Fortunately, we can draw on our personal experiences as we consider this "deeper game." Let's use our experiences with high school sports in North America as an example. When students in high school play on a varsity basketball team, we know their participation may affect their status in the school and the way teachers and fellow students treat them. We know it may have implications for their prestige in the surrounding community, for their self-images and their self-esteem. We know that it may affect even their future relationships and opportunities in education and the workforce.

Building on this knowledge enables us to move further into this deeper game associated with sports. For example, we might study the cultural significance of the great importance we place on varsity sports and top athletes. What does that say about our schools and communities, and about our values? And we might study how varsity programs are organized and how they are related to the way many people think about masculinity and femininity, about achievement and competition, about pleasure and pain, about winning and fair play, and about many other things

important to those who endorse and promote the programs. We might look at the impact of new forms of corporate sponsorships on the organization of high school sports and examine what students think about the corporations whose names and logos are on buses, gym walls, and uniforms.

In other words, sports are more than just games and meets; they are also **social phenomena** * that have meanings that go far beyond scores and performance statistics. In fact, sports are related to the social and cultural contexts in which we live our lives; they provide stories and images that many of us use to explain and evaluate these contexts, as well as events in our lives and the world around us.

People in the sociology of sport study the connection between sports and the social and cultural contexts in which they exist, as well as the deeper meanings and stories associated with sports in particular cultures. Then they use their studies to develop an understanding of (1) the society in which sports exist, (2) the social worlds that are created around sports, and (3) the experiences of individuals and groups associated with sports.

Sociology is very helpful when it comes to looking at sports as social phenomena. It provides concepts, theoretical approaches, and research methods for describing and understanding human behavior and social interaction as they occur in particular social and cultural contexts. Sociology gives us the tools we need to examine social life *in context*, in its "social location." These tools enable us to "see" behavior as it is connected with history, politics, economics, and cultural life. In this book we will use sociology to "see" sports as a part of social and cultural life and to describe and understand social issues related to sports.

As we do this, it is important that we know what is meant by the terms *culture* and *society*.

---

*Social phenomena are occasions or events involving social relationships and collective action, and having relevance in the social lives of particular collections of people.

Culture consists of the "ways of life" people create in a particular society. These ways of life are complex; they come into existence and are changed as people in a society come to terms with and sometimes struggle over how to do things, how to relate with one another, and how to make sense out of the things and events that make up their experiences. The ways of life that we refer to as culture are not imposed by some people on others; rather, they are creations of people interacting with one another. And they consist of all the socially invented ways of thinking, feeling, and acting that emerge in particular groups as people try to survive, meet their needs, and achieve a sense of significance in the process.

Sports are parts of cultures. Therefore, sociologists often refer to sports as **cultural practices.** Like other cultural practices, sports are human creations that come into being as people struggle to decide what is important and how things should be done in their groups and societies. This is why sports have different forms and meanings from one place to another and why they change over time: people never come to once-and-for-all-time definitions of the ways things should be in their lives. For example, traditional martial arts and Sumo wrestling in Asia are very different in both form and meaning from individual sports such as boxing and wrestling in North America. And basketball's form and meaning has changed considerably since 1891, when it was developed at a YMCA in Massachusetts as an indoor exercise activity for men who didn't want to play football outside during the winter. Canadian James Naismith, who invented basketball as part of an assignment in a physical education course in the U.S., would not recognize his game if he saw Shaquille O'Neal slam dunk during the Olympics as a billion people watched on satellite television. It is important to know about these cultural and historical differences when we study sport as a social phenomenon.

As you read this book, keep in mind that sports have different forms and meanings from place to place and time to time. This is the case because sports are **social constructions.** In other words, sports are activities that human beings give form and meaning to as they interact and live their lives with one another. Because sports are social constructions, sociologists study them in connection with social relationships and social, political, and economic processes. Thus, sociologists ask questions about why particular groups and societies have selected certain physical activities and designated them as sports, why sports are organized in certain ways, why different groups and societies associate certain meanings with sports and sport participation, and who benefits from the organization and definition of sports in society.

In this book, the term **society** refers to a collection of people living in a defined geographical territory and united through a political system and a shared sense of self-identification that distinguishes them from other collections of people. Thus, Canada and Japan are different societies, and they have different cultures, or ways of life. Canada and the United States are also different societies, but although they have different cultures, there are some important cultural similarities between them. Sports in Japan have forms and meanings that we can understand only in connection with Japanese history, society and culture. The same is true for other sports in other societies.

In summary, sports are cultural practices that differ from place to place and time to time. How they are defined, organized, and integrated into social life varies from group to group. The types of sports played in a particular group or society, the ways they are organized, the resources dedicated to sports and sport programs, the people who get to play sports, the conditions under which sport participation occurs, the individuals who sponsor and control sports, the rewards that go to participants, the definition of an "athlete," and the meanings associated with sport participation—all are determined through social interaction. This means that to understand sports we must view them as social phenomena. And the analytical tools sociology provides will help us do this as we discuss major issues related to sport in society in the chapters that follow.

ABOUT THIS CHAPTER

This chapter describes the sociology of sport as a subfield of physical education and sociology and explains what is meant by the term **sports** as it is used in the following chapters. Throughout this book I generally will use the term *sports* rather than *sport*. I do this to emphasize that the forms and meanings of sports vary from place to place and time to time. I want to avoid the inference that "sport" has some type of essential and timeless quality apart from the contexts in which people develop, plan, package, promote, program, and play sports activities.

This chapter focuses on four questions:

1. What is the sociology of sport?
2. Why study sports as social phenomena?
3. What is the current status of the sociology of sport as a field of study?
4. What are sports, and how are they related to similar activities, such as play, recreation, games, and cultural spectacles?

The answers to these questions will be guides for understanding material in chapters 2 to 16.

WHAT IS THE SOCIOLOGY OF SPORT?

This question is best answered at the end of the book instead of the beginning. However, you should have at least a brief preview of what you will be reading for the next fifteen chapters.

Most people in the sociology of sport agree that the field is the subdiscipline of sociology that studies sports as parts of social and cultural life. The focus of much of the research and writing in this field is on what many of us refer to as "organized, competitive sports." The people who do this research and writing utilize sociological concepts, theories, and research to answer questions such as the following:

1. Why have certain activities (rather than others) been selected and designated as sports in particular groups?
2. Why have sports in particular groups and societies been created and organized in certain ways?
3. How do sports and sport participation get included in our personal and social lives, and how do they affect who we are, how we are connected with other people, and how we define those connections?
4. How do sports and sport participation affect our ideas about our own bodies, about what is "natural" and "unnatural," about masculinity and femininity, social class, race and ethnicity, work, fun, ability and disability, achievement and competition, pleasure and pain, deviance and conformity, aggression and violence?
5. How are the organization and meanings of sports connected with social relations, material conditions, and the dynamics of power in groups and societies?
6. How are sports related to important spheres of social life, such as family, education, politics, the economy, the media, and religion?
7. How can people use their knowledge about sports and what sports could and should be as a basis for changing them to make social life more fair and democratic?

What Are the Differences Between the Sociology of Sport and the Psychology of Sport?

One way to understand the sociology of sport is to contrast it with another discipline that also studies sports. Let's take psychology as a comparison discipline.

Psychologists study behavior in terms of attributes and processes that exist *inside* individuals; they focus on motivation, perception, cognition, self-esteem, self-confidence, attitudes, and personality. Psychologists also deal with interpersonal dynamics, including communication, leadership, and social influence, but they usually

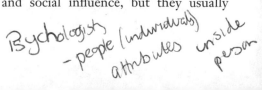

Psychologists
- people (individuals)
   attributes inside person

discuss these things in terms of how they affect attributes and processes that exist inside individuals. Therefore they might ask a research question like this: "How is the motivation of athletes with certain personality characteristics affected by different leadership styles used by coaches?"

Sociologists study behavior in terms of the social conditions and cultural contexts in which human beings live their lives; in other words, they focus on the reality *outside and around* individuals. Therefore, sociologists deal with how people form relationships with one another and create social arrangements that enable them to survive and exert some control over how they live their lives. Sociologists also ask questions about how behavior, relationships, and social life are related to characteristics that people in particular groups define as socially relevant. This is why they often deal with the social meanings and dynamics associated with age, gender, race, ethnicity, disability, and social class. A sociologist might ask a question like this: "How do prevailing cultural definitions of masculinity and femininity affect the way sport programs are organized and who participates in sports?"

When it comes to the application of their knowledge, psychologists focus on the personal experiences and the personal troubles of particular individuals. Sociologists focus on group experiences and social issues experienced by entire categories or groups of people. For example, when dealing with burnout among young athletes, psychologists most likely would look at factors that exist *inside* the athletes themselves. Since stress has been identified as an "inside factor" related to burnout (Smith, 1986), psychologists would focus on the existence of stress in the lives of individual athletes and how stress might affect motivation and performance. They might use strategies to help individual athletes manage stress through goal setting, personal skills development, and the use of relaxation and concentration techniques.

Sociologists, on the other hand, would be likely to focus on how sport programs are organized and how athletes fit into that organization; they also would concentrate on athletes' relationships with parents, peers, and coaches. Since burnout often occurs when athletes feel their lives are so controlled by others that they have no power to make the decisions they feel are important in their lives (Coakley, 1992), sociological intervention probably would emphasize the need for changes in the way sport programs and athletes' relationships with others are organized. Sociologists would suggest changes in "outside factors," such as the conditions and context in which sport participation occurs. They would design these changes to empower athletes and give them more control over important parts of their lives.

As you can see, both approaches have potential value (see Gould, 1996). However, some people may see the sociological approach as too complex and too disruptive. They may conclude that it is easier to change individual athletes and how athletes deal with external conditions than to change the external conditions in which athletes live their lives. This is one of the reasons those who have power and control in sport organizations have not widely used sociological approaches. These people are often hesitant to use any approach that might lead to recommendations calling for shifts in the way they exercise power and control within their organizations. Parents and coaches also might be wary of approaches that call for changes in the structures of their relationships with athletes, especially since they have developed those structures for reasons they think are important!

Using the Sociology of Sport

The insights developed through sociological analyses are not always used to make changes in favor of the underdogs (the people who lack power) in society. Like any science, sociology can be used in many different ways. For example, it can assist people in positions of power as they try to control and enhance the efficiency of particular social arrangements and organizational

Calvin and Hobbes   by Bill Watterson

Sociologists study the aspects of sports that Calvin identified; the rules, organization, ranks, and authority systems. Sociologists also study gender relations in sports, the issue identified by Susie.

structures. Or, sociology can assist people who lack power as they attempt to change social conditions so they have more autonomy and greater opportunities to make choices about how they will live their lives.

In other words, sociologists must decide how they are going to "do" sociology and what they want the consequences of their work to be. Sociologists cannot escape the fact that social life is complex and that the interests of different groups of people in society are not always the same; sociologists must recognize that social life is at least partly shaped by who has power and who does not. Therefore, using sociology is not a simple process that always leads to good and wonderful conclusions for all humankind. This is the reason we must think critically about what we want sociology to do for us when we study sports.

As a result of my own thinking about sports in society, I have written this book to help you use sociology to do the following:

1. Think critically about sports so you can identify and understand social problems and social issues associated with sports in society.
2. Look beyond game scores and performance statistics to see sports as social phenomena having relevance for the ways people feel, think, and live their lives in society.

3. Learn things about sports that you can use to make informed choices about your own sport participation and the place of sports in the communities and societies where you live.
4. Think about how sports might be transformed in your schools and communities so they do not contribute to ideas or conditions that systematically disadvantage some categories of people while privileging others.

Controversies Created by the Sociology of Sport

As we have noted, the conclusions sociologists reach sometimes create controversy. This occurs because those conclusions often call for changes in the organization of sports and the structure of social relations in society as a whole. These recommendations often threaten certain people, including those in positions of power and control in sport organizations, those who benefit from the ways sports are organized currently, and those who think the current organization of sports is "right and natural," regardless of its consequences. These are the people with the most to lose if changes are made in social relations and social organization. After all, people with power and control in existing social structures know that changes in those structures could jeopardize their positions and the privilege that comes with them. This leads many of these people to favor approaches to sports that explain problems in terms of the characteristics of individuals rather than in terms of social conditions and social organization. If theories blame problems on individuals, the solutions will emphasize better ways of controlling people and teaching them how to adjust to the world as it is, rather than emphasizing changes in the way that world is organized.

We can illustrate the potential for controversy that results from a sociological analysis of sport by looking at some of the research findings on sport participation among women in many countries around the world. Research shows that women, especially women in low-income households, have lower rates of sport participation than other categories of people do. The research also shows that the reasons for this are many. Most obvious is that women are less likely than men to have the resources they need to initiate and sustain sport participation, and less likely to have opportunities to become involved in sports on a regular basis. Women don't control the facilities where sports are played, or the programs in those facilities. The demands of women's jobs combined with the demands of homemaking may lead them to have less free time than men; they also have less access to transportation and less overall freedom to move around at will and without fear, and they may be expected to take full-time responsibility for the social and emotional needs of family members—a job that is never completed or done perfectly! Furthermore, the sport programs that do exist in societies around the world are grounded primarily in the values and experiences of men; they are controlled by men, and geared to the way men have learned to think about their bodies, their relationships to other people, and the way the world operates. To the extent that this is the case, many men may choose not to support women's participation, by taking care of the children, for example. Furthermore, many women may not see

sports as appropriate activities for them to do or take seriously, and the men in their lives may encourage them to continue thinking this way.

It is easy to see the potential for controversy associated with these conclusions of sociologists about sport and sport participation among women. On the basis of these discoveries a sociologist might suggest that sport participation opportunities be increased for women, that resources for women's programs be increased, that women and men share control over sports, and that new variations of sports based on the values and experiences of women be developed. Other suggestions would call for changes in gender relations, family structures, the organization of work, the distribution of resources in society, and the way children are cared for; they would call for expanded definitions of femininity and masculinity, and new forms of social organization that were more sensitive to how women in particular groups and societies live their lives. Sociological recommendations would *not* call for giving sport-related pep talks to the women themselves, or simply telling women that sports are wonderful and they should make sport participation a priority in their lives.

When sociologists make recommendations about how to increase sport participation among women or how to achieve gender equity in sport programs, they may not get positive responses from certain people. In fact, their recommendations may threaten those who benefit from the way sports and social life are now organized. And they also may threaten those who just believe that sports and social life were simply meant to be as they are now, regardless of who benefits and who doesn't. This is the reason some see the sociology of sport as too critical and negative. But the study of sports as social phenomena forces us to take a critical look at the social conditions that affect our lives on and off the playing field, and doing this can help us understand more about the world in which we live. Even when this makes some people uneasy, we should not abandon the task.

WHY STUDY SPORTS AS SOCIAL PHENOMENA?

Sports Are a Part of People's Lives

Studying sports seems to be a logical thing for sociologists to do. Sports clearly have become an important part of the social and cultural profiles of many societies around the world. As we look around us we see that the Olympic Games, soccer's World Cup, the Tour de France, the tennis championships at Wimbledon, and American football's Super Bowl are now worldwide events capturing the interest of billions of people as they are televised by satellite in two hundred or more countries. Children around the world grow up with vivid images of televised sports and sport figures, they play video games based on these sports, and they are encouraged to participate in sports by parents, teachers, and the elite athletes who often are presented as role models in their lives.

People of all ages connect with sports through the media. Newspapers in most cities devote entire sections of daily editions to the coverage of sports. This is especially true in North America, where space given to sports coverage frequently surpasses space given to the economy, politics, or any other single topic of interest. Radio talk shows about sports capture the attention of millions of listeners every day in certain countries. Satellites and Internet technology now enable millions of people around the world to share their interest in sports. Consequently, sport information is no longer limited by newspaper and network television editors.

People around the world now recognize high-profile sport teams and athletes, and this recognition fuels everything from product consumption to tourism. For example, during the 1990s Chicago Bulls hats, shirts, posters, jackets, and other memorabilia became precious commodities in China and other parts of Asia, as well as around North America and Europe. Japanese travelers during the 1990s paid thousands of yen per person to take special tours to Chicago, where they attended a Bulls game after being photographed

Some athletes have become national and international celebrities, in part because of widespread media coverage of sports as well as the use of athletes by corporations to market products. Sports are a large part of the news that people attend to in their daily lives. Does this coverage distract attention from significant social issues? Sociologists consider this question. (Dennis Coakley)

outside the United Center arena in front of a sculpture of Michael Jordan. People schedule not only their vacations, but also their weekends and other free time around playing and watching sports. Even when individuals don't have an interest in sports, the people around them may insist on bringing them to games and talking with them about sports, to such a degree that they are forced to make sports a part of their lives.

Sport images are such a pervasive part of life in the U.S. that many young people during the mid-1990s were more familiar with the tattoos and body piercings of Chicago Bulls player Dennis Rodman than with President Clinton's nationwide program for putting police in their neighborhoods, even though new forms of neighborhood policing would have a greater impact on their lives than the navel pins or tattoos that would make them look like Rodman. At the same time, lawyers and judges were deciding who owned the right to profit from the sale of T-shirts with images of Rodman's tattoos on them. Such celebrity highlighting is another way that sports enter our lives. Clearly, the attention given to certain athletes today has turned them into celebrities at least, if not cultural heroes. This sort of status is what caused a furor in Canada when hockey star Wayne Gretzky was traded to a U.S. team.

Of course, the U.S. is not the only country in which sports pervade social life so extensively. In many countries, soccer evokes religious-like fervor. For example, when the stadium used by Ajax, a premier soccer team in Amsterdam, was being replaced by a new facility, a local cemetery purchased the turf from the old playing field so deceased fans could have their ashes scattered over the grass on which their heroes once played. The fee for this service included the provision of a plaque in the Ajax colors of red and white; each plaque, placed along a sideline of the simulated "field," contains the name of a dearly departed fan.

People around the world increasingly talk about sports—at work, at home, in bars, on dates, at dinner tables, in school, with friends and family members, and even with strangers at bus stops, in airports, and on the street. Relationships often revolve around sports, especially among men, and among an increasing number of women as well. People identify with teams and athletes so closely that what happens in sports influences their moods and overall sense of well-being. In fact, people's identities as athletes and fans may be more important to them than their identities related to education, work, or even family.

Overall, sports and sport images have become a pervasive part of the everyday lives of human beings, especially those living in countries where resources are relatively plentiful and the media are widespread. For this reason, they are logical topics for the attention of sociologists and anyone else concerned with social life today.

Ties Between Sports and Cultural Ideology

Studying sports as social phenomena is also appropriate because sports are closely tied to **cultural ideology** in society. Cultural ideology consists of the general perspectives and ideas that people use to make sense out of the social world, to figure out what their place is in that world, and to determine what is important or unimportant and what is right and natural in the world (Hall, 1985). We could say that cultural ideology is a window into the underlying logic of the way people live their lives in a particular society.

Cultural ideology does not come in a neat package, especially in the case of highly diverse and rapidly changing societies, such as the United States, for example. Different groups in societies develop their own perspectives and ideas for making sense of the social world, and they may not always agree with one another. In fact, different groups may struggle over whose way of making sense of the world is the best way, or the right way, or the moral way. This is where sports enter the picture. Sports consist of activities and situations that either embrace or challenge particular ideologies. As sports are created by people, they may develop around particular ideas about the body and human nature, about how people should relate to each other, about expression and competence, about human abilities and potential, about manhood and womanhood, and about what is important and unimportant in life. These ideas usually support and reproduce what might be called the dominant ideology in a society, but this is not always the case. Dominant ideology is built on the perspectives and ideas favored and promoted by dominant and powerful groups in a society; dominant ideology serves the interests of those groups (Theberge and Birrell, 1994).

Let's focus on gender ideology in North America to show sports' connection with cultural ideology. In North American culture there are many different perspectives and ideas about gender, about masculinity and femininity, and about relationships between men and women. As sports were developed and became increasingly organized, they often contained a **gender logic** that was consistent with dominant forms of gender ideology in the culture as a whole. This gender logic usually worked to the advantage of men, while it disadvantaged women. Therefore, when people participated in sports, they often learned that "common sense" led to the conclusion that women were "naturally" inferior to men in any activity requiring physical skills and cognitive strategies.

This conclusion about male superiority and female inferiority even informed the vocabulary used in connection with many sports. For example, when someone threw a ball correctly, many people would say that he or she threw "like a boy" or "like a man." And when someone threw a ball incorrectly, many would say that he or she threw "like a girl." The same was true when running or other physical skills were assessed: if the skill was done right, it was done the way a boy or man would do it; if it was done wrong, it was done the way a girl or woman would do it. In fact, people generally understood that doing sports, especially sports that were physically demanding, would make a boy into a man. This ideology created confusion when people saw women who were excellent athletes. According to the traditional dominant gender logic, people often saw the competent woman athlete as a "dyke," or lesbian. The belief was that heterosexual femininity and excellence in sports, especially physically demanding and heavy contact sports, could not go together.

This gender logic became such a central part of many sports that some coaches of men's teams even used it to motivate players. These coaches would criticize male players who made mistakes or did not play aggressively enough by "accusing" them of "playing like a bunch of girls." Thus, according to the gender logic of sports, being a female meant being a failure. This "logic" clearly served for many years to privilege boys and men in sports and disadvantage girls and women, who were never considered to be equal to males when it came to allocating resources and providing opportunities and encouragement to play sports. Although this gender logic has been challenged and discredited in recent years, enough people still use it in some form that traditional systems of privilege for boys and men are maintained and girls and women are regularly disadvantaged.

The traditional gender logic used in sports has tended to promote or reproduce dominant gender ideology in the society as a whole, which also has privileged men and disadvantaged women in economic, political, legal, and educational spheres of life. Similarly, the gender logic in many sports over the years has reproduced ideas about masculinity, promoting the notion that manhood is based on being hard, tough, aggressive, and willing to endure pain without showing weakness.

However, cultural ideology is never established "once and for all time"; people constantly question and struggle over it. They challenge the cultural logic used by others, and they even may mount challenges that produce changes in deeply felt and widely accepted perspectives and ideas. In the case of gender ideology, sports have been a "social place"* for mounting such challenges to dominant ideas about what is natural and feminine. The history of these struggles over the meaning and implications of gender in sports is complex, but recent challenges by both women and men who do not accept the logic widely used in the past have led to important revisions in dominant cultural ideology. Women athletes have illustrated clearly that one can be powerful and a woman at the same time, that women are capable of noteworthy physical achievements surpassing those of the vast majority of men in the world, and that ideas about what is "natural" when it comes to gender should be questioned. We will discuss issues related to gender logic in sports in nearly every chapter, but especially chapter 8. The box on page 11, The Body and the Sociology of Sport, presents issues related to what we consider "natural" when it comes to the body.

Studying sports as social phenomena is important because sports are sites for many important ideological struggles. For example, ideas about social class are built into dominant forms

---

*Sociologists often refer to the "social places" or "social locations" where significant social occasions or developments occur as **sites**.

REFLECT ON SPORT   The Body and the Sociology of Sport

Until recently, most people have viewed the body as a fixed, unchanging fact of nature. They have seen the body in biological terms rather than social or cultural terms. But an increasing number of people in different academic fields now recognize that we cannot fully understand the body unless we consider it in social and cultural terms (Cole, forthcoming; Heller, 1991; Loy et al. 1993; Shilling, 1994). For example, medical historians recently have shown that the body and body parts have been socially defined in different ways through history and from one cultural group to another; and they have shown that these definitions are important because they affect medical practice, government policies, social theories, and the everyday experiences of human beings (Laqueur, 1990).

Changes in the ways bodies have been socially defined (or "constructed") over the years have had implications for how people think about sex, sex differences, sexuality, ideals of beauty, self-image, body image, fashion, hygiene, health, nutrition, eating, fitness, racial classification systems, disease, drugs and drug testing, violence and power, and many other things that affect our lives. In fact, body-related ideas have even affected the way people in some countries view desire, pleasure, pain, and the quality of life. For example, nineteenth-century Europeans and North Americans used insensitivity to pain as a physiological indicator of general character defects in a person, and saw muscular bodies as indicators of criminal tendencies and lower-class status (Hoberman, 1992). Today, however, partly in connection with how sports have been defined, people in those societies see the ability to ignore pain as a physiological indicator of strong character, instead of a sign of deviance and defective character. They now regard a muscular body as an indicator of self-control and discipline rather than criminality.

When it comes to sports, the physical body is social in a number of ways. This is explained by sociologist John Wilson (1994: 37–38) in the following way:

> [In sports] social identities are superimposed upon physical being. Sport, in giving value to certain physical

attributes and accomplishments and denigrating others, affirms certain understandings of how mind and body are related, how the social and natural worlds are connected. The identity of the athlete is not, therefore, a natural outgrowth of physicality but a social construction . . . . Sport absorbs ideas about the respective physical potential of men versus women, whites versus blacks, and middle-class versus working-class people. In doing so, sport serves to reaffirm these distinctions.

In fact, sport science has invented new ways to see bodies as complex performance machines with component parts that can be isolated and transformed to enhance specialized competitive performances (Hoberman, 1992; Turner, 1984). This, in turn, has led to an emphasis on monitoring and controlling bodies. This body monitoring and controlling takes forms such as weigh-ins, body fat percentage measurements, tests for aerobic capacity, muscle size measurements, muscle biopsies, responses to various stressors, measurements of anaerobic capacities, hormone testing, drug taking, drug testing, blood boosting, blood testing, diet regulation and restriction, vitamin regulation, and on and on. In the future there will likely be brain manipulations, hormonal regulation, DNA testing, and genetic engineering (Hoberman, 1992). Therefore, the body is cultural in the sense that it is now "read" and understood in terms of performance outcomes rather than in terms of how people experience and enjoy their bodies. In many sports today, pain rather than pleasure has become the indicator of the "good body," and limiting the percentage of body fat has become such a compulsion that bodies are starved to be "in good shape."

This new way of thinking about the body in cultural terms has challenged traditional Western ideas about the separation of mind and body. It also has raised new questions and issues in the sociology of sport. Some people in the sociology of sport are now working with colleagues in other disciplines who share interest in the body. They are asking critical questions about (1) how our ideas about what is "natural" are formed, (2) how the body is trained, disciplined, and manipulated in sports, and (3) how sport

Continued

scientists are using technology to probe, invade, monitor, measure, test, evaluate, and rehabilitate the body as a performance machine. These are crucial questions, although asking them makes many people associated with sports uncomfortable, because the answers often challenge the way many sports have been organized and played, the way excellence has been defined, and the way rewards have been allocated in sports.

of sports in many cultures; in other words, many sports are associated with a **class logic.** This class logic serves as a basis for explaining economic success and failure, leading to favorable conclusions about the character and qualifications of those who are wealthy and powerful, and to negative criticism of poor people and those who lack power in society. We will discuss this in chapter 10, among others.

Many sports also encourage a **race logic** related to dominant ideas about links between the color of a person's skin and sport-related physical skills. Using this race logic, people often associated dark skin with physical and athletic prowess, and especially with positions on teams for which physical demands are greater than intellectual demands. Like other forms of cultural ideology, this race logic can be a powerful force in social relations. We will discuss this issue in chapter 9.

People also associate what we might call **character logic** with sports in certain countries. In other words, they have organized sports around particular beliefs about what character is and how it is developed and proved. And many people assume that participation in sports teaches people valuable lessons and therefore develops character. We will discuss this crucial issue in connection with questions related to "socialization and sports" in chapters 4 to 7.

As we think about sports and cultural ideology, we must remember that ideology is complex and sometimes inconsistent, and that sports come in many forms and have many different meanings associated with them. Therefore, sports connect with ideology in various and sometimes contradictory ways; we saw this in the example of the ways sports are sites for simultaneously reproducing *and* challenging dominant gender ideology in society. Furthermore, sports come in many different forms, and those forms can have many different social meanings associated with them. For example, baseball is played by similar rules in both Japan and the U.S., but the meanings associated with baseball, with games, and with athletes' performances are different in the two cultures. This is the case because sports are cultural practices as well as games, a fact that makes it difficult to generalize about the consequences of sports in society. Sports have the social potential to do many things. This is another reason for studying them as social phenomena.

Sports Are Connected with Major Spheres of Social Life

Another reason to study sports as social phenomena is that they are clearly connected to major spheres of social life, including the family, the economy, media, politics, education, and religion. We will discuss these connections in various chapters in this book, but it is useful to highlight them at this point.

SPORTS AND FAMILY   Sports are closely related to the family. In North America, for example, millions of children are involved in a variety of organized sport activities. It is primarily their parents who organize leagues, coach teams, attend games, and serve as "taxi drivers" for child athletes. Family schedules are altered to accommodate practices and games. These schedules

"This won't take long will it?"

Families and family schedules often are influenced by sports involvement. Sometimes this involvement disrupts family life and interferes with family relationships (top); sometimes it brings family members together in enjoyable ways (bottom).

also may be affected by the patterns of sport involvement among adult family members. The viewing of televised sport events sometimes disrupts family life and at other times provides a collective focus for family attention. In some cases relationships between family members are nurtured and played out during sport activities or in conversations about these activities.

SPORTS AND THE ECONOMY The economies of most countries, especially wealthy postindustrial countries, have been affected by the billions of dollars spent every year for game tickets, sports equipment, participation fees, athletic club membership dues, and bets placed on favorite teams and athletes. The economies of many local communities have been affected by the presence of major sport teams. Most countries use public monies (taxes) to subsidize teams and events. Some athletes make impressive sums of money from various combinations of salaries, appearance fees, and endorsements. Corporations have paid up to $2.6 million for a single minute of commercial time during the telecast of the Super Bowl in the U.S.; they have paid well over $60 million to be international Olympic sponsors, entitled to have their corporate names associated with the Olympic name and symbol for four years. Sports stadiums, arenas, and teams are now named after corporations instead of people or images with local cultural or historical relevance. Sponsorships and commercial associations with sports have been so effective that many people around the world now believe that without Coca-Cola, McDonald's, Nike, and other transnational corporations, sports would not exist.

Finally, the fact that per capita income around the world in the mid-1990s was only $3,500 per year, while a few athletes in the U.S. were making from $5 million to $30 million per year in salary and more than $10 million per year in endorsements, indicates that sports are cultural practices deeply connected with the material and economic conditions in society.

SPORTS AND MEDIA Television networks and cable stations often pay hundreds of millions of dollars for the rights to televise major games and events. NBC in the United States paid the International Olympic Committee (IOC) $2.3 billion for the rights to the Summer Games of 2004 and 2008 and the Winter Games of 2006; it also paid $1.27 billion for the rights to televise the 2000 Games in Sydney and the 2002 Games in Salt Lake City. People in sport organizations that depend on spectators are keenly aware that without the media their lives would be different. Also, the images and messages presented in mediated sports emphasize certain ideological themes related to social life, and they influence

Many sports images in today's urban landscape are actually advertisements for products and services. Corporations have found sports and sport figures to be effective tools for delivering messages that promote corporate interests. Sociologists are concerned with connections between sports and the economy. (Kimberly Gunn)

the ways people see and think about sports. For example, television's use of zoom lenses, special camera angles, filters, isolated coverage of action sequences, slow-motion replays, diagrammatic representations of action, commentary intended to enhance drama and excitement, and "delayed live" coverage all serve to change the ways people "see" sports. For those who don't play sports or attend games in person, the mediated versions of sports are the only versions they know.

Over a few decades, the media have converted sports into a major form of entertainment in many societies. Satellite technology makes it possible for the images and messages associated with a single competitive event to be witnessed simultaneously by billions of people. Athletes become global entertainers in the process, and powerful corporations sponsor these media events to imprint their logos in people's minds and promote a lifestyle based on product consumption. This certainly raises issues related to values, power, and culture.

SPORTS AND POLITICS People in many societies link sports to feelings of national pride and a sense of national identity. Despite frequent complaints about mixing sports and politics, most North Americans have no second thoughts about displaying national flags and playing national anthems at sporting events, and some may quickly reject athletes and other spectators who don't think as they do about the flag and the anthem. Political leaders at various levels of government promote themselves by associating with sports as both participants and spectators. International sports have become hotbeds of political controversy in recent years. And most countries around the world have used sports actively to enhance their reputations in global political relationships. Furthermore, sports themselves involve political processes associated with issues such as who controls sports and sport events, the terms of eligibility and team selection, rules and rule changes, rule enforcement, and the administration of sanctions. Sports and sport organizations are political, since they have to do with the exercise of power.

SPORTS AND EDUCATION Sports have become integral parts of school life for many students around the world, although sport participation most often occurs in physical education classes. But in North America, and especially in the U.S., high schools have exclusive varsity sport teams, and some of these teams attract more attention among students and community residents than academic programs do; at the same time, many of these schools have eliminated or are in the process of eliminating physical education for their student bodies as a whole. Some U.S. universities even use their varsity teams to promote the quality of their academic programs, making or losing large amounts of money in the process. They may even have public relations profiles built on (or seriously damaged by) the reputations of their sport programs.

SPORTS AND RELIGION There is a relationship between sports and religion. For example, local churches and church groups in both the United States and Canada are some of the most active sponsors of athletic teams and leagues. Parishes and congregations have been known to revise their Sunday service schedules to accommodate their members who would not miss an opening kickoff in a professional football game for anything—even their religious services. Religious rituals are increasingly used in conjunction with sport participation, and a few large nondenominational religious organizations have been created for the sole purpose of attracting and converting athletes to Christian beliefs. Other religious organizations have used athletes as spokespersons for their belief systems in the hope of converting people who strongly identify with sports.

In summary, there is no shortage of reasons for studying sports as social phenomena: they are part of our everyday lives, they influence cultural ideology, and they are connected with major spheres of social life.

WHAT IS THE CURRENT STATUS OF THE SOCIOLOGY OF SPORT?

The Sociology of Sport Is a New Field of Study

Prior to the 1980s, few sociologists in North America or around the world devoted much attention to sports as social phenomena. This lack of attention was the result of various combinations of the following factors:

1. *The social significance of sports in the past.* Organized sports as we know them today have become a pervasive part of social life only recently. It took the invention of television and increasing affluence in industrial societies to make organized sports such a popular and visible part of contemporary life. Now that sports are prominent in so many people's lives, physical educators and sociologists pay more attention to them as social phenomena. When you are interested in what people feel, think, and do, it is difficult to ignore events like the Olympics, which now capture the attention of billions of people.

2. *Intellectual biases in Euro-American cultures.* The cultures of European and North American societies traditionally have made clear-cut distinctions between play and work, and between physical and intellectual activities. The priority given to the work ethic led people to define play and sports as nonserious because they were nonproductive; they were not worthy of the attention that people gave to activities defined as serious and productive. Additionally, because sports were physical rather than intellectual activities, people viewed them as lower forms of culture unworthy of serious scholarly attention. Although this approach to physical culture has changed among many sociologists and physical educators, it still leads some people to question the merits of studying sports, and it still exerts a negative effect on the status of the sociology of sport in Europe and North America. To the extent that intellectual traditions in other cultures emulate Euro-American traditions, these intellectual biases have had global impact as well.

3. *Intellectual traditions in physical education and sociology.* The study of sports as social phenomena seldom has been defined as an activity that would benefit the professional

Publication Sources for Sociology of Sport Research

JOURNALS DEVOTED PRIMARILY TO SOCIOLOGY OF SPORT ARTICLES

International Review for the Sociology of Sport (quarterly)
Journal of Sport and Social Issues (3 issues per year)
Sociology of Sport Journal (quarterly)

SOCIOLOGY JOURNALS THAT SOMETIMES INCLUDE ARTICLES ON OR RELATED TO SPORTS

American Journal of Sociology
American Sociological Review
British Journal of Sociology
Sociology of Education
Theory, Culture and Society

SPORT SCIENCE AND PHYSICAL EDUCATION JOURNALS THAT SOMETIMES INCLUDE ARTICLES ON OR RELATED TO SOCIOLOGY OF SPORT TOPICS

Avante
Canadian Journal of Applied Sport Sciences
Exercise and Sport Sciences Reviews
Journal of Physical Education, Recreation and Dance
Journal of Sport Behavior
Journal of Sport Sciences

Physical Education Review
Quest
Research Quarterly for Exercise and Sport
Sport, Education and Society
Sport Science Review
Women in Sport & Physical Activity Journal

JOURNALS IN RELATED FIELDS THAT SOMETIMES INCLUDE ARTICLES ON OR RELATED TO SOCIOLOGY OF SPORT TOPICS

Adolescence
Aethlon: The Journal of Sport Literature
The British Journal of Sport History
International Journal of the History of Sport
Journal of Human Movement Studies
Journal of Leisure Research
Journal of the Philosophy of Sport
Journal of Popular Culture
Journal of Sport and Exercise Psychology
Journal of Sport History
Leisure Sciences
Olympika: The International Journal of Olympic Studies
Sporting Traditions
The Sports Historian
Youth & Society

---

careers of scholars. In physical education, the primary focus has been on motor learning and physical performance; studying sports as social phenomena has been given a lower priority. Sociologists often have seen the study of sports more as a hobby than as a serious career interest. These intellectual traditions have faded in recent years, but they still exist in some sociology and many physical education/kinesiology departments in Europe and North America.

A good indicator of the growing acceptance of the sociology of sport is the number of journals

that now accept and publish research using sociological perspectives to study sports. Some of these journals are identified in the box above.

Organizational Support for the Sociology of Sport

Professional associations in both sociology and physical education now sponsor regular sessions in the sociology of sport at their annual conferences. The field also has its own professional association, the North American Society for the Sociology of Sport (NASSS). Organized in 1978, this association has held annual conferences since 1980 and has sponsored the *Sociology of Sport Journal* since 1984. The Sport Sociology Academy, one of ten disciplinary academies in the National Association for Sport and Physical Education, conducts business and organizes sessions included in the annual conferences of the American Alliance for Health, Physical Education, Recreation and Dance. The International Sociology of Sport Association (ISSA) holds conferences in connection with the International Sociological Association, and it publishes the quarterly *International Review for the Sociology of Sport*. With this type of organizational endorsement and support, it seems that the sociology of sport will continue to grow as sports continue to become increasingly significant in society.

Future growth also will depend on whether the sociology of sport can prove itself useful as a tool for understanding social life in ways that can help make the world a better place. However, agreeing on what is "better" is not always easy.

Disagreements in the Sociology of Sport

Not everyone who studies sports as social phenomena is primarily interested in learning about human behavior, social relations, culture, and ideology. Some people are concerned more directly with learning about sports. Their involvement in the sociology of sport focuses on understanding how sports are organized and how changes in that organization might influence sport experiences for both athletes and spectators. The goal of these scholars is often to improve sport experiences for current participants and make sport participation a more attractive and accessible activity for those who do not currently participate. They also may want to help athletes improve their performances, help coaches be more supportive of athletes and more successful in competition, and help sport organizations grow and operate more efficiently.

These scholars, whether trained in physical education or trained in sociology, generally refer to themselves as **sport sociologists.** They tend to see themselves as part of a subdiscipline in the larger field of **sport sciences;** they are more concerned with sport science issues than with general sociological issues.

Scholars concerned primarily with general social and cultural issues usually refer to themselves as sociologists who study sports. Their work in the sociology of sport is often connected with other interests in leisure, everyday life and popular culture, social relations, and the social world as a whole.

Not everyone associated with the sociology of sport sees the field in the same way. People differ in what they prefer to study, how they do their research, what types of questions they ask, what theoretical perspectives they use, and what goals they identify for their research. For example, some people in the field see themselves as **scientific experts** who serve as consultants to those who can afford to buy their expertise. Others dislike this approach because it aligns the sociology of sport with people who have the power and money to hire experts—and people with power and money seldom want to ask tough critical questions about sports and the way sports are organized.

Those who favor the "scientific expert" model argue that the future of the sociology of sport depends on scholars in the field establishing reputations as researchers, getting large research grants, using research money to fund graduate assistants and recruit young scholars into the field, and using the knowledge produced in their research to maintain a professional image that can be marketed and sold to sport organizations or other groups interested in sports.

Other sociologists favor what might be called a "critical transformation" model over the "scientific expert" model. They focus primarily on improving the human condition by making social life more fair and democratic. They argue that if research in the sociology of sport serves only to reproduce what already exists in society, then scholars in the field become mere "efficiency experts" who sell their expertise to people with power and resources. These "critical sociologists" also argue that if scientific research and knowledge serve primarily people with power and wealth, science and scientists may become agents of control and oppression rather than agents of human freedom and emancipation. Therefore, they use research primarily to understand and solve problems in the lives of those who lack power and resources.

Such political debates about the focus and "applications" of science are not unique to the sociology of sport; they occur among professionals in other fields as well. But they often appear first in sociology because sociology is less closely tied to and supported by powerful interests in society. For example, political scientists often work for and are supported by governments; economists often work for and are supported by business and large public agencies; and psychologists often are involved in personal testing and supported by clinical practice. These external sources of support provide resources, but they also focus the work of these scholars on "the interests of the state," on "production and profit," and on helping people cope with and adjust to the status quo. This is not to say that these are unworthy ends, but there are others that also need attention.

Sociologists usually have little to lose by asking critical questions about sports. This enables them to explore alternative ways of looking at and organizing sports, and to consider projects that challenge the status quo and deal directly with problems and issues affecting the lives of people who lack power or who have been socially marginalized in particular societies. Of course, the downside of not having regular sources of external support is that sociologists are not as likely to get big research grants or consulting jobs. Those asking critical questions about sports usually do not have the money to fund large grants or hire consultants.

All of us in the sociology of sport have to make choices about how we will do our work and what we want the consequences of our work to be. Science is not so neutral and value free as we have been led to believe. The entire notion of being a "scientific expert" is tied to issues of power and control. Knowledge is a source of power in our complex world, and power has an impact on how knowledge is produced. In other words, doing research to build knowledge in the sociology of sport has political implications, because it has an impact on how people see sports and how they think about their own lives and the world around them. Unless people in the sociology of sport think about these things when they do their work, they will limit their understanding of the many meanings people give to sports in their lives and the impact that sports and sport participation have on individuals, communities, and societies.

WHAT ARE SPORTS?

For anyone reading this book, this question may seem elementary. We have a good enough grasp of the meaning of sports to talk about them with others. However, when we study sports systematically, it often helps to have a clear and precise definition of what we're talking about. For example, can we say that two groups of children playing a sandlot game of baseball in a Kansas town and a pickup game of soccer on a Mexican beach are engaged in sports? Their activities are quite different from what occurs during games in the Little League World Series, or in Yankee Stadium, or in soccer's World Cup tournament. These differences become significant when parents ask if playing sports is good for their children, or when community leaders ask if they should fund sports in city parks, or when school officials ask if sports contribute to the educational missions of their schools.

Students ask me if jogging and jump roping are sports. How about weight lifting? Hunting? Backpacking? Scuba diving? Darts? Automobile racing? Rhythmic gymnastics? Ballroom dancing? Chess? Should any or all of these activities be called sports? In the face of such a question, it becomes obvious that we should think about the social organization, social dynamics, and social implications of certain activities to determine which ones are similar enough to be grouped

Is Ultimate (Frisbee) a sport? How do sociologists decide what to include in their study of sports? How do members of a society decide what is a sport? These are important questions in the sociology of sport. (Bob Byrne, Ultimate Players Association)

together when we do sociological research. For this reason, many scholars in the sociology of sport have decided that a precise definition of **sports** is needed, so that we can study sports as distinct from other activities having different social dynamics and social implications.

People in the sociology of sport generally agree that in many cultures at this point in history it makes sense to define sports in the following way:

> *Sports are institutionalized competitive activities that involve vigorous physical exertion or the use of relatively complex physical skills by individuals whose participation is motivated by a combination of personal enjoyment and external rewards.*

Parts of this definition are clear, but other parts need explanation. First, it is quite easy to understand that sports are *physical activities.*

Therefore, according to this definition, chess would not be a sport, since playing chess depends on cognitive abilities rather than physical ones. Automobile racing might be physical enough to qualify as a sport under this definition, but such a decision is somewhat arbitrary, since there are no objective rules for how "physical" an activity must be to qualify as a sport. Pairs ice dancing is considered a sport in the winter Olympics, so why not add ballroom dancing to the summer games? Is it physical enough to be a sport?

Second, sports are *competitive activities* according to this definition. Sociologists realize that competitive activities have different social dynamics from cooperative or individualistic activities; they know that what happens when two girls pass a basketball to each other and shoot baskets at a hoop mounted on their garage is sociologically different from what happens when the U.S. women's basketball team plays Brazil's national team in the Olympics. So, it makes sense to separate them for research purposes.

Third, sports are *institutionalized activities.* **Institutionalization** is a sociological term referring to the process through which behaviors and organization become patterned or standardized over time and from one situation to another. Institutionalized activities have formal rules and organizational structures that people use to frame and guide their actions from one situation to another. When we say that sports are institutionalized activities, we are distinguishing what happens when two skiers decide to race each other down their favorite ski slope while they are vacationing in Colorado from what happens when skiers race each other in a World Cup giant slalom event that has been highly organized according to strict rules laid down by the International Federation of Skiing. When it comes to defining sports, sociologists would say that the process of institutionalization includes the following:

1. *The rules of the activity become standardized.* This means that sports have rules that are

not simply produced by a single group getting together on an informal basis. These rules are based on more than spontaneous expressions of individual interests and concerns. In sports, the rules of the game define an official set of behavioral and procedural guidelines and restrictions.

2. *Official regulatory agencies take over rule enforcement.* When the physical performances of teams or individuals are compared from one competitive event to another, it may be necessary for some regulatory agency to sanction games and meets and to ensure that standardized conditions exist and rules are enforced. Regulatory agencies could include everything from a local rules committee for a children's softball league to the highly organized central office of the National Collegiate Athletic Association (NCAA).

3. *The organizational and technical aspects of the activity become important.* When competition is combined with external rule enforcement, an activity becomes increasingly *rationalized*. This means that players and coaches come to develop strategies and training schedules to improve their chances for success within the rules. Additionally, shoes, uniforms, and other types of equipment are developed and manufactured to enhance performance and maximize the range of experiences available through participation.

4. *The learning of game skills becomes formalized.* This occurs for two major reasons. First, as the organization and the rules of the activity become more complex, they must be presented and explained to people in systematic ways. Second, as the concern with being successful grows, participants at various skill levels begin to seek guidance from experts. Teaching experts or coaches are often supplemented by others such as trainers, dietitians, sport scientists, managers, and team physicians.

Finally, according to this definition, sports are *activities played by people for a combination of per-sonal enjoyment and external rewards.* This means that participation in sports involves a combination of two sets of motivations. One set is based in the internal satisfactions associated with expression, freedom, spontaneity, and the pure joy of participation; the other set is based in external satisfactions associated with displaying physical skills in public and receiving approval, status, or material rewards for performing well. When we define sports in this way, we can distinguish them from pure **play** and from **dramatic spectacle.** An example of pure play would be three four-year olds who, during a recess period, spontaneously run around a playground, yelling joyfully while they throw playground balls in whatever directions they feel like throwing them in. Of course, it makes sociological sense to distinguish this type of behavior, motivated *exclusively* by personal enjoyment, from what happens in sports. An example of dramatic spectacle would be four professional wrestlers paid to entertain spectators by staging a cleverly choreographed tag-team match in which the ring and the referee are performance props. It also makes sociological sense to distinguish this type of physical activity, motivated *exclusively* by a desire to perform for the approval of others, from what happens in sports.

Does this mean that sports do not involve play or spectacle? No, it means that sports, according to this definition, involve combinations of both. It is the combination of intrinsic enjoyment and the desire to display physical skills, and the effort to preserve some sort of balance between these two factors, that distinguish sports from either play or dramatic spectacle. People who define sports in this way might complain when physical activities are not "organized enough" to enable them to know what's going on; they also might complain when they see activities that are so carefully organized for entertainment purposes that they seem to be "fake."

In summary, many sociologists feel it is important to define sports in order distinguish them from other activities that are sociologically dissimilar. This is a practical approach to defining sports, but it has potentially serious problems associated with it. For example, when we focus our attention on institutionalized, competitive activities, we may overlook physical activities in the lives of many people who have neither the resources to formally organize those activities nor the desire to make their activities competitive. In other words, we may spend all our time considering the physical activities of relatively select groups in society, because those groups have the power to formally organize physical activities and the desire to make those activities competitive. If this happens, we can create the impression that the activities of these select groups are more important parts of culture than the activities of other groups. This, in turn, could contribute to the marginalization of groups who have neither the resources nor the time to play organized sports, or who are not attracted to competitive activities.

Ironically, this outcome would reinforce the very ideas and organization that may have disadvantaged these groups in the first place, and we would be doing this in the name of science! But if we are aware of this potential problem, we still can ask critical questions about how sports have become what they are in particular societies and what social purposes they serve. We also can ask questions about how sports are connected to power, privilege, and social relations, and about

Many sociologists define sport precisely, so that they can distinguish situations such as organized wrestling meets from both the informal play of children and the spectacle of professional wrestling. High school and college wrestling are sociologically different both from wrestling that might go on in a family room, and from a highly hyped match that pits Hulk Hogan against the British Bulldog. (Bob Jackson, Colorado Springs *Gazette*)

the changes needed to involve more people in the determination of what sports could and should be in society. However, when we ask such questions we may begin to wonder if there is another way to deal with the definition of sports, a way that does not give priority to organized sports. This has led some scholars to seek an alternative approach to defining sports.

An Alternative Approach to Defining Sports

Instead of using a single definition of sports, some scholars ask two definition-type questions about sports in a particular society: (1) What gets to count as a sport? and (2) Whose sports count the most? Asking these questions does not limit the analysis of sports in ways that might happen when a precise definition is used. In fact, asking these questions forces researchers to dig into the social and cultural contexts in which ideas are formed about physical activities. The researchers must explain how and why some physical activities come to be defined as sports and then included as culturally important activities in the social life of a particular group or society.

Those who use this alternative approach do not describe sports with a single definition. When they are asked, "What is sport?" they say, "Well, that depends on whom you ask, when you ask, and where you ask." They explain that not everyone has the same way of looking at and defining sports, and that ideas about sports vary over time and from one place to another. For example, they might note that many people who grew up at the end of the nineteenth century in England would be horrified, confused, or astonished by what people in the U.S. today consider to be sports. And people who watch NFL football games today would look at many activities that were considered sports in nineteenth-century England and say they were not "real" sports because participants did not train, compete according to schedules, play in leagues, or strive to set records and win championships. And who knows what people in the year 2100

will think of what many of us define as sports today?

Those who use this alternative approach to defining sports also note numerous cultural differences in how people identify sports and include them into their lives. In cultures that emphasize cooperative relationships, the idea that people should compete with each other for rewards might be defined as disruptive, if not immoral; and for people in cultures that emphasize competition, physical activities and games that have no winners may seem pointless. These cultural differences are important to understand. Instead of letting a definition of sport shape what should be studied, those who use this alternative approach would do research based on what the people in particular cultural settings thought was important in their own lives.

The assumption underlying this approach is that sports themselves are "contested activities." In other words, there is no universal agreement about the meaning, purpose, and organization of sports; there is no universal agreement about who will participate in sports, about the circumstances under which participation will occur, or about who will sponsor sports or the reasons underlying sponsorship. All these things vary over time from group to group and society to society. The most important sociological issue to recognize when using this approach is that people in particular places at particular times struggle over *whose* ideas about sports will get to count as *the* ideas in a group or society. A guide for thinking about these issues is in the box titled Sports as Contested Activities on pp. 24–25.

Struggles over whose ideas get to count when it comes to the forms and meanings of sports are much more common than you might think. Consider the different ways *sports* might be defined and the different meanings associated with those definitions in connection with the following decisions:

- Whether children younger than six years old should be allowed to play *sports*, and how youth *sports* ought to be organized and what they ought to mean.

encourge who, what

- Whether money from a local youth *sport* program ought to be given to a group teaching young girls to jump rope or to a group forming a new roller hockey league at a local skating rink.
- Whether a youth *sport* director in a community *sport* program ought to budget funds for a competitive dancing program for children.
- Whether a state high school activities association ought to include cheerleading as an official high school *sport*.
- Whether skateboarding and hacky sack ought to be included in a university intramural *sport* program.
- Whether aerobics and Tae Kwon Do ought to be added to an intercollegiate *sport* program.
- Whether tenpin bowling, ballroom dancing, darts, or women's softball ought to be recognized as Olympic *sports*.
- Whether a permit to use a *sport* field in public park ought to be given to a group that wants to throw frisbees freely for a couple of hours or to a softball team that plays in a community *sport* league.
- Whether synchronized swimming events ought to be covered in the *sports* section of a city newspaper, or in the lifestyle section.
- Whether an editor ought to assign a *sport* reporter to a cheerleading clinic attracting hundreds of local girls or to a press conference with boxer Mike Tyson.
- Whether the headline on the front page of the *sports* section ought be about a local woman who just climbed Mount Everest or about an NFL game played by a team located in a city sixty miles away.
- Whether a corporate *sport* sponsorship should be awarded to a beach volleyball league or to a fitness walking program for older people.

- Whether Hulk Hogan should be approved as a nominee for a "*sports*man of the year" award.
- Whether it is more important to preserve traditional folk games (*sports?*) in local communities or to build expensive facilities so some people can play the *sports* they see on satellite TV.

Some of these issues may seem strange, but they raise important questions about what activities get to count as sports in certain societies at certain points in time. And they also raise questions about the usefulness of a single definition of sports. For example, if sports are institutionalized, competitive physical activities played to achieve internal and external rewards, then why aren't competitive dancing, aerobics, jump roping, cheerleading, and synchronized swimming always considered to be sports? They all fit the definition. The fact that they are not considered sports when it comes to important issues like sponsorships, funding, and formal recognition raises two questions: what gets to count as a sport in a society, and who determines what gets to count as a sport?

Answering these questions requires a careful analysis of the cultural context in which decisions are made in everyday life. Consider the following scenario as an illustration of this point.

Let us say that street roller hockey is growing in popularity among middle-class boys and some girls in many suburban communities around the United States. At the same time, various forms of jump roping are growing in popularity among African American girls living in low-income areas of big cities and small southern towns.

Now, think about answering the following questions. Which of these two activities would be most likely to get to count as a sport in U.S. culture? Would the answer to this question depend on funding or media sports coverage? How would these things be determined, who would determine them, and whose interests would be served in the process?

REFLECT ON SPORT

Sports as Contested Activities

When sociologists say that sports are "contested activities," they mean that through history people have differed in their ideas about what sports could and should be. These differences have led to struggles over the following three primary, interrelated issues.

1. What is the meaning, purpose, and organization of sports?

   The struggles over this issue have focused on things such as the following:

   - What activities will be defined as "official" sports?

   - What will be the relative importance of different types of physical skills in those activities? Will strength and speed, for example, be more important than flexibility and balance?

   - How will the sport experience be evaluated? Will emotional enjoyment or achievement be more important? Will fun and physical pleasure be more important than performance outcomes? How will "fun" be defined by sport participants?

   - What types of performance outcomes will be important and how will success be defined, measured, and rewarded? Will the most valued rewards be intrinsic or extrinsic? Will they go to the person who completes an event, the one who achieves a personal best, the one who outscores or dominates others in terms of scores or some other measure, or the one who lives through the experience without being seriously injured or killed?

   - How will excellence be defined—in terms of one's abilities to be tough, aggressive, and dominate others; in terms of all-around abilities to do different things well; or in terms of being able to maximize enjoyment for self and others?

2. Who will participate in sports and under what conditions will this participation occur?

   The struggles over this issue have focused on things such as the following:

   - Will females and males be involved in the same sports? Will they play at the same time or be segregated by sex? Will some sports be considered girls' and women's sports and others considered boys' and men's sports? On what basis will these distinctions be made? Will rewards for achievement be the same for females and males?

   - Will sport participation be open to people regardless of their social class and wealth? Will the rulers and the ruled, the wealthy and the poor, the powerful and the powerless play together? Will they be segregated, and for what reasons? Will participation opportunities be equal? Will participation be subsidized by sponsors?

   - Will skin color or ethnicity be related to participation? Will blacks and whites, and people from different ethnic backgrounds, be encouraged to play together? Will they be segregated? Will some be banned from certain

Answering these questions could be tricky, and it would require careful consideration of issues related to U.S. society and culture. Being considered a sport often depends on issues related to resources, organization, social "connections," and visibility. In the quest to be counted as a sport, roller hockey would draw on the resources of middle-class families, whereas jump roping would be less able to count on financial support

from participants' families. In the absence of family funding, would local governments in cities and small towns provide funds to promote and support jump roping as a sport? Under what conditions might this happen? My guess is that it would be unlikely and would occur only if the girls were seen as a threat to community safety and government agencies saw a need to "keep them off the streets."

sports? Will the meanings given to skin color influence participation patterns?

- Will age be a factor in whether people are encouraged or discouraged from participating in sports? Will expectations vary for people of different ages? For what reasons might they vary?

- Will able-bodied people and the disabled have the same opportunities? Will they play together or be segregated? For what reasons will integration or segregation occur, and who will benefit from what is decided?

- Will gay men and lesbians be included in sports in the same way heterosexual people are? Will homosexual persons be encouraged to participate in all sports?

- Will athletes be in control of the conditions under which they play sports? Will they have the rights and the power to change those conditions to meet their own needs and interests? Will they be paid? Will they be rewarded in noncash terms? How much will players be rewarded and how will this be determined?

3. How will sports be sponsored, and what will be the reasons for sponsorship?

The struggles over this issue have focused on things such as the following:

- Will sports be sponsored by public agencies and organizations for the sake of the "public good"? Who will determine the public good, and how will they define what it means?

- Will sports be sponsored by nonprofit groups and organizations? Will the reasons for their sponsorship be related to their organizational philosophies, to the interests of all group members, or to the interests of some group members over others?

- Will sports be sponsored by private commercial organizations? Will their sponsorships be designed for the benefit of athletes and communities or for the purpose of maximizing profits and increasing their power in society?

- To what extent will sponsors control the sports and the athletes they support? What will be the legal rights of sponsors relative to those of athletes and others involved in sports?

As you can see, sports are indeed contested activities! These are just a few of the things people struggle over in connection with sports. And these struggles never result in permanent resolutions. Struggles are renewed constantly as interests change; as power shifts; as the meanings associated with age, skin color, ethnicity, gender, and disability change; and as economic, political, and legal forces take new and different forms.

This means that any definition of sport we develop tends to restrict the scope of our study. This may be helpful sometimes, but we always should use our definition with caution.

Other issues also would come into play. The middle-class people associated with roller hockey might have had years of experience when it comes to forming organizations, becoming officially recognized, getting volunteers to run things, and setting up press conferences; such experience might be in shorter supply in low-income areas in cities and small towns, as might available volunteers. The same could be true when it came to the social "connections" needed to reserve the spaces and facilities for events, to enlist sponsors to fund events, and to get the media to cover events.

If either roller hockey or jump roping could get newspaper or television coverage, it would be a key factor in the quest to count as a sport in the culture as a whole. Which activity would be most likely to get this coverage? On what basis would

What gets to count as a sport in society? Discussions of this question show that sports cannot be understood apart from cultural values and power relations in a society. As ideas about gender have changed over the past three decades, physical activities such as rhythmic gymnastics are now considered to be sports, despite resistance from some who believe that "real" sports must reflect "manly" attributes. Women athletes and spectators have more power in society today than they have had in the past. (Colorado Springs *Gazette*)

newspaper editors and programming people for television companies make their decisions? Would they be more interested in activities played by boys and men or in those played by girls and women? Would they be more interested in activities involving speed and physical contact or in activities involving coordination and cooperation? What dominant values and priorities in U.S. culture would influence their decisions? How did those values and priorities come to be? Whom do they favor? Whom do they disadvantage?

The issues raised by asking what gets to count as sport are challenging. They force us to look at the cultures in which people live their lives and make decisions about what is important (See the box titled Sports as Contested Activities, pp. 24–25).

SUMMARY

CONCLUSION: WHY STUDY SPORTS?

Sociology is the study of the social arrangements people create as they live together and make sense of their lives. Sociologists are concerned with social issues, social relationships, social organization, and social change. Their overall goal is to enable people to understand, control, and change their lives so human needs among all categories of people are met at both individual and group levels.

Sociologists study sports as parts of culture. They look at sports in terms of their importance in people's lives, how they are organized, and their connections to cultural ideology and major spheres of social life. Research in the sociology of sport helps us understand sports as social phenomena, but beyond that, often leads to the discovery of problems based in the structure and organization of sports or of society itself. When this happens, the recommendations sociologists make may threaten those who want sport activities and programs to remain as they are now. Therefore, sociology sometimes creates controversies.

The sociology of sport is a new field with roots in both sociology and physical education. It is likely to grow in the future because it is supported by professional organizations and a body of literature in academic journals. However, growth also depends on whether those of us in the field are able to make meaningful contributions to the way people live their lives.

Complicating the issue of future growth is the fact that not everyone in the field agrees on how to "do" sociology of sport. Some use a *scientific expert model* to guide their work, while others use a *critical transformation model*. Those using the scientific expert model emphasize questions of organization and efficiency, while those using the critical transformation model emphasize fairness and the empowerment of those who lack resources or have been pushed to the margins of society. Differences between these two approaches raise important questions about the production and use of scientific knowledge. Many of us in the field are currently debating these questions.

Some scholars in the field define sports as activities involving (1) the use of physical skill, prowess, or exertion, (2) institutionalized competition, and (3) the combination of intrinsic and extrinsic reasons for participation. Such a definition can be problematic unless it is seen as a limited tool for distinguishing different forms of socially important activities in people's lives. A sociologist who takes a single definition of sports too seriously can focus attention primarily on the lives of people who have the resources and the desire to develop formally organized and competitive physical activities. For this reason, some scholars recommend that instead of using a single definition of sports, sociologists should ask what gets to count as sports in different cultures at different points in time. This question focuses attention on the relationship between sports and power and privilege in society, and leads more directly to the consideration of issues related to transforming social life so that more people have access to the resources they need to make their lives meaningful.

SUGGESTED READINGS

Coakley, J., and E. Dunning, eds. Forthcoming. *Handbook of sport and society.* London: Sage (*forty-two chapters on the ways sports are studied as social phenomena, and on the sociology of sport in various countries and regions around the world*).

Frey, J., and D. S. Eitzen. 1991. Sport and society. *Annual Review of Sociology* 17: 503–22 (*a concise overview* of the sociology of sport with attention given to the prominence of sport as a part of contemporary societies).

Guttmann, A. 1988. *A whole new ballgame: An interpretation of American sports.* Chapel Hill, NC: The University of North Carolina Press (*although this book focuses on the U.S., it presents a thoughtful history of the changing approaches to sport in U.S. culture*).

Morgan, W. J., and K. V. Meier, eds. 1988. *Philosophic inquiry in sport.* Champaign, IL: Human Kinetics (*especially the eight articles and bibliography in Part I, The nature of sport, play, and game*).

Wilson, J. 1994. Playing by the rules: *Sport, society and the state.* Detroit: Wayne State University Press (*especially chapters 1 and 2, in which the author defines sports and describes major sociological concepts used in the sociological study of sports*).

Yiannakis, A., T. D. McIntyre, and M. J. Melnick, eds. 1993. *Sport sociology: Contemporary themes.* Dubuque, IA: Kendall/Hunt (*Unit I, "The emergence and development of the sociology of sport", provides three articles detailing the history of the field, major research issues, and controversies in the field*).

2

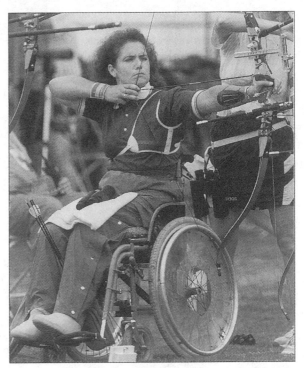

(Elise Amendola, AP/Wide World Photos)

Using Social Theories
What can they tell us about sports in society?

It is legitimate to ask ourselves how sports can truly contribute to the improvement of modern society. We are all concerned on this account because sports can degenerate into manifestations which dishonor the noble ideals which they can promote. . . .

Pope John Paul II (1989)

Sports are a tremendous force for the status quo. . . . They do distract millions from more serious thoughts—as do . . . all other "escape" entertainments. As mass entertainment, they are definitely antirevolutionary.

Leonard Koppett, sports reporter and columnist (1994)

Hockey is our national glue. It defines Canada and Canadians. We have so few people in such a large land . . . . But hockey holds us together.

Roy Green, host of *Toronto's Talk* radio program (1996)

Sport is a women's issue because female sport participation empowers women, thereby inexorably changing everything.

Mariah Burton Nelson, writer and former professional basketball player (1994)

Students sometimes become either bored or confused when sociologists talk about theory. Social theories are often explained in ways that make them seem unrelated to people's lives. I don't want this to happen in this chapter, so I will talk about theories in a down-to-earth, practical, and personal way.

The goals of this chapter are to do the following:

1. Explain what is involved in theorizing about social life.
2. Describe and critique major theoretical approaches used by sociologists who study sports.
3. Provide examples of research inspired by these theoretical approaches.
4. Compare the policy implications of major theoretical approaches.

THEORIES IN SOCIOLOGY

Whenever we ask why our social world is the way it is and then imagine how it might be changed, we are "theorizing" (hooks, 1992). Theorizing involves a combination of description, reflection, and analysis. When we theorize, we aren't required to use big words, complex sentences, and long paragraphs. In fact, the best theories are those we can understand and then use to make sense out of the world and empower ourselves as we deal with the world.

Most of the theorizing sociologists have done over the past 150 years has been motivated by a desire to synthesize information about the social world and develop general explanations for how and why social life is organized in particular ways. Underlying this motivation has been the belief that if we could identify the key forces that drive and shape social life, we could become masters of our own destiny. In other words, if we developed a valid and reliable theory about how the social world works, we could outline rational strategies for organizing societies in progressively efficient and satisfying ways.

This hope that humans could make the world better and more controllable through the use of knowledge and science was the foundation of the Enlightenment period in the eighteenth century, and marked the beginning of what we call "modernism" in Western societies. **Modernism** is an approach to life based on the idea that humankind can achieve progress through the use of rationality, science, and technology. Modernism gave rise to the belief that people could use social science to discover the knowledge needed to make societies more efficient, just, and harmonious. And as knowledge accumulated, human beings could bring societies closer and closer to perfection.

Most sociologists traditionally have wanted to be a part of this process of collecting information, testing theories, and eventually discovering scientific "truths" about how the social world works and how it might be controlled. Many have searched for "social laws" and "cause-effect relationships" that would explain all social life—regardless of time, place, and culture. These sociologists have tried to find the building blocks of social life by identifying the types of relationships and organizational structures that enable people to live satisfying lives in groups and societies. This search for the general foundations and building blocks of all societies has taken sociologists in different directions depending on their assumptions and viewpoints, as you will see in the following sections of this chapter.

But not all sociologists have joined in the search for a general theory of social life. Some have argued that it is not possible to develop a theory that explains all social life, and that the search for such a theory leads sociologists to ignore the diversity, complexity, and contradictions that are clearly a part of everyday life. Others argue that the quest for a general theory of society distracts sociologists from focusing on specific problems and identifying practical ways for people to solve problems fairly as they live their lives together. Finally, some sociologists have abandoned the search for a general theory of social life because they realize there are many different perspectives or standpoints from which to study and understand the world.

My point in this section is that sociologists in the 1990s use many different theoretical approaches as they ask questions and think about social life, and as they study sports. This means that people in the sociology of sport take many different directions when it comes to theorizing and doing research on sports. But before I discuss social theories and sports, I want to provide additional reasons for the many different theoretical approaches used in sociology and the sociology of sport. *Why* are there so many?

Theoretical diversity in sociology reflects the diversity and complexity of social life itself. Societies are complex phenomena. They have their own histories, dynamics, and cultures. And they can be viewed from many different perspectives. The diversity of theoretical approaches used in sociology today results from the recognition that no single perspective can tell us all we need to know about social life. Some very important changes in our world have promoted this recognition.

First, feminist scholars and women around the world have made convincing arguments that theories based primarily or solely on men's experiences and perspectives do not tell the whole story about social life. They note that theories ignoring the experiences and perspectives of 50 percent of the world's population are incomplete at best and dangerous at worst. These scholars have explained how social life and theories about social life are influenced by the relative power of men and women in society and by *who* does the theorizing about society. This has led to new theoretical approaches in science as a whole, but especially in sociology.

Second, global social changes have forced social scientists from North America and northern and western Europe to realize that their theories about social life are based on a "Eurocentric viewpoint" that is irrelevant to other parts of the world. As people around the world have become more interconnected, the peoples of Asia, Latin America, and Africa have contributed new ways of understanding social life. These new theoretical approaches are grounded in the experiences and perspectives of peoples who have not experienced industrialization or have experienced it in forms quite different from those found in Europe and North America. Some of these new theories have been developed out of the experiences of those who have lived under the colonial rule of Euro-American nations. And it is easy to understand that theories about social life developed by the colonized would be different from theories developed by the colonizers.

Third, new communications technologies have created a rapidly changing and diverse stream of computer-based and media-generated images and simulations that have altered our sense of what is real and what isn't. These mediated and image-based forms of reality have led some sociologists to develop new theoretical approaches that enable them to consider dimensions of social life outside traditional social boundaries and fixed social structures.

Fourth, sociologists who realize that science itself is a part of culture have begun to reject theories they feel have maintained the power and privilege of an elite few rather than making social life more fair for everyone. These sociologists have worked to develop new theoretical approaches that focus on specific problems and generate knowledge that disadvantaged people can use to gain more control over their lives. These approaches are very different from the approaches most sociologists have used in the past.

THEORIES ABOUT SPORTS AND SOCIETY

Through the 1970s most sociologists used one of two general theories of social life—functionalist theory and conflict theory—to guide their analyses of sports in society. Each of these theoretical approaches is based on different assumptions about the foundation of social order in society, each leads to different questions about social life and about sports, and each leads to different conclusions about the importance and consequences of sports in society. The differences between functionalist theory and conflict theory are outlined in table 2–1 on pp. 38–40 and explained in the next two sections.

Functionalist Theory: Sports Are an Inspiration

Functionalist theory is based on the idea that we best can study society by using a "systems" approach. Sociologists who use functionalist theory assume that society is an organized system of interrelated parts held together by shared values and processes that create consensus among people.

According to functionalist theory, the driving force underlying all social life is the tendency for any social system to maintain itself in a state of balance so it continues to operate efficiently. This balance is achieved "naturally" as groups of people develop consensus, common values, and coordinated organization in the major spheres of social life (such as the family, education, the economy, government, religion, leisure, and sport). The theory assumes order itself to be natural. When behaviors or forms of organization contribute to this balance, they are described as **functional.** And when certain behaviors or forms of organization upset this balance, they are described as **dysfunctional.**

Functionalist theory also assumes that social change is dysfunctional unless it occurs in a

One assumption underlying functionalist theory is that social order depends on consensus and common values. Functionalists assume that established social institutions such as sports contribute to consensus and common values. (USA Volleyball)

gradual, evolutionary manner. When sociologists use functionalist theory they emphasize research questions focused on factors that promote or disrupt social stability, social structure, and social organization.

When sociologists use functionalist theory to explain how a society, community, school, family, or other social system works, they focus attention on how each part in the system contributes to the system's overall operation. For example, if Canadian society is the system being studied, a person using functionalist theory will be concerned with how the Canadian family, economy, government, education, religion, and sport are related to each other and how they all work together in contributing to the smooth operation of the society as a whole. The analysis will focus on the ways in which each of these different spheres of social life helps to keep the larger social system operating efficiently.

According to functionalist theory, the following four things must happen if a social system is to operate efficiently:

1. First, there must be methods for teaching people in the system the basic values and rules they are supposed to live by. And since tension and frustration are created when people must conform to specific values and rules, there also must be opportunities for people in society to release this tension and frustration in harmless ways.
2. Second, the system must contain social mechanisms for bringing people together and establishing cohesive and integrated social relationships.
3. Third, there must be methods for teaching people in the system what goals are important and how they should go about achieving those goals.
4. Fourth, the social system must contain built-in mechanisms for responding to social and environmental changes occurring outside the system, while preserving order inside the system.

According to functionalist theory, these four things represent the building blocks of social order in any society. And when sociologists use functionalist theory to study sports, they focus their attention on how sports function to help meet these four *system needs*.

FUNCTIONALIST THEORY AND RESEARCH ON SPORT Theories always influence the questions we ask in our research. Sociologists using functionalist theory usually have asked questions about how sports "fit into" social life and contribute to stability and social progress in communities and societies. Their questions have led them to search for ways sports contribute to the four basic needs of social systems, and their studies generally have fallen into the following four categories:

1. *Studies of the relationship between sport participation and the development of good character.* These studies examine whether sports provide socialization experiences through which people learn the values and rules of society, and whether sports provide settings in which people can release tension and frustration in safe ways so that order and stability in society are preserved. We discuss this issue and examples of these studies in chapters 4 to 7.
2. *Studies of sports and social integration in groups, communities, and societies.* These studies examine whether sports bring people together and create the unity and integration that functionalists assume to be the basis for order and efficiency in society. We discuss this issue and examples of these studies in chapters 9 and 13.
3. *Studies of sport participation and achievement motivation.* These studies examine whether sports teach people to be committed to social progress as it is defined in their society, and whether sport participation teaches the importance of working hard to achieve social progress. We discuss this issue and examples of these studies in chapters 4 and 10.

4. *Studies of sports participation and the develop-ment of abilities needed to defend society against external threats.* These studies examine whether sport participation creates survival skills and prepares people to help their soci-eties survive in the face of external social and environmental changes. Although the issue of sports and military readiness has not been studied for some time, we discuss the general issue of health and wellness in a number of the following chapters.

In summary, functionalist theory focuses attention on how sports satisfy the needs of so-cial systems. Those using functionalist theory often study how sports contribute to personal growth and the preservation of social order at all levels of social organization. This is why a func-tionalist approach is often popular among people who have a vested interest in preserving order and stability in society. These people want soci-ology to tell them how sports contribute to the communities in which they live. They are inter-ested in seeing how sports provide valuable lessons for young people and opportunities for people of all ages to release tension and frustra-tion in harmless ways. They want to see how sports strengthen "social togetherness" by giving everyone in their group or society something to share. They also want to know how sports can provide models for setting and achieving goals in their group or society. And finally, they tend to see sports as activities that improve health and fitness and keep their country prepared to de-fend itself economically and militarily. These people like functionalist theory because it leads to the conclusion that *sports are an inspiration for both individuals and societies.*

Throughout the world, people have used a functionalist approach to make decisions about sports and sport programs at both the national and local levels. Those using it have encouraged the development and growth of organized youth sports, the continued funding of varsity sports in high schools and colleges, the growth of sport opportunities for girls and women, the use of

sports in military training, and the promotion of the Olympic Games to maintain international goodwill. We are exposed constantly to analyses of sports based on a functionalist approach as we read about sports in the newspapers and watch sports on television. This widespread use of functionalist theory makes it important for us to be aware of its limitations.

LIMITATIONS OF FUNCTIONALIST THEORY The *first* problem with functionalist theory is that it usually leads to exaggerated statements about the positive effects of sports. This occurs because it is based on the assump-tion that social systems tend to reject any form of social organization that does not contribute to overall order and efficiency. Therefore, ac-cording to functionalists, if sports were dysfunc-tional in social systems, they would not have ex-isted for so many years in many societies. However, this conclusion ignores cases where sports continue to exist even though they create negative consequences for some groups of peo-ple in a society. For example, the gender logic that has been perpetuated in connection with sports certainly has worked to the disadvantage of girls and women in society, just as the class logic perpetuated by sports has worked to the disadvantage of those who are poor. This con-clusion that sports would not exist if they were dysfunctional also ignores cases where sports distort values and norms and destroy motivation among some people, create tensions and frus-tration and social friction, interfere with the set-ting and achieving of important goals, and di-vert people's attention away from crucial social problems in the system.

The *second* problem is that functionalist the-ory is based on the assumption that the needs of all groups within a society are the same as the needs of the society as a whole. The existence of real conflicts of interest within a society is incon-sistent with the functionalist assumption that all social systems are naturally held together in a state of balance. Therefore, when people use functionalist theory to study sports, they have a tendency to overlook cases where sports benefit

TANK MᶜNAMARA®   by Jeff Millar & Bill Hinds

Sociologists who have used functionalist theory to guide their analysis of sport in society often have ignored the possibility that sports may generate conflict by supporting the interests of some groups in society over others. The women in this cartoon might prefer to use conflict theory or some form of critical or feminist theory to study and understand sport in society.

some groups more than others within a community or society. This limits an understanding of social life, and it discourages a detailed discussion of social change and the ways sports are related to processes of change in society.

The *third* problem is that those using functionalist theory are so concerned with discovering how sports serve basic system needs that they disregard the idea that sports are "social constructions" created and defined by members of society to promote their own interests and the interests of the groups to which they belong. Therefore, functionalist approaches overlook how sports might promote the interests of those with power and wealth, and thereby contribute to disruptive forms of social inequality in societies.

In sociology, the general theory that draws attention to social problems, changes, and inequalities in society is called **conflict theory.**

Conflict Theory: Sports Are an Opiate

Most people living in societies that have market economies (the U.S., Canada, England, Australia, and many others) don't like conflict theory, because it doesn't fit with dominant ideas about how societies should and do work. Sociologists using conflict theory do not view society as

a relatively stable system of interrelated parts held together by common values and consensus; instead, they view it as an ever-changing set of relationships characterized by inherent differences of economic interests.

Social order, according to conflict theory, exists because some groups of people have resources enabling them to coerce and subtly manipulate others to accept their view of the world as the correct view. This means that anyone using conflict theory is concerned with "class relations." **Class relations** refers to social processes revolving around who has economic power, how economic power is used, and who is advantaged or disadvantaged by economic factors in a society. Studies of class relations focus on processes of change and the consequences of social inequality in society, rather than on what is required to keep society stable and orderly.

Conflict theory is based on an updated version of the ideas of Karl Marx. Although it can be used to describe and understand any situation in which masses of people lack resources and have little control over their lives, it usually has been used to study countries having market economies—that is, all countries that have capitalist economic systems.

According to conflict theory, sports are determined or shaped by economic factors and the needs of capital in market economies. The process through which this occurs goes like this:

1. All market (or capitalist) economies require the development of highly efficient work processes through which an ever-increasing amount of consumer goods can be mass produced.
2. To meet this need for efficiency, it is necessary for societies to create large industrial bureaucracies.
3. Within industrial bureaucracies, the vast majority of workers end up performing highly specialized and alienating jobs.
4. Because of the lack of control and lack of excitement on the job, workers are constantly searching for activities offering a combination of escape and tension-producing excitement.
5. Within societies with market economies, these workers are subtly coerced and manipulated (primarily through media advertising) to seek the satisfaction they need through consumerism and mass entertainment spectacles.
6. Under these social conditions, sports emerge as especially popular forms of entertainment spectacles for two reasons. First, sports can be tied to product consumption through the promotion and sale of equipment, tickets, and items linked to teams and players (for example, official NFL clothing, Air Jordan athletic shoes, and University of Miami coffee cups). Second, sports can be organized to emphasize values and processes that privilege the economically powerful while turning others into efficient and obedient workers.

According to conflict theory, sports ultimately promote the interests of people with economic power in societies with market economies. This is because sports keep workers emotionally focused on escapist activities that distract them from the need to make changes in the way social life is organized. Thus, conflict theorists say that sports are distorted forms of physical exercise shaped by those possessing power and resources in capitalist societies. Those using conflict theory see sports as an *opiate*, not an inspiration.

CONFLICT THEORY AND RESEARCH ON SPORTS Sociologists who use conflict theory usually ask questions about how sports perpetuate the power and privilege of elite groups in society, and how sports serve as tools of economic exploitation and oppression. Research inspired and guided by conflict theory generally falls into the following categories:

1. *Studies of how athletes become alienated from their own bodies.* These studies examine whether competitive sports leads athletes to define and experience their own bodies as tools of production, as machines designed to produce entertainment and profits for others rather than feelings of pleasure for themselves (Brohm, 1978). These studies also examine whether athletes might use performance-enhancing drugs because they are victims of profit-making sport systems that make winning all-important. We discuss this issue and examples of these studies in chapters 4 to 7.
2. *Studies of how sports can be used to coerce and control people so they will not question the way social life is organized.* These studies examine whether sports focus popular attention on games and scores rather than on finding solutions to social, economic, and political problems in society. We discuss this issue in most of the following chapters.
3. *Studies of sports and the development of commercialism in society.* These studies examine whether sports are used to promote capitalist expansion in either of two ways: by creating profits for large corporations and wealthy people, or by serving as an advertising medium to encourage people in society to use consumption as an indicator of self-worth and quality of life. These studies also

examine issues of social inequality in society and ways sport might reflect and perpetuate inequality. These issues are discussed in chapter 4 and chapters 10 to 13.

4. *Studies of sports and various forms of nationalism and militarism.* These studies examine whether sports create superficial, irrational, and potentially harmful feelings of nationalistic pride, and whether sports might be used to justify violence in society, especially violence initiated by the state for the purpose of protecting the interests of economically powerful groups. We discuss these issues and examples of studies in chapter 7.

5. *Studies of sports and racism and sexism.* These studies examine whether sports divide people by race and gender, perpetuate racial stereotypes and distorted definitions of masculinity and femininity, and create racial and gender inequities in society. We discuss these issues and examples of studies in chapters 8 and 9.

In summary, conflict theory focuses attention on how powerful people use sports to promote attitudes and relationships enabling them to maintain their power and privilege. Like functionalist theory, it is based on the assumption that social life is driven and shaped by specific societal "needs," although conflict theory emphasizes the "needs of capital" rather than general "system needs." Conflict theory also focuses attention on how sports reflect and perpetuate the unequal distribution of power and economic resources in societies. This leads to an emphasis on the negative consequences of sports and the conclusion that radical changes are needed in sports and society as a whole. In fact, the goal of most conflict theorists in the sociology of sport is to bring about the development of a humane and creative society so that sports can become sources of expression, creative energy, and physical well-being. But until this happens, conflict theorists will continue to conclude that *sports are an opiate.*

Most beginning students in the sociology of sport aren't comfortable with conflict theory. It doesn't fit with dominant ideas about sports in society as a whole, and students say it is too negative and too critical of their sports and their societies. Many students, especially those who accept sports and society as they are organized currently, prefer functionalist theory, because it does not lead to conclusions that threaten the structure of either sports or society. However, conflict theory has been very useful in calling attention to the problems in sports and the need for changes in sports and society as a whole.

LIMITATIONS OF CONFLICT THEORY
Conflict theory, like functionalist theory, has weaknesses. *First*, it assumes that all social life is driven and shaped only by economic factors, by "market needs." Conflict theory focuses on the relationship between the economic "haves" and "have-nots" in society. It assumes that since the "haves" own the means of production in market economies, they possess economic power and use that power to control and exploit the labor of "have-nots." It also assumes that the "have-nots" are destined to be the victims of economic exploitation and live lives characterized by powerlessness and alienation. These assumptions lead people who use conflict theory to focus exclusively on economic factors when they study sports. However, many sports, especially those emphasizing recreation and mass participation, cannot be explained totally in terms of the interests of economically powerful people in society.

Second, conflict theory ignores the importance of gender, race, ethnicity, age, sexual orientation, and other factors when it comes to explaining how people identify themselves, relate to others, and organize social life. Conflict theory is based on the Marxist assumption that all history and social organization revolves around economic factors. Therefore, those who use conflict theory to study sports do not acknowledge that inequalities in society might be related to something other than struggles between social classes.

Table 2–1 Functionalism, conflict theory, and critical theory: a summary and comparison

Functionalism	Conflict Theory	Critical Theory	Feminist Theory	Interactionist Theory
I. ASSUMPTIONS ABOUT THE SOCIAL ORDER				
Social order is based on consensus, common values, and interrelated subsystems.	Social order is based on coercion, exploitation, and subtle manipulation of individuals.	Social order is negotiated by people within constraints imposed by historical forces, cultural ideology, and the material conditions of social life.	Social order reflects the values, experiences, and interests of men through history.	Social order depends on shared meanings created and maintained by people as they define the world around them, make decisions, take action, form relationships, and reflect on who they are and how they are connected to their social worlds.
II. MAJOR CONCERNS IN THE STUDY OF SOCIETY				
What are the essential parts in the structure of social systems? How do social systems continue to operate smoothly?	How is power distributed and used in society? How do societies change, and what can be done to promote change?	How is social life produced and reproduced through social relationships and cultural practices? How do people become agents for making society into what it could and should be?	How does social life reflect gender relations in society? How do gender relations impact the lives of men and women?	How are meanings and identities created through communication and social interaction? How do meanings and identities serve as a foundation for human understanding, individual behavior, social relationships, and culture?

Continued

III. MAJOR CONCERNS IN THE STUDY OF SPORT

How does sport contribute to basic social system needs, such as pattern maintenance and tension management, integration, goal attainment, and adaptation?	How is sport related to alienation, coercion and social control, commercialism, nationalism and militarism, sexism, and racism? How is sport used to maintain the interests of the power elite?	What "gets to count" as sports in a society? How have sports been defined and organized in certain ways? How are sports connected to processes of development and change in society?	How do sports reproduce existing forms of gender relations? How might sports become sites for challenging/opposing dominant ideas about masculinity and femininity?	What does it mean to be an athlete? How do people come to think of themselves as athletes? How are sport cultures and subcultures created and maintained, and what are their characteristics?

IV. MAJOR CONCLUSIONS ABOUT THE SPORT-SOCIETY RELATIONSHIP

Sport is a valuable social institution benefiting society as well as individual members of society. Sport is basically a *source of inspiration* on personal and social levels.	Sport is a distorted form of physical exercise shaped by the needs of capitalist economic systems. Sport lacks the creative and expressive elements of play; it is *an opiate*.	Sports are social constructions created in connection with social and power relations in society. Sports are sites at which the status quo can be reproduced or transformed. Sports are cultural practices that can repress or liberate, control or empower.	Dominant sport forms tend to reproduce traditional ideas about masculinity and femininity, although sports can be sites for challenging these ideas, especially those concerning femininity.	The formation and maintenance of an athlete's identity depends on reaffirmation through social interaction. Behavior in sports is best understood within the context of sport subcultures and in connection with the identities formed in these subcultures.

Continued

Table 2-1 Continued

	Functionalism	Conflict Theory	Critical Theory	Feminist Theory	Interactionist Theory
V. GOALS OF THE SOCIOLOGY OF SPORT	To discover ways in which sport's contribution to personal growth and the maintenance of social order can be maximized at all levels.	To promote development of a humane and creative society so that sport can be a source of expression, creative experiences, and physical well-being.	To discover how sports and sport forms in society are influenced by social relations, and to identify alternative sport forms that represent the interests of more people and enable previously underrepresented people to participate meaningfully as citizens in society.	To identify and promote sport forms that fit the values and experiences of women in a society, to use sports as sites for challenging and transforming current forms of gender relations, and to make sports more inclusive and equitable in society.	To describe in rich detail the social worlds that make up sports and serve as the contexts for developing identities, making decisions about what is important, and taking action on the basis of those definitions and decisions.
VI. MAJOR WEAKNESSES	Exaggerates positive consequences of sport; assumes that sports exist because they serve positive functions for all of society. Ignores differences and conflicts in society; assumes sports serve equally the needs of all people in society. Ignores economic and political issues in the creation of sports by people in society.	Deals with historical and economic factors in a deterministic way; ignores factors other than capitalism in analyzing sports in society. Focuses too much on men's high-performance spectator sports; overemphasizes the extent to which sports are shaped and controlled by the wealthy and powerful.	Does not provide a unified, clearly explained framework for understanding society and social processes. Provides no explicit guidelines for determining when sports either reproduce or transform the status quo. Has in the past been slow to inspire research on real-life sport experiences in society.	As a form of critical theory, comes in many different forms, which can be confusing. Can be confusing, because different forms of feminist theory have different assumptions about the origins, dynamics, and consequences of gender relations in society.	Does not identify how meanings, identities, and interactions in sports are related to material conditions and the social structure of society as a whole. Pays little attention to how sport choices are constrained by meanings associated with gender, race, ethnicity, disability, and age. Has in the past been focused on the mind and ignored the body and physical experiences.

Struggles related to gender, race, ethnicity, age, religion, sexual orientation, physical ability (being able-bodied or disabled) often are given low priority or ignored by conflict theorists.

Third, conflict theory ignores cases where sport participation consists of experiences that empower individuals and groups, even in capitalist societies. Many testimonials from athletes indicate that sports do more than alienate people from their own bodies, despite the fact that some athletes do take harmful drugs and use their bodies as tools of production. In fact, sport participation is sometimes a personally creative and liberating experience. Furthermore, sports may serve as sites for challenging and resisting the interests of economically powerful groups, and in some cases they could even be sites for transforming the way power is distributed in an organization or community (Birrell and Theberge, 1994a, b; Donnelly, 1988).

Therefore, the major problem with conflict theory is that it leads people to see sports as determined solely by economic forces and the needs of capital in society (Messner, 1984). However, things are seldom so simple. Even though sports are used as instruments of economic control and expansion in society, they also may be personally empowering activities and sites for resisting and even transforming how social life is organized in groups and communities. Other theoretical approaches have tried to take into account and explain the complexities of sports as social phenomena.

Critical Theories:
Sports Are Social Constructions

Most people in the sociology of sport no longer debate the relative merits of functionalist and conflict theories. Sociologists have not completely abandoned these theories, but they now are using various forms of what they refer to as *critical theories* to describe and understand the everyday realities of sports in the lives of individuals, groups, and societies. Columns 3 and 4 respectively in table 2–1 present critical theory generally and one specific type of critical theory: feminist theory.

People using critical theories assume that behavior and social life are limited by historical, social, and material conditions, but they do not assume that all social life is driven and shaped by a unified set of factors that exist outside of people's relationships with one another. Those using critical theories attempt to take into account the complexity and diversity of social life as they ask research questions and do studies for the purpose of making the world better—not more rational and efficient, but more fair, open to diversity, and democratic. Critical theories tend to focus on explaining particular problems and situations rather than seeking one "universal" explanation of social life.

Critical theories focus on *power* in social life; they consist of various approaches designed to understand where power comes from, how power works in different situations and in different aspects of people's lives, and how power shifts as people struggle over the many issues that affect their lives.

Critical theories are also about *action and political involvement*. All forms of critical theory have grown out of efforts to make social life more fair and open to diversity, and they have been used to guide the development of practical programs that promote equity, fairness, and openness. Most people who use critical theory are interested in explaining that all human relationships are grounded in political struggles over how social life should be defined and organized. These struggles occur in all aspects of people's lives. For example, they involve economic struggles over labor law, rights of workers, property ownership, and power structures in organizations; and they involve personal and legal struggles over family violence, child and spouse abuse, and women's control over their own bodies. In the case of sports, they involve struggles over basic questions such as these: What activities get to count as "sport"? How is it that sports have come to involve aggression, competition, and the rational pursuit of goals through the use of performance technology? Why is excellence in sports defined in terms of measurable achievements in highly specialized activities that have little to do with general fitness or life off the playing field?

Those using critical theory realize that dominant forms of sport in most societies have been socially constructed in ways that privilege some people over others, and they want to expose this fact and examine it in ways that will open the door for thinking about alternative ways of defining, organizing, and playing sports.

Critical theories come in many different forms. This makes them difficult to summarize. They encompass a variety of approaches to understanding social life, including those used by neo-Marxists, feminists, and people who do cultural studies.* We discuss feminist theories in the box on pp. 44–46. Most of these approaches have grown out of a desire to avoid the economic determinism of conflict theory and the pretentious quest of functionalist theory to explain all social life by discovering universal "social laws."

Critical theories have been used increasingly in the sociology of sport because more people recognize that they cannot explain sports simply in terms of the production needs of a market economy or the needs of all social systems to seek balance and equilibrium. Sociologists have turned to theoretical approaches allowing them to recognize that sports are created and organized by human beings as they use their power and resources in cultural struggles over values and how social life is organized.

Critical theories can be confusing because they are based on three ideas: (1) that agreement and conflict exist simultaneously in social life, (2) that agreement and shared values are never

permanent in any society because they depend on never-ending processes of negotiation, compromise, and coercion between various groups, and (3) that the bases for conflicts in any society change from one location to another as there are changes in historical circumstances and the political and economic organization of social life. This means that according to critical theories, the relationship between sports and society is never set once and for all time: sports change as historical conditions and political and economic forces change; sports change with new developments in government, education, the media, religion, and the family; and sports change with new ideas about masculinity and femininity and about race, ethnicity, age, sexual orientation, and physical ability. Therefore, critical theories help us ask questions such as the following. Why were sports in the past different from the way they are now? Why do sports take different forms in capitalist societies than in communal societies? Why were women not allowed to play certain sports in the past? Why were most sports racially segregated in the past, and how have patterns of racial and ethnic segregation changed over time? Why in certain societies have specialized sports and sport organizations developed around issues of sexuality (the Gay Games), mental and physical ability (the Special Olympics and the Paralympics), and age (the Senior Olympics and Senior Golf, among others)?

When people use critical theories to study sports, their analyses proceed along the following lines:

1. We cannot understand or analyze sports apart from the specific historical and cultural circumstances in which they exist; therefore, we must study sports in context.
2. The definition and organization of sports vary over time and from one group to another; therefore, we must study sports by identifying whose ideas about sports are most important when it comes to using resources to develop sports.

---

*People in cultural studies are concerned with the processes through which people's actions and interactions create, reproduce, and change cultural practices and the ideologies and beliefs underlying those practices.

Critical theorists believe that sports may be sites for challenging and even transforming society. This T-shirt, designed on behalf of Lithuania's men's basketball team, is an example of how athletes can use sports to challenge oppressive political structures. Such challenges are rare, but they do happen. (Jay Coakley)

3. The definition and organization of sports will usually reflect the rest of society, but it is also possible for sports to become sites for challenging, resisting, and even transforming the way social life is organized; therefore, we must study sports as more than simple "reflections of society." (See a detailed explanation of this point in the box titled "Sports Are More than Reflections of Society." on p. 49).

4. People socially construct sports continually, as they cope with the realities of everyday life in their own changing families, groups, communities, and societies; therefore, we must study sports in connection with various forms of social relations, as well as the overall processes of social development in societies.

Critical theories are designed as tools for the critical examination of society and the way it operates. However, the ultimate goal of research based on critical theories is *change*. In the sociology of sport, this means that critical theorists focus on (1) what sports *could be* in society, (2) how sport opportunities vary from one group to another, (3) how sports could be changed to reflect the interests of more people in society, and (4) when and how sports could become sites for promoting changes in how people interact with one another and how social life is organized.

The best way to explain critical theories is to show how people actually use them in the sociology of sport. We do this in the following section.

CRITICAL THEORY AND RESEARCH ON SPORTS Critical theory inspires research that focuses on *why* sports have taken certain forms and been organized in certain ways in particular groups, communities, and societies. For example, when studying a country like the United

REFLECT ON
SPORT

Feminist Theories
A Critical Look at Gender and Sports

All feminist theories are critical theories. They are based on a combination of the lived experiences of women and evidence that women have been systematically devalued, exploited, and oppressed in many societies. Feminist theories are also tied to a strong commitment to develop programs of social action that will improve conditions for women. Feminist theories have grown out of a general dissatisfaction with intellectual traditions that ignored women and failed to recognize the extent to which men's values and experiences had shaped science and the production of scientific knowledge.

Although all feminists are committed to changing the way social life is organized, they don't all agree on the changes needed. *Liberal feminists* identify discrimination and unequal opportunities as the issues in greatest need of attention. Their goal is to promote "full and equal participation for girls and women" in all spheres of social life, including employment, education, politics, and sports (as noted in Lenskyj, 1992b). In the case of sports, liberal feminists focus on the issue of fair and equal access for women to participate as athletes and share in the rewards available to athletes, to coach at all levels of competition, and to gain positions in the power structures of sport organizations. According to Helen Lenskyj, "Liberal feminists would probably agree with the statement, 'If it's good for males, it's good for females, too'" (1992b: 1).

Radical feminists, on the other hand, believe that problems go much deeper than issues of discrimination and equal opportunity. They argue that if fairness and equity are the only issues addressed and if success is measured only by women's participation in activities and organizations created by and for men, feminists will end up reproducing the very orientations toward social life and social relationships that led women to be devalued and exploited in the first place. Radical feminists say that since many activities and organizations have been shaped to represent and promote the power and privilege of men, there must be goals that go beyond equal participation opportunities; they would *not* agree with the idea that "if it's good for men, it must also be good for women" (Vertinsky, 1992). In

the case of sports, radical feminists would question the merits of wanting to play and work in sport activities and organizations where aggression, competition, goal orientation, and rational efficiency are the most important standards for evaluating organizational success and individual qualifications.

Most radical feminists do not dismiss the approach or the goals of liberal feminists. They do not claim that liberal feminists are going in the wrong direction, but they do argue that liberal feminists do not go far enough in their analysis of sports or social life. Radical feminists contend that to fully understand the history and social significance of organized sports in our lives, we must understand how sports have been and continue to be ordered along gender lines. They would support this contention by reminding us that organized sports were developed in England at a time when many people feared that home life was controlled by women and that boys raised by women would not learn to be tough enough to control colonized peoples around the world, fight wars, and expand capitalist economies. This fear of the "feminization of social life" also fueled the development and sponsorship of organized, competitive sports in other societies during the nineteenth century. Sports were intended to emphasize and teach "manly" values and behaviors.

Organized, competitive sports became associated with making boys tough, creating men who fit dominant definitions of masculinity, and demonstrating that men's bodies could endure and engage in violence in ways that made them superior to women's bodies. Boxing, rugby, football, and other contact sports were not only used widely in military training, but also seen as proof that men were naturally superior to women and that power, aggressiveness, and the ability to physically dominate others were uniquely male qualities grounded in biology itself (Messner, 1992).

Over the years, women were systematically excluded from contact sports and discouraged from participating in most strenuous physical activities because their bodies were seen as incapable of aggression, physical power, and stamina. Of course, the more important implications of this exclusion and discour-

If sports in today's society have been constructed primarily to reflect the values and experiences of powerful men, should women strive to participate in sports that emphasize aggression and physical domination? Would all feminists consider this high school wrestling match between a young woman and a young man a sign that gender definitions and gender relations are changing for the better? (Kirk Speer, *Colorado Springs Gazette*)

agement were the definition of women's bodies as naturally inferior to men's bodies, and the perception that it was women's biological destiny to be controlled by men (Bryson, 1991). This ideological rationale for the development of organized sports also existed in other cultures, including the United States and Canada.

Feminists also note that when physical strength has practical utility in employment and when force and violence are widely used in society, the balance of power between men and women is likely to favor men. And in a society where physical strength is not needed in the economy and displays of force and violence are controlled, men will seek other means of maintaining a rationale for their superiority. This rationale is at least partially provided by football, boxing, ice hockey, and other sports defined as "manly" or "aggressive."

These sports are promoted and popularized partly because they perpetuate the belief that force and aggression are important parts of life and that men are fundamentally and naturally superior to women because they are more forceful and aggressive (Bryson, 1991; Nelson, 1994).

Feminists describe sports as "gendered" activities. The fact that organized sports were developed to emphasize competition, efficiency, and performance ranking systems and to devalue supportiveness, kindness, responsiveness, and caring contributed to their "gendered" character. To say that sports are "gendered" activities and that sport organizations are "gendered" structures is to say that they have been socially constructed out of the values and experiences of men. It also means that certain "masculine values and

Continued

experiences" are highly regarded and used as standards for evaluating everything from organizational success to the qualifications of all participants, whether athletes or athletic directors. When you are aggressive, forceful, and committed to achieving competitive success efficiently, you are seen to be "qualified" as an athlete, coach, or administrator; but when you are supportive and focused on being responsive to others, you are qualified only to be a cheerleader, host the next booster club luncheon, or work in public relations. In the gendered world of sports, being supportive, kind, caring, and responsive to others doesn't count for much, and it certainly doesn't make you qualified to do anything more important than be a volunteer on the hospitality committee.

In light of this analysis of sport, critical feminist theories lead people in the sociology of sport to ask the following questions when they do their research:*

> To what extent have the character and structure of dominant sport forms in most societies been formed by the ways people think about gender and about masculinity and femininity?
>
> Would sports *as we know them today* in much of the world even exist if gender were not an organizing principle for sport activities and organizations?
>
> How are certain forms of masculinity and the power and privilege of men in society connected with the packaging, promotion, and playing of today's most popular sports?
>
> How have the images, symbols, and ideologies associated with dominant sport forms in particular societies led to a "gendering" of sport participants, activities, and organizations?
>
> How has the devaluation and exclusion of women been built into the structures and operational dynamics of sports and sport organizations?
>
> How have athletes and coaches constructed gendered personas or personal images that enable them to "fit" into sports and sport organizations without being defined as deviant or threatening?

These are "boat-rocking" questions, and it is easy to see why many people, both men and women, feel threatened by the feminists who ask them. This is the reason there has been such a concerted effort over the past ten to fifteen years to portray feminists as social demons. These efforts have been so successful that many college students today would forfeit an A in a sociology class before they would ever describe themselves as feminists, much less radical feminists!

But despite the bad rap given to feminism, these are crucial questions to ask in the sociology of sport. They make us aware of many important issues that we must address in our thoughts and research (see Birrell, forthcoming; Birrell and Cole, 1994; Birrell and Theberge, 1994a, b; Hall, 1996; Hargreaves, 1994; Nelson, 1991, 1994). For example, why have many men in American sports resisted the spirit of Title IX for over twenty years? Why have strong and powerful women athletes been accused of being lesbians unless they design athletic fashions, wear long fingernails, and travel with their husbands? Why are men's locker rooms full of homophobia, gay-bashing vocabulary, and comments that demean women? Why do we constantly read about doctors warning women that vigorous exercise might not be good for their health, while forty thousand young men get carried off football fields every year with serious knee injuries? Why are sexual harassment and sexual assault low-priority issues in most sport organizations? Why has an openly gay football player never been featured on the cover of *Sports Illustrated?* And why are so many women's intercollegiate teams called "Lady this" and "Lady that"?

We will explore many of these questions in different chapters in this book, but we leave others for you to consider on your own—if you don't mind using critical feminist theory to guide your thoughts. What do you think?

---

*Most of these questions are paraphrased versions of general questions listed in Joan Acker's (1992) discussion of "gendered institutions" in societies today.

States, critical theorists would be interested in the way *excellence* has been defined in dominant forms of sport. If excellence is defined in terms of setting records and winning championships instead of showing general abilities across a wide variety of sports, they would want to know how and why such a definition came into existence. They also would want to know about alternative definitions of excellence and how people might view and evaluate those definitions. Finally, they would try to explain how and why one definition of excellence came to be accepted over others, and in their explanations they would note who benefits most from the dominant definition of excellence, and who benefits least. They would outline the consequences of that definition, and compare them to the possible consequences of other definitions.

Summaries of actual studies emphasize this point in different ways.

Example 1: Creating alternatives to dominant forms of sport Susan Birrell and Diana Richter (1994) combined two forms of critical theory (feminist theory and cultural studies) to study how a specific sport experience was socially constructed by a group of women playing on certain teams in slow-pitch softball leagues in two communities. For four years the researchers did intensive interviews and observations that focused on how the feminist consciousness of these women might inform and structure their sport experiences, their interpretation of those experiences, and the integration of sport experiences into their lives.

Birrell and Richter reported that the women in their study were concerned with developing and expressing skills, playing hard, and challenging opponents, but that they wanted to do these things without adopting orientations characterized by an overemphasis on winning, power relationships between players and coaches, social exclusion and skill-based elitism, an ethic of risk and endangerment, or the derogation of opponents. In other words, the women attempted to create alternative sport experiences that were "process oriented, collective, supportive, inclusive, and infused with an ethic of care" (p. 408). Transformations in the way teams were organized and the way games were played came slowly over the four-year research period; many women found it difficult even to try an alternative to the sport forms that had been created out of men's values and experiences, the forms that were presented to them as *the* ways to do sports. But as changes occurred on their teams, the women experienced a sense of satisfaction, enjoyment as softball players, and a reaffirmation of their collective feminist consciousness and feelings of political empowerment.

Birrell and Richter's study shows that sports are not so much "reflections of society" as "social inventions" of people themselves. The definition and organization of sports are grounded in the consciousness and collective reflection of the participants themselves, and this means that people can alter sports through their own efforts. In other words, sports are social constructions; people can define them and include them in their lives to serve many different purposes. This research finding makes a significant contribution to our overall understanding of sports in society.

Example 2: The social construction of masculinity in sports Michael Messner (1992) used a form of critical feminism to study the ways in which masculinities were socially constructed in connection with men's athletic careers. Open-ended, in-depth interviews were conducted with thirty former athletes from different racial and social class backgrounds to discover how gender identities developed and changed as men lived their lives in the socially constructed world of elite sports. Messner noted that the men in his study began their first sport experiences with already-gendered identities; in other words, when they started playing sports they already had certain ideas about masculinity. They had not entered sports as "blank slates" ready to be "filled in" with culturally approved masculine orientations and behaviors.

As their athletic careers progressed, these men constructed orientations and relationships, and had experiences consistent with dominant ideas about manhood in American society. Overall, their masculinity was based on (a) trying to make a public name for themselves and make money in the process, (b) relationships with men in which bonds were shaped by homophobia (a fear of homosexuality) and misogyny (a disdain for women), and (c) a willingness to use their bodies as tools of domination regardless of consequences for health or general well-being. This socially constructed masculinity not only influenced how these men presented themselves in public, but also influenced their relationships with women and generated a continuing sense of insecurity about their "manhood."

Messner also found that the consequences of sport participation in the lives of the men he interviewed were complex and sometimes confusing. For example, sport participation brought many of the men in his study temporary public recognition, but it also discouraged the formation of needed intimate relationships with other men and with women. Sport participation enabled the men to develop physical competence, but it also led to many serious injuries and chronic health problems. Sport participation opened some doors to job opportunities for these men, but opportunities also varied depending on the sexual preferences and the racial and class backgrounds of the men. Sport participation provided these men guidelines on how to "be a man," but the involvement and success of women in sport also raised serious questions for those who had learned that becoming a man necessarily involved detaching oneself from all things female.

Overall, sport participation for the men was a process through which they enhanced their public status, created nonintimate bonds of loyalty with each other, perpetuated patriarchal relationships with women, and constructed masculinity in a way that privileged some men over others. Even though the men sometimes challenged this process, transformations of sports and sport experiences were difficult to initiate because dominant forms of sport in the U.S. have been constructed to perpetuate the notion that male privilege is grounded in nature and biological destiny. Messner's work calls attention to the fact that gender is a social construction and that sports offer fruitful sites ("social locations") for studying the formation of gender identities.

Example 3: Sport rituals and social life in a small town Anthropologist Doug Foley (1990a) studied the connection between sport events and community socialization processes in a small Texas town by using field methods (observation, participant observation, and informal and formal interviews) over a two-year period. His analysis was guided by a form of critical theory that he describes as "performance theory." One of his goals was to examine the extent to which sports might be used by certain community members as sites for challenging and making changes in the capitalist, racial, and patriarchal order that defined social life in their town.

Foley thought that as he studied sports he would find progressive practices challenging the dominance of a small elite group that controlled the town's economy. But he found few such challenges connected with sports. There were a handful of athletes, cheerleaders, and local townspeople who challenged certain traditions and ways of doing things, but they produced no real changes in who had power and how things were done in the town. This discovery led Foley to conclude that high school sports in general and high school football in particular were important community rituals in the town he studied, but that they ultimately reproduced existing inequities related to gender, race, ethnicity, and income.

Foley's study shows that sports are tied to the economic, political, and cultural systems in a community, and that it can be very difficult to use sports as sites for challenging and changing the way social life is organized.

In summary, these overviews of how critical theories are used in research emphasize that *sports are more than reflections of society*. Of course,

REFLECT ON SPORT

Sports Are More than Reflections of Society

In the sociology of sport it is sometimes said that sports are reflections of society. This idea may be helpful to someone who is just beginning to study sports as a part of social life. But it is not very helpful to the person who really wants to take an in-depth sociological look at sports. The problem with assuming that sports are reflections of society can be demonstrated by shifting our attention away from sports and onto another sphere of social life: *the family.*

Like sports, families are reflections of society. But our personal experience tells us that everyday family life is more than that. Real families are the creations of people interacting with one another in a variety of ways depending on their abilities, resources, power, and definitions of family life. Of course, the opportunities and choices available to the members of any particular family are influenced by factors in the larger society, including laws, economic conditions, government policies, and general beliefs about how husbands and wives and parents and children should relate to one another. This means that there will be similarities among many families in the same society. However, it does not mean that all families are predestined to be alike or to be mere reflections of society.

Society serves only as a context within which individuals produce, define, and reproduce specific family practices; families are not so much units determined or shaped by society as sets of relationships that come to be in society. This is why each family has its own unique "way of life": *people create families.*

At times, families become sites (social locations) for raising questions about how family life should be organized. And some of these questions force people to rethink larger issues related to cultural values and the organization of society as a whole. In this way, what we do in our families becomes part of a process of cultural production, the impact of which goes far beyond family life. For example, when people in the U.S. asked questions about marriage and family, there were discussions that ultimately led to changes in divorce laws. These discussions also encouraged people to rethink their ideas about relationships, gender, the rights of women, parent-child relationships, and even how communities and community services

should be organized. In other words, families have always been much more than reflections of society. They are the creations of human beings, and sites for producing and transforming the ways of life that comprise culture.

This means that human beings are agents for social change, not just in their immediate family lives, but in the larger social settings in which they live. Through the things that human beings do in their families they produce and/or reproduce the culture of which they are a part.

So it is with sports and those of us connected with sports. Sports are reflections of society, but that tells only part of the story. They are more accurately seen as the creations of people interacting with one another. No voice comes out of the sky and says, "I am society, and this is the way sports should be." Of course, social conditions have an impact on the structure and dynamics of sports, but within the limitations set by those conditions, people can change sports or keep them the way they are. In fact, it is even possible for people to create and define sports in ways that are uniquely different from dominant forms of social life in a particular society, and in the process, turn sports into sites for the transformation of the very culture of which they are a part.

This is a helpful way of thinking about sports in society. It recognizes that sports can have both positive and negative effects on participants, that *people define and create sports* in their own lives, and that sports are involved in either reproducing culture or standing in opposition to dominant ideology and forms of social relations in society.

This means that sports are very important in a sociological sense. Instead of just being the mirrors that reflect society, they are the actual "stuff" out of which society and culture come to be what they are. When people understand this they become aware of their capacity as "agents" of cultural production. This awareness helps them realize that they are not destined to have sports like those of the past or live on a planet where culture revolves around the images promoted by Coca-Cola, Nike, or Budweiser. This culture is mine, and ours. Don't you agree?

like other spheres of social life, sports share things in common with the social settings in which they exist. But according to critical theories, sports have never been developed in a neatly ordered and rational manner, and there are no simple rules for explaining sports as social phenomena. Instead, the structure and organization of sports in any society vary with the complex and constantly changing relationships in and between groups possessing varying amounts of power and resources. In addition to being concerned with how sports come to be what they are in society, critical theorists are concerned with how sports affect the processes through which people develop the orientations and beliefs they use to explain what happens in their lives. They want to know how and when sports become sites for encouraging changes in the way people see and interpret the social world around them.

LIMITATIONS OF CRITICAL THEORIES
Critical theory comes in many different forms, so it is much more flexible and much less pretentious than either functionalist or conflict theory. Its major limitation is that none of its variations provide clear guidelines for determining when sports reproduce dominant forms of social relations in society and when they become sites for resistance and the transformation of social relations (Critcher, 1986). Although recent research has focused on the ways in which sports become sites for oppositional forces in society, research using critical theories provides few examples of when this has occurred in the past and little information on the circumstances under which it might occur in the future. Also, the many variations of critical theory often make it confusing to use, and they certainly make it difficult for students to understand without doing extensive reading.

Interactionist Theories:
Sports Are Meaningful Interaction

Many sociologists use various forms of interactionist theory. These theories are useful because they provide frameworks in which people can study meaning, identity, and social relationships in sports. Interactionist theories are based on the assumptions that human behavior involves choices and that choices are based on meanings or "definitions of the situation" that people create as they interact with others. According to an interactionist approach, we humans don't simply respond in an automatic fashion to the world around us; instead, we choose to behave in certain ways in anticipation of the impact we think our behavior will have on ourselves, the people around us, and the social world in which we live. The final column in table 2–1 presents aspects of interactionist theory.

According to interactionists, as we behave and as we see the impact of our behavior on ourselves and others, we develop a sense of who we are and how we are connected to the rest of the social world. This sense of who we are is our *identity*. Identity forms as we interpret the connections between our lives and the social world, and then identity influences our choices as we relate to others and "construct" our social worlds. In other words, identity is a basis for *self*-direction and *self*-control in our lives. Identity is never formed once and for all time, because it emerges out of our relationships with other people, and those relationships are constantly changing as we meet new people, as people change, and as we face new situations.

Those who use interactionist approaches to behavior are concerned with understanding how human beings define and give meaning to their social worlds and how those meanings become the basis for identities. When interactionists do research, they generally focus their attention on the meanings that people assign to things and events in their world and how those meanings become the "realities" people use as contexts for making decisions about who they are and for understanding the implications of their own behaviors and the behaviors of others.

Interactionists see meaning, identity, and relationships as "social creations." They see behavior in terms of emerging processes, not cause-effect relationships. They define human beings as choice makers, not as "responders" to stimuli. Therefore, they study real-life situations and processes as they are created by people interacting with each other. Interactionists do not do experiments designed to discover cause-effect relationships, because they don't believe that we can explain human behavior by using cause-effect models. Therefore, when they study behavior and social events, they are open to the possibility that human beings can behave in surprising and unconventional ways. Two interactionist theorists put it this way:

> Nothing has to happen. Nothing is fully determined. At every step of every unfolding event, something else might happen (McCall and Becker, 1990).

However, interactionists also recognize that behavior reflects the resources people possess and the constraints and opportunities people face as they live their lives in society. Interactionists realize that under certain circumstances, the behaviors of many different people are likely to be similar; but they also realize it doesn't have to be that way because human beings have minds of their own.

As with critical theories, the best way to learn about interactionist theories is to review research based on them. We do this in the following section.

INTERACTIONIST THEORIES AND RESEARCH ON SPORTS When interactionists study sports, they usually focus on how people develop meanings and identities associated with sport participation, and how those meanings and identities influence their behavior and relationships with others. The goal of this research is to reconstruct and describe the reality that exists in the minds of the people being studied. This is slightly different from research based on critical theory, where the goal is to understand how cultural ideologies are produced, reproduced, and challenged, and how ideologies are related to social issues and problems.

Interactionists use research methodologies designed to gather information on how people see their social worlds and their connections to those worlds. Therefore, they do studies that involve participant observation and in-depth interviews. These are the best methods for understanding how people define situations and use those definitions as a basis for identifying themselves and making choices about their behavior. The best way to explain research by interactionists is to give some examples. I could choose many, but I will highlight three of my favorites.*

Example 1: The complex process of becoming an athlete Sociologists Peter Donnelly and Kevin Young (1988) used a form of interactionist theory to guide their collection and analysis of ethnographic, observational, and interview data on mountain climbers and rugby players. Their analysis enabled them to develop a model showing that becoming a serious athlete involves problematic, long-term processes of identity construction and confirmation. According to their findings, becoming a mountain climber or rugby player involved more than simply receiving encouragement and rewards from other people and being exposed to opportunities to climb mountains or play rugby. Instead, it involved long-term processes through which individuals (1) acquired knowledge about their sport, (2) became associated with a group of recognized athletes in their sport, (3) learned the norms and expectations shared by group members, (4) earned the acceptance of group members, and (5) experienced repeated confirmation and reconfirmation of their identities as climbers or rugby players as they interacted with group members.

Donnelly and Young's study shows that becoming a serious athlete involves more than a single decision or event, and more than the influence of a particular person or set of persons. Instead, it involves extended interactive processes through which people come to identify

---

*These three examples are adapted from Coakley (1993a, b).

themselves as athletes. This identity is gradually formed as they become knowledgeable and accepted members of particular sport groups or subcultures.

Example 2: The meaning of Little League baseball Sociologist Gary Alan Fine (1987) used an interactionist approach in a study of the sport experiences of 10- to 12-year-old boys on ten teams in five different youth baseball leagues. Over a three-year period, he collected data through a combination of participant observations, informal conversations, and interviews. Fine's analysis showed that the boys on each team developed their own systems of meanings and understandings to assess their baseball experiences and guide their interaction with teammates through the season. Fine called these systems of meanings and understandings **idiocultures.** These idiocultures were important because they served as the contexts in which the boys interpreted and made sense out of their Little League experiences. For example, Fine found that the boys used idiocultures as "experience filters" through which they redefined and transformed the idealized rules and moral lessons coaches and parents presented to them during the season. Instead of taking the rules and lessons at face value, the boys changed them in ways that fit their own immediate needs, primarily needs for acceptance among peers. Coaches and parents did not notice these changes, because the boys were very good at presenting themselves in ways that led the adults to think that the boys understood and internalized everything they said.

The boys didn't completely ignore the moral talk offered by adults or see it as useless, but they did transform it to fit their own definitions of the situation. For example, Fine found that while parents and coaches talked about the importance of effort and sportsmanship, the boys were concerned primarily with being socially accepted by their peers (social acceptance is developmentally important for 10- to 12-year-olds). And according to team idiocultures, social acceptance by the

boys' peers generally depended on being able to present themselves to others as "men" in a traditional moral sense. This led many of the boys to choose behaviors that expressed independence and established distance between themselves and anyone defined as weak and submissive, such as girls and younger children. Being identified with girls or younger children was defined as disastrous by the boys, so most of them mimicked stereotypical models of traditional masculinity. They presented themselves as tough and ready for anything.

Most coaches encouraged this tendency, because they could use it to motivate the boys to play in aggressive ways. The coaches used aggressive behavior as proof of a player's motivation, effort, and "hustle." Therefore, Little League experiences perpetuated definitions of masculinity that valued toughness, risk taking, and dominance, and devaluation of girls as weak and unable to stand up physically to boys. This was not something that the adults wanted to happen, but it occurred as the boys defined their experiences in their own terms in the context of how Little League baseball was organized in their communities.

Fine's study shows that sports and sport participation can affect young people in many different ways, depending on how sports are organized and what developmental issues are important in the lives of participants. In sociological terms, Fine shows that sport socialization is a complex process.

Example 3: The meaning of pain in an athlete's life Sociologist Tim Curry (1992) examined biographical data on the sport career of an amateur wrestler. He collected case study data through three two-hour interviews over a two-month period. These interviews followed several years of observing the college wrestling team on which this young man (in his early twenties) participated. Curry's analysis clearly outlines the social processes through which many athletes come to define pain and injury as normal parts of their sport experiences.

Interactionists study the meaning and identities associated with sports and sport participation. Meanings associated with youth sports vary from one cultural setting to another, and so do the lessons players learn in connection with participation. (Jay Coakley)

Curry's report showed that this young wrestler initially learned to define pain and injury as a routine part of sport participation simply by observing other wrestlers and interacting with people connected to the sport. As he progressed to higher levels of competition, he became increasingly aware of how the endurance of pain and injury were commonplace among fellow athletes and former athletes who had become coaches. Over time this young man learned what it meant to be a wrestler, and what was required to have others define him as a wrestler.

For example, over time he learned the following: to "shake off" minor injuries, to define special treatment for minor injuries as a form of coddling, to express desire and motivation by playing while injured or in pain, to avoid using injury or pain as excuses for not practicing or competing, to use physicians and trainers as experts who could keep him competing when not healthy, to define pain-killing antiinflammatory drugs as necessary performance-enhancing aids,

to commit himself to the idea that all athletes must pay a price as they strive for excellence, and to define any athlete unwilling to pay the price or to strive for excellence as morally deficient. As he participated in wrestling this young man applied all these things to himself; in fact, they became his identity guidelines.

Despite his identity as a wrestler, a combination of spine and knee injuries, and repeated injuries that disfigured his ears ("cauliflower ear" is common among longtime wrestlers) led this young man to stop wrestling. But because he was defined as a model of dedication and commitment, he became a role model for younger wrestlers.

The experiences associated with this young man's wrestling career clearly illustrate the way in which painful and potentially self-destructive experiences can be defined as positive in the life of an athlete, especially a male athlete. Athletes in certain sport groups may even come to use these experiences as proof of self-worth and evidence of a special form of character that separates them from others who are less dedicated and committed. But the important thing about this study is that it shows how meanings and identity associated with sport experiences are grounded in social interaction processes.

LIMITATIONS OF INTERACTIONIST THEORIES The strength of interactionist theories is that they have generated informative studies of meaning, identity, and interaction. However, one weakness of these theories is that many of these studies focus almost exclusively on personal definitions of the situation and on interaction dynamics without identifying the ways in which meanings and interaction processes are related to the social structure of society as a whole (which is a goal of critical theories). Therefore, interactionist theories have not done a very good job of explaining how what happens in sports is connected with the material conditions and the structured forms of inequality in the societies in which sports exist. For example, when interactionist theories are used in the sociology of sport, full attention is given to meanings and interaction as a basis for identity and for the construction of sport itself. At the same time, little or no attention is given to the ways that people's sport lives and their choices about sport participation are limited by constraints associated with social class, gender, disability, sexuality, and age.

Another weakness of interactionist theories is that they do a poor job of explaining behaviors grounded in processes other than rational problem solving and choice making—things generally associated with the mind, not the body. They tend to give no attention to the body and physical experiences in social life (Glassner, 1990; McCall and Becker, 1990). This is important to note as we think about the usefulness of interactionist theories in the sociology of sport. Interactionists studying sports have begun recently to incorporate the body and physical experience into their studies of meanings, identities, and interaction in sports (Curry, 1992, 1996; Hasbrook and Harris, 1996; Johns, 1997).

USING SOCIOLOGICAL THEORIES: A COMPARISON

Many people think that theories don't have practical applications. This is not true. Many of our own actions are based on our predictions of their consequences for ourselves and those around us. And our predictions are based on our *personal theories* about social life. Our personal theories may be incomplete, poorly developed, based on limited information, and biased to fit our own needs, but we still use them to guide our behavior. The better our theories are, the more accurate our predictions are, and the more effective we become in managing our relationships with others and controlling the situations in which we live our lives. When people make decisions about sports, when they make policies, and when they fund or cut money from sport programs, they usually base their decisions on personal theories about sports and their connections to social life.

None of the theories and theoretical approaches discussed in this chapter is perfect, but each can be useful as we attempt to move beyond our own limited personal perspectives when we try to study and understand the social world. As opposed to our personal theories, sociological theories are based on a combination of systematic research and deductive logic. Sociological theories are presented for the review of other sociologists in the form of book and journal publication. They are often the products of more than one person, and they are usually refined and improved over time as people test their implications in research.

Even when people are not familiar with theories in the sociology of sport, they still base their decisions on personal ideas and theories about how sports and social life work. Since many people use a "systems model" to understand how the social world works, their view of sports fits with a view guided by functionalist theory. In other words, they assume that society is held together by shared values, and they see sports as contributing to the order and stability of society.

Which theoretical perspective would be most useful if we wanted to study and understand the social and cultural significance of the growing number of urban murals that show sport figures from local teams? (Jay Coakley)

This is the viewpoint that many students have when they take courses in the sociology of sport, and it leads many of them to feel comfortable with questions, ideas, and research based on functionalist theory and uncomfortable with questions, ideas, and research based on other theoretical approaches. A summary of the practical implications of each of these theories may make this point more clear.

Applications of Functionalist Theory

Functionalist theory leads people to promote changes in sports that emphasize traditional values in a society. If individualism, competition,

and success are important values in society, a person using functionalist theory would call for changes leading to increases in individual achievement, winning records, and overall participation in sports. Since functionalist theory generally leads to the conclusion that sports build the kind of character valued in the society as a whole, it also leads to policy recommendations for more organized competitive programs, more structured sport experiences, more supervision of athletes, more coaching education programs, the development of more training centers for top-level athletes, and increased drug testing to control the behavior of athletes. In the case of youth sports, functionalist theorists generally would recommend more developmental programs, coaching certification requirements, and a sport system that builds skills leading to success at elite levels of competition. Functionalist theory leads people to look for and do research on how sports contribute to the development of individuals and society as a whole.

Applications of Conflict Theory

Conflict theory leads to concerns with economic factors, class inequality, and the need for changes in the actual structure of sports. These changes would emphasize making athletes and spectators more aware of how they are manipulated and oppressed for the profit and personal gains of the economic elite in society. Conflict theorists would argue that problems in sports exist because power does not rest in the hands of those who would and do play sports themselves. They would support policies and programs through which economic profit motives could be controlled or eliminated in sports and athletes themselves could be given more control over sports and the conditions of their sport participation. They would support sports with more emphasis on play and less emphasis on business so that sport participation could become more liberating and empowering. Conflict theorists would endorse players' unions and any athlete

How does a community regulate access to sport facilities? Who makes the rules? Whose interests are served by the rules? How can sport and sport participation be made more democratic? These are questions that interest me when I study sports as social phenomena. Therefore, I usually find critical theories more helpful than other theoretical perspectives. (Suzanne Tregarthen/Educational Photo Stock)

organizations that could serve as vehicles for making radical changes in the overall organization of sports. Their policies ultimately would discourage the development and growth of spectator sports, and promote the idea of games for the players themselves; they would eliminate profit, and highlight play.

Applications of Critical Theories

Critical theories lead to concerns about how sports either reproduce or transform the societies in which they exist. They emphasize that changes in sports depend on more than simply shifting the control of sport to the participants themselves. Critical theorists emphasize that most athletes and spectators are aware of who controls sports in their societies and have learned not only to accept those systems of control, but to define them as correct. Therefore, their policy recom-

mendations would call for increases in the number and the diversity of sport participation alternatives available in society, and increases in the choices available to participants in any sport. Their goal would be to provide as many people as possible with the opportunities to create and maintain forms of sport participation that enhance personal development and create critical abilities leading to transformations in sports and society as a whole. They would see sports as sites for challenging the dominant ideology in a society, and they would call for changes in sports that would encourage such challenges.

Feminist theories, as forms of critical theory, emphasize the need for gender equity and the need to critically assess the extent to which the ideology and organization of sports must be changed to include recognition of the values and experiences of women in society. Most feminist theorists believe that unless ideological and organizational changes are made, there will never be true gender equity.

Applications of Interactionist Theories

Interactionist theories focus on the meanings and interaction dynamics associated with sports and sport participation. They emphasize the complexity of human behavior and the need to understand behavior in terms of how people themselves define situations through their relationships with others. Interactionists would call for changes in sports that reflect the perspectives and identities of those who play sports. Many of them would argue that the best way of effecting these changes is to restructure sport organizations so that all involved, especially athletes, have opportunities to raise issues about the purposes and conditions of sport participation. Therefore, they would call for sport organizations to be changed to make them more democratic and less autocratic and hierarchically organized.

SUMMARY

IS THERE A BEST THEORETICAL APPROACH TO USE WHEN STUDYING SPORTS?

As someone who studies sports in society, I'd like to think that knowledge in the sociology of sport is cumulative and progressive, and that we can build on what we know today so that we can know more tomorrow. This is a reasonable goal, but it needs to be qualified, because sports are cultural practices subject to redefinition and transformation as social relations change and as other changes occur in the social world. Thus our knowledge about sports is always in danger of being irrelevant or obsolete; we have discovered that there are always new ways of looking at and analyzing any social phenomenon, including sports.

Sociology provides a number of theoretical frameworks that we can use to understand the relationship between sports and society, and each takes us in a different direction. In this chapter we have focused on four of those frameworks: *functionalism, conflict theory, critical theory,* and *interactionist theory.* The purpose of the chapter was to show that each framework has something to offer in helping us understand sports as social phenomena. For example, *functionalist theory* offers an explanation for positive consequences associated with sport involvement in the lives of both athletes and spectators. *Conflict theory* identifies serious problems in sports and offers explanations of how and why players and spectators are oppressed and exploited for economic purposes. *Critical theories* suggest that sports are connected with social relations in complex and diverse ways, and that sports change as power and resources shift and as there are changes in social, political, and economic relations in society. *Feminist theories* have taken a critical approach that emphasizes the extent to which sports in their present forms are gendered activities that privilege men and disadvantage women. *Interactionist theories* suggest that an understanding of sports requires an understanding of the meanings, identities, and interaction associated with sport involvement.

It is also useful to realize that each theoretical perspective has its weaknesses. *Functionalist theory* leads to exaggerated accounts of the positive consequences of sports and sport participation; it mistakenly assumes there are no conflicts of interests between groups within society; and it ignores powerful historical and economic factors that have influenced social events and social relationships. *Conflict theory* is deterministic, over emphasizes the importance of economic factors in society, and it focuses most of its attention on top-level spectator sports, which make up only a part of sports in any society. *Critical theories* provide no explicit guidelines for determining when sports are sources of opposition to the interests of powerful groups within society, and are only beginning to generate research on the everyday experiences of people involved in struggles to define and organize sports in particular ways. *Interactionist theories* do a poor job of relating what goes on in sports to general patterns of social inequality in society as a whole, and they generally ignore the body and physical experiences when they consider issues of meaning, identity, and relationships.

Apart from critical feminist theory, none of these theoretical approaches has encouraged a systematic consideration of gender relations in the study of sports. However, this will change in the future, as feminist theories continue to raise issues that encourage people to rethink the way they use these and other theoretical frameworks in their study of social life.

Which theory or theoretical framework will lead to the truth about sports? This depends on the goal of the person asking the question. If the goal is simply to understand more about sports as social phenomena, it would be wise to use all or some combination of the multiple approaches. However, if the goal is to use an understanding of sports as a basis for becoming involved and making changes in sports and social life, then the individual must take more care in choosing a theoretical framework. As we have seen in this chapter, each framework has different implications for action and change, for policies and program organization.

In my experience, I have found all the frameworks discussed in this chapter useful. I have used interactionism to guide much of my own research, but I also think that a combination of certain forms of critical theory and feminist theory offers the best framework for understanding sports and engaging in political action in the U.S. and many other societies. I am much more interested in increasing choices and alternatives for people in sports than in trying to make sports a more efficient means of maintaining the status quo in society or in dismantling sports altogether. I think that many aspects of the status quo in societies are in need of change, and that sports can be useful sites for making people aware of what changes are needed and the forms they might take.

Creating alternative ways of doing sports requires an awareness of the values underlying dominant forms of sport in society today, and a vocabulary for thinking about creative possibilities for the future. A combination of critical and feminist theory is especially helpful in critically assessing those values and providing the vocabulary we need to critically examine sports and develop new sport forms that can offer human beings new possibilities for organizing their connections with each other.

SUGGESTED READINGS

It is difficult to classify books and articles strictly in terms of the theoretical frameworks they represent. Many use a combination of perspectives. However, in the list below, each reference is classified according to the major framework used to draw conclusions about the relationship between sport and society.

FUNCTIONALISM

Booth, D., and J. Loy. Forthcoming. Functionalism sport and society. In J. Coakley and E. Dunning, eds., *Handbook of sport and society*. London: Sage (*overview of the role of functionalism and research informed by functionalism in the sociology of sport*).

Lever, J. 1983. *Soccer madness*. Chicago: University of Chicago Press (*analysis of the relationship between soccer and Brazilian society*).

Luschen, G. 1981. The interdependence of sport and culture. In J. W. Loy et al., eds., *Sport, culture, and society* (pp. 287–295). Philadelphia: Lea & Febiger (*classic functionalist explanation for how sports are connected with cultural values and how they serve system needs in society*).

CONFLICT THEORY

Brohm, J.-M. 1978. *Sport: a prison of measured time*. London: Ink Links (*essays on how sport is distorted by economic and political forces in contemporary society*).

Hoch, P. 1972. *Rip off the big game*. New York: Doubleday (*analysis of how sport is distorted by capitalism*).

Rigauer, B. Forthcoming. Marxist theories. In J. Coakley and E. Dunning, eds., *Handbook of sport and society*. London: Sage (*overview of the role of*

Marxist theory and research informed by Marxism in the study of sport; special emphasis on sport as a form of work in capitalist societies).

CRITICAL THEORY

Birrell, S., and C. Cole, eds. 1994. *Women, sport, and culture.* Champaign, IL: Human Kinetics (*twenty-four papers using critical feminist theory in analyses of issues related to ideology, sport organization, the transformation of sports, media and gender, and the politics of sexuality*).

Foley, D. E. 1990. *Learning capitalist culture.* Philadelphia: University of Pennsylvania Press (*insightful use of a form of critical theory to analyze a field study of social life in a small town; sport rituals are central in the analysis*).

Hall, M. A. 1996. *Feminism and sporting bodies: Essays on theory and practice.* Champaign, IL: Human Kinetics (*overview of feminist approaches to the study of sport and culture; discusses feminist theories in connection with other forms of cultural theories*).

Hargreaves, J. 1994. *Sporting females: critical issues in the history and sociology of women's sports.* London: Routledge (*critical analysis of female sports from the nineteenth century to the 1990s; explores the connection between sports, the body, and identity in culture, with special emphasis on British culture; received the 1995 NASSS Book of the Year Award*).

Hargreaves, J., and I. MacDonald. Forthcoming. Gramscian/cultural studies. In J. Coakley and E. Dunning, eds., *Handbook of sport and society.* London: Sage (*overview of the role of critical theory and research informed by Gramsci and Cultural Studies in the study of sports*).

Messner, M. 1992. *Power at play: sports and the problem of masculinity.* Boston: Beacon Press (*use of critical feminist theory to guide a study of men's sport experiences; this is the best critical analysis of masculinity I have found*).

Messner, M., and D. Sabo, eds. 1992. *Sport, men, and the gender order: critical feminist perspectives.* Champaign, IL: Human Kinetics (*the eighteen papers in this anthology use a combination of critical and feminist theory to understand different aspects of sports*).

Morgan, W. J. 1994. *Leftist theories of sport: A critique and reconstruction.* Urbana, IL: University of Illinois Press, (*thoughtful critique of critical theory, followed by a conceptually reinforced reconstruction of a critical theory of sport that can be used to make sports more humane*).

Sage, G. H. 1990. *Power and ideology in American sport: a critical perspective.* Champaign, IL: Human Kinetics (*clearly written, informative critical analysis of dominant sport forms in the United States; excellent book to use as an introduction to critical theory*).

Sage, G. H., ed. 1993. Sociocultural aspects of sport and physical activity: a critical perspective. *Quest* 45(2):Special Issue (*eight papers that critically assess sports and offer suggestions for making sports more democratic, just, and humane*).

INTERACTIONISM

Adler, P. A., and P. Adler. 1991. *Backboards & blackboards: college athletes and role engulfment.* New York: Columbia University Press (*insightful study using an interactionist framework to explain identity formation processes among intercollegiate male athletes in a big-time sport program*).

Coakley, J., and A. White. 1992. Making decisions: Gender and sport participation among British adolescents. *Sociology of Sport Journal* 9(1):20–35 (*study showing how sport participation decisions among working-class adolescents are mediated by a combination of meanings attached to past experiences, current resources, self-definitions, and cultural forces*).

Donnelly, P. Forthcoming. Interpretive approaches to the study of sports. In J. Coakley and E. Dunning, eds., *Handbook of sport and society.* London: Sage (*overview of the role of interactionist and other interpretive approaches to studying sports*).

Schmitt, R. L., and W. M. Leonard. 1986. Immortalizing the self through sport. *American Journal of Sociology* 91(March):1088–111 (*study showing how the collective memory of athletic accomplishments is created through interaction among sport fans and then used to socially construct the identities of individual athletes*).

Stevenson, C. L. 1990. The early careers of international athletes. *Sociology of Sport Journal* 7(3):238–53 (*informative interactionist analysis explaining the complex process through which people go as they make decisions leading to involvement in elite amateur sports*).

FIGURATIONAL THEORY

Sociologists who use figurational theory to study sports in society are usually associated with Eric Dunning and the University of Leicester in England. Figurational theory grows out of the work of Norbert Elias, a German sociologist who felt that social life consists of a complex network of inter-dependencies among human beings. Figurational research identifies these interdependencies and studies the dynamic processes associated with them. I have not described this complex and important theoretical perspective, but the following references can be used to learn more about it.

Dunning, E., J. A. Maguire, and R. E. Pearton, eds. 1993. *The sports process: A comparative and developmental approach*. Champaign, IL: Human Kinetics (*twelve papers focusing on the making of modern sports, the diffusion and development of modern sports, and modern sports cultures; the editors discuss all papers in terms of a figurational approach*).

Dunning, E., and C. Rojek, eds. 1992. *Sport and leisure in the civilizing process: critique and counter-critique*. Toronto, Ontario: University of Toronto Press (*focuses on the strengths and weaknesses of figurational theory*).

Elias, N., and E. Dunning. 1986. *Quest for excitement*. New York: Basil Blackwell (*uses figurational theory to guide discussions of sport as a form of pleasurable excitement that counterbalances the stress-tensions in the rest of people's lives*).

Murphy, P., K. Sheard, and I. Waddington. Forthcoming. Figurational/process sociology. In J. Coakley and E. Dunning, eds., *Handbook of sport and society*. London: Sage (*overview of the role of figurational sociology in the study of sport and society*).

chapter

3

(K. N. Heinz/USOC Archives)

A Look at the Past

How have sports changed throughout history?

Of the thousands of evils which exist in Greece there is no greater evil than the race of athletes. . . . Since they have not formed good habits, they face problems with difficulty. They glisten and gleam like statues of the city-state itself when they are in their prime, but when bitter old age comes upon them they are like tattered and thread-bare old rugs.

Euripides, Greek dramatist (fifth century BC; in Miller, 1991)

In each . . . epoch of human history, sports are integrally related to the political and social structures dominant at the time.

William Baker, historian (1988)

A woman . . . has plenty of oxygen-carrying power for simple household tasks . . . . [S]he has ample development for . . . light office and factory work. But men should keep her away from the

heavier tasks, both out of chivalry and good sense.

Dr. Donald Laird, M.D., *Scientific American* (March 1936)

Just as the dominant class writes history, so that same class writes the story of sport, including the sports them-selves and the rules of all the federations, clubs, and olympics. The dominant class controls how books and mass

media portray (or ignore) sports . . . .

James Riordan, social histo-rian and former soccer player (1996)

They who laid the intellec-tual foundations of the West-ern world were the most fanatical players and orga-nizers of games that the world has ever known.

C. L. R. James, West Indian writer and cricket player

To understand sports as social phenomena in today's world, we should have a sense of what sport activities were like in past times and different places. Therefore, the purpose of this chapter is to briefly summarize information on sport activities in different cultural and historical settings. The material I present will focus on (1) the ancient Greeks, (2) the Romans, (3) the Middle Ages in parts of Europe, (4) the Renaissance through the Enlightenment in parts of Europe, and (5) the Industrial Revolution through recent times, with special emphasis on the United States.

This material shows that for each of these times and places, our understanding of how sport activities have been defined, organized, and played depends on what we know about the social lives of the people who created, played, and integrated into their everyday experiences those activities. It is especially important to know how people used their power and resources as they struggled with one another to shape physical activities that fit their needs and interests.

When we view sports in this way, we don't get bogged down with sequences of dates and events. Instead, we focus on how sport activities reflect relationships between various groups of people at particular times and places. This will be the focus throughout this chapter.

AN OPENING NOTE ON HISTORY

When we think about history, most of us think about chronological sequences of events that build on each other and gradually lead to a better, or more "modern," society. Even the terminology used in many discussions of history leads us to think this way. For example, historical accounts are often full of references to societies that are traditional or modern, primitive or civilized, underdeveloped or developed, preindustrial or industrial. This terminology leads people to think that history is moving in a particular direction, and that as it moves in that direction, things are improving and getting more modern and developed. In other words, history is frequently presented as linear and progressive—always following a straight line and moving forward.

This approach enables some people to feel superior by allowing them to conclude that they are the most modern, civilized, and developed people in history. But this perspective does not lead to an accurate analysis of history. For example, in the case of sports there are literally thousands of "histories" related to the development and organization of physical activities among thousands of groups of people in different places around the world. These histories involve patterns of changes that many people would not describe as progressive. And it is important to remember that the definitions of progress different people use are themselves products of their cultural experiences.

Historical evidence suggests that physical activities of one sort or another have existed in all cultures. But the forms of these activities and the meanings people gave to them were the results of people interacting with one another and determining what sports should be like, who should play them, and how various sport activities should be integrated into their lives. To say that sport activities over the years have evolved to fit a pattern of progress or modernization is to distort the life experiences of people all over the world (Gruneau, 1988). People around the world may be playing more and more of the same kinds of physical games today, but not because sports are "developing" to fit some grand scheme for how physical activities should be organized. Nor does this fact imply that sports mean the same thing in different societies and cultural groups. Instead, similarities around the globe reflect the people who have power in the international arena and how they use that power to define, organize, sponsor, and promote particular sports and sport forms.

One clear illustration of the importance of power relations in sports is the process through which new events are added to the Olympic Games. New events usually reflect the interests of those groups or organizations that can influence the decisions of the International Olympic Committee. This is the reason events and games from Africa, Latin America, and vast parts of Asia are not included in the Olympics. It is also the reason beach volleyball was included as a new sport in the 1996 Summer Games in Atlanta. Beach volleyball represents the interests of sport groups, corporate sponsors, and media organizations from wealthy countries. To call this progress is to make a political statement, not a historical one—although Coca-Cola, Nike, and Cuervo Tequila (one of the sponsors of beach volleyball in the U.S.) would want you to think otherwise.

So as you read this chapter, don't conclude that it is a story of progress. Instead, read it as a series of stories about people of different times and places struggling over and coming to terms with what they wanted their physical activities to be and how they wanted to include them in their lives. Certainly, there is some continuity in many of these interactional processes and struggles in particular cultures, but continuity does not always mean that the structure and organization of sports equally represent the interests of all people in a culture. Human history does not follow some grand plan of progress. When progressive things do happen, it is because people have made them happen at a particular time, and these people usually realize that unless they keep an eye on things, the progress will be only temporary.

This chapter is *not* meant to be an overall history of sports. Such a history would look at the development and organization of physical activities across all continents from one cultural group to another over time. This would be an ambitious and worthy project, but it is beyond the scope of this book. The times and places I have chosen to review in this chapter are limited to the "Western world"; we must be careful not to conclude that they somehow represent either the entire world or the most important part of the world. This chapter is just one look at a few past times and places.

SIDELINES

©1982 M.T.F.-T.W.S.-Lakewood, CO

"How can you stop to shoot pool on the way home when it won't be invented for another ten million years?"

....

In early human history there were no sports as we define and play them today. People used their physical abilities for survival. Physical activities occasionally were included in community and religious rituals, but their purpose probably was to appease the gods, rather than to occupy leisure time or build character.

....

SPORTS VARY BY TIME AND PLACE

People in all cultures have engaged in playful physical activities and used human movement as a part of their ritual life. As we look at cultural variations, it is necessary to remember that few cultures have had physical activities that were characterized by organization, competition, and record keeping. This shows that even people's definitions of sports—and the meanings people attach to physical activities—are influenced by social and cultural factors.

In prehistoric times there were no sports as we know them today. Physical activities were tied directly to the challenge of survival and the expression of religious beliefs. People hunted for food and sometimes used their physical abilities to defend themselves or establish social control and power over others. Archaeological evidence suggests that people on each continent of the globe created unique organized forms of physical challenges for the purpose of appeasing their gods, by acting out events having important symbolic or real meaning in their everyday lives. These activities, even though they may have taken the form of games, were inseparable from sacred rituals and ceremonies. In fact, they usually were performed as forms of religious worship, and sometimes their outcomes were determined by religious necessity rather than the physical abilities of the people involved (Guttmann, 1978).

The first forms of organized games around the world probably emerged from this combination of physical exercises and religious rituals. From what we can tell, these games were connected closely with the social structures, social relations, and belief systems of the societies in which they existed, and they usually re-created and reaffirmed dominant cultural practices in those societies. But this was not always the case. Sometimes they served as sources of protest or opposition against dominant ways of thinking about and doing things in particular groups or societies.

Variations in the forms and dynamics of physical activities from time to time and place to place remind us that any cultural practice, even sports, can serve a variety of social purposes. This raises the question of how the definition and the organization of sports in any society promote the interests of various groups within that society. Since sport activities are created by people who operate within the constraints of the social world in which they live, not everyone has an equal say in the way activities are defined and organized. Those with the strongest vested interests and the most *power* in a group or society generally will have the greatest impact on the way sports are defined, organized, and played in that group or society. Sport activities will not totally reflect the desires of powerful people, but they will represent the interests of the powerful more heavily than they represent the interests of other groups in society.

This approach to studying sports in history calls attention to the existence and consequences of social inequality in societies. Social inequality has always had a significant impact on how sport activities are organized and played in any situation. And the most influential forms of social inequality are those related to wealth, political power, social status, gender, age, and race and ethnicity. We will pay special attention to these in the following discussions of times and places.

GAMES IN ANCIENT GREECE: BEYOND THE MYTHS (1000 BC TO 100 BC)

The games played by the early Greeks (circa 900 BC) were grounded in mythology and religious beliefs. They usually were held in conjunction with festivals involving a combination of prayer, sacrifices, and religious services, along with music, dancing, and ritual feasts. Competitors in these early games were from wealthy, respected Greek families. They were the only ones with the money and time to hire trainers and coaches and travel to the various games. Events clearly were based on the interests of young males. They consisted primarily of warrior sports, such as chariot racing, wrestling and boxing, javelin and discus throwing, foot racing, archery, and long jumping. Violence and serious injuries were commonplace in comparison to today's sport events (Elias, 1986; Kidd, 1984). The sport activities Greek women, children, and older people engaged in were occasionally included in the festivals, but they were never incorporated into the games held at Olympia.

The locations and dates of the Greek festivals also were linked to religious beliefs. For example, Olympia was chosen as one of the festival sites because it was associated with the achievements and activities of celebrated Greek gods and mythological characters. In fact, Olympia was dedicated as a shrine to the god Zeus about 1000 BC. Although permanent buildings and playing fields were not constructed until about 550 BC, the games at Olympia were held every four years. Additional festivals involving athletic contests were also held at other locations throughout Greece (Corinth, Delphi, and Nemea), but the Olympic Games became the most prestigious of all athletic events.

Women were prohibited from participating in the Olympic Games. They could not even enter the playing areas or the stadium as spectators. However, women held their own games at Olympia. Dedicated to the goddess Hera, the sister-wife of Zeus, these games grew out of Greek fertility rites. And according to some estimates, the Heraean Games even predated the exclusively male Olympic Games. Unfortunately, serious women athletes often risked their reputations in the eyes of males when they engaged in sports. Physical prowess did not fit with definitions of heterosexual femininity among the Greeks, so questions were raised about the sexuality and sexual orientations of strong and physically skilled women, and even of the goddesses in Greek mythology (Kidd, 1984).

The discrimination against women who participated in sports was rooted in a patriarchal family structure in which females had no legal rights and only limited opportunities for experiences outside their households. Although some women from well-to-do Greek families did become regular participants in the games at certain sites, their involvement was limited to a few events and their achievements were not promoted and publicized like the achievements of male athletes.

As the visibility and popularity of the games at Olympia grew, they took on political significance. As success in the games became connected with the glory of city-states, physically skilled slaves and young men from lower-class backgrounds were charged to become athletes or hired by wealthy patrons or government officials to train for the Olympics and other games. Victories brought these slaves and hired athletes cash prizes in addition to their living expenses. Victories also earned them reputations that they could convert into cash rewards when competing in the other popular Greek games. These male athletes saw themselves as professionals to such an extent that during the second century BC, they organized athletic guilds similar to the players' associations and unions in some professional sports today. Through these guilds they bargained for athletes' rights and "to have a say in the scheduling of games, travel arrangements, personal amenities, pensions, and old-age security in the form of serving as trainers and managers" (Baker, 1988).

Greek athletes specialized in particular events to such an extent that they made poor soldiers. They engaged in warrior sports, but they lacked the generalized skills of warriors. Furthermore, they concentrated so much on athletic training that they ignored intellectual development. This evoked widespread criticism from Greek philosophers, who saw the games as brutal and dehumanizing, and the athletes as useless and ignorant citizens.

Sports in Greek culture influenced art, philosophy, and the everyday lives of many people, especially those wealthy enough to train themselves, hire professionals, or travel to games. However, Greek games and contests were different from the organized, competitive games that we call sports today (Guttmann, 1978; see also the box on pp. 80–81). First, they were grounded in religion; second, they lacked complex administrative structures; and third, they did not involve the measurements and record keeping that characterize sport as we defined it in chapter 1. However, there is one major similarity: they reflected and re-created dominant patterns of social relations in the society as a whole. The power and advantages that went along with being wealthy, male, and young in Greek society served to shape games and contests in ways that limited the participation of women, older people, and those without many economic resources. In fact, the definitions of excellence used to evaluate performance even reflected the abilities of young males. This meant that the abilities of others were by definition substandard (Kidd, 1984). We can see similar things in some organized sports today.

ROMAN SPORT EVENTS: SPECTACLES AND GLADIATORS (100 BC TO 500 AD)

Roman leaders used sport activities to train soldiers and provide mass entertainment spectacles. They borrowed events from Greek games and contests, but they geared athletic training to the preparation of obedient military men. They were critical of the Greek emphasis on individualism and the development of specialized physical skills that were useless in battle. And they packaged their sport activities in ways that would appeal to spectators.

Through the first century AD, Roman sport events increasingly took the form of circuses and gladiatorial contests. Chariot races were the most popular events during the spectacles. Wealthy Romans recruited their slaves as charioteers. Spectators bet heavily on the races, and when they became bored or unruly, the emperors passed around fruit and bread to keep them from getting too hostile. In some cases, free raffle tickets for attractive prizes were distributed throughout the crowd to keep riots from starting

SIDELINES

"Why don't we settle this in a civilized way? We'll charge admission to watch!"

....

Dominant forms of sport in many societies have been created by and for men. These sports often have celebrated a particular form of masculinity emphasizing aggression, conquest, and dominance.

....

when people became overexcited. This tactic not only pacified the crowds, but also allowed the emperors to use sport events as occasions to celebrate themselves and their positions of power. Government officials outside of Rome did the same thing during local events to maintain control in their communities.

As the power and influence of the Roman Empire grew, sport events and spectacles became increasingly important as diversions for the masses. By 300 AD, half of the days on the Roman calendar were public holidays. Many workers held only part-time jobs, and unemployment was extremely high. Activities other than the standard chariot races, boxing matches, and other contests were needed to keep events interesting. Bearbaiting, bullbaiting, and animal fights were added to capture spectator interest. Another addition involved forcing men and women into the arena to engage in mortal combat with lions, tigers, and panthers. And sometimes condemned criminals were dressed in sheepskins and thrown in with partially starved wild animals. Gladiators, armed with a variety of weapons, were pitted against one another in gory fights to the death. According to Baker (1988), these spectacles achieved two purposes for the Romans: they provided "entertainment for an idle populace while at the same time disposing of the socially undesirable." "Undesirable" people included thieves, murderers, and Christians.

Some Romans criticized these spectacles as tasteless activities, devoid of cultural value. However, the criticisms were not based on concerns for slaves, troublemakers, or Christians. They were based on the idea that no good could come out of events at which people from the upper and lower social classes mixed and fraternized with one another while watching "common people" being maimed and killed. In other words, the objections were based on prejudice against the lower classes. Other than some outspoken Christians, few people objected to the spectacles on moral or humanitarian grounds.

The objections coming from the Christians had little effect on the fate of the events. In fact, the demise of Roman sport spectacles went hand in hand with the fall of the Roman Empire. As the Roman economy went deeper and deeper into depression, and as wealthy people moved away from cities, there were not enough resources to support sport spectacles (Baker, 1988).

Women were seldom involved in Roman sport events. They were allowed in the arenas to watch and cheer male athletes, but few had opportunities to develop their own athletic skills. Within the Roman family, women were legally subservient to and rigidly controlled by men. Like Greek women, they were discouraged from pursuing interests beyond the confines of the household.

Although folk games and local sport activities existed throughout the Roman Empire, we know little about how they were organized and played and what they meant in people's lives. The spectacles did not capture the interest of everyone, but they certainly evoked considerable attention in major population centers. Roman sport events differed from organized sports today in that they sometimes were connected with religious rituals, and they seldom involved the quantification of athletic achievements or the recording of outstanding accomplishments (see box on pp. 80–81).

TOURNAMENTS AND GAMES DURING THE MIDDLE AGES: SEPARATION OF THE MASTERS AND THE MASSES (500 TO 1300)

Sport activities during the Middle Ages usually took two forms: local games played by peasants, and tournaments staged for knights and nobles. The games emerged from the combined influence of local peasant customs and the Roman Catholic Church. The tournaments, however, emerged from the demands of military training and the desire for entertainment among the feudal aristocracy and those who served them.

Some of the local games of this period have interesting histories. As Roman soldiers and government officials moved throughout Europe during the fourth and fifth centuries, they built bathing facilities to use during their leisure time. To loosen up before their baths, they engaged in various forms of ball play. Local peasants picked up on the Roman activities and gradually developed their own forms of ball games. They often integrated these games into local religious ceremonies. For example, the tossing of a ball back and forth sometimes represented the conflict between good and evil, light and darkness, or life and death. As the influence of the Roman Catholic Church spread through Europe during the early years of the Middle Ages, these symbolic rituals were redefined in terms of Roman Catholic beliefs; sport and religion were integrally connected.

During most of the medieval period, the Roman Catholic Church accepted peasant ball games. In fact, local priests encouraged games by opening church grounds on holidays and Sunday afternoons to groups of participants. So the games became a basic part of village life. People played them whenever there were festive community gatherings. They were included with the music, dancing, and religious services held in conjunction with seasonal ceremonies and saints' feast days. An interesting note is that these local ball games contained the roots for many contemporary games, such as soccer, field hockey, football, rugby, bowling, curling, baseball, and cricket.

The games played in peasant villages had little structure and few rules. Local traditions guided play, and these traditions varied from one community to the next. Baker (1988) provides an interesting description of a thirteenth-century "futball" game played in England on Shrove Tuesday, the day before the beginning of Lent:

> [At the town of Derby] teams from the two parishes of St. Peter's and All Saints squared off. The three miles of countryside separating the parishes constituted the "field" of play. The size of the teams was not fixed; anyone living in the parishes played. There were no written rules. The purpose of the game was simply to kick, carry, or throw the ball against the opponents' goal—a

prominent gate in the parish of St. Peter's, an old waterwheel in All Saints' parish. Inspired by local pride and Shrovetide ale, villagers kicked, bit, and mauled each other. Some took the opportunity to even old scores.*

During the Middle Ages, the upper classes paid little attention to and seldom interfered in the leisure of peasants, because they saw peasant games and festivities as safety valves defusing mass social discontent (Baker, 1988). The sport activities of the upper classes themselves were distinctively different from those of the peasants. Access to equipment and facilities allowed the nobility to develop early versions of billiards, shuffleboard, tennis, handball, and jai alai. Ownership of horses allowed them to develop various forms of horse racing (while their stable hands developed a version of horseshoes). On horseback, they also participated in hunting and hawking. Their ownership of property and possession of money and servants had an impact on their sports.

Through a good part of the medieval period, the most popular sporting events among upper-class males were tournaments consisting of series of war games, designed to keep knights and nobles ready for battle. Early versions of tournaments differed very little from actual battlefield confrontations. Deaths and serious injuries occurred, victors carried off their opponents' possessions, and losers often were taken as prisoners and used to demand ransoms from opposing camps. Later versions of tournaments were not quite so serious, but they still involved injuries and occasional deaths. Gradually, the warlike nature of tournaments was softened by colorful ceremonies and pageantry, and entertainment and chivalry took priority over military preparation and reaping the fruits of victory.

Throughout the medieval period, women were less apt than men to be involved in physically active games and sport activities. Their

restricted opportunities were grounded in a combination of religious dogma (the Roman Catholic Church taught that women had inferior status) and a male-centered family structure. A woman's duty was to be obedient and submissive. This orientation did not change much through the Middle Ages. However, peasant women were involved in some of the games and physical activities associated with the regular rounds of village events during the year. Among the aristocracy, gender relations were patterned so that men's activities and women's activities were clearly differentiated. Aristocratic women did little outside the walls of their dwellings, and their activities seldom involved rigorous physical exertion for the purpose of self-entertainment. Women in the upper classes sometimes engaged in "ladylike" games and physical activities, but because they were subject to the control of men and often viewed as sex objects and models of beauty, their involvement in active pursuits was limited. Feminine beauty during this time was defined in passive terms: the less active a woman was, the more likely she was to be perceived as beautiful. Therefore, in meeting the expectations for beauty, a woman avoided all but very limited involvement in physical exercise.

Medieval tournaments and games were not much like today's organized sports, even though they contained the roots of many of today's sport activities in Europe and North America. They lacked the specialization and organization of today's competitive sports. They never involved the measurement and recording of athletic achievements, and they were not based on a commitment to equal and open competition among athletes from diverse backgrounds (see box on pp. 80–81). Guttmann (1978) has vividly described this latter point:

> In medieval times, jousts and tournaments were limited to the nobility. Knights who sullied their honor by inferior marriages—to peasant girls, for instance—were disbarred. If they were bold enough to enter a tournament despite this loss of status, and were discovered, they were beaten and their weapons were broken. Peasants reckless

---

*Material reprinted from *Sports in the Western World* by permission of the author and the publisher, University of Illinois Press, Urbana, IL, 1988.

enough to emulate the sport of their masters were punished by death.*

Many of the characteristics of medieval sport activities carried over to the Renaissance and Enlightenment periods.

THE RENAISSANCE, REFORMATION, AND ENLIGHTENMENT: GAMES AS DIVERSIONS (1300 TO 1800)

The Renaissance

Wars throughout Europe during the fourteenth and fifteenth centuries encouraged some monarchs, government officials, and church authorities to increase their military strength. To do this, they often enacted new rules prohibiting popular peasant pastimes. Those in authority saw the time peasants spent playing games as time they could spend learning to defend the lands and lives of their masters. But despite the pronouncements of bishops and kings, the peasants did not readily give up their games. In fact, the games sometimes became rallying points for opposition to government and church authority.

About the same time that peasants were being subjected to increased controls in many locations, the "scholar-athlete" became the ideal among many of the aristocrats and the affluent. In fact, they saw the "Renaissance man" as someone who was "socially adept, sensitive to aesthetic values, skilled in weaponry, strong of body, and learned in letters" (Baker, 1988).

Throughout the Renaissance period, women had relatively few opportunities to be involved in sport activities. Although peasant women sometimes played physical games, their lives were restricted by the demands of work both inside and out of the home. They often did hard physical labor, but they were not encouraged to engage in public activities that called special attention to their physical abilities and accomplishments.

Upper-class women sometimes participated in activities like bowling, croquet, archery, and tennis, but because women were seen during this time as "naturally" weak and passive, their involvement was limited. Some of these "Renaissance women" may have been pampered and put on the proverbial pedestal, but their lives were tightly controlled by men who maintained their positions of power partially by promoting the idea that women were too fragile to leave the home and do things on their own.

The Reformation

During the Protestant Reformation, a growth in negative attitudes regarding games and sport activities adversely affected the participation of both men and women, especially in locations where either Calvinism or Puritanism was popular. For example, between the early 1500s and the late 1600s, the English Puritans worked hard to eliminate or control leisure activities, including games and sports, in everyday life in England. The Puritans were devoted to the work ethic, and according to one social historian (Malcolmson, 1984), this is how they viewed sports:

> [Sports] were thought to be profane and licentious—they were occasions of worldly indulgence that tempted men from a godly life; being rooted in pagan and popish practices, they were rich in the sort of ceremony and ritual that poorly suited the Protestant conscience; they frequently involved a desecration of the Sabbath and an interference with the worship of the true believers; they disrupted the peaceable order of society, distracting men from their basic social duties—hard work, thrift, personal restraint, devotion to family, [and] a sober carriage.

The primary targets of the Puritans were the games and sports of the peasants. Peasants didn't own property, so their festivities occurred in public settings and attracted large crowds; thus, they were easy for the Puritans to attack and criticize. And the Puritans did their best to eliminate them—especially festivities scheduled on Sunday afternoons. It was not that the Puritans objected so much to the games themselves; they disapproved of the drinking and partying that accompanied the games and did not like the idea of promoting physical pleasure on the Sabbath.

---

*Copyright ©1978 by Columbia University Press. Used by permission.

REFLECT ON SPORT

Lessons from History: Distorted Views of Sports among Native Americans

The history of sports is noteworthy as much for what it does not tell us as for what it does tell us. This is especially true when it comes to the physical activities, games, and sports of native peoples from what is now the United States. In the prologue of his book, *American Indian Sports Heritage*, educator Joseph Oxendine (1988: xxi–xxiii)* explains why this is so. This is what he says:

> Several major difficulties accompany the task of presenting American Indian sports in historical perspective. Foremost among these is the lack of adequate recorded history. Of course, there is no written history of the American Indian prior to the arrival of Columbus in 1492. It was another two to three centuries before significant cultural information was recorded about the Indian. Consequently, most of the relevant literature has been produced within the past two centuries, a period during which Indian culture was being greatly influenced by nonIndians. Nevertheless, Indian oral history and mythology have contributed importantly to the body of information about sports and games. In addition, archaeologists and anthropologists have been able to establish hypotheses about traditional Indian culture, including sports, on the basis of playing implements, ball courts, eyewitness reports, and other evidence that has become available during recent years. Over the past two centuries, reporting on Indians and Indian sports has been seriously distorted. The 19th century, for example, was a very atypical period for Indians, given the almost constant rash of "Indian wars." In addition, the nonIndian population of this country increased rapidly and constantly pushed westward into traditional Indian lands. Along with the general mistreatment of Indians, this caused Native American lifestyles to bear less and less resemblance to traditional patterns.
>
> It became practically impossible, furthermore, for nonIndians to observe Indian games and ceremonies in the Indians' traditional form and significance. When they did enter the Indians' midst, it was usually as an oddity, either not able or not wishing to participate fully in the activities. . . . [Furthermore, being watched by nonIndians certainly] tended to restrain the behavior of Indians who were aware that they were being watched and studied. By the time sizable numbers of Indians had acquired a facility with the English language, their rituals, games, and ceremonies had been appreciably altered.
>
> Several Indian games were essentially religious rites; they were more religion than *play* in today's meaning of the term. . . . As such, nonIndians were not usually allowed to view these activities in their traditional form. Consequently, complete and accurate descriptions of these activities have not been reported in the literature.
>
> Despite the many diversities among the tribes and in addition to the communications problems, there were commonalities that transcended most traditional Indian cultures. . . . [M]any games and practices tended to be universal and were found in most tribes. These games and customs were transmitted through normal communication

• •

The sport activities of the affluent were less subject to Puritan interference. Activities like horse racing, hunting, tennis, and bowling took place on the private property of the wealthy, making it difficult for the Puritans to enforce their prohibitions. As in other times and places, power relations had much to do with who played what activities under what conditions.

Despite the Puritans and despite social changes affecting the stability and economic structure of English village life, many peasant people maintained their participation in games and sports. This was especially the case in locales where Martin Luther's ideas had been more influential than John Calvin's. However, some traditional peasant activities were adapted so they could be played in less public settings.

During the early 1600s, King James I formally challenged the Puritan influence in England by issuing *The King's Book of Sports*. This book, reissued in 1633 by Charles I, emphasized that Puritan ministers or officials should not discourage lawful recreational pursuits among the English people. Charles I and his successors ushered in a new day for English sporting life. They revived traditional festivals, and actively promoted and supported public games and sport activities. A few sports, including cricket, horse racing, yachting, fencing, golf, and boxing, became highly organized during the late and interaction that took place among tribes during their centuries of residence in this hemisphere.

In recent years, a major problem in reporting on Indian sports performers has been the lack of a systematic way of identifying persons as Indians. During the last two decades, Indians have participated in practically all sports in all parts of the country, both as amateurs and as professionals. Although some have been identified or recognized as Indians, others have not. The lack of a uniform identification system, as well as a central record-keeping mechanism, makes the task of highlighting Indian athletic performance particularly difficult. In former years it was relatively easy to identify a Native American. Today's increasing interaction among races, including assimilation and other social developments, makes such identification less clear. Some Indians, both full-blood and mixed-blood, have welcomed such identification, whereas others have not.

Oxendine's analysis tells us important things we should know about history when we study the sociology of sport. It says that people's ideas about what they want sport to be and how they include it in their lives are often influenced by social, political, and economic forces that are far beyond their control. Oxendine's analysis reminds us that if we want to understand the social importance of a historical event such as the establishment in 1983 of the Iroquois National Lacrosse Team (see chap. 14 in Oxendine), we need to know

about Native American cultures in general, about the history and organization of the six nations of the Iroquois Confederation, about the relations between Native Americans and the U.S. government, and about the experiences of Native American men and women as they have struggled to honor their cultural heritage and survive in a society where powerful others consistently have tried to strip them of their dignity, language, religion, and customs.

History is much more than a chronological series of events, and we can view it from many different perspectives. Therefore, when we study the history of sports we must be aware of whose perspectives are being represented and whose are being ignored or described by "outsiders." In the U.S. there is a scarcity of information about the sports of people from ethnic minority groups. This is the case, for example, for Hispanic Americans and Asian Americans, and until Arthur Ashe's (1993) three-volume work, was true for African Americans as well. This scarcity has diminished our awareness of the diversity of sports and sport forms that has characterized U.S. history.

* From *American Indian Sports Heritage* (pp. xxi–xxiii) by J. B. Oxendine, 1988, Champaign, IL: Human Kinetics. Copyright © 1988 by Joseph B. Oxendine. Reprinted by permission.

• •

1600s and the 1700s, although participation patterns reflected and reproduced social class divisions in society.

In colonial America, Puritan influence was strong from the time of the founding of the colonies until the eighteenth century. Many of the colonists were not playful people; hard work was necessary for survival. However, as the lifestyles of the colonists became established and as free time became available, Puritan beliefs became less important than the desire to make games from the past a part of life in the new colonies. Town laws prohibiting games and sports gradually were abandoned, and traditional leisure activities, including sports, grew in popularity.

During this time, the games of Native Americans were not affected by the influence of the Puritans. Native peoples in the East and Northeast continued to play games that had been a part of their cultures for centuries. In fact, sport and sport participation has many histories across North America. The material in the box on pp. 70–71 above explains how and why the history of sports among Native Americans has been distorted.

The Enlightenment

During the Enlightenment period (1700 to 1800), many games and sport activities in parts of Europe and North America started to resemble sport forms that we are familiar with today (Guttmann, 1978). With some exceptions, they were no longer grounded in religious ritual and ceremony; they involved some specialization and some degree of organization; achievements sometimes were measured; and records occasionally were kept. Furthermore, the idea that events should be open to all competitors, regardless of background, became increasingly popular. This very commitment to equality and open participation gave rise to world-changing revolutions in France and the United States.

However, sport activities during the Enlightenment period were different from high-profile sport forms of today in at least one important respect: they were defined strictly as diversions, that is, as interesting and often challenging ways to pass free time. People did not see them as having any utility for athletes in particular or society in general. No one seriously thought that sports and sport participation could change how people developed or acted, or how social life was organized. Therefore, there were no reasons for people to organize sport activities for others or to build sport organizations to oversee the activities of large networks of participants. People formed a few sport clubs, and they occasionally scheduled contests with other groups, but they did not feel compelled to form leagues or national and international associations. All this began to change during the Industrial Revolution.

THE INDUSTRIAL REVOLUTION: THE EMERGENCE OF STANDARDIZED SPORT FORMS (1780 TO THE PRESENT)

It would be an oversimplification to say that the organized, competitive sports of today are simply a product of the Industrial Revolution (Gruneau, 1988). They clearly emerged during the process of industrialization, but they were actually "social constructions" of people themselves—people who were trying to play their games and maintain their sport activities while they coped with the realities of everyday life in their rapidly changing families and communities.

It is difficult to pinpoint the beginning of the Industrial Revolution. It is not marked by a single event, but started with the development of factories and the mass production of consumer goods. It was associated with the development of cities and an increased dependence on technology. It involved changes in the organization and control of work and community life and was generally accompanied by an increase in the number of middle-class people in the societies in which it occurred. The Industrial Revolution first began in England around 1780. Shortly after that time it became a part of life in other European countries; in the United States and Canada, it started around 1820.

The Early Years: Limited Time and Space

During the early years of the Industrial Revolution, it was difficult for all people except the very wealthy to maintain their involvement in games and sport activities. Those who worked on farms and in factories had little free time. The workdays, even for many child workers, were often long and tiring. People who lived in cities had few open spaces in which they could play sports. Production took priority over play in the plans of industrialists and city leaders. Parks did not exist. Furthermore, working people were discouraged from getting together in large groups outside the workplace. Those in authority perceived such gatherings as dangerous because they wasted time that could be used for work, and because they provided opportunities for workers to organize themselves and challenge the power of the owners of the means of production.

In most industrializing countries, the clergy also endorsed the containment of popular games and gatherings. Ministers preached about the moral value of work and the immorality of play and idleness. Many even banned sports on Sundays and accused anyone who was not totally committed to work of being lazy. In the religious belief systems of the time, work was a sign of goodness. Not everyone agreed with this way of looking at things, but working people had few choices. For them, survival depended on working long hours, regardless of what they thought about work, and they had little power to change these definitions of work or what they needed to do to survive.

In most countries, games and sport activities existed during this period despite the Industrial Revolution, not because of it. People in small towns and farm communities still had opportunities to participate in games and sport activities during their seasonal festivities, holidays, and public ceremonies. But most city people had few opportunities to organize their own games and sports. The only exceptions to this were those few people who could use newly acquired family fortunes to maintain lives of leisure. But for the working classes, sport involvement seldom went beyond being spectators at new forms of commercialized sport events. Although there were variations from one country to the next, urban workers watched a combination of cricket, horse racing, boxing and wrestling, footraces, rowing and yachting races, cockfighting, bullbaiting, and circus acts, among other things.

It seems that the rules against getting together in large crowds were suspended when people were participating in controlled commercialized spectator events. A fear of riots had led to restrictions on many neighborhood events that might have attracted crowds, but organized commercial events seldom met objections in most industrial societies, even when they attracted large groups; these events were controlled and organized to benefit the interests of the powerful.

Some sport participation among urban workers did occur, but it was relatively rare during the early days of the Industrial Revolution. In the United States, for example, it was usually limited to activities like bowling and billiards, and these were played mostly by males. The constraints of work and the lack of material resources made it difficult for working-class people to engage in anything but informal games and sport activities. There were some exceptions, but they were rare.

Similarly, African American slaves, who constituted 20 percent of the U.S. population during the early 1800s, had few opportunities to engage in any games or sports beyond what the slaveholders permitted. The dancing and other physical activities Africans performed in the slave quarters emphasized cooperation and community spirit—qualities required for their survival (Wiggins, 1994). These activities took forms based on a combination of memories of Africa and efforts to deal with the experience of slavery. According to former slave and noted abolitionist Frederick Douglass, the games and holidays the slaveholders permitted "were among the most effective means . . . of keeping down the spirit of insurrection among the slaves" (quoted in Ashe, 1993:10).

Around the middle of the nineteenth century, things began to change. During the first part of the century, people in parts of Europe and North America had become concerned about the physical health of workers. Some of this concern was grounded in an awareness that workers were being exploited, and some was grounded in the recognition that weak and sickly workers could not be productive. So people began calling for new open spaces and sponsored "healthy" leisure pursuits. Fitness became highly publicized, and there was an emphasis on calisthenics, gymnastics, and outdoor exercises. In the U.S., for example, these fitness activities did not necessarily include sports, but they definitely excluded hanging around in pool halls, bowling alleys, and bars. Furthermore, the Emancipation Proclamation and the Civil War made it possible for 4.5 million ex-slaves to pursue many different sport activities.

The emergence of formally organized, competitive sports would require more than increased freedom and calls for healthy leisure activities, but this was the time during which their foundations were established. In discussing more recent issues related to sport in society, we will focus in the next section on events in the United States.

The Later Years: Changing Interests, Values, and Opportunities

From the late nineteenth century until now, there has been a growing emphasis on rationality and control in American society as a whole. For example, during the 1800s, common interests in sport activities led to the establishment of organized clubs that sponsored and controlled sport participation. Club membership usually was limited to wealthier people in urban areas and college students at the exclusive Eastern schools. However, the clubs did sponsor competitions that often attracted spectators from all social classes. And the YMCA, founded in England in 1844 and a few years later in the U.S., did much to change the popular notion that physical conditioning through exercise and sports was anti-Christian (Ashe, 1993).

The games and sport activities of the people in lower income groups did not usually occur under the sponsorship of clubs or organizations, and seldom received any publicity. The major exception to this pattern was baseball. Middle- and working-class male participation in baseball was relatively widespread, and after the Civil War, baseball games were organized, sponsored, and publicized in many communities throughout the East and Midwest. Leagues were established at various levels of competition, and professional baseball became increasingly popular. Professional women's teams existed, but they seldom received the sponsorship they needed to grow in popularity. And African Americans developed teams and leagues around the country, despite the racism that prevented them from playing in many communities in the south.

As sport activities became more organized, they generally reinforced existing class distinctions in society. Upper-class clubs emphasized achievement and "gentlemanly" involvement—an orientation that ultimately provided the basis for later definitions of amateurism (which originated in England). These definitions of the "amateur" then became tools for excluding working-class people from the sport events organized to fit the interests of upper-class participants (Eitzen, 1988). The activities of the working classes, by contrast, were much more likely to emphasize folk games and commercialized sports—a combination that ultimately led to professionalization. This two-phased development of amateurism and professionalization occurred in slightly different ways in England, Canada, the U.S., and a number of European countries.

THE SEEDS OF NEW MEANINGS Underlying the increasing organization of sport activities during the second half of the nineteenth century was a growing emphasis on the seriousness of sports. Instead of defining them simply as enjoyable diversions, people came to see organized sports as tools for achieving economic progress and social development. Many people linked sport participation with economic productivity, national loyalty, and the development of admirable character traits, especially among males. This new way of looking at organized sports was grounded in a wide array of changes in every segment of industrial society: the economy, politics, family life, religion, education, science, philosophy, and technology.

THE GROWTH OF ELITE, COMPETITIVE SPORTS IN THE UNITED STATES: 1880 TO 1920

Power and wealth in action. The years between 1880 and 1920 were crucial for the development of elite, competitive sport forms in the United States (Cavallo, 1981; Mrozek, 1983). During this time, very wealthy people developed lives of leisure in which sport activities played a major part. In fact, the rich used participation in certain sports to prove to the world that they were successful enough to have the luxury of "wasting" time by engaging in frivolous, nonproductive activities (Veblen, 1899). Although the wealthy often used sports to reinforce status distinctions between themselves and the rest of the population, they also influenced how sports were played and organized by others, especially those in the middle class who aspired to enter the ranks of the rich and powerful.

The leisure activities of the wealthy at the turn of the century included sports. Systems of gender exclusion in sports have varied through history, and from one sport to another. Sports played by girls and women during the nineteenth and twentieth centuries often involved balance and coordination, which were defined as "ladylike" qualities, and they often included nets or other barriers so that there would be no physical contact between female players. (H. Armstrong Roberts)

The influence of the upper classes affected various dimensions of sports: sport norms for players and spectators, standards for facilities and equipment, and the ways people in other social classes defined sports and integrated them into their leisure patterns. Specifically, wealthy people used their economic resources to encourage others to define sport as a consumer activity to be played in *proper* attire, using the *proper* equipment in a *proper* facility, and preceded or followed by *proper* social occasions separated from employment and the workplace. Through this process of "encouragement" and developing consensus about the forms and meanings of sports (referred to as *hegemony* by many sociologists; see chap. 4, p. 110), sports became closely tied to the economy in an interesting way: they involved widespread consumption and a commitment to rules and productivity, while at the same time being popularly defined as forms of "nonwork" separate from the economy.

The emergence of these ideas about how sports "should be" played was important because it enabled people with power to reproduce their privilege in society without overtly coercing workers to think and do certain things. Instead of maintaining their privilege by being nasty, people with economic power promoted sport forms that were entertaining and fun, but at the same time reinforced the values and orientations that were good for capitalist business expansion. This is a good example of the way sports are both "political" and "economic" activities, even though most people see them as just fun physical activities and events.

During the period from 1880 to 1920, opportunities for sport involvement among middle- and working-class people grew, especially for white boys and men. Labor unions, progressive government legislation, and economic expansion combined to improve working and living conditions—except among many blacks, who faced new forms of racism and segregation beginning in the mid-1880s as a white backlash to Reconstruction occurred. The efforts of unions and social reformers gradually led to increases in the free time and the material resources available to many working-class people. This process was complemented by the expansion of the middle class, a collection of people with at least some leisure resources. The spirit of reform around the turn of the century also was associated with the development of parks, recreation programs, and organized playground activities for city people, especially children.

Ideas about sport participation and "character development." Early in the twentieth century, opportunities for sport involvement increased, but the kinds of opportunities available to most people were shaped by factors beyond the interests of the participants themselves. Important changes in how people thought about human behavior, individual development, and social life led to an emphasis on organized, competitive sports as "character-building" activities.

Until the latter part of the nineteenth century, most people believed human behavior was unrelated to environmental factors. They believed that fate or supernatural forces dictated individual development, and that social life was established by a combination of God's will, necessity, and coincidence. However, these ideas began to change as people became aware of the links between the environment and behavior and of the possibility to intentionally change how social life was organized.

This new perspective was a crucial catalyst in the growth of modern sports; it made sports into something more than just enjoyable pastimes. Gradually, sports came to be defined as potential educational experiences—experiences with important consequences for both individuals and society as a whole. This change, based on the functionalist theory that was dominant at the time, provided a new basis for organizing and promoting sport participation. For the first time in history, people saw sports as tools for positively changing behavior, shaping character, building unity and cohesion in an ethnically diverse population, and creating national loyalty.

People began to think about the meaning and purpose of sports in new and serious terms. For example, some religious groups, later referred to as "muscular Christians" (see chap. 15), suggested a link between physical strength and the ability to do good works; they promoted sport involvement as an avenue for spiritual growth. Others saw sports as tools for teaching immigrant children lessons that would make them into contributing members of a corporate-bureaucratic-democratic society; they promoted organized playground programs that used team sports to undermine traditional ethnic values and replace them with an Americanized way of looking at the world. Those interested in economic expansion tended to see organized sports as tools for generating profits and introducing untrained workers to activities emphasizing teamwork, obedience to rules, planning, organization, and production; they promoted sports for the purpose of creating good workers who could tolerate stressful working conditions.

In large part, organized sports became important because they could be used to train loyal and hardworking bodies dedicated to achievement and production for the glory of God and country. Sports were socially constructed and defined in ways that people believed would promote this

In the 1920s the women's suffrage movement was strong, and many women pushed the boundaries of gender. Attempts to challenge and transform society included playing what then were defined as "men's sports." Women's soccer and baseball games often drew large crowds, even though some people believed that participation in these sports was contrary to nature and morality. (Sally Fox)

type of character development. In the U.S., this was done through new "Americanized" sports like football, baseball, and basketball. Soccer, very popular among many central and southern European immigrants at the turn of the century, was believed to perpetuate potentially dangerous links with "foreign" cultures. Therefore, those who wanted to encourage new American identities among immigrants viewed soccer negatively. And it has taken soccer nearly eighty years to make a partial comeback in the U.S.

Organized sports and ideas about masculinity and femininity. The new belief that sport participation built character was applied primar-

ily to males. Those who organized and sponsored new programs thought they could use organized sports, especially team sports, to tame what they perceived as the savage, undisciplined character of young, lower-class males. Their intent was to create orderly citizens and cooperative workers. They used sports for young males from middle-class backgrounds, on the other hand, to counteract what many believed was the negative influence of female-dominated home lives, turning "overfeminized" males into assertive, competitive, achievement-oriented young men who would make good leaders in business, politics, and the military. In these ways, contemporary sports were heavily grounded in the desire of those in the dominant social classes to exercise control over the working classes, while at the same time preparing their own sons to inherit their positions of power and influence.

Although an increasing number of women participated in sport activities between 1880 and 1920, many sport programs ignored females. Organizers and sponsors did not see females' participation in organized sports as an important factor in their character development. They sometimes included young girls with boys in the organized games in playground programs, but discouraged sex-integrated sport activities for children nearing the age of puberty. There were strong fears that if boys and girls played sports with one another they might become good friends, and that if they were friends, their relationships would lose the mystery that led people to be interested in getting married and having children. (We may laugh at such a "theory" today, but I've recently heard people say similar things about possible problems of allowing women to play on football and wrestling teams).

While boys were taught to play a number of different sports on the playgrounds after the turn of the century, girls often were given shady places where they could rest and preserve their energy. Medical doctors warned that playing sports would sap the energy needed to conceive and bear healthy children. And Luther Gulick, the primary shaper of the YMCA's philosophy on recreation at that time, wrote, "It is clear that athletics have never been either a test or a large factor in the survival of women; athletics do not test womanliness as they test manliness." Gulick also felt that strenuous activity was harmful to the minds and bodies of females. This was the "gender logic" of the time.

Therefore, organized activities for girls often consisted of domestic science classes designed to make them good homemakers and mothers. When playground organizers did provide opportunities for girls to play games and sports, they designed activities that would cultivate "lady-like" traits, such as poise and body control. This is why so many girls participated in gymnastics, figure skating, and other "grace and beauty" sports (Hart, 1981). Another goal of the activities was to make young women healthy for bearing children. Competition was eliminated or controlled, and the activities emphasized personal health, the dignity of beauty, and good form. In some cases, the only reason games and sports were included in girls' activities was to provide the knowledge they would need in the future to introduce their sons to active games.

Limited opportunities and a lack of encouragement did not stop women from participating in sports, but they certainly restricted the extent of their involvement. Some middle- and upper-class women engaged in popular physical exercises and recreational sport activities, but apart from a limited number of intercollegiate games and private tournaments, they had few opportunities to engage in formal competitive events. The participation of girls and women from lower income groups was restricted to informal street games, a few supervised exercise classes, and field days in public schools. Ideas about femininity were changing between 1880 and 1920, but Victorian attitudes and numerous misconceptions about the physical and mental effects of strenuous activities on females prevented the "new woman" of the early twentieth century from enjoying the same participation opportunities and encouragement males received (Lenskyj, 1986). In fact, medical beliefs did more to subvert the health of women during these years than to improve it (Vertinsky, 1987).

Organized sports and ideas about skin color and ethnicity. After the Civil War, African Americans in the U.S. became increasingly involved in sports. Much of their participation occurred in segregated settings, but participation with whites gradually increased until the 1880s, when new forms of segregation and racism emerged to slow the changes that were upsetting a society built on white privilege. Whites in both the North and the South became increasingly uncomfortable with changes in race relations and drafted Jim Crow laws that clearly divided people into the categories of "white" and "black" and restricted the rights and opportunities of blacks.

The widespread belief among whites that blacks were intellectually and physically inferior led many whites to view black athletes as a curiosity. But as black athletes gradually demonstrated their skills in certain sports, whites developed increasingly detailed genetic explanations for black achievements. The more blacks achieved in sports, the more whites used those achievements as "proof" that blacks had animal-like characteristics that made them socially inferior. This powerful form of "race logic" became deeply ingrained in U.S. culture.

White ethnics (Irish, Italians, Germans, and others) during this time also experienced forms of discrimination that limited their sport participation and forced them to play their native games in ethnically segregated clubs. Public schools became the settings in which many young men from these ethnic groups came to learn Americanized sports and enjoy participation to such an extent that they often excelled in them.

Organized sports and ideas about age and disability. Aging involves biological changes, but the connection between aging and sport participation depends on the social meanings given to those changes. Because developmental theory around the turn of the century emphasized that development occurs during childhood and adolescence, sport programs were created and sponsored for young people, not for older ones. The theories suggested that older people were already developed: they were "grown up," and their characters could no longer be developed.

Medical knowledge at the time also discouraged older people from engaging in sports. Many believed that strenuous activities might put too many demands on the heart and other muscles. This did not stop older people from participating in certain forms of sport activities, but those activities seldom were sponsored by public or private programs. Furthermore, when participation did occur among older people, it was usually in age-segregated settings.

People with most forms of physical or mental disability during this time were either denied the opportunity to participate in or actively discouraged from engaging in most physical activities, especially sports. People were unsure about the effects of strenuous exercise on their behavior or physical well-being. Definitions of mental and physical disability often gave rise to fears and prejudices; therefore, those who were not able in mind and body were either isolated or seen as unworthy of any serious attention related to their development.

1880 to 1920—a key period. Although opportunities for participation in organized, competitive sports were not equally distributed by social class, gender, skin color, age, or ability during these years, participation increased dramatically. This was the case in most industrializing societies. In most Western cultures, the organizational attributes we associate with today's high-profile organized sports became clearly established during this time. The games people played featured a combination of secularism, a growing commitment to participation among competitors from all socioeconomic backgrounds, increased specialization, rationalization, bureaucratization, quantification, and the quest for records. As the box on pp. 80–82 explains, these are some of the sociologically relevant characteristics that have become the foundation for what many people define as sports today.

Since 1920, the resources devoted to what many people define as sports have increased in many societies around the world. Technology has been used to change sport experiences for both participants and spectators, and tremendous growth has occurred in sport-related industries and government sponsorship of sports. But many of today's struggles about what sports are and how they should be integrated into people's lives were visible in some form eighty years ago.

The Characteristics of High-Profile, Organized, Competitive Sports

The organized, competitive sports so popular in many parts of the world today are very different from the games and sport activities played before the Industrial Revolution. Allen Guttmann's study of sport activities through history shows that today's *dominant form of sports* (DFSport) has seven interrelated characteristics that have never before appeared together in sport forms. These characteristics are as follows:

1. *Secularism.* Today's DFSport is not directly linked to religious beliefs or rituals. It is a means of entertainment, not worship; it is played for personal gains, not the appeasement of gods; it embodies the immediacy of the material world, not the mysticism of the supernatural.

2. *Equality.* Today's DFSport is based on the ideas that participation should not be regulated by birthright or social background, and that all contestants in a sport event should face the same set of competitive conditions, regardless of who they are or where they come from.

3. *Specialization.* Today's DFSport is dominated by the participation of specialists and the spectators who watch them. Athletes often dedicate themselves exclusively to participation in a single event or position within an event. Positions often are defined and distinguished from one another by skills and responsibilities. Equipment, such as shoes and clothing, is specialized to fit the demands of particular activities.

4. *Rationalization.* Today's DFSport consists of complex sets of rules and strategies. Rules specify goals and how athletes should pursue goals; they also regulate equipment, playing techniques, and the conditions of participation. Strategies inspire rationally controlled training methods that affect the experience of sport participation and the evaluation of athletes.

5. *Bureaucratization.* Today's DFSport is controlled through the establishment of complex organizations on the international, national, and local levels. The people in these organizations oversee and sanction athletes, teams, and events. They

Organized competitive sports today are characterized by an emphasis on quantification, among other things. Everything that can be defined in terms of time, distance, or scores is measured and recorded. The clock is key in sports. (Bob Jackson, *Colorado Springs Gazette*)

make up and enforce rules, organize events, and certify records.

6. *Quantification.* Today's DFSport features an abundance of measurements and statistics. Everything that can be reduced to a time, distance, or score is measured and recorded. Standards of achievement are discussed in clearly measurable terms, and statistics are used as proof of achievements.

7. *Records.* Today's DFSport involves an emphasis on setting and breaking records. Performances are compared from one event to another, and records are published for individuals, teams, leagues, events, communities, states, provinces, and continents. Most important, of course, are world records.

One or more of these traits have characterized sport forms of previous historical periods, but not until the nineteenth century did all seven appear together. This does not mean that today's organized, competitive sports are somehow superior to the games and activities of the past. It means only that they are different in the way they are organized. Sociologists are concerned with these differences because they have implications for the choices of participants and the ways they experience participation.

Table 3–1 summarizes Guttmann's historical analysis of sports in terms of these characteristics. It illustrates that today's dominant form of sports is indeed different from the sports played by people in times past. However, it does not explain why the differences exist.

Finally, we should remember that not all sports today have these seven characteristics. Sports are social constructions, and many people seek alternatives to today's dominant form of sports, which are marked by these seven characteristics.

Table 3–1 Historical comparison of organized games, contests, and sport activities*

Characteristic	Greek games and contests (1000 BC to 100 BC)	Roman sports events (100 BC to 500 AD)	Medieval games and tournaments (500 to 1300)	Renaissance and Enlightenment games and sport activities (1300 to 1800)	Modern sports
Secularism	Yes & no	Yes & no	Yes & no	Yes & no	Yes
Equality	Yes & no	Yes & no	No	Yes & no	Yes
Specialization	Yes	Yes	No	Yes & no	Yes
Rationalization	Yes	Yes	No	No	Yes
Bureaucratization	Yes & no	Yes	No	No	Yes
Quantification	No	Yes	No	Yes & no	Yes
Records	No	No	No	Yes & no	Yes

*This is a modified version of a table developed by Guttmann (1978). I have dropped Guttmann's information on primitive sports, added information on sports during the Renaissance and Enlightenment, and changed column titles.

Calvin and Hobbes   by Bill Watterson

As social life becomes increasingly rationalized and bureaucratized, so do sports. Even Calvin, who values spontaneity and personal expression, sometimes defines fun in terms of measurable indicators defined by those he calls "experts." Does the emergence and use of sport science influence how some people define sport experiences?

SINCE THE 1920S: THE STRUGGLES CONTINUE Major cultural links between sports and American society had been established by the 1920s. The desire to make or raise money had led to the creation and marketing of spectator sports on the professional and intercollegiate levels. Entertainment had become at least as important as the development of moral character in the sponsorship of sports. The most heavily promoted sports were football, baseball, and basketball. Each was native to the United States; each celebrated a form of masculinity emphasizing aggression, domination, and emotional control; and each was used to generate profits, patriotism, and national loyalties. Commercial interests had promoted an emphasis on competition, winning, and record setting.

Basic organizational structures for professional sports had been established. Colleges had formed athletic conferences and a national association governing intercollegiate sports. There were numerous other national associations connected with a wide variety of amateur and professional sports, and the Olympics had been revived and held on six different occasions: once in Greece, four times in western Europe, and once in the United States.

By the 1920s there already had been investigations of problems in intercollegiate sports, and some had accused college football of being too violent, too professionalized, and unrelated to educational goals. Powerful economic and political interests controlled major league baseball. It had already had serious labor problems, and had faced a highly publicized gambling scandal in the 1919 World Series.

Universities and local governments had constructed lavish stadiums and field houses for the purpose of showcasing their men's teams. Newspapers promoted and sensationalized sport events to boost their circulation; radio broadcasts brought sports into people's homes and maintained spectator interest in both urban and rural areas.

High school and college athletes had become a primary focus of attention within many schools, and the "dumb athlete" stereotype had become popular in many colleges and universities. Interscholastic teams were elitist and sexist. Schools generally ignored the participation interests of female students, providing them with sport "field days" at best. Some women struggled to make changes in these "traditions," but they had little success. With rare exceptions, sports at

During this century sports clearly have been linked to political ideologies, and sport events often have been settings for the display of political symbols. Political symbols sometimes are associated with gender and racial images. We will discuss the racial images in this photograph of the 1936 Olympics, and a related photograph, in chapter 9. (USOC Archives)

all levels of participation were racially segregated. However, blacks had formed and sponsored their own teams in many communities (Ashe, 1993; Ruck, 1987). Black athletes received widespread attention only when it was in the financial interests of whites to provide coverage.

Coaching had emerged as a specialized, technical profession, and coaches were hired to supervise teams and maintain winning records. The control of teams had shifted from the players to coaches, managers, owners, and top administrative staff members. These professionals used principles of scientific management to teach strategies and train athletes. Some athletes even took substances they thought would enhance their performance. There was a heavy emphasis on obedience to authority, both on and off the field. Control over the lives of athletes had become an important issue because of

the commercial and reputational consequences of events; it was easier to sell "clean" events and "clean" athletes than to sell "tarnished" events and athletes.

Rules had become standardized on a national level, so that commercially attractive intersectional competitions could be held. Sponsoring organizations kept records and statistics, frequently publishing them in newspapers and discussing them in radio broadcasts. The broadcasters used flair and exaggeration to dramatize events and enhance their own images and reputations.

Thus, sports in the 1920s contained the seeds of today's sports. There were differences, of course: fewer teams and leagues, no television, no instant replays, no domed stadiums or artificial turf, no corporate ownership of professional teams, and no agents bargaining for bigger player contracts. Things certainly have changed over the past eighty years—but sport itself continues to be socially constructed through the struggles of various groups to integrate physical activities into their lives in ways that meet their interests. Therefore, sports remain organized and competitive; they remain integrally linked to commercial interests; and they remain tied to an emphasis on the importance of winning and on their supposed character-building consequences.

In other words, sports continue to be contested activities, and people continue to struggle over how they could and should be defined and organized (see box in chap. 1, p. 24). For example, some people change rules in their sport leagues so they can have more fun; others form groups that have no formal rules and organization. Some people push to expand women's opportunities in sports; others call for women to develop alternative sport forms emphasizing partnership rather than domination (Nelson, 1991). People still confront issues of racial exclusion, disabled people fight for resources for their events, and gay men and lesbians have their own Gay Games. Professional athletes organize themselves into unions and even call strikes to gain more control of the conditions of their own sport involvement; owners lock players out and collude with one another to maintain their power.

These things all happen in social, political, and economic contexts that limit alternatives and influence the choices made by individuals and groups. The sociology of sport is concerned with these struggles and these contexts.

SUMMARY

LOOKING AT SPORT AT DIFFERENT TIMES AND IN DIFFERENT PLACES

Throughout history, games and sport activities have been integrally related to social relations and forces in societies. As these relations and forces have changed and as power has shifted, there have been changes in the organization and meanings of games and sport activities, and in the people who participate in and sponsor them.

In ancient Greece, games and contests were grounded in mythology and religious beliefs. They focused on the interests of young males from the wealthier segments of society. As the outcomes of organized games took on political implications beyond the events themselves, athletes were recruited from the lower classes and paid for their participation. This process of professionalization was accompanied by developments similar to those associated with professional sports today.

Roman sport events emphasized mass entertainment. They were designed to celebrate and preserve the power of political leaders and to pacify masses of unemployed and underemployed workers in Roman cities and towns. Many athletes in Roman events were slaves recruited for the events, or "troublemakers" coerced into jeopardizing their lives in battle with one another or with wild animals. These sport spectacles faded with the demise of the Roman Empire.

Sport activities in Europe during the Middle Ages clearly reflected and reproduced gender and status differences in medieval societies. The peasants played local versions of folk games in connection with seasonal events in village life. The knights and nobles engaged in tournaments and jousts. Other members of the upper classes, including the clergy, often used their resources to develop numerous games and sport activities to occupy their leisure time.

This pattern continued through the Renaissance in parts of Europe, although the Protestant Reformation generated negative attitudes about any activities interfering with work and religious worship. Peasants felt the impact of these attitudes most sharply, as they seldom had the resources to avoid the restrictive controls imposed by government officials who were inspired by Calvinist or Puritan orientations. The games and sports of the wealthy generally continued within the safe confines of their private grounds. The Enlightenment was associated with increased political rights and freedom to engage in diversionary games and physical activities.

During the early days of the Industrial Revolution, the influence of the Puritans faded in both Europe and North America, but the demands of work and the absence of spaces for play generally limited sport involvement to the wealthy and people in rural areas. This pattern began to change in the United States from the middle to the late nineteenth century, when the combined influence of labor unions, progressive legislation, and economic expansion led to the creation of new ideas about the consequences of sport participation and new opportunities for involvement. However, opportunities for involvement were shaped primarily by the needs of an economy emphasizing mass production and mass consumption. It was in this context that people developed what we now refer to as organized, competitive sports.

Sports have never been so pervasive and influential in the lives of people as they are in many societies today, and never before have physical activities and games been so closely linked to profit making, character building, patriotism, and personal health. Organized sports in the United States have become a combination of business, entertainment, education, moral training, masculinity rituals, technology transfer, declarations of identity, and endorsements of allegiance to countries and corporate sponsors. However, sports are also activities through which people seek physical challenges and exciting expressive experiences seldom available in the rest of their lives (Elias and Dunning, 1986). All these things have combined to make organized, competitive sports important social phenomena, in the past, the present, and probably the future.

SUGGESTED READINGS

Ashe, A. 1993. *A hard road to glory.* 3 vols. New York: Amistad (*an overview and analysis of the history of sport participation among blacks in the U.S.; little attention is given to black women's participation in any form of sport activity*).

Baker, W. J. 1988. *Sports in the western world.* Urbana, IL: University of Illinois Press (*a survey and analysis of European and North American sports starting with the ancient Greeks and ending with contemporary commercial sports*).

Cahn, S. K. 1994. *Coming on strong: Gender and sexuality in twentieth-century women's sports.* New York: The Free Press (*focuses on the struggles women have engaged in as they have become increasingly involved in sports since the turn of the century*).

Cavallo, D. 1981. *Muscles and morals: Organized playgrounds and urban reform, 1880–1920.* Philadelphia: University of Pennsylvania Press (*excellent discussion of how sports became connected with American values around the turn of the century*).

Dunning, E., and K. Sheard. 1979. *Barbarians, gentlemen and players: A sociological study of the development of rugby football.* New York: University Press (*uses sociological concepts to explain the development of one of Britain's most popular sports*).

Elias, N., and E. Dunning. 1986. *Quest for excitement.* New York: Basil Blackwell (*a historical overview of how sport and leisure are linked to the civilizing process in Western societies*).

Goodman, C. 1979. *Choosing sides: Playground and street life on the Lower East Side.* New York: Shocken Books (*a critique of the efforts of playground organizers who used organized recreation programs to subvert the street games of immigrants in New York City around the turn of the century*).

Gruneau, R. 1983. *Class, sports, and social development.* Amherst, MA: University of Massachusetts Press (*Chap. 3 contains a social history of sport and social development in Canada*).

Gruneau, R. 1988. Modernization or hegemony: two views of sport and social development. In J. Harvey and H. Cantelon, eds., *Not just a game.* Ottawa, Ontario: University of Ottawa Press (*a concise critique of conceptual approaches to the history of sport; read this article before reading any of the "historical accounts" of sport events in this list*).

Guttmann, A. 1978. *From ritual to record: The nature of modern sports.* New York: Columbia University Press (*a comparative analysis of the characteristics of sports in different historical periods*).

Guttmann, A. 1988. *A whole new ball game: An interpretation of American sports.* Chapel Hill, NC University of North Carolina Press (*a readable interpretation of sports within the social context of U.S. history;*

includes chapters on sports and Native Americans, Puritans, and Southerners, among other topics).

Guttmann, A. 1991. *Women's sports: A history.* New York: Columbia University Press (*an overview of women's sport participation in ancient civilizations through the present, with special emphasis on the nineteenth and twentieth centuries*).

Kruger, A., and J. Riordan, eds. 1996. *The story of worker sport.* Champaign, IL Human Kinetics (*an overview and ten accounts of the history of the worker sport movement, which, between 1912 and the late 1940s, provided for workers around the world an alternative to sport forms emerging in connection with capitalist economic expansion*).

Mandell, R. 1984. *Sport: A cultural history.* New York: Columbia University Press (*a discussion of the cultural importance of sport through history in Western Europe and North America; analysis generally is grounded in a functionalist approach to the sport-society relationship*).

Mrozek, D. J. 1983. *Sport and American mentality, 1880–1920.* Knoxville: The University of Tennessee Press (*an excellent social historical analysis of the origins of modern sports in the United States*).

Ruck, R. *Sandlot seasons: Sport in black Pittsburgh.* Urbana, IL: University of Illinois Press (*a unique look at the sporting life and the meanings of sport in the community life of blacks in Pittsburgh in the early twentieth century*).

Wiggins, D. K., ed. 1995. *Sport in America: From wicked amusement to national obsession.* Champaign, IL: Human Kinetics, (*nineteen essays focusing on sport activities from colonial times to the 1990s*).

4

(Danielle Hicks)

Sports and Socialization
Who plays and what happens to them?

In gym, when we start . . . basketball or volleyball, most of the girls go to the benches and just talk. All the guys are on the court . . . . That's why I think most of the guys from my school figure the girls can't play sports.

David, high school student (1996)

Whatever else you learn in school, I would like you to master at least two "life sports" . . . . [that] can bring you comfort and pleasure for the rest of your life. . . . [T]he lessons of sports cannot be duplicated easily; you quickly discover your limits but you can also build . . . a positive sense of yourself.*

Arthur Ashe, activist and tennis player, *My Dear Camera* (Ashe's advice to his daughter before his death, 1993)

I signed my first contract when I was nineteen years old. From that minute on, I was a professional. But it took me every second of every minute before that to make me a player.*

Shawn Kemp, NBA player (1996)

The professional [athlete]. . . is for all practical purposes terminally adolescent . . . . [T]he longer the exposure to the professional [sport] environment . . . the further athletes will drift from an ability to understand and cope with the demands of the real world.*

Tom House, psychologist and former major-league pitcher (1989)

What do kids know about us? They only know that we play sports. They don't know who we are as people. You don't learn the important things about life by watching a person play football.

Emmitt Smith, NFL player (1996)

Sports and socialization is a popular topic today. In fact, whenever we discuss the following questions, we are talking about "sports and socialization" issues:

- Why are some people fanatically interested in playing and/or watching sports while others don't seem to care about sports?
- How and why do some people see themselves as athletes and dedicate themselves to playing particular sports?
- When and why do people stop playing sports, and what happens to them when they do?
- What impact do sports and sport participation have on people's lives, characters, relationships, careers, the way they think, and what they do?

Since so many people are interested in these questions, many of us in the sociology of sport have done research to attempt to answer them. But the search for answers has taken people in different directions depending on the theoretical frameworks they have used to guide their thinking about sports and sport participation. I will deal with this issue in the first section of this chapter.

After looking at how definitions of socialization influence research, I will consider three issues important in the sociology of sport:

- the process of becoming involved and staying involved in sports
- the process of changing or ending sport participation
- the impact of being involved in sports

As I discuss these issues, I will note how sociologists have answered the questions listed above. As you read the chapter, you will see that most of our answers are incomplete, and that others are so complex that discussions about them will carry over into other chapters.

The chapter ends with a description of new approaches to socialization, approaches based on theoretical frameworks that emphasize socialization as a community and cultural process rather than an individual and personal process.

WHAT IS SOCIALIZATION?

Socialization is an active process of learning and social development that occurs as people interact with one another and become acquainted with the social world in which they live, and as they form ideas about who they are, and make decisions about their goals and behaviors. Human beings are not simply passive learners in the socialization process. Instead, they actively participate: they influence those who influence them, they make their own interpretations of what they see and hear, and they accept, revise, or reject the messages they receive about who they are, what the world is all about, and what they should do as they make their way in the world. Therefore, socialization refers *not* to a one-way process through which society molds and shapes people, but to an interactive process through which people actively connect with others and *make decisions* that shape their own lives and the social world around them.

This definition of socialization, which I use in my research, is based on a combination of *critical* and *interactionist* theories. Therefore, not all sociologists would agree with it. Those using functionalist or conflict theory approaches, for example, would define socialization differently.

A Functionalist Approach to Socialization

When people used *functionalist theory* to guide their research, they defined socialization as a process through which society molded and shaped people, especially young people, so they fit into and contributed to its operation. Those in the sociology of sport used this functionalist definition widely through the 1970s. It assumed that human beings were passive learners who, as they grew up in their families and went to school, learned the rules they should follow and the roles they should play in order to contribute to society. Because of this assumption, we say that functionalists used an *internalization model* of socialization (see Coakley, 1993a, b), that is, a model according to which people responsively internalize the rules and roles of the society in which they live.

When researchers used an internalization model, they focused attention on three things: (1) the characteristics of those being socialized, (2) the people and social institutions that *did* the socializing, and (3) the specific outcomes of socialization. In most studies of sports and socialization, the researchers focused on athletes as the people being socialized. Those doing the socializing were fathers, mothers, brothers, sisters, teachers, coaches, peers, and occasionally, certain "role models." The most central and influential socializers were and still are referred to as **significant others.** The social institutions that did the socializing were education, religion, the government, the media, and sport itself. The outcomes of sport socialization that functionalists widely studied included personal attitudes, values, and skills that the researchers considered "functional" for the society as a whole.

Those who used a functionalist approach often studied who and what *caused* people to participate in sports, and how participation prepared young people to fit into and become contributing members of society as they grew up. Until recently, most socialization research used this approach. Hundreds of studies using quantitative research methods were done. Thousands of questionnaires were sent to people, especially children and high school students. Those who played certain organized sports were compared statistically with those who didn't play organized sports. Researchers presented data in these studies in complex tables, computed statistics to assess relationships between variables, and discussed findings in connection with hypotheses about the "benefits" of sports in society.

Some of these studies based on a functionalist approach have helped us to understand certain aspects of sport participation, but many reported inconsistent findings. Over the years they presented mixed information on the causes and benefits of playing sports, and they told us little about sport socialization as an ongoing process in people's lives. They gave us fuzzy snapshots of socialization, rather than clear videos with audio commentary.

A Conflict Theory Approach to Socialization

At the same time that functionalists were studying socialization (up through the early 1980s), *conflict theorists* were doing their own studies. Like the functionalists, they used an internalization model. However, they saw socialization as a process through which passive human beings were shaped by economic forces to become compliant workers and eager consumers of goods and services. Many conflict theorists assumed that people with economic power directed these economic forces for the purpose of maintaining their privileged positions in society. This approach led conflict theorists to focus on unique research issues such as these: (1) how sports were organized to produce work-based, militaristic, sexist, and racist orientations among players and spectators; (2) how people from low-income and working-class backgrounds had few opportunities or choices to play sports on their own terms and in their own ways; (3) how athletes, especially those from poor, minority backgrounds, lacked rights and usually became passive victims of a profit-driven, win-at-all-cost sport system, and (4) how people in positions of power controlled the conditions of sport participation to make money and maintain their own interests.

Therefore, studies by conflict theorists emphasized the ways elitist, oppressively organized sport programs and autocratic, military-style coaches produced athletes who were obedient, politically conservative, and willing to engage in violence to achieve goals approved by those with power in the society. These studies also focused on how sport participation usually was terminated due to injuries, or because athletes no longer contributed to economic profits for those who controlled sports.

New Approaches to Socialization

While the studies functionalists did often leave their readers confused and uncomfortable with the idea that we are all products of society and its "system needs," the studies by conflict theorists left us angry and uncomfortable with the idea that we are all pawns of economic forces and the interests of rich and powerful people. This is why many of us in the sociology of sport looked for new ways to define and study socialization.

Since the early 1980s, researchers increasingly have based their work on various combinations of critical and interactionist theories, and they are now more likely to define socialization the way I defined it at the beginning of this section. This new approach has led to qualitative rather than quantitative studies. That is, researchers now want detailed descriptions of sport experiences as they occur in the larger context of people's lives; they also want more information on the meanings associated with sport participation as a cultural experience. Questionnaires are still used, but more sociologists are using in-depth interviews and field observations to obtain the data they need to study socialization processes.

The rest of this chapter will explain and connect old and new approaches to sports and socialization.

BECOMING INVOLVED AND STAYING INVOLVED IN SPORTS

According to research based on functionalist theory, we know that sport participation is related to (1) people's abilities and characteristics, (2) the influence of family and friends on them, and (3) the availability of opportunities to play sports and experience success as they play. These are the snapshots of socialization into sports. However, a fuller description of the ongoing process of becoming and staying involved in sports emerges when we obtain stories from people about their sport participation. These are the "videos" we need to understand more fully why people play sports.

These stories, usually uncovered through in-depth interviews or long-term observations and strategic conversations, indicate that sport participation is not simply the result of outside influences. Instead, it is part of the larger processes that make up people's lives, and it occurs as people make decisions about their lives in connection with these processes. Because these processes are *ongoing*, people make decisions about sport participation continually, *not* once and for all time. As social conditions change, so do people's decisions. And as a person stays involved in sports, the person's reasons for participating on one day may be different from the reasons for participating the next day, or the next. When there is no reason, the person may discontinue or change his or her sport participation.

We can best understand the process of becoming and staying involved in sports by looking at examples of research. The studies summarized below give us sociological videos of how people integrated playing sports into their lives on an everyday basis. These videos may be fuzzy and blurred here and there, but they help us get a sense of the processes occurring in people's lives.

Example 1: The process of becoming an elite athlete Chris Stevenson is a physical educator interested in how people become athletes. As he interviewed and collected stories from elite athletes about how they were introduced to their sports and became committed to sport participation, he noticed that these stories sounded like descriptions of "careers." In other words, they seemed to have "a beginning, a development, and ultimately an end" (1990b). And an observer could understand these careers only as continual experiences that had varying degrees of importance in the athletes' lives over time. Being an athlete and playing sports was more important to an individual at some points than at others, depending on what was going on in the rest of the person's life.

In one of his studies, Stevenson interviewed twenty-nine Canadian and British international athletes. At first he was struck by the diversity of

Participation in sports usually is sponsored through important social relationships. This young man's participation in football is tied to his father's sponsorship. But his continued participation will depend on his own development of a commitment to the sport. Commitment depends on more than sponsorship; it emerges as an individual's identity develops and he or she establishes social connections related to sport participation. (Jay Coakley)

the stories the athletes told him. But then he detected two underlying processes in the stories. *First,* there was the process of **sponsored recruitment,** a term Stevenson used to explain how his interviewees had been introduced to sports bit by bit over time, through important relationships in their lives. Their entry into and participation in specific sports then was sponsored through those relationships. Thus, they made their decisions to try a sport in connection with support and encouragement that oc-

curred over time in their relationships. *Second,* there was the process of **developing a commitment** to sport participation. This process occurred as people did three things: (1) assessed their potential for achieving success in their sports, (2) formed a "web of personal relationships" connected with their participation, and (3) gradually established personal reputations and identities as athletes in their sports. Thus, their staying in sports depended on how these young people altered personal priorities and made choices about the ways they would include sport participation in their lives. Over time, their participation depended on their active and thoughtful efforts to develop desired identities as athletes. As this happened, and as these young people received recognition and respect from those important in their lives and in their sports, they became more deeply committed to sports and to being athletes.

Stevenson found that these processes did *not* occur automatically; the young people themselves helped them happen. Becoming and staying involved in sports was a problematic process. The young people realized that they could not take social support for playing sports and being athletes for granted: resources could disappear, and changes in other parts of their lives could force them to alter the importance of sport participation. Therefore, they made decisions to stay involved in sports day after day, and as they stayed involved, they influenced those who influenced and supported them. This is why we must see the socialization process as *interactive,* and the person being socialized as an active agent in the process.

Example 2: The process of being accepted as an athlete Peter Donnelly and Kevin Young are sociologists who also are interested in sports and socialization. As previously noted (see chap. 2, p. 51), they have studied sports as "social worlds" where people develop their own ways of doing things and relating to one another. They have paid special attention to how people become a part of those worlds. In their research, they have zoomed in and taken a closer look at some of the things Stevenson studied.

On the basis of stories that Donnelly collected from rock climbers and Young collected from rugby players, they determined that playing sports occurs in connection with processes of identity formation (1988). They explain that entering and becoming a part of a particular sport world depends on (1) acquiring knowledge about the sport, (2) associating with people involved in the sport, (3) learning how those people think about their sport and what they do and expect from each other, and (4) becoming recognized and fully accepted into the sport group as a fellow athlete.

This description of sport socialization extends our understanding of what is involved in "developing a commitment" to a sport. Donnelly and Young discovered that becoming involved in a sport depends on learning to "talk the talk and walk the walk" so that one is identified and accepted as an athlete by others who are athletes. This identification and acceptance does not happen once and for all time; it is a continuous process. When we lose touch and are no longer able to talk the talk and walk the walk, acceptance wanes, our identities are difficult to maintain, and overall support for our participation becomes weak. We are not "athletes" forever.

To replicate part of what Donnelly and Young found in their study, just observe a sport group such as skateboarders ("street skaters," "ramp skaters," or "curbheads"), in-line skaters, or beach volleyball players. They each have their own special vocabularies and ways of referring to themselves and what they do. They use terms not found in dictionaries. They also have unique ways of thinking about and doing their sports, and they have special understandings of what they can expect from others in their group. New participants in these sports may be tested and "pushed" by the "veterans" before being accepted and defined as true skaters, riders, or volleyball athletes. Vocabularies may change over time, but this process of becoming accepted and

gaining support for participation exists in basketball, hockey, gymnastics, golf—in every sport, in fact. Many people have discovered that if an individual does not establish social "connections" and acceptance, that person's sport participation may not be very regular or long term.

Example 3: To participate or not to participate Anita White is a sport sociologist who is now the national director of sport development at the British Sports Council. Before she began working at the Sports Council, Anita and I did a study of sport participation patterns among British adolescents in a working-class area east of London. Our goal was to provide coaches and program organizers information about why some young people participated in Council-sponsored sport programs, while most did not.

Our in-depth interviews with thirty-four young men and twenty-six young women indicated that participation or lack of participation in sports was the result of decisions based on a combination of factors. In the lives of British teenagers, these factors included these things: (1) their ideas about how sport participation was related to other interests and goals in their lives, (2) their desires to develop and display competence in ways that would get them recognition and respect from others, (3) social support for participation and access to the resources needed for participation (time, transportation, equipment, and money), (4) memories of past experiences with physical activities and sports, and (5) the general cultural images and messages about sports that they had in their minds.

We found that young people played sports when it helped them extend control over their lives, become what they wanted to be, and present themselves to others as competent. We also found that young women were less likely than young men to see sport participation as having these effects in their lives. Therefore, young women participated in organized sports less often and less seriously.

The young people in our study did not simply respond to the world around them; instead, they actively thought about how they saw sports fitting with the rest of their lives, including their self-conceptions and what they wanted out of life. Then they made decisions accordingly. Their sport participation patterns shifted over time depending on their access to opportunities, changes in their lives, and changes in the way they saw themselves and their connections to the world. Therefore, socialization into sport was a *continuous process* grounded in the social and cultural contexts in which the young people lived.

The stories we heard in our study showed that people make decisions to participate in sport for different reasons at different points in their lives. This fits with theories telling us that developmental tasks and challenges change as we move through childhood, adolescence, young adulthood, and adulthood. Therefore, when seven-year-olds make decisions about sport participation, they take into account issues different from those of fourteen-year-olds or forty-year-olds. And when seven-year-olds make decisions about sport participation today, they do so in a different cultural context than the one seven-year-olds experienced in 1970. Likewise, forty-year-olds who consider trying sports for the first time today find conditions for forty-year-olds different from those in the 1970s. (Just ask a grandparent about this, especially your grandmother).

Additionally, sport participation decisions at all points during the life course and through history are tied to the perceived cultural importance of sports and the links between playing sports, general social acceptance, and the achievement of personal goals. Therefore studies of socialization into sports must take into account the ways in which sport participation patterns are connected with developmental *and* cultural issues.

These studies show us three short videos about becoming involved and staying involved in sports. They show that sport participation is grounded in decision-making processes involving self-reflection, social support, social acceptance, and cultural issues. People never make

decisions about sport participation once and for all time. They make them day after day as they consider how sports are related to their lives. In fact, they sometimes make them moment by moment, when coaches are making them run wind sprints! And their decisions are mediated by the social and cultural contexts in which the people live. Therefore, social meanings attached to gender, class, race, age, and physical abilities influence decision-making processes. And these social meanings are influenced by political, economic, social, and cultural forces.

CHANGING OR ENDING SPORT PARTICIPATION

Questions about becoming and staying involved in sports often are followed by questions about changing or ending involvement. Much of the research on this latter issue has been guided by "role theories" inspired by functionalist theory, or "alienation theories" inspired by conflict theory (see Coakley, 1993b).

Over the years, researchers using *functionalist approaches* were concerned with identifying who was dropping out of sports and what could be done to keep them in sports, so they could learn all the lessons sport participation could teach them. This was a popular topic when millions of baby boomers were flooding playgrounds and elementary schools, and parents wanted to know how to control and build character in their children. This research also focused on how to build sport programs that were "feeder" systems moving athletes to increasingly higher levels of competition. This still is a popular topic among people in sports, since they have an interest in creating "winners" on interscholastic, international, and professional teams.

Researchers using *conflict theory approaches* focused on the possibility that rigidly organized, win-oriented programs turned children off to participation. These programs, along with autocratic, command-style coaches, alienated many young athletes, often to the point of dropping out. Older athletes dropped out because of

Many factors can cause people to drop out or shift their participation from one sport to another. Identity changes, access to resources, and life course issues are also involved. As circumstances change, so do our ideas about ourselves and about sports and sport participation. (Travis Spradling, *Colorado Springs Gazette*)

alienation caused by exploitation. Research explored how athletes in elite sports were victims of exploitation and how highly specialized, long-term sport participation itself could be a socially alienating experience causing athletes to drop out and to have serious personal problems when they did.

After reviewing dozens of these studies, I've concluded that they tell us the following important things:

- When people drop out of particular sports, they don't drop out of all sports forever, nor do they cut all ties with sports; in fact, many play different and less competitive sports or move into other sport roles, such as coach, program organizer or administrator, or sports businessperson.

- Dropping out of sports is usually part of a process involving changes and transitions in the rest of a person's life (changing schools, graduating, getting a job, getting married, having children, etc.).
- Dropping out of sports is not always the result of victimization or exploitation, although negative experiences can and do influence decisions to change or end participation.
- Problems may occur for those who end long careers in sports, especially those who have no identities apart from sports or who lack the social and material resources they need to make transitions into other careers and social settings.

Recent studies, especially those seeking stories from people who have changed or ended their sport participation, have built on these findings and extended our understanding. Here are two examples of these studies.

Example 1: Burnout among young athletes
My work with coaches combined with an interest in identity issues led me to do a study of young people who, after being age-group champions with the potential to succeed in their sports, had made the decision to quit playing their sports (Coakley, 1992). Since the term *burnout* often was used to describe this phenomenon, I decided to interview some former elite athletes identified by themselves or others as cases of burnout; all were adolescents. I wanted to see what burning out involved.

Data from fifteen in-depth interviews with young former athletes, all but one from individual sports,* led me to conclude that burnout was grounded in the organization of the high-performance sports in which these young people had played (Coakley, 1992). It occurred when the young people felt they had lost control over their lives and had no identity apart from sports. The athletes associated this combination of having no control and being a unidimensional person with high levels of stress and a drop in the fun they had in their sports. As stress increased and fun decreased, they burned out.

This study showed that stress and fun were connected with how sport programs were organized and how sport experiences were connected with developmental issues during adolescence. When being a young athlete, especially a highly successful one, interferes with developing desired identities apart from sports, and precludes the athlete's establishment of the autonomy and independence so important during adolescence, burnout is likely. Teaching young athletes how to manage stress may be important in preventing burnout, but it is just as important to find ways to empower athletes and change the social organi-

---

Individual sports are all sports that do not involve the simultaneous, coordinated action of team members. In this study, individual sports included tennis, figure skating, skiing, gymnastics, and swimming.

zation of the sport contexts in which they train and compete (Gould, 1996).

Example 2: Getting out of sports and getting on with life Konstantinos Koukouris (1994) is a physical educator from Greece who wanted to know how and why people who have been committed to sports decide to end or seriously reduce their participation. After analyzing questionnaire data from 157 former athletes in track and field, rowing, and volleyball, Koukouris identified 34 who ceased or reduced sport participation between the ages of 18 and 24. In-depth interviews with these people enabled him to construct case studies illustrating the process of "disengaging from sports."

Stories told by the athletes indicated that they voluntarily decided to end or change their participation. They often did this over a period of time, during which they stopped playing and then started again more than once; they didn't go "cold turkey" as they cut their sport involvement. The decision to end or change sport participation was associated primarily with the need to get a job and support themselves, but also with realistic judgments about their own sport skills and their chances to move to higher levels of competition. As they graduated from high school or college, they were faced with the expectation that they should be responsible for their own lives. As they got jobs, they didn't have the time needed to train and play sports at a serious level, and as they spent money to establish adult lifestyles, they didn't have enough left to pay for serious training. Furthermore, sport programs enabling them to train were not available, or were organized so rigidly that training didn't fit into their new adult lives.

As serious training ended, these young adults often sought other ways to be physically active or connected with sports. They sometimes had problems, but as they faced new challenges, most of them grew and developed in positive ways, much like people who had never been serious athletes. Disengagement from serious sport training was inevitable, necessary, and usually beneficial in the lives of young adults.

Calvin and Hobbes   by Bill Watterson

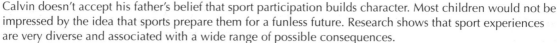

Calvin doesn't accept his father's belief that sport participation builds character. Most children would not be impressed by the idea that sports prepare them for a funless future. Research shows that sport experiences are very diverse and associated with a wide range of possible consequences.

Research shows that people's ending or changing of their sport participation often occurs in connection with the same processes that underlie their becoming and staying involved in sports. Just as people are not simply "socialized into sport," neither are they simply "socialized out of sport." Changes in participation are grounded in decision-making processes tied to the lives, life courses, and social worlds of those involved. Researchers have discovered that it is difficult to explain changes in sport participation without knowing about the circumstances surrounding the changes; about identity issues and the resources the athletes have to make transitions to other activities; about developmental and life course issues; and about the cultural contexts in which people maintain identities, gain resources, and make transitions (Brown, 1985; Greendorfer and Blinde, 1985; Messner, 1992; Ogilvie and Taylor, 1993; Swain, 1991). Some people have problems when they "retire" from sports, but to understand those problems, we require information about how sports fit into their lives and about whether playing sports limited or expanded their experiences, relationships, and resources. If it limited them, problems are more likely; if it expanded them, they usually do fine—in fact, they may do so well that we can assume

that sports built their character. This brings us to the next section.

BEING INVOLVED IN SPORTS: WHAT HAPPENS?

Seeking Proof That Sports Build Character

Beliefs about the consequences of sport participation vary from culture to culture. But the notion that playing sports builds character has been and continues to be widely accepted in many cultures. In fact, this form of **character logic** has been used as a basis for encouraging children to play sports, funding sports programs, building stadiums, promoting teams and leagues, and sponsoring events such as the Olympic Games. This often unquestioned belief that sports are inherently character building has led people to ignore important things about sports and sports experiences.

It wasn't until the 1950s that researchers began seriously to test the validity of the character logic used in connection with sport participation. Again, functionalist theory and, to a lesser extent, conflict theory guided most of the studies. Researchers focused on how sport participation was associated with character traits, political attitudes, moral development, rates of delinquency and deviance, grades in school, academic aspirations and achievements, popularity and social status, career success, and upward social mobility. The functionalists generally collected data on achievement and success, while the conflict theorists investigated political attitudes and problems athletes experienced or caused.

These studies provided a diverse series of "socialization snapshots" comparing the characteristics of athletes (i.e., "participants") in organized, competitive sports with nonathletes (i.e., "nonparticipants"). These snapshots have continued to help us make tentative conclusions about what happens to people as they play certain sports. We will discuss many of these conclusions in the following chapters, as we cover topics such as youth sports, deviance, aggression, gender relations, race and ethnic relations, class relations and social mobility, and religion. However, much of the research has produced very little consistent evidence that sport participation is a useful and dependable character builder. This, of course, has proved frustrating for those who would like to document the character logic of sports and identify patterns of positive consequences of playing sports (Beller and Stoll, 1995; Berlant, 1996; Miracle and Rees, 1994; Papp and Prisztoka, 1995).

The inconsistent findings of many socialization studies are primarily due to three faulty assumptions researchers often make (McCormack and Chalip, 1988).

- Faulty Assumption 1: *All* sports, especially organized, competitive sports, involve powerful character-shaping experiences for *all* athletes.
- Faulty Assumption 2: Athletes passively internalize most if not all of the "character-shaping lessons" *inherently contained* in sport experiences.
- Faulty Assumption 3: The character-shaping lessons learned in sports are *so unique* that people who don't play sports miss out on them altogether in their nonsport experiences.

Over the years, these faulty assumptions have led many researchers to overlook the following important things as they have studied sports and socialization:

- Sports are organized in vastly different ways across programs, teams, and situations, and therefore offer many *different experiences* to participants; that is, not all sport participation carries the same socialization messages. (I explain this point in the box describing Power and Performance versus Pleasure and Participation, on pp. 98–100).
- People who choose or are selected to participate in sports are often different to begin with from those who do not make the choice or get selected to participate; that is, sports may not *build* character so much as *select* people with particular character traits.
- Different people define their sport experiences in different ways, even when they are in the same programs or on the same teams; that is, we all have our own ways of making sense of what we do and applying it to our lives.
- The meanings people give to specific sport experiences may even change over time as they grow older and change the way they look at themselves and their lives; that is, we "edit" our pasts as we change the way we look at our lives in the present.
- Socialization ultimately occurs through the social relationships that accompany sport participation, not through the mere fact of participation itself; that is, playing sports is less important than the relationships created in connection with sports.
- The lessons learned in sports can also be learned in other activities by people who are not athletes or regular sport participants; that is, in such activities as learning to dance, participating in the science fair, or even playing video games.

Due to these faulty assumptions and oversights, studies that have compared so-called "athletes" with so-called "nonathletes" have not told us much. Not everyone who plays organized competitive sports has the same experience, and those

REFLECT ON SPORT

Power and Performance versus Pleasure and Participation:
Different Sports, Different Experiences, Different Consequences

Sport experiences vary depending on how and under what conditions sports are organized and played. To assume that all sports are organized around the same goals and emphasize the same orientations and behaviors is a mistake. In North America, for example, there are highly organized competitive sports, informal sports, adventure sports, recreational sports, extreme sports, alternative sports, cooperative sports, folk sports, contact sports, artistic sports, team sports, individual sports, and so on; and there are various combinations of these types!

However, at this time it seems that the dominant sport form in many societies is organized around what I will call a **power and performance model.**

Power and performance sports include all those sports that are highly organized and competitive; generally, they emphasize the following:

- the use of strength, speed, and power to push human limits and aggressively dominate opponents in the quest for victories and championships
- the idea that excellence is proved through competitive success and achieved through intense dedication and hard work combined with making sacrifices, risking one's personal well-being, and playing in pain
- the importance of setting records, defining the body as a machine, and using technology to control and monitor the body
- exclusive participation based on physical skills and competitive success
- hierarchical authority structures in which athletes are subordinate to coaches and coaches are subordinate to owners and administrators
- antagonism between opponents; opponents defined as "enemies"

Of course, becoming involved in and playing sports organized around these factors would be different from becoming involved in and playing sports organized around other concerns.

Although power and performance sports have become the "standard" for determining what sports should be in many countries, they have not been accepted by everyone. In fact, some people have maintained or developed other forms of sports grounded in

Power and Performance Sports involve the use of strength, speed, and power to dominate opponents in the quest for competitive victories. (Bob Jackson, *Colorado Springs Gazette*)

a wide range of values and experiences. Some of these are "spin-offs" or revisions of dominant forms, while others represent alternative or even oppositional sport forms. These alternative and oppositional forms are diverse, but many are organized around what I will call a **pleasure and participation model.**

Pleasure and participation sports represent a diverse collection of different physical activities, but they generally emphasize the following:

- active participation revolving around a combination of different types of connections—connections between people, between mind and body, and between physical activity and the environment

Pleasure and Participation Sports may involve competition, but the primary emphasis is on connections between people and personal expression through participation. (Susanne Tregarthen/Educational Photo Stock)

- an ethic of personal expression, enjoyment, growth, good health, and mutual concern and support for teammates and opponents
- empowerment (not power) through experiencing the body as a source of pleasure and well-being
- inclusive participation based on an accommodation of differences in physical skills
- democratic decision-making structures characterized by cooperation, the sharing of power, and give-and-take relationships between coaches and athletes
- interpersonal support around the idea of competing *with*, not against, others (opponents are not enemies, but those who test each other)

These two sport forms certainly do *not* encompass all the different ways that sports might be organized and played. In fact, many sports played today, contain elements from both forms and reflect many different ideas about what is important when we engage in physical activities. But power and performance sports seem to be dominant today, in the sense that they receive the most attention and support.

Why are power and performance sports dominant today? My answer to this question goes like this:

Sports are parts of culture, and people with power and resources usually want sports in their cultures to be organized and played in ways that promote their interests. They want sports to fit with how they see the world. They want sports to celebrate the relationships, orientations, and values that will "reproduce" their privileged positions in society. At this point in time, power and performance sports fit the interests of people with power and resources.

Let me explain further why this is so. Powerful and wealthy people in societies around the world maintain their privileged positions through many means. Some may use coercive strategies through their control of military force, but most use cultural strategies designed to create the belief that power and wealth are distributed in legitimate and acceptable

Continued

ways in society. For example, in countries with monarchies, the privilege of the royal family usually is explained in terms of their birthright. The monarchies exist as long as people in the society believe that birthrights represent legitimate claims to wealth and power. This is the reason church and state have been so close in many societies with monarchies: kings and queens have used their association with powerful external forces such as a God or gods to legitimize their power and wealth.

In democratic countries, most people use "merit" as a standard when judging whether power and wealth is legitimate. Thus, power and wealth in democracies can be maintained only when most people believe that rewards actually go to those who have earned them. When there is widespread inequality in a democratic society, those with power and wealth must promote the idea that they earned their privileged positions through intelligence and hard work, and that poverty and powerlessness is the result of a lack of intelligence and hard work. One way to promote this idea is to emphasize *competition* as a "natural" part of social life, and as a fair means to determine who gets what in the society. If people believe this, then they will believe that those with power and wealth deserve what they have.

This connection between power relations and an emphasis on competition helps us understand why power and performance sports are so widely promoted

and supported in North America. These sports are based on a cultural logic that celebrates winners and idealizes the domination of some people over others. These sports also promote the idea that the only fair and "natural" way to distribute rewards is through competition, and that those with the most power and wealth deserve to have more privileged positions than others because they have competed successfully.

This is how power and performance sports have come to be dominant in democratic societies in which there are extensive inequalities between people. In fact, we can explain the global expansion of these sports in similar ways. This is the reason powerful and wealthy transnational corporations spend billions of dollars annually on the sponsorship of power and performance sports. Their interests go far beyond the money related to sports. More important is the creation of widespread agreement that life should involve competition, that rewards should go to winners, that winners deserve power and wealth, and that ranking people on the basis of power and wealth is not only fair, but "natural."

Pleasure and participation sports, as well as other sport forms that challenge or oppose the cultural logic that underlies power and performance sports, may be popular among some people, but they will not receive much sponsorship and support from those with power and wealth in democratic societies. It's just not culturally "logical." What do you think?

• •

who don't play may be involved in other physical activities and may experience character-developing challenges in the things they do (Mielke and Bahlke, 1995). The mere fact that people do or do not play sports tells us little about their overall lives and how they go about developing their sense of who they are and how the world works. This is the reason hundreds of studies have not provided evidence that sport participation builds character or teaches certain lessons. Fuzzy snapshots make it difficult to understand what occurs

in the dynamic socialization processes connected with sport participation.

It is important for us to realize that the mere failure of research to find consistent, measurable effects of sport participation on character traits *does not mean* that sports have no impact on people's lives. As most of us know, *sport participation does affect people* in ways related to who they are and how they live their lives. And we have strong evidence from many sources to prove this. Ironically, this evidence does not come from studies listed in traditional sports and socialization bibliographies. Instead, it comes from studies using new approaches to sports and socialization. We will discuss these studies below. But first, let's consider why so many people maintain the belief that "sports build character."

"Sports Build Character": If It Isn't True, Why Do People Believe It?

Although research has not supported the belief that sports competition builds character, many people accept this belief in some form. I think that their acceptance is related to one or more of the following five factors.

1. Their perception is influenced by a "halo effect" that leads them to assume that if athletes do great things on the playing field, they must be great people. It is much easier for people to see skilled athletes as heroes when they think this way, and they tend to ignore information that would tarnish or defame their heroes, even though much of what they hear about athletes strongly suggests that sport has not built character.

2. They are unaware of the selection processes in sport that lead people with certain character traits to become athletes and to remain on teams. Highly competitive sports are organized to attract and select people with high levels of self-confidence and other attributes valued by those who select athletes. Those with low self-confidence usually do not try out for teams, and those with traits not valued by coaches are cut from teams. We can illustrate the effect of this selection process in sport by discussing physical traits rather than character traits. For example, if high school basketball players are taller than other students, is this so because basketball builds height? Obviously not. Coaches select tall people. However, we should recognize that tall people may improve their ability to use their height as they play basketball. The same is true with character traits: sports give people settings in which to use them in new ways.

3. They focus their attention on successful top-level athletes and then generalize about what happens in sports as a whole. Of course, using such a limited and biased "sample" of sport participants leads to faulty conclusions. This is like studying people with doctoral degrees and making conclusions about education, or studying millionaires and making conclusions about capitalism: it guarantees positive findings and excludes information from the 99 percent who played sports but didn't make it to the top.

4. They overlook the possibility that athletes may be perceived as different from others only because sports provide them with a stage on which to display the traits they have developed in the course of normal maturation. This often occurs when parents and other adults see young people publicly display their abilities in sports. Without opportunities to see their children perform in nonsport situations, they often conclude that the "character" the children display in sports is the product of sport participation itself. However, what usually happens is that sports provide people public opportunities to display traits that they have developed over a number of years and across a variety of different experiences.

5. They focus their attention on limited media portrayals of athletes in which athletes tend to look and sound knowledgeable and self-confident. They may conclude, without any supporting evidence, that this knowledge and self-confidence exhibited by athletes extend to all areas of life outside the sport arena.

The tendency to maintain the character logic leading to the conclusion that sports build character may be grounded in deeper political and cultural issues as well. For example, this logic leads people to expect athletes to be role models, to condemn athletes when they fail to exhibit model behavior, and to ignore problems related to the structure and organization of sports. This diverts attention away from the need to assess sports critically. In the process, it enables those who benefit from sports to maintain their privileged positions, and it prevents sports from being changed in ways that might change the socialization experiences of sport participants.

The character logic of sports also leads people to define *character* in terms of traditional male attributes. This creates a definition of the ideal person that works to the disadvantage of the female half of the world's population. Let me explain further.

Dominant forms of sports have been shaped and organized in connection with the values and experiences of men in society. In fact, for many men, playing sports has been used as a proof of masculinity. Coaches even urge their male athletes to "go out and prove who the better men are." This means that according to the character logic of sports, especially *power and performance sports*, women must be aggressive, unemotional, willing to play in pain, and willing to sacrifice their bodies for the sake of a victory, to be seen as having "character." In other words, to show character they must be "male-like" in terms of traditional definitions of masculinity. However, if they do not strive to dominate opponents, are sensitive to others, show emotion, are sensitive to the risk of injury, and prize health over competitive success, they are seen as lacking character as it has been defined in the power and performance sports that are dominant today.

The meaning of *character* in many sports is tied to a long history of male participation and female exclusion (see chap. 3). This way of thinking has created serious problems both in and out of sports. Women are told that to get ahead in the occupational world, they must demonstrate they are qualified, but men have defined qualifications to fit the way they have done things for years. This means that a woman is qualified only to the extent that she does her job like a man. The problems this has caused for women outside of sports should alert us to the negative implications of saying that sports build character when sports have reflected special interests throughout

history, interests connected with the power and status of men with resources.

NEW APPROACHES TO SPORTS AND SOCIALIZATION

Sports and sport participation do have an impact on people's lives. We are learning more about this impact through three types of research that sociologists and others are now doing:

1. Research on sport experiences as explained through the voices of sport participants; that is, stories from those who play or have played sports.
2. Research on the social worlds that are created around sports and then become the contexts in which people define sport experiences and make them part of their lives; that is, stories about what life in particular sports actually involves.
3. Research on sports as sites for the formation of ideology and struggles over ideological issues; that is, stories about how popular ideas in sports are applied to people and situations outside of sports.

These three types of research have led many people in the sociology of sport to rethink socialization issues. Now most of us in the field see sports as *sites for socialization experiences, not causes of socialization outcomes.* In other words, sports are social locations rich in their potential for providing memorable and influential personal, social, and cultural experiences, but *sports do not cause patterned changes in the character traits of athletes or spectators.*

A summary of some of this research illustrates its usefulness in helping us understand what happens in sports and in connection with sports in society.

Real-Life Experiences: Sport Stories from Athletes

As previously noted, we need socialization videos, not snapshots. Here are some examples of work that is especially helpful in understanding how

The moral socialization that occurs with sport participation depends greatly on the meaning given to sport experiences and the cultural messages associated with them. These cultural messages sometimes have been different for girls than for boys. These differences reflect dominant definitions of gender in a culture. (Jerilee Bennett, *Colorado Springs Gazette*)

sport participation influences people's lives:

Example 1: The moral lessons of Little League Sociologist Gary Alan Fine (1987) spent three years studying boys in Little League baseball. As I noted in chapter 2, Fine focused on the moral socialization that occurred as the boys interacted with one another, their coaches, and their parents. He found that the moral messages coaches and parents presented to the boys were based on the perspectives of adults, while the boys heard and interpreted these very messages from their perspectives as eleven-year-old males concerned with peer acceptance. Thus, socialization was a two-way interactive process in which the learners played key roles in what and how they learned. What happened to the boys as they played baseball resulted from a combination of adult influence, developmental factors, and the social reality of being eleven-year-old boys in U.S. culture during the early 1980s. Far from merely being "socialized through sport participation," the boys defined and gave meaning to their experiences and then included them in their lives on their terms.

Among other things, the boys learned to define masculinity in terms of displays of toughness and dominance, and to express disdain for females and any boys seen as weak or unwilling to take risks on or off the playing field. They also learned other things, but their emerging ideas about manhood were influential in how they saw themselves and their connections to the world. Of course, Fine realized that their playing baseball did not "cause" their definitions of masculinity; baseball was simply one site, among many, where boys developed ideas about themselves as males. What made baseball significant was that these emerging ideas about being tough and aggressive received support and endorsement from coaches, parents, and peers; in fact, these people actually promoted the ideas in connection with strategies and player evaluations. The impact of the ideas was accentuated because they were consistent with general cultural messages the boys received in the rest of their lives. The situation was not so much that the boys became "gendered" by sports as that sports became sites for the gendering processes that occurred in society as a whole.

According to other studies, these "gendering" processes are a pervasive part of sport experiences for boys and girls (Hasbrook, 1995). Data show that as males play sports, most gradually learn to accept pain, physical risks, and injuries as normal (Curry, 1993; Curry and Strauss, 1994; Nixon, 1994a, b; Young et al., 1994). This type of body socialization occurs in connection with the norms and standards used by *both* men and women in high-performance sports to evaluate self and others. But for males, it is also related to how they define and express themselves as men (Nixon, 1996b; Young et al., 1994). Girls and women in high-performance sports have similar socialization experiences, and over time, they learn to define and talk about pain, risk, and injury much as their male counterparts do (Donnelly, 1993; Nixon, 1994a; Theberge, 1993; Young and White, 1995). But this is the case because high-performance sports have been socially constructed in connection with the values and experiences of men; in fact, such sports usually celebrate all those things that men use to establish status among each other. To be accepted in these sports, women often accept the mindset and the "performance ethic" that comes with them. Thus, the body socialization women experience is tied to their identities as high-performance athletes, but not to their identities as women. For men, it is tied to both. Again, this illustrates that we can understand sport socialization only in connection with the overall cultural context in which people live their lives.

Example 2: Lessons in the locker room Sociologist Nancy Theberge (1995) spent two years studying a top-level women's ice hockey team in Canada. As she observed and interviewed team members, she noted that the experiences and orientations of the players were related to the fact that men controlled the team, the league, and the sport itself. Within this overall sport structure, the women on the team developed a very professional approach to their participation. They focused on hockey and were serious about being successful on the ice. In the process, they developed close connections with one another. The team became a community with its own dynamics and internal organization. It was within the context of this "constructed community" that the athletes learned things about hockey, about themselves, and about one another. The definitions and meanings that these players gave to their hockey experiences and the ways they linked them to their lives emerged as they interacted with one another on and off the ice.

Theberge noted that the locker room was one of the places where team members worked out the definitions and meanings of sport participation through interaction, and where team bonding took place. The emotional climate of the locker room, especially *after* a practice or game, encouraged talk that focused on who the athletes were as people and how they saw their connections with the rest of the world. This talk gave shape and meaning to what they did on the ice, to their sport experiences. But it also served as a means for expressing feelings and thoughts about men, sexuality/homosexuality, male partners and female partners, and families. The women talked and joked about men, but didn't degrade or reduce them to body parts in their comments. They made references to sex and sexuality in their conversations, but the substance of references promoted inclusiveness rather than hostility or stereotypes.

Theberge's study, like many others, shows us that playing sports is a social as much as a physical experience. *The socialization that occurs in sports occurs through social relationships.* Theberge focused on relationships between the athletes themselves, but relationships with coaches, managers, trainers, friends, family members, sport reporters, and even fans are also important. If we want to know what happens in sports, we need to understand what happens in those relationships. They are the sites that give meanings to the things that happen on the playing field, whether they are wonderful plays or terrible mistakes. This is true for young and old, gay and straight, black and white, wealthy and poor, men and women, amateur and professional.

Example 3: Media stories about experiences Sociologists are not the only ones concerned with the impact of sport experiences in people's lives. Journalists and biographers also provide useful information for understanding what happens in sports. This information may not be guided by social theories, and it may not be presented or analyzed in critical terms, but it can be useful if we read it critically. For example, Rick Telander, a long-time *Sports Illustrated* writer who now writes for the *Chicago Sun-Times*, wrote a book called *Heaven is a Playground* (1988), in which he describes the sport experiences of young black males living in a low-income Brooklyn neighborhood. Telander has a sociology degree, and he was sensitive to the need to view and report on the lives of these young men in the social context in which they lived. His descriptions emphasize that what young people learn in sports depends on who they are, where they come from, why they are playing, whom they play with, whom they meet while they play, and what happens in and around the place where they play. Similar things are highlighted in both the documentary film *Hoop Dreams* and the book of the same name (Joravsky, 1995); both focus on four years in the lives of two young men from a Chicago neighborhood. Their experiences were clearly related to the time and place in which they lived and played basketball. When viewed with a sociological eye, these sources give us vivid stories that help us understand sports and socialization.

Social Worlds: Living in Sports

Sports are not only physical activities, games, teams, and organizations; they also are **social worlds.** *Social world* is a term used in interactionist theory to refer to a way of life and an associated mindset that revolve around a particular set of activities and envelop all those people and relationships connected with the activities. I use this term to explain that we can't understand who athletes are, what they do, and how sport influences their lives unless we view them in two contexts: (1) the social world of their sport, and (2) the overall culture in which the sport world exists. Unless we know about these contexts, we have difficulty making sense of sport experiences and their impact on people. This is especially the case when we study people who live much of their lives in connection with a particular sport; for them the social world around their sport is their entire world.

Studies of social worlds revolving around sports provide useful information about socialization processes and experiences. Here are a few examples:

Example 1: Learning to be a Hero Sociologists Patti and Peter Adler spent nearly ten years studying the social world of a high-profile college basketball team. Much of their data, presented in the book *Backboards and Blackboards* (1991), focuses on how the self-conceptions of college student-athletes changed as they played college basketball. The Adlers found that the young men, nearly 70 percent of whom were African Americans, usually became so engulfed in their athlete roles after they entered the social world of this team that the roles deeply affected how they viewed themselves and how they allocated time to basketball, social life, and academic matters. This "role engulfment" occurred as the young men made increasing commitments to identities based exclusively on playing basketball. These commitments were consistently and clearly reinforced by coaches, students, fans, community members, the media, and teammates. Thus, the social world of the team and intercollegiate basketball became the context in which they viewed the rest of the world, set goals, and evaluated and defined themselves.

The Adlers felt that during the time these young men played basketball, they learned something about setting goals, focusing their attention on specific tasks, and making sacrifices to pursue their goals. But the Adlers found nothing to suggest that the athletes carried these lessons over into the rest of their lives. It seemed that the social world of basketball was so separate from and unrelated to other parts of their lives that the lessons they learned in that world stayed there.

Other research suggests that this lack of carryover between sports and the rest of life may be more common among men than among women, since the social worlds that revolve around women's intercollegiate sports are not so isolated from the rest of the athletes' lives (Meyer, 1990; see also chap. 14 in this text, p. 449). Therefore, gender and gender relations, among other forms of social relations (class, race/ethnic, etc.), influence the meanings attached to sport experiences and the integration of those experiences into people's lives.

Example 2: Realizing image isn't everything Anthropologist Alan Klein spent seven years studying the social world of competitive bodybuilding in California. In his book *Little Big Men* (1993), he explains that a good part of the lives of the bodybuilders revolved around issues of gender and sexuality. Bodybuilders, both male and female, learned to project images of power and strength to the rest of the world while they experienced serious doubts about their own identities and self-worth. The social world of bodybuilding seemed to engender a desperate need for attention and approval from others, especially fellow bodybuilders. Ideas about masculinity within the social world of bodybuilding were so narrow and one-dimensional that male bodybuilders developed homophobic attitudes and went to great lengths to assert their heterosexuality in public. Also, the focus on body size and hardness created such insecurities that the men learned to present and even define themselves in terms of exaggerated caricatures of masculinity—like comic-book depictions of men. Overall, these were powerful socialization experiences in their lives. However, due to gender relations in the culture at large, these experiences played out in slightly different ways among men and women bodybuilders.

Example 3: Living in the shadow of a man's world Sociologist Todd Crossett (1995) spent a good part of fourteen months traveling and living in his pick-up truck while he studied the social world of women's professional golf. He found that being on the LPGA tour creates and, in fact, requires a complete mindset revolving around the commitment to using physical competence as a basis for evaluating self and others on the tour. He describes this mindset as "an ethic of prowess." This ethic of prowess exists partly because the women are very concerned about neutralizing the potentially negative effects that dominant ideas about gender could have if they entered the social world of women's professional golf. One golfer he interviewed said that much of what she did in her life was a response to the notion that "*athlete* is almost a masculine noun" in this society. The impact of being a pro golfer was summarized by one woman, who said, "We are different than the typical married lady with a house full of kids in what we think and do." Crosset's study emphasizes that we can understand the meaning of this statement only in the context of the social world of the LPGA. *And,* we can understand the social world of the LPGA only in the context of gender relations in late-twentieth-century U.S. culture.

Example 4: Surviving in a ghetto Sociologist Loic Wacquant (1992) spent three years studying the social world of boxers in a ghetto gym in Chicago. His observations, interviews, and experiences as a boxer helped him uncover the social logic and meaning that underlies the life and the craft of boxing. He explains that the social world of the boxing gym is very complex: it is created in connection with the social forces in the black ghetto and its masculine street culture, but it also shelters black men from the full destructive impact of those forces. In order to learn the "social art" of boxing, the men at the gym engaged in an intense regime of body regulation focused on the physical, visual, and mental requirements of boxing. They had to "eat, drink, sleep and live boxing," and in the process, they developed what Wacquant described as a "*socialized lived body*" that was at the very core of who they were and what they did. This experience of living in the social world of

the boxing gym separated them from their peers and kept them alive as they tried to make sense out of life in dangerous neighborhoods devoid of hope or opportunity. For these men, boxing was indeed a powerful socialization experience.

Example 5: Sport worlds portrayed in the media Joan Ryan (1995) and Christine Brennan (1996) are journalists who have studied and written about the social worlds of elite, competitive women's gymnastics and men's and women's figure skating. Their research methods and writing styles are different from those of sociologists, but they contribute to what we know about the experience and impact of being involved in these two sports. For example, Ryan's descriptions of the social world of elite women's gymnastics provides a basis for understanding why girls and young women in that world frequently develop disordered eating behaviors. Although these behaviors are not explicitly taught by parents, coaches, or fellow athletes, the young women often come to see them as part of being a gymnast, part of life in the social world of gymnastics. And as we know from a few highly publicized cases, they can be fatal. This is body socialization in an extreme form.

These studies of social worlds show that sports are *sites* for powerful forms of socialization. A full understanding of socialization processes and experiences requires a knowledge of those worlds, and the connection between those worlds and the culture as a whole. Once we understand a sport world in a "deep" way, once we are able to penetrate it using sociological tools, the things that athletes think and do become meaningful and understandable to us, regardless of how they appear to outsiders (Goffman, 1961).

Ideology: Sports as Sites for Struggling Over How We Think and What We Do

Past socialization research often looked at what occurred in the lives of individuals or small groups. But as researchers have combined critical theories with new theoretical approaches, including cultural studies and poststructuralism,* they have begun to study *socialization as a community and cultural process*. Their research goes beyond looking at the experiences and characteristics of athletes. Instead, it focuses on sports as sites where people in society create and learn "stories" that they can use as they make sense out of the world and their lives. The stories that revolve around sports and athletes have their own vocabularies and images; their meanings shift depending on the settings in which people tell them and hear them, and they often identify important cultural issues in people's lives. Researchers try to identify these stories and then determine how they fit into the culture and how people use them in connection with what they think and do.

Researchers also are concerned with whose stories about sports become dominant in the culture, since there are so many stories that could be told about sports. For example, the stories told by NBC Sports and by the corporate sponsors during the 1996 Olympic Games represented highly selective versions of what was happening in Atlanta and in the lives of the athletes. Other stories and images that didn't fit the interests of NBC and the corporate sponsors were not presented in the television coverage. Of course, the media do not dictate what we think, but the stories and images presented in the media often provide the context in which we think, and they frame the topics of the conversations we have in our lives and the stories we create and use to make sense out of the world. This is an important way in which socialization occurs in connection with sports.

Research on this form of socialization is difficult to do, because it requires a knowledge of history and a deep understanding of the settings in which sports and sport "stories" come to be a part of people's lives. But this research is important, because it deals with the influence of sports in the culture as a whole, rather than just in the lives of individuals and small groups.

Research on socialization as a community and cultural process is partly inspired by the ideas of Italian sociologist Antonio Gramsci. When Gramsci was imprisoned by Italian fascists from 1927 to 1937 he spent time thinking about why people had not revolted against repressive forms of capitalism in Western societies. Gramsci concluded that it was important to understand how people throughout a society formed their definitions of common sense and their ideas about how society ought to be organized socially, politically, and economically. He thought that one of the most effective ways for those with power to influence popular definitions of common sense and win the support of people throughout a society was to control the pleasurable pastimes in people's lives. Gramsci suspected that the members of a society use the cultural messages associated with everyday pleasures in their lives as they form ideas about the organization and operation of society as a whole. Therefore, if dominant groups in a society could influence the language, images, and messages tied to the sources of fun and excitement in their lives, they could defuse the extent to which people might disagree with them or oppose their ideas about how society should be organized. If they were lucky, they

---

*Poststructuralism is a theoretical and methodological perspective that assumes that culture today is based more on the production of symbols and rapidly changing media and computer images than on the production of material commodities. Structuralists, including conflict theorists and some critical theorists, consider material production and material reality to be the key dynamic around which culture is created and maintained. Those using a poststructuralist perspective focus on language, including both written and spoken discourse, because they assume that social life in today's postmodern culture is constantly negotiated, constructed, challenged, and changed through language and discourse. Much research done by poststructuralists today deals with the media in its many forms, and focuses on how images, identities, symbols, and meanings are fabricated through the media, and then serve as the contexts for our material lives. Part of poststructuralists' purpose is to disrupt these media-generated discourses in ways that increase critical sensibilities in the culture as a whole.

When a corporation spends money to have its name, logo, and products associated with sports, it is looking for more than sales. In the long run, its executives hope that people will believe that a good part of their enjoyment of sports depends on the corporation. If this happens, people are more likely to support what the corporation wants. (Jay Coakley)

could even use pleasurable pastimes as contexts for winning agreement with their ideas, to such an extent that they could maintain their power and influence.

This, of course, is part of the hegemonic process of how ideologies are produced and reproduced in societies. According to an analysis based on a Gramscian version of critical theory, forms of popular culture such as sports are ideal sites for telling stories that people might use to formulate their ideas about what is important in life and what life is all about. Sports, then, are important social phenomena, because they are contexts in which people often learn the vocabulary and ideas that inform how they see and evaluate themselves and the rest of the world.

It seems that the large corporations that spend millions of dollars to sponsor sports and advertise in connection with sports agree with Gramsci's critical analysis. For example, why would Coca-Cola spend over $500 million in connection with the 1996 Olympics in Atlanta

and be willing to spend similar amounts in the years 2000 and 2004? Is it because powerful executives at Coke like sports? Is it because their association with the Olympic rings can make them money? Yes, both of these things are important. But a still more important factor is that Coke, General Motors, and other corporations can use the Olympics and other sports as vehicles for delivering cultural messages they want people in the world to hear and agree with. They want people to think that competition is the best way to allocate rewards in life and that successful people and companies really deserve their power and privilege. They want people not only to drink Coke and drive Chevy trucks, but to develop an approach to life that associates pleasure with consumption and status with things and corporate logos. They want people to say, "These large companies are important in our lives, because without them we would not have the sports we love so dearly." They want people to think that enjoyment and pleasure in life depends on the corporations and their products. They want to establish consumption as a way of life, as the foundation for culture itself. Their profits and power depend on it, and their marketing people know it. They are selling a whole way of life, and an ideology in which people express their identity through competitive success and consumption. To the extent that people in society adopt this way of viewing the world and their relationship to it, corporate interests become dominant in society. Many sociologists refer to this process of forming consent around a particular ideology as the process of establishing **hegemony.**

The cultural messages associated with sports have become a part of most of our lives. It is difficult to determine how these messages are heard around the world, but it is clear that major corporations see sports as important vehicles for delivering them. This is why so much sponsorship money goes to sports. Giving people pleasures creates gratitude, if not agreement. People in corporations know that their interests depend on establishing "ideological outposts" in people's heads. And sports, as activities that give so many people pleasure, seem to be avenues through which these outposts can be built, outposts from which the corporations also can send other messages about the world.

RESEARCH EXAMPLES This approach to socialization is difficult to understand unless we see it in action. I summarized three examples of studies using this approach in chapter 2, in the section on critical theories. I will mention each again here, since they are good examples of new approaches to sports and socialization.

In Doug Foley's ethnography (see p. 48), his findings showed that high school football was important in the lives of many individuals in the small town he studied. However, the stories created around football and those who played it, coached it, cheered for it, and watched it reaffirmed established ways of thinking and doing things. In the process, sports became a means for maintaining forms of social inequality that make life good for a few and difficult for many

in the town. For example, even though a young *mexicana* could become popular as a cheerleader, and a young *mexicano* from a poor family could be a star on the team, this had no effect on the political and economic standing of women, Mexican Americans, or low-income people in the town. Inequalities related to gender, ethnicity, and social class were not challenged by what people experienced in connection with football. Instead, the cultural basis for those inequalities was reproduced, even though individual lives sometimes were changed in connection with sports.

Mike Messner's (1992) interviews with former elite male athletes showed that sports were sites where these athletes created identities that influenced how they presented themselves in public, how they related to women, and how they defined and evaluated themselves (see pp. 47–48). These identities and the stories associated with them then became part of popular culture in the U.S. and reproduced dominant ideas about manhood. Messner concluded that as people struggle over issues related to gender, sports have an impact because they provide vocabularies and images that perpetuate ways of thinking and doing things that privilege men over women and some men over others.

Susan Birrell and Diana Richter's (1994) observations of women's softball teams showed that it is possible for sports to be sites for creating experiences and relationships that actually challenge dominant ways of things and doing things in U.S. culture (see p. 47). The stories that emerged in connection with the women's experiences came with vocabularies and images that empowered the players in their own feminist terms. What they experienced was different from what others experience who play sports grounded in traditional masculine values. This study showed that sports don't always reproduce dominant ways of thinking and doing things. Sometimes sport forms or people in sports clearly "push the limits" of what is traditionally accepted and acceptable in society. When this happens, more space is created for

Nike-sponsored images of Michael Jordan are found around the world; this one is on a building in Paris. Nike and other corporations have worked hard to sever the Jordan persona from connections with African American experiences. This allows people to comfortably ignore the legacies of colonialism and racism that still affect people's economic, political, and social lives today. (Jay Coakley)

people to play sports, and some people change how they think about what is important in life and how social relationships can and should be organized.

Other studies also have approached the issue of socialization through the concept of ideology. They have focused on how popular images connected with sports become cultural symbols as they are represented in the media and everyday conversations. For example, David Andrews (1996) has used cultural studies and poststructuralism (see footnote on p. 108) to study the stories created around Michael Jordan since 1982, and the links between those stories and

racial ideology in U.S. culture. His analysis of commercials and other media coverage show how the "Jordan persona" was severed from African American experiences and culture so that white America, seeking evidence that it was color-blind and open to all, would identify with him. Andrews uses historical information about race and current depictions of the "Jordan persona" to argue that even though Jordan's persona is colorless, we cannot understand his status and impact as a cultural icon without knowing about how racism operates in the U.S.

Andrews' research, as well as studies done by others using similar approaches, emphasizes that *none of us lives outside the influence of ideology* (Andrews, 1996a, b; Birrell and Cole, 1990; Messner and Solomon, 1993; Paraschak, 1997). This research is based on the premise that sports, because they are popular sources of pleasure in people's lives, are avenues through which people learn and question ideology. Although this type of research is in its infancy, it holds the promise of showing us how sports influence the collective consciousness in a culture and how people could disrupt that influence if it promoted stereotypes and exploitation.

WHAT SOCIALIZATION RESEARCH DOESN'T TELL US

We can't expect a few studies to tell us all we want to know about sports and socialization. We have many research snapshots and a few short research videos enabling us to describe and understand parts of socialization in and out of sports. But there is little information on how these processes operate in the lives of people from various ethnic groups and different social classes. In North America, research on Asian Americans, Latinos, Native Americans, and French-Canadians in sports is especially needed. And we need studies of sport participation in high-income and low-income communities, and among wealthy and poor individuals and families.

We also need research on sport participation careers among young children and on how those careers are linked to overall social development, especially among girls and children from ethnic minority backgrounds. We need research on older people, especially those considering or trying sports for the first time or the first time in a long while.

We need research on how people make participation decisions about different types of sports. Sports come in many forms, and my guess is that experiences related to power and performance sports would be quite different from experiences related to pleasure and participation sports (see pp. 98–100).

If we knew more about each of these topics, we then could provide sport participation opportunities that fit into the lives of a greater number of people, and could make sports more democratic and less subject to the commercial forces that make it exclusive and elitist (Donnelly, 1993, 1996).

We also need stories about the emotions connected with socialization into sports. Few sociologists have considered emotions in their research. But most of us know that decisions about sport participation are clearly connected with our feelings, fears, and anxieties. For example, decisions may be tied to what people in sports refer to as "psyching up": the emotional experience of forming expectations for what they will encounter in sports. These expectations are based on past memories, as well as images about sports that exist in the culture as a whole.

Stories about the emotional side of sports have been collected by social psychologists who have studied "flow experiences" among athletes. "Flow" occurs when we become so engrossed in what we are doing that we lose track of time and get carried along by the activity itself (see Csikszentmihalyi, 1991). The "runner's high," "peak experiences," and "that game when everything just seems to click," are examples of flow in action. Even though flow is a personal experience, it is tied to sociological issues such as how activities are organized and how much control participants have over their involvement in those activities. But we need more stories in order to test our guesses about emotions and decisions about sport participation.

Finally, we need stories about how the language used in certain sports influences sport participation decisions. My guess is that young women in U.S. high schools are less likely than their male counterparts to try out for and stay on varsity teams because the "language of sports" in many schools is based on traditional masculine images and orientations (Jansen and Sabo, 1994; Segrave, 1994; Trujillo, 1995). For example, does talk about sports being a form of "warfare" requiring aggression, toughness, and the desire to dominate others make varsity sports less attractive to women than to men? Are fifteen-year-old girls as likely as boys to be interested in playing sports so they can be members of a "Letter-*man*'s Club"? Are little girls less likely to see sports as important in their lives after hearing a coach reprimand players by saying they played "like a bunch of girls" (see Landers and Fine, 1996)? Sociologists, especially those interested in gender equity, want to know these things. Stories about these issues are difficult to obtain, but they are needed.

On the practical side of things, we should remember that what we learn from stories about sports and socialization will make us more responsive and supportive friends, parents, coaches, teachers, managers, and administrators. Then we can create sports offering a wider array of challenging and satisfying experiences.

SUMMARY

WHO PLAYS AND WHAT HAPPENS?

Socialization is a complex, interactive process through which people form ideas about who they are and how they are connected to the world around them. This process occurs in connection with sports as well as with other activities and experiences in people's lives. Research indicates that playing sports is a social experience as well as a physical one. Becoming involved and staying involved in sports occurs in connection with processes of decision making and identity formation. The same is true for changing or ending sport participation. People do not play sports in social and cultural vacuums; as they consider alternatives and play sports, they make decisions and form identities. This occurs in connection with other social processes related to age, social class, gender, ability/disability, and race/ethnicity.

The belief that sports build character is grounded in a faulty character logic widely used in most wealthy, postindustrial societies. We know that when people live much of their lives in and around sports, their characters and behaviors, positive or negative, are related to sport

participation in some way. This is no surprise! But research suggests that we can make few generalizations about patterns of character development or behavior in connection with sport participation. It seems that sport participation is most likely to have positive character effects when it is associated with the following:

- increased opportunities for testing and developing new identities
- increased knowledge of the world and how it works
- new experiences going beyond sports
- formation of new relationships apart from sports
- clear lessons about how sport experiences can be used as a basis for dealing with challenges outside of sports
- expansion of how others define, see, and deal with a person (that is, as more than just an athlete)
- expansion of opportunities to develop competence and become responsible in activities apart from playing sports

On the other hand, when playing sports constricts or limits a person's life and developmental opportunities, we can expect negative socialization consequences. Again, this is no surprise. But what we must remember is that none of these things occurs automatically in connection with sport participation, and when they do occur, their impact is mediated by the cultural context in which people live their lives.

The faulty character logic used in connection with sports not only limits our awareness of problems associated with playing sports, but it also leads to an idealization of character that privileges certain men and disadvantages most women.

When we consider sports and socialization, it is helpful for us to know that different sports involve different experiences and consequences. For example, what occurs in connection with *Power and Performance Sports* is quite different from what occurs in connection with *Pleasure and Participation Sports*. The visibility and popularity of power and performance sports today in many societies are related to issues of power and ideology: these sports fit the interests of those with the power and wealth needed to sponsor and promote sports.

New approaches to sports and socialization emphasize research on (1) the everyday experiences of people who play sports, (2) the social worlds created around sports, and (3) community and cultural processes, especially in connection with the ideological messages associated with sports in society. As we listen to the voices of those who participate in sports, look in depth at how they live their lives in connection with sports, and pay special attention to the ideological messages associated with sports, we will learn more about socialization. Researchers increasingly see sports as *sites for socialization experiences, not causes of socialization outcomes.* They know that sports provide memorable and influential personal, social, and cultural experiences, but they also know that *sports in general do not cause patterned changes in the character traits of athletes or spectators.* We have learned from past studies, but the new approaches offer promise for new understandings of sports and socialization.

SUGGESTED READINGS

Note: In addition to the following references, I would suggest that readers consult the studies summarized in this chapter; many have good discussions of socialization issues, and bibliographies that identify other useful sources.

Coakley, J. 1993. Socialization and sport. In R. N. Singer, M. Murphey, and L. K. Tennant, eds., *Handbook on research in sport psychology* (pp. 571–86). New York: Macmillan (*a general overview of sport socialization research, including research on socialization through sports*).

Coakley, J. 1993. Sport and socialization. *Exercise and Sport Sciences Reviews* 21 (169–200) (*a critical review of sport socialization research, with an emphasis on the need for interactionist models and qualitative methodologies*).

Coakley, J. 1996. Socialization through sports. In O. bar-Or, ed., *The child and adolescent athlete* (pp. 353–63). Vol. 6 of *The Encyclopaedia of Sports Medicine*—a publication of the IOC Medical Commission. London: Blackwell Science (*an overview of research on the impact of sport participation in people's lives; a focus on new research approaches to studying socialization*).

Coakley, J., and P. Donnelly, eds. Forthcoming. *Inside sports: Research on athletes and sport experiences.* Routledge, London. (*twenty-two articles that summarize key research projects on socialization and sports; written especially for beginning students*).

Donnelly, P. Forthcoming. Interpretive approaches to the sociology of sport. In J. Coakley and E. Dunning, eds., *Handbook of sport and society.* London: Sage (*an overview of the emergence and development of interpretive sociology; examples of research using interpretive approaches, and discussion of the impact of interpretive approaches on research in the sociology of sport.*)

Fine, G. A. 1987. *With the boys: Little League baseball and preadolescent culture.* Chicago, IL: University of Chicago Press (*insightful analysis of the processes of moral socialization that occur on youth baseball teams; uses an interactionist perspective and shows how young boys are involved in their own socialization*).

Foley, D. 1990. *Learning capitalist culture.* Philadelphia: University of Pennsylvania Press (*an ethnographic study looking at sports and socialization in the context of an entire community's way of life; Foley deals with issues of class, gender, and ethnicity as he focuses on the local high school and its football team*).

Klein, A. 1993. *Little big men: Bodybuilding subculture and gender construction.* Albany, NY: SUNY Press (*an inside look at training experiences associated with competitive bodybuilding; focuses on how gender and gender relations are involved in what happens during training and competition, and what happens to the athletes themselves*).

Kohn, A. 1986. *No contest: the case against competition.* Boston: Houghton Mifflin (*a readable, thorough review of research on competition; a critique of the role of competition in society*).

Miracle, A. W., and C. R. Rees. 1994. *Lessons of the locker room: The myth of school sports.* Amherst, NY: Prometheus Books (*an excellent overview of research on what happens to participants in high school sports in* the U.S.; discusses the implications of research findings for school policy).

Ogilvie, B., and J. Taylor. 1993. *Career termination issues among elite athletes.* In R. N. Singer, M. Murphey, and L. K. Tennant, eds., *Handbook of research on sport psychology* (pp. 761–75). NY: Macmillan (*a comprehensive overview of research on the conditions and experiences of leaving competitive sports; emphasizes psychological research, but includes sociological references*).

Ryan, J. 1995. *Little girls in pretty boxes: The making and breaking of elite gymnasts and figure skaters.* NY:

Doubleday (*a powerful and disconcerting journalistic account of the experiences of girls in the social world of these two elite sports; focuses on relationships between athletes and parents and coaches, and the social and physical consequences of sport participation*).

Telander, R. 1988. *Heaven is a playground.* NY: A Fireside Book, Simon & Schuster (*a journalistic account of the experiences of young African Americans living in a low-income neighborhood in Brooklyn; focuses on participation on a basketball team; this looks at inner-city experiences from a slightly different perspective than that used in the filming of* Hoop Dreams).

5

The whole complexion of children's sports has changed. Organized sports have replaced free play and the sandlot . . . [O]rganized sports have brought on "overuse" injuries . . . unknown in freeplay and sandlot sports [in which] hurt or sore athletes generally went home and didn't return to play until they felt better. But children in organized sports often overtrain and play when hurt.

Lyle J. Micheli, M.D., Director of Sports Medicine, Boston Children's Hospital (1990)

(Colorado Springs Gazette)

Sports and Children
Are organized programs worth the effort?

Parents' lives are so crammed [that] many of them find organized sports, with its adult scheduling, the best way to be involved in their kids' lives.

Mike Weiss, journalist and youth sport coach (1994)

Yes, it's expensive. [But I] want to give him every advantage . . . I know I overspend . . . but he's always wanted to be a baseball player, and to attain that takes money.

Single mother of a twelve-year-old son, Washington, DC area (1995)

Sometimes the preparation is so hard, so intense . . . [t]he crying, the screaming. . . . We are not in the gym to be having fun. The fun comes at the end, with the winning and the medals.

Bela Karolyi, gymnastics coach (1992)

If there were no sports, life would be easier because you wouldn't have to go play games every other day. . . .

Fifth-grade student, Colorado Springs (1991)

When, how, and to what end children play sports is an issue that concerns families, neighborhoods, communities, and even national and international organizations. When sociologists study this issue, they focus on how the experiences of children vary with the types of programs or settings in which they play sports. Since the early 1970s, the research of sociologists and others has had a major impact on how people think about youth sports, especially sports emphasizing competition (Donnelly, 1993). Parents, coaches, and program administrators today are much more aware of the questions and issues that they must consider when evaluating organized youth sport programs. And many (though not all) of the programs today have used research findings to create and change programs so that they serve the interests of children.

This chapter will deal with five major topics:

1. the origin and development of organized youth sports
2. major trends in youth sports today
3. differences between informal, player-controlled sports and formally organized, adult-controlled sports
4. commonly asked questions about youth sports, including these:

   • When are children ready to play sports?
   • Do youth sports affect parent-child relationships?
   • Do boys and girls play sports differently?

5. Recommendations for changing children's sports

Throughout the chapter, this question will guide our discussion: Are organized youth sports worth all the time, money, and effort put into them? I asked this question many times as my son and daughter moved through childhood, and I continue to ask it as I talk with parents and work with coaches and policymakers who have made extensive commitments to youth sports.

ORIGIN AND DEVELOPMENT OF ORGANIZED YOUTH SPORTS

During the latter half of the nineteenth century, people in Europe and North America realized that the social environment influenced the behavior and character of children. They then took it upon themselves to control that environment as much as possible, making many efforts to organize children's lives so they would develop into productive adults in rapidly expanding capitalist economies.

It wasn't long before sport activities were organized for young boys in schools, on playgrounds, and in church groups. The organizers hoped that sports, especially team sports, would teach boys from working-class families how to cooperate and work productively together. They also hoped that sports would turn boys from middle- and upper-class families into strong, assertive, competitive men by providing them with experiences offsetting the influence of their home lives, which many men felt were dominated by women and women's values. At the same time, girls were given quiet games and other activities that would turn them into good mothers and homemakers. Most people believed that domestic skills were much more important than sport skills in girls' lives, and they organized the school curriculum and playground activities to teach those skills.

Of course, there were exceptions to these patterns, but this was the general framework out of which most organized youth sport programs developed after World War II, especially in North America. As the first wave of the Baby Boom generation moved through childhood during the 1950s and 1960s, organized sports grew dramatically. They were funded by a combination of public, private, and commercial sponsors. Parents also entered the scene, eager to have their sons' characters built on the playing field. Fathers became coaches, managers, and league administrators. Mothers became chauffeurs and short-order cooks so their sons could be on time for practices and games.

Most programs were for boys between eight and fourteen years old, and emphasized competition as preparation for adult life in the world of work. Until the 1970s, girls' interests in sports were largely ignored in most countries. Girls were relegated to the bleachers during their brothers' games and, in the U.S., given the hope of becoming high school cheerleaders. Then the women's movement, the fitness movement, and government legislation prohibiting sex discrimination (Title IX in the United States) all came together to stimulate the development of new programs for girls (see chap. 8). During the 1970s and early 1980s, these programs grew rapidly, to the point that girls had nearly as many opportunities as boys. However, their participation rates have remained lower than those for boys—for reasons we will discuss later in this chapter (and in chap. 8).

Participation in organized youth sports is now an accepted part of growing up in most high-tech, rich societies, especially among the middle and upper classes, where resources enable adults to sponsor, organize, and administer many programs for their children. Most parents now encourage both sons and daughters to participate in sports; in the U.S., nearly half of all ten-year olds say they play or want to play organized sports outside of school (Ewing and Seefelt, 1990). Some parents question the merits of programs in which heavy emphasis is placed on winning and not enough attention is given to the overall development of children. Other parents look for the win-oriented programs, hoping their children will become the winners. And others encourage their children to do various noncompetitive sports outside of organized programs. Researchers seldom have studied these noncompetitive sports, in either mainstream recreational or alternative forms, and so we know little about when, how, and to what end children play them.

Organized Sports and Changes in the Family

Over the past half century, an increasing amount of children's free time and sport participation has occurred in organized programs supervised by adults (Adler and Adler, 1994). This change is related to a combination of five factors.

First, the number of families with both parents working outside the home has increased dramatically since the 1960s. This has created a growing demand for after-school and summer-time programs in which children might be constructively entertained and supervised by adults outside the home.

Second, since the early 1980s, there have been significant changes in what it means to be a "good parent." Good parents, in the minds of many people today, are those who can account for the whereabouts and behavior of their children twenty-four hours a day. This expectation has never existed in the past, but over the past two decades it has led many parents to seek organized programs in which their children are supervised by adults. Organized, adult-controlled sports have been especially popular among these programs. When children play organized sports, parents know where they are, and they assume the children are having fun and getting their characters built at the same time.

Third, there has been a growing belief that informal child-controlled activities often get out of hand and provide occasions for children to get into trouble. In fact, adults sometimes view children as threats to social order unless they are controlled by adults. They see organized sports as one of the best ways of keeping children with a lot of physical energy constructively occupied, out of trouble, and under adult control.

Fourth, many parents have come to see the world as a dangerous place for children. They regard organized sports as safe alternatives to "hanging out" or playing informal activities away from home in settings that have no adult supervision. Parents now say they want to control their children for the sake of the children themselves, for the sake of protection.

Fifth, the visibility of high-performance and professional sports has increased people's awareness of organized sports as a part of culture. As

Parents today are expected to account for their children's whereabouts and behavior twenty-four hours a day. Organized sports provide structured, adult-controlled activities that enable parents to meet this expectation. This is one reason that organized youth sport programs are so popular. (Jay Coakley)

children watch sports on television, listen to parents and friends talk about sports, and hear about the wealth and fame of popular athletes, they become increasingly interested in playing those sports that others define as official and important. For this reason, organized sports with adult coaches become attractive to many children. And when parents hear children say they want to be gymnasts or basketball players, they often look for the nearest organized program and sign up their kids. Participation in the programs results as much from what children want as from what parents want; organized youth sports are popular partly because children enjoy them and see them meeting their needs for acceptance and identity.

As a result of these five factors, more children than ever are in organized sports. But parents have found that organized programs for their children are not cheap. The amount of money parents spend on participation fees, equipment, and other things defined as necessary in many programs has skyrocketed in recent years (Wee, 1995). For example, my students and I interviewed parents of elite youth hockey players from Washington, Oregon, California, and Alaska who were in Colorado for a major tournament and discovered that families spent between $5,000 and $16,000 per year for fees, equipment, travel, and other expenses related to their sons' hockey participation. As they informed us about their expenses, many of them shook their heads and said, "I can't believe we're spending this much, but we are."

When children play organized sports, parents often become personal chauffeurs and team bus drivers; they may serve as coaches, referees, and umpires; they prepare special meals; they alter work and vacation schedules to do these things and to attend competitions; and they write regular checks to pay for everything their children need to stay involved. Regardless of how difficult this is, many parents feel they must keep their children in organized sports if they are to live up to their responsibilities in today's society. As long as this approach to parenting is popular, organized sports will remain a major part of many children's lives.

The downside of this approach is that parents in working-class and lower-income households may be defined as failures due to their inability to pay the financial price for controlling their children as others do. In this way, organized sports for children become linked to ideological and political issues and the debates about "family values" in the society at large.

MAJOR TRENDS IN YOUTH SPORTS TODAY

In addition to their growing popularity, youth sports are changing in at least two socially significant ways. *First*, youth sport programs have become increasingly privatized; this means that more of them today are sponsored by private and commercial organizations, and fewer are sponsored by public, tax-supported organizations. *Second*, youth sport programs increasingly emphasize the "performance principle": participants today, even in low-key, recreational programs, are encouraged to evaluate their experiences in terms of developing technical skills and progressing to higher personal levels of achievement in one or more sports. These two major trends have an impact on who participates in youth sports and what kinds of experiences children have when they do participate. I will explain this in the following sections (and in the box on p. 121).

The Privatization of Youth Sports

Privatization is an interesting and sometimes alarming trend in youth sports today. At the same time that organized sports have become more popular, there has been a decline in the number of publicly funded programs with free and open participation policies. When local governments face budget crises, various social services, including youth sports, often are cut back or eliminated. In the face of cutbacks, local parks and recreation departments and other public agencies sometimes have tried to maintain youth sport programs by imposing participation fees to cover expenses. But many have been forced to drop programs altogether.

In response to this turn of events, concerned parents with resources often have organized privately sponsored leagues for their children. These leagues depend on fund-raising, participation fees, and corporate sponsorships. They offer many of the same kinds of sport opportunities that have existed in public programs. However, they are expensive, and they tend to attract children from middle- and upper-middle-income families. Even when there is a willingness to waive fees for children from low-income families, few participate.

Commercial sport providers also have entered the youth sport scene in growing numbers since the decline in public programs has occurred. The programs they offer are usually selective and exclusive, and children from many low-income and single-parent families have few opportunities to play in these privatized organized sports. To the extent that low-income and single-parent families are more prevalent among minorities, privatized programs of all types are increasingly characterized by racial and ethnic segregation and exclusion. In communities where this occurs, it accentuates differences between the haves and the have-nots, and between people from different racial and ethnic groups. In this way, youth sports are reproducing the same economic and ethnic inequalities that exist in the larger society. This, in my estimation, is a dangerous trend.

Emphasis on the "Performance Principle"

The **performance principle** has become increasingly important in many organized youth sport programs. With some exceptions, programs have put more and more emphasis on progressive skill development and competitive success. Private programs generally emphasize the performance principle to a greater degree than public programs do, since they often market themselves as "centers of athletic excellence." Such an approach attracts parents willing to pay high membership, participation, and instructional fees. Another way to sell private programs

REFLECT ON SPORT

Organized Youth Sports and the Goals of Sponsors:
How Do Politics Affect Sport Participation?

The purposes of organized youth sports often vary with the overall goals of their sponsors. Forms of sponsorship differ from one country to another, but they generally fall into one of the following four categories:

1. *Public, tax-supported community recreation organizations.* This includes parks and recreation departments and community centers that traditionally have offered a range of free or low-cost organized sport programs for children in local communities. These programs are usually inclusive and emphasize overall participation and general physical skill development as it relates to health and enjoyment.

2. *Public nonprofit community organizations.* These include the YMCA, the Boys and Girls Club, the Police Athletic League (PAL), and community-based service clubs that traditionally have provided a limited range of free or low-fee organized sport programs for children. The goals of these programs are diverse, including everything from providing children from particular neighborhoods a "wholesome, Christian atmosphere" for playing sports to providing so-called "at-risk" children with activities to keep them off the streets.

3. *Private nonprofit sport organizations.* These include organizations such as the nationwide Little League, Inc., or local organizations operating independently or through connections with larger sport organizations such as national federations. These organizations usually offer more exclusive opportunities to selective groups of children, generally those with special skills from families

who can afford relatively costly participation fees.

4. *Private commercial clubs.* These include gymnastics, tennis, skating, and soccer clubs, along with other "sport clubs." These organizations often have costly membership and participation fees and tend to emphasize intense training, progressive and specialized skill development, and elite competition.

Since each of these sponsors exists for a different purpose, the youth sports they provide are likely to appeal to different people and offer different types of experiences. Therefore, their impact on children and families is also likely to vary. This makes it difficult to generalize about what happens in organized youth sports.

As more people call for cutbacks in government spending on social services, one of the first things to be dropped or scaled back is the public, tax-supported youth sport program—the type in category 1 above. Wealthy people seldom object to this policy approach, since they can afford to pay for their own sport programs. But cutting back public programs has a range of effects. *First*, it often limits the opportunities available to children from low-income families and funnels them into one or two sports. *Second*, it creates a market for private, commercial programs that cater to those with the money needed to pay for their services.

This is the way political conditions and changes in society have an impact on who participates in organized youth sports and the type of participation opportunities available. Many communities continue to face the question of whether tax money should be used to provide organized youth sports. What do you think?

· ·

to parents who can afford what they think is best for their children is to promise great results by highlighting successful athletes who have trained in particular programs, and successful coaches and instructors working in the programs.

Parents of physically skilled children often are attracted to organized programs emphasizing the performance principle. They sometimes define fees and equipment expenses, which can be shockingly high, as *investments* in their children's future. They are concerned with skill development, and as their children get older, use performance-oriented programs as sources of information about college sports, scholarships, and ways to contact coaches and sport organizations. They approach their children's sport participation in a rational manner, and see clear connections between childhood sport participation and future development, educational opportunities, and success in adult life.

The general emphasis on performance in youth sport programs also has encouraged *sport specialization* among children. Private and commercial programs often encourage exclusive attention to a single sport, because it is in the interest of program organizers to capture year-round commitments to membership. In commercial clubs there are salaries to pay, rental payments to make on facilities, and other year-round expenses, and they need membership fees through the year to pay for these things. Therefore, they encourage year-round commitments and participation, and justify their encouragement in terms of the performance principle: they claim that meeting performance goals and moving up to higher levels of competition requires a year-round commitment to a particular sport.

Popular acceptance of the performance principle has given rise to a growing number of "high-performance" training schools, clubs, and programs for child athletes. Gymnastics, figure skating, ice hockey, soccer, tennis, and other sports have programs boasting an explicit emphasis on making children into headline-grabbing, revenue-producing sport machines. This extreme emphasis of the performance principle is alarming, and it is attracting more interest among sociologists (Coakley, 1992; Donnelly, 1993) and others, including journalists (Brennan, 1996; Ryan, 1995). Children in high-performance training programs work at their sports for long hours week after week and year after year; they compete regularly and often generate revenues (directly and indirectly) for their coaches and families; they appear on commercial television, they attract people to expensive arena

seats to watch them perform, and they are used to endorse products. In a sense, they become child laborers, and this occurs outside government regulations that might protect their interests, bodies, health, and overall psychosocial development. Child labor laws prevent adults from using children as sources of financial gain in other occupations and in the film and advertising industries, but there are no enforceable standards regulating what child athletes do or what happens to them. Coaches need no credentials, parents can live off the children's earnings, coaches can build careers on their performance, and commercial events can be scheduled around their talents as adults see fit. And the results are sometimes frightening.

I thought of this when Kim Zmeskel, a national team gymnast from the U.S., was asked in 1991 at age fifteen about how she had competed with chronic stress fractures since she was nine years old. She calmly said, "It's nothing unusual for a gymnast. Our trainer told us that if they took a bone scan, they'd find stress fractures all over our bodies." In 1996, fourteen-year-old Dominique Moceanu, a U.S. hopeful for a 1996 Olympic medal, couldn't participate in the national Olympic trials because of stress fractures that plagued her body; she was only one of many with such problems. Many children in these high-performance programs just pop dozens of antiinflammatory pills and other painkillers to keep making their coaches and parents happy and proud about how they perform in hours of daily practices and regular competitions.

Are there ethical issues involved in this? Are children being used and abused? Are children being harmed physically, psychologically, and socially? Sociologists, some parents, and others now are asking serious questions about how the performance principle, carried to an unregulated extreme, can impact the health and development of children.

While sociologists have been asking questions, young people occasionally have taken affairs into their own hands and rejected organized

As publicly funded youth sports are cut back or eliminated, participation opportunities increasingly are provided by private clubs whose membership fees may be beyond the means of many families. Additionally, there is usually a heavy emphasis on the performance principle in such programs. (Travis Spradling, *Colorado Springs Gazette*)

sports in favor of informal sports allowing them to engage freely in physical activities on their own terms without being controlled by adults. Certain groups of skateboarders, snowboarders, and others are good examples of this. Because organized sports are the norm in certain societies for the first time in the history of childhood, some people refer to these informal activities as "alternative sports"—alternatives, that is, to organized sports. Alternative sports encompass an infinite array of physical activities done individually or in groups. Their growth and popularity are in part a reaction by children against the highly structured emphasis on the performance principle in organized sports (see Beal, 1995).

DIFFERENT EXPERIENCES: INFORMAL, PLAYER-CONTROLLED SPORTS VERSUS ORGANIZED, ADULT-CONTROLLED SPORTS

Since the late 1970s, my students and I have talked with many children about their sport experiences and watched children play sports in different settings. We've learned that individual children define and interpret personal experiences in many different ways. But we've also discovered that experiences among children differ depending on whether sports are informally organized and controlled by the players themselves or whether they are formally organized and controlled by adults (see Coakley, 1980, 1982, or 1983a).

Our findings indicate that informal, player-controlled sports are primarily *action-centered,* while formal, adult-controlled sports are primarily *rule-centered*. This means that when children get together and make up their own games, they create rules that promote movement and excitement. When children play sports organized and controlled by adults, there is an emphasis on learning and following rules so that games and game outcomes can be considered "official" within the larger structure of a league or tournament. We will summarize further findings in the following sections.

Informal, Player-Controlled Sports

We have conducted our observations of informally organized, player-controlled sports in back yards, parks, vacant lots, and school playgrounds; we have conducted our interviews with children in connection with observed game situations. The observations and interviews have indicated consistently that when children get together and play on their own, they are interested in four things:

1. *action*, especially action leading to scoring
2. *personal involvement* in the action
3. *a close score* (that is, a challenging or exciting contest)
4. *opportunities to reaffirm friendships* during games

The number of players in these informal games range from two to twelve or more. Usually the players know one another from games played on previous occasions. In most cases, they form the teams quickly. Skill differences and *friendship* patterns are the criteria used to choose teams. Getting games started and keeping them going is usually a complex operation that depends on how good the players are at managing interpersonal relationships and making effective decisions.

The games and game rules often resemble those used in organized programs, but they contain many modifications to maximize *action*, scoring, and *personal involvement* while *keeping the scores close* at the same time. For example, for the sake of *action*, free throws are eliminated in basketball, throw-ins are kept to a minimum in

soccer, yardage penalties are dropped from football, and the pitcher's mound in baseball and softball is moved closer to the batter so that weak batters can hit the ball. Similar types of action-producing rules are found in other informal games. Further proof of the importance of *action* is the extremely high scores in most of these games.

Personal involvement is often maximized through a number of clever rule qualifications and handicap systems. For example, the children sometimes use restrictive handicaps to keep highly skilled players from dominating games. Other forms of handicaps allow advantages to less skilled players. Furthermore, less skilled players often use special rules in their own favor. They are the ones most likely to use "do-over" or "interference" calls to get another chance or compensate for the effects of their mistakes on the outcomes of games. This saves them personal embarrassment and preserves their integrity as "contributing" members of their teams. It also serves to *keep the game scores close*. The overuse of these special rules is usually discouraged informally, through jests or teasing.

The *personal involvement* of each of the players is also promoted by unique game rules. For example, in baseball there may be a rule against called strikes so that everyone has a chance to hit—which means that fielders then have chances to make catches and other action-packed plays are possible. In football, every team member may be eligible to receive a pass on any play. When children are asked to name the biggest source of fun in their games, they almost always refer to hitting, catching, kicking, scoring, or some other form of *action* in which they are personally involved. Children seek to be a crucial part of what is going on in the games.

The keeping of order in informal games depends on the extent to which players are committed to maintaining *action*. Usually, the more children are personally involved in the game, the more they are committed to maintaining *action*. Tactics to control behavior are used most often to keep players from disrupting *action* in the games. Players may joke around, and even ignore rules, but these forms of deviance are ignored unless they interfere with the flow of *action*.

Our observations of these games uncovered many different performance styles and moves, and these are accepted as normal if they don't disrupt *action* in the games. The players with the greatest skill are those who have the most freedom to use creative styles and moves, because they usually can do so without upsetting game *action* or interfering with the *personal involvement* of other players.

Prestige and social status among players is important, because it determines which individuals become involved in decision-making processes during the games. The older players or those with the greatest skills usually have the highest status, although status sometimes is given to others who are especially good at solving problems. Arguments, even though they do occur, are usually handled in creative ways, and don't often have a major impact on the flow of *action* in the games. When children play together often, they become skilled at solving conflicts.

A WORD OF CAUTION These generalizations about informal sports do not describe all occasions when children create their own games. Problems in informal games do occur. Bigger and stronger children may exploit smaller and weaker ones. Girls may be patronized or dismissed when they try to play with groups of boys. And those children excluded from games may feel rejected by their peers (Evans, 1988).

Additionally, the dynamics of games usually vary with the availability of play spaces and equipment. For example, when a large group is using the only basketball court in the neighborhood, the games will exclude many who want to play; the team that wins will take on challengers rather than giving up the court to others; and those with less-developed skills will not be given special concessions when it comes to participation. "Taking turns" is rare when there are more players than spaces to play. But when there are many courts and only a few players, the goal is often to accommodate everyone's interests so

Informal games usually emphasize action, personal involvement, close scores, and the reaffirmation of friendships. (Tini Campbell)

that nobody will leave and force the game to end. This is a major reason why the informal games of children in low-income areas with few facilities and resources are often different from the games played by children in higher-income areas where facilities are more plentiful and there is no competition for space (Carlston, 1986).

Clearly, then, external conditions in the society as a whole have important effects on the way children play informal games. The majority of the children we observed and interviewed in our projects have been from neighborhoods where competition for space is not a major issue.

Formal, Adult-Controlled Sports

Our observations of formally organized, adult-controlled sports and interviews with children in these sports indicate that even though the children value action and personal involvement, they are likely to be serious and concerned with performance quality and game outcomes. Most apparent in these games is that the action, personal involvement, and behavior is strictly regulated by specialized *rules*. These *rules* are enforced by adult coaches, managers, umpires, referees, scorekeepers, timekeepers, and other game officials.

The children in these sports also are concerned with the formal *positions* they play on their teams. For example, they often refer to themselves in terms of those *positions*, and may even take pride in describing themselves as "defensive halfbacks" or "offensive ends," as "centers" or "left wingers," as "catchers" or "right fielders." The importance of *positions* is also emphasized by coaches and spectators, who often encourage players to "*stay in position*" during games. This happens regularly in basketball, soccer, hockey, and other sports in which players are constantly on the move.

The actual play of organized sports is governed by time schedules, the weather, and the setting of the sun. Individual playing time for participants varies according to skill levels. Most often, the smaller, visibly timid, and less skilled children sit on the sidelines. Although everyone usually gets into games for at least a short time, those whose playing time is low often maintain only a token interest in games. While these substitutes are on the sidelines, they are usually bored with the whole situation or interested in things unrelated to the games. Highly skilled players are most likely to exhibit strong interest in the games and express disappointment when they are taken out of the lineup. When taken out, they often stay close to coaches and wait or ask to be put back into the games.

A consequence of adult control and organization is the visible absence of arguments and overt displays of hostility between players from opposing teams. The few arguments we've seen over the years have been between adult officials (or spectators and officials) and between members of the *same* team. Arguments between children in organized sports are rare, and they are usually connected with a player's inability to remember game *rules*, stay in *position*, play a *position* efficiently, or carry out team strategies developed by adults.

Adult control and formal organization (that is, *rules* plus *positions*) not only hold the group together but limit visible displays of affection and friendship during the games. This makes it difficult to determine who is friends with whom, but since adults control the games, the interpersonal relationships among players have little to do with how they play the games.

The major purpose of game *rules* is the standardization of competition and the control of player behavior. *Rules* and rule enforcement regularly cause breaks in the action, but players don't seem to resent these breaks. The only signs of displeasure come when delays are caused by penalties called against a player's team. *Rule enforcement (social control)* in these games is based on the self-control and obedience of players, but it ultimately rests in the hands of adults: coaches, referees, and game officials. These adults usually apply the *rules* universally; which means that they don't make exceptions, even though there might be differences in players' abilities and characteristics. The freedom of the players is restricted by the *rules* and the strict applications of the rules by coaches.

Compliance with *rules* and coaches' expectations is extremely high in organized sports. Deviance occurs more often because players forget or don't know what to do than because they blatantly disregard the rules. On the playing field, rule infractions usually are accompanied by formal sanctions, even if they don't have an effect on game action or outcomes. Off the field, *rules* vary from one team to another, and violations usually involve "joking around" or exhibiting a lack of interest in the game or the team. Responses to these behaviors also vary. Coaches and parents use verbal and nonverbal sanctions. They use the game *rules*, team *rules*, and sanctions to control behavior and preserve the organization of the game and the values underlying the authority of referees and coaches.

Our observations and the interviews indicate that children in organized sports are serious about their games. They want to win, although they are not usually obsessed with winning. Those most concerned with winning are highly skilled players and members of the most successful teams. Although they have other goals, the principal goal of participation is to have fun; however, they always know their win-loss record and their place in the league standings. Players are most likely to be disappointed when they don't get the playing time they want. Playing time is related to children's reputations among peers, so it is very important.

Status on organized teams depends largely on the coaches' assessments of players' physical skills and value to the team. The better players are sometimes given more responsibility and more latitude in determining what they do during games. Physical skills and approval from coaches are the basis of status and autonomy among the players. And approval from coaches comes most often when players follow team *rules*.

Finally, the games in organized sports are extremely stable: they don't end until the *rules* say they are over, regardless of the quality of play or the satisfaction of the players; and players don't leave without permission from a coach or referee. Adults' whistles, along with verbal encouragement, commands, and advice, are ever present in these games.

Analysis of Differences

The personal experiences of children in each of these two sport forms are very different. Informal sports are generally *action centered*, whereas organized sports are *rule centered*.

Which of these experiences is more valuable in the development of children? The answer to this question is important not only to the children involved, but also to the adults who invest so much time, money, and energy into organized programs.

After doing years of research on this issue, I believe that each experience makes different contributions to the lives of children, and neither is without problems. However, people traditionally have overrated the contributions of participation in organized sports, and underrated the contributions of participation in informal sports.

Playing informal sports clearly involves the use of interpersonal and decision-making skills.

Children must be creative to organize games and keep them going. They encounter dozens of unanticipated challenges requiring on-the-spot decisions and interpersonal abilities. For example, long-time sports journalist Leonard Koppett (1994) has said, "The most important part of [informal sports] is learning how to set up the game, choose sides, agree with your peers, make compromises, figure out answers, [and] submit to self-directed rulings so that the game can continue." He adds that these experiences have "important civilizing functions" that aren't found in adult-controlled organized sports.

Patricia and Peter Adler's (1994) five-year study of children's after-school activities led them to conclude that informal sports provide experiences involving cooperation, planning, organizing, negotiating, problem solving, flexibility, and improvisation. Their examples of how children go about doing these things are impressive. Although we do not know how and to what extent the learning that occurs in these informal sports carries over to other settings, we can assume that children are influenced by their experiences.

Playing organized sports, on the other hand, involves a different set of experiences. Organized sports demand that children be able to manage their relationships with adult authority figures. Children also learn the rules and strategies used in activities that are highly visible and important within the culture, and through their participation they often gain status that carries over to the rest of their lives. When they play organized sports they see bureaucracy and hierarchy in action, and they become acquainted with forms of rule-governed teamwork and adult models of work and achievement (Adler and Adler, 1994).

Joe Paterno, long-time football coach at Penn State University, said over twenty years ago, "Kids want the opportunity to do things for themselves. . . . [T]hey're just sick and tired of having adults organize things for them." However, many children seem to contradict Paterno's statement. They seem to enjoy playing organized sports and see them as worthwhile, both while they play and long after they stop playing.

In organized sport programs for children, it is the adults who . . .

determine and enforce the rules,

plan strategies and call plays,

solve problems,

and wait anxiously for results. (Jay Coakley)

A possible negative outcome of too much participation in organized sports is that "adult-organized activities may prepare children for passively accepting the adult world as given" (Adler and Adler, 1994). If this is true, children may grow up thinking they are powerless to change the worlds in which they live. According to the Adlers (1994), who spent eight years studying after-school activities among children, there is hope in informal sports: "activities that children organize themselves may prepare them for creatively constructing alternative worlds." This distinction may not be as clear-cut as the Adlers infer, but it does give us something to think about as we study youth sports.

THREE QUESTIONS ABOUT YOUTH SPORTS

When Are Children Ready to Play Sports?

Readiness questions are hot today. Parents want to know if they should sign their three-year-olds up for T-ball teams, put their five-year-olds on swim teams, and let their eight-year-olds participate in state gymnastics competitions. Some want to give their children an early start on an imagined path to athletic glory; others don't want their children to fall behind peers in skills development; still others just want their children to have healthy fun and feel good about their bodies.

Answers to readiness questions are available in the fields of motor learning, physical education, exercise physiology, psychology, and sociology. When sociologists talk about readiness they give different answers, depending on what the term *sports* means. If *sports* refers to physical play, there is one answer; if the term refers to organized physical activities, there is another; and if it refers to organized competitive games, there is yet another answer. The three answers and their explanations follow.

Answer 1: It's never too early for physical play It's never too early for children to begin playing in physical ways. Body knowledge is an important part of our lives, and we begin learning about our bodies shortly after birth. Body learning occurs in the normal process of growing up and dealing with the physical environment. How children play and what they learn depends primarily on the freedom and encouragement they have to use their bodies and explore the environment. The more freedom and encouragement they have, the more they learn.

This sounds simple, but cultural factors influence how people think about body learning and physical play. For example, preferred childrearing practices often call for restrictions on the physical movements of infants and children, and various cultures justify these restrictions in cultural terms. Definitions of what is normal when it comes to how children use their bodies vary with different cultural ideas about morality, gender, sexuality, and even definitions of physical space. This means that physical activities have a cultural dimension that influences how they are defined and included in children's lives. The definitions people attach to physical activities often influence how they hear and apply answers to the question of when children should begin various forms of physical play.

We can illustrate these points about cultural influence by taking a look at physical play among North American children. Most children in North America are encouraged to be physically active from birth. Of course, parents and other adults influence patterns of physical play when they put children in different environments and give them access to different play objects. Parents and adults who define physical skill development as important tend to encourage forms of physical play that involve less emphasis on expression and more emphasis on practice and achieving performance goals. Such adults might encourage their children, even very young children, to keep practicing physical movements until they "get them right."

This cultural emphasis on *performance over expression* could restrict the range of physical experiences in children's lives, and could encourage children to define physical pleasure in terms of achieving goals rather than feeling good about movement itself. If this happened, it could lead to a society in which many children were physically inactive, while others were active primarily in goal-oriented physical activities. It also could lead children to be concerned with "being perfect" in what they did and in what they might attempt in the future. This seems to have occurred to some degree in North America. However, it is not clear exactly how cultural processes affect specific forms of physical play among children. This topic is difficult to study, but studies are needed.

Answer 2: Any child in school is ready for organized physical activities Children should begin playing in organized programs when this enables them to expand the range of their physical experiences beyond what they can do on their own. Children as young as three or four years old can be organized into groups in which they are encouraged to join peers in expressive physical play. In fact, a benefit of organized programs is that they provide children with safe physical environments and with adults who can intervene when egocentric behaviors, common among preteen children, interfere with play.

Organized physical activities are appropriate for children as young as five or six years old. However, the activities should encourage physical expression and creativity, along with the development of basic movement and coordination skills. The best organized programs are run by people committed to listening to children and allowing them freedom to use their bodies on their own terms. Then organization becomes liberating, rather than suffocating or oppressive. Children are usually good at distinguishing freedom from oppression and knowing when organization enables them to expand their physical experiences and when it restricts them. When it comes to noncompetitive organized physical activities, children themselves often can answer our question about readiness; we just have to listen.

Answer 3: Organized sports before age 8 and competition before age 12 must be matched with children's needs and abilities The readiness to play organized sports is a different matter. It's not until the age of eight or nine that children begin developing the cognitive abilities they need to understand and play sports, especially competitive sports. And these abilities are not *fully* developed until children reach twelve years

of age. Anyone who has ever watched two teams of eight-year-old soccer players knows what this means. Most preteen children play what I call "beehive soccer": after the opening kick, there are twenty bodies and forty legs surrounding the ball, and they follow the ball around the playing field like a swarm of bees following its queen. Everyone is out of position, and they usually stay that way for the entire game. Meanwhile, coaches and parents on the sidelines loudly plead with children to "Stay in position!" and yell demands to "Get back where you belong!"

But in most sports, determining where you belong is difficult, because positions change depending on where teammates and opponents are relative to the location of the ball. Understanding the concept of "position" requires the ability to mentally visualize the ever-changing placements of teammates and opponents over the entire field, assess their relationships to each other and to the ball, and then decide where *you* belong. But the ability to do this complex form of thinking and "role taking" is seldom developed before the age of twelve, and children don't even begin developing this ability at all until they are eight or nine.

Parents and coaches often are frustrated when children fail to understand positions and follow strategies. When adults don't know about cognitive and psychosocial development during childhood, they may accuse children of not trying hard enough, not thinking, or having a bad attitude. This, in turn, frustrates children who *are* trying and thinking as best they can at their stage of development.

"Beehive soccer" and its equivalents in other sports can be avoided in two ways. One is good; the other creates problems. *First*, the actual games children play can be altered to focus on skills and expression rather than competitive processes. This is a good strategy consistent with children's abilities. *Second*, children can be tediously conditioned to respond in certain ways to certain situations during competitive games and matches. This is not a good strategy. Coaches who opt to condition children have practices in which they create various game situations and then have each player rehearse individual tactical

"I know this is starting early, but I can't let him get too far behind the other kids if he's ever going to make a team in high school."

responses to each situation. Doing this with every player for even a few basic strategies makes practices tedious and boring. It may win a few games, but it often destroys much of the action and personal involvement that children value in sports. This is a problem, and it causes some children to wonder if sports are really fun.

Children are not born with the ability to compete or cooperate with others, nor are they born able to mentally visualize complex sets of social relationships between teammates and opponents. They must learn these things, and the learning depends on a combination of social experience and the development of abstract thinking and interpersonal abilities. This learning cannot be forced; it can occur only as children move from a stage in which they see the world from their own limited viewpoint to a stage in which they can see the world from a "third-party perspective"—that is, one that goes beyond their own view and the view of any other single person they know (Coakley, 1985b). This third-party perspective gradually emerges between the ages of eight and twelve years in most children. Therefore, organized sports for preteens should be controlled in ways that accommodate this gradually emerging ability; the highest emphasis should be on cooperation and confidence. Children must learn to cooperate before they compete with one another; if they don't know how to cooperate, competitions can get nasty and brutish.

Most sociologists raise serious questions about the readiness of children for high-performance sports for which competition is the name of the game. When ten-year-olds travel ten thousand miles and play ninety hockey games a year, when nine-year-olds leave home and devote fifty-two weeks a year to live and train with coaches, when eleven-year-olds go from seasons of competition to training camps to off-season training sessions without a break during the year, we must wonder whether children are pretending to be ready for sports just to make the adults they depend on for love and affection happy with them. When are young people ready to put their bodies on the line and make the sacrifices necessary to achieve excellence as it has

been defined in today's high-performance sports? Well after age twelve, in my opinion! In fact, I think sixteen-year-olds may be pushing the readiness issue in many cases. If the adults who run these programs weren't blinded by the money and status they receive in connection with these wonder kids, they too would be concerned. But the social world of elite sports often swallows up these adults, so that they focus on performance goals, not children (cf. Ryan, 1995).

A LOOK BACK AT THE ORIGINAL QUESTION People who ask the question, "When should children play sports?" generally live in cultures in which scientific approaches to childhood development are popular, and people have the time and resources to organize children's activities. Youth sports are a luxury. They cost money and they take time, so many people cannot afford them. This is true even among certain groups of people in high-tech, rich countries like the U.S. and Canada. Many children around the world include movement and physical play in their lives as they learn how to be boys or girls in their cultures, or to fit into class and occupational structures. "When to begin sports" is not even a relevant question for them or their parents; gender and class set strict boundaries for how they move and what they play.

Do Youth Sports Affect Parent-Child Relationships?

We've all heard horror stories about the extreme behaviors of some "Little League parents." Fortunately, these stories are not representative of all parents. Sports do not bring out the worst in most parents; parents usually have good intentions and want the best for their children.

Informal sports seldom involve relationships between parents and children, except that parents can provide support and take an interest in what their children do when they skateboard, play street games, choose sides in the local park, or make up games in the back yard. These activities often require the passive approval of parents, but not their direct support and involvement. Organized sports, on the other hand, require time, money, and organizational skills,

Adults have changed games so that children can play them at younger and younger ages. This can be a problem if the adults also expect children to be able to understand competition and team play at younger and younger ages. Such understandings begin to form at around eight years of age, but are not well established until age twelve. This five-year-old has no cognitive understanding of the dynamics and organization of a team sport. (Suzanne Tregarthen/Educational Photo Stock)

and these usually come from parents. Therefore, playing organized sports becomes a family affair, and may impact parent-child relationships.

It is clear that family schedules are affected when a child participates in organized sports—any parent knows this (Chafetz and Kotarba, 1995). But surprisingly few sociologists have done research on how youth sport participation affects family *relationships*. Some former youth sport participants may have happy family memories, but we must not jump to the conclusion that whenever parents and children are involved in something together, they get along in positive ways. Sports are not always fields of happy dreams. Parents may act in ways that damage re-

lationships with children, and they may become so emotionally involved with sports that what they think is encouragement is seen by the children as a form of pressure.

Family relationships may be damaged when children believe that their parents' attention to them depends on their playing sports and being good athletes. Young people sometimes find themselves facing a triple-bind dilemma: (1) if they quit sports, their parents will withdraw support and attention; (2) if they play sports but do not perform well, they will get negative feedback from their parents; (3) if they do perform well, they will be treated like "little pros" instead of children. The Alanis Morisette song *Perfect*, from the mid-1990s, describes part of this dilemma and how deeply children can feel it.

In Mike Messner's (1992) interviews, former elite athletes described similar dilemmas. Many men in Messner's study (see chap. 2) remembered that early sport experiences enabled them to connect with their fathers, who were otherwise away from home and emotionally distant from them. The boys wanted to please and receive attention from their fathers, but they often found that the togetherness they had in sports did not involve real intimacy; nor did it carry over into nonsport settings. Despite this, many of the men remembered feeling that they had to stay in sports and become good athletes to maintain connections with their fathers.

Many parents today are aware that they should not make parent-child relationships dependent on children's sport participation or performance. However, they may unintentionally lead their children to make such connections. To see how this can happen, put yourself in the $130 top-of-the-line athletic footwear of an eleven-year-old in an organized sport program:

> As an eleven-year-old, you clearly remember that before you became a skater, football player, soccer player, etc., your parents were good to you and told you they loved you. But now things are different. In the past, they always let you know how hard they worked for the ten-dollar allowance they gave you and told you that money did not grow on trees. But now that you play sports, they do not hesitate to spend from $300 to $1,000 per season to outfit you in the best sport gear and pay entry fees and instructional fees that can amount to thousands of dollars. After years of hearing how busy your parents were and how they needed a vacation, they now are giving up weekends to drive you to games, meets, and practices. They even changed the family vacation schedule to accommodate your playoff games. They now fix special dinners five nights a week so you can get to practice on time. They come home from work a little early to see your practices or games. They make it a point to ask how things are going at practice and they give pep talks about sports.

At the same time, they did not attend the quarterly PTA meeting when your latest art project was displayed, and they complained about how it was impossible for them to miss work to attend a parent-teacher conference to discuss your schoolwork. Of course, they continue to tell you that education is important. But you see that their behavior indicates something different: what happens at school is not nearly so crucial as what happens in your game next Saturday.

Under such conditions, most eleven-year-olds conclude that playing organized sports is much more important than their parents say it is. If parents are not careful about the content of these unspoken messages, their children will think that being an athlete is a prerequisite for continued parental interest and concern. This is upsetting for most eleven-year-olds, and can damage a parent-child relationship.

Sociologists need to study further how the participation of children in organized sports affects family relationships. In some cases, participation has brought parents and children together; in others, participation has caused problems. Brothers and sisters may enjoy playing sports with each other; conversely they may resent the devotion of attention and resources to another family member. Researchers need to discover when and why these things happen. But researchers also must be open to the possibility that participation has no *systematic impact* on family relationships. It may be that sports provide family members additional settings to display what is already deeply grounded in their interpersonal relationships. Again, research should explore this possibility.

Do Boys and Girls Play Sports Differently?

The answer to this question is yes. But as we identify the differences and explain why they exist, we begin to see that asking "gender difference" questions may lead us to overlook important issues related to behavior, sports, and culture. For example, when we look for gender differences, we often ignore all the overlap in how boys and girls play sports, and all the

Parental support is important to children. But might children sometimes define that support as a form of pressure? Does it pressure a boy to continue playing football if his mother wears a shirt that shows a picture of him in his football uniform? Only the boy on the field could tell us. (Jay Coakley)

differences that exist among boys and among girls.

My students point out the problems with using gender difference questions to guide research whenever they read and respond to findings in these studies. For example, when students see descriptions of the characteristics of boys' informal sports and girls' informal sports, a number of them quickly point out that the gender-specific lists do not accurately describe *their* experiences. At first, I was inclined to tell them that they were exceptions, and the lists were generally accurate. After a while I felt uncomfortable with this response, because it was leading stu-

dents to either see themselves as weird or question the validity of the lists. Furthermore, it was cutting me off from learning about their experiences.

So I changed my approach and began to ask them about their experiences. As they talked and everyone listened, we saw that many different things have an impact on how children play sports. After a while, we started to see gender issues in connection with a wide range of reasons for why people play sports the way they do. Gender did not disappear, but it became meaningful only in how it was linked to other factors in people's lives. In other words, when explaining how children played sports, we saw that a girl's gender was less important than her having parents who controlled her life and wanted her close to home after school, or being in a low-income family and having to baby-sit a younger sibling. And a boy's gender was less important than his having a father who played catch with him nearly every day and always let him go to the well-kept local park after dinner so he could play baseball with his friends. When boys had parents who were overprotective and wanted them close to home or demanded they care for younger siblings, this had an impact on when and how they played sports. And when girls had fathers who played catch with them and let them go to the well-kept local park to play baseball after dinner, this too had an impact on when and how they played sports. Gender was important only in connection with these other factors that set limits or opened possibilities in children's lives.

The "gender difference lists" that are so popular today tend to obscure these influential factors or to see them as gender-dependent, which they are not. The focus on *difference* leads us to lose sight of *experience*. But this does not mean we should ignore gender in our research. Gender is indeed important in children's lives. Asking gender-difference questions can help us gather concrete information about inequities that exist in society. But unless we move beyond those questions, we end up perpetuating the

REFLECT ON SPORT   **Gender Differences versus Experiences:**
What Should We Study?

Many sociologists today use "experience questions" rather than "gender difference questions" when they study behavior. So instead of asking, "What are the differences between boys and girls in the ways they play sports?" we ask, "How and why do children play the way they do?" Asking our research question in this way enables us to avoid seeing the world in terms of two "opposite" sexes, when, in fact, boys and girls share well over 96 percent of their biological traits and are capable of seeing and doing things in many ways that have nothing to do with the few biological differences that do exist.

This does not mean that we ignore gender when we ask "experience questions." For example, when we study children's experiences, we begin to see how children become "gendered" in ways that impact when and how they play sports, and to what end. We look at the gendering process in the lives of all children rather than asking a "difference" question that forces us to see boys and girls as "opposites" despite all their similarities.

"Gender difference questions" are *loaded*, because they lead us to ignore important things about variations in human experiences and behaviors when we do research. In the sociology of sport, these questions sometimes prevent us from seeing and explaining all the *variations* in girls' play behaviors and experience, and the *variations* in boys' play behaviors and experiences. Instead, we do study after study looking for boy-girl differences; then, after we find them, we conclude that boys and girls are indeed different and look for reasons for the differences.

Over the short term, the strategy of asking "difference questions" in our research adds something to our

knowledge of behavior and how the world works, but over the long term, it takes us in big circles and leads us to reaffirm the very gender assumptions that prompted our "difference questions" in the first place. This happens because "gender difference questions" force us to conceptualize our research in terms of a set of assumed either-or differences, and then search for evidence that fits our assumptions.

"Experience questions," on the other hand, are much more useful in the long run because they force us to focus our research attention on real-life experiences and why they happen. So we ask, "How do children play?" Then, after we have identified patterns in children's play experiences, we ask other questions, like this one: "When children are on their own after school, why do some play competitive sports in relatively large groups while others don't play sports at all, or play noncompetitive sports, or play sports in small groups?" These questions force us to explore issues that go beyond assumed male-female differences in experience.

This approach makes some people uncomfortable, because they've learned to see the world in terms of a two-category, male-female classification system. For their entire lives they have used that system to explain why people do what they do. Once a person gets into this way of viewing the world, it is difficult to change. But maintaining this view means bypassing the complexity and variation of human experiences across all women and across all men. Eventually, this view presents problems for those who use it. When they use it in research, it raises serious questions about the accuracy of what we call "knowledge." What do you think?

· ·

same differences that led to the inequities to begin with! (See the discussion in the box entitled Gender Differences versus Experiences: What Should We Study? above).

With this in mind, here is what we know about the question. Research indicates that girls

and boys often have different types of early childhood experiences when it comes to physical activities (White et al., 1992). Parents, especially fathers, play with their sons more often and in more physically active ways than they play with their daughters. In general, the physical activity messages young boys receive often differ from the messages girls receive, both inside and outside family settings (Beal, 1994; Caplan, 1981; Chafetz, 1978; Greendorfer, 1993; Hargreaves, 1994; Hasbrook, 1996, 1997; Lenskyj, 1986; Lewis, 1972a,b; Nelson, 1991).

One of the results of these messages is that before most children take their first physical education class or play their first organized sport, they have clear ideas about their physical skills and potential. Boys are likely to see themselves as being physically skilled more than girls do, even though gender differences in actual skill levels are small or nonexistent (*JOPERD*, October 1990:9). Boys are more likely than girls to think they are better than they actually are when it comes to sport skills. This has an effect on their self-confidence and their willingness to use and test their bodies in active ways and voluntarily participate in physical activities. Girls learn to minimize the physical space they occupy, sexualize their bodies through modifying their appearance and movement, and accept the notion that boys are physically superior to them (Hasbrook, 1993). At the same time, boys learn to present themselves as physically big and strong, act in ways that claim physical space around them, and expect to exert power and control over girls (Hasbrook and Harris, 1997).

Physical self-concepts come to be related to gender because many people expect different levels of sport-related skills from girls and boys. And when boys show skills and girls don't, people continue various forms of differential treatment. This may be one of the reasons why some physical education teachers have different expectations for girls than for boys. These expectations may be one of the reasons boys' ball games often dominate the space on elementary school playgrounds, "while girls play less vigorous games in smaller groups" (White et al., 1992). Of course, there are some teachers who actively discourage such gender-based patterns, but it is often difficult to change them, because they are deeply rooted in the culture as a whole.

At this point, we know more about gender as it relates to patterns in informal games (Lever,

1976, 1978, 1980) than about its influence in organized sports. However, it is likely that many parents and coaches have gender-based expectations for children in organized programs. When we attempt to explain these expectations, it is difficult to tell when they are based on (a) realistic assessments of the actual experiences girls bring to the programs, (b) well-intentioned but paternalistic concerns about protecting girls from stress and challenges, or (c) sexist beliefs about the supposed physical inferiority of girls.

Some people argue that motives for differential treatment are irrelevant, and that differential treatment is always wrong because it perpetuates inequalities and subverts the potential of all girls and women. However, this argument is based on the assumption that boys are always treated the "right" way, a debatable assumption. Undoubtedly, if girls have fewer opportunities and fewer challenges to become physically competent through sports, they are being shortchanged. And if girls are "protected" so they don't develop a sense of physical empowerment, they are being cheated. But on the other hand, if adults are more sensitive to the feelings and physical well-being of girls, then boys are being shortchanged; and if adults are less apt to force girls into competitive sports, while not giving boys a choice, then boys are being cheated.

We know that among most children today, the social popularity of boys depends much more than the popularity of girls on athletic abilities and achievements. The Adlers discovered this when they did their study of children. But the Adlers also note the following:

> Preadolescent boys' and girls' social worlds are . . . different in some ways and similar in others. While we have noted that boys and girls stratify themselves in popularity according to different factors . . . , there is more similarity to the friendship structures and interactions across gender than up and down the status hierarchy. Boys and girls are thus both competitive and cooperative, hierarchical and leveling, and they compose their peer societies into stratified groups that are fundamentally comparable (1996:136).

Therefore, when discussing differences in how boys and girls play sports, we also must consider the rest of children's lives, or else we will exaggerate gender differences and overlook what real lived experiences are all about.

RECOMMENDATIONS FOR CHANGING CHILDREN'S SPORTS

Changing Informal Sports

Informal (alternative) sports are unique because they are *not* controlled by adults. In fact, many children opt for such sports because they want to avoid the organized structures of adult-controlled teams and programs. Therefore, the goals of adults should be to (1) enable children to play informal sports as safely as possible, and (2) take an interest in these sports so they can serve as a reference point in the adult-child relationships that all children need to grow up knowing they are valued in their communities.

This means that instead of simply passing laws to suppress informal sports such as skateboarding or in-line skating, adults should work with young people to provide safe settings for them to create their own activities. As we have seen from recent media coverage of the "X Games" (extreme sports), the skills that young people develop in their own activities can be very impressive. Although there are problems with the "X Games" in particular, children do need their own "space" in which they can find ways to be creative and expressive in sport forms that they themselves control.

Changing Organized Sports

There are a wide variety of organized sport programs for children. This is especially true in countries that have no centralized state authority through which youth programs are funded, controlled, and administered. Programs vary from one sport to another, from community to community, and from league to league. However, those in charge could improve conditions in most programs, maximizing positive experiences and minimizing negative experiences for participants. This is true in other countries as well as in North America.

In making recommendations for changes, most people agree that organized programs should be set up to meet the needs of the children who participate in them. This means that children themselves are a valuable source of information. Since children have fun by emphasizing action, involvement, close scores, and friendships in the games they create for themselves, it makes sense that organized programs also should emphasize these things. In the following discussion, we provide examples of using the informal games of children to recommend change in organized sport programs.

INCREASING ACTION In their own games, children emphasize action. Much activity occurs around the "scoring area," and scoring is usually so frequent that it is difficult to keep personal performance statistics. Organized sports, although they do contain action, emphasize rules to promote order, standardized conditions, and predictability. The strategy of many organized teams is to *prevent* action, rather than stimulate it. Parents and coaches sometimes describe high-scoring games as undisciplined "free-for-alls" caused by poor defensive play. The desired strategy in the minds of many adults is to stop action: to strike out the batter, stall the game when you are in the lead, use a safe running play for a 3-yard gain, and wait for just the right shot. These tactics may win some games, but they limit the most exciting aspects of any game: action and scoring.

Recommendations. It's usually easy to increase action and scoring in organized sports, as long as adults do not view game models as sacred and unchangeable. Bigger goals, smaller playing areas, and fewer rules are the best means to increase action. Why not double the width of soccer and hockey goals, make all players eligible to receive a pass in football, or use a 6-foot basket in a half-court basketball game? Many adults resist changes they see as altering game models—that is, the models adults use. They want children to play the "real thing." But children are more interested in having fun than in doing it just like the pros.

INCREASING PERSONAL INVOLVEMENT
Children don't sit on the bench in informal games; they use rule qualifications and handicap systems to maximize their involvement and promote action. Smaller or less skilled players may not contribute to the action as much as others do, but they play the whole game. If they are treated badly or don't get included, they leave without being branded as quitters by their parents or given lectures on commitment.

In organized games, playing time is often seriously limited for all but the most skilled players, and the substitution process is a constant source of problems for the coach and pressure for players. Specialization by position further restricts the range of involvement. For example, when ten-year-olds describe themselves as left defensive tackles or center fielders or left wingers or center halfbacks, it is a sure sign that the range of personal involvement is limited.

Recommendations. Coaches and other leaders could extend personal involvement in organized sport programs by rotating players to different positions and by coordinating group substitutions with opposing teams. They could alter team size to allow more players on the field, or reduce rosters so that there were more teams with fewer subs. Batting lineups for baseball and softball could include all team members, regardless of which ones were playing the nine or ten positions in the field. In ice hockey, the games could be played across the width of the rink and portable dividers and lightweight goals could be used; this would allow three times as many teams to compete at the same time. In basketball, the first-string teams could play a half-court game at one basket, while the second-string teams played each other at the other basket. A combined score could determine the winner. These or many other similar changes would increase personal involvement.

CREATING CLOSE SCORES "Good games" are those for which the outcomes are in doubt until the last play; double overtime games are the best. Lopsided scores make games uninteresting.

Children realize this, so they keep their games close.* Since motivation partially depends on how people perceive their chances for success, a close game usually keeps players motivated and satisfied. Just like adults who use handicaps to keep the competition interesting in golf and other sports, children adjust their games to keep them close.

In organized games, lopsided scores are common and team records are often very uneven. Keeping players motivated under these circumstances is difficult. Coaches appeal to "pride" and "respect" to keep players motivated in the face of lopsided scores, while they urge their teams and players to take big leads during games.

Recommendations. Adults who control organized youth sports are usually hesitant to make changes affecting outcomes of games, but they might consider some possibilities. For example, they could encourage close scores by altering team rosters or by using handicap systems during games. The underdog could be given an advantage, such as extra players or the right to use five downs or five outs or a bigger goal. Numerous changes could keep games close; but when game models are viewed as unchangeable, they don't get discussed.

MAINTAINING RELATIONSHIPS In player-controlled sports, the reaffirmation of friendships is important; it influences how teams are chosen and the dynamics of problem-solving processes during games.

Organized sports may provide useful contexts for making friends, but players need more opportunities to nurture relationships.

Recommendations. Coaches and managers could ask groups of players in organized sports to plan game strategies or coach practice sessions. They could encourage players to talk with opponents, help them when they were knocked

---

*Close scores may be sacrificed when close friends want to be on the same team; playing with friends is sometimes more important than having evenly balanced teams.

Calvin and Hobbes   by Bill Watterson

Gender ideology and gender relations often influence children's decisions to play sports.

Calvin has learned that hanging around girls can damage a boy's reputation, although Susie thinks this attitude is stupid.

Calvin doesn't think of himself as a wimp, but he is pressured by the class bully to play sports to prove that he is not a sissy.

Calvin has his doubts about playing a game that constrains action and creativity.

down, and congratulate them when they did something commendable. Too often, relationships between opposing players are cold and impersonal. Players should learn that games have a human component that they can recognize during play.

Most important, players should be expected to enforce most of the rules themselves during games. Through self-enforcement, they would learn why rules are necessary and how any collective action depends on taking other people and the expectations of others into consideration. Self-enforcement of rules would also help to control the largest financial expense and administrative headache in most organized programs: the hiring and training of officials. Many people argue that self-enforcement would never work (although it does work in tennis)—but if organized programs do not teach young people how to control themselves so that playing a game without referees is possible, then those programs are not worth our time and effort. Too many coaches and players blame officials for anything that goes wrong during a game. They see rules as coercive restrictions rather than necessary guidelines.

Changing High-Performance Sport Programs

Many of the worst problems in youth sports occur in high-performance programs. To deal with these problems, sociologist Peter Donnelly (1993) has called on sport governing bodies to do two things: (1) change their policies, procedures, and rules to account for the rights and interests of children, and (2) create less controlling sport environments designed to promote children's growth, development, and empowerment (p. 120). Because people in sport organizations may have vested interests in keeping things as they are now, Donnelly advocates some form of child labor laws that can be applied to high-performance youth sports and enforced when the health and well-being of children is in jeopardy.

Journalist Jane Ryan (1995) picked up on Donnelly's points when she studied girls in elite gymnastics and figure skating. She has argued, "Child labor laws should address all labor, even that which is technically nonpaid, though top [child athletes do sometimes] labor for money" (p. 13). And she concludes with strong words:

> Since those charged with protecting young athletes so often fail their responsibility, it is time the government drops the fantasy that certain sports are merely games and takes a hard look at legislation aimed at protecting elite child athletes (p. 15).

Amen!! This is a suggestion that we should all take seriously. When the livelihoods of adults depend on the work or performance of children, the children need formal protection.

PROSPECTS FOR CHANGE

Important changes have been made in many organized youth sport programs in recent years. Most often, these changes have reflected recommendations based on a functionalist approach to sport (see chap. 2). In other words, they involve efforts to increase efficiency and organization in youth sports. This means that there are now more training programs for coaches, more formal rules regulating the behavior of parents and spectators, more rules for what is expected from players and coaches, more promotional brochures and advertising in the local media, more of an emphasis on performance and skills development, and more contacts with other organized programs in the same sport to ensure state and regional play-offs.

As organized youth sports become increasingly affiliated with national organizations and sport governing bodies, the chances that these bodies will consider changes that involve alterations in game models become increasingly slim. Changes may be considered at local levels, but even local sport programs are not likely to make changes in official game models. Such changes would threaten their relationships with the influential state and national organizations that many of the players' parents have paid to join.

Changes are also slow to come because many adults who administer and support organized sport programs have vested interests in keeping them as they are. They know the programs are not perfect, but they are afraid changes in them will eliminate many of the good things they have accomplished in the past.

One factor that could produce significant changes in many private youth programs is *burnout.* Burnout is a dreaded phenomenon among parents who have given long-term support to the participation of one or more of their children. They do not want sons or daughters to drop out or burn out after years of successful and often expensive participation. If burnout becomes common, or if more than a few parents expect it to be a problem, program organizers and coaches may be willing to consider structural changes that would alter the experiences their young people have in sport.

Coaching Education as a Means of Producing Changes

Coaching education programs will continue to grow into the next century. Existing programs in many countries provide coaches with information on how to (1) deal with young people responsively and safely, and (2) be more effective in organizing their practices and teaching skills to young people. Most coaching education programs emphasize putting the needs of athletes ahead of winning, but none of them teach coaches how to critically assess the sport programs in which they work with young people. None of them have information on how to make structural changes in the programs themselves, or on creating alternatives to existing programs. Coaching education materials generally are based on the assumption that existing sport programs are pretty good, but they could be better if coaches only knew more about applied sport science.

Although coaching education is important, I worry that some programs ultimately will foster what we might call a "technoscience approach" to youth sports. Such an approach emphasizes issues of control and skill development, rather than an overall understanding of young people as human beings. If this happens, coaches will become "sports efficiency experts" rather than teachers who provide young people with opportunities to become autonomous and responsible decision makers who control their own lives.

At this point, most coaching education programs have contributed to responsible coaching in youth sport programs. But as we examine coaching education programs and critically assess their place at all levels of sport, it would be good to remember that the former East Germany had one of the most efficient and highly respected coaching education programs in the world. But its program was based on a "technoscience approach," and did little to contribute to the overall development of young people as human beings. The East German experience reminds us that without critical self-reflection, the application of sport science knowledge to coaching will not necessarily make sports or the world any better. But *with* critical self-reflection, coaching education could lead to many positive changes in sports programs for people of all ages.

SUMMARY

ARE ORGANIZED YOUTH SPORT PROGRAMS WORTH THE EFFORT?

According to the official policy handbooks of organized youth leagues, all participants should come out of organized programs as models of virtue and good character. However, this does not happen. The consequences of participation are mixed—some positive, some negative. This is the case because every sport participation environment is different in terms of the experiences it offers to young people (see chap. 4, pp. 98–100).

Organized programs obviously serve a vast number of young people, especially those coming from all but the lowest socioeconomic groups in wealthy, postindustrial countries. For some of those young people, the programs provide opportunities to develop physical skills, self-confidence, and status among their peers. And in areas where play groups are scarce for one reason or another, they assist children in making friends and getting together in group activities. On the other hand, there are problems associated with organized sport programs. Some parents use bribes and pressure to push their children to achieve; some coaches interfere with the development of young people by being authoritarian and abusive; for some players, sport becomes a crutch that prevents them from developing other dimensions of themselves; for others, sport is boring and tedious. And there are also cases of parents arguing with coaches; referees being attacked by parents, coaches, or spectators; children being injured by the violent tactics of opponents; and adults being more concerned with game scores than with the interests of children. As we saw in the last chapter, when sport participation expands a child's experiences, relationships, and identities, it contributes to development; when it constricts and limits, it subverts development.

Research and media coverage have helped people realize that organized sports are not perfect. The most frequent targets of popular criticism have been insensitive coaches and the win-at-all-costs philosophy that seems to underlie certain programs. But the origins of problems in organized sports are not so easily identified. Eliminating a few insensitive coaches and preaching about how fun is more important than winning will not do much to change the experiences of the children in those programs. Many more changes are needed.

Of course, no program can guarantee that it will make children into models of virtue, but those organizing programs can change them to cut down on the number of problems. What this means is that organized sport programs for children are worth the effort—when the adults controlling them put the interests of children ahead of the organizational needs of the programs and their own needs to gain status through their association with child athletes.

SUGGESTED READINGS

Adler, Patricia, and Peter Adler. 1994. Social reproduction and the corporate other: The institutionalization of after-school activities. *The Sociological Quarterly* 35(2): 309–28 (*an analysis of qualitative data collected over a five-year period; summarizes findings on the socializing influences of after-school activities, including sports; distinguishes between child-controlled and adult-controlled activities*).

Cahill, B. R., and A. J. Pearl, eds. 1993. *Intensive participation in children's sports*. Champaign, IL: Human Kinetics (*articles by Coakley and Donnelly provide sociological analyses of issues associated with children playing high-performance sports; articles by Gould and Weiss are also informative from a psychological perspective*).

Coakley, J. 1992. Burnout among adolescent athletes: a personal failure or social problem? *Sociology of Sport Journal* 9(3): 271–85 (*reports findings from in-depth interviews of fifteen adolescents identified as "sport burnouts"; presents a model of burnout that is an alternative to psychological, stress-based models*).

DeKnop, P., B. Skirstad, L.-M. Engstrom, and M. Weiss, eds. 1996. *Worldwide trends in youth sport*. Champaign, IL: Human Kinetics (*background material on comparative research; excellent information about youth sports in twenty countries; summarizes research on youth sports in terms of global patterns, trends, problems, and policies*).

Fine, G. A. 1987. *With the boys: Little League baseball and preadolescent culture*. Chicago: University of Chicago Press (*an in-depth study of ten teams showing how boys create their own ways of experiencing organized sport*).

Gould, D., and M. Weiss, eds. 1987. *Advances in pediatric sport sciences: behavioral issues*. Champaign, IL: Human Kinetics (*twelve articles on practical issues related to children's involvement in youth sports*).

Morris, G. S. D. 1980. *How to change the games children play*. 2d ed. Minneapolis: Burgess (*describes a model that can be used to analyze, change, and create games for children; contains useful guidelines for teachers, parents, and some youth league coaches*).

Ryan, J. 1995. *Little girls in pretty boxes: The making and breaking of elite gymnasts and figure skating.* New York: Doubleday (*an in-depth journalistic account/exposé of the lives of U.S. girls and young women in elite gymnastics and figure skating*).

Smoll, F. L., R. A. Magill, and M. Ash, eds. 1988. *Children in sport.* 3d ed. Champaign, IL: Human Kinetics (*twenty-two papers by leading researchers;*

good papers on the history and development of youth sports in North America and on psychological issues and social processes related to youth sports).

Weiss, M. R., and D. Gould, eds. 1986. Sport for children and youths. Champaign, IL: Human Kinetics (*thirty-seven papers from the Olympic Scientific Congress sessions on youth sports; six papers on youth sport in different countries*).

6

(Mark Reis, *Colorado Springs Gazette*)

Deviance in Sports
*Is it getting out of control?**

Want proof we've abandoned all pretense of a civil society? . . . In today's billion-dollar sports business, winning is the only thing. If players act like freaks or worse on the court or off, no one seems to care. Least of all those in the stands whose own behavior emulates their idols'. Fans . . . [have] become sideline guerrillas.

Linda Chavez, USA Today editorialist (1996)

I go out there and get my eyes gouged, my nose busted, my body slammed. I love the pain of the game; it makes me feel alive.

Dennis Rodman, NBA player (1996)

Simply, I had grown tired of losing. I didn't cheat because the Joneses did or because it made me a big man, I did it because I didn't want to get beat anymore. That's all.

Tates Locke, college basketball coach (1985)

The increasing number of rapes and criminal assaults of women by football players seems to indicate that players can be poorly socialized or downright hostile toward women without being adversely affected on the field of play.

Rick Telander, sports journalist (The Hundred-Yard Lie, 1989)

. . . it was just a case of loving to play. . . . We all just took shots or painkillers or whatever they offered you and went right back out there, because we wanted to play football.

Ralph Cindrich, attorney-agent, former NFL linebacker (1996)

*This chapter is coauthored with Robert Hughes.

Cases of deviance among athletes, coaches, agents, and others connected with sports have attracted massive attention in recent years. Media coverage of on-the-field rule violations and off-the-field criminal behavior has led some people to conclude that deviance in sports is out of control.

In fact, the *Los Angeles Times* reported that during 1995 in the U.S., there were newspaper stories on 350 intercollegiate and professional athletes, nearly all men, who were implicated in 252 cases of crimes and criminal charges. The cases of criminal assault outnumbered those of any other type of offense, and most of the assault cases involved women as victims. Drug possession and use were the next most frequently mentioned charges. During the late 1990s, some major U.S. newspapers began to run regular sidebars listing athletes who had been arrested or charged with crimes during previous weeks, and in 1996 there was even a Web page (<http://www.onhoops.com/badboys.html>) that summarized the arrests of pro basketball players!

Publicity given to criminal charges has been accompanied by continuing publicity on issues of behind-the-scenes drug use among athletes. Stories since the early 1990s have disclosed records documenting the systematic use of performance-enhancing drugs in the East German sports system, official cover-ups of positive drug tests during the 1984 Los Angeles Olympic Games, rumored drug use by Chinese swimmers and runners, positive drug tests among U.S. athletes in a number of sports, the use of "masking drugs" to distort test results, the development and use of undetectable "designer drugs," and the continued use of undetectable human growth hormones and "blood doping" procedures by athletes around the world.

Because traditional popular beliefs have emphasized sport participation as a character-building experience, these highly publicized cases of deviance among athletes, coaches, and others in sports have shocked and disappointed many people. In their disappointment, some have concluded that the moral and ethical fabric of society itself is eroding. In light of this extreme conclusion, the purpose of this chapter is to look at the issue of whether deviance is indeed out of control in sports. We will focus on the following four questions as we deal with this issue:

1. What is deviance, and what problems do we face when we study deviance in sports?
2. Are deviant behaviors, both on the field and off the field, a serious problem among athletes, coaches, and others connected with sports?
3. Is there a connection between playing on certain men's sport teams and the incidence of assault and sexual assault by male athletes?
4. Why do some athletes use performance-enhancing substances, and is it possible to control the use of these substances, including drugs, in sports?

These questions direct our attention to important issues in the study of society and social behavior.

PROBLEMS RESEARCHERS FACE WHEN STUDYING DEVIANCE IN SPORTS

The study of deviance in sports presents special problems for three reasons:

1. **What is normal in sports may be deviant outside sports.** Athletes are allowed and even encouraged to behave in ways that are prohibited or defined as criminal in other settings. For example, much of the behavior of athletes in contact sports would be classified as felony assault if it occurred on the streets; boxers would be criminals outside the ring. Ice hockey players would be arrested for some behaviors they define as "normal" during their games. Racing car drivers would be arrested for speeding and careless driving, according to the definitions of deviance used off the racetrack. Athletes in high-risk sports such as speed skiing and motocross racing are encouraged to engage in behaviors that are clearly discouraged and defined as deviant in nonsport settings. However, even when serious injuries or deaths occur in sports, criminal charges usually are not filed, and civil lawsuits asking for financial compensation are generally unsuccessful.

The use of hatred as a source of motivation in sports clearly contradicts the norms most people use to guide their behavior in families, religious congregations, classrooms, and work settings. Apart from sports, these widespread norms emphasize getting along with and being supportive of others. But in many sports, an emphasis on being hostile toward and overcoming others is defined as normal. In fact, this emphasis is so widely accepted that when athletes cause injuries to others, they are not sued for damages. The reason for this is the widespread belief that people enter sport participation with an assumption of risk and that the experience of risk is central to playing sports.

Studying deviance in sports is difficult, because athletes, especially elite athletes, are expected to ignore social expectations that might interfere with their developing their physical skills. As they train and practice, attend camps and clinics, play in year-round leagues, and focus their attention on sports, they may ignore expectations related to family, friends, work, and general social development. This extreme form of commitment would be defined as deviant in connection with many other activities. But in sports, it is widely accepted and even praised and rewarded, even when it interferes with people's overall social development and causes serious inconvenience and hardship for their close friends and family members (see Retton, 1992).

These examples show that when it comes to studying deviance, sports are "different." Engaging in extremely compulsive or self-destructive behaviors, risking one's health and well-being, inflicting pain and injury on others, and using the end (winning) to justify the means (violating rules)—these practices are not so quickly condemned in sport as they are in other activities. We tend to view the motives of people in sports, especially athletes, as positive, because their behaviors are directed toward the achievement of success for their team, school, community, country, or corporate sponsor. Therefore, those behaviors, even when they clearly overstep accepted limits, may be ignored or even praised, rather than condemned. It seems that different rules may apply to those who entertain us in sports and keep alive certain ideas about performance, excellence, achievement, and what it means to be male or female in society today.

2. Deviance in sports often involves an unquestioned acceptance of norms, rather than a rejection of norms. It is important to note that much of the deviance in sports does *not* involve a *rejection* of commonly accepted norms and expectations for behavior. Instead, it involves an *overacceptance of* and *overconformity to* norms and expectations. For example, most North Americans see playing football as right and good. Young men are encouraged to "be all they can be" as football players. They are encouraged to increase their weight and strength so they can play well and make valuable contributions to the reputations of their schools and communities. When young men go too far in their acceptance of these expectations for getting bigger and stronger, when they become so committed to playing football and excelling on the field that they use certain drugs, they become deviant. This type of deviance is dangerous, but it is grounded in completely different social dynamics from those operating in the deviance of young people who give up all hope for the future, reject commonly accepted rules and expectations, and use substances like heroin to deaden their awareness of the world.

We must take into account this difference between what some sociologists call **positive deviance** and **negative deviance** when we study sports. Sports, especially those emphasizing power and performance, often call for extreme forms of behavior that border on the deviant. As we will discuss later in this chapter, athletes may cross those borders in what they see as a "normal" course of sport participation. This is not to say that positive deviance should be accepted or

It is difficult to use certain theoretical frameworks to study deviance in sports, because athletes are often encouraged in and rewarded for behaviors that would not be accepted in other settings. For example, some of the behaviors that are acceptable in boxing, hockey, football, and other sports would get you arrested or sued if you acted in that way outside of sport competition. (*Colorado Springs Gazette*)

condoned in sports; *it should not*. But it does present special problems when we try to understand sports in society.

3. Training and performance in sports have become "medicalized." Training and performance are seen increasingly in medical and "sport science" terms. Many people now regard special medical treatments reserved in the past for those who were sick or in poor health as tools for coping with the everyday challenges of training and competing in sports, especially in power and performance sports (as described in chap. 4, p. 98). As this has happened, the use of biochemistry and pharmacology has become "normalized" in sports and among athletes. Many people associated with sports now believe that ingesting the performance-enhancing substances developed by scientists and those claim-

ing to be scientists is a normal part of being an athlete. In fact, the language and research of so-called "sport science" has been used to promote this process. Just go to a "health food" store in the U.S. to see all the performance-enhancing substances that anyone interested in improved sport performance can legally purchase and use—or count the ads for performance-enhancing substances in any recent issue of a "muscle magazine." The motto for many seems to be "strength and high performance is just a swallow away"! Of course, this process is encouraged by corporations that use athletes to endorse products and thus present athletes' bodies as the highest examples of health and well-being (Hoberman, 1995). In the meantime, it has become much more difficult to determine just what behaviors are deviant and what behaviors are simply normal parts of the new, scientific training.

Unfortunately, many discussions and studies of deviance in sports don't take into account these three characteristics of sports behavior. Researchers often base their analyses on theories and conceptual frameworks that ignore (1) how people define behaviors in sports, (2) the differences between positive and negative deviance, and (3) the medicalization of sport training and performance. Therefore, many analyses routinely condemn athletes as deviants, focus only on negative deviance, and ignore the way sports have changed with the combined influence of science and corporate interests. As we will argue in the next section, these analyses add little to either our understanding of deviance in sports or our understanding of sports as a part of culture.

DEFINING AND STUDYING DEVIANCE IN SPORTS: THREE APPROACHES

Most sociologists agree that deviance involves behavior that violates social norms or rules, but they don't agree on how to identify rules and violations of rules. Some sociologists, whom we refer to as *absolutists*, search for an absolute set of rules or ideals and then use them to evaluate behaviors as either right or wrong; they say we should separate the rule followers from the rule violators in sports. Others, whom we refer to as *relativists*, claim that norms and rules reflect the interests of whoever has the most power in a group, and that deviance is any behavior labeled wrong or bad by these people; they say the determination of deviance in sports is relative and arbitrary. Because these approaches are widely used in the sociology of sport, we will examine each more closely. Then we will offer an alternative approach for defining and studying deviance. This alternative, which we identify as a *critical normal distribution approach*, is based on the idea that deviance can involve overconformity as well as underconformity, and that deviants are not always morally bankrupt failures or pitiful victims of the system.

The Absolutist Approach: It's Either Right or Wrong

When sociologists use certain theoretical frameworks, they define deviance in terms of how actual behavior compares with a designated norm or ideal. The greater the difference is between the actual behavior and the norm, the greater the deviance is. The problem with this approach is that definitions of ideals in any social setting often either reflect biases related to gender, social class, race, and other factors, or are based on some arbitrary distinction between right and wrong. Because different people have different conceptions of ideals in sports, this approach creates considerable confusion. For example, if I think the ideal in sports is to engage in fair play and you think the ideal is to win, then I will see any violation of the rules as deviant, while you will see some violations as "good fouls" that contribute to winning. If I regard sports as a form of play in which intrinsic satisfaction is the primary reason for participation and you regard sports as "war without weapons," fought for external rewards such as trophies and cash prizes, then I will see aggressive behavior as deviant, while you will see it as a sign of courage and commitment. Because we don't see eye to eye on the ideals of sports, we will not define and identify deviance in the same way.

Despite the confusion created by this absolutist approach, most people use it to discuss deviance in sports. When the behaviors of athletes, coaches, management, or spectators do not contribute to what an individual considers to be the ideals of sports, that individual identifies those behaviors as deviant. In other words, "it's either right or wrong." And when it's wrong, the behavior and the person who engages in it are seen as problems.

This is the traditional structural-functionalist approach to deviance, and it is not very effective in producing an understanding of deviant behavior or in formulating programs to control deviance. It assumes that existing value systems and rules are absolutely right and should be accepted the way they are, so that the social order is not threatened. This leads to a "law and order" orientation emphasizing that the only way to establish social control is through four strategies: establishing more rules, making rules more strict and inflexible, developing a more comprehensive system of detecting and punishing rule violators, and making everyone more aware of the rules and what happens to those who don't follow them.

This approach also leads to the idea that people violate rules only because they lack moral character, intelligence, or sanity, and that good, normal, healthy people wouldn't be so foolish as to violate rules. Therefore, people who reject rules and don't live up to expectations are deviants, and all deviant behavior involves the rejection of rules and norms or a refusal to comply with them. This approach does little to help us understand much of the deviance in sport, and it provides a poor basis for developing programs to control deviance in sport. We will say more about this throughout the chapter.

The Relativist Approach: It All Depends on Who Makes the Rules

According to this approach, no behavior and no person is inherently deviant. Instead, deviance is defined through a labeling process in which some behaviors (or people) are identified as bad, undesirable, or unacceptable on the basis of rules made by people in positions of power. Those who use this approach assume that all people act in their own interests, and that people in power use their position and influence to make sure *their* definitions of what is good or bad become the *official* definitions of what is normal or deviant in the society as a whole. Of course, relativists also assume that those who lack power in society are at a real disadvantage, because they don't have anything to say about the content or enforcement of rules. Therefore, the behavior of people who lack power is labeled as deviant more often than that of people with power. To make matters worse, people who

lack power don't have the resources to resist being labeled as deviant when their behavior does not conform to the standards of the rule makers.

This approach is usually used by conflict theorists when they study deviance in sports. They assume that rules in sports organizations reflect the interests of owners and sponsors and ignore the interests of athletes. Therefore, they see deviance among athletes as the result of rules that not only discriminate against them but also force them to deny their own interests and follow the expectations of those in power, even though their health and well-being may be harmed in the process. This approach views athletes as victims whose only hope is tied to either disagreeing with the rules or rebelling against them.

Anyone using this relativist approach has a problem, because it leads to the conclusion that all deviance in sports is simply the result of exploitation and labeling on the part of those who have power. This conclusion is difficult to defend when many forms of deviance that exist in big-time intercollegiate and professional sports also exist in less formal sport settings, where the athletes themselves are often in positions of power and control. For example, the statement that anabolic steroid use in elite track and field is the result of rules through which athletes are forced to risk their health for colleges, countries, and corporate sponsors does not hold up, since similar forms of drug use exist among athletes who are not subject to coercive tactics employed by outside forces that control sports.

In other words, it is unlikely that all bad things in dominant sports today would disappear if athletes were in charge. This, however, does not mean that athletes should not have more control over the conditions of their sport participation; they should. But our point here is that since much of the deviance in sports involves overconformity and overacceptance of existing rules among athletes, it is unrealistic to expect that most athletes would have the critical insights needed to change how sports are played. Athletes certainly need to play a crucial role in making changes in sports, but those using a relativist approach are hoping for too much to think that all the causes of deviance in sports would automatically disappear if athletes made the rules.

Those using a relativist approach have another problem: they do not identify any behavior as objectively deviant. To them, nothing is bad or wrong in itself. But without an objective definition of deviance, behaviors such as the use of violence or the taking of performance-enhancing drugs are seen simply as outgrowths of alternative definitions of right and wrong accepted as normal by members of certain groups that value and admire violence and drug use. When deviance is defined in this way, efforts to control or change behaviors are often dismissed as biased or oppressive. Instead, a relativist approach emphasizes two ways to control deviance in sport:

1. Change the distribution of power in sports so that athletes are no longer victims of the exploitation and labeling processes used by those who currently have power in sports.
2. Change the political and economic systems that create tendencies among athletes to engage in destructive and dehumanizing behaviors when they play sports.

The relativists argue that when social systems become more humane, so will the behaviors of those within the systems. This is why those who use this approach often talk about the need to change society as a whole in order to control deviance in sports. This may be an admirable long-term goal, but deviance is grounded in things other than exploitation and labeling processes. Therefore there are good reasons to explore other factors related to deviance and other means of controlling those behaviors that jeopardize the health and well-being of those who play sports.

An Alternative Approach: Deviance Can Be Negative or Positive

The absolutist and relativist approaches provide insights about deviance, but neither explains much of the deviance in sports. The absolutists define deviance as a failure to conform, and see rule violators as disruptive and morally bankrupt. The relativists define deviance as behavior that violates the interests of people with power, and see rule violators as exploited victims. One of the main flaws in these approaches is that both ignore deviance that involves an overconformity to rules and expectations. Another flaw is that neither takes into account the norms used in sport cultures and the ways athletes use these norms to evaluate themselves and others.

It is clear that most people who violate rules in sports can't be classified either as morally bankrupt or as victims. For example, it is not accurate to say that young people lack moral character when they go overboard in accepting and overconforming to ideas about what it means to be an athlete. Nor is it accurate to define all athletes who engage in deviance as passive victims of an exploitative sport system. Of course athletes don't control all the conditions of their sport participation, but they do play an important part in the creation and maintenance of the norms that guide their own decisions and behaviors in sports.

Our understanding of deviance in sports could be expanded if we assumed two things: (1) that norms and rules are created in connection with complex and changing forms of social relations in society, and (2) that behaviors in any social setting will tend to be distributed along a continuum that conforms to a normal bell-shaped curve (fig. 6-1). When we use this "critical normal distribution approach," we see that most behavior falls into a normal range of acceptability in connection with any particular norm. Deviance occurs when behaviors fall outside this range of what is acceptable on *either side* of a "normally accepted range of behavior." Therefore, deviance can involve either underconformity or overconformity.

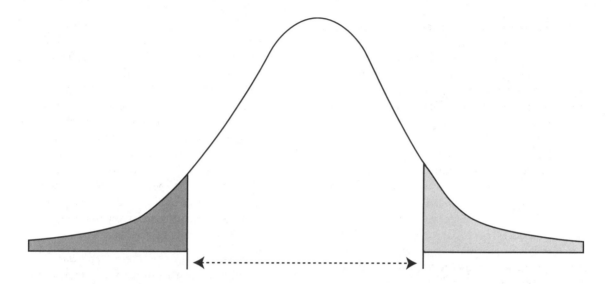

POSITIVE DEVIANCE
Overconformity;
supra-normal behavior based on
unquestioned acceptance of norms

NORMALLY ACCEPTED RANGE OF BEHAVIOR

NEGATIVE DEVIANCE
Underconformity;
sub-normal behavior based on
a rejection of norms

FIGURE 6-1 A "critical normal distribution approach" to understanding deviance in sports.
Note: Most behavior in sports falls within a normally accepted range in society. Deviance occurs on either side of this range. Negative deviance in society and in sports involves varying degrees of underconformity while positive deviance involves varying degrees of overconformity. Negative deviance is frequently discussed and often studied in society and most people in sports focus their attention on negative deviance. Positive deviance is often ignored and seldom studied. But it has become very common in many sports and can be dangerous to athletes. People in sports often ignore it because it frequently leads to success and victories.

Underconformity describes behavior that does not measure up to commonly accepted rules or standards of behavior; it is behavior grounded in a rejection or lack of awareness of rules. Underconforming behavior is **negative deviance.**

Overconformity describes behavior that goes so far in following commonly accepted rules or standards that it interferes with the well-being of self or others; it is behavior grounded in an uncritical acceptance of rules. Overconforming behavior is **positive deviance.**

Remember that positive deviance is still deviance; it is often as dangerous and disruptive as

negative deviance, and it can be more difficult to control than negative deviance. We can explain the differences between these two types of deviance further by noting that in their most extreme forms, negative deviance leads to **anarchy** (a condition of lawlessness in a group or society), while positive deviance leads to **fascism** (unquestioned conformity to an ideal embodied in a rigid belief system or a charismatic leader). Both anarchy and fascism are dangerous.

RESEARCH ON POSITIVE DEVIANCE Keith Ewald and Robert Jiobu (1985) illustrated the usefulness of the concept of positive deviance in their study of adult men seriously involved in one of two sport activities, bodybuilding or competitive distance running. After collecting information from both groups, they concluded that members of each group displayed classic characteristics of deviance in the form of addiction-like overconformity to the norms in their sports. Many of the bodybuilders and distance runners pursued goals in their sports to such an extent that their family relationships, work responsibilities, and/or physical health were affected negatively. Yet they did not question what they were doing or why they were doing it.

Other studies have identified similar forms of positive deviance: self-injurious overtraining among distance runners (Nash, 1987); unhealthy eating behaviors and weight control strategies among women athletes in intercollegiate and other elite amateur sports;* extremely rigid and exclusive dedication to training and competition among ultramarathon bicyclists (Wasielewski, 1991) and triathletes (Hilliard and Hilliard, 1990); and uncritical commitment to playing sports with pain and injury.†

When we use a critical normal distribution approach to define and study deviance in sports, we see how important it is to distinguish behavior showing a lack of concern for or rejection of norms and rules from behavior showing an uncritical commitment to and overacceptance of norms and rules. This approach also forces us to critically examine the value systems that exist in various forms of sports. For example, the value system in most high-performance sports encourages overconformity to a set of norms or guidelines that athletes use to evaluate themselves and others as they train and compete (Donnelly, 1996; Ingham, 1996; Johns, 1997). Because of

this, much of the deviance among athletes (and coaches) involves unquestioned and unqualified acceptance of and conformity to the value system embodied in what we will call the **sport ethic.**

THE "SPORT ETHIC" AND DEVIANCE IN SPORTS* The "sport ethic" is the cluster of beliefs that many people in power and performance sports have come to use as the dominant criteria for defining what it really means, in their social worlds, to be an athlete; this sport ethic constitutes the core of high-performance sport culture. Information from and about athletes and coaches has led us to conclude tentatively that the following four beliefs make up the sport ethic:

1. *An athlete makes sacrifices for "the game."* The idea underlying this dimension of the sport ethic is that "real athletes" must love "the game" above all else and prove it by subordinating other interests to their sport. To prove they care about their sport, athletes must have the proper attitude, be committed to their sport, live up to the expectations of fellow athletes, and make sacrifices to continue participating. In other words, being an athlete involves meeting the demands of others in the sport and the demands of competition without question. This is the spirit underlying the notion that athletes must make sacrifices, that they must be willing to "pay the price" to stay involved in their sport. Coaches' pep talks and locker room slogans are full of references to this guideline.
   An example of this dimension of the sport ethic is provided by a six-foot, two-inch 248-pound linebacker who, after ten knee operations in six years, played his last game at Syracuse University. He told a *USA Today* reporter (Wieberg, 1994) the following: "I've told a hundred people that if I got a chance to play in the NFL, I'd play for free. It's never been about money. It's never been about anything but playing the game."

*See Donnelly, 1993; Franseen and McCann, 1996; Johns, 1992, 1996, 1997; Overdorf and Gill, 1994; Sundgot-Borgen, 1993a, b; also see Wilmore, 1996 for a review of thirty-five studies.
†See Curry, 1993; Curry and Strauss, 1994; Nixon, 1991, 1993, 1994a, b, 1996a, b; Young et al., 1994; Young and White, 1995.

*This section is adapted from Hughes and Coakley (1991).

Phil Jackson, NBA Coach of the Year in 1996, emphasized this point when he said, "Whether they're willing to acknowledge it or not, what drives most players is not the money or the adulation, but their love of the game" (1996). These quotations, and numerous similar ones from other athletes, illustrate that athletes make sacrifices for "the game" because they love it. In fact, this love of the game and willingness to make sacrifices is part of what it takes to be defined as a real athlete in a power and performance sport.

2. *An athlete strives for distinction.* The Olympic motto, "Citius, Altius, Fortius" (swifter, higher, stronger), captures the meaning of this dimension of the sport ethic. "True athletes" constantly seek to improve, to get better, to come closer to perfection. Winning symbolizes improvement and establishes distinction; losing is tolerated only because it's part of the experience of learning how to win. Breaking records is the ultimate standard of achievement in sports. This is because "real athletes" are a special group dedicated to climbing the pyramid, reaching for the top, pushing limits, excelling, exceeding or dominating others, and trying to become Number One.

   This dimension of the sport ethic was illustrated in 1996 when Dominique Moceanu, the fourteen-year-old gymnast on the U.S. Olympic team, explained why she was competing with a 4-inch stress fracture in her right leg: "What else can I do? I have to bite my teeth somehow and make it through. This is the Olympics you're talking about here. This is a big meet, the biggest in anyone's life." In her quest for distinction, this fourteen-year-old clearly conformed to the sport ethic; in fact, she declared that she wouldn't even think of doing otherwise.

3. *An athlete accepts risks and plays through pain.* According to the sport ethic, an athlete does not give in to pressure, pain, or fear. The voluntary acceptance of risks to health and well-being is a sign of physical courage and dedication among athletes. This guideline also emphasizes moral courage as the ability to sustain physical performance under pressure even when the risk of injury is low. The idea is that an athlete doesn't back down from any challenge, that standing up to challenges involves moral and physical courage. Being an athlete means that one willingly confronts and overcomes the fear and the challenge of competition, and accepts the increasing risk of failure and injury as one moves to higher levels of performance.

   We have dozens and dozens of examples of this dimension of the sport ethic in our files. As the 1996 NFL season began, a linebacker asked about how he dealt with pain replied, "You take bottles of Advil and then you go out and smash some more heads" (*USA Today*, September 5, 1996). Typical is the case of an NFL player who played an entire season with knee and ankle injuries. His coach praised him by saying this: "Besides talent, everyone is aware [that he plays] hurt all the time. That says a lot for his character" (Adams, 1994). Of course, coaches look for a person who is willing to take risks and play through pain; athletes see this as part of their identity as athletes.

4. *An athlete accepts no limits in the pursuit of possibilities.* Finally, the sport ethic stresses "the dream," and the need to pursue it without question. An athlete doesn't accept a situation without trying to change it, to overcome it, to turn the scales. "Real athletes" believe that sport is a sphere of life in which anything is possible, *if* a person is dedicated enough. They feel obligated to pursue dreams without reservation; they ignore external limits as they focus on the attempt to achieve success. Of course, external rewards may influence athletes, but their pursuit of possibilities is driven primarily by what they believe they must do as athletes, apart from money.

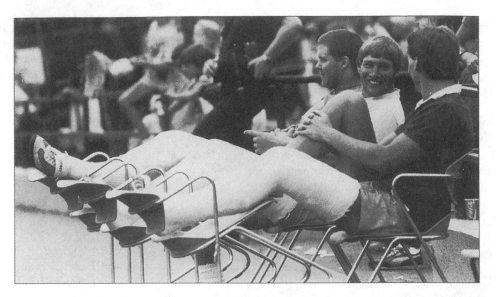

Athletes who conform to the norms of the sport ethic take risks to prove their moral and physical courage. Of course, this can lead to high rates of injury in certain sports, especially when athletes engage in positive deviance by overconforming to the norms. (Bobette, Brecker, University of Colorado Media Relations)

This dimension of the sport ethic was clearly illustrated by Buddy Lazier, who won the 1996 Indianapolis 500 in 1996 while driving the entire race with a broken back. Despite his injury, he trained four hours a day, seven days a week. After the race his father said, "He absolutely never said quit. He was not going to be robbed of this opportunity" (Ballard, 1996). Buddy conformed to the sport ethic in accepting no limits in pursuing his dream; surgery on the crushed disks pressing on his nerves waited until after the race.

These four norms that make up the sport ethic are part of the mindset and culture of athletes in power and performance sports. At first glance, they resemble slogans hanging on locker room walls or written in self-help and motivation books. People who play sports, especially at elite levels, use these norms as guidelines to evaluate themselves as athletes and others who claim to be athletes. This is part of the overall partici-

pation experience in certain forms of sport; athletes are expected to accept and live by these norms (see the box titled Just Do It: The Sport Ethic in Nike Ads, on pp. 155). Forms of negative deviance that occur when athletes reject these norms or underconform to them are often mentioned by coaches and media commentators as problems in sports. An unwillingness to make sacrifices for "the game," a refusal to strive for distinction, play through pain, and fight though limits are identified as forms of deviance. Few people ever refer to the positive deviance that occurs when athletes and others in sports blindly and uncritically accept these norms and overconform to them. However, overconformity to the sport ethic can cause as many serious problems as underconformity.

Unfortunately, many people in sports *do* overconform to the sport ethic. In fact, today's sport heroes are often those who unquestioningly follow the ethic to the point of risking their own safety and well-being. Media commentators glorify athletes who overconform to the sport

REFLECT ON SPORT

Just Do It:
The Sport Ethic in Nike Ads

Nike summed up the meaning of the sport ethic in an ad the company placed in the 1996 *Sports Illustrated* Olympic Preview Issue. In fact, their definition of "an athlete" is almost exactly the same as the one Bob Hughes and I discovered after years of talking with athletes about the meaning of sport and sport participation in their lives. We first described the sport ethic in 1991. Here is the text from the 1996 Nike ad that was timed to run in connection with the Atlanta Games:

WHO THE HELL DO YOU THINK YOU ARE? ARE YOU AN ATHLETE?

Because if you are, then you know what it means to want to be better, to want to be the best. And

if you are, then you understand it's not enough to just want to be the best. You can't just sit around and BS about how much you want it. Show me how much you want it. . . . Dare to do what it takes to be the best. And then, whether you win, lose, or collapse on the finish line, at worst you'll know exactly who you are.

IF YOU CAN'T STAND THE HEAT, GET OUT OF ATLANTA.

The marketing people at Nike understand the mindset of the elite athlete; they also know that elite athletes are dedicated to following the norms of the sport ethic. I can't prove it, but I think their ad encourages overconformity to the sport ethic. What do you think?

ethic; they praise athletes who play with broken bones and torn ligaments (especially when they win medals and boost TV ratings), who have surgery after surgery in order to come back and play "the game," who take out opponents with "big hits," and who request or submit to injections of huge doses of painkilling drugs at halftime. Spectators also glorify athletes who are willing to overconform to the sport ethic. According to Dr. Robert Huizinga, a former NFL team physician and past president of the NFL Physicians Society, many sport fans today "want people to play hurt, and when someone doesn't play hurt, he's no longer our hero" (cited in King, 1996). Therefore, it is not surprising that many athletes go overboard in their acceptance of the sport ethic and overconform to its norms without question or qualification, even when overconformity creates problems, causes pain, disrupts family life, jeopardizes health and safety, or even shortens life itself. This type of deviance is dangerous even though it is widely ignored.

WHO IS MOST LIKELY TO ENGAGE IN POSITIVE DEVIANCE? Not all athletes overconform to the sport ethic, but many do. There are two general reasons for this frequent overconformity to the sport ethic:

1. Athletes find their experiences in sports so exhilarating and thrilling that they want to continue participating as long as possible; they love their sports, and will do almost anything to stay involved.
2. The likelihood of being chosen or sponsored for continued participation in sports increases when athletes overconform to the sport ethic. Coaches often praise athletes who engage in positive deviance and make them models on their teams; the athletes may use overconformity to the sport ethic to prevent coaches' accusations that they lack "desire" and "hustle."

Because of these general factors, many athletes have come to use positive deviance to define and evaluate their sport experiences. Nike even has used it in TV commercials by high-lighting athletes who throw up, shed blood, collapse from exhaustion, and break bones as part of regular training and competition. ("Just doing it" is fine, but "just doing it" till you vomit, bleed, lose consciousness, or need surgery is a problem!) Most athletes don't see overconformity to the sport ethic as deviance. Instead, they see it as confirming and reconfirming their identities as athletes and their membership in select sport groups. This can be very important to them, especially when their continued participation and success in sports take on significant personal and social meanings.

Of course, not all athletes are equally likely to overconform to the sport ethic. Those most likely to do so include the following:

1. Those athletes who have low self-esteem or are so eager to be accepted by their peers in sport that they will make whatever sacrifices they think others want them to make.
2. Those athletes who see achievement in sport as their only way to get ahead, make a name for themselves, and become important in the world.

In other words, athletes whose identities or future chances for success and significance are completely tied to their sport are most likely to engage in positive deviance. This, too, needs to be explored through research, but we hypothesize that this form of deviance is slightly more prevalent among men than among women (only because at this point in time, men are more likely to use sport as an exclusive identity and/or mobility source), among low-income minority athletes in revenue-producing sports (for similar reasons), and among those whose relationships with significant others have been based exclusively on their continued involvement and success in sport.

As people's identities become dependent on participation in power and performance sports, they seem to tend to use overconformity to the sport ethic to demonstrate their worthiness for continued membership and status within their sport groups. It is an athlete's vulnerability to group demands, combined with the desire to gain or reaffirm group membership through overconforming to these demands, that is a critical factor in the incidence of positive deviance.

Along these lines, some have suggested that one of the qualities of certain winning coaches (such as Bela Karolyi, for example) is their ability to create environments that keep athletes in a perpetual state of adolescence. This leads athletes to strive continually to confirm their identities and eliminate self-doubts by engaging in behaviors that please their coaches and teammate-peers. When this dependency-based commitment occurs, overconformity to the sport ethic becomes increasingly common, and many young people become willing to sacrifice their bodies and play with reckless abandon in the pursuit of affirmation and approval. When coaches encourage this, intentionally or naively, they themselves become promoters of dangerous forms of deviance.

POSITIVE DEVIANCE AND GROUP DYNAMICS Special bonds between athletes often form when they collectively conform to the norms of the sport ethic; when they overconform and demonstrate their unqualified commitment to the sport ethic under conditions of stress and challenge, the bonds may become extraordinarily powerful. These powerful bonds give rise to special feelings of unity and uniqueness, especially in groups of elite athletes in the same sports. This is the reason athletes often emphasize the camaraderie and togetherness they experience when they play sports. For example, after his first retirement, Magic Johnson said, "It's not the playing part I miss most, it's just being one of the boys."

These special feelings of unity and uniqueness that are created as athletes collectively conform and overconform to the sport ethic tend to separate athletes from other people, even those fans who view the athletes with awe and admiration (see also Lyng, 1990; Wacquant, 1995). When this occurs, many athletes, especially those in power and performance sports, have a tendency to look down on or even disdain nonathletes: those outside their special athletic fraternity, who do not and cannot understand what it's like to be an athlete, to make sacrifices for the game, to strive for distinction, take risks, play with pain, and ignore limits in the pursuit of dreams. The desire to remain inside this special athletic fraternity and continue sharing unique feelings of togetherness with athlete-peers serves to promote even more positive deviance.

When this process occurs, athletes often develop excessive pride that gives rise to a form of arrogance or an inflated sense of power (Higgs, 1995). Some athletes come to think they live their lives in a special zone that exempts them from following community rules. Although research is needed on this issue, we would hypothesize that the **hubris** (pride-driven arrogance) often associated with long-term overconformity to the sport ethic creates conditions and group dynamics that encourage such forms of negative deviance as assault, sexual harassment, sexual assault, binge drinking, drunken driving, academic cheating, theft, and property destruction. This possible connection between positive and negative deviance comes to mind when we hear an NFL football player say, "Hey, I have no problem sharing women with my teammates. These guys go to battle with me" (cited in Nelson, 1994: 144). It also seems to be operating when male athletes don't report a date rape or gang rape by teammates.

Dealing with these forms of negative deviance is especially difficult when the athletes who engage in them are viewed with awe and admiration by many in the community, even police and judges, in some cases! The athletes' hubris may make them feel above community standards, and the awe and admiration community members feel may interfere with the enforcement of community standards in the case of athletes, especially high-profile athletes. Of course, as we have seen in recent years, this can be a dangerous combination.

The point of this section is that much of the deviance in sports is *not* motivated primarily by the desires to win or to make money. Instead, it is motivated by the desires simply to *play*, to *be an athlete*, and to *maintain membership in an elite athletic fraternity*. This is not to say that winning and money are irrelevant to athletes; they are important and powerful motivators. But we must remember that many athletes who realize they will never win championships or make money from their athletic accomplishments frequently engage in positive deviance. These athletes, just like their more talented and money-making peers, are motivated by the belief that being a "real athlete" means taking risks, making sacrifices, and paying the price to be all you can be. This means that the roots of positive deviance go deeper than individual desires to win or make money. In fact, these roots are grounded in the very values promoted through the sport ethic itself. Therefore, we can see much of the deviance in sports most accurately as a social issue rather than just a personal problem of individual athletes. For this reason, it is especially difficult to control, and fines and jail sentences do little to slow it down.

CONTROLLING POSITIVE DEVIANCE IN SPORTS Positive deviance presents special social control problems in sports. Coaches, managers, owners, and sponsors—all of whom exercise control within sports—often benefit when athletes blindly accept and overconform to the sport ethic. These people often see athletes who willingly engage in positive deviance as a blessing, not a curse. The fact that athletes often use their overconformity to the sport ethic as proof of their personal commitment and courage works to the advantage of all those interested in winning records and high TV ratings. This is why there is a widespread unwillingness among the controllers of sports to discourage athletes who engage in forms of positive deviance (even when it involves using performance-enhancing substances, as we will explain later in this chapter).

The issue of social control is further complicated by the tendency to promote extreme overconformers to the sport ethic into positions of power and influence in sports. Because these people have proved they are willing to "pay the price" and use the sport ethic without reservation, they are seen as ideal candidates for certain jobs in sports, especially jobs in which they train or serve as examples for athletes. This creates a situation in which deviance and ethical problems among athletes are rooted in the organization of sport itself, in athletes' relationships with one another and with coaches and managers.

By itself, the sport ethic is not a problem. Of course, we must make sacrifices, take risks, endure pain and pursue dreams when we play certain types of sports; in fact, conformity to the sport ethic is what makes sport participation a unique and exciting activity in many of our lives. It is only when the norms of the sport ethic are accepted uncritically, without question and qualification, that problems occur. This point was made by Alberto Salazar, the great marathoner who coached middle-distance runner Mary Decker Slaney as she tried to qualify for the 1996 Olympics. Slaney had undergone nineteen sport-related surgeries and was living in constant pain at the time. Salazar noted that her overconformity to the sport ethic was a "two-edged sword." He explained that

> . . . [t]he greatest athletes want it so much, they run themselves to death. You've got to have an obsession, but if unchecked, it's destructive. That's what it is with [Slaney]. She'll kill herself unless you pull the reins back (in Longman, 1996).

As this example shows, when the sport ethic is not critically assessed by coaches, athletes, media commentators, and fans, there is a tendency for sports to become corrupted by the commitment and excitement they inspire. In other words, sports, like many exciting activities that captivate interest and capture commitment, contain the seeds of their own corruption. Controlling this "inside" corruption may be the biggest challenge facing those concerned with deviance in sports today.

Everyone in sports must work together to discourage overconformity to the sport ethic. This does not mean that we should ignore negative deviance, or that underconformity and the rejection of rules and regulations is not a problem in sports. But underconformity is regularly identified as a problem; positive deviance is more subversive, because it is widely ignored as a problem. For example, when a fourteen-year-old gymnast is late for practice, a coach can see this negative deviance and correct it quite easily. However, when the same gymnast engages in unhealthy eating behaviors in an effort to maximize her performance, many coaches, parents, and gym owners don't see this positive deviance, or don't want to interfere with the mind-set of a champion—until, of course, stress fractures interfere with competition and weight loss puts their athlete and daughter in a hospital.

Control of positive deviance depends on athletes, coaches, commentators, and fans to raise questions constantly about the meaning and organization of sports, and about behaviors that go beyond conformity to the sport ethic. In the absence of these questions, sports will become spectacles that threaten health and well-being and depend on the use of painkilling drugs, rather than pleasurable activities that promote health and well-being and depend on the use of physical skills.

The continuation of any social activity or organization depends on awareness of the consequences of both underconformity and overconformity. In the case of sport, this means that people need to strike a balance between accepting rules and questioning rules. The more everyone in sports is involved in questioning and qualifying norms and rules, the closer they will come to controlling forms of positive deviance, even though the control will never be perfect or permanent. Control of positive deviance also will lead to control of negative deviance, because the separation between athletes and other people will diminish; athletes will be less likely to feel above the law, and the community will be less likely to put athletes above the law.

RESEARCH ON DEVIANCE AMONG ATHLETES

Systematic studies of deviance among athletes are rare; studies of positive deviance are especially rare. Instead of doing systematic studies, media people and some sociologists often take lists of cases of athletes' alleged misconduct from newspaper accounts, pick the behaviors they dislike the most, and then talk about the decline of fair play in sports and the decline of values in society. This approach, however, doesn't tell us much about whether deviance is out of control in sports, whether there is more deviance today than there was in the past, whether deviance involves overconformity or underconformity, or whether it is rooted in factors inside or outside of sports. Usually, these investigations conclude that deviance is caused by athletes with weak character and a lack of discipline, or that it is the result of TV, money, or societal pressures to be Number One. Few investigations discuss the possibility that deviance is related to the actual structure of certain sport forms and to specific dynamics of sport involvement itself.

In reviewing accounts of deviant behavior among athletes, it is important to distinguish on-the-field and sport-related deviance from off-the-field, away-from-sport deviance. They are related to different types of norms and rules, and they have different causes and consequences.

On-the-Field and Sport-Related Deviance

Sport-related deviance includes norm violations that occur while people prepare for or participate in sports. Commonly reported examples are things like cheating (such as using the spitball or corking a bat in baseball), gambling, shaving points, throwing games or matches, engaging in unsportsmanlike conduct, fighting, taking performance-enhancing drugs, and generally finding ways to avoid rules. Some people claim that these types of deviance have become a serious problem in most sports because of pressures to perform and win that have been

heightened by increased commercialization and television coverage.

Most historical reviews, however, suggest that deviance in the form of cheating, dirty play, fighting, and the use of violence are *less* common today than they were in the days before television coverage and big salaries and prize money (Donnelly, 1988; Dunning, 1993; Dunning and Sheard, 1979; Elias and Dunning, 1986; Maguire, 1986, 1988; Murphy et al., 1998; Scheinin, 1994). These reviews note that sports today are more rule governed than they were in the past, and that instances of on-the-field deviance are more likely to be punished by official sanctions within sports and criticized by observers outside of sports. Therefore, it may be a mistake to blame today's deviance in sports on money and TV, as some people are inclined to do.

Actually, it is very difficult to track and study rates of on-the-field deviance among athletes, because rules change over time and rules are enforced in different ways at different points in time. Research does suggest that athletes in most sports interpret rules very loosely during games, and that they often create informal norms that stretch official rules (Shields and Bredemeier,

When winning becomes the sole measure of achievement, athletes may resort to deviance to keep opponents from the victory stand.

1995; Bredemeier and Weiss, 1993; Donnelly and Young, 1985, 1988; Stephens and Bredemeier, 1995). But this is not new; athletes have done this ever since sports have been organized and umpires and referees have been enforcing rules. In fact, athletes in organized sports traditionally have played to the level permitted by umpires and referees;—players still adjust their behaviors according to how tightly refs are calling a game. But this does not mean that the players are ignoring rules, or that deviance is necessarily out of hand. Nor does it mean that we ought to ignore identified forms of deviance.

The impression that rates of on-the-field and sport-related deviance are going up may exist because there are more rules today than ever before, and sports are more rule governed than they have been in the past. A look at the rule books of various sport organizations clearly shows that there are literally thousands of rules today that did not exist fifty years ago in sports. For example, the National Collegiate Athletic Association (NCAA) and other organizations controlling the lives of athletes have hundreds of rules and regulations listed in official handbooks; every year the list of rules grows longer and longer. International sport organizations now ban about three thousand drug substances. There are more ways than ever before of becoming deviant in sports! Furthermore, the forms of surveillance used today and the increased emphasis on rule enforcement means that more rule violators get caught today; especially when violations involve negative deviance.

Finally, there is evidence that in certain sports, especially those emphasizing outcomes and the domination of opponents, athletes simply come to expect and engage in a certain amount of on-the-field intentional rule violation ("good fouls"), cheating, and aggression (Pilz, 1996; Shields et al., 1995). This type of mind-set seems to be more prevalent at higher levels of competition and to increase with time spent participating in a sport; it is also more common among men than women, and is especially strong among members of winning teams and among

nonstarters. This finding is consistent with other research suggesting that playing most forms of power and performance sports does not promote moral development and moral decision making (Shields and Bredemeier, 1993).

However, in the absence of good historical data, our sense is that most forms of on-the-field and sport-related rule violations are not significantly more frequent today than they were in the past, and they are not out of control. Deviance does exist, it is a problem, and it ought to be studied and controlled in sensitive and informed ways. The specific form of sport-related deviance that may be more prevalent today is the use of banned performance-enhancing substances. This is clearly a serious problem, one we will discuss in detail later in the chapter.

Off-the-Field, Away-from-Sport Deviance

Certain cases of off-the-field deviance receive widespread media attention. When athletes are arrested in bar fights, charged with drunken driving, named in sexual assault cases, found using or dealing "street drugs," caught with altered transcripts (to remain eligible in high school or college sports), or linked to criminal activity, they make headlines and the evening news. But systematic research on these forms of deviance tells us only part of what we want to know to assess the extent of the problem. At present, we have data from a number of studies of delinquency and sport participation among high school students, a few studies of academic cheating and a few studies of excessive alcohol use among high school and college athletes, and an emerging but small collection of studies of sexual assault rates among intercollegiate athletes.

DELINQUENCY RATES Research findings on delinquency and sport participation generally contradict attention-grabbing headlines about athletes. For example, when rates of off-the-field delinquent and deviant behavior among varsity athletes have been compared to rates among other students, the rates for athletes almost always have been found to be lower than those for other students *from similar backgrounds*. With only a couple of exceptions (Stark et al., 1987), this general finding seems to hold up for athletes in different sports, athletes in different societies, and both boys and girls from different racial and social class backgrounds.*

Of course, these findings may reflect the fact that students with histories of deviant behavior do not usually try out for sport teams, or that coaches cut them when they do try out, or that athletes receive preferential treatment that keeps them out of court and jail when they are deviant. But until we know more about off-the-field behaviors, it is difficult for us to argue that athletes have higher rates of delinquency than comparable "nonathletes." Sport participation may not change people into models of virtue, but it doesn't seem to turn them into delinquents either.

ACADEMIC CHEATING The charge that college athletes use academic cheating to stay eligible has never been examined thoroughly enough for us to draw definite conclusions. If we compared them with members of fraternities and sororities, we probably would find that athletes choose courses and complete coursework much as some of these other students do.

Fraternity and sorority members, whose academic career patterns have not often been critically studied, tend to come from upper-income backgrounds, and often are able to use their advantaged positions, family and peer connections, and experiences to succeed in school and careers. They have the "social capital" needed to avoid scrutiny and to present themselves to others as upstanding and deserving students. Student-athletes from lower-income and minority backgrounds, on the other hand, are often the object of studies, and are routinely criticized for failing to live up to the academic ideal of attending college to pursue intellectual truth. They do not have the social capital needed to routinely challenge this criticism and make the case that they are deserving students.

Possible differences between the academic behaviors of student-athletes and those of other identifiable groups of students have not yet been documented enough for us to make definitive conclusions. Such documentation would include comparisons with other groups of students, such as fraternity members and students who work, and careful qualitative assessments of the academic experiences of a range of students from different backgrounds.

ALCOHOL USE AND BINGE DRINKING As most of us know from our own experience, underage and excessive alcohol consumption in high school and college is not limited to athletes. But some data indicate that athletes, especially male athletes, might engage in more alcohol abuse and binge drinking than other students. For example, a study of 17,500 students in 140 U.S. colleges indicated that 61 percent of men who participated on intercollegiate teams and said that sports were important in their lives engaged in episodes of binge drinking, while the rate among male students not involved in sports was 43 percent (Naughton, 1996b; Wechsler, 1996). The rates were 50 percent among women athletes who said sports were important, and 39 percent among women not in sports. In fact, intercollegiate athletes in this study had the highest rates of binge drinking of any student subgroups investigated. Another study found that among white, middle-class high school students, the young men on high school teams had higher rates of *both* regular alcohol use *and* total abstinence than other students (Carr et al., 1996). Patterns among young women athletes were not different from patterns among other students.

These research findings are important because alcohol use in high school and binge drinking in college may be related to other forms of negative deviance, especially those engaged in by groups of young people. More studies are needed to see if the group dynamics of alcohol use and binge drinking are related to the dynamics

---

*See Buhrmann, 1977; Landers and Landers, 1978; Miracle and Rees, 1994; Rankin, 1981; Sabo et al. 1993; Schafer, 1969; Segrave, 1986; Segrave and Chu, 1978; Segrave and Hastad, 1982; Segrave et al., 1985; Thorlindsson, 1989.

TANK McNAMARA®

by Jeff Millar & Bill Hinds

Are athletes treated differently than others by law enforcement and criminal justice officials? This comic strip suggests that they are, but there is no evidence to prove that this occurs systematically. Data on the dynamics of privilege are always difficult to collect.

underlying overconformity to other group norms among athletes. Getting drunk or binging with fellow athletes may not be very different, sociologically speaking, from playing with a serious injury so as not to let teammates down: "Have another five shots of tequila—it's what us teammates who make sacrifices and take risks together are doing tonight; are you a part of this special group or not?" Again, research is needed to see if and why this is the case.

SEXUAL ASSAULT Recent cases of sexual abuse, assault, rape, and gang rape in which male athletes are the offenders have created a growing sense of urgency about the need for systematic studies of these forms of deviance. Commentaries, theoretical analyses, and empirical studies have begun to focus on whether participation in certain sports is related to misogyny (hating or detesting women), high rates of physical and sexual assault, and the occurrence of rape and gang rape. Sexual assault and rape rates among male athletes in certain sports are reportedly high,*

---

*See Bohmer and Parrot, 1993; Crosset et al., 1995; Koss and Gaines, 1993; Lenskyj, 1992b; Loy, 1992; Melnick, 1992; Moore, 1991; Nelson, 1991, 1994; O'Sullivan, 1991; Toufexis, 1990.

but systematic empirical research on this form of off-the-field deviance is scarce. We need studies done with care and precision to determine the extent of the problem and why it exists. Researchers must exercise sensitivity and responsibility; victims' rights must be respected, and male athletes must not be made scapegoats for what is clearly a society-wide problem.

What do we know at this time? Research in anthropology shows that when men become emotionally bound together in all-male groups that demand unqualified allegiance and emphasize physical dominance, they often express their sense of togetherness through a systematic demeaning of women (Sanday, 1990). This pattern is apparent in *certain* military units, fraternal organizations, and sport teams. In a creatively designed study using qualitative methods, Tim Curry (1991) found that locker-room talk among men on two "big-time" intercollegiate sport teams at a large U.S. university "generally treated women as objects, encouraged sexist attitudes toward women and, in its extreme, promoted rape culture" (p. 119). However, Curry had no information on the actual behavior of these men outside the locker room. The reasons men in certain all-male groups demean women are not clear, but this behavior may be partially grounded in the dynamics associated with overconformity to group norms, as we suggested in our earlier discussion of positive deviance: women may be defined as "outsiders" who do not deserve respect because they don't know what is required in the world of "men's sports."

Other social scientists have made sound arguments that many sports consist of cultural practices that perpetuate a gender order privileging men and subordinating and degrading women (see, for example, Messner and Sabo, 1992). But the link between certain sport forms, male bonding, a rape culture, rape, and gang rape needs to be further explored and explained through research.

Using self-reports collected in one university from introductory sociology students and a range of intercollegiate athletes across all four years, Koss and Gaines (1993) found that sexual assault seemed to be associated with participation in revenue-producing sports. However, this study has serious methodological limitations and cannot be used as a basis for any generalizations. The best published study available when this chapter was written is one by Todd Crosset, Jeff Benedict, and Mark McDonald (1995). They used official sexual assault reports filed at the judicial affairs offices and campus police departments of 30 U.S. universities, 25 of which had top-ranked teams in men's basketball or football. They found that male college student-athletes, especially those in men's basketball and football, were implicated in a disproportionately high number of sexual assault cases, especially those reported to judicial affairs offices. But the patterns varied from school to school.

As you can see, it isn't easy to gather data on this topic; nor is it possible to make definitive conclusions on the basis of a few studies. We need a range of studies—studies using self-reports, official statistics, interview data from victims and offenders, ethnographic data on student groups, and data from focus groups composed of men alone, women alone, and men and women

together. In the meantime, there is a need to address all forms of sexual assault as a social issue, a campus problem, and a problem for athletic teams, as well as for other all-male groups on college campuses and in other organizations.

The point of this section is that most forms of off-the-field deviance among athletes do not seem to be out of control. Research suggests that athletes aren't very different from their peers from similar social backgrounds. There are possible exceptions to this: excessive alcohol use, binge drinking, physical and sexual assault rates, and cases of rape and gang rape among athletes may be relatively high. Research is needed to establish if and why athletes measure higher on these forms of negative deviance than other groups and individuals in society as a whole (See Benedict and Klein, 1997).

Finally, it is interesting that while some people claim that off-the-field deviance among athletes is getting out of control, others claim that sport participation can be used to control deviant behavior among young people. Although this latter claim needs further testing, it is worth discussing (see the box titled Is Sport Participation a "Cure" for Deviant Behavior?, pp. 164–66).

Why Focus Only on Deviance Among Athletes?

This chapter focuses almost exclusively on deviance among athletes. This is an important issue and we want to cover it in some detail. However, athletes are not the only people in sports who violate norms. Here are a few other examples of deviance related to sports:

- *coaches* who hit players, treat them inhumanely, use male players' insecurities about masculinity as a basis for motivating them, sexually harass women in and out of sports, subvert efforts to provide women with equal participation opportunities in sport, and violate NCAA or other organizational rules
- *high school and college program administrators* who ignore or try to subvert Title IX

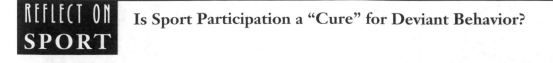

Is Sport Participation a "Cure" for Deviant Behavior?

Off-the-field deviance among athletes may decrease if athletes are taught a philosophy of nonviolence, respect for self and opponents, self-control, confidence in their abilities, and responsibility. This can happen in a variety of sports, even those involving heavy physical contact. (*Colorado Springs Gazette*)

Trying to determine the relationship between sports and deviance can be confusing. On the one hand, we hear that sports keep kids off the streets and out of trouble, and build character in the process. On the other hand, we hear about numerous athletes getting into trouble and clearly demonstrating that years of sport participation have not kept them from being deviant. How do we make sense out of this conflicting information? Fortunately, research can help.

A study by sociologist Michael Trulson* suggests that only *certain types of sports and sport participation* can lower delinquency rates among young people. After obtaining parents' permission, Trulson took thirty-four young men aged thirteen to seventeen who had been classified as delinquents, tested them for aggression and personality adjustment, and divided them into three groups matched on important background char-

acteristics. For six months, each group met three times a week for one-hour training sessions with the same instructor. Group 1 received traditional Tae Kwon Do training taught with a clearly given philosophy emphasizing respect for self and others, the importance of physical fitness, self-control, patience, perseverance, responsibility, and honor; meditation and self-reflection time was combined with the philosophy. Group 2 received "modern" martial arts training emphasizing free-sparring and self-defense techniques; the coach provided no philosophy in connection with the physical training. Group 3 received no martial arts training, but jogged and played basketball and football under the instructor's coaching and supervision.

Trulson's findings indicated clear-cut changes among the young men in Group 1. After six months they had fewer delinquent tendencies, were less anxious and less aggressive, had improved self-esteem and social skills, and agreed more closely with commonly held values. Those in Group 2 had increased delinquent tendencies, and were more aggressive and less well-adjusted than they had been when the study began. Those in Group 3 showed no change on delinquent tendencies and most personality measures, but their scores on self-esteem and social skills improved over the six months.

THE MORAL OF THE STORY.

It appears that certain types of sport participation might indeed keep kids out of trouble. However, this is most likely to happen when young people play sports in connection with a clearly expressed emphasis on the following: (1) a philosophy of nonviolence, (2) respect for self and others, (3) the importance of fitness and control over self, (4) confidence in physical skills, and (5) a sense of responsibility. Trulson's study is important because it shows that when these five things are absent, we cannot expect sport participation to keep young people out of trouble. Simply getting kids off the streets is just the beginning. If kids play sports with an emphasis on hostility towards others, using aggression as a strategy and bodies as tools, dominating others, and letting referees and coaches make calls they should be making for themselves, we *cannot* expect rates of deviance to decrease.

Changing behavior is a complex process, and to do it in connection with sport participation requires a clear-cut program of intervention in the lives of young people. This doesn't mean that all sport teams must be turned into treatment exercises, but it does mean that playing sports can't be expected to turn around people's lives unless the meaning and experience of sport participation connects them with other people in supportive and positive ways.

A WORD OF CAUTION

A study by sociologist Eldon Snyder[†] suggests that when athletes form special bonds with each other, become arrogant about their unity and uniqueness, and become subjectively separated from the rest of the community, their sport participation may become a take-off point for deviant behaviors. Snyder did a qualitative analysis of a case in which nine varsity athletes at a large university were arrested after committing dozens of burglaries over the course of two years. Seven of the athletes were on the men's swim team, one was on the track and field team, and one was a former member of the women's swim team (and currently dating one of the men); they all came from middle-class families.

Snyder examined all the records, testimony, and court documents in the case, including statements by the athletes, their parents, their lawyers, and others. He did *not* conclude that sport participation had caused these young people to be deviant. But he did cautiously conclude that playing sports together had created the bonds and dynamics out of which the deviant behavior of this group of college student-athletes emerged. Snyder has no final explanation for why these young people did what they did, but he notes that sport participation certainly did not serve as a deterrent to deviance.

This general conclusion is consistent with Peter Donnelly's[†] research showing that certain forms of binge deviance are relatively common in the lives of elite athletes, especially after major competitions, at the end of their seasons, and following retirement (Donnelly, 1993). Donnelly interviewed recently retired national-level athletes in Canada and found that when these dedicated athletes had a break in their training they often felt, as one former athlete explained, that they "had to make the most of it. Go for it. Do everything to the max!" The former athletes told stories about their off-field behaviors: "When you partied, you just partied your face off. . . . You knew that you would have to get into the grind tomorrow or the next day." And one said that after the season a number of them went on a binge by "eating, popping, drinking, injecting, and sniffing everything that wasn't nailed down."

A FINAL NOTE

These studies show that neither virtue nor deviance is *caused* by sports and sport participation. Sports are simply sites where young people often have powerful and exciting physical and social experiences. When sports are carefully organized so young people can

Continued

receive thoughtful guidance from adults who are sensitive to the things young people need to feel good about themselves and connected to the rest of the community, good outcomes are likely. But when sport participation separates athletes from the rest of the community, we should beware of the possibilities. The bonds formed among athletes can take them in many directions, including deviant ones. Sport programs such as Midnight Basketball are effective only when they enable people to live more satisfying lives in the community; just taking people off the streets for a few hours a week so they can bounce basketballs does little

more than provide temporary shelter. What do you think?

*Trulson, M. E. 1986. Martial arts training: a novel "cure" for juvenile delinquency. *Human Relations* 39(12):1131–40.
†Snyder, E. E. 1994. Interpretations and explanations of deviance among college athletes: A case study. *Sociology of Sport Journal* 11 (3): 231–48.
‡Donnelly, P. 1993. Problems associated with youth involvement in high-performance sport. Pp. 95-126 In B. R. Cahill and A. J. Pearl, eds., *Intensive participation in children's sports* (pp. 95–126). Champaign, IL: Human Kinetics.

legislation in the United States, operate sport programs that do not provide athletes with proper health and accident insurance, or ignore infractions violating university or NCAA rules (Frey, 1994); *The NCAA Register,* for example, presents a multipage monthly collection of reports of "institutional deviance" on the part of NCAA schools.

- *sport team owners* who stretch or violate antitrust laws, collude with each other to hold down player salaries, and deliberately mislead city officials and voters in connection with stadium bond issues and stadium construction issues
- *sport administrators* (including those on the International Olympic Committee and related organizations) who take bribes and gifts in return for favors, and who violate public trust and organizational principles by making decisions clearly based on their personal interests (see Jennings, 1996)
- *team managers and player personnel staff* who use racist criteria for evaluating athletes and hiring staff and coaches
- *media promoters and programmers* who deliberately distort and misrepresent sport events

so they can generate high television ratings or newspaper sales
- *agents* who mislead athletes, misrepresent themselves, or violate rules as they solicit college players
- *spectators* who endanger athletes by throwing objects on the field of play, verbally attack athletes, fight with one another, destroy property in anger after losses and in "joy" after wins, place illegal bets on sports, and forge and sell autographs of athletes

We will discuss some of these and other examples of deviant behaviors in other chapters.

PERFORMANCE-ENHANCING SUBSTANCES: A STUDY OF POSITIVE DEVIANCE IN SPORTS

Stories about athletes using performance-enhancing substances are no longer shocking. But many people do not know that drug use in sports has a long history. Athletes have taken a variety of substances over the years, and substance use has never been limited to elite athletes (Hoberman, 1995; Hoberman and Yesalis, 1995; Todd, 1983, 1987). These points raise the following important questions about this form of deviance in sports:

1. If the use of performance-enhancing substances is not new, how can we now say it is caused by money, television, an overemphasis on winning, or deterioration of values among today's athletes?
2. What are performance-enhancing drugs, who identifies them, and on what basis are they banned in different sports?
3. Why are athletes tested for drug use, and what dangers are associated with the testing of athletes?
4. What theoretical approach to deviance is most helpful in developing programs for controlling this serious problem?

History and Causes of Substance Use Among Athletes

Evidence indicates that athletes have sought and used performance-enhancing drugs for centuries.* Athletes in Greece and Rome used a variety of potions and substances, including hallucinogenic mushrooms, believed to improve physical performance. Strychnine and brandy was the potion of choice among European distance skaters in the 1700s and distance runners during the 1800s (strychnine is a dangerous "upper" used to stimulate the nervous system). Heroin was used as a painkiller by boxers before 1900, and as early as 1886 a cyclist died after using a mixture of heroin and cocaine. Many athletes in different sports used this mixture, called a *speedball*, in the late 1800s. Other drugs, including opium, alcohol, caffeine, strychnine, ethyl ether, and nitroglycerine, also were used during this period. Cyclists in the 1930s and British soccer players in the 1950s used amphetamines in combination with cocaine.

This brief review is not intended to give the impression that all athletes through history have

_____
*See Donohoe and Johnson, 1986; Goldman, 1984; Goldman, Bush, and Klatz, 1992; Hoberman, 1992, 1995; Hoberman and Yesalis, 1995; Todd, 1983, 1987; Voy, 1991.

been drug users. Most athletes have not used performance-enhancing drugs, although many at elite levels of competition have experimented with and used a wide variety of different substances believed to enhance performance (Hoberman, 1992; Jennings, 1996; Rozin, 1995; Voy, 1991). But the use of these substances is not new; this is important to remember as we try to explain why athletes use them today.

Historical evidence also shows an increase in the use of performance-enhancing drugs in the 1950s (Hoberman, 1992, 1995; Todd, 1987; Voy, 1991). This was due to two factors: (1) the development and official use of amphetamines in the military during World War II, and (2) advances in biology and medicine that led to the laboratory isolation of human hormones and the development of synthetic hormones, especially hormones fostering physical growth and development.

Experiences with amphetamines during the war alerted many physically active young men to the possible use of these drugs in other settings, including sports. Athletes in the 1950s and 1960s fondly referred to amphetamines as "bennies" (slang for benzedrine, a potent "upper"). Research on the use of synthetic hormones in sport had been done as early as the 1920s, but it wasn't until the 1950s that testosterone, steroids, and growth hormones from both humans and animals became more widely available. They didn't become very widely used, however, until weight training and strength conditioning programs were emphasized in certain sports. When athletes realized that muscle growth and lean body mass could be extended significantly, they became increasingly interested in specialized weight training programs, planned diets, vitamin supplements, and a variety of newly developed chemical substances. As might be expected, the growth of bodybuilding also has been closely connected with substance use, especially the use of hormones and hormone derivatives.

When Harold Connelly, the 1956 Olympic hammer-throw champion, testified before a U.S.

Senate committee in 1973 that the majority of athletes he had known "would do anything, and take anything, short of killing themselves to improve athletic performance," he was probably describing what many athletes through history would have done. The reason drug use has increased so much since the 1950s is not that sports or athletes have changed but that drugs believed and known to enhance physical performance have become so widely available. If today's drugs had been available in past centuries, it is likely that athletes would have used them as much as athletes do today (Hoberman, 1992; Todd, 1987). This makes it difficult to blame all drug use on the profit motive, commercial interests, television, or the erosion of traditional values.

This **substance availability hypothesis** must be examined more closely, but it clearly fits with the model of positive deviance presented in this chapter. The use of drugs and other substances by athletes is generally not the result of defective socialization or lack of moral character. After all, users are often the most dedicated and committed athletes in sports! Nor are the users helpless victims of coaches and trainers who lack moral character, although coaches and trainers who push the sport ethic without question may indirectly encourage the use of performance-enhancing substances. Instead, most substance use and abuse is clearly tied to an overcommitment to the sport ethic itself. It is grounded in overconformity—the same type of overconformity that occurs when injured distance runners continue training even when training may cause serious injuries, when young female gymnasts cut their food intake to dangerous levels, and when American football players risk their already injured bodies week after painful week in the NFL.

Apparently, many athletes enjoy playing their sports so much that they will do whatever it takes to stay involved and live up to the expectations of their athlete peers. Of course, being winners helps them avoid cuts or elimination, but winning is usually secondary to just playing and

being accepted as an athlete. And as long as even a few athletes are willing to take performance-enhancing substances to gain the edge they need to continue playing at their level of participation, others will conclude that they also must use similar substances to stay competitive, even if it's against their better judgment. These dynamics, all connected with overconformity to the sport ethic, seem to operate at various levels of sports, from the local gyms of bodybuilding to the locker rooms of professional sport teams, and among both women and men across a wide variety of sport events, from the shot put to the 100-meter sprint.

The implications of the drug availability hypothesis and the positive deviance model become especially clear when we examine efforts to define, test for, and control the use of performance-enhancing substances and other forms of positive deviance.

Defining, Identifying, and Banning Performance-Enhancing Drugs

Defining what constitutes a drug is tougher than it seems (Goode, 1988). Drugs can include anything from aspirin to heroin; they may be legal or illegal, harmless or dangerous, natural or synthetic, socially acceptable or unacceptable, commonly used or exotic. Furthermore, they may produce real physical changes, psychological changes, or both.

The International Olympic Committee, for example, defines drugs in terms of the following definition of *doping*:

> [Doping is] the administration of or use by a competing athlete of any substance foreign to the body or any physiological substance taken in abnormal quantity or taken by an abnormal route of entry into the body with the sole intention of increasing in an artificial and unfair manner his/her performance in competition. When necessity demands medical treatment with any substance which, because of its nature, dosage, or application, is able to boost the athlete's performance in competition in an artificial and unfair manner, this too is regarded by the IOC as doping (USOC, 1992).

TANK McNAMARA®

by Jeff Millar & Bill Hinds

Definitions of doping are confusing and inconsistent. Athletes in some sports today must closely monitor everything they ingest to avoid unintentionally violating the rules of national and international governing organizations. The more rules there are, the more ways there are to be deviant.

This definition may sound good, but it leaves many questions unanswered. What is a substance "foreign" to the body, and why are the "foreign" substances of aspirin and ibuprofen not banned while the "natural" hormone testosterone is banned? What are an "abnormal" quantity and an "abnormal" route of entry? Why are megadoses of vitamins not banned, while small amounts of many decongestants are banned? Why can athletes be stripped of medals when they take medications without intending to enhance performance? And with new scientific discoveries being made every day and applied to sports, what is artificial and what is unfair? Why are needles permitted to rehydrate athletes, but considered dangerous and artificial when used to infuse red blood cells into athletes? Why isn't the electronic stimulation of muscles banned? Isn't it artificial? Why are biofeedback and other psychological technologies defined as "natural" and "fair" while certain forms of herbal tea are defined as "unnatural" and "unfair"? Are vitamins natural? Amino acids? Caffeine? Human growth hormone? Gatorade? How about other artificial foods now stacked floor to ceiling in U.S. health food stores and sold with the promise of performance en-

hancement? And is it "natural" to deprive yourself of food to make weight or meet the demands of a gymnastics coach who measures body fat every week and punishes athletes who eat "normal" diets?

Are big-time college football players deviant when saline solutions are dripped into their veins through intravenous needles in a pregame locker room to minimize the threat of dehydration on a hot playing field? Isn't this a performance-enhancing procedure? Is it normal, safe? How about twelve-year-old gymnasts who pop a dozen antiinflammatory pills every day so they can train through pain? Are they deviant? How about Brett Farve, the NFL quarterback who became addicted to painkillers after being regularly injected by team physicians during the 1995–96 NFL season? Why do we call athletes heroes when they use an IV procedure to play in ungodly heat or take large injections of painkilling drugs to keep them training and playing, and then condemn the same athletes when they take drugs to help them build muscles damaged by overtraining or to help them relax and recover after their bodies and minds have been pushed beyond limits in the pursuit of dreams? Why do many athletes see the use of drugs as a noble act of commitment and dedication, while many spectators see it as a reprehensible act of deviance, yet pay big money to watch athletes do superhuman things requiring extreme training regimes and strategies?

These and hundreds of other questions about what is artificial, natural, foreign, fair, and abnormal show that any definition of doping will lead to endless debates about the technical and legal meaning of terms (Hoberman, 1992: 261). While these debates proceed in classrooms and courtrooms, physicians, pharmacists, chemists, inventors, and athletes continue to come up with new and different aids to performance, chemical and otherwise. And this "endless game of scientific hide and seek" shows no sign of letting up (Hoberman, 1992: 101). In fact, we can expect it to get more heated and controversial as scientists manipulate the brain and nervous system and try to use genetic engineering to improve athletic performance. How will we define, identify, and deal with deviance in light of all these possibilities? According to Australian sociologist Jim McKay (1990), "The argument that drugs are 'unnatural' pales in comparison to the array of biological, biochemical, social, biomechanical, psychological, environmental, and technological regimens which manipulate athletes' bodies" in today's high-performance sports. Drug use among athletes seems to be only one of many issues related to technology and athletes' bodies; sooner or later we will have to deal with all these issues.

Further complicating decisions about which drugs to ban is confusion about their effects on athletic performance. Ethical and legal considerations have constrained researchers wanting to study the impact of super-high doses and multiple combinations of substances used ("stacked and cycled") by athletes. It wasn't until 1996 that *The New England Journal of Medicine* published a study documenting what thousands of athletes have known for over three decades: high dosages of testosterone do increase muscle mass and strength to a significant degree, and they may not have serious negative side effects

when used with care over the short term (Bhasin et al., 1996). But until this study was published, official medical statements contradicted what some athletes claimed and knew about the effects of steroids. This is the reason many athletes have ignored "official statements" about the consequences and dangers of doping (Fish, 1993).

Sport organizations defend the withholding of information by saying they don't want athletes to know too much about drugs because knowledge might encourage use. However, many athletes now get information in "underground" publications that claim to provide a sound basis for making informed choices about substance use (Di Pasquale, 1992a). Most athletes in international sports such as the Olympics also realize that the IOC and other sport organizations withhold information because they don't want to jeopardize the billions of dollars that corporate sponsors and TV networks pay for what they want to present to the world as a clean and wholesome event (Jennings, 1996).

Most arguments for banning the use of performance-enhancing substances are at least partially based on the belief that these substances are dangerous to the health of athletes. Although this is true in some cases, it is tough to argue this point to athletes who are already asked and told to make sacrifices, pay the price, and take many health risks as they strive for distinction in their sports. For example, when athletes who have dedicated between four and fifteen years of their youth to make a national team are told that taking certain hormones could shorten their lives by a few years or do damage to their livers or their hearts, they don't listen very closely. Such messages don't scare many of them; they know that being an athlete means taking chances and often suffering injuries in the process. And when they are not encouraged to question the mind-set that promotes other dangerous forms of overconformity to the sport ethic, how can they be convinced to avoid substances that may negatively affect their health? After all, they know that participation in power and performance sports is itself a threat to their health (Waddington, 1998)!

Finally, some people ask why drugs should be banned in sports when they are widely accepted in society and used to improve performance or treat conditions that interfere with performance at home or on the job. The majority of adults in most wealthy, high-tech societies use tranquilizers, pain controllers, mood controllers, antidepressants, decongestants, diet pills, birth control pills, caffeine, nicotine, or alcohol. Testosterone, human growth hormone, DHEA,* and creatine† are being used increasingly by some doctors in health-related hormone therapies designed to improve strength and counteract the decremental effects of aging (Cowley, 1996). In fact, if people really did say no to drugs, life in most Western societies would change dramatically.

These facts give rise to an important question. Why bother to control athletes in ways that other people are not controlled? After all, do colleges have a policy against using caffeine to aid late-night studying for a test? Do teachers make students sign an oath to avoid taking drugs that might enable them to do their coursework? Do employers tell executives not to use hormone (testosterone) therapy to keep them fit for work? Why should athletes have to do these things when others competing for valued rewards do not?

In the meantime, it remains very difficult even to begin to define, identify, and ban drugs and doping procedures used in sports. This brings us to the issue of drug testing.

As governing bodies add items to the banned substance list, some athletes seek still other substances to aid training and performance. As of early 1997, these were some of the substances preferred by some world-class athletes in the U.S. Herbs and nutritional supplements are now being used instead of or in combination with various hormonal substances. (Jay Coakley).

Drug Testing in Sports

BACKGROUND AND HISTORY The creation and enforcement of rules regulating drug use among athletes has always been the responsibility of individual sport associations, federations, leagues, and conferences. And every organization has a different drug control policy history.

The IOC, for example, first defined and banned doping in 1967. The first drug tests in international sport were administered at the 1968 Olympic Games in Mexico City, but they were done for research purposes and no athlete was punished for testing positive. In 1968 there

---

*Dehydroepiandrosterone (DHEA) is a hormone available in "health food" stores. It is a product of the adrenal glands, and it stimulates the production of testosterone. Athletes and people over age forty take it to maintain lean body mass. At this time it is not a banned substance for athletes.
†Creatine is a compound produced by the liver, kidney, and pancreas. It facilitates the renewal of anaerobic energy reserves, delays the onset of fatigue during intense exercise, and cuts recovery time between workouts (Granjean and Reimers, 1996).

were no accurate tests for detecting anabolic steroids; few sports leaders were aware of how many athletes were using steroids, and most medical experts naively claimed that steroids had no significant effect on performance (Todd, 1987). These first regulatory drug tests were prompted by suspicions about drug-related deaths among cyclists and soccer players and by rumors about widespread drug use among athletes in Eastern Europe.

The absence of tests for steroids opened the door for rapid increases in the number of athletes using them. According to an unofficial poll taken by Jay Sylvester, a member of the U.S. track team in 1972, 68 percent of all track and field athletes used some form of anabolic steroid in preparing for the 1972 Games in Munich (Todd, 1987). Accurate tests to detect steroid use were developed in 1973, and they were first administered on an experimental basis at the 1974 Commonwealth Games. No athletes were punished, even though about 20 percent of the competitors in the sample tested positive.

During the 1976 Olympic Games in Montreal, 8 out of 275 athletes tested positive for steroids, but at that time many already had switched from synthetic steroids to pure testosterone. This was ironic, since anabolic steroids originally were developed and used in medical treatment because they were safer than testosterone. However, because testosterone is a natural substance in the human body, it created detection problems for the testers. According to the policy used then in Olympic sports, a positive test for testosterone meant that an athlete's urine contained more than a 6:1 ratio of testosterone to epitestosterone ("T/E ratio" or "tet/epitet ratio"), both of which are naturally occurring hormones in men and women (normal T/E ratios are about 2:1 or less). Many athletes manipulated their use of hormones so that they would not surpass this ratio.

Drug tests done in 1980 indicated that over 20 percent of the U.S. athletes who would have competed in the Moscow Olympic Games (if there had been no boycott) tested positive for the use of exogenous (not "naturally" produced) testosterone, according to the T/E ratio definition of doping. In 1982 the IOC added testosterone to its list of banned substances. During the next year, fifteen male athletes from the United States tested positive for steroids at the Pan American Games in Caracas, and a dozen others packed up and returned home before competing in their events when they heard about the testing. This attracted attention and led to numerous investigations of drugs in sport by sport organizations, journalists, and others. The popular press was full of drug reports. The investigations suggested that drug use existed among many athletes in a wide range of amateur and professional sports.

The USOC stepped up its testing efforts during the 1984 Olympic trials, although there were no punishments for eighty-six athletes who tested positive. But the athletes used the test results to learn more about how to avoid detection, and many steroid users turned to unbanned masking drugs, switched to the use of human growth hormone (hGH), or controlled their testosterone use more carefully (Todd, 1987). The reason for the switch to hGH was that growth hormone could not be detected through standard testing methods. Testosterone was allowed as long as the T/E ratio was not beyond 6:1. However, both hGH and testosterone are more dangerous and powerful than anabolic steroids (Donohoe and Johnson, 1986). Additional rumors in the mid-1980s suggested a few athletes may have even experimented with "monkey juice," the growth hormones of monkeys and apes (Todd, 1987). During the Los Angeles Games in 1984, a number of positive drug tests were never made public, and the records of these tests were mysteriously shredded when discovered by the press. Also, tests were not done for testosterone or caffeine, blood boosting policy was kept unclear, and athletes routinely used cleverly evasive methods of providing testers with "clean urine" (Jennings, 1996). Overall, the testing in 1984 was a sham that may have been influenced by an interest in selling the games to image-conscious corporations. Of course, the sale of the games has continued at a record pace!

The outcomes of the drug-testing programs for the 1988, 1992, and 1996 Summer Olympic Games in Seoul, Barcelona, and Atlanta followed similar patterns: only a few athletes tested positive amid rumors of widespread use. Evidence suggests that the rumors are at least partially true. Testing done after the completion of the Seoul Games revealed at least fifty men using anabolic steroids and twenty positive drug tests that were never made public; after the Barcelona Games, hundreds of athlete urine samples were found to contain evidence of drug use (Jennings, 1996). Athletes probably are using various forms of anabolic steroids, other hormones, and substances such as EPO* in a wider range of events than ever before; usage is no longer limited to weight lifting and other so-called strength sports.

Many people believe that the relatively small number of positive tests in recent Olympic Games has been due not only to cover-ups, but also to the use of masking drugs to distort test results, a more careful and knowledgeable determination of usage cycles and dose amounts among athletes, the use of customized "designer drugs" that escape detection in the tests, and the use of hGH, EPO, and other substances that can't be accurately detected by the tests. Also, some athletes have now become so experienced in the use of testosterone that they take it in doses that keep the detectable amount below allowable limits, which have occasionally been raised to a 10:1 T/E ratio—over 500 percent of what is normal in the human body! In order to stay close to but not exceed the 6:1 ratio, some athletes, especially women, now take strength- and speed-boosting doses of testosterone through skin patches and via skin cream (Hornblower, 1996). As long as they stay under 16:1, they do not test positive.

Other sport organizations have different histories of drug testing from that of the IOC. Every organization has its own policies, procedures, and "banned substances list." And each organization's policy is influenced by unique sets of internal political issues and external factors, such as the policy positions of players' associations, the availability of money to conduct tests, and the legal limits of testing in certain situations.

The effectiveness of drug testing in high-profile power and performance sports such as those in the Olympic Games is compromised because people associated with these sports like the benefit of performance-enhancing drugs. Charles Yeselis, a drug expert and professor of health policy at Penn State University, explains that these drugs give sports "world records, bigger-than-life human beings with tremendous physical capacities they could not attain without drugs. That sells television minutes and endorsements" (cited in Rozin, 1994). And as we saw in the Atlanta Games and have seen in other events since then, television and commercial endorsements shape sports in dramatic ways; while they may not cause the taking of drugs, they do impact the enforcement of drug policies.

TESTING AS A DETERRENT Drug testing is controversial. One of the main arguments against it is that it doesn't prevent athletes from using drugs. In the face of testing, athletes have used numerous evasive tactics. Critics of the ban on steroids also argue that it not only criminalizes the use of a helpful drug but also forces athletes to obtain drug supplies in the black market and isolates users from the supervision and guidance of physicians (Courson, 1988; Bender, 1988). According to Mauro Di Pasquale, editor of the journal *Drugs in Sports*, the policy of banning substances and testing athletes has failed because it has "led to the use of more dangerous drugs" (Di Pasquale, 1992b: 5).

---

*Erythropoietin (EPO) is a form of protein that stimulates the formation of red blood cells and therefore boosts the oxygen-carrying capacity of an athlete's blood. EPO has been used by a growing number of athletes, especially in endurance sports, as an effective and relatively safe alternative to "blood doping," which involves drawing blood from an athlete weeks prior to a competition, separating the oxygen-rich red blood cells, storing them, and then reinfusing them into an athlete's circulatory system just prior to competition. At this point, neither blood doping nor EPO can be detected accurately through standard drug tests.

A practical argument against testing is that it cannot detect all the substances athletes use to enhance their performance. Athletes are often one step ahead of rule makers and testers. By the time the sport organizations ban substances and the testers calibrate tests to detect newly banned substances, the athletes have moved on to something else, or have found new ways of masking the presence of banned substances in their systems. Meanwhile, the list of banned substances is growing to catalog length and athletes are being overwhelmed with confusing rules.

Other arguments against drug testing are based on legal issues and social considerations. Mandatory testing and testing without cause not only violates a person's right to privacy but sets precedents that could lead people to see testing as permissible in other spheres of life. Privacy issues are very important because future tests may call for blood as well as urine samples, and may involve DNA analysis. Because athletes are used as models, testing in sports could lead many other people to consent to testing in their personal lives. This would not only open the door to oppressive forms of social control in everyday life, but also encourage the use of social stigma to mark people whose bodies have been labeled as "impure" or "contaminated" (Black, 1996; Cole, Denny, and Coakley, 1993).

Arguments in favor of drug testing also reveal interesting dimensions of the drug use problem in sports. Many people feel that performance-enhancing drugs should be banned from sports because they allow athletes to perform beyond their "natural" abilities and give them an unfair advantage over opponents. They say that this destroys the basis for competition and threatens the health and well-being of athletes even to the point of causing permanent physical damage or death. Others, using a hard-line "law and order" approach, favor testing because they define drug use as immoral behavior that "must be severely punished. Period. End of discussion."

When these people are told that current testing programs are not effective, they call for more comprehensive tests that are administered regularly without warning, mandatory for everyone (no excuses), and 100 percent effective and accurate (so that athletes have faith in them and won't think others are escaping detection). But such a testing program would be so expensive that it would bankrupt most sport organizations, and it would probably be illegal in certain countries. Furthermore, many athletes have become skeptical about testing policies and programs. They realize that international sports are heavily influenced by political and economic interests that cloud the validity and reliability of tests. They also know how bureaucratically complicated drug testing processes can be, and that mistakes can occur at any one of a number of points in those processes. This has been illustrated through court cases in which the accuracy and fairness of drug testing procedures has been called into question. Finally, they know that some of their peers, fellow athletes willing to overconform to the sport ethic, will continue seeking new ways to push their bodies to new limits in the pursuit of dreams.

Controlling Substance Use in Sports

Today's athletes, like their counterparts in the past, seek continued participation and excellence in sports. And when they push the sport ethic too far and overconform to norms promoting sacrifice and risk in the pursuit of distinction and dreams, they are not likely to define the use of performance-enhancing substances as deviant. Even Ben Johnson, the Canadian sprinter who lost his gold medal for the 100-meter sprint in the 1988 Seoul Olympics, said this in 1993: "You can never clean it up. People are always gonna be doing something. They feel good about themselves, and they feel it's right to do it" (cited in Fish, 1993). Johnson's point is made in another way by a physician who works with athletes; he observes that "athletes don't use drugs to escape reality—they use them to enforce the reality that surrounds them" (Di Pasquale, 1992).

In light of these points, the explanations of deviance and the strategies for controlling it offered by absolutist and relativist approaches are not very helpful. Most athletes do not use performance-enhancing substances because they lack character, intelligence, or sanity. Nor do they use them because they are victims of biased and coercive rules. The solutions offered by these theoretical approaches are also unsatisfactory. Tougher rules and increased testing have not and will not control the problem; nor will simply letting athletes make the rules control it.

As long as athletes are encouraged to accept the norms of the sport ethic without question or qualification, they will continue to voluntarily try anything or take anything to remain in sports. Overreactions to drug use and oversimplified solutions will not make athletes stop using substances they see as important tools of their trade. Drug use can be controlled only if and when enough people involved in sports critically assess the norms of the sport ethic in ways that lead them to set limits on conformity to those norms.

In light of this approach, recommendations for controlling substance use in sport should begin with the following changes:

- To avoid hypocrisy, the use of so-called "legal" performance-enhancing drugs and procedures that may harm the health of athletes should be eliminated. Painkillers, massive injections of vitamin B-12, blood boosting and the use of EPO, playing with pins in broken bones or with high-tech "casts" to hold broken bones in place during competition, and playing with special harnesses to restrict the movement of injured joints may be as harmful to health as taking anabolic steroids, and these practices also must be regulated and controlled if we are to begin to limit the use of performance-enhancing drugs.
- Rules must be put into place that clearly indicate that risks to health are undesirable and unnecessary in sports. Turning fourteen-year-olds who compete in gymnastics with training-induced stress fractures into national heroes and corporate poster children

"Is this what those hormones are supposed to do, Carl?"

The negative side effects of various combinations of substances are difficult to identify. But controlled studies of banned substances are difficult to do, if not unethical.

for corporate sponsors disguises the problem of positive deviance in sports.

- No athlete should be allowed to play while hurt or injured until certified as "well," *not* simply "able to compete," by a physician chosen by someone *outside* the athletic program in which the athlete is involved. Outsiders are necessary to avoid medical opinions mediated by pervasive organizational overconformity to the sport ethic.
- Norms emphasizing an awareness of one's limits must be developed so that courage is defined as the ability to accept the discipline necessary to become well, not the willingness to disregard the consequences of injuries.
- The goals of sport science must be reframed to emphasize the growth and development of athletes through the expansion and continuation of the sport experience for participants at all levels of involvement. Training advice must be informed by this goal, or sport scientists become high-tech panders. For example, sport psychology should be used to help athletes understand the consequences of their choices to participate in sports, and to reduce the extent to which guilt, shame, and

pathology influence participation and training decisions; this is the alternative to the technique of "psycho-doping," which encourages overconforming deviance by making athletes more likely to give body and soul to their sport without carefully answering questions about why they are doing what they are doing.

- The process of questioning and qualifying the sport ethic must be made formal in sports and sport organizations, and it should involve all sport participants. Unless this happens, forms of positive deviance will continue to occur. Athletes, coaches, and others associated with sports must continually develop and assess guidelines that discourage overconformity to the sport ethic; these guidelines should emphasize pleasure, health, and development, as well as performance.
- Drug education should be part of larger *deviance and health education* programs for coaches, managers, administrators, and athletic directors, in additional to athletes.

A switch to *deviance and health education* is important because it focuses attention on important issues often ignored in standard drug education programs. For example, such a program would involve the following:

- creating norms regulating the use of new and extremely powerful forms of technology and medical knowledge that go beyond the use of drugs
- questioning and critically examining the value systems and norms used to guide behavior in sports, and then setting limits on conformity while also controlling underconformity
- redefining the meaning of sport experiences in light of the availability of new forms of performance-enhancing technologies
- becoming more aware that the behavior of athletes is based on choices and that to avoid self-destructive and meaningless choices, athletes must have valid and reliable information and be full participants in rule-making processes in sports.

"Deviance and health education" would involve a critical examination of how sports are defined, organized, promoted, and played. This approach to social control is based on critical theory rather than functionalism or conflict theory (see chap. 2). It assumes that rules and relationships are the creations of people and that constructive changes are possible when people critically examine the values, norms, and social conditions affecting their choices and their lives.

As it is now, we face a future without any clearly defined ideas about what achievement in sports means in light of new financial incentives to set records and win events, the new importance of sport participation in the lives and identities of many young athletes, new technologies that clearly enhance performance, and new forms of corporate sponsorship that make image as important as ability. Our guidelines must be new as well; using old guidelines with more coercive enforcement methods will not work. There are new issues now that call for new responses. Widespread involvement in this process is needed, or else powerful entities such as transnational corporations will appropriate sport culture and the bodies of athletes as sites for delivering their messages about success, performance, efficiency, winning, and laboring in pain for the sake of achieving goals.

SUMMARY

IS DEVIANCE IN SPORTS OUT OF CONTROL?

The study of deviance and sports presents an interesting challenge. This is the case because deviance among athletes often involves overconforming to norms, rather than underconforming or rejecting norms. Widely used conceptual frameworks in sociology often ignore this form of deviance; in fact, they don't offer many helpful recommendations for controlling the full range of deviant behavior in sports. When deviance is defined as failing to measure up to an ideal and grounded in a lack of moral character (the absolutist approach), an analysis of deviance in sport runs into problems. Ideals are difficult to identify, and athletes may violate norms because they go overboard in their acceptance of them, not because they lack character.

It also doesn't help much when deviance is defined as a result of labeling processes through which powerful people impose their definitions of good and bad on those without power (the relativist approach). Describing rule violators as victims is seldom accurate, and changing the rules and the rule makers is not likely to decrease positive deviance in sports.

A critical normal distribution approach seems to be most useful when explaining much of the deviance in sports today. Such an approach distinguishes negative deviance, or extreme underconformity, from positive deviance, or extreme overconformity. This distinction is important, because the most serious forms of deviance in sports are created by behaviors in which athletes, coaches, and others clearly overconform to norms. For example, when being an athlete is defined in terms of making sacrifices, striving for distinction, taking risks, playing with pain, and focusing on dreams, extreme overconformity is bound to be a problem if no limits are set on expectations. It is the unqualified acceptance of these norms that accounts for much of the deviance in sports.

Research strongly supports this explanation. Most on-the-field and sport-related behaviors among athletes fall within a normal range of acceptability, and when they fall outside this range, they often involve overconformity with the norms of the sport ethic. Off-the-field deviance often makes headlines, but most evidence indicates that rates of deviance among athletes are not higher than those among comparable people who don't participate in sports. There is one likely exception to this, a serious one: the reported high rates of physical and sexual assault. However, it does not seem that deviance in sports is generally out of control.

The use of performance-enhancing substances is another form of deviance that is reportedly widespread despite new rules, testing programs, educational and treatment programs, and strong punishments for violators. Historical evidence suggests that recent increases in rates of use are primarily due to the increased availability of substances rather than to changes in the values and characters of athletes or the victimization of athletes. Most athletes through history have sought ways to remain athletes and improve their skills, but today the search is more likely to lead to drugs because more drugs are available. Science and medicine have not slowed this process, because they have been used to control athletes' bodies rather than to enable athletes to control themselves and their lives through the critical assessment of new technology (McKay, 1990).

Despite expanding lists of banned substances, athletes have generally stayed one jump ahead of the rule makers and testers. When one drug is banned, athletes use another, even if it is more dangerous. If a new test is developed, athletes switch to an undetectable drug, or use masking drugs to confuse testers. The use of hGH, blood doping, and other new procedures still escape detection, and new tests are problematic, since they will be challenged as violations of privacy rights and/or cultural norms in many societies.

Controlling positive deviance requires a serious reexamination of norms in many sports. A balance must be struck between accepting and questioning norms and rules; people in sports must critically qualify norms and rules, and set limits on conformity so that athletes who engage in self-destructive behaviors are not presented as heroes. Everyone in sports should question existing norms and create new norms related to the use of medical science and technology. The meaning of sport experiences requires redefinition if positive deviance is to be controlled. After all, what would happen if someone discovered how to safely stimulate the brain to produce natural hormones that would increase size and strength and dramatically change performance potential?

An effective transformation of sports also requires that all participants be involved in a continual process of critical reflection about the meaning and organization of sports. Control of deviance requires a critical examination of the values and norms in sports, as well as a restructuring of the organizations controlling and sponsoring sports. This critical examination should involve everyone, from athletes to fans.

SUGGESTED READINGS

Bredemeier, B. J. L., and D. L. L. Shields. 1993. Moral psychology in the context of sport. In R. N. Singer, M. Murphey, and L. K. Tennant, eds., *Handbook of research on sport psychology* (pp. 587–99). New York: Macmillan (*a review of theory and research on morality and sport; I have not covered this literature in this chapter, but it is helpful in understanding issues related to deviance*).

Crosset, T. W., J. R. Benedict, and M. A. McDonald. 1995. Male student-athletes reported for sexual assault: Survey of campus police departments and judicial affairs offices. *Journal of Sport & Social Issues* 19 (2): 126–40 (*contains original data from U.S. universities and provides an overview and critique of published accounts of sexual assault and sports; very helpful in discussions of this topic*).

Davis, L., and L. Delano. 1992. Fixing the boundaries of physical gender: Side effects of anti-doping campaigns in athletics. *Sociology of Sport Journal* 1 (1): 1–19 (*an insightful analysis of how antidrug media campaigns in the U.S. during the 1980s often used fixed ideas about gender to promote fears about the effects of steroids on bodies*).

Di Pasquale, M. G. 1992. *Drugs in Sports* (*this new journal contains no sociological analysis, but is an invaluable source of information about performance-enhancing substances and technologies. It is not an underground publication, but it is not endorsed by most sport organizations*).

Donohoe, T., and N. Johnson. 1986. *Foul play: Drug abuse in sports.* New York: Basil Blackwell (*a clearly written overview of the history of drug use by athletes; thorough discussion of major drugs currently being used; focus is primarily on world-class amateur sport*).

Eitzen, D. S. 1998. Sport and social control. In J. Coakley, E. Dunning eds., *Handbook of sport and society.* London: Sage (*although not dealing directly with deviance, this article does outline useful information on the various ways sports are related to the dynamics of social control in society*).

Hoberman, J. 1992. *Mortal engines: The science of performance and the dehumanization of sport.* New York: The Free Press (*an insightful analysis of the use of sport science in the quest of extending human limits; reading this book will leave you wondering about the benefits and dangers of science*).

Hoberman, J. 1995. Listening to steroids. *The Wilson Quarterly* 19 (1, Winter): 35–44. Hoberman, J., and C. Yesalis. 1995. The history of synthetic testosterone. *Scientific American* (February): 60–65 (*this and the other Hoberman article connect the use of steroids to larger medicalization processes occurring in the late nineteenth century; they predict that instead of being banned in the future, steroids will be used by all of us to improve our everyday lives*).

Jennings, A. 1996. *The new lords of the rings.* London: Pocket Books (*a well-researched, journalistic account of the many forms of deviance associated with Olympic sports in the 1980s and 1990s*).

Miracle, A. W., and C. R. Rees. 1994. *Lessons of the locker room: The myth of school sports.* Amherst, NY: Prometheus Books (*Chap. 5, pp. 101-25, "School sports and delinquency" (pp. 101–25), provides a thorough overview of research on sport participation in U.S. high schools and deviant behavior*).

Snyder, E. E. 1994. Interpretations and explanations of deviance among college athletes: A case study. *Sociology of Sport Journal* 11 (3): 231–48 (*an insightful study of college athletes involved in a series of larcenies; suggests that the group dynamics of team membership and the thrill of collective risk taking is related to the mind-set underlying this form of deviant behavior*).

Todd, T. 1987. Anabolic steroids: the gremlins of sport. *Journal of Sport History* 14(1):87–107 (*a historical analysis of the use of drugs by athletes, with special reference to the recent use of steroids and efforts to control their use*).

Voy, R. 1991. *Drugs, sport, and politics.* Champaign, IL: Leisure Press (*an overview of drug usage in sports, a critique of doping control policies in amateur sports, and recommendations for drug control policies; highly critical of current efforts to control performance-enhancing substances among athletes*).

It happens all the time, everywhere I go. There always are people wanting to get in a fight with me.

Dennis Rodman, NBA player (1996)

I think we have some warriors. I think they are ready for the battle.

Tara VanDerveer, coach, USA National Women's Basketball Team (1996)

(Jay Coakley)

Aggression in Society
Do sports control or encourage aggressive behaviors?

Serious sport has nothing to do with fair play. It is bound up with hatred, jealousy, boastfulness, disregard of all rules and sadistic pleasure in witnessing violence. In other words, it is war minus the shooting.

George Orwell (1950)

Boxin' doesn't jus' teach you violence. I think, boxin' teaches you discipline an' self-respect. . . . Anybody who feels that it teaches you violence is a person tha's really a, a real incompetent mind I think. Someone tha' their min's thinkin' real low.

Twenty-four-year-old professional boxer (quoted in Wacquant, 1995)

The greatest feeling I get playing baseball right now is knowing that I can go out and be a warrior for the Lord. I can go out . . . and say my prayer and then be a very aggressive, warrior-like pitcher, glorifying Him. . . .

Randy Johnson, major-league baseball player (1996)

I've never, ever sent a "Get Well" card [to a player I've injured] . . . . Hey, it's a man's game. If you can't play, get out and play tennis.

Bryan Marchment, National Hockey League player (1995)

Some people argue that sports and sport participation provide players and spectators with opportunities to let off steam, release feelings of aggression, and develop coping strategies in the face of stressful and highly emotional situations. And they conclude that sports ultimately serve to control and moderate aggression and violence in society. Others argue the opposite. They say that sports and sport participation create frustration, arouse aggressive tendencies in players and spectators, teach people to use aggressive tactics in their lives, and support a general culture of violence among certain groups of people. And they conclude that sports ultimately promote aggression and violence in society.

The major purpose of this chapter is to explain and critique these two arguments. We will begin by defining aggression, violence, and intimidation, and then examine the idea that sports provide a safe outlet for aggression. Next, as we assess the argument that sports promote aggression, we'll examine the patterns of aggression that exist in sports, and the connections between aggression, gender, and ethnicity. Finally, we will turn our attention to aggression among sports spectators, and the ways that spectator violence might be discouraged and controlled.

WHAT IS AGGRESSION?

Contradictory statements and conclusions about sports and aggression often occur for at least four reasons. *First,* many people don't define important terms in their discussions. They often use words such as *physical, assertive, tough, competitive, intense, intimidating, risky, aggressive, violent,* and *destructive* interchangeably. *Second,* those making the statements may not distinguish players from spectators, even though the dynamics of aggressive behavior in these two groups differ. *Third,* they often lump all sport forms together, regardless of organization, purpose, and the amount of physical contact involved. In fact, we cannot group pleasure and participation sports with power and performance sports when it comes to discussing aggression. *Fourth,* people

drawing conclusions may not distinguish the short-term effects of playing or watching sports from the long-term effects on patterns of aggressive behaviors among individuals and groups; this is important, because people's immediate responses to sport-related situations do not always predict what they will do long after games and events are over.

In this chapter I will use definitions of concepts that will enable us to precisely identify behaviors that occur in connection with sports. The term *aggression* will refer to behavior that *intends* to destroy property or injure another person, *or* is grounded in a *total disregard* for the well-being of self and others; the consequences of aggression may be physical or psychological. This definition allows us to distinguish aggressive behavior from other behaviors that we might describe as assertive, competitive, or achievement oriented. I assume that there is a difference between being aggressive and simply being assertive or trying hard to win or achieve other goals.

The term *violence* will refer to acts of *physical* aggression. *Violence* is defined as physical assault based on total disregard for the well-being of self and others, or the intent to injure another person or destroy property. The term *intimidation* will refer to verbal or physical behaviors that threaten violence or coercion for the purpose of controlling others against their wishes or interests. *Intimidation* usually does not cause physical harm, but often is designed to produce psychological consequences, enabling one person to physically overpower or dominate another.

These definitions will help focus our discussion, but they will not eliminate all conceptual problems. For example, there are various types and levels of aggressive actions that can occur in sports (Silva, 1983). Players can intend aggressive actions to produce various things: psychological intimidation, physical intimidation, injuries taking an opponent out of a game for a few minutes, injuries eliminating an opponent from an entire game, injuries ending an opponent's season, or injuries permanently disabling an opponent. Most athletes recognize the differences between these actions; some may feel justified in being aggressive to a certain point but not beyond that point, while others may see any action as justified as long as it is within the rules of the game. The way athletes feel usually varies from sport to sport, from one level of competition to the next, and over time, depending on rules, rule-enforcement, and the cultural context in which players make decisions about their sport participation.

It will be helpful for you to keep these definitions and conceptual distinctions in mind as you read and critique my discussion of sports and aggression.

DO SPORTS CONTROL AND MODERATE AGGRESSION IN SOCIETY?

Those who argue that sports serve to control aggressive behavior in society generally base their case on

1. assumptions about human instincts
2. ideas about how frustration is "released" through sport participation
3. information describing what people learn during sport participation

We will discuss each of these three arguments for this case that sports control aggression.

Human Instincts and Aggression

Some people still believe that all forms of aggressive behavior are grounded in instincts. Theoretical support for this belief is often based on the works of Sigmund Freud and other psychoanalysts. According to Freudian theory, all humans possess a *death instinct*, sometimes referred to as the "death wish." This death instinct takes the form of destructive energy in a person's psyche. If this energy is not released intentionally, eventually it will build up and be released involuntarily, in the form of aggression against self (the extreme form of which is suicide) or others (the extreme forms of which are murder and warfare). The only way to control this potentially destructive energy

is to release it safely through an aggressively expressive activity. This safe form of release is called a *catharsis*, and its operation resembles what happens when steam is slowly released from a pressure cooker: it keeps the pot from blowing up.

Even though Freudian theory leaves unanswered many questions about the nature and operation of the death instinct and the aggression it generates, some people have applied it to sports. Their conclusion is that playing and watching sports allows players and spectators to safely release, or "drain off," innate aggressive energy; that is, sports, especially contact sports, provide a catharsis for instinct-based aggressive tendencies that inevitably build up over time in human beings.

Many ethologists have used a combination of Freudian and evolutionary theories to make a similar case (Ardrey, 1961, 1966; Lorenz, 1966; Morris, 1967, 1981). Ethologists are scientists concerned with the biological foundations of animal behavior; they usually study the behavior patterns of insects, fish, birds, or nonhuman animals in their natural habitats. Using their

"*Now that we've invented violence, we need a sport to use it in.*"
....
The existence of violence in sports is not new. But this does not mean that violence is a part of nature or an inevitable part of sports.

....

research to explain human behavior, some have suggested that aggression is a product of evolution, and that without aggressive instincts, no species (including humans) would survive. Some have assumed that humans can safely release aggressive energy through playing and watching sports (Lorenz, 1966).

Peter Marsh (1978, 1982), a British social psychologist, has expanded the ideas of both Freud and the ethologists to argue that sport events serve as occasions for "ritual confrontations" between fans. After observing the behavior of young, male soccer fans in England, he concluded that such confrontations are relatively harmless, symbolic displays of aggressive energy. They are highly structured and predictable, and they serve to control the extent to which the fans express aggression in other spheres of life. In fact, Marsh argues that if the aggressive behaviors associated with soccer were suppressed, the rates of violent crime and fighting behavior in nonsport settings would increase.

The assumption underlying all three of these arguments is that humans are instinctively aggressive and that sports, especially contact sports, provide safe "outlets" for aggressive behaviors that people *must* express in some form. This assumption is often built into the language that sportspeople use when they describe their own sport participation. For example, Mike Ditka, an NFL player in the 1970s, an NFL coach in the 1980s, and an NFL TV commentator for football and then a coach once more in the 1990s, explained in these words:

> There's no question about it. I feel a lot of football players build up a lot of anxieties in the off-season because they have no outlets for them. . . . I'm an overactive person anyway and if I don't get rid of this energy, it just builds up in me and then I blow it off in some other way which is not really the proper way (cited in Fisher, 1976).

In Ditka's mind, participation in heavy contact sports is a safe "outlet" protecting the rest of society from potentially destructive expressions of his "natural" aggressive energy. In fact, he might say that in his present role of coach, he releases his aggressive energy as he watches football games and vicariously experiences the aggressive behaviors of players on the field. Ditka probably believes that for both participants and avid observers, football serves as a catharsis, to purge aggressive energy.

PROBLEMS WITH INSTINCT THEORY
The use of instinct theory to argue that sports control and moderate aggression in society suffers from the following four weaknesses.

First, research does not support the notion that aggressive behavior in humans is the product of biologically based destructive energy. Studies of behavior among insects, fish, birds, reptiles, and mammals have suggested that some aggression among *nonhuman species* may be grounded in instincts—but these studies are of little help in developing a theory of *human* aggression. Human behavior is much more complex than the behavior of other species, because it is grounded in a combination of culture, self-reflection, and ever-changing definitions and meanings. This means not that biology is irrelevant, but that the influence of biology in human behavior does not occur through instincts. In fact, even if someone could make a convincing case that humans do have aggressive instincts, this would tell us little about human behavior. We would still have to explain why rates of aggression vary from one group to another, why they vary over time in any single group, why aggression is highly correlated with certain social conditions, and why most human beings have to be coerced or socialized to behave in aggressive and violent ways. In fact, research suggests that the tendency for humans to cooperate is more common than any tendency to be aggressive (Kohn, 1986).

A *second* problem is that instinct arguments often assume that all sports are effective outlets for the presumed aggressive energies of both players and spectators. However, it is quite certain that different sports provide different opportunities to engage in aggressive behaviors. For example, some sports involve no direct physical contact between opponents, and provide few opportunities for players to engage in actual aggressive behavior. Much of what occurs in most sports, even in many power and performance sports, would be a poor substitute for real aggression. Furthermore, many athletes define their sport experiences in ways that de-emphasize or eliminate expressions of aggression. This is the dominant pattern in pleasure and participation sports, which have the goal of connecting with others as challenges are faced, rather than overpowering and dominating others in aggressive ways.

A *third* problem with instinct theory is that research does not support the idea that sport participation provides a catharsis for supposed instinct-based aggressive energy. Contrary to the predictions of instinct theory, numerous studies show that contact sports exist and thrive in the same societies that have high rates of aggression and violence. If sports served as a catharsis for aggressive energy, the studies would show the exact opposite!

Instead of allowing people to release the pent-up energy that instinct theorists say is the foundation of all aggression, contact sports seem to be expressions of the same cultural patterns and orientations that underlie warfare and high rates of murder, domestic violence, and assault. For example, in a carefully designed comparison of ten peaceful societies and ten societies with long traditions of fighting many wars, anthropologist Richard Sipes (1975, 1996) found that contact sports were popular in 90 percent of the warlike societies and in only 20 percent of the peaceful societies. This clearly contradicts the notion that contact sports serve a cathartic function for players or spectators.

Other studies have shown that homicide rates in the United States increase immediately after television broadcasts of highly publicized boxing matches (Phillips, 1983), and that military activity is positively related to the popularity of contact sports in countries participating in the Olympic Games (Keefer et al., 1983). Historical research in England shows a similar pattern: the level of violence in dominant sport forms has gone hand in hand with the level of violence in a particular society (Dunning, 1993). Sports do not seem to be "draining off" aggressive energy.

The *fourth* problem with instinct arguments is that they continually refer to the aggressive behavior of men, ignoring women and the ways presumed aggressive instincts and impulses might be released in the behavior of women. Women are not involved in warfare, group violence, or heavy contact sports to the same extent as men; what, then, are the outlets for their presumed aggressive instincts? If women turn aggressive energy inward, their suicide rates should be much higher than the rates for men—but this is not the case. If women are releasing their aggressive impulses in other ways, maybe men should use them as role models; it might make the world a safer place for all of us.

In summary, the instinct argument provides no valid support for the notion that sport participation can serve as a cure for violent behavior among athletes or spectators. However, this argument remains popular; many people still use what I call the "language of catharsis" in their everyday conversations about human behavior. We often hear references to "aggressive tendencies" and "releasing pent-up feelings of aggression"; the speakers fail to realize that the theoretical model on which they base their statements is faulty and invalid.

Frustration and Aggression

Some have argued that since aggression is frequently the result of frustration, and since frustration is "released" through sports, people would be less aggressive if they played and watched sports more frequently. Of course, it would be convenient if this were true—if we could deal with all of our feelings of frustration in such a way, and aggression could be controlled by having everyone play and watch sports. But there is no evidence that playing racquetball, soccer, or any other sport for an hour eliminates the sources of frustration in a person's life and makes the person less aggressive in the process. Playing sports may make us physically tired, and it may temporarily relieve feelings of frustration, but no matter how hard someone plays, the situation or person that was the source of frustration today will still be there tomorrow. Playing sports does not change the frustrating behaviors of other people or the sources of frustration at home or work.

How about the possibility that vigorous physical exercise in sports makes people less violent by producing physiological or biochemical changes in the body? This is an interesting possibility. People frequently say they "feel better"—more relaxed and less stressed—after vigorous physical exercise. Some even say they feel as though they have "released" tensions in their bodies. And in fact, research shows that among some people, vigorous exercise is associated with reductions in (1) muscular tension, (2) certain forms of anxiety, and (3) depression (Morgan, 1984). However, researchers do not know what causes these changes. Are they direct outgrowths of the *physiological and biochemical* consequences of exercise, or does strenuous physical exercise simply serve as a "time out" in the daily schedules of people who are temporarily bored, busy, or mildly depressed about how things are going in their lives? Furthermore, researchers do not know if any of the physical and psychological changes that accompany vigorous exercise actually reduce the occurrence of aggressive behaviors.

If the intent to do harm or inflict injury on others does decline after a person plays sports, this probably occurs because intense involvement in any activity can put *time* between a person and the frustrating conditions in the rest of life. During this period of time, people can calm themselves down or outline rational, nonaggressive strategies for dealing effectively with the sources of frustration in their lives. But the type of activity may not matter; playing a game of chess, meditating, or reading a good book could be as helpful as sports, *if* people became intensely involved in these activities. Of course, sports often are played *with friends;* this means that they provide social occasions in which frustrated people can receive advice from others on strategies for dealing with the sources of frustration at home or work. So in addition to providing a "time out," playing sports *may* involve social interaction that is likely to discourage the use of aggression in response to frustrations.

My guess is that we often see playing sports as a way to relieve frustration mainly because it involves intense concentration and often produces physical exhaustion. For most of us, participation in sports puts us in a setting separate from the more serious concerns of our daily existence; gyms, tracks, or golf courses often are worlds of their own. This, along with the heavy focus on physical movement and physical challenges, and the social interaction that often occurs while we participate, makes sport refreshingly unique in most of our lives. As a woman who recently took up boxing explains, "You're hitting a bag. You're not . . . in front of a television or reading a magazine. All that frustration from work, you're getting rid of it" (in Coleman, 1996). Of course, she does not claim that boxing eliminates the sources of frustration in her life, or that it makes her less aggressive; she just says boxing makes her feel less frustrated when she leaves the gym. And unless her fellow boxers tell her to punch her boss's lights out, she is likely to think of nonaggressive ways of handling things at work tomorrow.

However, not all people leave the gym less frustrated than they were when they came in. For example, those who use sports as a means of *proving* themselves rather than *expressing* themselves often discover that playing sports actually creates frustration in their lives. When these people lose or play poorly, they may leave the gym or playing field with more aggressive feelings than they had when they began their sport participation.

Just as there is nothing magic or automatic about playing sports and getting rid of frustrations, there is no evidence that *watching* sports

There is no evidence supporting the widespread belief that players in heavy contact sports experience a catharsis, or draining off, of aggressive energy that will make them less aggressive in other settings. (Rick Bowmer, AP/Wide World Photos)

serves to eliminate frustrations in the lives of spectators (Smith, 1983). Watching sports may temporarily distract people from the things causing them to be frustrated, but this does not necessarily make them more mellow and less aggressive in the rest of their lives.

In summary, it is difficult to argue that people can control aggression by using sports to release or eliminate frustrations. However, there is some support for the notion that sports can serve as a valuable "time out" separating people from the sources of frustration in their lives. We do not know at this point whether this makes them less aggressive. Nor do we know if this occurs on a collective level, so that rates of aggression in society as a whole would decline if sport participation were more widespread. Most existing evidence points against this possibility.

Learning to Control Aggression by Playing Sports

Another popular belief is that sport participation teaches people to control aggressive responses in the face of stress, defeat, hardship, and pain. In making this case, people often assume that the lessons people learn through enduring such negative conditions in sports will carry over to the rest of life and enable them to behave nonaggressively despite other types of adversity they might encounter.

Some research findings support this idea, but they must be interpreted carefully and critically. For example, Nosanchuk (1981) interviewed forty-two students in three traditional karate *dojos* (studios), and found that training in karate was negatively associated with scores on an aggressive fantasy test. However, the training emphasized nonviolence, mastery of skills, and self-defense; using karate as an offensive weapon was not allowed in the training. Similarly, in a study summarized in chapter 6 (pp. 164–66), Trulson (1986) found a decrease in aggressive tendencies among male juvenile delinquents who had received training in the philosophy and techniques of Tae Kwon Do. The philosophy emphasized respect for self and others, confidence, physical fitness, self-control, honor, patience, and responsibility. Trulson also found that similar young men who received training in Tae Kwon Do *without* the philosophy actually measured higher on aggressive tendencies after a training period, and that young men who participated in running, basketball, and football with standard adult supervision didn't change at all in terms of their aggressive tendencies.

One of the most provocative studies on this topic was done by French sociologist Loic Wacquant (1995). For over three years Wacquant trained and "hung out" at a traditional, highly structured, and reputable boxing gym in a black ghetto area in Chicago. During that time he observed, interviewed, and documented the experiences and lives of over fifty men who trained as professional boxers at the gym. He not only learned the craft of boxing, but also became immersed in the social world in which the boxers trained. He found that the particular social world formed around this gym was one in which the boxers learned to value their craft and become dedicated to the idea of being a professional boxer; they also learned to respect their fellow boxers and to accept the rules of sportsmanship that governed boxing as a profession. In a neighborhood where poverty and hopelessness promoted intimidation and violence all around them, these boxers accepted taboos on fighting outside the ring, avoided street fights, and internalized the controls necessary to follow a highly disciplined daily training schedule.

When Wacquant asked about the connection between boxing and violence, the responses he got tended to challenge popular beliefs. Here are three of them:

> Boxin' doesn't jus' teach you violence. I think, boxin' teaches you discipline an' self-respect an' it's also teachin' you how to defen' yourself, so, it's really great to box. It's a lot of fun. Anybody who feels that it teaches you violence is a person tha's really a, a *real incompetent mind* I think. Someone tha' their min's thinkin' real low (a twenty-four-year old night security guard from a black neighborhood who had trained at the gym for eight years and boxed as a middleweight, 1995: 494–95).

> It's a skill, it's a sport to be better than a person. I don't think violence and all, (shakes his head vigorously) I don't agree with that. I tell ya the truth: ever since I started boxing, I've been more of a mellow person. I've been more relaxed. Like I said, I'm not, all my aggressions are taken out. In the gym I work out, I come home, someone come up to me and say "yer an asshole," I'm like, (with a smirk) "you're right!" You know, I'm *mellowed out*. I'm way mellowed out (A twenty-four-year old light-heavyweight who was a truck driver from a white ethnic neighborhood, 1995: 498).

> Man, the sports commentators an' the writers and stuff, they don't know nuthin' abou' the boxin' game. *They ignorant.* I be embarrassed to let somebody hear me say (chuckles in disbelief), "Boxing teach you violence". . . . Tha's showin' *their* ignorance. For one thin', they lookin' at it from a spectator point of view. . . . on the *outsi' lookin' in*, but [the boxer's] *insi' lookin out* (A twenty-eight-year old lightweight, part-time janitor, seven years in the ring, 1995: 489).

I do not include these quotations here to promote professional boxing, a sport I think ought to be banned for health reasons. However, the statements, along with other information in the studies by Nosanchuk, Trulson, and Wacquant, suggest that participation in sports, even martial arts and boxing, can encourage individuals to control their aggression. But this control depends greatly on the conditions under which sport participation occurs. *If the*

Does participating in a sport such as boxing help some people learn to control the expression of aggression? This depends greatly on the conditions under which sport participation occurs, but it is possible. (Bob Jackson, *Colorado Springs Gazette*)

social world formed around a sport promotes a mind-set and a culture emphasizing nonviolence, self-control, respect for self and others, physical fitness, patience, and responsibility, then athletes *may* learn to control aggressive behavior. Those most likely to benefit seem to be young men who need structured challenges and firm guidance dedicated to making them respect themselves when they avoid aggression and violence.

However, such conditions do not regularly exist in many sports around the world. Instead, the mind-set that many athletes take on, and

the sport cultures in which they play, emphasize hostility, physical domination, and a willingness to sacrifice physical well-being for the sake of competitive success. This mind-set and the social world that forms in connection with it seem to promote aggression; control under these conditions would be likely only when there was a good chance that aggressive behaviors would bring penalties that interfered with winning.

Another obstacle that might prevent athletes from learning to control aggressive behaviors, even under the conditions identified in the studies described above, is the **hubris,** or pride-driven arrogance, that is sometimes created as athletes see themselves as separate from and superior to those who do not pay the price they pay to participate in their sports. This hubris can subvert the humility athletes need if they are to refrain from demonstrating their toughness through putting others down. And hubris also tends to attract challengers, those who would knock the arrogant athlete down a notch. For example, it is probably Dennis Rodman's hubris that leads him to find that "there are always people wanting to get in a fight with me" (cited in Leray, 1996). We discussed hubris in chapter 6, but it is clearly relevant in this discussion of aggression as well.

More studies are needed, especially those that dig into the social worlds of athletes in particular sports and outline the meanings athletes attach to their behaviors and to the place of aggression in their worlds. In the meantime, we should remember that the mere fact that a football player refrains from attacking a referee after a bad call does not mean that he has learned to control aggression when dealing with all authority figures in all situations. And the fact that a hockey player does not fight during a game does not mean the player will use the same restraint on the street after a game. Even if athletes do learn to control aggressive behaviors during a game or contest, we cannot assume that this control automatically carries over into the rest of life; carryover seems to depend on very specific conditions.

In summary, there is some evidence suggesting that athletes can, under special conditions, learn to control the expression of aggressive behaviors through their involvement in sports. There is no evidence that this occurs for spectators. For the most part, when athletes show control on the field, their behavior is based more on concern for winning games than on concern for the well-being of others. Of course, controlling aggression for any reason is good. But if an athlete is motivated solely by a concern for winning games, it is very doubtful that the nonagressive behavior will carry over into nonsport situations.

DO SPORTS PROMOTE AGGRESSION IN SOCIETY?

Those who argue that certain forms of sports increase rates of aggression in society generally base their case on the following beliefs:

1. Playing and watching competitive sports generates frustrations that give rise to aggressive behaviors.
2. Playing and watching certain types of sports leads people to define aggression and violence as useful tools for managing relationships and achieving success.
3. Power and performance sports, so common in many societies, emphasize dominance, and thereby perpetuate the notion that men are naturally superior to women because of their ability to be aggressive and violent.

We will discuss each of these points to evaluate the argument that sports promote aggression.

Sport Experiences, Frustration, and Aggression

Some athletes may love to play their sports so much that they never get frustrated when they play, even when they lose or play badly; and some spectators may be so taken in by the beauty of sports or the efforts of athletes that they feel no frustration when they watch a game or match. However, few people fit into these categories. Usually, athletes and spectators *are* concerned with outcomes, and they *do* see sports as a means of proving something to themselves or others. This means that frustration often accompanies sports participation (Dunning, 1993).

Although frustration does not always lead to aggression, it is most likely to do so when (1) the frustration gives rise to the emotion of *anger*, and (2) the situation contains *opportunities, stimulus cues,* and *social support* for aggressive

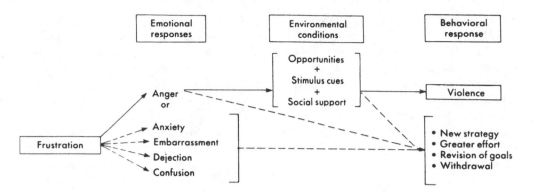

FIGURE 7-1   The link between frustration in the sport experience and the aggressive behavior of athletes.

behavior.* Figure 7-1 illustrates this chain of events. Just follow the solid line in the figure to see when aggression may occur in connection with the frustration experienced in sports. The broken lines indicate all of the possible nonaggressive responses that may follow frustration. These broken lines tell us the following things:

1. Anger is not the only emotion that a person may feel in connection with frustration; athletes may experience many other emotions that would lead to nonaggressive behaviors.
2. Even when it does occur, anger can be controlled or expressed in a wide range of nonaggressive behaviors.
3. The combination of anger, opportunities to be aggressive, stimulus cues (that is, things that can be used as tools for violence), and social support for aggression increase the likelihood of aggressive behaviors, but players still may choose nonaggressive behaviors for many reasons, including a fear of penalties and concern for the welfare of themselves and others.

Players are most likely to experience the emotion of *anger* when they feel they are victims of unfair calls by referees or unfair tactics by opponents (Mark et al., 1983). *Opportunities* to be

aggressive are most frequent in heavy-contact sports. *Stimulus cues* are strongest in sports in which athletes use equipment that can be associated with violence and transformed into weapons. And *social support* exists when athletes and spectators define their status and personal worth in terms of the ability to physically dominate others. Therefore, violence is most likely to be a problem in certain sports. For example, we would expect relatively high rates of violence in men's ice hockey, where physical contact affords opportunities, where hockey sticks can be defined and used as weapons, and where norms among athletes and many spectators celebrate toughness and a willingness to fight, seek retribution, and intimidate opponents (Gruneau and Whitson, 1993). Football also provides players with opportunities and social support to be violent, but stimulus cues are less apparent—except when the players see helmets as weapons. Baseball, although it involves little physical contact, provides pitchers with opportunities for violence, and baseballs in the hands of pitchers can be defined and used as weapons. However, social support for throwing at a batter's head or body is not exceptionally strong, since most players realize they too are potential targets each time they come to bat; in addition, most spectators are uncomfortable with the idea of throwing a rock-like object at a human being's head at 100 miles per hour.

---

*This framework builds on the research of Berkowitz, 1969.

As you think about other examples, remember that the combination of anger, opportunities, stimulus cues, and social support does not automatically lead to violence. This combination only increases the likelihood that violent forms of aggression will occur.

Figure 7-1 is also helpful in explaining aggressive behaviors among *spectators*. For frustration among fans to give rise to aggression, the following three things must happen:

1. There must be enough identification with players or teams to provide the basis for frustration in connection with their fate on the field of play.
2. When fans become frustrated, anger must be the dominant emotion they feel.
3. Opportunities for aggression, stimulus cues, and social support for acting aggressively must be present.

In many cases, individual spectators may not identify with players or teams to the extent that is necessary to produce frustration. However, when their identification is strong enough and when their frustration is followed by anger, the aggression of spectators is best prevented by the absence of opportunities, stimulus cues, and social support for aggressive actions (see Russell et al., 1988–89).

This frustration-aggression model has led to policies that (1) separate spectators from opposing teams during and after games, (2) prevent spectators from bringing to the arena objects that they can throw from the stands, and (3) emphasize an orderly flow of people around the arena. Contact between angered losers and exuberant winners creates obvious opportunities for violence. Objects that people can throw, such as bottles and cans, can become stimulus cues for violent behavior when an official makes a "bad call" or when players and coaches do not live up to expectations. And the absence of explicit behavioral guidelines for spectators increases the probability that some groups of fans will create their own ideas about how they should express their anger.

In summary, the playing and watching of sports does regularly generate frustration. Frustration *may* lead to aggression, but this occurs only under certain conditions. Rules in sports and sport facilities have been designed to limit the opportunities, stimulus cues, and social support for aggression among players and spectators. For example, use of the hockey stick, football helmet, or baseball as weapons brings heavy penalties in most cases. Even the use of intimidation has been regulated in some sports, although this is difficult to do.

Those who benefit from the popularity of certain sports are sometimes hesitant to make rules that discourage spontaneous displays of emotions by players and spectators. Most of us who enjoy sports would not like to see all such displays discouraged, even though we object to aggression on the field and in the stands.

Finally, there is little evidence that aggression resulting from sport-related frustration actually carries over into nonsport settings. There are cases of bar fights and domestic violence that might be related to such frustration, but there is no systematic research enabling us to say when and how often such carryover might occur.

Sport Participation and Learning to Use Aggression as a Strategy

NONCONTACT SPORTS In certain forms of noncontact sports, participants may intimidate their opponents verbally, but physical intimidation and violence is rare. When violence does occur, it is usually off the field of play, and generally punished with fines or other severe sanctions. For example, tennis players have been fined for slamming a ball to the ground in protest or talking to an official or opponent in a menacing manner. Players in noncontact sports are seldom, if ever, rewarded for aggressive behaviors. Therefore, it is doubtful that playing or watching these sports teaches people to use violence as a strategy on or off the field. If athletes in these sports act violently off the field, their actions may be related to events tied to their sport careers, the repressive control systems used by their coaches (or parents), their personal lives, or many other factors. But the violence is not likely to be grounded in what they have learned during sport participation.

Intimidation may be used in some noncontact sports. However, little has been written about the forms this intimidation takes or how it might be related to general forms of aggression outside sport settings. Some athletes say they use hatred to motivate themselves during competition, but it is not known if this is done in a way that might carry over into nonsport relationships and behaviors. For example, sprint cyclist and 1996 Olympic silver medalist Marty Nothstein uses the language of aggression and hatred when he describes how he approaches a race. He says, "I am really aggressive out there. I pretty much hate the guy I'm racing. It wouldn't matter if it were my brother. . . . I want to destroy the guy. End it quick. Boom. One knockout punch" (in Becker, 1996). Of course, cycling does not allow him to physically destroy or punch a competitor, and most cyclists don't have opportunities to express such feelings directly to those they race against. Does Nothstein carry these feelings off the track after a race? I doubt it, but we know little about this form of emotional compartmentalization in sports and its implications for behavior. Research is needed.

CONTACT SPORTS: MALE ATHLETES
Athletes in power and performance sports involving heavy physical contact often learn to use intimidation and violent behavior as strategies. It is widely believed that both can be used to win games and build high-profile personal and team reputations that strike fear in opponents and inspire awe among spectators. Evidence shows that male athletes in contact sports readily accept rule-violating behaviors and certain forms of violence, and that as the amount of contact increases in a sport, so does this acceptance (Bredemeier and Shields, 1983, 1984b, 1985; Pilz, 1996; Silva, 1983; Weinstein et al., 1995). Athletes often see intimidation and violent behavior as permissible, as long as they do not seriously disrupt the flow of action in the games or lead to injuries that affect players after games are over. Athletes routinely

"When are you gonna learn when it's necessary to use unnecessary roughness?"
....

In men's contact sports, players sometimes learn physical intimidation and violent behaviors as strategies. Both have been used to win games and build reputations.

....

disapprove of "cheap shots" done solely to hurt other players, but many have no reservations about hurting opponents in connection with legal tactics in a game. They don't intend to hurt, but they may not avoid hurting someone as they do what they feel they have to do to "take the guy out," "break up the double play," "stop the drive to the basket," etc. At this point, issues get fuzzy, since aggression is defined as involving *intent* to do harm. Intent is hard to prove, and it is often irrelevant, when athletes so totally and routinely ignore the well-being of others that injuries become inevitable and widespread. For this reason, I think it is necessary to define aggression to include actions based on a clear disregard for others, as well as on the intent to injure.

In heavy contact sports such as boxing, football, ice hockey, and rugby, intimidation and violence have become widely used as strategies for winning games, promoting individual careers, and increasing drama for spectators and profits for sponsors. For example, a professional hockey player explains, "[S]ometimes when you're losing or your team is flat, you need to rough it up a bit to give the other team a message . . . [Y]ou have to fight . . . [and] I'd like to think I helped our team to win some games because I did rough it up . . ." (cited in Swift, 1986). As long as this orientation exists among players, and as long as rules permit its expression in a sport, players will use violence and intimidation.*

Another hockey player, known for his aggressive style of play, explains, "I do whatever it takes. Whatever it takes to stop the other guy. Whatever it takes to win" (in Scher, 1993). He says that his goal is often to provoke another player to fight, but "I don't think I've ever intentionally tried to hurt someone—unless I got hurt myself. Then I try to get even." A football player also known for his aggressive style protested with the following words after the NFL fined him $30,000 in 1993 for "two acts of flagrant unnecessary roughness involving the use of his helmet":

> They're saying what I do is dirty and cheap, but I've played this way forever. I signed a million-dollar contract because of it. People cheer when I make a big hit. I mean, that's what I do (in Telander, 1993).

The same player also noted, "[on the field,] I don't see players, I see situations." And he explains his feelings when he makes a hit that devastates an opponent in terms that certainly imply aggressive intent:

> It's unbelievable. An orgasm. Euphoria. I don't know if you can put it into words. There is just a feeling of . . . power. For that split second of time you own that person. You are better. For just one moment, you know where you stand (in Telander, 1993).

The use of fines has been relatively effective in reducing brawling and certain forms of flagrant fouls, but players still may be encouraged by peers and coaches to engage in aggression on the field of play. For example, Pat Riley, a highly suc-

cessful NBA coach, has made it clear to his players that he will fine anyone who doesn't give a hard foul to an opponent driving to the basket, and that if they help an opponent up after knocking him to the floor, they will be fined $1,500 (Reilly, 1995). This, of course, is one of the ways that aggression comes to be an integral part of the game for many male athletes in contact sports. The message is clear: Be aggressive or get out. Not everyone associated with sports agrees with this message; many feel that Riley is out of line for fining his players when they are not aggressive. But others pay Riley $45,000 per appearance (in 1996 dollars) so that he can tell corporate executives how to be successful in business (O'Brien and Wolff, 1996).

Another example of the way aggression and aggressive strategies have been incorporated into the very structure of certain heavy contact sports is the existence of players who act as designated "enforcers" or "goons" or "hit men" on teams. These players are expected to intimidate, provoke, or injure opponents. They are paid to intimidate and to be violent. As one legendary NHL "enforcer" explains, "If I can make a highly skilled player . . . want to whack me instead of concentrating on getting a good shot, that's half the battle" (in Scher, 1993).

These "enforcers" and their aggressive acts are well known to other players. For example, one hockey player recently described a player on another team this way: "His job is to hurt people. He goes for the knees a lot. He takes runs at you, and really all he's trying to do is hurt you and knock you out of the game" (in Scher, 1993). In recent years ice hockey players have begun to ask questions about this strategy, because some of the game's most skillful and popular players have been sidelined by serious back injuries resulting from constant hits from behind. But there are still players who have based their careers on a willingness to inflict injuries on fellow players.

The role of "enforcer" has nothing to do with frustration or anger generated during a game. This is explained very clearly by a hockey player known for his fighting and violent behavior:

---

*The belief that fighting behavior can be used to win games is especially strong in hockey, but research by George Engelhardt (1993, 1995) shows that this belief does not fit the facts in the NHL.

I don't know if I ever really get all that mad. You have to have a clear head when you fight. You don't want to be swinging wildly. You try to aim at the nose or the chin, someplace where . . . it'll cause damage. Broken nose, broken jaw. . . . There's no sense getting into a fight if you're not trying to hurt them (cited in Swift, 1986).

The use of violence in men's contact sports is no secret, and it is not new. Journalists have described it, sociologists and psychologists have tried to explain it, and athletes have bragged, complained, and testified in court about it (Bloom and Smith, 1996; Goldstein, 1983; King, 1996; Morra and Smith, 1996; Scheinin, 1994; Smith, 1983). And whenever an athlete dies or is paralyzed by an aggressive act, the media run a series of self-righteous stories on violence in sports, asking if we've gone too far, if there is a need to pull in the reins, if violence is rampant in sports and in society. Although players do not always feel comfortable with the amount of violence in their sports, they generally have come to accept it. Even those who don't like it may use it reluctantly as a way of improving or maintaining their positions on teams and their popularity with spectators.

It seems that many boys and men in contact sports, even at beginning levels of competition, learn that they will be evaluated on their ability to use violence in combination with physical skills (Vaz, 1982; Weinstein et al., 1995). Those who identify with violent professional players will be even more aggressive in their own games (Smith, 1974). As they become more immersed in the social world of heavy contact sports, they are encouraged to be aggressive by peers and teammates, and sometimes by coaches and parents (Smith, 1983; Bloom and Smith, 1996). In fact, their character may come to be defined in terms of their ability to do violence on the field. For example, many rookies at top levels of competition are subjected to aggressive treatment by teammates and opponents to "see if they have what it takes to be one of us." Learning to "take it and give it back" in aggressive ways is, in a sense, an expression of conformity to the sport ethic, and over-

Establishing an identity as an athlete may involve being willing to take risks and to do violence to others. This young man displays symbols on his helmet showing that he is willing to use intimidation, if not violence, to dominate others. (Jay Coakley)

conformity to this aspect of the sport ethic is common. This overconformity gives rise to a language or discourse that extols a willingness to "put it all on the line," to "sacrifice," to "give your body," to "never back down," to "show what you're made of," to "be tough." As some young men try to earn identities as athletes, their behavior becomes increasingly and consistently more aggressive. By the time they reach top levels of competition, they seemingly don't even give violence a second thought during a game. In fact, many male athletes come to see aggression as a "natural" part of their sport and a "natural" part of who they are as athletes. As a result, they often resist efforts to reduce aggression on the field.

Of course, sports, even contact sports, do not have to be played this way—but external efforts to control aggressive behaviors are made very cautiously. Team owners, coaches, television commentators, and sponsors seldom say a discouraging word. Rules may be enacted to make certain forms of aggression illegal, and players who break the rules may be fined. But violent incidents are replayed in numerous slow-motion shots during and after games, and then included in special videotapes sold to fans who want to see the aggressive acts, filmed with high-speed cameras and zoom lenses, over and over again. To intensify the drama associated with aggressive action, some videos even have the actual sounds of bodies colliding, bones and tendons snapping on impact, and players gasping in effort and pain.

The underlying message in these videos is this: "This is really what the game is about; see it up close and personal, so you can get a feel for the violence and the crazy men who engage in it." For example, the narrative in *The Hidden NFL*, a video used to recruit new subscribers to *Sports Illustrated*, proudly announces, "We have revealed a side of pro football that is savage." The footage of game action along the line of scrimmage (referred to as the "pit") is introduced with this statement: "There is more violence per square foot in the pit than anywhere in sport." And as if these words don't praise violence enough, the narrator continues, "It is only through [special video technology] that the savagery of these raging struggles can actually be seen." An interview with a player then confirms the reality of the violence being presented; he proudly declares: ". . . there's things going on in there that would be illegal off the football field. I mean you can literally kill someone with the things we're doin' in there." As he talks, it is easy to see the hubris underlying his description of what he does on the football field; he knows he is set apart because of his willingness and ability to do violence.

Of course, confusion occurs when these very players are fined for their violent behavior (King, 1996). It seems that those who control certain sports are ambivalent about the issue of violence: they say they are against it and fine players who are especially violent, but they also produce and sell for a profit special videos that highlight the exact aggressive acts they have fined! It appears that in some cases, violence increases spectator enjoyment (Bryant et al., 1997; DeNeui and Sachau, 1996; Zillman, 1996), and that those who profit from that enjoyment allow and even encourage violence on the playing field.

Do violent strategies learned in sports carry over to the rest of life? This is the question we asked at the beginning of this section. Research clearly shows that many male athletes in heavy contact sports learn to accept and use violence and intimidation as strategies during competition. But does this learning carry over into the rest of their lives? Does sport participation make them more aggressive people? It would seem that most athletes are capable of distinguishing between the playing field and other types of interaction settings. And most realize that the aggressive strategies they use in their sports are not appropriate in the classroom, in a bar, or on the streets. However, the violent off-the-field reputations of some athletes, along with a number of highly publicized court cases involving athletes charged with violent acts, suggest that this is a possibility—especially in the case of athletes in elite, heavy contact power and performance sports. As John Niland, a former lineman for the Dallas Cowboys of the NFL, says, "Any athlete who thinks he can be as violent as you can be playing football, and leave it all on the field is kidding himself" (in Falk, 1995).

Research on the carryover issue is difficult to do, and it must be carefully designed. Even if data show a high rate of off-the-field aggression among athletes, this does not mean that they learned their aggressive behavior patterns in sports. It is possible that people who choose to play heavy contact sports are more likely than others to see aggression as an appropriate way to deal with life events. But their playing of contact sports may not make them any more aggressive than they would have been if they had not played

TANK MᶜNAMARA®

by Jeff Millar & Bill Hinds

.... Data on sexual assault are often confusing. Although sexual assault is a problem that goes far beyond sports in U.S. culture, research on the social worlds created around sports may provide deeper understanding of the cultural dynamics underlying assaultive behaviors. Ignoring the problem or explaining it away, as this team spokesman is trying to do, will only confuse things more.

....

sports. Furthermore, athletes with reputations for being aggressive on the playing field might receive extra encouragement from people outside of sports to be violent on the streets. They may even be challenged to get involved in fights because of their reputations in sports. If this is the case, researchers must be careful in deciding whether the off-the-field behavior patterns of athletes are learned in sports and then carried over into other situations, or are grounded in other factors.

Research by Gordon Bloom and the late Michael Smith (1996) helps us begin to deal with these questions. In their study, older players in elite, highly competitive ice hockey programs approved of violence in settings apart from sports and engaged in violence when they played other sports more often than those who played hockey in less competitive recreational programs and those who did not play hockey at all. But the older athletes in the elite, highly competitive hockey programs had lower rates of fighting with family members than did the recreational players and those who did not play hockey. Unfortunately, Bloom and Smith did not take into account the possibility that men who are already

aggressive might select themselves into highly competitive ice hockey programs. Nor could they identify what it is about elite, competitive hockey that might lead men to approve of aggression or to be more aggressive in other sports. And why were they less likely to fight with family members?

More research is needed. But my guess is that studies will not tell us much unless they focus on issues related to sport participation, identity, group dynamics among and around athletes, ideological issues, and social factors associated with the incidence of violence. We need to know more about the social worlds created around certain sports and certain groups of athletes, and about the connection between those social worlds and other aspects of community life. The aggression and violence learned in certain sports does not inevitably carry over to other relationships and settings. Instead of looking for carryover, perhaps we should look for "cultural connections" between sport worlds and the ideas and relationships that encourage the incidence of aggression. Those "cultural connections" are likely to involve gender, ethnic, and class relations, among other factors.

How is violence connected with ideas about masculinity and race? We cannot separate carryover questions about sports and violence from the cultural connections between sports and the formation of popular ideas about gender and race. According to many social scientists, dominant forms of sports in most societies have been constructed in ways that not only celebrate aggression, but also tie the expression of aggression to dominant forms of masculinity (see Bryson, 1987; Connell, 1987a, b; Messner, 1992, 1994; Messner and Sabo, 1992; Sabo, 1994; Weinstein et al., 1995). The ability to "do" violence has become a part of gaining respect as a "man" within many male groups. This is especially true in certain sports. Sociologist Mike Messner explains:

> Young males come to sport with identities that lead them to define their athletic experience differently than females do. Despite the fact that few males truly enjoy hitting and being hit, and that one has to be socialized into participating in much of the violence commonplace in sport, males often view aggression, within the rule-bound structure of sport, as legitimate and "natural" (p. 67).

In fact, Messner explains that many male athletes learn not to see injurious acts as violence, even when they are done with intent to hurt, as long as they are within the rules of the game and as long as they are not motivated by anger.

This orientation makes contact sports especially dangerous places to be, but many men choose to be there because they have learned to define masculinity in terms of being tough enough to participate in the give-and-take of violent confrontations. Some even have learned to use a language that labels unaggressive men as "pussies," "ladies," "fags," or "wimps." In fact, these misogynist and homophobic labels may be used by some men in sport to indicate that someone does not have what it takes to be one of them, to be a part of the *male* world of sport. And when the give-and-take of violence leads to injury and pain, some men learn to "suck it up" and stay in the game, not just because of what it means to be an athlete, but because of what it means to be a

man in their social world. In fact, those men who are desperate to avoid labels that challenge their masculinity can be encouraged to do extremely violent things on the playing field. Of course, as long as men do not question this self-destructive way of defining masculinity on and off the playing field, aggression will remain linked with gender.

Issues of masculinity often overlap with racial issues when it comes to aggression in sport. For example, Messner's study led him to conclude that some black male athletes capitalize on the racist stereotypes held by whites by presenting a "bad-assed" image to intimidate competitors. This is explained by one of the men he interviewed:

> I'm tall, I'm thin, I'm a black person with a shaved head, and I'm fearful [looking]. You have to intimidate mentally . . . [Y]ou've got to talk shit in this game, you have to say, . . . "If you come close to me, I'm gonna hurt you!"

This statement illustrates how race and masculinity get tied together for some athletes, and it also shows that the connection between gender and race relations can encourage the incidence of violence in sports.

The connection between sports and violence in society as a whole seems to depend on whether sports perpetuate ideas about masculinity and race that permit and promote violence in off-the-field relationships and situations (Young and Smith, 1988). As we noted in chapter 6, the norms and group dynamics in certain all-male sport groups encourage athletes to demean and humiliate others who don't come close to matching what they see as their own unique, elite status. Under certain conditions, women and gay men become targets of such humiliation. Still, even when violent behaviors occur in connection with these norms and group dynamics, we cannot necessarily say that they are carried over from the strategies learned in sports. It would be more accurate to say that the violence is grounded in complex processes related to the hubris developed among athletes, the general separation of athletes from the rest of the community, and social relations revolving around gender, sexual orientation, and race.

Overall, I think it is necessary for all of us to critically assess how men play dominant forms of heavy contact sports. We should raise questions about how those sports can be made safer, how aggression in the sports can be controlled more effectively, how athletes can be encouraged to focus on skill development while still respecting the well-being of teammates and opponents, and how athletes can be connected meaningfully with the rest of the community. But a close examination of the carryover hypothesis requires that we also look beyond sports and consider questions about identity, masculinity, and racism in society.

CONTACT SPORTS: FEMALE ATHLETES
Information on violence among girls and women in contact sports is scarce. When sociologist Michael Smith (1983) reviewed research on this topic in the early 1980s, he concluded that women's participation in contact sports was steadily increasing, and that women in those sports did engage in aggressive behaviors. However, the studies did not enable him to make conclusions about whether aggression among women athletes was increasing over time or about the dynamics underlying the aggression.

Since the early 1980s, research findings on this issue have been confusing. This is the case partly because researchers have gathered data from women participating in a wide variety of sport programs at different levels of competition. Women's programs have undergone many changes over the past twenty-five years; they have become more competitive, they are more likely to involve an emphasis on power and performance, and the stakes associated with success have increased considerably. And women athletes vary greatly in terms of how they link sport participation to their identities and how their achievements are perceived and rewarded by others. At this point we know that as the level of competition gets higher, and as women become increasingly immersed in the social world of elite sports, they become more tolerant of rule violations and aggressive behaviors on the playing field. But this pattern is less clear among women than it is among men (Nixon, 1996a, b; Shields and Bredemeier, 1995; Shields et al., 1995). And we know next to nothing about whether such orientations carry over to and inform behaviors outside of sports.

We do know that women can be aggressive in and outside of sports, but generally have lower rates of aggression than men in most comparable situations. Research suggests that "there is no known biological reason that women cannot be as physically aggressive as men"—in other words, there's nothing about a woman's biology, brain, or hormones that prevents aggression from occurring (Dunn, 1994). But most girls and women become involved and learn to participate in sports in ways different from those of most boys and men. As they compete at higher and higher levels, women seem to become similar to men in the way they embrace the sport ethic and use it to frame their self-definitions as athletes. Like men, they are willing to take risks, make sacrifices, pay the price, and play with pain and injury. But unlike men, women do not link toughness, physicality, and aggression to their gender identities; the ability to do violence is seldom linked to femininity. For example, coaches do not try to motivate women by urging them to "go out and prove who the better woman is" on the field. Women athletes do not see their ability to be aggressive in sports as an indicator of their femininity and womanhood. And at this point in time, women seem to be less likely than men to act as if they "own" an opponent they have just defeated in a race or game; they don't seem to use expressions of control and dominance the way some male athletes do.

What we need are studies to see if elite women athletes develop the same forms of hubris (pride-based arrogance) that many elite male athletes seem to develop, and if so, how they link it to their identities and how they express it on and off the field. Do they do "in-your-face dominance dances" over opponents they intentionally knock down in contact sports? Do they talk trash, and is their trash talk filled with references to dominating and controlling

Both men and women are capable of aggressive behaviors. However, they may not link those behaviors to their identities in the same ways. What vocabulary and discourse do women boxers and women in other contact sports use to explain their involvement and achievements in sports? Do they use references to domination and control to the same extent that men do? (Ken Regan, Camera 5)

opponents? Do their vocabulary and discourse about sports, sport achievements, and relationships to others on the playing field contain references to domination and control? If so, does this carry over to nonsport relationships and settings? Research suggests that this is not the case (Nelson, 1994; Theberge, 1995; Young and White, 1995), but more information is needed.

Sports, Violence, and the Gender Order

"Men are naturally superior to women." This statement will arouse anger among many people today. But some still believe it, and when the believers defend their position, they often turn to sports to get "proof" of so-called male superiority. For example, J. Carroll, a physical educator in England, has argued that women are by nature tender, nurturant, and compassionate, and that when women participate in sports they go

against nature and destroy the political and military values that define what he thinks sports and masculinity are all about (Carroll, 1986). For this reason, Carroll even argues that women ought to be excluded from playing sports; he doesn't want to defy "Mother Nature."

The irony in this approach is that if gender differences in behavior were really grounded in biology and nature, there would be no need for them to be taught and preserved through sports; they would just "come naturally" to males and females. But the behaviors of males and females don't come naturally, so those who believe in so-called "natural" differences often use sport examples to emphasize the physical power and strength of men. Sociologist Michael Messner discovered this when he asked a thirty-two-year-old man in a professional job what he thought about the recent promotion of a woman to a high position in his organization. The man replied with these words:

> A woman can do the same job I do—maybe even be my boss. But I'll be *damned* if she can go out on the [football] field and take a hit from Ronnie Lott (1992: 168; note that Lott was a football player with a reputation for hitting others very hard).

Messner noted that even though this man could not "take a hit" from the NFL defensive back (Lott) either, he identified with Lott as a man, and then he used that identification to explain that men were superior to women because of men's ability to do violence.

This way of thinking about men and gender relations is strongly related to child abuse, spouse abuse, rape, gang rape, assault, and murder in societies around the world. The idea that power, strength, and a nature-based tendency to be aggressive are the basis for male privilege and superiority has been challenged by many people, but sports continue to be used to promote this idea in the minds of many men *and* women. This is the reason some men celebrate sports in which aggression is commonplace. They want to keep alive the notion of "difference" because it privileges them in the gender order. These are usually the same people who reject rules against fighting and other forms of violence by saying, "We can't turn our sport into a girls' game." For example, when rules were passed recently to partially limit fighting in hockey, Tie Domi, a hockey player with a reputation for being aggressive, complained:

> If you take out fighting, what comes next? Do we eliminate checking? Pretty soon, we will all be out there in dresses and skirts (1992).

Domi's point is that unless men can do violence in hockey, there will be nothing that makes them different from women, and nothing is worse than being like women—except perhaps being gay.

The other side of the gender order issue is that women who enter sports and play them as aggressively as men show that women can be tough and strong. On the one hand, this contradicts the traditional idea that women are frail and vulnerable, and it disrupts the aspect of male dominance expressed in Domi's statement. On the other hand, when women include violence in their sports, they reaffirm an aspect of the power and performance approach to sports that has developed around the values and experiences of men. This can be a problem, because values and experiences that have emphasized the use of aggression to dominate others in and out of sports have worked to the disadvantage of many women. In fact, they have led to behaviors that put women in hospitals and domestic violence shelters. This means that women should be careful not to buy into the same aggressive orientations used by some men in sports; it is important for women to find ways to be strong and tough without being aggressive and violent. Nancy Lieberman-Cline, a TV sportscaster and former pro basketball player, raised this issue in 1996 when she said, "I think the biggest problem in women's athletics is that we look at the guys and want to do it their way. . . . It worries me to see these girls impressed by the fighting. . . ."

We will say more about these issues in later chapters, but here it is important to see that some people have used sports with high rates of aggression as "proof" that men are superior to women because of their ability to do violence. Does this help set the stage for high rates of certain forms of violence in society as a whole? It probably does, but the influence of sports in this process is clearly tied to the dynamics of the gender order as a whole in society.

Aggression in the forms of violence and intimidation occurs in certain sports, especially those involving physical contact. Aggression originates in some combination of (1) frustration coupled with anger, opportunities, stimulus cues, and social support; (2) strategies used by athletes and encouraged by peers, parents, coaches, spectators, and sponsors; and (3) definitions of masculinity emphasizing violence as a basis for becoming a man and being superior to women. However, at this point, evidence indicating that athletes use violence in nonsport settings *because of* their experiences in sport is weak. This is not to say carryover never happens, but we have no

The connection between violence and masculinity runs deep in some cultures. This connection often carries over into sports in symbolic and expressive forms. Among certain groups of men, the willingness to engage in violence is a basis for status among peers. (Jay Coakley)

convincing proof that it occurs regularly or in an identifiable pattern.

Another variable that might be related to aggression in sports is the great insecurity associated with being an athlete on a highly competitive sport team. The idea that "you're only as good as your last game" is widespread. This means that each player's personal feelings of worth and status as a team member are constantly threatened in many sport settings. Under these circumstances, athletes are often willing to take extreme measures to "prove" themselves, even if the measures involve violence. Therefore, violence becomes a means for athletes to prove their worth and establish membership on their teams. In the case of men, it also becomes a way to reaffirm their masculine identity. This is the reason injuries that force a player to quit during a game often become defined as indicators of personal failure. But if the player remains in the game, injuries become "badges of courage"; for men, they also become badges of "manhood."

Within the social context of the team, the willingness to face and use violence and to endure its consequences creates an intense drama and excitement that can facilitate strong emotions among the members of a team. The sharing of these emotions creates bonds that athletes perceive as special. In fact, some ex-athletes talk about their sport experiences and relationships with old teammates in the same way that war veterans talk about old military buddies and battlefield relationships. Despite the pain and injuries they still may carry with them, they claim that the risks and relationships associated with sport participation made them feel alive and aware in ways that nonathletes simply cannot understand. As long as athletes feel this way, they will continue to define violence as behavior that adds to their lives rather than restricting, limiting, and sometimes ending their lives.

SPORTS AND AGGRESSION AMONG SPECTATORS

Do sports influence or incite aggressive behaviors among spectators? This question is important, because sports and sport events capture considerable public attention in communities around the world; spectators number in the billions. To answer this question, we must distinguish between watching sports on television and attending events in person.

The Effects of Watching Sports on Television

Most sport watching occurs in front of the television. Television viewers may be emotionally expressive during games and matches. They may even get angry. But they are not likely to be aggressive with the friends and family members watching with them. When TV viewing occurs in more public settings such as bars or pubs, most viewers are supportive of one another and restrict their emotional expressions to verbal comments. When they do express anger, they nearly always direct it at the characters in the mediated event, not at fellow viewers. Coaches, referees, and players are the targets of hostile remarks, and the emotional intensity of the remarks often is defused by other people who make humorous statements, or try to calm their emotional friend, or order another round of drinks. Even when fellow viewers define emotional displays as too loud or inappropriate, their efforts to settle a fan down are supportive rather than aggressive. When fans from opposing teams are in the same bar, there are usually other sources of mutual identification that keep them from identifying each other as targets of aggression. And they tend to confine expressions of their differences to verbal comments.

Only rarely do fans express anger and other emotions associated with watching sports in a bar or other public place in the form of aggression or violence. When such expression does occur, it usually takes the form of a "celebratory riot" on the streets (Murphy et al., 1990). These riots, some of which have been very destructive, occur after victories in championship games marking the end of long seasons or tournaments. However, as communities have learned to anticipate these potentially destructive displays, preventive measures have been used to limit and control them. Team officials and high-profile team members make pregame statements that encourage emotional control. These statements often associate "good behavior" with allegiance to the team and the community it symbolizes. A strategic police presence on the streets and appropriately nonaggressive policing methods also have become effective and widely used tactics. In most situations, this combination of internal, fan-based control and external, community-based control has been effective in discouraging celebratory riots among fans watching events on television.

VIOLENCE AS MEDIA ENTERTAINMENT AND ENTERTAINERS AS MODELS It is well known that people who watch sports enjoy action, drama, suspense, conflict, and highly motivated performances by athletes (Bryant et al., 1994; DeNeui and Sachau, 1996; Coakley, 1989). But we should be cautious about using this fact to conclude that media audiences hope to see violence, or that watching violence in

sports makes them more violent in their personal lives. It is doubtful that more than a small number of media spectators would be entertained by regularly watching random or blatantly irrational displays of violence in sports. The shock value of such incidents may be high, and people may talk about them in their accounts of games, but most do not see them as entertaining in themselves. For example one car accident offers drama; accident after accident with death after death would evoke more outrage than excitement.

When studying this issue, Michael Smith (1983) asked young hockey fans in Canada, most of whom watched games on TV, what they thought about the fighting in professional hockey games. Of the 756 young people interviewed, 60 percent of those who played hockey and 87 percent of those who did not wanted *less* fighting in professional games. Only 2 percent of the entire sample wanted more fighting. Of course, when fights do occur in televised sports, they attract attention. But this does not mean that viewers are automatically incorporating violence into their own lives, or that they approve of violence in a moral sense, or even that they look forward to seeing violence in future sports coverage.

The experience of watching sports on television is tied to a complex combination of social, emotional, and cognitive processes. For example, viewers are entertained by suspense (Bryant et al., 1994), and suspense is increased when play is rough and players are giving their all in a closely contested game or match. It is likely that many spectators view roughness and certain forms of aggression in sports as an indication of real commitment and desire on the part of the players, of their wholehearted efforts to achieve victory. But I hypothesize that when aggression and violent acts interfere with goal achievement or disrupt action, most spectators do not define them as entertaining. Therefore, when a player on a fan's favorite football team makes a bone-breaking legal tackle that stops the opposition from scoring the winning touchdown, the fan voices support for the effort and the action; but when the same player brutally hits someone with a cheap shot or starts a fight that leads to a penalty and disrupts the game for ten minutes, the TV fan is not entertained. The average fan is looking for dramatic suspense and highly motivated, goal-directed action, not violence for the sake of violence.

TV sports announcers realize these things and work hard to provide commentary that emphasizes drama, roughness, and suspense during the events. Their orchestrated excitement generally contributes to a positive entertainment experience, even when viewers know that the commentary contains exaggerations and questionable statements about what is actually occurring on the field of play or in the minds of players. Viewers want to be entertained, and generally appreciate excited announcers and emotion-packed commentary, even when the game is pretty ordinary. However, this does not mean that they are entertained simply by watching or hearing commentary about aggression and violence.

Finally, research shows that watching aggression in sports does not have short- or intermediate-term effects on the way people play sports themselves, unless the viewers strongly identify with aggressive players and then play in situations in which they have opportunities to imitate their models (Smith, 1983). This form of imitation seems to occur often enough for it to be a problem in certain sports, and there is a need to discourage violence among both potential models and potential imitators (Young and Smith, 1988). There is also some evidence that short-term effects may exist when people who are already angered, view aggressive acts on TV; these results may not be reliable, however, because they were obtained in lab studies rather than in everyday life settings (Russell et al., 1988–89). There may be long-term general effects of watching aggression in sports, but they are difficult to identify in research. Watching certain sports may be associated with aggressive behavior in society, but it probably doesn't cause this behavior. As I noted earlier in the chapter, the

"Hey, watch it, pal! You stepped on my foot."

The language used in association with sports often refers to violence, but we do not know if such language actually incites violent behavior.

causes of violence are more likely to be grounded in gender, racial or ethnic, and class relations than in watching athletes tackle one another in televised games.

The Effects of Attending Sport Events in Person

Spectators attending sport events, especially noncontact sport events such as golf, tennis, swimming, gymnastics, bowling, track and field, and figure skating, are generally well-behaved. They may be emotionally expressive, but cases of overt aggressive behavior directed at fellow fans, players, coaches, referees, ushers, or police are very rare. The attack and wounding of Monica Seles in 1993 stands out as one of the only incidents in such sports of spectator violence beyond the hostile words or minor pushing and shoving that may result when, for example, one fan drops a drink into another fan's lap. Those who watch contact sports are more vocal and emotional, but they too are usually not violent.

Studies of fan behavior show that "the typical sports fan manages his or her emotions admirably. He or she may yell and stomp the ground, but, after the game, he or she will usually be no more vicious than after an exciting movie or a stimulating concert" (Zillman et al., 1983). This pattern generally has existed through recent history (Guttmann, 1986). However, media reports of violent behavior at sport events around the world have led many people to conclude that spectator violence is quite common and very serious. There is no doubt that when deaths, injuries, and property damage occur, the actions of spectators should cause grave concern. But considering the number of events held every week, the record of behavior among sport fans is surprisingly nonviolent. It seems that the vast majority of fans focus on the event and have fun with those sitting around them. As they watch, they generally conform to and enforce informal norms that discourage behaviors interfering with their enjoyment. Aggressive acts that would disrupt games, matches, meets, or races also are discouraged under most circumstances. But there *are* exceptions to these patterns, which we will discuss below.

When spectators do engage in violence, their behavior is related to three sets of factors:

1. the action in the sport event itself
2. crowd dynamics and the situation in which the spectators watch the event
3. the historical, social, economic, and political context in which the event is planned and played

VIOLENCE AND ACTION IN THE EVENT Research indicates that spectator violence is related to the actions of players during an event. If players' actions are *perceived* as violent, spectators are more likely to engage in violent acts during and after games (Berkowitz, 1972a; Smith, 1983). This point is important, because the perceptions of spectators often are influenced by the ways in which events are promoted. If an event is promoted for its potentially violent content, spectators are more likely to perceive violence during the event itself, and then they are more likely to be violent themselves. This leads some people, including me, to argue that promoters and the media have a responsibility to advertise events in terms of the action and drama expected, not the blood and violence.

Another important factor in the event is the action of the officials. If referees or umpires make calls defined as unfair by the vast majority of spectators, the likelihood of violence increases (Mark et al., 1983; Murphy et al., 1990). Research on this issue is needed, but it seems that when fans believe a crucial goal or a victory has been "stolen" by a clearly incompetent or unfair call by an official, they are more likely to engage in violent acts during or following the event. This is the reason it is important to have competent officials at crucial games and matches, and the reason it is important for them to control game events so that actions that may be perceived as violent are held to a minimum. The knowledge that fan aggression may be precipitated by a crucial call late in a close, important contest puts heavy responsibility on the shoulders of the officials.

VIOLENCE, CROWD DYNAMICS, AND SITUATIONAL FACTORS The characteristics of a crowd and the immediate situation associated with a sport event also influence behavior patterns among spectators. Spectator violence is likely to vary with one or more of the following factors:*

- the size of the crowd and the standing or seating patterns among spectators
- the social composition of the crowd (age, sex, socioeconomic characteristics, and racial/ethnic mix are often important)
- the importance of a victory or the meaning of the event for one or both opponents
- the history of the relationship between the teams and groups of spectators attending the event
- the system of crowd control used at the event (police, attack dogs, or other security measures)

---

*See Armstrong and Harris, 1991; Giulianotti et al., 1994; Goldstein, 1988–89; Guttmann, 1986; Murphy et al., 1990; Pearton, 1990; Smith, 1983; Taylor, 1992; Wann, 1993; Williams et al., 1984.

- the amount of alcohol consumed by the spectators
- the location of the event (that is, a neutral location versus the home site of one of the opponents)
- the motivations among spectators for attending the event
- the extent to which the team and its success symbolize important aspects of fan identity—class identity, ethnic or national identity, regional or local identity, club or gang identity, etc.

We will not discuss each of these factors in detail, but the following comparison of two game situations illustrates how many of them might be related to the incidence of spectator violence.

The *location of an event* is important because it has implications for the form of transportation used by spectators. This means that an NFL football game played in San Francisco between the 49ers and the Miami Dolphins is very different from a soccer game played in Manchester, England, between Manchester United and Liverpool. Few Miami fans can attend the game in San Francisco, and those who do make the trip are likely to keep a low profile because they don't have many allies from Miami around them. Furthermore, Candlestick Park in San Francisco is best reached by car, which means that spectators go to the game in small groups and, in most cases, will not be drinking heavily during the drive. Game tickets cost thirty to sixty dollars each so those going to the game are middle-class or upper-middle-class citizens who probably have much to lose if they are arrested.

On the other hand, it is only a 20-mile train ride from Liverpool to Manchester. The soccer teams in both these cities have existed for about one hundred years, and the rivalry between them has a long tradition; some fans may feel they have scores to settle from past games and encounters. When they play each other, thousands of fans for the visiting team fill dozens of train cars to make the trip to the game. Game tickets are reasonably priced, so many spectators are

young working-class men. In fact, soccer has special meaning among many of these men, and relatively few women attend games. Large groups of young male fans arrive together in the train station of the host city. Drinking may be heavy; fans wear scarves and "colors" to identify team loyalties; and many of them, especially young males looking for action, want to make their presence known as they arrive and make their way to and into the stadium.

This sets up a completely different set of crowd dynamics from those in San Francisco. The crowd dynamics at the soccer game in Manchester are more likely to foster violence than the crowd dynamics at the NFL game in San Francisco.

The *system of crowd control* used during events also may influence spectator behavior. For example, some British soccer stadiums have been fortified to look and feel more like jails than sport facilities. Although there are efforts to change this at many stadiums, the security systems of the past often included 12-foot fences, barbed-wire barriers around the stadium and between sections within the stadium, tightly segregated seating that restricted movement, one-way turnstiles and gates that often were guarded or locked, police patrols around the field and through the stands, and few amenities to meet the needs and interests of the spectators. This approach to crowd control not only makes the spectators, most of whom are working-class males, feel like outsiders, but it also fosters a siege mentality that encourages defensiveness, if not violent confrontations. One observer has commented, "Build a cage to hold a person and that person is likely to act like a caged animal" (Guttmann, 1986).*

---

*The causes of violence at British soccer games, and at games in Europe and South America, are far too complex to explain in this chapter. Those interested in this phenomenon should consult the following: Adang, 1993; Armstrong, 1994; Buford, 1991; Giulianotti, 1994; Giulianotti et al., 1994; Haynes, 1993; Murphy et al., 1990; Pearton, 1990; Pilz, 1996; Roversi, 1994; Taylor, 1992; Williams et al., 1984. Spectator violence is a complex phenomenon, and these sources offer varied and sometimes contradictory explanations for why it occurs and what it involves.

Crowd size and composition also influence crowd dynamics. This is not to say that big, homogeneous crowds are especially prone to violence. However, when a crowd is made up almost exclusively of young, working-class men, many of whom are looking for action and memorable experiences, and when the stadium is packed with people representing opposing teams, officials reasonably should be prepared for confrontations, if not violent incidents. These incidents can take numerous forms: celebratory riots among the fans of the winning team, fights between fans of opposing teams, random property destruction carried out by fans of the losing team as they leave town, panics incited by some perceived threat unrelated to the event itself, isolated attacks on a referee who makes an unpopular call, or planned confrontations between groups using the event as a convenient place to face off with each other as they seek to enhance their status and reputations, or as they reaffirm their ethnic, political, class, national, local, or gang identities.

Whenever thousands of people get together for an occasion intended to generate collective emotions, it is not surprising that crowd dynamics and circumstances influence the behavior of individuals and groups. This is especially true at sport events, and sometimes violence among spectators is the result. After it starts, this violence can be particularly destructive, because it is fueled by what some social psychologists call *emotional contagion*. This is especially the case in panic situations. In other words, when circumstances are confusing, people look to one another for cues as to how to feel and how to behave. As they see others acting in extreme ways, they may follow suit, if they think extreme behavior is warranted.

VIOLENCE AND THE OVERALL CONTEXT IN WHICH THE EVENT OCCURS
Sport events do not occur in social vacuums. When spectators attend events, they bring with them the histories, issues, controversies, and ideologies of the communities and societies in which they live. They may be racists who want to harass those they identify as targets for discrimination. They may come from ethnic neighborhoods and want to express and reaffirm their ethnicity. They may resent negative circumstances in their lives and want to express their bitterness. They may be members of groups or gangs in which status is gained partly through fighting. They may be powerless and alienated and looking for ways to be noticed and defined as socially important. They may be young men who believe that manhood is achieved through violence and domination over others. Or they may be living lives so devoid of significance and excitement that they want to create a memorable occasion they can boastfully discuss with friends for weeks and years to come. In other words, when thousands of spectators attend a sport event, their behaviors are grounded in factors far beyond the event and the stadium.

When conflict and violence are widespread in a community or society, sport events are likely to be characterized by related forms of conflict and violence. For example, some of the worst spectator violence in the United States has been grounded in racial tensions aggravated by highly publicized rivalries between high schools whose students come from different racial or ethnic backgrounds (Guttmann, 1986). Where housing segregation has led to heavily segregated schools, the racial and ethnic conflicts within communities have contributed to confrontations before, during, and after games. Gangs, some of whose members have weapons, sometimes stake out territories around a sport stadium, so that sport events become scenes for displays of gang power. Similarly, when the "ultras," organized groups of fans now prevalent in Italy, attend soccer games, they often use acts of aggression as expressions of their loyalty to their peers and the teams they follow (Roversi, 1994).

In his classic book *Power and Innocence: A Search for the Causes of Violence* (1972), Rollo May observes that all human beings need some means of achieving a sense of personal significance. Significance, he says, is best achieved when people are in control of their lives. But

Crowd violence has not been a major problem at most sport events, but when it happens, there is a need for controlled intervention to prevent serious injuries. (John Leyba, *The Denver Post*)

when people are powerless and without resources, "violence may be the only way individuals or groups can achieve a sense of significance." This may partially explain the violent behavior of young, predominantly male soccer fans around the world. At least some of these young spectators probably perceive violence as a means of temporarily achieving a sense of significance. After all, violence forces others to take notice and respond to the perpetrator's existence. This is certainly not the only factor underlying violence among fans, but it is part of a historical, social, political, and economic context that we must understand when explaining violence among spectators.

Controlling Spectator Violence

Effective efforts to control spectator violence must be based on an awareness of each of the three sets of factors discussed above.

First, the fact that violence gives birth to violence indicates a need to minimize violence among players during events. If fans do not define the actions of players as violent, crowd violence will decrease. Furthermore, fans' perceptions of violence are likely to decrease if events are not hyped as violent confrontations between hostile opponents. Players and coaches could be used to make public announcements that defuse hostility and emphasize the skills of the athletes involved in the event. High-profile fans for each team could make similar announcements. The use of competent and professionally trained officials is also important. When officials maintain control of a game and make calls the spectators see as fair, they decrease the likelihood of spectator violence grounded in anger and perceived injustice (Mark et al., 1983). These referees also could meet with both teams before the event and calmly explain the need to leave hostilities in the locker rooms. Team officials could organize pregame unity rituals involving an exchange of team symbols and displays of respect between opponents. These rituals could receive media coverage so that fans could see that athletes do not view opponents with hostility.

Second, those who hope to control violence among spectators must be aware of crowd dynamics and the conditions that can precipitate violence. Preventive measures are important. The needs and rights of spectators must be known and respected. Crowd control officials must be trained properly to intervene in potentially disruptive situations without increasing the chances for violence. The consumption of alcohol must be regulated realistically. Facilities should be safe and allow for spectators to move around. But there also must be ways of limiting contact between hostile fans of opposing teams. Exits should be accessible and clearly marked, and spectators should not be herded like animals before or after games.

Third, anyone seeking to curb spectator violence must be aware of the historical, social, economic, and political issues that often underlie it. Restrictive law and order responses to crowd violence may be temporarily effective, but they will not get at the real causes of many forms of violent behavior. Policies dealing with issues of inequality, economic difficulties, unemployment, a lack of political representation, racism, and distorted definitions of masculinity in the community and in society as a whole are needed. These are the factors often at the root of conflict and violence. Also needed are real efforts to establish connections between teams and the communities in which they are located. These connections can be used to defuse potentially dangerous feelings or plans among groups of spectators or community residents. This does not mean that teams merely need better public relations. There must be *actual* connections between the teams, the facilities, and the communities in which they exist. Players and coaches need to be engaged in community service. Owners must be visible supporters of community events and programs. Teams must develop special programs to assist in the development of local neighborhoods, especially those around the stadium or arena.

The goal of these guidelines is to assist in the creation of antiaggression norms among spectators. This is difficult to do, but not impossible. And over the long run it will be more effective than using metal detectors, moving games to distant locations away from either team's home, hiring scores of police, patrolling the stands, using video cameras for surveillance, or scheduling games in the early morning on Saturdays and Sundays so that crowds will be sparse. Of course, some of these latter tactics can be effective but they destroy part of the enjoyment of attending events, and they restrict attendance access for many people. I see them as last resorts or temporary measures taken only to provide time to promote the development of new spectator norms.

There is no clear indication that watching sports on television makes people more violent or more accepting of violence in their own lives. This issue is difficult to study, because watching television sports is only a small part of people's lives, and violence is usually only a small part of what occurs in a televised sport event. However, there is a need to study how people actually interpret the action they see in televised sport events and how they relate those interpretations to situations and relationships in their own lives. The fact that people respond to and talk about violence in an event does not mean they accept or morally permit violence in everyday life. More research is needed on this issue.

The effects of going to a sport event are also difficult to pinpoint. Although spectator violence is relatively rare, it does occur. When it occurs, it seems to be related to (1) what happens on the playing field, (2) crowd dynamics and the situation at the event itself, and (3) the overall historical, social, economic, and political context in the community and society. When spectators become regularly violent in a particular community or society, this is probably related to issues far beyond the sport event and the stadium. Regular violence signals other serious problems calling for responsive social policies affecting opportunities and relationships within the society. Some specific ways of controlling spectator violence include limiting violence on the playing field and managing crowd dynamics in responsive and sensitive ways.

Because cultural context is so important to an understanding of spectator violence, it is necessary to compare violence across groups, situations, and cultures. We need more comparative research, but it is very difficult to gather good data on both the groups that engage in violence (Giulianotti, 1995) and the history, structure, and dynamics of spectator violence in the societies being compared (Giulianotti and Williams, 1994; Murphy et al., 1990; Redhead, 1993).

SUMMARY

CURE OR CAUSE?

Many people have discussed the relationship between sports and aggression. Those who argue that sports are a cure for violence in society have little research evidence to support their case. Neither playing nor watching sports seems to "drain off" the energy that might lead to violent behavior. But under certain circumstances, sport participation may help people separate themselves from sources of frustration in the rest of their lives. If this separation gives them the time they need to redefine and cope effectively with these sources of frustration, then they may become less

violent. But this possibility needs to be explored in research. Athletes also may learn to control violent behavior during games, especially the types of violence leading to penalties. But it is doubtful that this learning has any long-term effects on behavior off the field unless it has been intentionally linked to a philosophy of nonviolence and respect for oneself and one's opponents.

Those who argue that sports are a cause of violence have more research to support their case, but they cannot show that what happens in sports has a *direct* impact on violent behavior in the rest of society. Sport experiences sometimes create frustration that leads to violence among both players and spectators; but for this to happen, the frustration must be followed by anger combined with opportunities, stimulus cues, and social support for violence. Male athletes in contact sports learn to use violence and intimidation as strategic tools, but we do not know if they carry these strategies over into nonsport settings. Among males, learning to use violence as a tool within a sport is frequently tied to the reaffirmation of a form of masculinity that emphasizes a willingness to risk personal safety and a desire to intimidate others. If males who participate in certain sports learn to perceive this orientation as natural or appropriate, then sports may intensify serious forms of nonsport violence, including violence against women and children and other forms of physical assault (Theberge, 1989). Furthermore, ideas about the so-called "natural superiority of men" often are grounded in beliefs that the ability to engage in violence is part of the essence of being a man; people often use references to sports violence to make this argument.

Female athletes in contact sports also engage in aggressive acts, but we know little about how those acts and the willingness to engage in them are linked to the identities of women athletes at different levels of competition. At this time, many women seem to prefer an emphasis on supportive connections between teammates and opponents, and on pleasure and participation in sports. Therefore, aggression and violence do not occur as often or in connection with the same dynamics in their sports as in men's sports.

Violence among spectators is influenced by violence on the field of play, crowd dynamics, the situation at the event itself, and the overall historical and cultural context in which spectators live. Isolated cases of violence probably are best controlled by improved crowd management, but chronic violence among spectators usually signals that something needs to be changed in the way certain sports are defined and played, or in the actual social, economic, or political structure of the community or society.

SUGGESTED READINGS

Bredemeier, B., and D. Shields. 1986. Athletic aggression: an issue of contextual morality. *Sociology of Sport Journal* 3(1):15–28 (*a clearly written conceptual discussion of how athletes define aggression in their own sports*).

Dunning, E. P., P. Murphy, and J. Williams. 1988. *The roots of football hooliganism.* Leicester, England: University of Leicester Press (*an in-depth analysis of the behavior of British soccer fans, based on many years of research*).

Giulianotti, R. 1995. Participant observation and research into football hooliganism: Reflections on the problems of entrée and everyday risks. *Sociology of Sport Journal* 12 (1):1–20 (*this is essential reading for anyone planning to study patterns of spectator violence using qualitative research methods*).

Giulianotti, R., N. Bonny, and M. Hepworth, eds. 1994. *Football, violence and social identity.* London: Routledge (*articles on key issues related to spectator violence, especially soccer hooliganism*).

Goldstein, J. H., ed. 1988–89. Violence in sport. Special issues of *Current Psychology: Research & Reviews* 7(4); 8(1) (*ten papers and two book reviews devoted to deviance, the media, boxing, and recent incidents involving British soccer fans—all with a focus on violent behavior*).

Gruneau, R., and D. Whitson. 1993. Violence, fighting and masculinity. In *Hockey night in Canada: Sport, identities, and cultural politics* (pp. 175–96). Toronto: Garamond Press (*insightful analysis of violence in sports with special attention to ice hockey; deals with social class, masculinity and gender relations*).

Guttmann, A. 1986. *Sports spectators.* New York: Columbia University Press (*a good overview of the behavior of spectators; includes an examination of the history of sports spectators and an in-depth analysis of important sociological, psychological, and economic dimensions of spectatorship*).

Murphy, P., J. Williams, and E. Dunning. 1990. *Football on trial.* London: Routledge (*a policy-based overview of spectator violence associated with soccer around the world; special emphasis is given to British spectators, and there is an interesting section on why there has been no equivalent of British soccer hooliganism in the United States*).

Sipes, R. G. 1996. Sports as a control for aggression. In D. S. Eitzen, ed., *Sport in contemporary society.* New York: St. Martin's Press (*an analysis of data on the relationship between the existence of combative sports and rates of violence in different societies*).

Smith, M. D. 1983. *Violence and sport.* Toronto: Butterworths (*a dated but excellent survey of the literature on this topic*).

Telander, R. 1989. *The hundred-yard lie.* New York: Simon and Schuster (*a critique of American college football; shows how violence becomes an institutionalized part of men's sports organized to emphasize power and performance*).

Young, K. Forthcoming. Sport and violence. In J. Coakley and E. Dunning, eds., *Handbook of sport and society.* London: Sage (*an overview of manifestations and explanations of sports violence among players and spectators; excellent analysis of issues related to policing sports violence*).

8

(Jay Coakley)

There was no other women when I started [playing hockey] seven years ago. . . . Some of the guys wouldn't even get on the ice when I was playing.

Kellee Sikes, twenty-four-year-old in "men's" hockey league (1996)

I paint my fingernails. I color my hair. I sometimes wear women's clothes. I want to challenge people's image of what an athlete is supposed to be. I like bringing out the feminine side of Dennis Rodman.

Dennis Rodman, NBA player (1996)

Gender

Is equity the only issue?

We feel that the Olympic Games must be reserved for the solemn and periodic exaltation of male athleticism, with internationalism as a base, loyalty as a means, arts for its setting and female applause as reward.

Pierre de Coubertin, founder of the modern Olympics (circa 1896)

The visibility of [women] athletes . . . represents a welcome change in our sense of what women can be and do. That's why I loved watching the Olympics—not for the soap-opera coverage, but for the sheer joy of seeing those wonderful, powerful women in action.

Ruth Conniff, managing editor, *The Progressive* (1996)

It is still the case that more men than women watch a sport like women's basketball. Ah, but women do watch the Olympics. . . . They prefer figure skating, where the women don't look like athletes, and gymnastics, where the athletes don't look like women.

Frank Deford, sports journalist/writer (*Newsweek*, 10 June 1996)

If you let me play—I will like myself more, I will have more self-confidence, I will suffer less depression, I will be 60 percent less likely to get breast cancer, I will be more likely to leave a man who beats me, I will be less likely to get pregnant before I want to, I will learn what it means to be strong—IF YOU LET ME PLAY SPORTS.

Voice of a young girl, Nike ad (1996)

Gender and gender relations has become the most popular topic in the sociology of sport since 1990. Sociologists now realize it is important to explain why sports traditionally have been defined as men's activities, why half the world's population traditionally has been excluded or discouraged from participating in many sports, how sports influence people's ideas about masculinity and femininity, and why the topic of sexual orientation and sports is so controversial. Although gender issues underlie many topics discussed in this book, a separate chapter is necessary to identify the full sociological significance of gender and sports.

When people discuss gender in the sociology of sport, they usually focus on two sets of issues: (1) participation and equity issues, and (2) ideological and structural issues. These are some of the major participation and equity issues:

- sport participation patterns among women
- gender inequities related to participation opportunities, support for athletes, and jobs in coaching and administration
- changes needed to achieve equal opportunities for girls and women in the future

Some of the important ideological and structural issues, are as follows:

- how sports are connected with ideas about masculinity and femininity
- the need for more flexible and inclusive definitions of masculinity and femininity to achieve real and lasting gender equity in sports
- the need for changing and diversifying how sports are organized, promoted, played, and portrayed to achieve real and lasting gender equity

My goal in this chapter is to discuss these two sets of issues and show that even though many people deal with them separately, they go hand in hand in real life. We cannot ignore either one if we are seeking fairness as we interact with others and as we "do" sports in our lives.

PARTICIPATION AND EQUITY ISSUES

Participation patterns among women

Writing in *Newsweek* magazine, Frank Deford noted in 1996 that what "has happened in the last generation to women in sports has been nothing short of revolutionary—and those who would seek to understand the 21st century woman dismiss [sports] at their peril." I would add that since the early 1970s, the single most dramatic change in the world of sport has been the increased participation of girls and women. This has occurred in many countries around the world, especially those with reasonably strong postindustrial economies. But even in traditional, labor-intensive, poor countries, women have begun to push for new opportunities to play sports on their own terms (Cohen, 1993). Despite resistance in some countries, girls and women around the world now participate in a variety of school, community, and club programs that didn't even exist twenty-five years ago.

WHY PARTICIPATION HAS INCREASED Five major factors account for recent increases in sport participation among girls and women in North America and other parts of the world:

1. new opportunities
2. government legislation demanding equal treatment for women in public programs
3. the women's movement
4. the health and fitness movement
5. increased media coverage of women in sports

New opportunities. The primary reason more girls and women participate in sports today is that there are more opportunities than ever before. Prior to the mid-1970s, many girls and women did not play sports for one simple reason: teams and programs didn't exist. Young women today may not realize it, but few of their mothers had the opportunities they now enjoy in their schools and communities. Teams and programs developed over the past two decades have uncovered and cultivated interests ignored in the past. Girls and women still do not receive an equal share of sport resources in most organizations and communities, but their increased participation clearly has gone hand in hand with the development of new opportunities. The majority of these new opportunities owe their existence to some form of political pressure or government legislation.

Government legislation. People tend to complain about government regulations, but literally millions of girls and women would not be playing sports today if it were not for liberal local and national legislation mandating new opportunities. Various policies and rules have come into existence as a result of concerted efforts to raise legal issues and apply pressure on political representatives. These efforts have been made by individuals and groups committed to the struggle to achieve fairness in sports. For example, in the United States, it took years of lobbying before Congress passed Title IX of the Educational Amendments in 1972. Title IX declared, "No person in the United States shall, on the basis of sex, be excluded from participation in, be denied the benefits of, or be subjected to discrimination under any educational program or activity receiving federal financial assistance." The men who controlled athletic programs in high schools and colleges objected to this "radical" idea and delayed the enforcement of Title IX for five years after it was passed into law. Many claimed that equity was impractical and burdensome. They apparently thought they were entitled to be "more equal" than women when it came to sports. And they passionately resisted equality by claiming they were now going to be victims of equality!

In 1984, after six years of enforcement and progress, the U.S. Supreme Court strengthened the resistance to Title IX. It ruled that the law did not apply to school athletic programs because the schools and the students were the true recipients of federal funds, not the athletic programs (even though the programs were sponsored by the schools). Consequently, eight hundred cases of alleged discrimination under investigation at the U.S. Department of Educa-

tion's Office for Civil Rights were dropped or narrowed (Sabo, 1988). It then took Congress another four years to pass (over President Reagan's veto in March 1988) the Civil Rights Restoration Act, which again mandated equal opportunity in *all* programs in any organization receiving federal money. This was helpful, but this act did not contain enough incentives for schools and other sport organizations to make positive changes; nor did it encourage people to challenge inequities in the courts.

Then, in 1992, the U.S. Supreme Court ruled that if schools intentionally violated Title IX, the injured parties could sue for financial damages. This ruling enabled many young women in schools and even women coaches to make schools and other public organizations accountable in establishing gender equity in sports. The result has been that people have become much more sensitive to the need to take girls and women into account when it comes to sports. People still resist the law, but they leave themselves open to lawsuits when they do. And this state of affairs has led a few men in Congress to suggest in 1996 that new rules are needed to protect current funding for the most traditional of all men's sports: football. Progress has been made, but the struggle continues (Bruce, 1993; Carpenter, 1993; Shaw, 1995; Staurowsky, 1996).

The Canadian experience has been similar (see Hall, 1996; Lenskyj, 1988). After a Royal Commission on the Status of Women was established in 1970, studies were done to document the existence of inequality, and conferences were held to identify issues and set priorities. In 1980, the Fitness and Amateur Sport Women's Program was established. It provided a combination of government-funded programs, training, and policy development opportunities for women. This program, along with other federal and provincial programs and pressures from feminist advocacy groups, led to the 1986 publication of *Women in Sport: A Sport Canada Policy*, which outlined national policy on women in sport. This document not only set the official goal of equality of opportunity for women at all levels of sport, but also called for a specific action-oriented program to achieve this goal. Thus Canada became the first noncommunist country to have an official policy on women in sport.

Other countries have followed (Hargreaves, 1994). But in many of them, especially those with traditional and/or religion-based cultures, change has been very slow. Official power in these countries rests in the hands of men, and they often see women's sport participation as disruptive of the social or moral order. Women in these countries have had to be persistent and politically creative to produce even minor changes.

The women's movement. The worldwide women's movement over the past thirty years has emphasized that females are enhanced as human beings when they have opportunities to develop their intellectual *and* physical abilities. This idea has encouraged women of all ages to pursue their interests in sports, and it has led to the creation of new interests among those who, in the past, never would have thought of participating in sports (Fasting, 1996). The women's movement also has helped redefine occupational and family roles for women, and this has provided more women with the time and resources needed for sport participation. As the ideals of the women's movement have become more widely accepted, and as male control over the lives and bodies of women has weakened, more women have been choosing to play sports. More change is needed, especially in poor countries and among low-income women, but the choices now available to women are less restricted than they once were.

A number of politically influential women's sport organizations have emerged in connection with the women's movement. In the U.S., for example, the Women's Sport Foundation has become an important lobbying group for change. WomenSport International is a new organization designed to assist people around the globe in their efforts "to bring about positive change for girls and women in sport and physical education." A group of women delegates from eighty countries met in Brighton, England, in 1994 to discuss "Women, Sport and the Challenge of Change," and unanimously passed a declaration of global gender equity principles. What has come to be known as the "Brighton Declaration" is now used by women in a number of countries to apply pressure on their governments and sport organizations to make new spaces for girls and women in sports. Lobbying efforts by representatives from these and other groups led to the inclusion of statements related to sports and physical education in the official Platform for Action of the U.N.'s Fourth World Conference on Women held in Beijing, China, in 1996. These statements called for new efforts to provide sport and physical education opportunities to promote the education, health, and human rights of girls and women in countries around the world. What started out as the radical thinking of a few now has become a widely accepted global effort to promote and guarantee sport participation opportunities for girls and women (Hargreaves, 1994).

The health and fitness movement. Since the mid-1970s, increased awareness of health and fitness has encouraged women to become involved in many physical activities, including sports. Although much of the emphasis in this movement has been tied to the traditional feminine ideal of being thin and sexually attractive to men, there also has been an emphasis on the *development of physical strength and competence.* Muscles have become more widely accepted as desirable attributes among women of all ages. Traditional standards still exist, as illustrated by many clothing fashions and marketing strategies associated with women's fitness. But many women have moved beyond those standards and given priority to physical competence and the good feelings that go with it rather than trying to look like anorexic models in fashion magazines.

Furthermore, many transnational corporations, such as Nike and Reebok, recently have jumped from the women's fitness and appearance bandwagon to the fitness and sport bandwagon. Even though their ads are designed to sell clothes, shoes, and even sweat-proof makeup, they present strong messages intended to "appeal to women's enthusiasm for sports as a symbol of female liberation and power" (Conniff, 1996). And they have encouraged sport participation in the process.

Increased media coverage of women's sports. Even though women's sports are not covered as often or in the same detail as men's sports (see chap. 12), girls and women now can see and read about the achievements of women athletes in a wider range of sports than ever before. Seeing women athletes on television and reading about them in newspapers and magazines encourages girls and women to be active as athletes themselves. As girls grow up, they often want to see what is possible before they experiment with and develop their own athletic skills. This is the case because many of them still receive mixed messages about becoming serious athletes; their vision of the athletic woman gets clouded by swimsuit models in *Sports Illustrated* and other powerful images emphasizing the "need" to be thin and sexually appealing to men. Under these cultural conditions, the media coverage of everything from professional women's basketball to synchronized swimming helps girls and young women conclude that sports are human activities, not male activities.

Media companies, like their corporate counterparts that sell sporting goods, have begun to realize that women really do make up half the world's population, and, therefore, half the world's consumers. NBC, the U.S. television network that covered the 1996 Summer Olympic Games in Atlanta, experienced great ratings success when it targeted women during its 175 hours of coverage. Many men complained about this new approach, since they liked it better when their interests were the only ones that mattered in sports media coverage. But we can expect to see the real existence of women athletes and spectators acknowledged in the media coverage of the future, and that coverage clearly will change the images that all of us associate with sports and athletic achievement. (Gunther, 1996)

In summary, it is clear that increased opportunities, government legislation, the women's

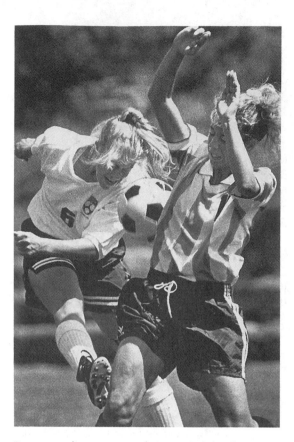

Recent media coverage of women's sports has shown young girls a wider range of sport participation than they have seen in the past. This is likely to encourage even more sport participation in the future. (*Colorado Springs Gazette*)

movement, the health and fitness movement, and increased media coverage given to women's sports and women athletes have combined to encourage sport participation among girls and women. These changes are part of the growing awareness that girls and women cannot be denied equal sport participation opportunities.

REASONS TO BE CAUTIOUS WHEN PREDICTING FUTURE PARTICIPATION INCREASES Increases in the sport participation rates of girls and women have not come easily. They are clearly the result of the dedicated efforts of many individuals and groups. Now we can look forward to continued positive changes. Or can we?

There are at least six reasons to be cautious when predicting the pace and extent of future sport participation increases among girls and women. These reasons include (1) budget cutbacks and the "privatization" of sport programs, (2) popular resistance to government regulations, (3) backlash among those who resent changes favoring strong women, (4) the underrepresentation of women in coaching and other powerful positions in sports, (5) a continued emphasis on "cosmetic fitness" in certain cultures, and (6) the trivialization of certain women athletes and women's sports.

Budget cutbacks and the privatization of sport programs. Many public programs in schools and communities are threatened by budget cutbacks. Boosting opportunities for girls and women is difficult when cutbacks are required (Shaw, 1995). Furthermore, programs for girls and women are often vulnerable to cuts themselves. They are less established than programs for boys and men, they seldom have the same administrative and community support, and they seldom have the revenue-generating potential of certain men's programs; overall, they often are seen as less important for the overall future of the sponsoring organizations (Staurowsky, 1995). As one woman said, "It seems like the only time women's programs are treated equally is when cuts must be made." According to Christine Grant, women's athletic director at the University of Iowa, this creates problems: "Women's sports were never equal in the first place, so when you cut equally, you're cutting women disproportionately" (quoted in Muscatine, 1991).

Another issue related to budget cutbacks is that sport programs for girls and women are often new programs, and they generally require *greater* financial support than longstanding and well-established programs for boys and men. This principle is widely recognized in the business world: new businesses always have high start-up costs, and investors realize that unless they absorb those costs, the new businesses are likely to fail. Therefore, budget cuts may cause women's programs to fail at a faster pace than

"All that we're asking is that you each lose ten pounds. Isn't that fair?"
....

In 1991 Brown University withdrew full athletic department funding from women's volley ball and gymnastics and men's golf and water polo. The cuts were about equal for men and women, even though 63 percent of total intercollegiate athletes at the university were men and 37 percent were women. In 1992 the women sued to restore funding under Title IX rules. Brown University lost the case, appealed and lost again in 1996. The university then filed an appeal with the U.S. Supreme Court and lost again (in mid-1997). The university said that its disparity in athletic opportunities for men and women students existed because women were not as interested as men in playing sports at an intercollegiate level. None of the courts have agreed with Brown's claim.

....

men's programs because they never have had the chance to develop name recognition and "market presence." Boys' and men's programs are less vulnerable because they have enjoyed decades of support and development, and are now in a position to seek and obtain private support to keep them going.

As public, tax-supported programs are cut, sport participation becomes increasingly dependent on private support and sponsorship. This trend is occurring in many communities and societies, and it often has a negative impact on the provision of sport participation opportunities for girls and women, especially those who live in low-income households. Although few public programs have been known for their special sensitivity to the sport needs and interests of girls and women, when public programs did provide participation opportunities, they were affordable and sometimes free.

When public programs are cut back or eliminated, people must buy sport participation from private providers. This presents few problems for females from wealthy backgrounds: they just buy what they want. In fact, private providers want their business and make efforts to attract it. "Free enterprise sports" are great for those with plenty of resources, but not very good for those on tight budgets; nor are they good for women, who generally have lower salaries and less discretionary money than men. Private providers are not interested in selling sport participation to those who can't buy it. When money talks, poor people are able only to whisper, and poor women often are silenced. Therefore, future participation increases may be unevenly distributed among girls and women; in fact, those who lack resources may even suffer participation setbacks (Hargreaves, 1994).

Resistance to government policies and legislation. When governments pass new policies or rules, people often debate what they mean in practical terms. For example, people have been debating the implications of Canada's national policy on women in sport ever since it was established in 1986, and gender equality and fairness still do not exist (Hall, 1996). Changes have been contested by those with vested interests in doing things according to old ways. As they have opposed changes, they often have questioned the right of the government to mandate

changes; they have lobbied for less "government interference." (Gunzelman, 1996).

The same is true in the United States. It took over twenty years of struggle to obtain the legal backing needed to enforce the principle of equal participation opportunities for women, and resistance to Title IX continues in many organizations. It takes time and effort to establish precedents for what Title IX means in practical terms in different organizations (Carpenter, 1993). And those precedents may be opposed by men who feel they are "victims" of equality for women (Staurowsky, 1996). These men make appeals to political sentiments for less government interference in everyday life. Of course, what those who have power and enjoy privileged positions see as "interference" is generally seen as "protection" by those without power and privilege. In the case of Title IX, powerful men who benefit from one hundred years of male privilege in sports say that government is interfering with the way life should be. And they continue to challenge and change the practical and legal meanings that have been given to Title IX. If they are successful, participation rates may be jeopardized.

Backlash among those who resent changes favoring strong women. In 1994, Mariah Nelson, a former pro basketball player and now a writer, published a book entitled *The Stronger Women Get, The More Men Love Football.* Her point is that when women gain the strength and resources enabling them to challenge the traditional gender order effectively,* some men, especially those privileged by that order, will do all they can to discredit strong women and reaffirm the need to return to the "good ol' days" when men were men and women yielded to their interests. In line with Nelson's thesis, we might predict that in the face of threatening changes in the

---

Gender order is a term that refers to the norms, historical traditions, legal definitions, and opportunity structures that define and describe the conditions under which men and women form gender identities, live their lives as men and women, and relate to each other.

gender order, some men would become passionate in their condemnation of lesbians; they might even make claims that lesbians were taking over sports and had to be stopped before the moral basis of society completely eroded. We also could predict that some men would turn to all-male groups to reaffirm traditional values that placed men in positions of moral and civil authority; for the same reason, they would look to strong male coaches as model leaders in society. And as Nelson's title suggests, we also could predict that football, hockey, and other "power sports" would become increasingly popular among some men in society.

In fact, these forms of backlash to changes in the gender order have been documented in U.S. culture (see Faludi, 1991). However, hypotheses on how they occur in sports are in need of testing. Nelson seems to be prophetic in her analysis. Her thesis may apply to *both* men and women who have learned to live with and benefit from the traditional gender order; some women who managed to get what they wanted in the past also might "love football" more today and see strong women athletes as a threat.

The effects of this backlash on sport participation among girls and women are not completely clear. But my guess is that it contributes to the mixed messages girls and women receive and even give to one another about sports, and fuels the trivialization of women's sports and strong women athletes. If this is occurring in fact, we can expect future increases in sport participation rates to become less dramatic than they have been in the recent past.

Underrepresentation of women in coaching and power positions in sports. Despite radical increases in the number of sport participation opportunities for girls and women since the mid-1970s, women have suffered setbacks in the ranks of coaching and sport administration in women's programs. For example, in the years immediately following the passage of Title IX in the U.S., there was an actual decline in the number and proportion of women head coaches and administrators (Parkhouse and Williams, 1986).

Of course, it is possible for men to do a good job in these positions, but unless girls and young women see women in positions of authority and power in their own programs, they will be reluctant to define sports and sport participation as important in their own futures. If women are not visible as leaders in sport programs, people tend to conclude that women's abilities and contributions are less valued than men's. This conclusion can limit sport participation among girls and women (Ligatom-Kimura, 1995).

Continued emphasis on "cosmetic fitness." There are competing images of female bodies in many cultures today. Many girls and women hear confusing cultural messages that they should be "firm but shapely, fit but sexy, strong but thin" (Markula, 1995). Although they do see images of powerful women athletes, they cannot escape the images of fashion models whose reputations depend on a body shape that women can match only by depriving themselves of the nourishment they need to be strong. These fashion images highlight thinness, bust size, waist size, lip shape, hairstyles, body hair removal, complexion, allure, and the clothes and accessories that together "make" the woman. Girls and women also hear that physical power and competence are important, but they see disproportionate rewards going to women who look young and vulnerable. They are advised to "get strong, but lose weight." They get the impression that muscles are good, but too many muscles are unfeminine. They are told that men now like competent women, but they see men who are attracted to the Dallas Cowgirls (cheerleaders) and the latest celebrity models with breast implants and workout videos, rather than to accomplished women athletes (see the box on pp. 218–220).

Despite highly publicized ads by sporting goods companies and other cultural messages saying that being strong and athletic is "in," powerful cultural messages promote the "beauty myth" (Hargreaves, 1994; Wolf, 1991). The "cultural pull" toward the beauty myth remains powerful for two reasons: (1) if women become too strong, this will disrupt the established

REFLECT ON SPORT

Cheerleaders
The "Sideshow" of American Sport?

Who are cheerleaders today? They are described variously as athletes, "acro-sport" athletes, tumblers, gymnasts, stunt performers, vocal pep leaders, entertainers, dancers, sex objects, and sideshows for men's power sports. Historical and cultural factors have contributed to all these descriptions. (Davis, 1994)

The very first cheerleaders in the late 1800's were men. Women weren't allowed because cheerleading was part of sports, and sports were "manly" activities separate from the world of the feminine as it was defined then.

The first women who became cheerleaders were considered rebels or deviants, invaders of male space. Up through the 1940s, they received warnings from educators that cheerleading was bad for their health and overall development as women. Laurel Davis (1994) tells of an educator who wrote in 1938 that women cheerleaders "frequently became too masculine for their own good," developed "loud and raucous voices," and often took to using "slang and profanity" because they hung out with rough and tough male cheerleaders.

But many women didn't listen to these warnings, and social definitions of both femininity and cheerleading continued to change. By the 1950s cheerleading was dominated by women, and most men had dropped out because they didn't like being associated with what was becoming a "girls' activity" (Davis, 1994). And by the 1970s, many people thought cheerleading was "naturally" suited for females, and females were "naturally" suited for cheerleading. In fact, some people even thought cheerleading was an activity in which girls could learn about real femininity and through which young women could show they were socially accepted in the highly gendered world of junior and senior high schools. How quickly things had changed!

Today, it is difficult to make generalizations about cheerleading. But whenever I see the "honey shots" of the made-up young women smiling and posing (for men?) on the sidelines of NFL games, and whenever I hear NBA fans make demeaning remarks about the bodies and overall looks of a team's dance team/cheerleader squad, I am reminded that many Americans still evaluate men in terms of what they do and women in terms of how they look. The bodies of women seem to be "fair game" for men who gaze at them, judge them, and then reject or accept them as unattractive or attractive according to dominant heterosexual standards.

In the most popular team sports in American society, men are the doers; they make the decisions, play the games, and get credit for their skills. Women are the spectators; they become part of a sport by standing on the sidelines as showpieces for the teams they represent or by entertaining fans when the men on the field need a rest. Their role is to provide emotional support for men, or simply to fill in breaks in the men's game that everyone came to see. Men must be aggressive and able to dominate others to be athletes; females must be good at providing support and nurturing emotional involvement among spectators to be cheerleaders. As Jim Lord, director of the Universal Cheerleaders Association, says, "the primary role of a cheerleading squad is to lead the crowd" (in O'Shea, 1995).

Of course, this depiction of cheerleaders must be qualified. High schools and universities select female cheerleaders on the basis of many attributes, including character, grades, popularity, spirit, voice, and gymnastic abilities. But physical attractiveness also may be considered. In fact, those who have many of the attributes needed to become cheerleaders but lack "looks" sometimes are encouraged to join the pep club and sit in the bleachers with the band. There they can provide support for the team without being individually seen and evaluated. What if coaches used "looks" as a criterion for selecting members of the football team? And do spectators use the same evaluative terms when they describe cheerleaders that they use when they describe male athletes? Or rather, do the terms suggest that male athletes are the show and cheerleaders are the sideshow of sports? In my experience, this frequently has been the case.

Some girls and women still accept this gender logic. For them, being a cheerleader is a more important basis for popularity than being an athlete. In the social world of men's professional sports, wriggling

Female cheerleaders have become an expected part of many sports in the U.S. Although a highly sexualized image of cheerleaders is presented regularly in connection with some men's professional sports, many young women at the high-school level view cheerleading as a sport in its own right. In both instances, however, cheerleading is an activity done by females to support males who are playing the sport everyone has come to see. (Jay Coakley (left); Dennis Coakley (right))

female centerfolds still capture the attention of cameramen and leering spectators between plays and during time outs. These women are showpieces who are expected to be alluring and sensuous. But at the same time, they are also expected to be pure, wholesome, and selflessly dedicated to the teams they support. In fact, if they use their bodies to make money for themselves (by posing for certain magazines), the men who have approved their existence will dismiss them without thinking twice. It seems that being alluring and
Continued

sensuous for men at a football game is wholesome, but doing so for your own financial gain is immoral. Now those are strange rules! I wonder who made them up?

We also can see the gendered aspects of cheerleading in the issues that surround cheering for women's sports in high school and college. Do cheerleaders cheer for both men's and women's teams? One sixteen-year-old high school cheerleader explains, "We said we would, but some cheerleaders were like, 'We're not cheering for girls' " (in Minton, 1995). This gendered attitude is widespread enough that it

has created tension between cheerleaders and women athletes in some schools. The women's teams want the same support that the men's teams receive, but people still see cheerleading in traditionally gendered terms, and the image of females cheering females doesn't fit with their gender logic. They still like to think of cheerleaders as "cute enough to date the quarterback." This, of course, reproduces the gender ideology that still works to the disadvantage of girls and women in sports. Progress depends on challenging and changing this ideology. What do you think?

gender order, threatening those men and women who benefit from the status quo; and (2) if women become too satisfied with their body images, they will not spend as much money on products whose sales depend on high levels of female insecurities about their appearance. The message in many ads is clear: "heterosexualized hard bodies" are valued, especially when they are displayed in the latest bodysuits, leotards, and other high-fashion sport gear (see Bolin, 1992a, b; Cole, 1993; Cole and Hribar, 1995; Hargreaves, 1994; Holmlund, 1994; MacNeill, 1994; White and Gillett, 1994).

Mixed cultural messages about female bodies are related to sport participation in two ways: (1) many women of all ages don't want to begin participating in physical activities and sports until they are thin enough to look "right" and to wear the "right" clothes, and (2) many women who do participate combine their physical activity with pathogenic weight-control behavior that lowers body fat but produces amenorrhea, deprives them of necessary nutrients, and increases the likelihood of stress fractures and other injuries. Studies show that an alarming number of women athletes use laxatives, diet pills, diuretics,

self-induced vomiting, binges, and starvation diets in conjunction with their training (Caldwell, 1993; Clark, 1993; Johns, 1992, 1996, 1997; Nativ et al., 1994; Noden, 1994; Overdorf and Gill, 1994; Ryan, 1995; Tofler et al., 1996; Wilmore, 1996). This increases the probability of injuries, jeopardizes health, and keeps alive the idea that women must either conform to the beauty myth or be rejected by men and by women who subscribe to the myth and use it to evaluate other females of all ages.

Finally, when the goal of being physically active is cosmetic fitness rather than physical competence, there is a tendency to drop out of sport programs when weight loss goals are achieved and appearance meets myth-based expectations. Of course, it is possible that those seeking cosmetic fitness actually will discover that sports are fun, but this is not assured. Some women seem to be on a never-ending quest to look like Barbie rather than to achieve pleasure in sports with a strong body. This limits sport participation.

The trivialization of certain women athletes and women's sports. "Okay, she's a good athlete, but she's not a 'real' woman." I regularly hear statements with this theme. They are based on

The Olympic Gymnast Barbie sends mixed messages to both girls and boys. Barbie is a model of cosmetic fitness. The beauty myth enters the lives of girls in many ways; this Barbie guarantees that sport is one of those ways. (Jay Coakley)

the assumption that unless women are clearly heterosexual (however that is determined!), or at least attractive enough to be sexually desired by heterosexual men, they are not real women (Birrell and Theberge, 1994; Kolnes, 1995). This way of thinking trivializes women athletes and what they do. It is grounded in homophobia, the irrational fear of homosexuality. In response to homophobia, many women athletes, including heterosexuals, will go to great lengths to "prove" they are "real women." They may go out of their way to emphasize traditional feminine attributes and even say in interviews that being an athlete is not nearly as important as eventually getting married, settling down, having children, and becoming a nurturing homemaker. Homophobia affects all women athletes, lesbian and straight alike; it creates fears, it pressures women to conform to traditional gender roles, and it silences and makes invisible the lesbians who manage, coach, and play sports (Crosset, 1995; Hargreaves, 1994; Nelson, 1994; Sabo and Messner, 1993).

"Okay, women play sports, but most of them don't play 'real' sports." I also hear statements like this. They are based on the assumption that "real" sports involve "manly" things like displays of aggression and physical dominance over others (Theberge, 1996). If sports involve not these things, but grace, balance, and coordination, one or both of these things occur: the sports are demeaned, or the bodies of the athletes are sexualized and evaluated from top to bottom. In either case, the physical skills of the athletes are ignored and women athletes are trivialized.

In the past, women athletes and women's sports also were trivialized by team nicknames or mascots inconsistent with physical competence. U.S. colleges and universities sometimes did this. For example, the Mercer (Georgia) University men's teams were called the Bears, while the women's teams were the Teddy Bears. Other examples were Blue Hawks and Blue Chicks, Wildcats and Wild Kittens, Boll Weevils and Cotton Blossoms, (see Eitzen and Zinn, 1989; Fuller and Manning, 1987). "Lady" or the suffixes "-ettes" or "-elles" also were used to describe women's teams, because it was important for women athletes to let everyone know that playing sports would not lead them to renounce their softness and femininity. The women knew they would never be funded if anyone thought that sports would masculinize them. But over time they discovered that nobody was seriously eager to fund the Wild Kittens either! So most teams have dropped the trivial nicknames and presented themselves as the athletes they are. But some people still think of them as "ladies" or Wild Kittens, and fund them accordingly.

Even though women now have become a crucial part of sport culture in many societies, these remnants of old ways of thinking about gender have prevented the formation of a clear image of the athletic woman in society. Donna Lopiano, director of the Woman's Sport Foundation in the U.S., made this point, noting, "We know how to make Charles Barkley a hero [in U.S. culture], but nobody has yet to figure out the simple image of the active woman today" (in Deford, 1996).

Lopiano's statement partly summarizes this section. Sport participation rates among girls and women will not continue to increase automatically. Just as the participation of men has been nurtured and developed for years through consistent support and in connection with clear popular images of men in sports, so must it be for women. Without continued support and encouragement, without powerful new images, some of the progress of the past could be jeopardized. However, we will never backslide to the extreme inequality that existed before 1970.

Gender Inequities in Sports

PARTICIPATION OPPORTUNITIES The types of sport participation opportunities available for girls and women reflect dominant definitions of femininity in a culture. Prior to the early 1970s, females were widely believed to be naturally frail and inclined toward graceful movements. So they were encouraged to participate in figure skating, ice dancing, gymnastics, swimming, tennis, golf, and other sports that people thought were unrelated to strength, power, and speed, which were widely believed to be "manly" traits. Girls and women did play

sports, but they never had the same opportunities men had.

Over the past fifty years, some of the women who have participated in sports have demonstrated clearly that notions of female frailty were grounded in ideology rather than nature. This led to gradual changes in popular ideas about what girls and women could and should do in sports. Today the vast majority of people in North America and many other regions agree that women should have the same participation opportunities as men (Sabo and Messner, 1993). However, some people say that women should not play sports involving direct physical confrontation and contact with opponents. Others say that equity is great as long as women don't wrestle, box, play on men's contact sport teams, or ask for the funds that men use to play their sports. It seems that girls and women encounter the strongest resistance when they play sports that traditionally have been the "flag carriers of masculinity" in particular societies (Bryson, 1990).

This resistance to equal participation opportunities continues to cause problems across a range of sports. For example, in many private golf clubs women cannot own memberships, even though they may make more money than their husbands. Even when they are club members, they sometimes cannot vote on club policies or participate in club governance; they might not be given weekend tee times until the afternoon, even though morning tee times are available and they have paid the same fees as men; they may be denied entry into eating areas and other rooms where men drink and play cards, and they often cannot pass their membership on to a daughter as they would to a son—unless she is married, and then it goes to her husband (Chambers, 1995). Of course, golf is tied to elitist white, male traditions, and private clubs are home to powerful white men who don't give up privilege without a fight, so it is not surprising that women have run into resistance there (nor is it surprising that forms of racial exclusion still exist in such clubs).

Inequities in participation opportunities also exist in many other settings, including interna-

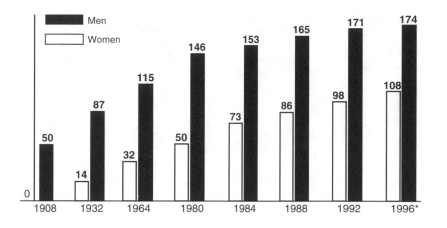

FIGURE 8-1 Number of Summer Olympic events open to women and to men.*
*Eleven events in 1996 were mixed, or open to both men and women. These eleven have been added to both totals for men and women. This procedure was also used for each of the other Olympics in this graph.

tional sports. For example, women still have fewer sports than men in the Olympics and other international events. Although important changes have occurred over the past two decades, women athletes remain underrepresented in international competitions. Information in figure 8-1 and table 8–1 illustrates that women in the modern Summer Olympic Games always have had fewer events than men have had, and there always have been fewer women participants than men. The International Olympic Committee (IOC), which from 1894 to 1981 was all-male, did not approve a women's 1500-meter run until the 1972 Games in Munich. It was not until the 1984 Games in Los Angeles that women had the opportunity to run the marathon. Women waited until 1988 to run the Olympic 10,000-meter race and until 1996 to run the 5,000-meter race; and women still do not have opportunities to compete in longer race-walking events. The men on the IOC justified this restriction of opportunities by claiming that women needed to be protected from such exhausting (and "unladylike") events.

Equity is sometimes difficult to achieve on the international level because of fundamentalist re-

ligious beliefs. For example, Islamic beliefs in some cultures forbid women from publicly exposing any surface of their bodies to the sight of men. Women in many Catholic countries traditionally have had few legal rights to pursue activities not approved by the men who control the resources in their societies, including resources supporting sport participation. Women in traditional cultures often face barriers that preclude or discourage sport participation, and certainly limit the extent to which any woman could take sport seriously enough to train at an elite level. These barriers are both normative (i.e., establishing ideas about what is and isn't appropriate) and structural (i.e., restricting access to opportunity and to the things they need to take advantage of the opportunity).

Women have relatively few participation opportunities at the professional level. Until recently, not many people believed that spectators would pay to watch women play anything but "ladylike" sports in which they competed alone or with nets separating the opponents and preventing physical contact between them. Norms in some countries began to change in the 1980s, but many people still wondered if spectators would

Table 8–1   Male and female athletes in the modern Summer Olympic Games, 1896–1996

Year	Place	Countries represented	Male athletes	Female athletes	Percent female
1896	Athens	13	311	0	0
1900	Paris	22	1,319	11	0.01
1904	St. Louis	12	617	8	1.3
1908	London	22	1,999	36	1.8
1912	Stockholm	28	2,490	57	2.2
1916	Olympics (scheduled for Berlin) cancelled (World War I)				
1920	Antwerp	29	2,543	64	2.5
1924	Paris	44	2,956	136	4.4
1928	Amsterdam	46	2,724	290	9.6
1932	Los Angeles	47	1,281	127	9.0
1936	Berlin	49	3,738	328	8.1
1940	Olympics (scheduled for Tokyo) cancelled (World War II)				
1944	Olympics cancelled (World War II)				
1948	London	59	3,714	385	9.4
1952	Helsinki	69	4,407	518	10.5
1956	Melbourne	71	2,958	384	11.5
1960	Rome	83	4,738	610	11.4
1964	Tokyo	93	4,457	683	13.3
1968	Mexico City	112	4,750	781	14.1
1972	Munich	122	6,077	1,070	17.6
1976	Montreal	88	4,915	1,274	20.6
1980	Moscow	81	4,238	1,088	20.4
1984	Los Angeles	140	5,458	1,620	22.8
1988	Seoul	160	7,105	2,476	25.8
1992	Barcelona	170	7,555	3,008	28.5
1996	Atlanta	197	7,059	3,684	34.0

Note: These data show 100 years of gradual progress toward the goal of gender equity. If this progress continues at past rates, my granddaughter hopefully will see a Summer Olympics in which one-half the participants are women.

pay to watch women play sports that went beyond the limits of dominant definitions of femininity. To keep women within those limits, sponsors occasionally have encouraged players to wear clothes accentuating sex appeal. This approach is still part of the marketing strategy in certain sports, although other sports have focused on abilities rather than appearance. It seems that not only are women's professional opportunities more scarce than those for men, but they sometimes come with conditions men don't face.

SUPPORT FOR ATHLETES There has *never* been equity in the support received by women athletes in the vast majority of North American high schools and colleges or other sport-sponsoring organizations around the world. Take American schools as an example. Historically, there have been serious inequities in the following areas:

- access to facilities
- quality of facilities, including playing surfaces, locker rooms, showers, and heating and cooling systems
- availability of scholarships
- program operating expenses
- provision and maintenance of equipment and supplies

- recruiting budgets
- scheduling of games and practice times
- travel and per diem expenses
- opportunity to receive coaching and academic tutoring
- numbers of coaches assigned to teams
- salaries for administrators, coaches, trainers, tutors, etc.
- provision of medical and training services and facilities
- publicity for individuals, teams, and events

Eliminating inequities in each of these areas has been the goal of Title IX and of all supporters of gender equity. The enforcement of equity guidelines has been complicated because opposition has been so strong. The opposition continues as we enter the twenty-first century, but positive changes have occurred, and a growing number of U.S. women athletes now receive support similar to that given to men.

An important barrier to achieving equity in many U.S. university programs is related to football. Football supporters argue that because football involves such violent contact and so many injuries, the teams must carry 85 to 140 members, even though only 11 team members are on the field at any one time. This means that football, as a part of the men's sport programs in the universities, uses a disproportionate share of scholarships and other resources. According to recent legal interpretations of Title IX, women's sport programs should be receiving a share of athletic department resources that matches the percentage of women in the student body: 50 percent women students should get 50 percent of sport resources. Since men's programs traditionally have used nearly all the money in the athletic departments of these universities, this means that equity depends on (1) increasing resources so that women's sports can be funded on a par with men's sports, (2) cutting football's resources, or (3) cutting resources for other men's sports. There has been strong resistance to the idea of cutting football's resources. So when money is tight, other men's sports are cut, or equity is "postponed."

When men's teams are cut, some men attack the meaning and spirit of Title IX rather than asking why a football team can't be cut back to a smaller size (for example, many university teams could be cut in half and still have more players than NFL teams). Thus, male athletes in sports other than football claim to be victims of women's interests, not football's interests. Of course, additional issues emerge when football is a revenue-generating sport that makes a net profit, as it was in about 20 percent of the 554 schools that had teams in 1995. When teams lose money, which occurs in about 33 percent of the schools with big-time programs, other issues are raised. But overall, the question is whether educational institutions should make decisions based on entertainment considerations even though this means sacrificing equity. Most U.S. universities have answered yes to this question, and some continue to say yes in the face of lawsuits (we will say more about this in chap. 14).

Inequities also exist in many community programs, but they often go undocumented unless a researcher digs through data from parks and recreation departments and other local groups. Access to facilities, the number of available programs, and the staff assigned to programs are the most likely areas of inequity.

Most people now realize that a lack of support for women athletes leads to a lack of interest in sports among females of all ages. This makes it difficult to argue that inequities are justified because women just don't want to play sports as much as men do. For well over a century, men have built their programs, shaped them to fit their interests and values, generated interest in participation, sold them to sponsors, and marketed them to potential spectators. And they have done this without having to share any public resources with women; in fact, they have even used the student fees of women to fund their programs. So it seems reasonable to argue that women deserve at least one hundred years of unquestioned support before anyone can justifiably claim that they don't have a strong interest in sport participation, or that their sports don't generate the spectator interest that men's sports do.

JOBS FOR WOMEN IN COACHING AND ADMINISTRATION The athletic lives of most women are controlled by men. While women's sport programs have increased in number and importance around the globe, women often have lost power over those programs. In North America, for example, there has been a significant decline in the number and proportion of women coaches and administrators in many sport organizations, especially the athletic departments of high schools and colleges. And according to *College Sports* magazine, the list of the "Fifty Most Influential People in College Sports in 1996" included only six women. This clearly indicates that gender equity does not exist in these organizations.

Data at all levels of competition show that women do not have equal opportunities when it comes to jobs in coaching and administration; the higher and more powerful the jobs are, the scarcer the women are. Note the following information on American intercollegiate sports (taken from Acosta and Carpenter, 1996):

- When Title IX became law in 1972, 90 percent of women's teams were coached by women; in 1978, when the enforcement of Title IX began, the proportion had dropped to 58 percent; in 1996, it had dropped even further, to only 48 percent.
- Between 1994 and 1996, 209 head coaching jobs for women's teams were added; female head coaches decreased by 9 during the same period, while male head coaches increased by 218. Men received the equivalent of all the new jobs plus 9 of the existing jobs that women had held two years before.
- Women's programs in 1996 had 1,003 more head coaching jobs than they did in 1986; men received 670 of those new jobs, and women received 333.
- In 1972, over 90 percent of women's athletic programs were headed by women; in 1996, only 19 percent had women directors, and about 1 in 4 had no women administrators.

- In schools where women's programs have women athletic directors, there is a higher proportion of women in coaching positions.
- The decline in the proportion of women coaches and administrators generally has been most dramatic at the highest levels of competition and in the highest-paying jobs.
- Women make up only 12 percent of the full-time sports information directors in universities; men have 88 percent of those jobs.
- Fewer than 2 percent of the coaches in men's programs are women, and most of those are coaches of combined teams in swimming, cross country, or tennis; a few are "academic coaches" on high-profile revenue-generating teams.

Table 8–2 presents longitudinal data on the proportion of women coaches for the ten most popular women's intercollegiate sports. The data show that only soccer has a higher proportion of women coaches in 1996 than it had in 1977. Six of the other nine sports show a twenty-year percentage point decline in the proportion of women coaches, while three sports—basketball, cross country, and golf—show slight increases over the last decade, after significant declines in the previous decade.

What would men say if women constituted over 50 percent of the coaches and 82 percent of the administrators in men's programs, while men held only 2 percent of the jobs in women's programs? They would be outraged! And they would certainly call for major affirmative action programs in an attempt to achieve fairness.

The coaching and administration situation is much the same in other countries and on a global level (see McKay, 1993 for Australia; Hargreaves, 1994, and White et al., 1992 for England; Hall, 1996, and Lenskyj, 1994a for Canada). Systematic data on coaches are not easy to collect from country to country, but it is clear that over 90 percent of the national team coaches in most countries are men. The International Olympic Committee (IOC), probably the most powerful administrative body in global sports, is made up of 99 men and only 7 women. There were *no*

Table 8–2 Percentage of women coaches for the ten most popular women's intercollegiate sports, 1977, 1987, and 1996*

Sport	1977	1987	1996	Percentage point change, 1977–1996
Basketball	79.4	59.9	64.3	−15.1
Volleyball	86.6	70.2	66.3	−20.3
Tennis	72.9	54.9	42.5	−30.4
Softball	83.5	67.5	65.0	−18.5
Cross Country	35.2	18.7	21.5	−13.7
Track	52.3	20.8	18.5	−33.8
Swim/dive	53.6	31.2	28.1	−25.5
Field hockey	99.1	96.8	97.2	−1.9
Golf	54.6	37.5	50.2	−4.4
Soccer	29.4	24.1	34.0	+4.6

*Modified from Acosta and Carpenter (1992a and 1996).

women on the IOC between the 1890s and the 1980s! Since then lip service has been given to increasing the number of women, but between 1990 and 1996, of 42 new appointments made, 40 went to men, nearly all of them white. The IOC takes pride in its goal of having women in 10 percent of the decision-making positions in national Olympic committees and international and national sport federations by the year 2000, and in 20 percent of them by 2005 (Davenport, 1996; Jennings, 1996). However, at this rate, equal representation will not come until our daughters are great-grandmothers. It seems that many men around the world have strong vested interests in keeping sport organizations the way they are now, and they often resist changes favoring gender equity.

Reasons for the underrepresentation of women in coaching and administrative positions in women's sports have been widely debated and studied (Acosta and Carpenter, 1992; Dubois, 1995; Pastore, 1994; Pastore et al., 1996; Wilkerson, 1996). As far as I can tell, the major reasons for this underrepresentation include the following:

- Men have effectively used well-established connections with other men in sport organizations to help them during the job search and hiring process.
- Compared to men, most women applicants for coaching and administrative jobs do not

yet have the strategic professional connections and networks that are important when they seek jobs in sport organizations.

- Job search committees often use subjective evaluative criteria, making it more likely that women applicants for coaching and administrative jobs will be seen as less qualified than men applicants.
- Few support systems and professional development opportunities exist for women who want to coach or be administrators, and for women already in coaching and administrative jobs.
- Many women have the perception that athletic departments and sport organizations have "corporate cultures" that don't provide much space for those who see and think about sports differently than the white men do who over many years have established their ways of doing and thinking about sports.

These factors affect which people will aspire to jobs in coaching and administration, be recruited in job search processes, be defined as qualified for jobs, be hired, enjoy their jobs, quit, and be promoted into jobs with more responsibility and higher pay.

Recent research suggests that during the hiring process, those people on search committees often seek, evaluate, and hire candidates they think will be successful as coaches and administrators in sport organizations emphasizing power and performance (Wilkerson, 1996). In other words, after looking at all the objectively measurable qualifications like years of experience and win-loss records, the search committees consider the qualifications of job applicants in more subjective terms. As they look at written applications and then interview candidates, they try to subjectively assess things like a candidate's abilities to recruit and motivate players, to command respect on the team and in the surrounding community, to build toughness and character among players, to maintain team discipline, and to interact effectively with others in the athletic department or sport organization.

Of course, none of these subjective assessments occur in a vacuum. They are influenced by people's ideas about men and women, by their ideas about how their sport programs are organized and what the goals of those programs ought to be, and by their ideas about sports and what is important in sports. Although people on search committees may not all have the same ideas about these things, most job searches for

SIDELINES

©1982 M.T.F.-T.W.S.-Lakewood, CO

....

Women traditionally have been expected to play support roles for men in sports, as well as in society at large. This is changing, but these roles are still present in the gender logic grounded in the cultural ideology of many societies.

....

coaches and sport administrators still occur in settings where subjective assessments of qualifications favor men over women. In other words, coaching and other forms of leadership in sports are seen in terms that are consistent with traditional ideas about masculinity: if you "coach like a girl," you are doing it wrong; if you "lead like a man," you are doing it right. Under these conditions, women get jobs only when they present compelling objective evidence of their qualifications, combined with other evidence that they can do things the way successful men have done them in the past.

Even when women do get coaching and administrative jobs, they are less likely than men to feel that the sport organizations in which they are working are organized to be open and inclusive, and this has a negative impact on their job satisfaction (Pastore et al., 1996). In other words, women often feel that the culture of most sport organizations leaves little space and provides little support for those who see the world from different vantage points than those of the white men who have shaped that culture over many years. This is the reason turnover among women in sport organizations is higher than turnover among men. And unless there are changes in the cultures of sport organizations, gender equity will never be achieved in the ranks of coaching and administration.

What Changes Are Needed to Achieve Gender Equity?

Equity is about who gets what. Gender equity in sports is important because access to valued opportunities and rewards is crucial when it comes to controlling what happens in your life and making changes in the world around you. But achieving gender equity in sports continues to be difficult. Appeals to fairness sound good, but they haven't been very effective. Everyone supports fairness, but many don't want to give up what they already have to achieve it. This certainly has been the pattern in sport programs in which men control most of the power and resources. Most men support the idea of gender equity, but few of them are willing to sacrifice men's past privilege in the form of participation, support, or jobs to achieve it.

This resistance has forced those interested in equity to ask governments for assistance. However, many governments have been slow to respond. In fact, between 1972 and 1988 in the U.S., there were over 1,025 official complaints about gender inequities filed with the U.S. Department of Education's Office for Civil Rights, and *not one* of them resulted in any cuts of federal funds at any of the schools. Recent U.S. court decisions have been more supportive of gender equity in sports, but court cases often involve costly legal fees and long-term commitments. So far, only a few women have been interested in going into debt and giving up years of their lives to see if they can force a sports program to be equitable. But now that women can sue for personal damages, this has begun to change: legal actions now are an effective means for achieving equity.

According to Donna Lopiano, executive director of the Women's Sport Foundation (WSF), equity can be achieved only through strategic political organization and pressure (1992). She has called for the development of grass-roots organizations to systematically support and publicize girls' and women's sports programs. As these organizations publicly recognize the achievements of female athletes and their sponsors, other people will begin to see the value of women's sports and join their efforts to achieve equity. The WSF currently facilitates this process with its resources.

Lopiano (1991) also has urged people in sport organizations to use the following strategies to promote gender equity:

- Confront discriminatory practices in your organization and become an advocate for women athletes and women coaches and administrators.
- Be an advocate and a watchdog, and insist on fair and open employment practices in your organization.

- Keep track of data in your organization and issue a "gender equity score card" every year.
- Learn and educate others about the history of discrimination in sports and how to recognize the subtle forms of discrimination that operate in sports today.
- Object to any policies that would result in a decrease in women's sport participation or participation opportunities.
- Package and promote women's sports as revenue producers, so there will be financial incentives to increase participation opportunities for women.
- Recruit women athletes into coaching, and establish internships and other programs to recruit and train women to enter jobs at all levels in your organization.
- Use women's hiring networks when looking for coaches and administrators in all sport programs.
- Create a supportive work climate for women in your organization, and establish policies to eliminate sexual harassment.

These are useful suggestions. They emphasize a combination of public relations, political lobbying, pressure, education, and advocacy. They are based on the assumption that increased participation and opportunities for women will not come without struggle, and that favorable outcomes depend on organization and persistence.

However, it is very important that those who struggle for gender equity in sports understand the origins of inequities and critically assess the ideology that has shaped dominant forms of sport in their society. If women become participants in existing sports and sport organizations without understanding the connections between sports, gender relations, and dominant definitions of masculinity in society, they will end up contributing to and recreating a set of ideas about social life that not only privilege men, but also guarantee that women will never achieve full equity in sports. Striving for equity in activities and organizations that have been shaped over the years by the values and experiences of men *will not* eliminate some of the most important problems women face as they play and work in sports.

Equity is an important goal, but participation in sports based on a commercialized, media-driven version of the power and performance model needs to be critically assessed. Many people in the sociology of sport have argued that real gender equity can never be achieved in sports activities and organizations exclusively shaped by the values and experiences of men interested in control and domination. They say that real equity requires the development of new models of sport participation, models shaped by the values and experiences of women and of men who do not see themselves in terms of dominant definitions of masculinity (Birrell and Theberge, 1994; Cole, 1994; Hall, 1996; Hargreaves, 1994; Kane, 1995; Lenskyj, 1994b; Lopiano, 1993; McDermott, 1996: Messner and Sabo, 1994; Nelson, 1994; Pronger, 1996).

SPORT PARTICIPATION, PERSONAL EMPOWERMENT, AND STRIVING FOR EQUITY Research in the sociology of sport suggests that playing sports can be a personally empowering experience for girls and women (Nelson, 1994; Taub and Blinde, 1993; Young and White, 1995). Being an athlete, especially a skilled athlete, can change the way a woman sees herself. It can make her feel physically stronger, more competent, and more in control of her life as an independent individual. This is important, because social life often is organized in ways that lead girls and women to see themselves as weak, dependent, and powerless (Cantor and Bernay, 1992; Hargreaves, 1994; McDermott, 1996; Young, 1990).

Sport participation also provides girls and women with opportunities to reconnect with the power of their own bodies. Many images of women in society present the female body as an object to be looked at, evaluated, and consumed. Some girls and women even learn to objectify their own bodies as they apply these images to themselves. Because identity and a sense of power are grounded in a person's body and body image, sport participation can help women overcome the feeling that their bodies are objects. Developing physical skills can give women the confidence that comes from knowing that their bodies can perform with physical competence and power. Furthermore, the physical strength often gained through sport participation goes beyond simply helping a woman feel fit; it also can make her feel less vulnerable, more independent, and more in control of her physical safety and psychological well-being (see Birrell and Richter, 1994; Blinde et al., 1993, 1994; Nelson, 1991, 1994; Theberge, 1995; Young and White, 1995).

Sport participation also can change the way a girl or woman relates to males. A young woman who began working out with weights and training to be a power lifter explains (cited in Richmond, 1986):

> I haven't been the same since. I love it. All of a sudden I find I'm stronger than anyone else in the place—all the girls and practically all of the guys. . . . The guys respected me right away, and that's important. They all act like they're so tough, then you go in and lift more than they can. They can't ignore that there's a girl over in the corner doing more than them, and they hang their heads.

A seventeen-year-old working-class woman interviewed in England expressed similar feelings about her own weight training (Coakley and White, 1992):

> I think mainly I want to be . . . equal with the blokes because I think too many girls get pushed around by blokes. They get called names and things. I think that's wrong. They say "a girl can't do this, a girl can't do that," and I don't like it at all. I'd rather be, you know, equal.

Although feelings of personal empowerment are not always associated with sport participation, they occur frequently enough for us to ask how they might be related to the achievement of gender equity in sports.

The answer is that feelings of empowerment can lead women to be more assertive in their efforts to gain leadership positions in sports and sport organizations. However, the mere fact that women feel personally empowered and/or hold

Sport participation seems to create strong feelings of camaraderie as well as a sense of personal empowerment among women, but it does not automatically create an awareness of social issues related to women in society as a whole. (USA Volleyball)

leadership positions does not guarantee that they will critically assess sports and work to change them so that they will not privilege most men over most women. Nor does this fact guarantee that women will become more concerned with gender issues in society as a whole. For example, after interviewing women intercollegiate athletes in U.S. universities, Elaine Blinde and her colleagues (1994) reached this conclusion:

> Women's participation in sport may challenge traditional notions of women's capabilities and provide positive role models for girls and women. However, sport does not appear to be an effective vehicle for developing the athlete's consciousness as a woman or encouraging activism regarding the concerns of women.

In fact, some women athletes have expressed negative attitudes toward feminists and feminism, and they make a point to distance themselves from social activism related to women's issues. In other words, those who play elite-level sports emphasizing power and performance are not likely to be "boat rockers" critical of the gender order (Blinde et al., 1993, 1994; Young and White, 1995). A possible reason for this is that women athletes may feel they have much to lose if they are associated with civil and human rights issues for women, because others might identify them as ungrateful or even question their sexuality (Crosset, 1995).

Similarly, women hired and promoted into leadership positions in major sport organizations generally are committed to advancing the status of power and performance sports in society. Like many men in those organizations, they seem to have no objections to sports that highlight aggression and competition, in which people are evaluated in terms of their ability to dominate others and ranked in hierarchical terms (Miller and Penz, 1991). Certainly, not all women in sport organizations are like this, but when women become cheerleaders for power and performance approaches to sports, and to life in general, they do little to further the cause of equity over the long run. In contrast, when women combine personal empowerment and leadership positions with critical analysis of sports, and then use their power to actually change the structure and organization of sports, real and lasting gender equity can be achieved (Lopiano, 1993). The problem is that the men who control many sport organizations may not be eager to hire women who put women's issues on the same level as sport issues.

It is not surprising that women who have spent years involved in sports based on the values and experiences of men are often hesitant to promote women's issues. However, it is possible that women's involvement in sports based more closely on the values and experiences of women and emphasizing pleasure and participation can encourage social awareness and even a feminist consciousness (Bailey, 1993; Birrell and Richter, 1994; Deem, 1986; Duquin, 1993; Hargreaves, 1994; Lenskyj, 1994c; Zipter, 1988).

MEN'S INTERESTS IN GENDER EQUITY

Gender equity is not just a women's issue; equity also involves opening up options for men to participate in forms of sports that are not based on dominant definitions of masculinity. Sports that emphasize aggression and domination often lead to self-destructive orientations in the form of chronic injuries, an inability to relate to women, fears of intimacy with other men, homophobia, and a compulsive concern with comparing oneself to other men in terms of what might be called "life success scores" (Messner, 1992; Messner and Sabo, 1994).

Some men understand that when they seek status and rewards in sports and sport organizations in which success is defined in terms of dominating other men, ultimately their relationships with each other as well as with women become constrained and distorted. Bruce Kidd, a former Olympic runner and now a physical educator and social scientist, has pointed this out:

> Through sports, men learn to cooperate with, care for, and love other men, in [many] ways, but they rarely learn to be intimate with each other or emotionally honest. On the contrary, the only way

many of us express fondness for other men is by teasing or mock fighting (1987: 259).

Men who want to get beyond the expression of fondness through teasing and mock fighting have good reason to join with those women concerned with critically assessing the structure and organization of dominant sport forms in their society (Pronger, 1996).

In conclusion, it is important to understand that gender equity in sports is a complex issue. One way to think about gender equity is to use the following guideline, suggested by a gender equity panel organized in 1993 by the National Collegiate Athletic Association (NCAA):

> An athletics program is gender equitable when either the men's or women's sports program would be pleased to accept as its own the overall program of the other gender.

If male athletes, coaches, administrators, and other personnel in men's programs would not consider trading places with their counterparts in women's programs, then gender equity probably does not exist.

But this guideline must be used with caution, because some people in women's programs would not accept certain aspects of many men's programs today. When men's programs emphasize power and performance so much that people associated with them become obsessed with control and domination, they are stressful places to play and work—unless one enjoys striving to dominate others. Thus, the "trading places" guideline is best used only for *material resources* such as opportunities, support, facilities, and salaries, *not* for the spirit that underlies the program. Achieving a more total form of gender equity requires more fundamental changes in how we think about gender and how we play sports. This brings us to the topic of ideological and structural issues.

IDEOLOGICAL AND STRUCTURAL ISSUES

The "Gender Logic" of Sports

Dominant forms of sport in most cultures are played and organized in ways that work to the advantage of most men and to the disadvantage of most women. When people participate in sports, they often learn a form of "common sense" that leads to the conclusion that women are "naturally" inferior to men. For example, the tendency, even today, of some people to say that a person "throws like a girl" when he or she does not throw a ball correctly indicates that this notion of female inferiority is built right into the way we think about gender and physical abilities.* And when a coach of a boys' or men's team uses the words "girls" or "ladies" to describe the team, they are not meant as a compliment. We called this gendered form of "common sense" *gender logic* in chapter 1 (pp. 9–10). To the extent that it still exists today, this gender logic clearly privileges boys and men and gives them power over girls and women both in and outside of sports.

Another aspect of the gender logic used in many sports is that men and women are naturally different, and that the natural characteristics of men are superior to the natural characteristics of women, except when it comes to giving birth and nurturing children. For many years this "logic" led women to be excluded from sports. Women were told by male doctors that if they played sports they would damage their uteruses and breasts, and experience other physical problems endangering their abilities to have children. Today's college students may laugh at these myths, because the information needed to refute them is widely available. But their mothers and grandmothers didn't have this information, nor do many of today's women in countries where literacy rates are low. For these women, myths about sport and the physiology of women have kept and still keep them out of sports.

The notion that men and women are "naturally" different has been used for many years to justify the exclusion of women from some or all sports. Many people felt that since women could never equal or surpass men's achievements, there was no reason to let women even get involved.

After all, if sports were primarily about setting records and dominating others, women would always be second class in power and performance sports. Unfortunately, this way of thinking about gender and sports still exists. Many people continue to compare women and men in terms of performance differences and then go on to say that differences will never disappear because men are simply physically superior to women. Of course, most of these people never wonder what kinds of physical skills athletes would need if sports had been shaped by the values and experiences of women instead of men. For example, if most sports had been created by and for women the motto for the Olympic Games would not be *Citius, Altius, Fortius* (faster, higher, stronger); instead, it might be "Balance, Flexibility, and Endurance" or "Physical Excellence for Health and Humanity"!

Another belief promoted by the gender logic underlying many sports was that men must protect women because men are naturally strong and aggressive and women are naturally weak and passive. As we've seen, this belief has clearly disadvantaged women when it comes to sports. In fact, over the past century, billions of women around the world have been "protected" by men who would not let them play certain sports considered to be too rough or demanding. This belief also has led to the conclusion that because women can't match standards set by men, women's sports are not interesting to watch. For the last fifty years, this conclusion has prevented or slowed the development of professional sports for women.

It has taken many years to break down these gendered forms of "common sense." But they still exist in blatant forms in many poor countries where access to education, especially among women, is restricted. *And* they still exist in more subtle forms in postindustrial societies where access to education is widespread. Consider, for example, why gymnastics and figure skating are so popular in many countries where old forms of gender logic are being questioned and challenged. Joan Ryan (1995), a journalist who has

---

*For a readable explanation of the myth that females cannot throw correctly, see Fallows, 1996; Williams et al., 1996.

covered these sports for over a decade, gives the following explanation:

> Talent counts [in gymnastics and figure skating], but so do beauty, class, weight, clothes and politics. The anachronistic lack of ambivalence about femininity in both sports is part of their attraction, harkening back to a simpler time when girls were girls, when women were girls for that matter: coquettish, malleable, eager to please. In figure skating especially, we want our athletes thin, graceful, deferential and cover-girl pretty. We want eyeliner, lipstick and hair ribbons. . . . [We like gymnastics and figure skating because the athletes are presented to us] free of the sticky issues of power, sexual orientation and aggression that encumber most other female athletes (pp. 5, 68).

This is also the reason youth is so important in these sports: the power of these athletes does not overshadow their vulnerability and their dependence on others, including mostly male coaches. As Ryan also notes, "there is no creature on earth more desperate for approval than a girl inching toward puberty. . . . She is the perfect clay with which coaches can create the perfect gymnast" (p. 208). So when Kerri Strug, the eighteen-year-old U.S. gymnast, ignored her injury and performed her vault during the 1996 Atlanta Games, it was the powerful male coach who swept her up and was photographed carrying her (*against her wishes*) to the medal stand. The photo was widely publicized, *in part* because it vividly reproduced the traditional gender logic underlying sports. Bela Karolyi, the coach, certainly understood this, and was able to use the situation to enhance his reputation as the strong man concerned with the injured gymnast he'd coached since she was a vulnerable ten-year-old girl. (The accompanying photo captures this incident, which reproduces the traditional gender logic that men are strong while women are vulnerable and depend on them.)

Jerry Solomon, the agent who controlled figure skater Nancy Kerrigan's commercial life, also understands and believes the gender logic underlying sports. He explains the basis for Kerrigan's popularity this way:

> They can show Nancy eating soup because she's so attractive and feminine. She's perfect for companies that want a female audience. She's not a jock type (in Ryan, 1995: 129).

Solomon, who is now married to Kerrigan, knows that the gender logic from the past is still alive in the U.S., even though it is more hidden today. He knows that powerful women athletes who challenge this logic still create uneasy feelings among many people; and he knows that that girlish and "doll-like" females attract massive attention. It is clear to him that many people do not question the traditional gender logic of sports, even today.

FROM GENDER LOGIC TO IDEOLOGY: SPORTS AS A CELEBRATION OF MASCULINITY As I noted earlier in this book, cultural ideology consists of the ideas people use to explain (1) how the social world works, (2) how they are connected to that world, and (3) what they should do as they live their lives in that world. Ideology is so deeply rooted in our cultural being that we seldom think about it, and almost never raise questions about it; we just take it for granted. As physical educator and social scientist Bruce Kidd bluntly reminds us, "Ideology is like B.O.; you never smell your own."

This tendency to ignore our own ideology and its impact on how we see things related to sports is especially common among those of us who have been involved with sports for most of our lives. Many men see sports as one of the most exciting and satisfying activities in their lives, and it is difficult for them to critically examine something they enjoy so much. Some women also find it difficult to critically examine sports. This is especially true for women who have watched sports, participated in them, and wished they could share some of the rewards enjoyed by male athletes. When sports have been important in your life, it is difficult to raise critical questions about how they are structured and organized.

When we take a critical look at dominant sport forms in many societies around the world, we see that they often involve dramas highlighting masculine virility, power, and toughness—those

This is a classic sport photo: the strong, decisive, and controlling man (coach Bela Karolyi) picking up the young, heroic, but vulnerable woman (Kerri Strug). Despite her objections (as she later explained) the man lifted and carried her to the victory stand, capturing glory for himself in the process. The photo illustrates both how much things have changed and how much they have stayed the same when it comes to gender and gender relations in sports: women now achieve notable successes in sports, but the sponsorship and control of men remains clearly evident. (Susan Ragan, AP/Wide World Photos)

attributes associated with dominant ideas about masculinity in those societies. Sport spectacles celebrate an interpretation of the world that privileges men and perpetuates the power they have to organize social life to fit their interests. This is the reason Bruce Kidd (1987) has described sports stadiums and domed arenas as "men's cultural centers." These multimillion-dollar facilities usually built with public money cater to the interests of men and host sports in which men "kill," "whip," "roll over," "punish," and "annihilate" other men while people cheer them on. The images associated with these sports are images of a manhood based on aggression, physical power, and the ability to intimidate and dominate others; they emphasize a concern with ranking people in terms of their ability to dominate. In this way, sports tend to reinforce and perpetuate ideologies (interpretations of social life) that favor the interests of men over the interests of women.

IDEOLOGY IN ACTION: THE SOCIAL CONSTRUCTION OF "SISSIES" AND "TOMBOYS" Sports emphasizing aggression and competition "fit" with the dominant definition of masculinity in many cultures; they do not fit with most ideas about femininity or with alternative definitions of masculinity. This has presented problems for many boys and men who don't have the interest or ability to be competitive in sports requiring physically aggressive behaviors. It also has presented problems for many women who aren't comfortable trying to aggressively dominate others and women who are such tough competitors that they don't fit with dominant definitions of femininity. The boys who avoid sports during childhood, especially sports involving physical toughness, often are called "sissies." The girls who excel in those sports are called "tomboys."

Boys labelled "sissies" often get teased and excluded from peer-group relationships and activities; they are *socially marginalized* because of their characteristics. They may even be defined as "abnormal" because they don't fit the dominant definition of masculinity in society, a definition

that many people think is based in "nature" or "the way God made us." As they get older, these boys often continue to be marginalized because they are seen as threats to the ideology that many people use to define "nature" and interpret how the social world works. Questions may be raised about their sexual orientation and terms like "fag," "gay," and "queer" are used to describe them, regardless of their sexual orientation.

When the dominant definition of masculinity in society is based on the assumption that in addition to being aggressive and competitive, all "real men" must be heterosexual, "gay" becomes a derogatory identity label and an abnormal lifestyle. This, of course, leads gay men to hide their identities and feelings when they play sports, and encourages all men to idealize extra-aggressive behavior so they won't be seen as gay. It also leads to frequent gay-bashing comments in locker rooms and on playing fields. In fact, a men's coach may question a player's heterosexuality when he makes a mistake or is not as aggressive as he is expected to be; the assumption is that when players are called "girls" or "fags," they will try extra hard to be aggressive and dominate the other "real men" they are playing against. This is one of the ways that a combination of misogyny (a disdain for women) and homophobia (a fear of homosexuality) gets built right into the structure and organization of dominant forms of sport in a society. If you have doubts about this, go to the locker room of a major college football or men's basketball team and listen to what the athletes say over the course of a season (see Curry, 1991, 1996; Disch and Kane, 1996).

Gay male athletes have responded to homophobia in a variety of ways (Pronger, 1990, 1996). Some simply put up with feelings of estrangement and aloneness as they enjoy participating in sports, some laugh inside at the irony of participating in activities that glorify a combination of domination and heterosexuality, some use sports as a hiding place where they can "prove" masculinity to themselves or others, and some organize events like the Gay Games or their

When NBA player Dennis Rodman claimed that he was getting in touch with his "feminine side," most people saw his behavior as a publicity stunt. But what if he were serious? This possibility makes many people uncomfortable, because Rodman would be challenging the cultural belief in "opposite" sexes and the belief that only "real" (heterosexual) men play sports. These beliefs have enabled people to ignore the fact that males and females are much more similar than they are different, even biologically. (Beth A. Keiser, AP/Wide World Photos)

local counterparts to bring together gay athletes to compete in sports.

Dennis Rodman, a high-profile NBA player who does not hide his desire to wear makeup and dresses, has challenged homophobia and traditional ideas about gender. Rodman's reputation as a tough, aggressive basketball player, and the publicity given to previous behaviors of his that many have defined as outrageous, set the stage for a curious public acceptance of what Rodman calls his "feminine side." Of course, some think he is crazy or perverted or both, but even they are aware that Rodman has pushed gender boundaries in ways that male athletes have not done so before.

Two transvestite volleyball stars in Thailand also have pushed gender boundaries. Their off-court practice of wearing makeup, long hair, blouses, skirts, and dresses kept them from being chosen for Thailand's national team, even though they were clearly among the best six players in the country in 1996. So they formed a transvestite team, nicknamed "Steel Women," and have continued to play on the elite level in southeast Asia. Their popularity and ability to entertain audiences certainly has challenged the prevailing gender logic of sports. But boys still try to avoid being called sissies, even though they may cheer for Rodman and the Steel Women.

When girls are labelled "tomboys," they don't experience the same social disapproval as boys labelled "sissies." Tomboys often receive praise. This is because behaviors associated with boys and men are highly valued and rewarded in society, even when they are exhibited by girls. For example, Amy Van Dyken, the U.S. swimmer who won four gold medals in the 1996 Games, described her experiences this way:

> When I was growing up it was always kind of bad to be called "tomboy" and now I think it's flattering for girls to be called tomboys. I want to be out there saying it's cool to be in sports. It's the thing to do (in Carter, 1996).

Van Dyken's statement is encouraging, but as girls get older and their bodies become sexualized in terms of dominant gender ideology, they still receive powerful cultural messages that being a tomboy is not nearly so important as being physically attractive and sexually desirable in the eyes of men. They also hear that sport turns boys into men, and they wonder what it does to girls. And sometimes their boyfriends encourage them to drop out of sports that are too rough or that interfere with the girls' being available for them (Coakley and White, 1992).

Different young women deal with these "femininity messages" and the traditional gender logic of sports in different ways. For example, those who continue to play physical contact sports sometimes discover that unless they are careful to act in "ladylike" ways, the label "tomboy" might change to the label "lesbian." For example, a woman who promotes boxing in England explained, "Most people think [women in boxing] must be lesbians because boxing is not a ladylike thing to do" (Longmore, 1994). It seems that women who aren't "soft" and "graceful" don't fit the dominant definition of femininity. But these women can lower their chances of being socially marginalized if they present themselves to others in ways that give "proof" that they are really "normal" (meaning *heterosexual*) women (Kolnes, 1995). They can do this with bows, ribbons, ponytails, makeup, dresses, hose, heels, boyfriends or husbands, engagement or wedding rings, and statements about wanting to eventually settle down and have children. If women athletes in power sports don't do these

things, some people will define them as threats to the dominant definition of femininity and even threats to their ideas about "nature" and morality. This happens regardless of the sexual orientation of the women themselves. In this way, homophobia gets built into sports and then serves to control all women, lesbian and straight (Griffen, 1993; Krane, 1996). This is shown in the box, Women Bodybuilders: Expanding Definitions of Femininity?" on pp. 240–241.

The gender logic of sports and of homophobia have combined to work in strange ways over the years. Women who grew up between 1910 and 1950 heard from doctors and other "scientific experts" that playing certain sports would turn them into physiological "monsters" and cause their genital organs to decay and their bodies to change into men's bodies (some of these warnings are listed in Birke and Vines, 1987; Lenskyj, 1986; Vertinsky, 1987). Women who grew up during the 1950s and 1960s heard that most women athletes were "dykes" or that vigorous exercise could damage the uterus and cause problems with childbirth. They also were warned that playing sports would lead to the development of bulging muscles and other characteristics that men would not find sexually attractive. Today's women still face the norm of "compulsory heterosexuality" that is a vestige of traditional gender logic. Is this part of the reason sports announcers now call attention to women athletes who have husbands and children? Dominant gender ideology in society, including its expression in the gender logic of sports and homophobia, runs deep and changes slowly, even when questioned and challenged. It's not so long ago that some coaches had "no lesbian" policies for their teams, and pro women athletes wore lycra uniforms to meet the ideological requirements framed by the gender logic of sports. Lesbians are increasingly accepted in sports and in the rest of society, but many are still apprehensive about others' responses to their identities. They know, for example, that homophobia led some universities to put "no sexual harassment" clauses in contracts for women coaches of women's teams.

They know that lesbians are feared more than men coaches, even though nearly all sexual harassment, abuse, and assault allegations name men as the perpetrators. If heterosexual men had behavior records like those of homosexual women, harassment, sexual abuse, and rape would not even be problems in society. Although they are problems, we have no "heterophobia" in society and sports. Why not? Because ideology sometimes keeps us from recognizing what is in front of us.

Need for Ideological and Structural Changes

The major point of this section is that real gender equity in sports requires a complete rethinking of our definitions of masculinity and femininity, and our ideas about the purposes and goals of sports and sport organizations. This is a challenging task, but I will outline some of the ways it might be approached.

ALTERNATIVE DEFINITIONS OF MASCULINITY We need additional definitions of masculinity in society. As things are now, dominant sport forms normalize the idea that masculinity involves aggressiveness and a desire to outdo or outperform others. In fact, some people associate men's behavior in sports with biological nature and conclude that traditional definitions of masculinity are "natural." Strong and aggressive men are lionized and made into heroes in sports, while weak or passive men are marginalized and emasculated (Jansen and Sabo, 1993). As boys and men apply this ideology to their own lives, they tend to view manhood in terms of things that jeopardize the safety and well-being of themselves and others (Fine, 1987; Wacquant, 1995). They may ride the tops of elevators, drive cars at breakneck speeds, play various forms of "chicken," drink each other "under the table", get into fights, use violence in sports as indicators of manhood, build muscles to an unhealthy degree, avoid interacting with women as equals, keep sexual scores in heterosexual relationships, rough up girlfriends or wives, rape, or kill "unfaithful" women. Or they may conclude that what you can get away with in life depends on

how big and tough you are, and how much you can get others to fear or depend on you. If they take this ideology far enough, they may get in the habit of "forcing their way" on others through physical intimidation or coercion.

Even though this ideology of masculinity can be dangerous and socially isolating, athletes are seldom criticized for using it to guide their behavior in sports. For example, I've never heard coaches scold athletes for hitting someone too hard or showing no feeling when they have blown out someone's knee or knocked someone unconscious, or paralyzed or even killed an opponent (as in boxing). Is it dangerous to teach young men not to hesitate to hurt people, or not to express remorse when they do? Does this destroy their ability to empathize with others and feel their pain? If you teach boys to be tough and to dominate others, will they be able to develop intimate and supportive relationships with other men or with women? How will they handle their relationships with women? Will their rates of assault and sexual assault be high?

The frightening record of men's violent and destructive behavior suggests that there is definitely a need to develop additional and alternative definitions of masculinity. The dominant definition of masculinity and the idea that "boys will be boys" is closely associated with serious problem behaviors in many societies around the world—in other spheres of everyday life as well as in sports (Miedzian, 1991). However, dominant forms of sport in today's society seem to prevent people from being aware of the need to raise questions about gender ideology. The sociology of sport has an important role to play in the raising of these questions.

ALTERNATIVE DEFINITIONS OF FEMININITY The experiences of many women athletes also suggest a need to develop additional definitions of femininity. This was highlighted in 1990, when two fathers of girls in an under-twelve soccer league in Texas demanded proof that the goalie on the opposing team was really a girl. They said she was too skilled as an athlete to be a girl, and they wanted her to prove she was

REFLECT ON SPORT

Women Bodybuilders
Expanding Definitions of Femininity?

Women bodybuilders today are described variously as powerful women, unfeminine freaks, the ultimate hard bodies, new women, "gender benders," entertainers, and sideshows for real sports. These descriptions vary with historical and cultural factors (Bolin, 1992a).

Until the late 1970s, there was no such thing as competitive women's bodybuilding. It didn't exist, because it so totally contradicted dominant definitions of femininity and what people saw as "natural" muscular development for women. But women bodybuilders consistently have challenged those definitions of femininity, pushed boundaries of social acceptance, and raised questions about what is "natural" when it comes to the bodies of women.

Many people in the recent past saw women bodybuilders as rebels or deviants, as freaks of nature. This was the case because most people in Western cultures saw gender in terms of differences that divide all humans into two distinct and mutually exclusive categories: females and males. According to this classification system, females are defined as the "weaker sex" and femininity is associated with being soft, petite, emotional, and in need of protection. In fact, the dominant standard of feminine beauty over the past century has been associated with vulnerability and weakness. Males, on the other hand, are defined as the stronger sex, and masculinity is associated with being hard, strong, rational, and the defender of women. In fact, masculine attractiveness traditionally has been associated with invulnerability and strength. And many people simply assume that "nature intended it that way."

Women bodybuilders have challenged this gender logic, and in the process have threatened many people's ideas about how the world works. According to dominant gender ideology, women bodybuilders are unfeminine, because they are "too muscular," and ugly, because their bodies aren't soft and vulnerable. But not everyone accepts this ideology. For those seeking alternative definitions of femininity, women's bodybuilding has provided new images that some

people find exciting. They like the idea of challenging traditional notions of "female frailty" and raising questions about the biology of gender difference. Women's bodybuilding has encouraged this process by showing that hardness and strength are not exclusively the attributes of males (Miller and Penz, 1991).

Despite the fact that women bodybuilders, like women athletes in other power sports, are what we might call "gender benders," they are not able to completely escape the constraints of dominant definitions of femininity. The first women bodybuilders were careful not to be too good at building muscles. They emphasized a toned, symmetrical body displayed through carefully choreographed graceful moves. Their goal was to somehow stay within the boundaries of femininity as determined by contest judges. But this presented problems, because definitions of femininity have never been set once and for all time. Definitions are constantly changing, and that made it impossible for judges to spell out what was "too muscular" or how much body symmetry was needed to look "feminine."

While judges tried to come up with a bodybuilding ideal that balanced muscularity and body symmetry, women bodybuilders tried to anticipate judges' standards and often challenged the standards used from contest to contest. The controversy surrounding this issue of defining standards is the central theme in *Pumping Iron II: The Women*, a movie about women's bodybuilding in the early 1980s.

This issue of trying to define femininity was frustrating to bodybuilders who were seeking muscularity during the early 1980s. For example, one woman stated that,

> When you compete, your muscularity is all, but the judges insist on [us] looking womanly. They try to fudge the issue with garbage about symmetry, proportion and definition. What they really want is tits and ass (Cammie Lusko, cited in Bolin, 1992b).

According to Anne Bolin (1992a, b), a bodybuilder and an anthropologist who has studied bodybuilding, the constraints presented by dominant definitions of femininity have led women bodybuilders to make clear distinctions between how they present themselves during competitive posing and what they do in their workout gyms. In other words, the women carefully separate their lives into "frontstage" and "backstage" regions (see Goffman, 1959). In the backstage region of the gym, they focus on bodywork and building muscles. Serious training overrides concerns about how gender is defined outside the gym. Femininity is irrelevant, and workouts are not "gendered" in any way—all bodybuilders, women and men, train the same way.

But when the women get ready for the "frontstage," they try to neutralize the stigma of having too many muscles. They do this by using what might be called "femininity insignias." In other words, they carefully construct a presentation of self that highlights the "look" of dominant femininity as it is defined today. They may dye their hair blonde, wear it in a long, fluffy style, and adorn it with a ribbon. They manicure fingernails and toenails and polish them, or glue on false fingernails. They have makeup professionally applied, carefully choose posing bikinis for color and material, wear earring studs, wear an engagement or wedding ring, shave all body hair, and perhaps use plastic surgery to soften the contours of their faces. When they pose, they walk on their toes, use graceful dance moves, and smile incessantly. And if possible, they try to be seen with husbands or male friends, and they cautiously flirt with male judges. They do all this to appear "natural" according to dominant definitions of femininity (this process is described in Bolin, 1992b). Of course, it isn't natural at all!

Women bodybuilders are not unique when it comes to their presentation of self. Any women in a power sport has two choices if she wants to avoid being socially rejected by some people:

1. work to change dominant definitions of femininity, or
2. neutralize the stigma associated with being muscular by creating an image that fits dominant definitions of femininity.

However, when woman bodybuilders walk on stage, the femininity insignias they inscribe on their bodies contrast with their muscularity to such an extent that it is difficult for anyone who sees them not to realize that femininity is a social construction rather than a biological fact. The contestants in women's events today are clearly more muscled than 98 percent of the men in the world, and they make it difficult to maintain the notion that women are the weaker sex or that femininity implies frailty and vulnerability.

Of course, the popularity of women's bodybuilding has not gone unnoticed by people who benefit from dominant definitions of femininity. These people have tried to appropriate the image of the "hard body" and redefine it as a sexy body, a body desired by men, a body dependent on men for sexual satisfaction, if not protection. They use airbrushed photos of hard bodies in sensual poses on exercise equipment to emphasize that staying "in shape" really does mean staying more heterosexually attractive than other women (Cole, 1993). Women bodybuilders often go along with this sexualized image of their bodies so that they can obtain publicity, endorsement contracts, and appearance fees. They are photographed leaning on or looking up to even more muscular men. But in the gym, they train in ways that clearly show that conventional femininity is grounded in culture.

I would argue that despite the use of femininity insignias and the fact that the "hard body" image has been commercially manipulated to get women to view one another as competitors in a heterosexual mating marketplace, women bodybuilders have opened up possibilities for some women to view the development of muscles and strength as a source of personal empowerment. These possibilities focus on personal change rather than the development of progressive politics among women collectively, but those personal changes raise questions about the limiting consequences of dominant definitions of femininity. Isn't this one of the things that sports should do? What do you think?

one by disrobing in front of a woman observer in the locker room. If this sounds bizarre, remember that women athletes in some international sport competitions still must submit to genetic tests to "prove" they are really women (Hood-Williams, 1995; Jennings, 1996).

Until there is widespread acceptance of alternatives to dominant definitions of femininity, women will continue to face problems in connection with playing sports. These problems can take many different forms. For example, some girls still do not receive the same kind of encouragement as their brothers to be socially independent and physically active in play activities and sports. As infants, they are handled more gently and protectively than boys. Boys are thrown into the air more often, given more toys requiring active play and the use of motor skills, and allowed to explore more of their physical environments before being "cautioned" and constrained by their parents. Girls are watched over more closely, even before they start to walk. This pattern of "protectiveness" and constraint continues through childhood, and limits girls' participation in sport activities (Beal, 1994; Coser, 1986).

In most North American families, young girls are not discouraged from playing sports, but may be treated differently than their brothers in at least three respects. *First,* girls are less likely to learn that physical activities and achievements in sport can or should be uniquely important sources of rewards in their lives. *Second,* fathers spend considerably *less* time in shared physical exercises and activities with daughters than with sons. *Third,* the play time of girls is more likely to be regulated and controlled by parents. For example, when a young girl asks one of her parents for permission to go and play, she often hears something like this: "It's okay for you to go play as long as you . . .

- stay in the house"
- don't leave the yard"
- don't go far away from the house"
- go with a friend"
- play with children I know"
- get back home at exactly 4 o'clock—no later!"
- don't do anything dangerous"
- keep your clothes clean"
- don't play rough or get hurt"
- don't get in fights or arguments with your friends"
- get back in time to set the table"
- take your little brother (or sister) with you"

This "conditional permission," even when it is justified by parental fears for the safety of their daughters, is an outgrowth of the dominant definition of femininity; it can subvert opportunities and motivation to play or organize complex competitive games involving physical skills. Such games require going outside the house, leaving the family yard, playing with large groups (including some children unknown to parents), getting dirty, having arguments and fights now and then, playing rough, and sometimes getting hurt. Furthermore, it is impossible to do these things when curfews are inflexible and younger brothers or sisters have to be watched.

It is no wonder that girls end up playing different kinds of games than those their brothers play (Lever, 1976, 1978). Boys do not have nearly as many parental constraints limiting their activities. This is one of the things enabling many of them to move quickly beyond their sisters in the development of sport skills.

Fathers reinforce these "femininity restrictions" when they treat their daughters as "Daddy's little girls." This protectiveness is well-intentioned, but it often constrains the play activities of girls and focuses girls' attention on catering to the needs of their fathers, an orientation that precludes the development of social independence. Mothers reinforce these femininity restrictions when they treat their daughters as "Mommy's little helpers." Of course, girls (and boys) should support and assist their parents. But when girls get locked into caretaking and nurturing roles and overly dependent relationships with either of their parents, they seldom have opportunities to develop competence in physical activities and sports. Alternative definitions of femininity would alert parents and others to the problems that now exist because of traditional femininity restrictions.

The need for alternative definitions of femininity is also illustrated through the following story told by a young lesbian as she described her gym class in school:

> Gym classes were segregated . . . I would play with the girls and they always said that I played "too rough." They said I could play with the girls with my left hand only, or play with the boys. So, of course, I decided to play with the boys . . . So we were in the gym one day and all the girls were lined up against the wall and there I was along with the boys playing [dodge ball]. The girls were really cheering for me and I had this really mixed thing that has stayed with me ever since. I wanted to wipe out every boy in that group and I did, by the way, I won. I was the last person standing. I wanted to win for them, for the girls, for them to see that it could be done. At the same time, what was mixed up with this was this incredible contempt for the girls because they were all in their little dresses and little shoes sitting passively on the side, cheering for me, and I didn't want to be one of them and yet I knew I was one of them (Whitfield, cited in Lenskyj, 1994c: 363).

This story portrays the feelings experienced by a lesbian who was lost between mutually exclusive definitions of femininity and masculinity that didn't include her. Interestingly, her sense of herself was more "natural" than the definition of femininity that held the girls in the class on the sidelines. If girls and women are going to feel good about being involved in all types of sports, there is a need for new femininities that recognize diversity as natural.

Gender logic, in sports and society at large, is not fixed in nature. Instead, it is constructed, challenged, revised, and even changed in dramatic ways through social interaction (Connell, 1995). In most cultures, the meaning of gender and its application in people's lives is symbolized and powerfully presented in bodily perfor-

mances that occur in sports. Many people have used men's achievements in power and performance sports as evidence of men's aggressive nature, their superiority over women, and their right to claim social and physical space as their own. Male athletes, they say, are tough, powerful, and big; they are symbolic proof of traditional gender logic. In this way sports have been sites for the reproduction of a traditional gender order. At the same time, however, the growing achievements of many women athletes have challenged gender logic and encouraged some people to think in new ways about masculinity, femininity, and gender relations.

In most cultures there remains a strong attachment to what might be called a "two-box gender classification system" in which men are men and women are women, and there is nothing natural in between. This system is so central to the way many people see the world that they feel they cannot change or abandon it. But it flies in the face of powerful evidence showing that neither anatomy nor hormones, neither chromosomes nor secondary sex characteristics can be used to divide the world neatly into two categories, one male and one female (Ferrante, 1995; Hood-Williams, 1995). Actually, people fall along a number of different continua related to these factors. In the past, when people's bodies or other traits didn't fit into these categories, they were defined as freaks of nature or perverts, even though they came by these traits in nature. People are challenging this approach today, and sports are one of the primary sites where they are doing so.

Changing the Way We "Do" Sports

Gender equity involves more than inventing new ways to "do" masculinity, femininity, and gender relations. It also depends on changes in the ways sports are organized, promoted, played, and portrayed. We need new types of programs, new vocabularies to describe those programs, new images that people can associate with sports, and new ways to evaluate success and the enjoyment of sport experiences. But at the same time, we need critical women and men to become a part of

Calvin and Hobbes   by Bill Watterson

Calvin does not accept the notion that a boy must play sports to prove he is not a wimp. But Susie reminds him that dominant ideas about gender are just as constraining for girls and women. Calvin has a difficult time responding to Susie, and he changes the conversation to a less serious level. Will he ever learn?

existing programs and work to change them from inside (see Lopiano, 1993).

One strategy for achieving gender equity is to actually develop new sport programs that change how we "do" sports. Some of the possibilities include the following:

1. new programs promoting lifetime sport participation, and emphasizing combinations of competition and partnership, individual expression and teamwork, health and skill development
2. new programs reflecting an ethic of care and connection between teammates and opponents (Duquin, 1993)
3. new programs providing coaching and administrative opportunities for women, thereby creating more experiences that generate feelings of empowerment among women and the opportunities to put those feelings into action, like those men have had for many years in sports
4. new programs that bring boys and girls and men and women together in shared sport experiences that break down traditional gender logic (Sabo and Messner, 1993)

But the creation of new sport programs should not be the only strategy used to achieve equity. New programs sometimes present political problems when it comes to gender equity issues. These are some examples:

1. When women's sport programs are structured differently from men's programs, it can be difficult to determine if there are equal opportunities for girls and women.
2. New sport programs that are different from those already in existence run the risk of being perceived as "second class," thereby perpetuating the gender logic of female inferiority.
3. New sport programs are more difficult to promote than programs based on existing models, and it is much easier to apply pressure for equal resources within schools and other organizations when asking for comparable programs than when asking for new programs (Donnelly, 1996a).
4. When some men participate in sports grounded in the values and experiences of women, they devalue them by saying they are not "real" because they don't involve

traditionally masculine approaches and orientations.

The point here is that efforts to create new sport programs run the risk of inadequate funding and the loss of some community support. On the other hand, the approach in which girls and women simply participate in dominant sport forms has risks as well: girls could be discouraged from playing sports, ideals related to how sports might be different from the way they are now could be compromised, and old problems tied to beliefs about male superiority could be reproduced (Theberge, 1996). In the long run, it may be most effective for those interested in promoting gender equity to maintain both approaches simultaneously (Lopiano, 1993). This means that those who strive to participate in existing sports and sport organizations should continue to be aware of alternatives for the future. Then, as they gain power in sports, they will have a vision of the possibilities for improving opportunities for both women and men. Likewise, those who envision new sport forms should recognize that women can use their participation in existing sports and sport organizations to establish credibility and gain access to power and resources.

All of us can encourage ideological and structural changes in sports by changing the way we talk about sports. We could eliminate what we might call the "language of difference and domination" associated with sports and sport participation (Kidd, 1987). For example, using "jock" to refer to athletes perpetuates the idea that sports are for men. Labels like "sissy," "tomboy," "fag," and "wimp" serve to inscribe gender into sports in ways that interfere with gender equity. Motivating young men by telling them to go out and prove their masculinity on the playing field has similar consequences. Calling young adult intercollegiate athletes "kids" perpetuates a hierarchical organizational structure in which some people control others in autocratic ways that work against the interests of women in sports. Use of locker-room language that bashes gays and de-

means women also subverts the achievement of gender equity; the listener who stands by and says nothing in response to this language perpetuates inequities. The use of military metaphors to describe what happens in sports is another way that sports are masculinized: "throwing long bombs" and "killing the opposition" are just two examples of metaphors that are based on the experiences of men, not women (Sabo and Jansen, 1992; Segrave, 1994; Trujillo, 1995).

Structural and ideological changes promoting gender equity also could be encouraged through rule changes in sports. For example, there is a need for rules to eliminate violence in sports like hockey, football, rugby, and soccer. Men will object to such rules by saying they make sports into "girls' games," and that men who would propose them should wear skirts, but such comments only prove that the rules are necessary. Rules promoting safety are needed in many sports, and there is a need for policies about not playing in pain and when injured. Sports also need more rituals that bring opponents together in ways that emphasize partnership rather than hostility and rivalry.

Gender equity depends on the redesigning of existing sports from both the outside and the inside, and the development of new sports reflecting the values and experiences of women and of those men who don't identify themselves in terms of the dominant definition of masculinity.

SUMMARY

IS EQUITY THE ONLY ISSUE?

During the last quarter of the twentieth century, sport participation among females increased significantly. This was primarily the result of a growth in opportunities fueled by government legislation, the women's movement, the health and fitness movement, and increased publicity given to women athletes.

Despite increases to this point, future increases in sport participation among girls and women will not be automatic. In fact, we have good reasons to be cautious when we predict increases. These reasons include budget cuts and privatization of sports, resistance to government policies and legislation, backlash in response to changes favoring strong women, a relative lack of women coaches and administrators, a strong cultural emphasis on cosmetic fitness among women, and continued trivialization of women athletes and women's sports.

More women than ever are playing sports and working in sport organizations, but gender inequities continue to exist in participation opportunities, support for athletes, and jobs for women in coaching and administration. Even when sport participation leads to feelings of personal empowerment among women, the achievement of complete and permanent gender equity is impossible without a critical analysis of gender ideology and the structure of sport itself. This critical analysis is important, because it not only gives direction to women's efforts to achieve equity, but also shows that there are reasons for men to join women who are trying to achieve equity.

The major point of this chapter is that gender equity in sports is integrally tied to issues related to gender ideology and the structure of sport itself. Gender equity will never be complete or permanent unless there are changes in the way people think about masculinity and femininity, and unless there are changes in the way sports are organized and played. Dominant sport forms in society are currently based on a "gender logic" that leads to the conclusion that girls and women are, by definition, inferior to boys and men. This gender logic includes beliefs about male-female differences that "naturalize" the superiority of men over women. Therefore, sports celebrate a form of masculinity that leads to the social marginalization of many men and women. And as this form of masculinity is celebrated through sports, homophobia and misogyny are built right into the structure of sports and sport organizations.

Because of this "gender logic" and the fact that sports have been shaped by the values and experiences of men, real and lasting gender equity depends on our changing dominant definitions of masculinity and femininity, and changing the way we "do" sports in our own experience. New sports and sport organizations need to be created, while existing ones need to be changed both from the inside and through outside pressure. Change in sports can be accomplished through a combination of strategies: using new ways to talk about sports; developing new rules to control violence and injuries and to foster safety for all players; and creating new rituals and orientations based on the pleasure and participation approach to sports rather than the power and performance approach. Unless ideology changes, gender equity will never be completely and permanently achieved. This is the reason those interested in gender equity in sports should be interested also in gender and gender relations issues outside of sports.

SUGGESTED READINGS

Birrell, S., and C. L. Cole, eds. 1994. *Women, sport, and culture.* Champaign, IL: Human Kinetics (*an excellent selection of twenty-four papers focusing on key research and theory related to ideological issues*).

Boutilier, M. A., and L. SanGiovanni. 1993. *The sporting woman.* Champaign, IL: Human Kinetics (*a comprehensive discussion of women and sport*).

Cahn, S. K. 1994. *Coming on strong: Gender and sexuality in twentieth-century women's sport.* New York: The Free Press (*a social history of women in sports in the U.S.; attention is given to the interactions of gender, race, class, and sexuality*).

Cohen, G. L., ed. *Women in sport: Issues and controversies.* Newbury Park, CA: Sage (*twenty-seven articles dealing with political, economic, historical, sociological, psychological, and physiological issues; the articles bring together theory and practice related to gender and sports*).

Crosset, T. 1995. *Outsiders in the clubhouse: The world of women's professional golf.* Albany: State University of New York Press (*an insightful account of qualitative research done on a unique social world; material on the impact of gender in the everyday lives of golfers and the golf tour*).

Festle, M. J. 1996. *Playing nice: Politics and apologies in women's sports.* New York: Columbia University Press (*a clearly written political history of women's sports in the U.S. since World War II; deals with issues such as the need to challenge prevailing gender norms in order to make progress).*

Hall, M. A. 1996. *Feminism and sporting bodies.* Champaign, IL: Human Kinetics (*a personalized examination of the history, current trends, and future of gender relations in sports; insightful discussion of feminist approaches to sports*).

Hargreaves, J. 1994. *Sporting females: Critical issues in the history and sociology of women's sports.* London: Routledge (*North American Society for the Sociology of Sport Book Award Winner in 1994; the most comprehensive analysis of women in sports available. I learned much from this book*).

Lenskyj, H. 1994. *Women, sport and physical activity: Selected research themes.* Gloucester, Ontario: Sport Information Research Centre (SIRC/CDS) (*a thorough and useful overview of literature on feminist theory and sociological, psychological, and physiological research on women and sport; excellent reference source*).

McKay, J., M. Messner, and D. Sabo, eds. Forthcoming. Men, masculinities and sport. *Masculinities* (Special issue) (*a collection of empirical and theoretical papers dealing with the body, violence, media, and with sport as a site for resistance and change*).

Messner, M. A. 1992. *Power at play.* Boston: Beacon Press (*an insightful, in-depth analysis of masculinity and sports*).

Messner, M. A., and D. F. Sabo, eds. 1990. *Sport, men, and the gender order.* Champaign, IL: Human Kinetics (*nineteen papers dealing with sports, masculinity, sexuality, and the gender order from feminist perspectives*).

Messner, M. A., and D. F. Sabo. 1994. *Sex, violence and power in sports.* Freedom, CA: The Crossing Press (*two male sociologists with long histories of sport participation look back at their personal experiences in sports in a critically self-reflective way; they raise questions about dominant definitions of masculinity as they look back, and then make suggestions for bringing about changes in the future*).

Nelson, M. B. 1991. *Are we winning yet? How women are changing sports and sports are changing women.* New York: Random House (*selected as winner of the 1992 Amateur Athletic Foundation's Book Award; a readable description and analysis of the everyday experiences of a diverse collection of women athletes*).

Nelson, M. B. 1994. *The stronger women get, the more men love football: Sexism and the American culture of sports.* New York: Harcourt Brace (*this is a regularly assigned book in my courses; Nelson uses her own sport experiences and her feminist awareness to deal with sports in a critical but sensitive manner*).

Pronger, B. 1989. *The arena of masculinity: Sports, homosexuality, and the meaning of sex.* New York: St. Martin's Press (*examines the experiences of gay athletes in straight sports, and sports in gay communities in North American cities; this is an interpretation of the gay and athletic experiences combined*).

9

I give out three scholarships myself, and they're all academic. Not athletic. I'm just so sick of athletics and blacks. All you ever hear is we run for 100 yards and we dunk.

Charles Barkley, NBA player (1995)

(Jay Coakley)

Race and Ethnicity

Are skin color and cultural heritage important in sports?

To people of all races, every time you walk in this place is like coming home. All the cultures of Los Angeles come together at Dodger Stadium.

Bill Russell, manager, Los Angeles Dodgers (1996)

In our extremely race-conscious society, all minority athletes enter the sports

arena burdened with a certain racial-ethnic baggage.

Harry Edwards, sociologist and activist (1993)

I truly believe [African Americans] may not have some of the necessities to be . . . a field manager or perhaps a general manager. . . . They are gifted with great

musculature. . . . They are fleet of foot. . . . [But] as far as having the background to become club presidents or president of a bank . . . I don't know.

Al Campanis, former vice president for player personnel, Los Angeles Dodgers (1987)

The crazy theories of black intellectual inferiority are alive and well. . . . [Coaches and] managers have to think, and the conventional wisdom among sports' ruling elite is that . . . blacks don't think as well as whites.

Arthur Ashe (1992)

Popular beliefs about race and ethnicity have a major impact on what happens in sports; and sports have become sites where people either challenge or accept dominant forms of racial and ethnic relations in a society. For example, I recently invited five children to be on a "youth sports" panel in my sociology course; all were ten to 12 years old, heavily involved in sports, and white. During the discussion with the college students, a sixth-grade boy known in his all-white elementary school for his sprinting and basketball skills was asked if he planned to try out for those sports when he went to junior high school. Surprisingly, he said no. When asked to explain, he said, "I won't have a chance because all the black kids at the junior high will beat me out." He went on to point out that he wasn't upset by this since he was a good soccer player and distance runner, too. He said he would try out for those sports instead of for sprinting and basketball. He also said he had never played with black kids while in elementary school.

About the same time this sixth-grader was using his ideas about race to make important sport participation decisions, a local white male high school graduate who was student body president, class valedictorian, and an equally talented football and basketball player was asked by a sportswriter which sport he planned to play in college. He was being heavily recruited in both sports by many top universities. He said, "I guess, right now, I'd take football because it's more unique to be a 6-6 quarterback . . . than a 6-6 *white* forward" (emphasis added). This young man was taking his whiteness and his ideas about race into account as he computed his odds for succeeding as a college athlete.

Both of these student-athletes had watched sports on television, listened to people talk about the abilities of athletes, and in the process developed their own ideas about race, physical abilities, and chances for success in various sports. Their "whiteness" had a major influence on their decisions about their athletic futures. In fact,

they voluntarily limited their options because of their skin color.

Not surprisingly, the social meanings associated with skin color and cultural heritage also influence sport participation decisions among people of color around the world and among ethnic group members in different societies. At an even deeper level, sports are sites in cultures where people formulate and put into action ideas about skin color and cultural heritage that they then carry over into the rest of society. They even may use sports to express their ethnicity and what they feel is their cultural destiny.

In light of these factors, the goal of this chapter is to look in depth at race and ethnicity in sports. Specifically, I will deal with the following topics:

1. The meanings of *race* and *ethnicity*.
2. The impact of racial ideology on racial and ethnic relations in sports, and the impact of sports on racial ideology.
3. Sport participation patterns for different racial and ethnic groups in the United States.
4. The reasons certain American sports have been racially desegregated.
5. The dynamics of intergroup relations in sports, and the ways sports might be used as sites for improving racial and ethnic relations.

CULTURE, SPORTS, AND THE MEANING OF RACE

Definition of Terms

Discussions about race and ethnicity can be very confusing when people use terms without defining them. In this chapter, **race** refers to a category of people regarded as socially distinct because they share genetically transmitted traits believed to be important in a group or society. When people talk about "races," they assume the existence of a classification system used to categorize all human beings into distinct groups on the basis of certain biological traits related to individuals' genetic heritages.

Ethnicity refers to the cultural heritage of a particular group. Ethnicity is *not* based on genetically determined physical traits; instead, it is based on characteristics related to culture and cultural background. An **ethnic group** is a category of people regarded as socially distinct because they share a way of life associated with a common cultural background.

Confusion is created when people use *race* and *ethnicity* interchangeably as they deal with issues related to human behavior. One reason some people use these terms interchangeably is that most racial and ethnic groups are assumed to be "minority groups." However, this is not always accurate. **Minority group** is a sociological term used to refer to a socially identified collection of people who experience discrimination, suffer social disadvantages because of discrimination, and have a strong self-consciousness based on their shared social experiences.

It is important to remember as you read this chapter that the definition of *race* focuses on biologically based traits and characteristics, while the definition of *ethnicity* focuses on culturally based orientations and behaviors, and the definition of *minority group* focuses on discrimination directed at a collection of people because they share traits or ways of life that other people define as inferior or unworthy. **Bigotry,** as we use the term in this chapter, refers to a person's use of a set of interrelated attitudes and beliefs to define an entire category of people as racially or ethnically different, and to treat those who fit into the category as inferior in some way.

Origins and Implications of the Concept of Race

The classification systems used to divide human beings into racial categories are based mostly on popular beliefs about human differences and the meanings attached to those differences; they are *not* based on real biological factors that enable us to divide all human beings into genetically distinct categories. The racial categories that people use today are cultural creations, not indicators of some deep underlying biological truth

about human beings and their similarities and differences. In a biological sense, the concept of race is so confusing that it is meaningless.

Over the past three centuries no one has ever developed a biological classification system that objectively divides humans into distinct racial groups. Scientists in Europe and North America tried beginning in the early 1700s to develop such a system. They used classifications based on mental characteristics, brain size, skin color, and various combinations of head shape, hair form, skin color, stature, and nose shape. These systems led scientists to "discover" dozens of races, subraces, collateral races, and collateral subraces (these are actual terms used in some racial classification systems). There were so many different groupings of people with so much overlap in characteristics that it was impossible to fit them into a few categories; instead, dozens of categories were needed. And even then, many collections of people fell between or around categories. This meant that racial classification systems were useless. They remain useless today.

Here is the problem people face when they try to develop a scheme for dividing the world into distinct racial groups on the basis of biological factors. Usually they pick a physical characteristic, such as skin color or some other "continuous trait" possessed by humans. A **continuous trait** is one that exists to some degree in everyone. In other words, everyone has more or less of it. Take height, for example. It's not that some people have height and others don't; people simply vary from short to tall. Height falls along a continuum, with the shortest person in the world on one end of the continuum, the tallest person on the other, and everyone else in between.

The same is true for skin color, which is also a continuous trait. Skin color varies from *snow white* to *midnight black*, with an infinite array of color shades in between. When you use a continuous trait such as skin color to identify so-called races, the trick is determining where you should draw the line to distinguish one racial category from another. Lines can be drawn anywhere and everywhere. You can draw two lines or two thousand lines; there are no biological rules for where you draw them or how many you draw. Even after you have drawn lines in particular places along the continuum, someone else can decide to draw them in other places! The decisions on where to draw the lines and how many lines to draw are social ones, not biological ones. This is the reason nearly all scientists have abandoned the search for a biology-based racial classification system.*

Even biologists and geneticists have abandoned traditional notions of race. As noted by Jonathan Marks, a biologist at Yale University, "Race has no basic biological reality. The human species simply doesn't come packaged that way" (in Boyd, 1996). Two prominent geneticists who have done research on DNA agree. Luigi Cavalli-Sforza from Stanford University explains:

> The characteristics we see with the naked eye that help us distinguish individuals from different continents are, in reality, skin-deep. Whenever we look under the veneer, we find that the differences that seem so conspicuous to us are really trivial (in Boyd, 1996).

Another geneticist, Kenneth Kidd of Yale University, has studied variations in the genes of people from forty-two population groups around the world and has made the following observation:

> We are beginning to get good data at the DNA level. The DNA data support the concept that you can't draw boundaries around races. *Genetically, I am more similar to someone from China or the Amazon Basin than two Africans living in the same village are to each other.* This substantiates the point that there is no such thing biologically as race (in Boyd, 1996, *emphasis added*).

However, people on the street have not abandoned racial classification systems. They continue to use their own systems, and systems vary from one culture to another; "black" and "white" are not the same in every culture because different cultures use different definitions of race! Thus, a person might be classified as "black" in the United States, but not in Brazil, or Haiti, or Egypt, where the meanings and uses of race are different. Human variation does exist, but traditional racial classification systems distort and oversimplify that variation (Begley, 1995; Marks, 1994).

The most popular racial classification system in the United States is based on widely shared social meanings associated with skin color. Some of these meanings are beginning to change, but traditionally, if people could not be identified as "all white," they were classified as "black," unless they had identifiable cultural backgrounds that led them to be classified in particular ethnic groups rather than in racial groups.

This "system" led to much confusion. For example, the record-breaking American decathlete Dan O'Brien has a black father and a white mother, and was adopted by a family in which his brothers and sisters were Mexican, Native American, and Korean. O'Brien says, "I feel black when I want to, I feel white the rest of the time. . . . [and] when I hang out with my friends, I'm just Dan" (in Patrick, 1991). Golfer Tiger Woods is one-fourth Thai, one-fourth Chinese, one-fourth African American, one-eighth Native American, and one-eighth white European; many in the U.S. refer to him as "black," while he refers to himself as "Cablinasian (*Ca*ucasian. *Bl*ack, *In*dian, *Asian*.)" But where do he and O'Brien fit in a racial classification system? And what does biology have to do with it?

To make matters even more confusing, race is defined in different ways in different cultures. For example, former tennis player Yannick Noah

---

*This conclusion needs to be qualified. Some recent attempts to use genetics to identify similarities and differences between humans have been useful, because they enable us to understand more about disease patterns and the adaptability of the human body. But the "races" identified through these attempts do not correspond even closely to racial definitions and classifications traditionally used by Europeans and North Americans in the past; in fact, they group blacks and whites together in new races defined in terms of genes that are medically relevant. For example, there is evidence of a "sickle cell race," but it includes Greeks, Italians, and Africans living close to the equator (see Begley, 1995).

explains that in his native France he is considered black, but in Africa he is considered white. And people who are socially defined as "blacks" in the United States would be defined as "whites" in some other cultures, or would be put into racial categories not even used in the United States. In Brazil, for example, people recently used 135 different terms when they were asked to classify their race, and only 4 percent said they were black, even though a U.S. definition of race would classify about half the Brazilian population as "black"! Also confusing is that racial classification systems do not all use skin color as the primary distinguishing trait.

This variation in definitions makes race meaningless as a biological concept. But race as a *cultural creation* has been and remains a powerful force in society and in people's lives. This makes race and race theories important topics for sociological analysis; racial ideologies over the past four hundred years have been powerful components of culture, and sociologists must take them into account if they are to understand behavior and social relationships. But when it comes to using racial classifications in our personal lives, we should recognize that the human race contains many combinations of changing physical similarities and differences, and that *traditional racial categories are based on social meanings given to those similarities and differences, not on biology.*

Connecting Ideas About Race with Sports

It is important for people who study sports to know about the biological meaninglessness of race (Hallinan, 1994). Many people, including some scientists, have tried to explain the physical abilities and achievements of athletes in racial terms, even though race is socially, not biologically, determined. They have used *social definitions* to divide people into what they consider to be biologically different groups of blacks and whites to do their studies and measurements. Usually, the exact genetic backgrounds of these people are never outlined, and it is assumed that

"That's another gold for the Swiss! After living in the Alps for generations those people must have developed a skiing gene that gives them a natural ability to twist around slalom gates."
....
Explaining white Swiss success in skiing in this way is just as faulty as explaining the success of many people of color in certain sports.

....

everyone in the black group is alike genetically, and everyone in the white group is alike genetically. This is a risky and foolish assumption to make.

Another risky assumption is thinking that we can explain athletic performances in a range of sports and across different positions in those sports simply by identifying biological traits in a group of people. For example, no researcher has even come close to being able to identify a select set of traits that would together explain Grant Hill's ability to see the floor and make great passes, Michael Jordan's ability to make jump shots at the buzzer, Shawn Kemp's ability to jump, Penny Hardaway's ability to handle the ball, Scotty Pippen's ability to steal the ball, Dennis Rodman's ability to rebound, Shaquille O'Neal's ability to dunk, Dikembe Mutumbo's ability to block shots, and Lenny Wilkens' ability to coach and develop strategies. To say that these different individuals, each excelling in different physical and mental skills, are great athletes or coaches because of something related to skin color makes no sense. It is like saying that nine boxes of nine different shapes and sizes all contain the same thing just because they are wrapped with the same color of paper. When people do this, they deny the uniqueness of each basketball player and the complexity of the physical and mental skills involved in basketball. Using skin color to explain performance records *across* many different sports makes even less sense. Performance in different sports depends on a wide range of *different* physical and mental traits and abilities, combined with the opportunities to develop and display them.

It is interesting that many people use "racial theories" to explain the success of people with black skin and the failures of people with white skin in certain sports; for example, "blacks are 'natural leapers'" and "whites have 'white man's disease.'" This is odd, because people with white skin have dominated most running and jumping sports for many years, even though people of color have long outnumbered white-skinned people in the world. When people with white skin consistently do well in a sport event, why do many people talk about their character, dedication, work ethic, dependability, and intelligence, rather than their "natural physical abilities"? And when blacks do well, why do many people focus on what they identify as their "natural athletic skills"? We offer answers to these questions in the next section, and in the box on pp. 254–57

RACIAL IDEOLOGY AND SPORTS: A CRITICAL ANALYSIS

The concept of "race" was developed in the 1700s, when white Europeans began to look for a system to explain why everyone in the world didn't look and act as they did. Since then there have been countless attempts to discover relationships between physique and character, between external physical characteristics and internal characteristics such as temperament, personality, intelligence, moral standards, criminal tendencies, and overall cultural vitality. These attempts have turned up empty, but they have resulted in a wide range of "pseudoscientific folklore and stereotypes" about the characteristics of people with certain shades of skin color (Hoberman, 1992).

Many white observers in the U.S. colonies and many of the other whites who colonized three-fourths of the world between the seventeenth and early twentieth centuries were convinced that people of color were primitive beings driven by brawn rather than brains. This belief was used to justify the colonization and subsequent exploitation of those peoples. White Europeans and Americans developed racial theories leading them to conclude that any expressions of physicality and physical skills among people with dark skin were signs of intellectual inferiority and arrested development. Such theories, wrongheaded as they were, fit neatly with an oversimplified Darwinian model of human evolution in which mental traits were seen to be superior to physical traits among humans and other primates. And this idea led to the next: that white-skinned people were superior beings who deserved to be in positions of power and control around the world (this belief is called social Darwinism). I will refer to this way of thinking as *race logic*.

This **race logic** that white-skinned people were intellectually superior while people of color were "animal-like savages" was very convenient to white colonial powers (Hoberman, 1992). While it led some whites to view blacks as uncivilized pagans who needed to be "civilized" and have their souls saved, and hence were the "white man's burden," it enabled other whites both to kill dark-skinned natives without guilt and to subjugate them. Because it was so convenient, this race logic eventually became institutionalized in the form of a complex racial ideology about skin color, intelligence, character, and physical characteristics and skills.

This ideology has been revised continually over the years to fit new circumstances, explain contradictions, and justify new forms of racial discrimination. For example, just after the Civil

REFLECT ON SPORT

Preserving Racial Ideology Through Sports

Skiers from Switzerland, a country half the size of South Carolina with a population one-thirtieth the size of that of the United States, have won many more World Cup championships than U.S. skiers. Even though this happens year after year, scientists don't look to biology to discover why the Swiss are such good skiers. Everyone already knows why: the Swiss live in the Alps, they learn to ski before they go to preschool, they grow up in a culture in which skiing is highly valued, they have many opportunities to ski, all their friends ski and talk about skiing, they see fellow Swiss skiers winning races and making money in highly publicized (in Switzerland) World Cup competitions, and their cultural heroes are skiers. Race logic focuses attention on these *cultural* factors when the athletes are white; thus, there has been no search for a "ski gene" among the white Swiss people.

Similarly, dominant race logic has not led to studies looking for a weight-lifting gene among Bulgarian men, a swimming gene among white U.S. women, a cross-country skiing gene among Scandinavians, a soccer gene among Italians, or a volleyball jumping gene among white Californians who hang out on beaches. There have been no claims that Canadians owe their success in hockey to naturally strong ankle joints, or instinctive eye-hand-foot coordination, or an innate tendency not to sweat so they can retain body heat in cold weather. Race logic doesn't lead people to look for or use genetic explanations for the successes of athletes packaged in white skin, even when the shades of "white" vary among these people.

But as soon as athletes with black skin excel or fail at a certain sport, regardless of where they come from in the world, many people start looking for genetic explanations consistent with dominant racial ideology. They want to explain the successes and failures of black athletes in terms of "natural" or "instinctive" qualities or weaknesses; when skin color is some shade of "dark," they ignore social and cultural factors. Race logic, however, leads them to assume that white-skinned athletes succeed because of tradition, training opportunities, dedication, and personal sacrifice, *not*

the genetic heritage of the entire white-skinned population of a region, a country, or the world.

The tendency to explain the achievements of athletes by skin color is firmly grounded in Western racial ideology. This ideology emphasizes *racial difference* and leads people to forget history and culture so that they can continue to attribute differences to biology. It seems strange to think that a single genetic trait or even a combination of traits could explain the successes or failures of a genetically diversified group of athletes from many areas around the world across a range of sports requiring different physical abilities and characteristics. But racial ideology has sent some people on a quest for such a trait or traits. Race logic clearly leads people to do some strange things that are hardly logical!

We know that success in sports depends on combinations of different cognitive, emotional, and experiential factors, in addition to many different physical factors. We also know that these factors shift from sport to sport. So why do so many people assume that the color of a person's skin has anything to do with success in sports? Why should skin color be related to other physical traits that have performance implications in certain sports? And why do dark-skinned and light-skinned athletes come in so many different sizes and shapes, even in the same sports? For example, great sprinters have been both tall and short, slender and muscular, emotional and unemotional, of high IQ and of low IQ—and until the 1960s, almost all great sprinters were white (George, 1994). If eight dark-skinned sprinters lined up for an Olympic finals race in the 100-meter dash, the event would be sociologically interesting, but no more biologically meaningful than the presence of white-skinned Swiss and Austrians in the finals of so many World Cup skiing events, or the domination by light-skinned Californians of beach volleyball around the world, or the fact that seventy-one minor- and major-league shortstops have come from the Dominican Republic.

Similarly, genetics doesn't have anything to do with the fact that the 1988 and 1992 U.S. Olympic teams in archery, badminton, canoeing/kayaking, cycling, equestrian events, field hockey, modern pentathlon, and yachting had only white athletes (*Atlanta Journal/Constitution*, 1 October 1995).

Some people, including Jimmy "the Greek" Snyder, a former sports analyst for CBS, have combined genetic and experiential factors to seek explanations for the success of African American athletes in certain sports. In 1988 Snyder suggested that African Americans make good ball carriers in football because blacks were "bred" during slavery times to have big, strong thighs. Snyder conveniently ignored millions of African Americans with skinny thighs, and he was ignorant of the historical fact that the control of white slavemasters over sexual behavior between black men and women was never extensive enough to shape the genetic traits of even a small portion of the U.S. African American population. In fact, so many white men forced black women into sexual intercourse during the slave era that many African Americans today have a white ancestor somewhere in their past. How do these "white genes" figure into biological explanations? Is this the reason African Americans are better football players than blacks from many other countries? And what other silly things might race logic lead some people to say?

Snyder's explanation of the achievements of African American football players is as ridiculous as saying that Californians are great volleyball players because their ancestors migrated west in covered wagons and all those who were not strong enough or couldn't jump up on the wagons died during the tedious journey. Therefore, California was settled by great white jumpers! Is this the reason U.S. volleyball teams have been dominated by white Californians who have great vertical jumps and amazing "hang times"? This question is beyond silliness. But it is very similar to questions and explanations about the relation of slavery to success in running, boxing, football, and basketball. Let us ask some questions of our own. Did Africans survive being chained on shelves during the long journey on slave ships be-

cause they could run fast and jump high? Did slave owners breed slaves to be fast runners and high jumpers? And wouldn't the fastest runners and best jumpers have escaped the slave traders in West Africa? Race logic leads people to overlook such questions.

DOES RACE LOGIC INFLUENCE AFRICAN AMERICANS?

Is it possible that dominant racial ideology influences African Americans' interpretations of their own physical abilities and potential as athletes? This is a controversial question. My guess is that many young black men and some black women in the United States today grow up believing that the black body is special and superior when it comes to physical abilities in certain sports. This belief could inspire some young people to think that playing certain sports and playing them better than anyone else in the world is part of their biological and cultural destiny. This inspiration might be especially strong if young black men looked ahead and saw two possible futures: unemployment and dead-end jobs on one hand, and the possibility of big money and respect from slam dunks, end-zone catches, or Olympic sprint victories in sports on the other hand. Even boxing might look better than a minimum-wage dead-end job!

Figure 9-1 outlines a hypothesized sociological explanation of the athletic achievements of black male athletes. A look at U.S. history shows us that dominant racial ideology has given rise to stereotypes that emphasize "black male physicality" and black athletic superiority. A long history of racial segregation and discrimination has limited life chances for black men and created among them a sense of desperation. At the same time, there have been growing opportunities for them to develop skills and achieve immense status and money in a few sports, and there has been widespread encouragement for them to take advantage of those opportunities.

When you put these things together, you can certainly understand why many African American males

Continued

might grow up with a powerful sense that it was their biological and cultural destiny to become great athletes in certain sports. They would focus on others who had fulfilled that destiny and then use them as models as they dedicated themselves to go where others had succeeded. And since public school sport programs offer coaching and opportunities to develop skills, they could live out this dedication to sports on a daily basis.

This combination of factors could form a powerful force in the lives of millions of young people. This force could drive a young black man to dedicate the very fabric of his being to achieving greatness in certain sports. Is this what has led to the notable achievements of African Americans in basketball, football, track, and boxing? Is this the reason African Americans have a longer and more impressive list of accomplishments in sports than all blacks living in Africa, even though black Africans outnumber black Americans by a ratio of over 20 to 1? Is this the reason African American women have been winning gold medals in the Olympics for many years, but it wasn't until 1996 that a black African woman won a gold medal? I don't know, but this explanation of the accomplishments of African American athletes makes much more sense to me than an explanation based on unidentified biological factors associated with skin color. After all, when a group of people feel destined to greatness in an activity, when their feelings are grounded in an ideology emphasizing the "naturalness" of their achievements, and when their social worlds are structured so that those feelings make sense in their lives, *it shouldn't be surprising when they achieve notable things.*

Ideology is powerful, especially when it is combined with other factors that lead it to be used as a framework for self-evaluation and self-motivation. Three centuries ago, white Europeans felt it was their biological and cultural destiny to explore and control other parts of the world. This sense of destiny was so powerful that it drove them to colonize over three-fourths of the globe! And genes had nothing to do with this frightening and notable achievement.

Unfortunately, racial ideology and the race logic that goes with it will continue to blind many to the fact that people of color around the world have *diverse* genetic traits, *diverse* cultural and experiential backgrounds, and *diverse* records of achievement in a *diverse* range of sports and other activities. Unless they critically analyze this ideology, many people will continue to use skin color as a predictor of how people's minds and bodies perform. Our challenge today is to realize that this ideology fuels hatred and ignorance around the world, and that we must drop our silly concerns about skin color and stop asking racist questions about sport performance. Until then, many people will continue to use sports to preserve a destructive racial ideology. What do you think?

....

War, a surgeon in New Orleans who treated "colored" soldiers wounded in the war noted that "at present, [my colored patients are] too animal to have moral courage or endurance" (in Hoberman, 1992: 44). His conclusions suggested that maybe "colored people" would eventually evolve into something less animal-like.

Then, when Africans and other people of color engaged in what were clearly courageous behaviors, most whites quickly pointed out that such behavior among blacks was a sign of ignorance and desperation, rather than *real* character. In fact, some white people went so far as to say that people of color did not feel pain in the same way whites did and that this permitted dark-skinned people to engage in superhuman feats. But those feats were seen as meaningless by whites who saw them as acts driven by animal

When these Four Social Conditions Are Added Together:

A Dominant Racial Ideology Promoting Stereotypes of
"Black Male Physicality"

+

A Long History of Racial Segregation and Differential
Treatment that Limits Socioeconomic Opportunities for
Black Men

+

The Sense of Desperation that Comes with the Feeling
that Life Chances Are Limited

+

Widespread Opportunities and Encouragement to Develop
Skills and Excel in a Few Sports

↓

The Intermediate Result Is This:

A Segment of the African American Community Believes
that It Is the Biological and Cultural Destiny of Black
Men to Be Great Athletes in Certain Sports

+

Young Black Men Are Motivated to Use Every Opportunity
to Develop the Skills They Need to Fulfill that Destiny

↓

The Hypothesis:

It Is This Sense of Destiny, Combined with Continued
Motivation and Opportunities to Develop Certain Sport
Skills, that Leads to Outstanding Performances Among
Black Male Athletes in Selected Sports

FIGURE 9-1 A sociological hypothesis for explaining the achievements of black male athletes.

instincts, not by civilized human heroism. Of course, when whites did extraordinary physical things, other whites claimed this was due to their fortitude, intelligence, moral character, and being civilized.

Whites in the United States and other colonized areas used this racial ideology to justify the physical mistreatment of African slaves. Later, they used it to explain the success of African American boxers and other athletes in the early part of this century. According to dominant race logic, black males were believed to have unique physical stamina and skills; however, white people also believed that those physical attributes were grounded in an absence of deep human feelings and intellectual awareness. In fact, many whites even thought the skulls of black people were so thick that they could not be bruised or broken by a white man's fist (Hoberman, 1992). Thus, when black boxers were successful, this race logic was used to explain their success.

For example, after Joe Louis, the legendary black heavyweight boxing champion, defeated Italian Primo Carnera in a heavily publicized fight before sixty thousand people in Yankee Stadium in 1935, sportswriters in the United States described him as "savage and animalistic." A major news service story sent all over the country began this way:

> Something sly and sinister and perhaps not quite human came out of the African jungle last night to strike down and utterly demolish . . . Primo Carnera. . . . (cited in Mead, 1985).

Noted sportswriter Grantland Rice referred to Louis's quickness as "the speed of the jungle, the instinctive speed of the wild." Before another Louis fight, *New York Times* sports editor Paul Gallico wrote a nationwide syndicated column in which he described Louis in this way:

> . . . the magnificent animal. . . . He eats. He sleeps. He fights. . . . Is he all instinct, all animal? Or have a hundred million years left a fold upon his brain? I see in this colored man something so cold, so hard, so cruel that I wonder as to his bravery. Courage in the animal is desperation. Courage in the human is something incalculable and divine.

Despite hundreds of these stories, Joe Louis remained dedicated to representing black Americans as an ambassador of goodwill to whites. But although he trained hard and presented himself as a gentleman, he was still described as "a natural athlete . . . born to listen to jazz . . . eat a lot of fried chicken, play ball with the gang on the corner and never do a lick of heavy work he could escape" (from a story in a New York paper, cited in Mead, 1985). Race logic can be powerful; it can shape what people see and how they interpret the world in black and white.

Using Myths to Maintain Racial Ideology

Published descriptions of Joe Louis and other African American athletes capture dominant

racial ideology as it was applied to sports in the United States in the middle of the twentieth century. But prior to these racist sports stories, whites used other methods of making themselves feel comfortable with their beliefs about their own superiority. For example, over the past two centuries, many whites in Europe and the U.S. have had difficulty accepting the idea that they might be physically inferior to people of color. Many whites have not believed Darwin's notion that brains are always superior to muscles, but the ancient Greek idea that strong minds and strong bodies come together in the same package. This has led them to wonder: Could it be that dark-skinned peoples are superior in some way to light-skinned people? Many whites have worried about this. In fact, they have worried so much at certain times that they have accepted a number of myths designed to restore faith in their own racial superiority.

A classic example is the myth of "Tarzan, King of the Jungle"—the *African* jungle. In 1914, Edgar Rice Burroughs wrote *Tarzan of the Apes*, the first of his twenty-four Tarzan novels, which constituted the biggest-selling series of novels of the century. His stories then found their way into comic books and movies read and seen by additional millions of people, including millions of children, and especially white children who were forming their ideas about race.

Tarzan stories were very popular through much of this century for many reasons. One reason was that white people in Western industrial societies found it very comforting and exciting to read about a white man with aristocratic British ancestry who used a combination of physical strength and intelligence to become "king of the African jungle," ruler of the "noble black savages" and physically imposing beasts living in "uncivilized" colonized territories on the "dark continent" (Hoberman, 1992).

This white Tarzan was a real model and cultural hero for whites who wanted proof that they deserved their racial privilege. In physical appearance, he resembled a combination of a

When Jesse Owens won four gold medals during the 1936 Olympics in Berlin, his achievement was used by some people to challenge Hitler's ideas about "Nordic supremacy." Ironically, in the U.S. the athletic achievements of Joe Louis as well as Jesse Owens were used to support the racist belief that blacks were more suited genetically for physical than for intellectual tasks. In 1936, Owens returned to a U.S. where schools and the military were racially segregated, where blacks sat in the back of the bus and were systematically denied voting rights, and where racial discrimination was an accepted part of the economy. (USOC Archives)

Roman gladiator and a Greek god, and even though the fictional Tarzan was raised and socialized by apes, he eventually exhibited inner, "*in-born* racial qualities" that enabled him to not only survive but even rise above the "primitive" and "uncivilized" conditions in Africa. Therefore, those who read about Tarzan could conclude that whites really were "naturally" superior to people of color.

Burroughs did *not* intend to contribute to the formation of racial ideology when he wrote his Tarzan novels. He mainly wanted to convince sedentary Englishmen living off the fruits of colonialism and imperialism to change their ways and get in good physical condition lest they become weak and vulnerable as a military force. But his stories caught on and became popular partly because his white readers lived in countries whose economies had been built on colonialization combined with slavery, and they had deep fears and insecurities about people of color and about white privilege.

Fears about racial differences are not dead; nor is white privilege. Race logic and racial ideology are still with us. In fact, some have suggested that the increasing importance of sport in

North America has gone hand in hand with curiosity and myths about racial differences (Hoberman, 1992). White people in the 1920s and 1930s admired Tarzan as a "great white hope," and some whites in the 1960s and 1970s followed in their footsteps by looking for great white male athletes.

The search for white athletes may be less prevalent today, but efforts to reaffirm racial ideology now take other forms, such as giving excessive attention to black athletes who fail to live up to social expectations. If enough attention can be focused on the moral failures and character weaknesses of O. J. Simpson, Mike Tyson, Magic Johnson, and other black athletes who have excelled physically in sports, there will be no need for Tarzan myths or great white hopes. These new strategies can preserve racial ideology and white privilege.

Race Logic in Sports: Recent Examples

Race logic is still manifested as bigotry against blacks in the United States and other countries. Even in the late 1990s, the young golfer Tiger Woods noted that despite his skills and record of achievement, his skin color prevented him from playing on certain top golf courses in the United States where informal policies of club segregation still exist. In fact, when the PGA scheduled its annual championship at the Shoal Creek Golf Club in Birmingham, Alabama, in 1991, the club founder proudly noted that there were no blacks in the club because they would make his fellow white members uncomfortable. He explained that club policy was simply a matter of personal preferences, not racial prejudice or discrimination (!). When the PGA looked into the matter, it found that such "preferences" existed all over the United States, not just in the South.

In 1993, major-league baseball investigated one of its owners for anti-semitism and racial bigotry. Among many other things, the owner had referred to one of her players on the Cincinnati Reds as her "million-dollar nigger." The white owners of baseball teams had a difficult time conducting the investigation because she had made bigoted remarks in their presence on many different occasions and they had never corrected or reprimanded her. So when they found her guilty, they had to admit indirectly that they had long allowed blatant racism to exist in their midst without taking action.

Expressions of race logic come in a variety of forms. For example, Bale and Sang (1996) point out that the emergence and success of Kenyans and Ethiopians in distance racing has been discussed and "explained in stereotypical and sometimes racist terms" among whites in Europe and North America. These authors note that the idea of the "natural" black athlete is deeply ingrained in what has become a form of global racism in predominantly white societies. People simply ignore the obvious fact that black athletes, like white athletes, are culturally produced. Bale and Sang (1996) rightfully suggest that instead of jumping to genetic conclusions, we must examine the racial myths that surround explanations of sport performance among black athletes. For example, in the case of Kenyan athletes, we must recognize that running is an integral part of a Kenyan body culture that we can understand only in the context of colonialism, the globalization of high-performance sports exported from predominantly white societies, and the history of and current conditions in Kenya itself.

Race logic also may be expressed in code forms such as this: "I'm sick and tired of those ungrateful, self-centered NBA players making all that money and ignoring us loyal fans; so I'm going to skip NBA games this year and watch hockey, where the players are hard working." Of course, this is *not* to say that all people who turn their attention from basketball to hockey are reflecting racial ideology. However, some whites may view and evaluate the performance and behavior of black basketball players, who look, talk, and act differently from them, through a different cultural lens from the one they use to view white hockey players, who look, talk, and act more like they do.

These examples raise one of the issues emphasized in this book: humans are so deeply immersed in their cultures that they often accept without thinking the ideologies that color their views of the world and the people in it.

Race Logic, Gender, and Social Class

Race logic is interconnected with gender logic in complex ways in the social world of sports. Sociologists are just now beginning to explain some of these interconnections (Birrell, 1989; Corbett, 1995; Messner, 1992; Majors, 1991; Smith, 1992). Current research suggests that the implications of race logic are different for black men than for black women. This is true partly because the bodies of black men have been socially constructed and viewed differently from the bodies of black women over the past four hundred years. For example, whites traditionally have grown up fearing the power of black male bodies, being anxious about the sexual capacities of those bodies, and being fascinated with their movements. Ironically, this has created a situation in which black male bodies have over the years become valuable entertainment commodities, on stage in music and vaudeville theater, and on athletic fields. Black female bodies, on the other hand, have undergone different social constructions (Corbett and Johnson, 1993). They've been sexualized, but not feared; they've been used for domestic chores, but not defined in ways that make black women athletes uniquely valuable entertainment commodities on athletic fields.

Sociologist Richard Majors (1986, 1991) has suggested that as black males have struggled to establish their masculinity in terms recognized in U.S. culture, some have developed a presentation of self described as "cool pose." Majors explains that black men in the United States have accepted the dominant definition of masculinity in American culture. They have bought into the idea that men should be strong breadwinners

and protectors in their families and dominant in their relationships with women. But the race logic used in the U.S. has limited their success in institutional spheres, such as education, politics, and the economy, where they might establish who they are as men in the terms that other males have used.

The social conditions that have limited the "life chances" of black men have over the years produced a combination of frustration, self-doubt, anger, and even emotional withdrawal from schools, families, and the mainstream economy. Black males in the United States have coped with these things "by channeling their creative energies into the construction of unique, expressive, and conspicuous styles of demeanor, speech, gesture, clothing, hairstyle, walk, stance, and handshake" (Majors, 1991: 111). These expressive styles are forms of interpersonal self-presentation that Majors describes as "cool pose."

Cool pose is all about achieving a sense of significance and respect through *interpersonal* strategies when one cannot achieve significance and success within *institutional* spheres. Cool pose is also about being "bad," about being in control, tough, and detached. Cool pose says different things to different people. To the white man it says, "Although you may have tried to hurt me time and time again, I can take it (and if I am hurting or weak, I'll never let you know)." It also says, "See me, touch me, hear me, but, white man, you can't copy me" (Majors, 1986: 184–85). In general, cool pose is one of the ways in which black males who face status threats in the culture have used physicality in the production of masculinity; this happens even among first- and second-graders in inner-city U.S. schools (Hasbrook and Harris, 1997).

Majors suggests that cool pose has become part of the public personas of many black males in the United States, and also an integral part of the sports in which many athletes are black men. Is this how "style" got to be such a big part of basketball (George, 1992)? Is this the reason some black athletes are known for their "talk" as much as their action on the playing field? Do black men use cool pose to intimidate white opponents? Does cool pose sell tickets and create spectator interest in college basketball, the NBA, and football? Do people come to see dunks and other moves inscribed with the personas of the men who perform them? Is this what Albert Belle brought to baseball and Deion Sanders brought to football? Is cool pose the result of what happens when black men face a combination of race logic, gender logic, and the realities of class relations in the American economy? Majors says yes, and I think he is onto something worth considering. I would add, might cool pose, expressed under certain conditions, turn white spectators off or prevent them from identifying with black athletes, especially when cool pose comes with a snarl rather than a disarming smile on the face of a black athlete?

When we discuss the incidence and implications of cool pose, it is important to remember that some forms of "coolness" are adopted by many groups of people who must cope with powerlessness. This is the reason many adolescents try to be "cool," and many white teens copy popular cultural expressions of "coolness" that originate among blacks. So "coolness" is not somehow unique to African Americans. However, the history of African Americans and the traditions that have influenced their resistance to racial oppression *are* unique. Like Majors, I would argue that cool pose among African Americans cannot be understood apart from that history and the strategies of black resistance to a culture that empowers whites and privileges their values and experiences (Langley, 1994). Furthermore, cool pose can be expressed in ways that work to the disadvantage of young black males; in fact, it may have as many disadvantages as advantages (Majors et al., 1994).

Race Logic and Stacking Patterns in Team Sports

We also can see the impact of racial ideology in sports in the patterns of positions played in team

sports by athletes from different racial and ethnic backgrounds. Traditionally, certain position patterns on racially desegregated sport teams have clearly reflected racial stereotypes about the abilities of white players and black players. One of the general patterns has been that black athletes seldom have played the so-called "thinking positions" in major team sports in the United States, and in some other countries where sport has been racially desegregated. It seems that for many years, the white people who controlled sport teams (recruiters, coaches, administrators, and owners) believed that blacks were especially good at running and catching footballs, but they could not be expected to quarterback the team or be leaders on defense. They thought that blacks were good at running after and catching fly balls in the outfield, but not suited for strategy positions such as pitcher and catcher. They thought that blacks could be strong inside rebounders and outstanding scorers in basketball, but that white guards were needed to bring the ball up the floor, call the plays, and set the defensive strategy.

Remnants of these patterns still exist in professional baseball and football, although they have shifted to reflect changes in coaching strategies and associated changes in responsibilities for players in different positions. For example, quarterbacks in college often run the ball more now than they did in the past, and they seldom call their own plays in the huddle; shortstops in baseball rarely make decisions about where outfielders should play for certain hitters; guards in basketball no longer call plays when they dribble the ball up the court. In all team sports in recent years, coaches have taken over many of the thinking tasks, such as calling plays and setting offensive and defensive formations. This has affected the extent to which racial ideology is expressed in player position patterns.

Sociologists have long been interested in these patterns and how they conform to the race logic in particular cultures. Since the early 1970s, these patterns have been identified in

Table 9–1 Percentage of blacks, whites, and other players in positions on NFL and major-league baseball teams, 1995–96.

Sport	Positions	Black (%)	White (%)	Other* (%)
NFL (1995–96)				
	Total Players	67	31	2
	Offense			
	Quarterback	9	91	NA
	Running back	91	9	NA
	Wide receiver	91	9	NA
	Center	16	84	NA
	Guard	35	60	NA
	Tight end	54	44	NA
	Tackle	52	46	NA
	Defense			
	Cornerback	100	0	NA
	Safety	87	13	NA
	Linebacker	74	26	NA
	Defensive end	78	20	NA
	Defensive tackle	64	30	NA
MAJOR-LEAGUE BASEBALL (1996)				
	Total Players	17	62	20
	Pitcher	7	76	17
	Catcher	1	73	25
	First base	21	70	9
	Second base	11	51	37
	Third base	13	70	17
	Shortstop	17	39	43
	Outfield	54	28	18

Source: Center for the Study of Sport in Society (*1996 Racial Report Card* compiled by R. E. Lapchick).
*In baseball, this includes Latinos from many different national and cultural backgrounds. In the NFL, this includes Pacific Islanders, Latinos, and Asian Americans.

numerous studies.* When players from a certain racial or ethnic group are either over- or under-represented at certain positions in team sports, we say that *racial stacking* exists.

---

*For documentation of the existence of stacking, see Berghorn et al., 1988; Best, 1987; Curtis and Loy, 1978a, b; Hallinan, 1991; Johnson and Johnson, 1995; Jones et al., 1987; Lapchick, 1984, 1988, 1989; Lavoie, 1989; Lavoie and Leonard, 1994; Leonard, 1977a, b, 1987; Maguire, 1988; Melnick, 1988; Williams and Youssef, 1972, 1975, 1979; Yetman and Berghorn, 1993; and Yetman and Eitzen, 1984.

Because discussions of stacking can be confusing for anyone unfamiliar with positions on certain sport teams, I've provided summary information and illustrations for two major professional spectator sports in table 9–1 and figures 9-2 and 9-3. We can partially summarize research on stacking patterns in these and other sports over the past thirty years as follows:

- Black players on major league baseball teams have been most heavily concentrated in the outfield positions; white players have been

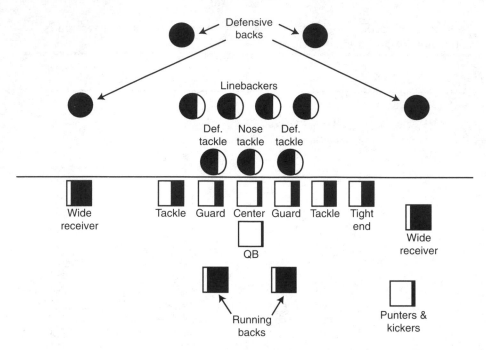

FIGURE 9-2 The football data from table 9-1 are portrayed here. The percentage of African American players in each of the offensive and defensive positions during the 1995–96 season is depicted by the black areas. As in baseball, African Americans are overrepresented in positions defined as requiring speed and quick physical reactions. Whites are overrepresented in positions that require leadership, decision-making skills, and dependability.

concentrated in the positions of pitcher and catcher, and in all the infield positions except first base.

- Black players on college and professional football teams have been most likely to play safety, cornerback, and end on defense and running back and pass receiver on offense; whites have been overrepresented at quarterback and guard on offense, and in the past, at one of the middle linebacker positions on defense.

- During the 1950s and 1960s, blacks in basketball were clearly overrepresented at forward; whites were overrepresented at guard and center. This pattern was less evident in the 1970s and generally disappeared in the 1980s, as basketball itself changed dramatically.

- In women's intercollegiate volleyball in the United States, blacks have been overrepresented at spiker and whites at setter and bumper (Eitzen and Furst, 1988).

- In Canadian hockey, French Canadians have been overrepresented at goalie, and English Canadians in defensive positions (Lavoie, 1989).

- Black West Indians and black Africans in British soccer have been clearly overrepresented in the wide forward positions, whereas whites have been disproportionately found at goalie and midfielder (Maguire, 1988; Melnick, 1988).

- Aborigines in Australian rugby have been overrepresented in the wide positions, whereas non-Aborigines have been

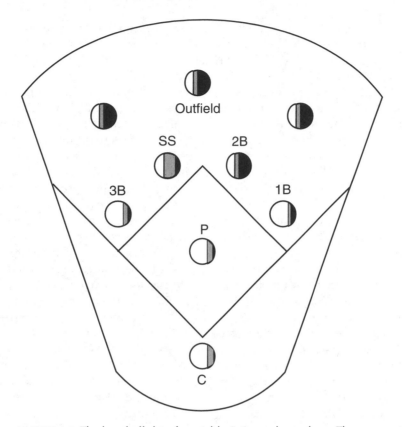

FIGURE 9-3 The baseball data from table 9–1 are shown here. The percentage of African American players in each position during the 1996 season is depicted by the black areas; the percentage of Latinos is shown in grey. African Americans remain concentrated in the outfield positions, whereas whites are overrepresented in the positions of pitcher and catcher. Latinos are slightly overrepresented at second base and strongly overrepresented at shortstop.

over-represented in the central team positions (Hallinan, 1988).

Why do stacking patterns exist? This question often leads to discussions that get tied up with the race logic that is widely accepted in the society as whole. When they exist, racial stacking patterns generally correspond with popular beliefs about skin color and such traits as intelligence, leadership and decision-making abilities, dependability, motivation and emotion, running and jumping skills, and what many people refer to as "instincts." The thinking and dependability positions generally have been stacked with white athletes; the speed and physical reaction positions have been stacked with black athletes. Even when white athletes have played the "speed positions," they have been described by many coaches and announcers as dependable and smart, and when black athletes have played the thinking and dependability positions, they sometimes have been described in terms of their "natural" physical attributes. Although this is not always the case, the patterns exist.

Stacking patterns in Canadian hockey have corresponded with dominant ethnic ideology and ideas about the characteristics of French Canadians (Lavoie, 1989); in British soccer they have corresponded with prevailing ideas about black West Indians and Africans (Melnick, 1988; Maguire, 1987); and in Australian rugby they have corresponded with prevailing ideas about Aborigines (Hallinan, 1988). The stacking of Latino players in U.S. baseball is clear, but more research is needed to discover whether patterns reflect the application of national and ethnic stereotypes, processes of recruiting and signing players from outside the U.S., or other factors (Gonzalez, 1996).

Of course, when people from a particular racial or ethnic group come to constitute the majority of players in a certain sport, and especially when they start to be hired as coaches, there is a decrease in stacking patterns based on dominant racial ideology. However, stacking patterns can be maintained and sometimes even intensified when the members of a racial or ethnic group become aware of how their futures in sport may be improved or hindered if they play certain positions. For example, young black athletes playing the thinking and dependability positions on all-black football teams in high schools sometimes have chosen to try out for the speed and physical reaction positions in college so that they will not be overlooked by the scouts and coaches of professional teams, who might be using traditional race logic as they evaluate them. These players choose to conform to stacking patterns, but they do so to cope with the consequences of racial ideology. Actually, self-stacking is very similar to self-segregation: it is a response to discrimination. This is the way racial ideology seeps into everyday life and then is perpetuated in certain sports. The ideology becomes a self-fulfilling prophecy.

It is important to remember that stacking patterns are related to race logic, and race logic differs in content and application from one culture to another and from one sport or situation to another in the same culture; it also changes over time. Recent research indicates that the process through which people come to play certain positions on sport teams is complex and ever changing (Lavoie and Leonard, 1994; Melnick, 1996; Melnick and Thompson, 1996). It reflects a combination of factors, including (1) historical traditions related to ethnic relations in society as a whole; (2) the history of a minority group's involvement in a particular sport; (3) the proportion of minority- and majority-group members in a sport and on particular teams; (4) the ethnic backgrounds of team coaches, general managers, and player scouts; (5) the degree to which different positions in a sport involve different skills and responsibilities; (6) the ways that positions are defined in connection with current offensive and defensive strategies; and (7) the perspectives used by those who identify and assess player skills and recruit players for teams. And as player recruitment becomes increasingly international in scope, the connections between race or ethnicity and the positions played on sport teams reflect global processes of labor migration combined with the racial ideologies, racial dynamics, national stereotypes, and ways sports are organized in different countries that import athletes (Chappell, Jones, and Burden, 1996; Maguire, 1991a, 1993, 1994).

Race Logic and Jobs in Coaching and Administration

At the very time that dominant racial ideology in the U.S. has turned black male bodies into entertainment commodities in certain sports, it also has restricted the entry of black men into management positions in sport organizations (Anderson, 1993; Lapchick, 1996). Arthur Ashe noted this in 1992 when he said, "The crazy theories of black intellectual inferiority are alive and well. . . . [Coaches and] managers have to think, and the conventional wisdom among sports' ruling elite is that . . . blacks don't think as well as whites." As figure 9–4 shows, the proportion of black men in top management and head coaching positions has never been close to the proportion of black athletes in the major professional (or college team sports) in the United States.

Apart from general racial issues in sports, the underrepresentation of blacks and other minorities in coaching and administration jobs has been one of the most widely publicized topics in sports since the mid-1980s. We will explore this issue further in chapter 10, but at this point we need to see how this pattern fits with a combination of race logic and stacking patterns in team sports. For example, coaches and managers are frequently former athletes who played the thinking-leadership-dependability positions in their sports, the positions that were central in the team's organizational structure (Kjeldsen, 1980; Loy et al., 1978; Loy and Jackson, 1990; Melnick and Loy, 1996). Athletes who have played less central positions, the positions calling for speed and physical skills more than leadership skills, don't get picked as coaches, because they did not show how bright and dependable they are when they were players. Unfortunately, this pattern underlying the recruitment of coaches works against many black athletes who have been stacked into the latter positions, and thus have had few chances to demonstrate their leadership abilities in ways that would lead athletic directors and team owners to regard them as good prospective coaches.

Another discouraging fact is that Latinos who play central positions on baseball teams are less likely than white players to be hired as coaches, even though they are *more* likely to play the central positions from which coaches are most often recruited. Apparently, playing central positions and demonstrating leadership skills on the field are not the only issues when it comes to defining minorities as good coaching prospects (Gonzalez, 1996). Other issues are involved, and they seem to be related to race and ethnicity in complex ways that have not yet been studied.

Because coaching abilities cannot be measured as objectively as playing abilities, the subjective feelings of those doing the hiring come into play when coach candidates are assessed (Lavoie and Leonard, 1994). An interesting fact is that the blacks or Latinos who do get hired as coaches have had "longer and more productive careers as players" than the whites who get hired (Rimer, 1996). In other words, the whites who are hired as coaches are more likely to have had mediocre or unimpressive playing careers; members of minority groups with similar careers are routinely passed over as coaching candidates.

SPORT PARTICIPATION PATTERNS GROUP BY GROUP

Sports in North America have long histories of racial and ethnic exclusion (Ashe, 1993; Corbett, 1995; Eisen and Wiggins, 1994; Shropshire, 1996). This has led to underrepresentation of both males and females of all minority groups. It has occurred at all levels of competition and management in most competitive sports, even in high schools and community programs. Prior to the 1950s, the organizations sponsoring sport teams and events seldom opened their doors to blacks, Latinos, Native Americans, or Asian Americans. When members of minority groups played sports, they usually played with one another in segregated games and events.

Blacks and Sport Participation

Before the early 1950s, most whites in North America consistently avoided playing with and against blacks; blacks were systematically excluded from participation in white-controlled sport programs and organizations. But blacks had their own baseball and basketball leagues. Occasional games with white teams were held behind closed doors, but they were not considered official, and did not affect the records of white teams. Because black teams sometimes beat even the best white teams and because whites rationalized the exclusion of blacks from

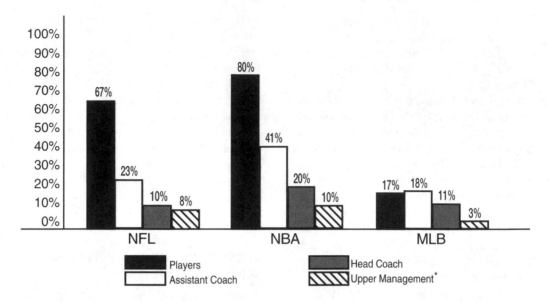

FIGURE 9-4 Ideology in action: percentage of blacks in the position of player, assistant coach, head coach, and upper management in the NFL, NBA, and major league baseball MLB (1996).

Note: Eleven NFL teams hired new head coaches during 1997; none hired a black coach even though experts agreed that four to six black candidates were qualified to be head coaches. This pattern also exists, in varying degrees, in women's professional basketball and in intercollegiate football, as well as in men's and women's basketball. Changes have occurred in men's basketball, but they have come slowly.

Source: 1996 Racial Report Card, Center for the Study of Sport in Society.

*Upper management includes CEOs, presidents, and vice presidents.

white leagues by the notion that blacks didn't have the character or fortitude to compete with whites, these games received no publicity in the white press.

Since the 1950s, the sport participation of blacks has been concentrated in just a handful of sports. Even in the 1990s, the 34 million African Americans are underrepresented or nonexistent in most sports at most levels of competition (*Atlanta Journal/Constitution*, 1995; Shropshire, 1996). This is often overlooked because those who watch boxing, track and field, college and professional football and basketball, and major-league baseball see many black athletes. But these make up only four of the forty-four men's and women's sports played in col-

lege, four of the dozens of sports played at the international amateur level, and five of the many professional sports in the United States. There is a similar pattern in Canada and in European countries with strong sporting traditions. Many people forget that there is a virtual absence of black athletes—male or female—in archery, auto racing, badminton, bowling, canoeing/kayaking, cycling, diving, equestrian events, field hockey, figure skating, golf, gymnastics, hockey, motocross, rodeo, rowing, sailing, shooting, alpine and nordic skiing, soccer, softball, swimming, table tennis, team handball, tennis, volleyball, water polo, yachting, and many field events in track and field.

African Americans are visible in a few high-profile sports in the U.S., but are underrepresented in most sports. The participation patterns and experiences of African American women in sports seldom have been studied, so we know little about the combined influence of gender logic and race logic in their lives. (Susan Ragan, AP/Wide World Photos)

The exceptions to this pattern stand out because they *are* exceptions. In fact, the underrepresentation of blacks in this long list of sports is much greater than the underrepresentation of whites in sports such as basketball and football: there are many more whites who play basketball and football in high school than blacks who play high school tennis or golf. And if the proportion of black race car drivers on the NASCAR circuit were as high as the proportion of whites in the NBA, it would be far greater than the proportion of blacks in the total U.S. population.

Throughout U.S. sports history, the participation of black females has been severely limited and has received little attention, apart from that given to occasional Olympic medal winners in track events. Black women suffer the consequences of dominant forms of gender logic and race logic. Apart from a handful of studies, we know little about the unique experiences of African American women athletes, even those participating in the 1990s (Corbett and Johnson, 1993; Green, 1993; Smith, 1992; Stratta, 1995).

Overall, sport participation rates in middle- and upper-middle-income white communities in the United States are much higher than those in the vast majority of predominantly black communities. Many people ignore this fact, along with the information I have just given. They seem to see only the black male athletes who make high salaries in high-profile sports. This exemplifies how dominant racial ideology influences what people "see" in their social worlds; *Hoop Dreams* myths affect whites as well as blacks.

Native Americans and Sport Participation

There are nearly 2.28 million Native Americans in the United States, and approximately 2% of the Canadian population is officially considered Native. Although officially classified as one minority group, Native Americans comprise many dozens of diverse cultural groups. Among native peoples, the differences between these cultural groups are important. However, most individuals and whites who are not Native American tend to think of them all as "Indians" and use stereotyped descriptions of their habits and dress. Popular ideas about Native Americans are different from racial ideology; they have their own history and have grown out of unique forms of ethnic relations.

Sports among Native Americans traditionally have combined physical activities with ritual and ceremony (Oxendine, 1988). Although Native Americans have made significant achievements in certain sports over the past century, public ac-

claim has been limited to those few who have been standout athletes on the football and baseball teams of government-sponsored reservation schools and training schools. For example, when Jim Thorpe and his teammates at the Carlisle School, a segregated government training school, defeated outstanding mainstream college teams in 1911 and 1912, they attracted considerable attention (Oxendine, 1988). Apart from a few successful teams and individual athletes in segregated government schools, Native American participation in most sports has been and continues to be limited. Where participation is not made impossible because of poverty, poor health, and lack of equipment and programs, it is discouraged by a combination of prejudice, government legislation and programs, lack of understanding (see box on pp. 272–273), and fears of being cut off from the cultural roots that are at the heart of personal identity for many Native Americans.

For example, Billy Mills, gold medalist in the 10,000 meters race at the 1964 Olympics, explained that becoming immersed in sport programs away from the reservation on which one grew up is

> . . . like walking death. . . . If you go too far into [Anglo] society, there's a fear of losing your Indianness. There's a spiritual factor that comes into play. To become part of white society you give up half your soul (cited in Simpson, 1996).

For a young Native American attending a school or watching games between schools with team names such as Indians, Redskins, Redmen, and Savages, and with mascots who run around and mimic white stereotypes of "Indian" behavior, playing sports involves giving up much more than half one's soul. For such a youth, to see a distorted or historically inappropriate caricature of a Native American on the gym wall of a school where students have no knowledge of local or regional native cultures means swallowing cultural pride, repressing anger against insensitive, historically ignorant non-Indians, and giving up hope of being understood in terms of personal feelings and cultural heritage.

Native American athletes also have experienced problems when their own cultural orientations have not matched those highlighted in the power and performance sports of many high schools. Naive teachers and coaches who work with Native American students on reservations have used systematic strategies to encourage them to abandon their traditional cultural ideologies emphasizing cooperation and replace them with an Anglo cultural ideology emphasizing competition. Coaches frustrated with the nonaggressive orientations of Native Americans on their football and basketball teams even have tried to instill a "killer instinct" in their players. For example, a high school football coach in Arizona complained that students at Hopi High School "aren't used to our win-at-all-costs, beat-the-other-man mentality. Their understanding of what it means to be a good Hopi goes against what it takes to be a good football player" (in Garrity, 1989). When the coach was asked how he handled the situation, he said,

> [I did] exactly what the missionaries tried to do— de-Indianize the Indians (quoted in Garrity, 1989).

It seems that when some Native Americans don't give up their cultural souls voluntarily when they play sports, some Anglo coaches may ask for them in the name of winning and cultural assimilation. Fortunately, not all Native American experiences match these; some Native Americans play sports in contexts where their ethnic identities are not only respected, but also supported by others (Blanchard, 1983; Paraschak, 1995; Schroeder, 1995).

Hispanics and Sport Participation

Hispanic is a generic term used by the U.S. government to group together all people whose ethnic roots can be traced to Spanish-speaking countries; *Latino* is a term sometimes preferred by those whose ancestors are from Latin America. Hispanic Americans generally encompass a wide range of diverse cultures often related by language, colonial history, or Catholicism. Mexican Americans constitute the largest Hispanic group in the United States, followed by Puerto Ricans, Cubans, other Central and South Americans, and people from Spain. There were about 27 million Hispanics in the U. S. as of 1995.

Sociologists have given little attention to any Latino group in North American sports. There have been a few papers dealing with stacking patterns, salary differences, and the numbers of Latino coaches and managers (Gonzalez, 1996; Leonard, 1988, 1995; Purdy et al., 1994; Rimer, 1996), but we know little about the actual experiences of Latino athletes. Even though the ancestors of Chicanos have resided in what is now the southwestern United States since before the Pilgrims set foot on Plymouth Rock, their experiences in sports have been largely ignored in the sport sciences.

Ethnic stereotypes about Latinos often vary in content and in the extent of their use from one region of the country to another, and they are not the same for all Latino cultural groups. For example, one major-league baseball scout explained that most Mexicans in major-league baseball are pitchers for the following reasons:

> Mexicans have bad foot speed. It's a genetic type thing. They have a different body type. Most have good hands and good rhythm. That's why they dance so well. Rhythm is important in baseball, it means agility (in Beaton, 1993).

Of course, millions of soccer fans who watched the Mexican national soccer team during the 1994 World Cup would take issue with the "bad foot speed" stereotype! Another baseball scout, a Latino himself, had a slightly different stereotype about Mexicans:

> Mexicans, because of their Indian blood, can run to New York and not stop. Just not fast (in Beaton, 1993).

REFLECT ON SPORT

Team Names, Logos, and Mascots:
When Are They Indications of Bigotry?

Using stereotypes to characterize Native Americans in the U.S. is so common that most people don't even realize they are doing it. This has occurred for so long that the stereotypes are now widely accepted as valid depictions of native peoples. When these stereotypes are used as a basis for team names, mascots, and logos, sports become a site for perpetuating an ideology that exploits, trivializes, and demeans the history and cultural heritage of Native Americans. This may not be the intent of those who use Native American images in this way, but it is often the result. When this is pointed out to them, many people try to excuse their ignorance and insensitivity by saying that using images in this way is just part of tradition.

Consider the following story from a statement by a group called the Concerned American Indian Parents:

> An American Indian student attended his school's pep rally in preparation for a football game against a rival school. The rival school's mascot was an American Indian. The pep rally included the burning of an Indian in effigy along with posters and banners labeled "Scalp the Indians," "Kill the Indians," and "Let's burn the Indians at the stake." The student, hurt and embarrassed, tore the banners down. His fellow students couldn't understand his hurt and pain.

This incident occurred in 1962, but this student's pain has not prevented hundreds of sport teams at the high school, college, and professional levels from using stereotypes of Native Americans for team names, logos, and mascots. The pain continues today (Banks, 1993; Davis, 1993). There are still "non-Indians" who dress in war bonnets and war paint and run around brandishing spears and tomahawks or pounding tom-toms. For example, Chief Wahoo, the mascot of the Cleveland Indians, is built on long-accepted stereotypes of Native Americans. Sadly, Chief Wahoo is only one of many examples of disrespectful caricatures used by American sport teams.

Many people don't realize that names like Redskins and mascots like Chief Wahoo tend to perpetuate stereotypes that have contributed to the powerlessness, poverty, unemployment, alcoholism, and dependency of many native peoples in the United States. What would people say if the mascot for the San Diego Padres were a fat, self-indulgent missionary who ran around swinging a rosary and waving a crucifix in a menacing or celebratory way? What if he led the fans in secular renditions of Gregorian chant as hitters came up with runners on base? What if fans did a "crucifix chop" as they chanted? Many Christians would object, and rightly so!

If teachers, administrators, and students in U.S. schools had a deep knowledge of the rich and diverse cultures of Native Americans and realized the discrimination native peoples currently face, they would not use names such as Indians, Redskins, Chiefs, Braves, Savages, Tribe, and Redmen for their teams; they would not allow Anglo students to entertain fans by dressing up as caricatures of Native Americans, and they would not allow fans to mimic Native American chants or act out demeaning stereotypes of war-whooping, tomahawk-chopping Native Americans.

Schools should not use any Native American name or symbol in connection with sport teams unless they do the following:

1. Sponsor a special curriculum to inform students of the history, cultural heritage, and current living conditions of the native group after which their sport teams are named. Unless 70 percent of the students can pass annual tests on this information, schools should drop the names they say are used to "honor" native people. There cannot be honor without knowledge.

2. Publish two press releases per year in which information about the heritage and current circumstances of the native peoples honored by their team names is described and analyzed; publish similar materials annually in school newspapers and yearbooks.

3. Once per year, during homecoming or a major sport event, sponsor a special ceremony designed by and for native peoples in the local area, with the purpose of informing students and parents about the people they say they honor with their team names.

If schools did these three things, they would be less likely to perpetuate some of the most destructive and vicious stereotypes in American history. Shouldn't schools be careful not to distort history through their own team names, logos, and mascots? Don't schools teach history? Of course they do. But those using names and mascots related to Native Americans often forget history and perpetuate misunderstandings and bigotry in the process. Traditions that insult others, like the old images of "little black Sambo" and "the Frito Bandito," should be abandoned—or at the least, those insulted should be compensated, just as the International Olympic Committee demands to be compensated when someone wants to use the symbol of the five rings and the name "Olympics."

If schools did the three things suggested, their students would think twice before using certain team names. For example, students would know that to many Native Americans, "redskin" is as derogatory as "nigger" for African Americans, or "spic" for Chicanos. Sadly, the capital city of the government that has broken hundreds of treaties with Native Americans still has a professional football team named "Redskins." From the cultural perspective of Native Americans, the use of this name, the use of stereotypes for mascots and logos, and the use of historically inaccurate images without permission simply symbolizes a long history of oppression.

Only when native peoples have a representative share of power and resources in the U.S. might the situation be right for using their names and images in association with sport teams. This is the reason the Irish do not object to Boston's use of the name "Celtics" or Notre Dame's use of "the Fighting Irish."

The poster pictured here was developed to make people question the use of Native American images in sports. If demeaning images of other ethnic groups were used in similar ways, there would be widespread objections. Native American Dennis Banks (1993) has asked for nearly thirty years, "Why do these people continue to make mockery of our culture [with tribal names and mascots in sports]?" Other native people want to know why professional teams that make millions of dollars using Native American images on everything from uniforms and hats to coffee cups and souvenir tomahawks don't build sport facilities on

(See chap.14, p 445, for photo illustrating a questionable use of a Native American image by a high school.) The National Conference, Minnesota-Dakotas Region.

reservations and fund programs to keep young Native Americans healthy enough that they can play sports. Maybe all those romanticized images on hats and gym walls have prevented people from seeing the reality of Native Americans today. What do you think?

Of course, these stereotypes about the genetic makeup of Mexican bodies are not applied to Cubans, whose success in baseball extends to many different positions, and whose success in many different sports requiring different physical abilities is legendary. Nor are they applied to baseball players from the Dominican Republic, who are overrepresented at the position of shortstop in major league baseball, or to Venezuelans, who play many different baseball positions. Other racial and ethnic stereotypes are used when people of color can be classified as black rather than Latin! Furthermore, the stereotypes about Mexicans ignore that Mexico itself is a multiracial society, with about 100 million people who have a combination of Spanish, English, German, French, Indian, and other central American ancestries.

It is clear that using ethnic stereotypes and racial ideologies to explain the success or failure of Latino athletes only creates confusion and perpetuates misinformation (Rodriguez, 1993). These stereotypes and ideologies are diverse, and they impact sport participation patterns and experiences in diverse ways. They remind us of the need for research on the cultural, political, economic, and social factors affecting the sport experiences of Latinos. In other words, we must focus on ethnic relations issues, not mysterious genetic predispositions and abilities. Recently anthropologists have done just that.

Anthropologist Alan Klein reported on his study of the experiences of Latin Americans in major-league baseball in his 1991 book *Sugarball: The American Game, the Dominican Dream.* Although Klein focuses his attention on the Dominican Republic and what happens there in connection with the baseball academies sponsored by major-league teams, he also notes that Dominican players who sign contracts and play in the minor or major leagues in North America often confront problems. They not only face significant cultural adjustments and language problems, but also must deal with others' behaviors based on ethnic stereotypes and a general lack of understanding of their cultural backgrounds.

Anthropologist Doug Foley gave special attention to Mexicano-Anglo relations in his study of rituals associated with high school football in a small Texas town. He describes the working-class Chicano males (*vatos*) who rejected sport participation but used sport events as occasions for publicly displaying their style (cool pose?) and establishing their social reputations in the community. He describes the way Mexicanos* protested a homecoming ceremony that gave center stage to Anglos and marginalized Mexicanos, the way Mexicano players defied coaches when Anglo players were given high-status positions on the team, and the resignation of the Mexicano coach in frustration because he could not appease powerful Anglo boosters and school board members and still maintain his ethnic integrity by challenging bigotry. Despite these examples of protest against prevailing Anglo ways of doing things in the town, Foley concludes that the rituals associated with high school football tend to perpetuate the power and privilege of Anglos. As long as Mexicanos saw things and did things the Anglo way, they were accepted. But the protests did nothing to make Anglos see or do things to fit the values and experiences of the Mexicanos.

There is a need for more research along the lines of the work by Klein and Foley so that we can better understand sport participation in light of patterns of ethnic relations in specific cultural settings. Research also is needed on Latinas, whose experiences have been highlighted only in connection with the success of a few tennis players, Nancy Lopez in golf, and Gina Fernandez in softball. Sport participation among Latinas has not been actively nurtured, in some cases because faulty generalizations about Latino families lead people to think that Latinas are physically passive

---

*This self-descriptive term was used by people with Mexican heritage in Foley's study.

and do not have family support for involvement in competitive physical activities (Jamieson, 1995). These generalizations will persist until research provides concrete examples of Latina sport experiences. This research must show how ethnicity combines with gender and social class in the lives of both Latinas and Latinos.

Finally, I suspect that Latino involvement in sports will receive increased attention in the future because Hispanics are the fastest-growing ethnic population in the U.S., and because leaders in commercial sports now are trying to attract Latino fans. This is the reason major-league baseball scheduled and played a game in Monterrey, Mexico during the 1996 season, and the reason baseball people are talking about locating a major-league team somewhere in Mexico (Monterrey or Mexico City). Also, the economic success of soccer in California and other parts of the U.S. will depend on whether organizers take into account the interests and orientations of Latino athletes and spectators. One banner proclaimed during a 1996 Major League Soccer game in San Jose Stadium in California: "You want us back? Get a Mexican player!" This fan wanted his Mexican roots acknowledged as he watched soccer, and his sentiment is shared by many others who see soccer as an international game tied to cultures that are a part of their own ethnic heritage, even when they are U.S. citizens. This does not mean they are not committed to their identity as Americans; it does mean they want their cultural heritage and uniqueness to be recognized and incorporated into their sport experiences in the U.S. and into the awareness of their fellow citizens.

At this point, it seems that professional soccer highlights the ethnic mix of U.S. society in ways that other sports have not done in recent years. Some predict this will doom the sport, because the popularity of spectator sports in the U.S. has been built around an emphasis on "Anglo American-ness" and a suppression of any "foreign" ethnic connection. This is one of the reasons soccer, which was widely played in the first half of the twentieth century in the U.S., lost favor in the 1930s and after World War II: it was associated with ethnic groups perceived as a threat to the core of Anglo American culture at that time. But times are changing, ethnic relations are changing, the expressions of ethnic identities are changing, and so might sports change. This would be encouraging for many Latinos in the U.S.

Asian Americans and Sport Participation

There were about 6.7 million Asian Americans as of 1996. Because of global migration patterns, the Asian population is rapidly expanding, and because of settlement patterns, most Asian Americans live on the West Coast and in selected cities around the U.S. The cultural heritage and the individual histories of Asian Americans are very diverse. To group them together is like grouping all Europeans together and making no distinctions between Irish Americans and Italian Americans. Although this diversity presents major challenges for researchers, there is a need in the sociology of sport for studies focusing on ethnic relations and sport participation patterns and experiences among various Asian American groups.

The success and popularity of Asian and Asian American athletes has raised important issues about the extent to which Asian American sport interests and experiences have been ignored in sociology and in society as a whole. The popularity of Los Angeles Dodger pitcher Hideo Nomo highlights how many Japanese Americans have embraced baseball, as both spectators and participants. Research is now needed on the impact, if any, of Nomo's popularity on ethnic relations in and around Dodger Stadium, and in the Los Angeles area. Have Nomo and other Asian and Asian American athletes had an impact on ethnic stereotypes, on beliefs about the characteristics and abilities of people with Asian ancestry, and on how Asian American people think about themselves and their connections with others?

The success of Chinese American tennis player Michael Chang and Japanese American figure skater Kristi Yamaguchi raise other issues about the willingness of Anglo Americans to embrace Asian American athletes as cultural heroes and spokespeople for products they endorse. Chang's image has been used and accepted more in China than in the U.S., although it has been used in the U.S. in connection with products and services that are associated with Pacific Rim nations. Yamaguchi certainly has been popular as an athlete, but some corporations have hesitated to have her endorse their products because they fear that many people in the U.S. will not identify with her. Research is needed on the ways in which the images of Asian American athletes are taken up and represented in the U.S.

We also need research on the dramatic rise in popularity of various martial arts in North America. Karate, judo, Tae Kwon Do, and other sports with Asian origins have become especially popular with U.S. children. Has participation in these martial arts had an impact on children's knowledge and awareness of Asian cultures, on ethnic relations in elementary schools, on the stereotypes used or challenged among children and others who participate in these sports? Or have these sport forms become so "Americanized" that their Asian roots are lost or ignored among participants?

The experiences and sport participation patterns of Asian Americans differ depending on their immigration histories. Chinese Americans whose families have lived in the U.S. for four or more generations clearly have different experiences from those of Vietnamese immigrants and their children. Research must be sensitive to these differences and the ways they influence sport participation patterns and experiences. Applied research is needed to assist coaches in high schools with Asian American students.

Anthropologist Mark Grey (1992) has dealt with some of these issues in his study of high school sports and relations between immigrants from southeast Asia and the established residents of Garden City, Kansas. Grey reports that despite beliefs about sports serving democratic functions in schools, sports at Garden City High School were organized so that participation could occur only in narrowly defined terms. The immigrant and minority students had to "fit in" with the dominant system of values and game orientations, and this system was grounded in the experiences of Anglo Americans. The school failed to provide these newcomers with sports they wanted to play, and when the immigrant students did not try out for football, basketball, baseball, and softball, they were seen as unwilling to become "true Americans." Over time, their failure to participate in the major high school sports led them to be socially marginalized in the school and community. The established community residents believed that "if *those people* really wanted to become Americans, they would participate in true American sports." When they didn't participate, new tensions were created and existing tensions were intensified. It is possible that this pattern also exists in other communities, although we don't know enough about it or about other possible patterns.

THE RACIAL DESEGREGATION OF CERTAIN AMERICAN SPORTS

The visibility of black athletes in high-profile spectator sports in the United States and other countries raises an interesting sociological question: Why have some sports been desegregated to such an extent that black male athletes are proportionately overrepresented relative to the size of the black population in the country as a whole? Three reasons may explain why. *First*, the organization of certain sports provides a unique context for desegregation at the player level. *Second*, built-in financial incentives encourage desegregation of certain sports. *Third*, black Americans have taken advantage of opportunities to develop their skills in certain sports where success depends on effort rather than money. Each of these reasons requires further explanation.

The Organization of Certain Sports

Unlike many other organizations, certain sport teams and leagues are set up to discourage discrimination against athletes from minority group backgrounds (Edwards, 1973). Consider the following characteristics of sports and sport teams:

1. Individual performances in sports can often be measured precisely and objectively, so it is possible to control subjective prejudices based on race or ethnicity.
2. Members of an entire team benefit when a teammate excels. This means that racial and ethnic prejudices are more likely to be controlled in sports organizations than in other organizations where individual achievements may not benefit fellow workers.
3. Superior performances by athletes lead neither to promotions in sport organizations nor to control over fellow players. This means that whites will be less threatened by the achievements of blacks in sports than by their achievements in settings where superior performances lead to power and authority over coworkers.
4. Team success in sports does not depend on friendships between teammates. This means that interracial relationships need not be maintained in off-the-field social situations, unlike relationships in many work organizations, where social obligations are an accepted part of the job.
5. Athletes have little power or authority in the organizational structure of a sport team. This means that playing sports does nothing to change the fact that blacks have little formal and legitimate power in the economy or the political world; being an athlete is therefore consistent with the relatively powerless status of blacks in the rest of society, and their in-

The sports that have been desegregated over the past fifty years have attracted African Americans. This participation is often strongly supported by parents, who see sport participation as one of the ways for their sons and daughters to participate more fully in community activities and programs, and to earn a living in the future. This mother is very proud of her son whose photo is included on the helmet pictured on her new shirt. (Jay Coakley)

volvement in sport is not seen as a threat to the status quo.

Because of these five factors, the white people who control sport teams can take advantage of the skills of any minority athletes without feeling threatened by the achievements of those athletes. Even so, it is difficult to change patterns of exclusion grounded in long-standing race relations.

This means that racial desegregation seldom has occurred unless there have been good reasons for whites to open doors and make opportunities available to black athletes. Money and the desire to win generally have been powerful reasons.

Money and Winning: Incentives for Desegregation

Money and winning can be powerful forces in sports. People generally believe that if revenues can be increased or win-loss records improved, change is worth it—even if the change is inconsistent with patterns of race relations. The history of desegregation in American sports clearly shows that when a winning season is necessary to generate money and profits, there is a tendency to recruit and play the best athletes, regardless of skin color. When sport team owners discovered they could make large profits in baseball, football, and basketball, they and their coaches abandoned their traditions of racial exclusion in favor of making money. Although some teams tried to remain competitive without recruiting black players, they dropped their policies when they discovered that winning could be difficult when they ignored the talents of skilled athletes.

Desegregation is a complex process grounded in a combination of social, legal-political, and economic forces. It usually occurs gradually and is promoted and restrained by many factors (Rayl, 1996). This is certainly true in the case of U.S. sports. But because money is such a powerful motivator in capitalist societies, it is not surprising that desegregation first occurred after the Civil War in the revenue-producing sports of horse racing and boxing, and then in the other major money-making sports in the middle of the twentieth century. In the U.S., black jockeys were plentiful before the turn of the century, but a racist press, a white jockeys' union, and laws making segregation mandatory (Jim Crow laws) forced blacks out of the public eye in horse racing and back into the less prestigious and less visible roles of trainer and stable attendant. Horse owners did not resist this change, because there were plenty of white jockeys, and because a race is won more by the horse than by the jockey.

In boxing, however, the individual fighter was solely responsible for victory. Segregation existed, but there were notable (and newsworthy) exceptions. White promoters and boxing managers saw blacks as potentially big money makers because they were box-office attractions. Given the race logic used by many whites through most of the twentieth century, even the rumor of a fight between a black man and a white one would sell newspapers, and an actual fight would generate ticket sales bringing handsome profits to white promoters and managers.

Desegregation was also financially motivated in professional and college team sports, where people other than the athletes themselves could make money. Desegregation started slowly, but as soon as powerful people in sports realized that black athletes could help them win games and boost profits, they questioned and changed traditions of racial exclusion. This is part of the reason the non-revenue-producing sports in U.S. colleges and universities seldom have black team members, and part of the reason 81 percent of all black men receiving athletic scholarships in the 305 Division I universities during the mid-1990s played basketball or football, the two college sports with the biggest revenue-generating potential. Ironically, the scholarships received by many white athletes from well-to-do families (in such non-revenue-producing sports as gymnastics, golf, swimming, tennis, soccer, and volleyball) are sometimes subsidized by revenue-producing teams whose success is due partly to the hard work and efforts of black athletes from lower-income families (Edwards, 1986). This results in a form of "reverse sport welfare" in which relatively poor students subsidize their wealthier white classmates in college sports! Even though white scholarship athletes in non-revenue sports seldom think of their athletic grants in this way, this is one of the reasons intercollegiate sports were desegregated.

If black athletes had not improved winning records and increased profits for those who controlled sports and sport-sponsoring organizations, the policies of exclusion that had restricted black participation for so long would not have changed as rapidly or as completely as they did in certain sports. When sports have made little or no money for their sponsors, there has been little interest in recruiting blacks or making opportunities to participate available in predominantly black neighborhoods. This fact, combined with a lack of opportunities in the job market, has led many young blacks to desperately pursue opportunities in those few sports where they exist. "Hoop dreams" are powerful when there is little else to dream about (Hoberman, 1997).

Perceived Opportunities and the Development of Sport Skills

Those who control sports are not the only ones influenced by financial factors and the desire for success. These things also influence all young people with athletic potential, and blacks are no exception. In fact, blacks are even more likely than whites to emphasize sports as a means of achieving prestige and economic success, because they perceive more barriers to achievement in other activities (Harris, 1994).

It is also important to note that blacks in the United States have excelled in sports requiring little expensive equipment and training. For example, basketballs are inexpensive, and the best coaching is widely available in public school programs. Furthermore, outdoor basketball courts are inexpensive to build and maintain. No grass is needed, and they can be squeezed into confined spaces. This is the reason basketball has come to be known as the "city game," and the reason it is the sport of choice among many black youths growing up in low-income urban areas where resources are scarce and opportunities to be noticed in other activities are rare (Axthelm, 1970; Joravsky, 1995; Telander, 1988).

Anthropologist Robert Sands, who has studied sprinters on college track teams, suggests that most sprinters today are black because black children growing up in urban areas run constantly. For black children, more than for white children, speed becomes play: "speed is everyday life, speed is the cultural password leading to success in sport participation and the possibility of future financial success" (1995). In other words, being fast is one of the traits needed to seek one's destiny as an athlete in sports such as boxing, track and field, basketball, and football.

As black men and women have become increasingly successful in a few highly visible sports, young blacks have focused their attention on developing skills in the same sports. This not only has contributed to the high proportion of blacks in certain sports, but also accounts for the tendency among many young black males to put all their motivational eggs into just a few sport baskets. Because they haven't had the chance to see payoffs connected with education, they conclude that running and jumping offer the best chances for fame and fortune. Therefore, many of them dedicate themselves to being the best runners and jumpers around. Unfortunately, outside of a couple of sports, occupational opportunities for runners and jumpers are very limited (see chap. 10).

Why Haven't All Sports Been Desegregated?

Desegregating any activity or organization is a complex process. In sports, desegregation has been influenced by the organizational structure of sports and sport teams, the payoffs associated with eliminating policies of exclusion, and the motivation among blacks to take advantage of opportunities to develop certain sport skills.

In discussions of race relations and sport, it is important not to equate desegregation with the elimination of bigoted racial ideologies or with the achievement of true racial integration. Desegregation involves opening doors; true integration occurs when there are unqualified invitations to come through the doors and join *all* the activities going on inside, regardless of where they are happening or who is

African Americans have excelled in sports requiring no expensive equipment or training apart from that available in public schools or other public programs. Basketballs are cheap, opportunities to play are plentiful, and good coaching is available in public schools. These are the reasons basketball is often described as the "city game." (*Colorado Springs Gazette*)

involved. Integration depends on deep changes in racial ideology.

Jackie Robinson, the first black man to play in modern major-league baseball, recognized the differences between desegregation and true integration when he once remarked that some of his racist teammates on the Brooklyn Dodgers tolerated him as a fellow athlete only because he "could help fill their wallets." He knew that those teammates never fully accepted him as a human being either on or off the field. The door to sport was opened for Robinson, but he knew there were no unqualified invitations to participate in everything going on inside sports, or in the rest of life outside of sports (Robinson, 1972).

Many things have changed in the fifty years since Jackie Robinson signed his first major-league contract, but racial bigotry still exists in sports. The mere fact that blacks have been accepted as athletes in certain sports does not mean that skin color has lost its relevance in all sports, or in the rest of society. It's one thing for people to say nice things about black athletes who run around football fields, basketball courts, and Olympic tracks, but it is quite another thing for them to be comfortable with racial integration off the playing field and across a wide range of social situations.

This point is important when we attempt to explain why some sports remain highly segregated, even as we move into the twenty-first century. Desegregation is most likely when sports involve little off-the-field social interaction, especially interaction between men and women.

However, when sports involve informal, personal, and mixed-gender social contact either on or off the field, desegregation comes slowly, if at all. This is the reason golf, tennis, swimming, bowling, and other sports learned and played in social clubs have been slow to open doors for blacks and other minorities. When sport participation is accompanied by informal social contact between family and friends and by intimate and personal interaction, dominant racial ideology among whites keeps doors closed or only partially open.

SPORTS AND INTERGROUP RELATIONS

Do sports enable people to transcend racial and ethnic differences? Are sports contexts in which personal prejudices can be broken down, dominant racial ideologies challenged, and intergroup relations improved on both personal and institutional levels?

Research shows that contact between people from different racial and ethnic groups can lead to favorable changes on a personal level when members of each group

- have equal status
- pursue the same goals
- depend on one another's cooperation to achieve their goals
- receive positive encouragement for interacting with one another in supportive ways

Even though these conditions exist in many sports, there are at least three reasons to be cautious before concluding that interaction in sports reduces prejudice:

1. When people are in the habit of using racial and ethnic ideologies to explain what happens in their worlds, they resist changing those ideologies.
2. Contact between members of different racial and ethnic groups in sports is often so superficial that it fails to break down prejudices, or challenge ideologies, or change people's behaviors, especially off-the-field behaviors.
3. The competition that occurs within and between teams may aggravate existing prejudices among players and spectators and lead them to perpetuate hostile and destructive ideologies.

Racial and Ethnic Ideologies Resist Change

When people use particular sets of ideas to interpret what goes on in the world, they often go to great lengths to defend and preserve those ideas, thinking that without them, the world would not make any sense. In sports, players from one racial or ethnic group may ignore players from other groups and selectively tune out information inconsistent with their preexisting ideas about race and ethnicity. When forced to interact with players who challenge those ideas, they may define those players as exceptions—not like other blacks, or whites, or Hispanics, and so on. This allows them to preserve negative racial ideologies while they play sports with teammates from other groups. When information clearly challenges ideologies, they just reinterpret the information so that it supports their negative stereotypes.

Social Contacts in Sports Are Superficial

Despite what many sport fans think, teammates don't have to be friends with one another to play well. Many teams with serious interpersonal problems among players have won championships. Success requires knowledge of teammates' playing abilities, but players can gain this knowledge without close personal interaction. In other words, people from different racial and ethnic groups don't become friends just because they are teammates.

When U.S. sports were first desegregated, black athletes led lonely lives. They coped with the racism and cautious acceptance of spectators, teammates, and coaches (Robinson, 1972). Off-the-field contacts with teammates were rare, and there were few opportunities for blacks and whites to share experiences and feelings (Charnofsky, 1968). As the number of black athletes has increased in certain sports, friendships between blacks and whites have become more common, but patterns of racial separateness and self-segregation still exist (Stratta, 1993, 1995). These patterns are most likely when whites have little awareness of race-related issues and problems, and when whites or blacks lack the experiences and the support that would make them feel at ease among people from different racial backgrounds.

Relationships depend on personal communication, and communication depends on acknowledging the reality of other people's experiences. Unless people are ready to listen to others, share their perspectives, and accept as valid what others say about their experiences, relationships don't happen. Sports provide *opportunities* for communication and forming relationships based on racial and ethnic awareness, but athletes don't seem to take advantage of these opportunities in a way that makes them more likely than other people their age to have friends from different racial or ethnic backgrounds (Chu and Griffey, 1982; Miracle, 1981; Thirer and Ross, 1981; Thirer and Wieczorek, 1984).

Social life in some U.S. schools involves little social mixing between students from different racial and ethnic groups, and sometimes even involves hostilities and conflicts (Jarvis, 1993). Sharing membership on a school team may override this pattern within the special sphere of the team itself, but it doesn't seem to override it when team members are in nonsport settings.

Competition Often Subverts Intergroup Cooperation

Competition in sports can destroy the common goals needed to challenge racial and ethnic prejudices. When athletes from different racial or ethnic groups are opponents, sports even can become sites for the creation or intensifying of stereotypes and negative ideas about race and ethnicity. This is the case for spectators as well.

This should not be surprising. Social psychologists long have used competition to create hos-

tility and negative attitudes between groups in their experiments (Kohn, 1986). They knew that competition consistently evoked negative feelings, and that when competitors were from different racial or ethnic groups, existing negative feelings would be intensified during competition.

These patterns also exist in sports. Sport competition can intensify emotions and generate hostile intergroup behavior during events. As one black student-athlete wrote in a paper on race and sport, "in the heat of sport competition, restraint gives way to raw emotion, and racism takes the place of sportsmanship." He noted that his statement was based on his experiences through years of sport participation. Race relations expert Richard Lapchick (1984), director of the Center for the Study of Sport in Society at Northeastern University, has noted that when black and white athletes meet in sport, they often carry "a great deal of racial baggage . . . [and] prejudices are unlikely to evaporate with the sweat as they play together. . . . Any display of negative behavior is likely to reinforce existing biases." When this happens, games may be defined in racial terms and even become racial battles.

The effects of competition are not always limited to the members of opposing teams. When teammates from different racial or ethnic backgrounds compete with one another for starting positions and other honors, their personal rivalries may be defined in racial or ethnic terms. When this occurs, coaches are faced with the challenge of defusing potentially dangerous situations. They serve as the mediators for what may be intense racial dynamics among players. For this reason, coaches in many sports need diversity training.

Is Change Possible?

People don't give up racial and ethnic beliefs easily, especially when they come in the form of well-established ideologies rooted deeply in their cultures. And people who have benefited from those ideologies will resist changes in the relationships and social structures that are built

African American men and women are seriously underrepresented in coaching jobs at the college and professional levels in U.S. sports. Ricardo Patton, head basketball coach at the University of Colorado in 1997, is one of a small but growing number of black male coaches in college basketball and football; black women coaches are especially scarce, regardless of the sport. (Jay Coakley)

on and reinforce their beliefs. This is the reason many expressions of racism and ethnic bigotry have remained a part of sports in the U.S. and other societies.

Sports may bring people together, but they do not automatically lead people to question the way they think about race or ethnicity or the way they relate to those from other racial or ethnic groups. For example, white team owners, general managers, and athletic directors in the U.S. worked with black athletes for years before they

ever hired black coaches; and it took concerted social and legal pressures to force those in power positions to act more affirmatively when it came to their hiring procedures. Blacks are still underrepresented in coaching and administration because people in power don't easily change the ideologies and the social structures undergirding their power (Shropshire, 1996). This probably accounts for the inclusion in the *College Sports* magazine list of the Fifty Most Influential People in College Sports in 1996 of only two African Americans (forty-one white men, six white women, and one team mascot made up the other forty-eight).

My purpose here is not to argue that sports are never sites for improving intergroup relations. Whenever racial and ethnic groups mix on relatively good terms, there is a chance for people to challenge negative ideas and find new ways of seeing and relating to one another. According to both athletes and spectators, there are cases when this *has* happened in sport, especially on the personal level. This is cause for hope. However, these good things do not happen automatically or as often as many think; nor do changes on the personal level automatically lead to changes on an organizational or institutional level. Challenging the negative personal beliefs of other people is one thing; changing the relationships and social structures that have been built on those beliefs is another thing. Both forms of change are needed, and neither occurs automatically just because sports bring people together in the same locker rooms and stadiums.

For intergroup relations to be improved through sports, those who control sport teams and sport events must make organized, concerted efforts to bring people together in ways that will encourage them to confront and challenge dominant racial ideologies and all the ways they have been manifested in relationships and organizations. These efforts must be initiated and supported by whites as well as members of ethnic minorities, or else they will fail (Oglesby, 1993). This is no easy task. But if it were attempted and did work, it would be significant, because sports attract so much public attention throughout today's societies. If sports served as sites for the regular challenging of dominant racial ideology and improving of racial and ethnic relations, they could serve as a model for change in other spheres of social life.

NOTEWORTHY EFFORTS Noteworthy efforts to challenge negative racial ideologies and their consequences have occurred. At the Center for the Study of Sport in Society at Northeastern University in Boston, Richard Lapchick and his multiracial, multiethnic staff have developed Project TEAMWORK, a program for improving intergroup relations in high schools and communities. Through this program, a trained, gender-mixed team of former athletes from diverse racial and ethnic backgrounds goes into schools and develops racial, ethnic, and gender sensitivity among students. Training sessions emphasize awareness of human rights and intergroup relations issues and how to deal with those issues in the school and the community in which the students live. The sessions also are designed to promote intergroup tolerance and respect among the students themselves.

Project TEAMWORK spends at least two weeks in target schools. Part of the goal is to form a "Human Rights Squad" with students trained and assigned to monitor intergroup relations in the school and initiate intervention strategies to control and defuse intergroup conflict. Between 1990 and 1996, Project TEAMWORK worked with nearly 130 thousand students in dozens of schools. Many students seem to be very aware of the destructive racial ideologies that exist in society; they see the consequences of those ideologies in their own lives, and want to do something to make race and ethnic relations better.

The Center for the Study of Sport in Society also publishes an annual "Racial Report Card" presenting data on racial and ethnic stacking patterns and the racial, ethnic, and gender composition of coaches, front-office staff, and executives in major professional team sports for men. The center uses the data to compute grades for each major sport league. When grades haven't measured up, citizens have applied public pressure for teams to act more affirmatively when it comes to player, coach, staff, and executive recruitment. Responses to this pressure have been slow, but they have occurred, and progress has been made.

The Commission for Racial Equality in Britain launched a campaign in England, Wales, and Scotland called "Let's Kick Racism Out of Football" in late 1993 and early 1994. The campaign was designed to generate widespread popular disapproval of white fans who directed racist attacks, abuse, and chanting at black (African, Afro-Caribbean, and Asian) fans and players before, during, and after soccer matches (Horne, 1996). The soccer clubs, the players, and many fans supported the campaign, which succeeded in reducing racial incidents in certain areas; it also offered support to those black fans and players who had been the targets of previous abuse (Donegan, 1994; Greenfield and Osborn, 1996).

"Hit Racism For Six" is another antiracism campaign in England. Organized in 1996 by social scientists through the Centre for Sport Development Research at Roehampton Institute in London, this campaign is directed at challenging longstanding traditions that have prevented blacks and Asians from participating in top levels of cricket, one of the most popular sports in England today (CSDR, 1996). The success of this campaign is yet to be determined as I write this chapter, but its existence certainly will raise popular awareness of racial issues, and it offers support to those who have felt until now that they were challenging racist ideologies on their own.

These and other approaches are desperately needed around the world. We need a new vocabulary to deal with the existence of diversity in social life and to promote affirmative action on both personal and organizational levels. We must get away from the notion that skin color or ethnicity signifies some sort of biological essence

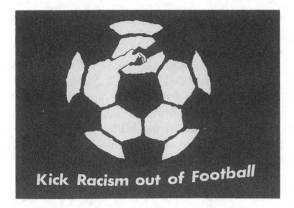

This slogan was used on shirts and posters in a 1990s campaign in Britain. The campaign raised public awareness of racism and emphasized the need for everyone to combat racism in sports. (Jay Coakley)

that shapes character and physical abilities. In connection with sports, we must realize that when we ask questions about so-called racial performance differences, we are merely reproducing a racial ideology that has caused hatred, turmoil, and confusion in much of the world for over two hundred years. Now we must ask questions about how people give meaning to physical and cultural characteristics and then use those meanings as a basis for their thoughts and their relations with others. But even framing questions this way requires a big shift in the way many people view the world.

Sport programs in high schools and colleges, and even at the professional level, need to sponsor racial and ethnic diversity training sessions. Everyone from team owners and athletic directors to the people in training rooms should attend these sessions. Coaches need these training sessions, and so do athletes. Even those who are already sensitive to diversity issues should be made aware that there is a formal commitment in their organizations to acting on those sensitivities.

The training sessions should familiarize everyone in sports with the history and implications of the dominant racial ideology and ethnic stereotypes in their society. That history must be told from the perspective of racial and ethnic groups, as well as from that of the dominant group. When the perspectives of racial and ethnic minorities are not used to guide efforts to "make things better" in society as a whole, those efforts often fail. When "making things better" means doing things to fit the interests of those with power and influence, real change is unlikely.

SUMMARY

ARE SKIN COLOR AND CULTURAL HERITAGE IMPORTANT?

Attempts to define race in biological terms have been futile; races are *socially* identified categories of people, rather than biologically distinct categories. The concept of race emerged in the eighteenth century and has been associated with confusion and turmoil ever since. The desire to classify all people of the world into distinct categories has been fueled by different factors at different points in history. The colonial expansion of Western societies was associated with the development of a racial ideology that claimed the intellectual superiority of light-skinned people over dark-skinned people. As part of this ideology, the physical abilities of dark-skinned peoples were reinterpreted as signs of arrested evolutionary development. Thus, people of color were seen as possessing physical prowess, but lacking the character, fortitude, intelligence, and spirit possessed by whites. White people used this race logic to justify colonization, slavery, and the exploitation of people of color around the world.

Race logic also influenced sport participation patterns and the interpretation of sport performance. White people considered black athletes to be less than human and often characterized them in physical terms, whereas they thought white athletes to be driven by inborn spirit and determination. However, many whites were uncomfortable with the possibility of black physiological superiority, and looked for examples to prove that whites could combine physical strength with their inherent intelligence to out-perform black people. The Tarzan myth and the search for great white athletes were associated with this desire by whites to "prove" their racial superiority. Race logic in sports and the racial ideology on which it is based continue to exist today, although they have been revised as times and circumstances have changed.

Race, gender, and class relations in American society have combined to create a context in which black males emphasize a personal presentation of self described as "cool pose." Cool pose is a stylized persona that has not only added to the commodity value of the black male body in sports, but also enabled some black male athletes to twist white race logic around and use it to intimidate opponents, especially white opponents, in sports.

Race logic has been and remains a factor underlying both racial stacking patterns and the absence of blacks in coaching and administrative positions in sports. It has promoted desegregation in those sports in which white team owners and managers could make money in connection with black and other minority athletes, but it has slowed the desegregation of sports that are learned, played, and sponsored in contexts where social, family, and gender-mixed relationships are part of the overall participation experience.

A combination of ideological, historical, and structural factors have influenced sport participation patterns among different racial and ethnic groups. But the sport participation of any minority group usually occurs under terms set by the dominant group in a community or society. Minority groups seldom have been able to use sports to challenge the power and privilege of the dominant group, even though individual minority-group members may experience great personal success in sports. This is probably the reason minority athletes become cultural heroes only when they present themselves as politically neutral "good guys" with understated racial or ethnic identities. Speaking out and challenging

race logic or expressions of racism in sports or society can be disastrous for black sports figures. Probably for this reason, only three sportspeople were listed in *Ebony* magazine's list of the 100 Most Powerful Blacks in the U.S. during 1996; and two of those figures were not athletes, but executives in sport organizations (Gene Upshaw, executive director of the NFL Players Association, and Leroy Walker, president of the USOC). Michael Jordan was the only athlete on the list, and even he has to be careful about exercising his power.

The racial desegregation of certain sports in the United States also has been influenced by the organizational characteristics of sports, strong financial incentives for recruiting blacks, and the desire of blacks to take advantage of any available opportunity to live the American dream of success. The importance of economic factors cannot be underestimated in the desegregation process. Only when winning has been tied to profits and when blacks have been able to contribute to winning have doors been opened willingly for black athletes.

The mere fact that some sports have histories of racially and ethnically mixed participation does not mean that racial and ethnic problems have been eliminated in those sports. In fact, intergroup harmony is never automatic in any setting, and it doesn't last long unless attention is paid to intergroup relations. Nor does it last long unless members of the dominant group are committed to the importance of racial and ethnic diversity. Sport is unique in the sense that it even may trigger a form of race awareness that makes skin color and certain cultural differences very important to many people. When this happens, race and ethnicity become "identity handles" used to differentiate athletes by potential, character, and physical abilities. This, of course, can be dangerous.

But sports also can be sites for challenging dominant racial ideology and transforming race and ethnic relations. This happens only if people in sports plan strategies to encourage critical awareness of racial ideology. They then must direct this awareness into changing existing relations. This necessarily involves a shift of focus, away from physical and cultural *differences* and onto a critical examination of the meanings associated with those differences and the forms of social organization that reflect those meanings and privilege some groups over others.

SUGGESTED READINGS

Ashe, A. R. Jr., 1988. *A hard road to glory: a history of the African American athlete.* New York: Warner Books (*this three-volume work traces the involvement of African Americans in sports from 1619 to the present; it contains a wealth of useful reference data; although it is short on analysis and information about women, it is the most comprehensive source of information on black Americans in sports ever compiled*).

Bale, J., and J. Sang, eds. 1996. *Kenyan running: Movement culture, geography and global change.* London: Frank Cass (*uses a combination of philosophy, history, sociology, and geography to examine myths around Kenyan running; views running as a body culture that is best understood in the context of colonialism, modern globalized sports, and the Kenyan nation-state*).

Brooks, D. D., and R. C. Althouse, eds. 1993. *Racism in college athletics: The African-American athlete's experience.* Morgantown, WV: Fitness Information Technology, Inc. (*twelve papers dealing with problems faced by African Americans in college sports. Papers provide historical material; discussion of recruitment, retention, and mobility issues; analysis of the intersection of race and gender in sports; and prospects for change in the future*).

Curry, T., ed. 1997. Race, ethnicity, and sport: Aspects of social inequality. *Sociological Focus* 30, 4 (*October, special issue*) (*a preface focuses on the cultural significance of Jackie Robinson and Tiger Woods, three papers provide general overviews of race/ethnic relations in the U.S., three papers provide more specific analysis of ethnic relations in Canada, Japan, and the U.K.*).

Edwards, H. 1969. *The revolt of the black athlete.* New York: The Free Press (*the first book written about black athletes by a sociologist; provides insights related to history and current issues related to race and sports*).

Eisen, G., and D. K. Wiggins, eds. 1994. *Ethnicity and sport in North American history and culture.* Westport, CT: Greenwood Press (*twelve historical analyses of how ethnicity influenced sports and how sports influenced ethnicity and ethnic relations in the U.S. between 1840 and 1990; deals with ethnic succession in sports, discrimination, assimilation, and resistance*).

Hoberman, J. 1997. *Darwin's athletes: How sport has damaged black America and preserved the myth of race.* Boston: Houghton Mifflin (*analysis of the connection between ideas about race and sport participation in the U.S.: the absence of opportunities and visible achievement in economics, politics, and education has encouraged many young black males to focus on what they can achieve through physical rather than intellectual prowess; the achievements of blacks in sports are used by whites to reaffirm racist ideas about the abilities and potential of blacks*).

Hoose, P. M. 1989. *Necessities: Racial barriers in American sports.* New York: Random House (*a response to the 1987 Al Campanis statement on ABC's* Nightline; *provides an easy-to-read overview of examples of racism in sports in the late 1980s*).

Jarvie, G., ed. 1991. *Sport, racism, and ethnicity.* Bristol, PA: The Falmer Press (*six of the eight papers in this anthology deal with racial and ethnic relations outside North America; papers offer good critical analyses*).

Klein, A. M. 1991. *Sugarball: The American game, the Dominican dream.* New Haven, CT: Yale University Press (*a study of intercultural relations as exhibited and informed by baseball; shows how baseball simultaneously generates among Dominicans pride, competition with the United States, and acceptance of North American interests*).

Lapchick, R., ed. 1996. *Sport in society.* Thousand Oaks, CA: Sage (*at least sixteen of the forty articles in this collection deal directly with issues of race or the experiences of black athletes in the U.S.; about half are written by Lapchick himself*).

Oxendine, J. B. 1988. *American Indian sports heritage.* Champaign, IL: Human Kinetics (*a much-needed book on a neglected topic; a good analysis of events prior to 1940s, but a weak analysis of what has happened since then*).

Paraschak, V. 1997. Variations in race relations: Sporting events for native peoples in Canada. *Sociology of Sport Journal* 14, 1: 1–21 (*analysis of native sporting practices in four different parts of Canada; results show that these practices cannot be understood apart from patterns of race relations that frame the everyday lives of native peoples*).

Shropshire, K. 1996. *In black and white: Race and sports in America. New York: New York University Press* (*written by a lawyer, this book critically assesses the past and current forms and manifestations of racism in sports; focuses on legal and other strategies for opening management and other power positions in sports to African Americans*).

Telander, R. 1988. *Heaven is a playground.* New York: A Fireside Book, Simon and Schuster (*first published in 1976, this is a personal account of a summer of playground basketball in Brooklyn; captures the futility of life in a low-income, inner-city neighborhood in which basketball offers an temporary alternative to street life*).

Verma, G. K., and D. S. Darby. 1994. Winners and losers: Ethnic minorities in sport and recreation. London: The Falmer Press (*a study of the sport participation of children from many ethnic minority backgrounds in England; good information on the intersection of ethnicity, religion, and gender*).

Wacquant, L. J. D. 1992. The social logic of boxing in black Chicago: Toward a sociology of pugilism. *Sociology of Sport Journal* 9(3): 221–54 (*read Telander's book first and then read this study—the comparison illustrates the difference between a journalistic account and a sociological analysis; excellent material on boxing, boxers, and the training gym in urban American culture*).

Wenner, L., ed. 1993. Mascots and team names. *Journal of Sport & Social Issues* 17: 1 (*this issue contains three papers dealing with the underlying processes and implications of using Native American images for team names, logos, and mascots*).

chapter 10

(*Colorado Springs Gazette*)

Social Class

Does economic inequality matter in sports?

If I [had gone to the right high school] . . . if I had that kind of exposure, that kind of coaching, that kind of compe- tition, I coulda been Michael Jordan.

Curtis Gates in Hoop Dreams (1995)

I know you won't believe me when I say this, but I wish kids, especially black kids, didn't dream so much about playing in the NBA.

Charles Barkley, NBA player (1995)

When men and women com- pete on the athletics field, so- cioeconomic status disappears. . . . It's the same way in the stands, where corporate pres- idents sit next to janitors . . . and they high-five each other when their team scores . . . which makes me wonder if [socioeconomic status] should matter at all.

Former U.S. President Ronald Reagan (1990)

A sport by sport breakdown of recent U.S. Olympic teams shows a movement split by both class and race. Although in theory anyone can earn a spot in the Olympics, the reality of the process is far different.

Atlanta Journal/Constitution (1 October 1995)

The golf industry was built on the basis of a white, male power structure. . . . We're going to have to allow women, minorities, and handicapped people to be a part of this industry.

Kerry Graham, president, LPGA teaching division (1992)

It has gotten too expensive for the average fan to go to sports events. Not just too ex- pensive to have a luxury box. Just too expensive.

Mike Lupica, sportswriter (1996)

It is widely believed that only performance counts in sports. Most people see sports as open to everyone, and they see success in sports as the result of individual abilities and hard work, not money and privilege. But when they are formally organized, sports depend on material resources. More than ever before, it now takes money to play certain sports and obtain the coaching necessary to develop sport skills. It also takes money to attend sport events in sport stadiums where spectators are increasingly segregated by how much they can pay for tickets or whom they know in the corporations that buy luxury boxes and club seats. It even takes money to watch sports on television when events appear on cable channels that have monthly subscriber fees. This means that sports and sport participation are closely connected with who has what in society. Money, wealth, and economic inequality do matter in sports.

When it comes to who has what in society, many people believe that skillful athletes can use sports to earn vast amounts of money or gain the experiences and connections that will lead ultimately to occupational success. This connection between sports and success has been repeatedly emphasized in rags-to-riches stories about highly paid athletes who came from low-income backgrounds. But these beliefs and stories often distract our attention from the ways sports can and sometimes do subvert economic achievement and success, and the ways sport participation is strongly linked with issues of social class and class relations in society.

This chapter deals with matters of money and wealth, connections between sports and socioeconomic factors, and issues related to social class and social mobility. Our discussion will revolve around the following questions:

1. How are sports related to matters of economic inequality and ideas about economic success and failure in a culture?
2. How is social class related to sport participation patterns in society?
3. To what extent do sports provide career opportunities for athletes and others who seek employment in sport organizations?

4. To what extent does sport participation contribute to the overall occupational success and upward social mobility* of former athletes?

SPORTS AND ECONOMIC INEQUALITY

Differences related to money and wealth, political position and influence, and social status are important in social life. Sociologists are concerned with these differences because they affect how people see themselves and others, how they interact with one another, and whether they can obtain what they want and need even when others resist them. In other words, sociologists see money and wealth, political position and influence, and social status as three important sources of *power* in society.

The processes through which these three sources of power become a part of the organization of social life and the everyday lives of people in society are called **class relations.** Because class relations are tied closely to economics and politics, and because they often involve a combination of intergroup tension, conflict, exploitation, and oppression, they attract considerable attention in sociology, including the sociology of sport.

Many people believe that sports and sport participation are open and democratic, that inequalities related to money, position, and influence don't spill over into the organized games we play and watch. Although this may be true in the case of some informally organized sport forms, it is *not true* in the case of formally organized sports.

Formally organized sports could not be developed, scheduled, or maintained without material resources (see chap. 1 and 3). The people who control those resources and use them to organize and sponsor sports generally give preference to

---

Social mobility is a term used by sociologists to refer to changes in wealth, education, and occupation over a person's lifetime or from one generation to the next in families. Social mobility can occur in a downward direction or an upward direction.

sport forms organized around their own values and interests. For example, the wealthy aristocrats who organized and sponsored the modern Olympic Games established a definition of "amateur" that gave an advantage to athletes from wealthy backgrounds around the world; athletes from less privileged backgrounds who used their sport skills to make a living were excluded from the games. Today the Olympics are associated with the logos of wealthy and powerful corporations that would not sponsor events unless they were consistent with the corporations' interests in expanding markets and making profits.

Elite and powerful groups in society always have had considerable influence over what types of activities will be organized into sports and how sports will be promoted, played, and defined. Even when grass-roots games and physical activities have become formally organized and developed into sport forms, they have not been widely sponsored or promoted unless they fit the interests of people with resources in society. Beach volleyball in the U.S. would not have become as visible as it now is unless it fit the marketing needs of Corona Beer and Cuervo Tequila. And the Olympics would not be what they are today without the sponsorship of transnational corporations that want to promote the worldwide consumption of everything from fast food and soft drinks to cars and computers.

But sponsoring sports is not only about expanding markets and making profits. It is also about promoting particular ideas about how social life should be organized and why economic inequality exists in society. This is why it is important that we understand the dynamics of class relations when we study sports.

The Dynamics of Class Relations

One way to understand the dynamics of class relations in connection with sports is to think about how age relations are involved in sports and sport participation. Consider this: Even though children are capable of creating their own games, organized youth sport programs have been developed by adults around the ideas and orientations that adults think should be emphasized in the lives of children and in the community as a whole. As we saw in chapter 5, the informal games organized by children emphasize action, personal involvement, stimulating competition, and relationships with their friends. But the youth sport programs organized and sponsored by adults tend to emphasize discipline, achievement, obedience to adult authority figures, conformity to rules established by adults, and learning to think and play according to the strategies developed by adults.

Because adults possess the *resources* needed to develop, schedule, and maintain organized youth programs, the sports in those programs reflect what adults think children should be doing and learning as they play. This does not mean that children don't have fun in organized sports, but it does mean that fun must occur within a general framework created and sustained by adults who use their resources to support the programs.

When the behavior of children in organized youth sports deviates from adult expectations, adults use their power to force compliance or convince children that it is in their best interest to play "the right way." When children play "the right way" and meet adult expectations, the adults say they possess "character" and reward them accordingly (Fine, 1987). This is the reason coaches obsessed with maintaining autocratic control over athletes (such as University of Indiana basketball coach Bobby Knight) are hailed as heroes by many adults in North America (Pyros, 1987). These coaches reaffirm the cultural belief that the world is a better place when adults have full control over young people, and when young people consent to that control. In this way, sport reproduces a form of age relations in which adult power and privilege is defined not only as good but as a "natural" and necessary aspect of social life.

Class relations work in similar ways. People with economic, political, and social power are able to organize and promote games and physical activities that fit their interests and foster their ideas about how social life should be organized. For example, these people can use their resources and social connections to play sports among themselves in exclusive clubs and in other settings inaccessible to others. When this happens, sports become tools with which members of elite groups can call attention to social and economic differences between themselves and others and promote the idea that people with money and influence are special in society.

Elite groups also can preserve their power and privilege in society by creating and sponsoring forms of organized sports that reinforce ideologies supportive of existing economic and political relationships in society. For example, high-profile, organized sports around the world now are presented in ways that emphasize competition, individualism, highly specialized skills, the use of technology, and dominance over opponents; they are not presented in ways that emphasize partnership, pleasure, participation, nurturance, and mutual support. This ties sports to an ideology of individual achievement, stressing that success is grounded in the ability to compete against others and is gained only by working hard and using the technology and equipment to outscore everyone else. As a recent ad for sport video games declares: "I am better than you, and I can prove it—I have a game."

This ideology gives rise to a form of **class logic** in which economic success (winning) becomes proof of individual ability, worth, and character. People who use this class logic to interpret their own lives often set out on an endless quest for individual economic achievement. Their success can be expressed by acquiring as many "things" as they can; "things" become symbols of their identity, status, and worth. A key component of this class logic is illustrated by a popular locker-room slogan often repeated by coaches in their pep talks: "When you're satisfied with your performance, you're finished." And when performances are measured by scores and records—the "bottom line"—class logic comes to emphasize achievement through individual competition and domination over others.

By extolling individual achievement combined with consumption and the use of technology, this class logic directly drives market economies and enables people with power in those economies to preserve and extend their wealth, position, and influence. When people in a society adopt a class logic that says, "You get what you deserve, and you deserve what you get," rich and powerful people tend to be defined as worthy winners, while the poor and powerless tend to be defined as lazy losers. The idea that you deserve what you get and you get it through competition clearly works to the advantage of those who have more than everyone else. In fact, it promotes the belief that money, wealth, and power are signs of ability, hard work, and strength of character.

This is the reason the rags-to-riches stories about athletes get so much publicity: they reaffirm a class logic that works to the advantage of those who already have power in particular societies and around the globe. In fact, this is one of the ways that sports are used to promote the idea that economic inequality in society is good (i.e., functional), natural, and morally correct. Because organized competitive sports depend on the sponsorship of people with wealth and power, they become effective tools for justifying and perpetuating certain forms of economic inequality. People learn that if they want to play sports, they must look to the wealthy and powerful to give them opportunities. This, of course, is part of the process of how sports come to be integrally tied to class relations in society.

Class Relations and Who Has the Power in Sports

It is difficult to determine who has power in sports and sport organizations. Sport decisions are made at many different levels, from neighborhood youth sport programs to the International Olympic Committee. Although sociologists are concerned with identifying the people who exercise power in various settings, they have not developed lists of such individuals in sports. But such lists do exist. For example, *The Sporting News*, a national weekly newspaper in the U.S., has attempted to identify the 100 Most Powerful

The inequality of social classes is sometimes reflected in sports. Upper-income groups often have used certain sports to maintain exclusive lifestyles emphasizing consumption and competition. When sports are connected to the lifestyles of particular status groups, they promote social class differences rather than equal opportunities. (Jay Coakley)

People in Sports every year since 1991. The list, published at the end of the calendar year, is based on the editors' estimates of which people during the year have had the greatest influence on elite-level sports in the U.S. (primarily) and around the globe. Although people from outside the U.S. are included, their rank generally reflects how much influence they have had on what happened in the world of sports from a U.S. perspective.

Table 10–1   The Top 25 in *The Sporting News* 100 most powerful people in sports, 1996

Rank	Name	Position	Organization	1991 Rank
1	Dick Ebersol	President	NBC Sports	3
2	Philip Knight	Chairman & CEO	Nike	74
3	Steve Bornstein	President & CEO	ESPN	
		President	ABC Sports	6
4	Mark McCormack	Chairman & CEO	International Management Group	11
5	Michael Eisner	Chairman & CEO	Disney (ABC, ESPN)	NR
6	Rupert Murdoch	CEO	News Corp.	NR
7	Ted Turner	Vice Chairman	Time Warner	15
	Gerald Levin	Chairman	Time Warner	NR
8	David Stern	Commissioner	NBA	1
9	Donald Fehr	Executive director	MLB Players' Association	12
10	Ronald Zarella and	V.P. (Sales/Marketing)	General Motors	NR
	Philip Guarascio	V.P. (Sales/Adv.)	General Motors	11
11	John Malone	President & CEO	Tele-Communications, Inc.	NR
12	Juan Antonio Samaranch	President	IOC	2
13	Robert Wright	President & CEO	NBC	25
14	Leigh Steinberg	Sports Attorney	(agent)	24
15	Jerry Reinsdorf	Chairman	Chicago White Sox & Bulls	98
16	Paul Tagliabue	Commissioner	NFL	5
17	David Falk	President & CEO	F.A.M.E. (agent org.)	23
18	Gary Bettman	Commissioner	NHL	66
19	James Dolan	CEO	Cablevision	NR
20	Jerry Colangelo	President & CEO	Phoenix Suns	
		Managing General Partner	Arizona Diamondbacks	NR
21	Richard Pound	Vice President	IOC	NR
22	Bud Selig	Chairman	MLB Executive Committee	
		Owner	Milwaukee Brewers	27
23	Jerry Jones	Owner	Dallas Cowboys	NR
24	Russ Granik	Deputy Commissioner	NBA	
		President	USA Basketball	33
25	Chase Carey	Co-COO	News Corp.	
		Chair & CEO	Fox Television Group	NR

Table Summary: The Top 25 consist of 9 media executives (6 of whom were not in the Top 100 5 years ago); 3 executives from corporate sponsors; 1 executive in a sport management company; 11 executives in sport organizations, including leagues, teams, and players' associations; and 2 agents. There are no women, no blacks, and no athletes in the Top 25; all are white men.

Table 10–1 lists the top 25 of the 100 most powerful people from the list for 1996, and it gives their previous rank positions in 1991. In 1996 the list included 88 white men, 9 black men, 3 white women, and 1 black woman. In fact, the top 25 most powerful were all white men—no women and no blacks. It is clear that in addition to wealth, dominant forms of gender logic and race logic also have an effect on who has power in sports. There were no coaches on the list, and only four athletes. The athletes were there primarily because of their endorsement contracts and the pervasiveness of their images in television commercials; if it were not for the media and major corporations, athletes would not have the mass audiences they have now. So not even the most highly paid athletes have influence in sports that matches those people who own and manage multi-billion-dollar transnational corporations, including media companies.

Five of the ten most powerful people in sports were owners or top executives in transnational media companies—a trend likely to continue indefinitely. The top ten in 1996 consisted of the following men.

- Number 1 was Dick Ebersol, president of NBC Sports. Ebersol not only negotiated the $3.57 billion purchase of broadcasting rights for the Olympic Games for 2000 through 2008, but also was the executive producer for the coverage of the 1996 Olympics, as well as many other major sporting events. As an editor from *The Sporting News* noted, "no one in sports affected more of what we saw, why we saw it and how we saw it than NBC's Ebersol . . . we weren't watching the Olympics; we were watching Ebersol's vision of the Olympics." Now Ebersol is in position to influence what TV viewers in the U.S. will see during the Olympics over the next twelve years. He will also make sure that NBC interests are considered in everything from Olympic site selections to which new sports are included in the games. During 1996, NBC Sports also covered baseball's World Series, Notre Dame football, the NBA All-Star game and playoffs, NFL football and Super Bowl XXX, Wimbledon, the French Open, the PGA tour and the U.S. Open, and the Breeder's Cup horse races.
- Number 2 was Phil Knight, chairman and CEO of *Nike*, which controls nearly 40 percent of the athletic footwear market. Nike's

sponsorship of athletes and teams shapes the sport images that people all over the world use to give meaning to what they see in the media and what they experience in their own sport participation. In fact, Nike's logo (the "Swoosh") is now a standard mark on the clothing of dozens of college and professional teams and of numerous high-profile athletes, from Michael Jordan in basketball to Tiger Woods in golf. The "Air Jordan" image is a creation of Nike that influences how children around the world see and think about basketball and basketball skills. Nike's image-making power was also clear in its $43 million contract with Tiger Woods. Nike images of girls and women in sports also have been influential. And all the images revolve around "the shoes" and the clothes.

- Number 3 was Steve Bornstein, president and CEO of ESPN, and president of ABC Sports (both ABC and ESPN are owned by Disney). ESPN is the number two sports network in the U.S.; it reaches about 70 percent of U.S. households. About 23 percent of all television sports watched in the U.S. are carried on ESPN channels. ESPN televises sports in over 160 countries and 19 languages worldwide. It has a massive production facility in Singapore that puts it in position to influence the media coverage of sports in Asia, where nearly 40 percent of the world's population resides. ESPNews, a new cable channel, was launched in 1996. ESPN Radio covered more events during the year. Bornstein also helped negotiate ABC's seven-year broadcasting contract with U.S. college football, a deal that virtually guarantees that there will be a national championship game in January 1999, and that it will be televised on ABC.
- Number 4 was Mark McCormack, chairman and CEO of International Management Group (IMG). IMG controls much of golf and tennis around the world; it not only owns and operates tournaments, but also lists

many athletes in these sports as its clients. IMG negotiates endorsement contracts, event sponsorships, and publicity for athletes and events. To recruit and maintain clients and serve as a consultant on event sponsorships, IMG has 69 offices in 28 countries, with plans to expand throughout Asia. IMG also owns sport academies that train athletes in tennis and baseball; their goal is to "create" the athletes they then will manage and "sell" to sponsors or sport teams. IMG guided Tiger Woods as he turned pro, and then negotiated his $43 million contract with Nike (of which IMG will take a percentage, customarily 15 to 20 percent).

- Number 5 was Michael Eisner, chairman and CEO of Disney. Eisner orchestrated Disney's $19 billion purchase of Cap Cities/ABC, which includes ownership of ESPN and ESPN2. Now Disney has cable access to viewers all around the world. Disney can highlight its teams, the Anaheim Mighty Ducks and the Anaheim (formerly California) Angels, and use them to generate business for Disneyland. As Disney-owned companies control more sports teams and events, sports will become a part of the traditional entertainment industry. Teams and athletes will be associated with Disney enterprises: we will see movies with Disney teams as "stars," cartoons will include images connected with Disney sport teams, and children will grow up associating Disneyland and Mickey Mouse with sports.

- Number 6 was Rupert Murdoch, majority owner of News Corporation, the parent company of Fox Sports and the Fox cable network, Sky Sports, and of other television companies and newspapers around the world. Murdoch's companies influence and, to an extent, determine media coverage of sports in much of Europe, Australia, Latin America, and Asia. In the U.S., Fox Sports has long-term contracts with major-league Baseball, the NFL, and the NHL; it also

covers other sports as it sees opportunities for profits. What Murdoch does influences everything from cricket in India to football in the U.S. and hockey throughout North America.

- Number 7 were Ted Turner and Gerald Levin, the vice chairman and chairman (respectively) of Time Warner, one of the three largest media organizations in the world. Together they control HBO Sports, all TBS properties (including the Atlanta Braves and Hawks, CNN, TBS, TNT, and SportSouth, the number one regional sports network in the U.S.). They launched CNN/SI, an all-sports news cable channel in 1996, and they are negotiating other major deals that will affect sports in the future.

- Number 8 was David Stern, commissioner of the National Basketball Association. Stern was able to reject efforts by powerful sport agents to restructure labor agreements in the NBA. He kept teams from using cable TV to broadcast their games that were not included in the NBA's media contracts, helped market the U.S. men's Olympic teams around the world, and developed the concept of the Women's NBA, which played its inaugural season in 1996.

- Number 9 was Donald Fehr, executive director of the Major League Baseball Players' Association. After nearly 4 years of labor-management conflict in baseball, Fehr negotiated a deal that safeguarded the interests of players into the next century. *The Sporting News* explained that "Fehr's ability to stonewall the owners should be remembered as one of the great stands in labor history."

- Number 10 were Ronald Zarrella and Philip Guarascio, vice presidents of General Motors in North America. As *The Sporting News* noted, "GM's involvement in sports is staggering. . . . GM's mark on sports is everywhere." The company sponsored everything from the Olympics to yachting to the Women's Sport Foundation. Forty percent of all vehicles sold in the U.S. during 1996 were light trucks and sport vehicles, and GM trucks and sport vehicles were heavily marketed in connection with sport events.

This list clearly indicates that economic wealth and power matters in sports. Those who control economic resources around the world make decisions that influence the visibility of sports, the ways they are organized, and the images and meanings associated with them. While these decisions do not ignore the interests of people around the world, their main purpose is to establish and expand the power and profitability of the organizations represented by the decision makers. Therefore, sports tend to revolve around the meanings and orientations valued by those with money and power, while they also provide enjoyable and entertaining experiences to people around the world. This is why some sociologists see sports as cultural vehicles for developing ideological "outposts" in the minds of people around the world: when transnational corporations become the primary providers of popular pleasure and entertainment, they are able to use pleasure and entertainment to deliver many other messages about what should be important in people's lives. This is a clear manifestation of class relations at work.

Sports as a Vehicle for Transferring Public Money to the Private Sector

The dynamics of class relations sometimes have ironic twists. This is certainly true in connection with the ways sports have been used as vehicles for transferring public monies collected through taxes into the hands of wealthy individuals and corporations in the private sector. For example, during the 1990s, about $8 billion of public money in the U.S. was used to build sport stadiums and arenas that then were turned into private revenue generators for wealthy individuals and powerful corporations owning professional sport team franchises.

Furthermore, the tax-free municipal bonds that cities sold to obtain the cash needed to build these facilities generally were purchased by wealthy investors. Thus, city and/or state taxes were collected from the general population to pay off the bonds, wealthy investors who bought the bonds received tax-free returns, and team owners used the facilities built by taxpayers to make large amounts of money for themselves or their corporations. According to a U.S. senator

....
Neither athletes nor coaches are the most powerful people in sports. Power is in the hands of the media executives, league administrators, and corporate leaders who negotiate TV contracts, sponsor events, and select locations for events.

....

who reviewed a study done by the nonpartisan Congressional Research Service, this method of financing stadiums through tax-exempt bonds "amounts to little more than a public housing program for millionaire team owners and their millionaire employees [athletes]" (in Welch, 1996). He also asked, "Do we [in the U.S.] have enough money to finance stadiums for [wealthy team] owners . . . at the same time we are cutting Head Start Programs [for low-income children]?" (in Brady and Howlett, 1996).

Ironically, this form of transferring public money into the hands of wealthy people all occurred during a decade when U.S. citizens called for fiscal responsibility and the elimination of "tax loopholes" traditionally used by wealthy people to avoid paying taxes on income and property.

Of course, it is true that jobs are created in connection with sport facilities, but those jobs also would be created if the facilities were privately financed. Furthermore, when cities spend public money to build sport facilities, they create far fewer jobs than they would create through other forms of economic development. For example, the same congressional study noted above found that *each new job* created in connection with the state-financed $200 million football stadium in Baltimore cost about $127,000. Meanwhile, the cost of creating one job through the Maryland economic development fund was about $6,250. So for each job created by the new stadium, twenty-one jobs could have been created if public money had been invested in other projects! Sport facilities do not employ many people; they sit empty most of the time, and most of the jobs they generate are low-paying seasonal jobs.

Sport team owners are not the only wealthy and powerful people who benefit when tax money is used to construct stadiums and arenas. New publicly financed sport facilities increase property values in urban areas in which major investors and developers can initiate projects from which they will benefit directly. For example,

when Atlanta hosted the Olympics in 1996, the major payoffs associated with the new construction and increased property values went directly to a small proportion of real estate developers and major corporations that were in position to use the millions of dollars of public money invested in the Atlanta area to their benefit. Of course, others benefited as money "trickled down" to the rest of the community from wealthy individuals and organizations associated with the Olympics and the Atlanta Committee for the Olympic Games. But the taxpayers who helped fund the Olympics will never see the benefits enjoyed by those whose power and wealth gave them the ability to take advantage of public investments. As journalist Andrew Jennings has noted, the emerging pattern in connection with hosting of the Olympics is that "the IOC will take its profits, the sponsors and television networks will make theirs and the local taxpayers will foot the bill" (1996: 293). This method of transferring public money to powerful individuals and corporations in the private sector is a clear manifestation of class relations at work in connection with sports.

SOCIAL CLASS AND SPORT PARTICIPATION PATTERNS

In all societies, who plays, who watches, and who consumes information about sports is clearly connected with class relations. Involvement with sports goes hand in hand with money, power, and privilege. People in high-income and high-status occupational groups have the highest rates of active sport participation, the highest rates of attendance at sport events, and even the highest viewing rates of sports on television. For example, Olympic athletes and officials always have come from more privileged groups in society (Beamish, 1990; Gruneau, 1976; Hall et al., 1991; Kidd, 1995). This was noted in connection with a recent analysis of U.S. Olympic teams across all sports:

A sport by sport breakdown of recent U.S. Olympic teams shows a movement split by both class and race. Although in theory anyone can earn a spot in the Olympics, the reality of the process is far different. Lack of funding and access at the developmental level creates a team and a system tilted toward segregation (Atlanta *Journal/Constitution*, 1995).

This pattern also exists in other top-level sports in the U.S. and other countries around the world.

Even the health and fitness movement, which often has been described as a grass-roots phenomenon in the United States and Canada, is confined primarily to people who have higher-than-average incomes and educations and work in professional or managerial occupations. People from lower income groups may do physical labor, but they don't run, bicycle, or swim as often as their high-income counterparts. Nor do they play as many organized sports on their lunch hours, after work, on weekends, or during vacations. This pattern holds true throughout the course of life, for younger and older age groups, among men and women, among various racial and ethnic groups, and among people with disabilities: social class is related strongly to access and participation, regardless of the category of people in question (see Donnelly and Harvey, 1996).

We also can explain this participation pattern in terms of class relations. The long-term impact of economic inequality on people's lives has led to connections between certain sports and the lifestyles of people with differing amounts of wealth and power (Bourdieu, 1984; Laberge and Sankoff, 1988). For the most part, these connections reflect patterns of sponsorship and access to opportunities for involvement. For example, wealthy people have lifestyles that routinely include participation in golf, tennis, skiing, sailing, and other sports that are self-funded and played at exclusive clubs and resorts. These sports often involve the use of expensive facilities, equipment, and/or clothing, and they have come to be associated with "class" as people with money and power define it. The people who engage in these

sports usually have considerable control over their work lives, so they have the freedom to take the time needed to participate, or they can combine participation with their work.

The lifestyles of middle-income and working-class people, on the other hand, tend to include sports that by tradition are free and open to the public, sponsored by public funds, or made available through public schools. When these sports involve the use of expensive equipment or clothing, participation occurs in connection with some form of financial sacrifice: buying a motocross bike means not taking a vacation this year and working overtime for a couple of months.

The lifestyles of low-income people and those living in poverty seldom involve regular forms of sport participation. When people spend so much of their time and energy coping with the challenges of everyday life, they have few resources left to develop sport participation traditions as part of their lifestyles. Furthermore, when hard work has not made them winners in the economy, they may have little interest in playing or watching sports popularly associated with an ideology claiming that poverty is associated with laziness and a lack of character. At the same time, those who are successful in the economy are so supportive of that ideology that they are willing to spend thousands of dollars each year to keep their club memberships, season tickets, and luxury boxes so they can reaffirm the cultural ideas that work to their advantage.

Homemaking, Child Rearing, and Earning a Living: What Happens When Class and Gender Relations Come Together in Women's Lives?

Women in family situations have been less likely than their male counterparts to be able to negotiate the time and resources needed to maintain sport participation. When a married woman with children decides to join a soccer team that schedules practices late in the afternoon, she may encounter resistance from members of her family. Resistance is certain if she traditionally has served her family as chef, chauffeur, and tutor.

"Time off for good behavior" is not a principle that applies to married women with children. On the other hand, married men with children may not face the same resistance within their families. In fact, when they play softball or soccer after work, their spouses may delay family dinners, keep dinners warm for when they arrive home, or even go to the games and watch them play.

Women in middle- and lower-income families most often feel the constraints of home-making and child rearing. Without money to pay for child care, domestic help, and sport participation expenses, these women simply don't have many opportunities to play sports. Nor do they have time to spare, or a car to get them to where sports are played, or access to gyms and playing fields in their neighborhoods, or the sense of physical safety they need to leave home and travel to where they can play sports. Furthermore, sports are often social activities occurring among friends. If a woman's friends don't have resources enabling them to participate, she will have even fewer opportunities and less motivation for involvement (Gems, 1993). Of course, this is also true for men, but women from middle- and lower-income families are more likely than their male counterparts to lack the network of relationships out of which sport interests and activities emerge.

Women from upper-income families often face a different situation. They have resources to pay for child care, domestic help, carryout dinners, and sport participation. They often participate in sport activities by themselves, with friends, or with other family members. They have social networks made up of other women who also have the resources to maintain high levels of sport participation. Women who have grown up in these families often have played sports during and since their childhoods and attended schools with good sport programs. They seldom have experienced the same constraints as their lower-income counterparts. While this is not to say they do not have any problems negotiating time for sport involvement, it is true that

their rates of successful negotiation are relatively high. Their opportunities are much greater than those of lower-income women, even though they may not be equal to those of upper-income men.

The sport participation of girls and young women also may be limited when they are asked to shoulder adult responsibilities at home. For example, in low-income families, especially those with only one parent, teenage daughters often are expected to care for younger siblings after school until after dinner, when their mothers get home from work. According to one girls' team coach in a New York City high school, "It's not at all unusual that on a given day there may be two or three girls who aren't [at practice] because of responsibilities at home" (Dobie, 1987). The coach also explained that child-care duties keep many girls from coming out for teams. His solution was to coordinate a cooperative child care program at practices and games so girls from low-income families could meet family expectations *and* play sports. But when coaches are not so creative or accommodating, some girls drop out of sports to meet responsibilities at home. Boys and girls from higher-income families seldom have household responsibilities that would force them to drop out of sports; instead, their parents drive them to practices, lessons, and games, and make sure they have all the equipment they need to participate in satisfying ways.

Getting Respect and Becoming a Man: What Happens When Class and Gender Relations Come Together in Men's Lives?

Boys and young men in low-income communities often see sport participation as a special and legitimate means of establishing a masculine identity. Sociologist Mike Messner notes that "the more limited a boy's options appear to be, and the more insecure his family situation, the more likely he is to make an early commitment to an athletic career" (1992: 40). It seems that for boys from low-income backgrounds, the stakes associated with sport participation are higher.

Messner's study of men who were former elite athletes indicated that males from lower-class backgrounds often saw sport participation as a means of obtaining "respect." This was not so much the case among males from middle-class backgrounds. One former athlete who later became a junior high school coach explained this in the following way:

> For . . . the poorer kids, [sports] is their major measuring stick . . . . They constantly remind each other what they can't do in the sports arena. It's definitely peer-acceptable if they are good at sports—although they maybe can't read, you know—if they are good at sports, they're one of the boys. Now I know the middle- and upper-class boys, they do sports and they do their books . . . But as a whole, [they put] less effort into [sports] (quoted in Messner, 1992: 57–58).

This coach was suggesting that social class factors create social conditions under which young men from lower-income backgrounds often have more at stake when it comes to sport participation.

What this coach didn't point out is that the development of sport skills often requires material resources that do not exist in low-income families. So unless equipment and training are provided in public school athletic programs, young men from low-income groups stand little chance of competing against upper-income peers who can buy equipment and training if they want to develop skills.

In fact, young people from upper-income backgrounds often have so many opportunities to do different things that they may not focus attention on one sport to the exclusion of other sports and other activities. For someone who has a car, nice clothes, money for college tuition, and good career contacts for the future, playing sports may be good for bolstering popularity among peers, but it is not perceived as a necessary foundation for an entire identity (Messner, 1992: 59). This often leads young men from middle- and upper-income backgrounds to disengage gradually from exclusive commitments

to playing particular sports and striving for careers as athletes. When these young men move through adolescence and into adulthood, opportunities may take them in a variety of directions; playing sports may be important, but not usually in the same ways that it is for young men from working-class and low-income families. This is clearly illustrated in the next section.

Fighting to Survive: What Happens When Class, Gender, and Race and Ethnic Relations Come Together?

Chris Dundee, a famous boxing promoter, once said, "Any man with a good trade isn't about to get himself knocked on his butt to make a dollar" (quoted in Messner, 1992: 82). What he meant was that middle- and upper-class males see no reason to have their brain cells destroyed in a quest to get ahead through a sport such as boxing. Of course, this is the reason boxers always come from the lowest and most economically desperate income groups in society, and the reason boxing gyms are located in low-income neighborhoods, especially low-income minority neighborhoods, where desperation is often most intense and life-piercing.

The dynamics of becoming and staying involved in boxing have been studied and described by French sociologist Loic Wacquant (1992, 1995a, c). As we noted in chapter 7, Wacquant spent over three years training and "hanging out" at a boxing gym in a black ghetto area in Chicago. During that time he documented the life experiences of fifty professional boxers, most of whom were African Americans. His analysis of those experiences shows that the motivation to dedicate oneself to boxing can be explained only in terms of a combination of class, race, and gender relations. Statements by the boxers themselves illustrate the influence of this combination:

> Right in the area where I lived it was definitely rough, it was dog-eat-dog. I had to be a mean dog . . . young guys wan'ed to take yer money and beat ya up an' you jus' had to fight or move out the

Although some sports clearly involve democratic participation, opportunities to participate in sports often are related to social class. Developing skills in certain sports requires material resources that are in short supply in many low-income and working-class neighborhoods. These boys are making the best of what they have: a street sign post and a deflated tetherball. (John Sutherland, *The Denver Post*)

neighbo'hood. I couldn't move, so I had to start fightin' (in Wacquant, 1992: 229).

I used to fight alot when I was younger *anyway so*, my father figure like, you know, [said] "if you gonna fight, well why don't you take it to a gym where you gonna learn, you know, a little more basics to it, maybe make some money, go further and

do somethin' . . . insteada jus' bein' on the streets you know, and fightin' for nothin" (in Wacquant, 1992: 229).

The alternative to boxing was often the violence of the streets. When Wacquant asked one boxer where he'd be today if he hadn't started boxing, he said, "Uh, prob'y in jail, dead or on the streets turnin' up a bottle" (1992:230). Other boxers said the following:

I figure if it weren't for the gym I might be doin' somethin' that I wouldn't wanna do . . . [l]ike you know, prob'ly *killin' somebody*, you know, stick up, you know drugs, anythin': you can't never tell! You never know what the world holds (1992: 230).

I figure well, the bes' thin' for me to do is chan' my life style 'cause I saw a lot of my frien's git hurt an' kill' from thin's that we were doin' . . . The gym show me that I coul' do somethin'. The gym show me that I can be my own man. The gym show me that I can do other thin's than the *gang bang, use drugs, steal, rob people, stick people up, or jus' bein' in jail* (1992: 230–31).

[If] I hadn't found boxin', I be in some trade school as a mechanic or some kind of a laborer, or maybe in a factory. 'Cause that's the only thing for me, (joyfully) I mean, *I'm lucky I found boxin'.* 'Cause you know I'll be (with a touch of bitterness) like the rest of the minorities in Chicago, y'know: jus' workin' in some factory or doin' somethin' laboral to make do (1995a: 519).

Wacquant explains that most boxers know that if they had *not* been born as poor minority persons and had been successful in school, they might never have put on boxing gloves. A trainer-coach at the gym explained the connection between social class and boxing when he said, "Don't nobody be out there fightin' with an MBA" (1995a: 521). In fact, Wacquant sees the men he studied as being tied to boxing in the form of a "coerced affection, a captive love, one ultimately born of racial and class necessity" (1995a: 521). And many of the boxers realized that despite their personal commitment to boxing, their sport involved exploitation. As one boxer noted, "fighters is whores and promoters is pimps, the way I sees it" (1995a: 520).

When Wacquant asked one boxer what he would change in his life, the answer he gave represented the feelings of many of his peers at the gym:

I wish I was born taller, I wish I was born in a rich family, I don't know, wish I was smart, an' I had the

brains to go to school an' really become somebody real important. For me I mean I can't stand the sport, I hate the sport, [but] it's carved inside of me so I can't let it go (1995a: 521).

Even though the boxers were attached to their craft, over 80 percent didn't want their children to become boxers. For example, one said,

No, no fighter wants their son [to box], I mean. . . . *that's the reason why you fight, so he won't be able to fight.* . . . It's too hard, jus' too damn hard. . . . If he could *hit the books* an' study an' you know, with me havin' a little background in school an' stuff, I could help him. My parents, I never had nobody helpin' me (1995a: 523).

These mixed feelings about boxing were pervasive; the men were simultaneously committed to and repulsed by their trade.

We can understand the motives underlying the sport participation of these men only in terms of the context in which they lived their lives and the gym's provision of a refuge from the violence, hopelessness, and indignity of the racism and poverty that had framed their lives since birth (Wacquant, 1995a).

Class Relations in Action: The Decline of High School Sports in Low-Income Areas

In chapter 5 we noted that publicly funded youth sports programs are being cut in U.S. communities facing government budget crises. The same thing is occurring with high school sports in school districts with high proportions of low-income families (Eitzen, 1995; see chap. 14 of this text also). Varsity sport programs are being cut back or dropped in a number of big-city and poor rural schools. When this occurs, fewer young people from low-income backgrounds have opportunities to participate in sports such as baseball and football, each of which requires playing fields that are relatively large and expensive to maintain. Meanwhile, basketball grows in popularity among low-income boys and girls because a school can offer basketball as long as it can maintain a usable gym (although maintaining a usable gym is getting to be a serious problem in some inner-city schools, where over-crowding has caused gyms to be turned into classrooms).

School sport programs in middle- and upper-income areas also may be threatened by financial problems, but when they are, they are usually saved by "participation fees" paid by athletes and their families. These fees, sometimes as high as $250 per sport, guarantee that opportunities to participate in varsity programs will continue for those young people born into families living in relatively wealthy areas. When we compare these programs to those in poor inner-city and rural areas, we see forms of what educator Jonathan Kozol (1991) has described as "*savage inequalities.*" These inequalities insidiously sub-vert the educational lives of young people living with the legacy of poverty and racism.

The impact of class inequality on sports was clearly noted by Arthur Agee, one of the two young men profiled in the film *Hoop Dreams*. When Arthur was forced to transfer from a pri-vate suburban school for which he could not af-ford the tuition to a public inner-city school in his neighborhood, he saw first-hand the differ-ences between suburban and city basketball. High schools in Chicago's public league didn't play at night or on weekends, as did the suburban schools; the city schools couldn't afford the over-time janitorial costs, so their games were played on weekday afternoons after school (Joravsky, 1995). Other differences were related to the quality of equipment and practice facilities, the availability of uniforms, the existence of junior varsity teams, the size of the gym and its seating capacity, locker-room facilities, transportation to away games, the number of coaches, the number and quality of referees, access to training-room support, and game attendance.

With funds being cut and coaches being laid off, people in poor neighborhoods realize that bake sales and car washes no longer can keep sports programs going. They now are looking to foundations and large corporations to sponsor high school sports. But corporations tend to sponsor only those sports that promote their im-ages; for example, they may support basketball rather than other sports, because basketball's popularity makes it effective in their marketing and advertising programs. If high school sports are funded by corporations, there will be in-creased emphasis on using selected sports to generate product visibility through media cover-age and high-profile state and national tourna-ments. Sports will continue to exist, but they will exist on terms that meet the interests of corpo-rate sponsors. When this happens, the link be-tween sports and class relations will become even more apparent.

In the meantime, young people from middle- and upper-income areas generally will have op-portunities to participate in a variety of sports; their resources will enable them to counteract the effects of budget cuts at schools or in public programs. Those who live and attend school in poor neighborhoods and communities will have fewer participation opportunities, inadequate and deteriorating facilities, less equipment, and less support. They may play sports, but they will have fewer choices; and the context in which they play will be heavily influenced by factors re-lated to social class.

Class Relations in Action: The Cost of Attending Sport Events

It is still possible to attend recreational sports for free. High school and many college events in the U.S. are affordable for most people, and in some communities the tickets for minor-league sports are reasonably priced. But tickets to most major intercollegiate and professional events are now beyond the means of many people, even those whose taxes are being used to pay for the facili-ties in which the events are played. The cost of attending these events has increased far beyond the rate of inflation over the past decade.

Table 10–2 shows that between 1991 and 1996, the average ticket prices for major-league baseball, the NFL, the NBA, and the NHL in-creased 30 percent, 42 percent, 37 percent, and

Table 10–2   Average ticket prices in 1991 and 1996 versus the five-year rate of inflation. *Five-year inflation rate, 1991–1996 = 15%*

	1991 Average Ticket Price	1996 Average Ticket Price	5-year Increase
Major League Baseball	$8.64	$11.20	+30%
National Football League	$25.21	$35.74	+42%
National Basketball Association	$23.24	$31.80	+37%
National Hockey League	$24.00*	$34.75	+42%*

Source: Team Marketing Report; U.S. Bureau of Labor Statistics.
*These are estimates, because no NHL data are available on the period prior to 1994.

42 percent, respectively. During the same time period, inflation was about 15 percent. The average ticket price to see a baseball game is relatively low, about $12. Tickets to NFL, NBA, and NHL games have an average cost of $36, $32, and $38, respectively (in 1996 U.S. dollars), and they are likely to increase further as new stadiums are built around the U.S. and Canada. The new stadiums all include expensive luxury boxes and sections of club seating where upper-income spectators have special services available to them: wait staff, special food menus, private restrooms, televisions, telephones, refrigerators, lounge chairs, temperature controls, private entrances with no waiting lines or turnstiles, special parking areas, and other things to make attendance at a game resemble going to a private club.

As ticket prices increase and as spectators are increasingly segregated by their ability to pay, social class and class relations become more evident in the stands. Very wealthy people, corporate executives, and those who know or do business with them sit in exclusive luxury boxes; those with slightly less money and influence sit in club seats; and others sit in regular seats in various stadium locations, depending on their ability to pay for tickets. The end result is that most working-class and low-income people never see the inside of the stadium, and those who do attend games are increasingly segregated by social class in the stadium itself. All at the games may cheer at the same times and experience similar emotions, but social class differences in the society as a whole are not transcended at the events; in fact, they are reaffirmed and made more apparent.

An interesting fact is that class relations partially account for the failure of attempts to organize fans so they can collectively have more influence over ticket prices and the prices of concessions at games. Those sitting in luxury boxes, club seats, and other exclusive seats are not eager to align themselves with those who cannot attend games or afford the high-priced tickets. In fact, they have used sports events and the seats they sit in as status symbols with their friends and business associates; they want class distinctions to be preserved in connection with spectatorship, and they are willing to pay, for example, over $1,000 a ticket for NBA courtside seats in New York and Los Angeles to conspicuously display their status. Attendance and seating at many events, from the opening ceremonies at the Olympics to the NFL Super Bowl, also is tied to conspicuous displays of wealth, status, and influence. As long as this is the case, efforts to organize fans will fail.

In summary, sports, sport participation, and sport spectatorship are closely tied to social class and class relations in any society. Because the existence of sports requires material resources, sport programs and events usually depend on the approval and support of those with power and influence. This creates a tendency for sport

Table 10–3   Approximate numbers and odds of playing in the pros during the mid-1990s*

| | NUMBER OF PLAYERS IN | | | PLAYERS ADVANCING | |
Sport	High School	College	Professional	HS to Professional	College to Professional
Football	928,134	51,162	1,400	1 in 750	1 in 37
Men's Basketball[†]	530,068	13,365	405	1 in 1316	1 in 33
Baseball[†]	438,846	22,575	700	1 in 625	1 in 32
Women's Basketball	445,869	9,000(est.)	80[‡]	1 in 5555	1 in 112

*Uses data from Leonard (1996: 292, table 1) the NCAA, and the National Federation of State High School Associations.
[†]The odds of playing in the pros are inflated for these sports because an increasing number of players in the NBA and MLB come from outside the U.S. Also, in baseball, many U.S. players do not play in college; instead, they go from high school to the minor leagues.
[‡]This number will increase when the WNBA begins playing. The odds in the future will improve as women's professional basketball grows.

programs and events to be organized in ways that recreate and perpetuate existing forms of class relations in a society. Furthermore, patterns of sport participation and spectatorship clearly reflect the distribution of resources and opportunities in a society.

OPPORTUNITIES IN SPORTS: MYTH AND REALITY

Do sports provide opportunities for satisfying and rewarding occupational careers? The general answer to this question is yes, but it must be carefully qualified in light of the following factors:

1. The number of career opportunities for athletes is severely limited, and they are short term.
2. Opportunities for women are limited.
3. Opportunities for African Americans and other minorities are limited.

We will discuss each of these qualifications in the following sections.

Opportunities Are Limited and Short Term

Young athletes often have visions of becoming professional athletes; their parents may have similar visions for them. But the chances for turning these visions into reality are quite low.

Statements about the chances of an individual becoming a college or professional athlete vary greatly because they are based on different methods of computation. For example, the chances for becoming a professional athlete may be computed for high school or college athletes in a particular sport, or for athletes from particular racial or ethnic groups, or for any person in a particular age group of the total population in a society.

The chances for high school and college athletes in football, men's basketball, baseball, and women's basketball to advance to the NFL, the NBA, major-league baseball (MLB), and the ABL, respectively, are given in table 10–3. The odds of making it from the high school level to the top pro level are 1 in 750 in football, 1 in 1,316 in men's basketball, 1 in 625 in baseball, and 1 in 5,555 in women's basketball. The odds for college players are 1 in 37 in football, 1 in 33 in men's basketball, 1 in 32 in baseball, and 1 in 112* in women's basketball.

As we consider these odds, we should remember three things: *First*, the odds for male

---

*I considered only the ABL when computing these odds. The WNBA had not yet begun its first season.

Table 10–4 Odds of 15- to 39-year-old males in the U.S. attaining professional athlete status in major professional team sports by race/ethnicity.

Sport	Caucasian	African American	Hispanic	Other
FOOTBALL	N = 467	N = 910	N = 14	N = 14
All groups*	111,111:1	50,000:1	3,333,333:1	3,333,333:1
Within group†	100,000:1	10,000:1	333,333:1	333,333:1
BASEBALL	N = 469	N = 112	N = 112	N = 7
All groups	111,111:1	500,000:1	500,000:1	10,000,000:1
Within group	100,000:1	50,000:1	50,000:1	500,000:1
BASKETBALL	N = 85	N = 320	N = 0	N = 0
All groups	500,000:1	166,666:1	—	—
Within group	500,000:1	20,000:1	—	—
HOCKEY	N = 630	N = 13	N = 7	N = 7
All groups	200,000:1‡	3,333,333:1	1,000,000:1	10,000,000:1
Within group	100,000:1‡	500,000:1	100,000:1	500,000:1
ALL FOUR SPORTS	N = 1660	N = 1355	N = 133	N = 28
All groups	33,333:1	33,333:1	333,333:1	1,666,666:1
Within group	25,000:1	5,000:1	50,000:1	166,666:1

*Includes all 15- to 39-year-olds in U.S. population in pool.
†Includes only members of one's own racial or ethnic group in pool.
‡Adjusted to account for the fact that at least 50% of Caucasian NHL players are from Canada, Russia, and Northern Europe.
Source: Adapted from data presented by Leonard (1996: 296, table 5).

basketball and baseball players have not been adjusted to account for the increasing number of NBA and MLB players who come from outside the U.S. *Second*, many MLB players never play in college, since they go from high school to the minor leagues. *Third*, there are professional opportunities outside the NFL, the NBA, MLB, the ABL, and the WNBA. Some young men and women who play in U.S. high schools and colleges play their sports in other countries or in minor leagues in the U.S., although the salaries they earn are usually a fraction of what players earn in the top leagues.

According to computations made by sociologist Wib Leonard (1996), the odds that an American man between the ages of 15 and 39 will be a professional athlete in the NFL, the NBA, the NHL, or major-league baseball are about 20,000 to 1—if the number of baseball and hockey players who come from outside the U.S. is taken into account. Leonard also has computed the odds of becoming a professional athlete for people from different racial and ethnic groups in the U.S. An adapted version of his data is in table 10–4. This table summarizes the chances of becoming a professional athlete in the four major professional team sports for 15- to 39-year-old males from different racial and ethnic groups in the U.S. The odds are based on the assumption that the numbers of pro players from each of these racial and ethnic groups stays constant from one year to the next.

Considering the *entire population* of 15- to 39-year-old men in the U.S., the best odds for African Americans are in football: 1 of every 50,000 men between 15 and 39 is a black football player. But when looking at the *within-group* odds, we see that 1 in every 10,000 African Americans is an NFL player. Note that the odds are worse in basketball, where 1 in 20,000 African American men in the 15- to 39-year-old age category is an NBA player. This is so because there are numerically fewer black NBA players than black NFL players (320, compared to 910).

The odds for becoming a professional athlete in an individual sport are especially poor. For example, rough estimates indicate that of every 750,000 women between 15 and 39 in the U.S., only 1 is a pro golfer, and that of every million, only 1 is a pro tennis player. These odds look even worse when we note that most of the women who play professionally in these sports do not win tournaments or place very high among the money makers. The odds are a little better for men, but not much.

Even though we can question the exact meaning of these attempts to compute the odds of becoming a professional athlete for a specific person, one thing is clear: *opportunities for making it to the top as an athlete are extremely limited*.

Professional sport opportunities are also short term, averaging three to seven years in team sports and three to twelve years in individual sports. This means that after a playing career ends, there are about *forty additional years* in a person's work life. Unfortunately, many people—including some athletes, coaches, and parents—ignore this fact.

Ideas about careers in professional sports often are distorted by misinterpretations in media coverage. The media focus on the best athletes in the most popular sports. The best athletes tend to have longer playing careers than others in their sports. If we follow certain sports, we hear some of the same names year after year, and we don't hear about or tend to forget the names of those who play for one or two seasons

SIDELINES

"His earnings on the pro tour have really dropped this year!"
....

Not all athletes achieve fame and fortune. Despite highly publicized coverage of salaries and prize money, many athletes do not earn enough to pay their expenses. Unless athletes in individual sports are seen by corporate sponsors as effective product representatives and spokespersons, they don't get the support they need to continue their participation.

....

before being cut or forced to quit for other reasons, especially injuries. For example, we hear about the long football careers of popular quarterbacks, but little or no coverage is given to the numerous players whose one-year contracts are not renewed after their first season. The average age of players on the *oldest* NFL team in 1996 was twenty-seven; this means that only a few players older than thirty are still in the league. Much more typical than thirty-three-year-olds contemplating another season are twenty-four-year-olds trying to deal with the ends of their careers as paid athletes.

Opportunities for Women Are Limited

Career opportunities for women athletes are growing, but they are still scarce relative to opportunities for men. Tennis and golf have provided some opportunities over the last fifty years. Today there are expanding opportunities in professional volleyball, basketball, skiing, bicycling, track and field, and rodeo. But the numbers of professional women athletes are very low, and only a few make big money. Pro volleyball and basketball leagues were established in the 1990s, but the number of teams in both sports is limited, and the pay for athletes is relatively low. We discuss the emerging status of women's professional basketball in the U.S. in the box on pp. 310–11.

What about other careers in sports? Are there jobs for women in coaching, training, officiating, sport medicine, sports information, public relations, marketing, and administration? The answer to this second question is a qualified yes in the case of women's sport programs, and a qualified no in the case of men's programs. As we noted in chapter 8, the majority of jobs in women's programs continue to be held by men, and women seldom have been hired for any jobs in men's programs. When men's and women's programs have been combined, few women have obtained top positions. For example, in 1996 women held only 17 of 305 chief athletic director positions in NCAA Division I college sport programs.

For a number of reasons, including the discriminatory gender logic that some people in sports still use, job opportunities for women have not increased as rapidly as women's programs have grown. This pattern exists in nearly all job categories, except for that of secretary in athletic departments and sport organizations. As one woman athletic director at a large university has explained, "If you're a man, you're assumed to be competent [according to the gender logic in the athletic department]. When you're female, you have to prove you're competent" (in Blauvelt, 1996).

This logic has an interesting variation in colleges and universities where those who coach women's teams, both men and women, make considerably less money than the men who coach men's teams. For example, a survey of athletic programs in the Big 12 Conference indicated that the average salary of the men who

were head coaches of men's teams was $69,400; the average salary of the men and women who were head coaches of women's teams was $44,500—a $24,900 difference. And this difference does not take into account the income that some coaches of men's teams make in team performance bonuses, endorsement deals, clinic fees, and television shows. So it appears that even men who coach women's teams can be adversely affected by the dominant gender logic in sports. Of course, the people who use this logic argue that those who coach men's teams should be paid more because it is more difficult to coach men's teams; but this argument is grounded more in memories of what sports were like in the past than in any systematic evidence from today.

Even employment patterns at the high school level appear to be influenced by discriminatory gender logic. As girls' programs have expanded and become more important, most of the coaching and administrative jobs have gone to men. Similar patterns exist in other sport-related employment settings, such as athletic clubs and community programs. Men are in most of the higher-paying jobs, even though the number of women participating in sports and physical activities has increased dramatically over the past two decades (Snyder, 1993).

We can expect that these patterns will continue to shift in the favor of women, but full equity is a long way off. Job opportunities for women will remain relatively limited, even though we will see more women as coaches, sports broadcasters, athletic trainers, administrators, and even referees. Changes will occur more rapidly in recreation programs, fitness club management, sportswear sales, physical therapy, public relations, community relations, and marketing. More women will be hired by sport clothing and equipment manufacturers and other sport organizations when women are identified as consumers of their products, and when the organizations must connect with the wider community for public relations and marketing purposes. But the gender logic used *inside* many sport organiza-

REFLECT ON SPORT

Women's Professional Basketball in the U.S.
Will It Succeed?

Before the mid-1990s, there were four attempts to establish professional women's basketball leagues in the U.S. The most successful attempt, the Women's Professional Basketball League, lasted three seasons, from 1979 to 1981. It included seven teams and highlighted well-known players such as Ann Meyers and Nancy Lieberman Cline, and a few well-known male coaches. The league enjoyed limited success, but did not make enough profits to continue past the 1981 season.

The league's failure was generally blamed on lack of interest among potential spectators. However, there may have been other more important reasons. The league was organized just like pro basketball for men. Games were played in large, high-rent facilities. All of the owners and coaches were men. Most of the coaches had annual salaries of $50,000 or more, whereas the players made between $5,000 and $20,000 (in 1980 dollars). Marketing strategies emphasized the male coaches rather than the women athletes. Promotions were expensive, because they were directed at all people interested in sports rather than those with specific interests in women's basketball. Marketing emphasized the physical attractiveness of the athletes rather than their basketball skills. Taken together, all these things may have doomed the WPBL to failure, because the league never tapped into potential spectator interest among people with personal connections to girls' basketball all over the United States.

In 1984, a six-team league was established with the name Women's American Basketball Association. The WABA played twenty-two games from October to December before financial troubles caused the league to discontinue its schedule. The National Women's Basketball Association, which played games between October 1986 and February 1987, experienced a similar fate. Then in early 1991, there was an attempt to initiate the Liberty Basketball Association. The league was introduced in an exhibition in connection with an NBA game. The players were dressed in Lycra unitards and the rims of the baskets were shortened to 9'2" so the women could dunk the ball and try to mimic the way men had come to play the game. However, sponsors and investors did not feel that spectator interest was high enough for them to continue their effort to establish the league.

But times are different today. The spectator appeal of women's sports in general and women's basketball in particular has been gradually building in the U.S. since the early 1980s. For example, attendance at NCAA Division I women's basketball games increased from just over 1.1 million in 1982 to over 4.1 million in 1996. Furthermore, the publicity and television coverage given to players from high-profile college teams and the 1996 U.S. Olympic team provided a new basis for promoting women's teams.

As I write this chapter, the eight teams in the American Basketball League are playing their first games. Although the league's budget is only $16 million and players' salaries average only $70,000 per year, many of those associated with the league feel the time is right for women's professional basketball. Ticket sales, television rights, licensed merchandise, and sponsorships are the major sources of revenues. Reebok is a founding sponsor of the ABL, but it is doubtful that its support will continue if other revenues are not generated to pay salaries and expenses. At this point, there are only eighty opportunities for women basketball players (versus 400 in the NBA). However, six of the eight head coaches are women, and there are at least twelve women assistant coaches in the league. Women are on the management staff of all teams, and many top management positions are held by women.

The status of the ABL depends in part on the success of the WNBA, a second league scheduled to begin playing games in 1997. The WNBA has deeper financial backing than the ABL, contracts with some of the highest-profile players of the mid-1990s, and national television contracts with NBC, ESPN, and Lifetime Television. The ABL began with limited

TANK McNAMARA®

by Jeff Millar & Bill Hinds

....

When one of the sponsors of the American Basketball League wanted the players to wear heavy makeup while filming a commercial, some of the players asked if the commercial was about their physical appearance or about their basketball abilities. They resisted using some of the makeup that the advertising company wanted them to use.

....

financial backing, contracts with fewer high-profile players, and regional television coverage of twelve Sunday night games through the Sports Channel Regional Network. The ABL's season runs at the same time as the men's NBA season, while the WNBA plans to play its games between mid-June and late August, to avoid overlap with men's basketball games.

One of the first problems faced by the ABL occurred when some of the high-profile players objected to the amount of makeup they were expected to wear while filming a Reebok commercial. It seems that women's sports still have not been able to shake the influence of traditional ideas about gender. Apparently some people are afraid that unless women athletes fit traditional ideas about heterosexual femininity, they will not be able to generate the spectator interest they need to survive. Of course, it has been this belief that has subverted support for women's sports at all levels for many years.

Even though problems will occur and the organization of the two first leagues will change over time, women's professional basketball will survive and eventually prosper. Women gradually will have more opportunities to play, coach, manage, and administer pro basketball. The social worlds and the organizational cultures that emerge in connection with the game will reflect the values and experiences of women rather than men.

The NBA has had well over fifty years to build its game, its reputation, and its fan base. Women's professional basketball will not need fifty years to be successful. The league(s) established during the mid-1990s will serve as the basis for increasing professional sport opportunities for women in the U.S. The expanding flow of basketball talent through women's teams in high schools and colleges will continue to elevate the quality of women's basketball and fuel expanding spectator interest. What do you think?

Opportunities for women in coaching and administration will increase when they become candidates for jobs in men's programs. If men are hired to coach and administer women's teams and programs, why aren't women hired to coach and administer men's teams and programs? (University of Colorado Media Relations)

(AIAW), many women coaches and administrators found it uncomfortable working in an organizational culture grounded in the values and experiences of men. Some women became alienated and detached from careers they had once loved. At the same time, many others were demoted, fired, or paid much less than men because they were no longer defined as "qualifed" in the terms used by those who controlled the NCAA-affiliated athletic departments.

Recent research shows that many sport organizations, including those in high schools and colleges, are not very good at supporting and retaining women coaches and administrators (Pastore, 1994). Professional development programs, workshops, and coaching clinics have not been widely sponsored for women employees, although some women's organizations, such as the Women's Sport Foundation in the U.S. and the Canadian Association for the Advancement of Women and Sport (CAAWS) in Canada, have stepped in to provide assistance and guidance for women working in sports. Barriers to career opportunities for women in sports are slowly being chipped away, but the forces that have limited opportunities in the past are still part of the ideologies and structures of many sport programs. As we noted in chapter 8, equity issues and ideological issues are tied together. Hiring more women is only one aspect of the changes needed to achieve real equity; the other is changing the cultures of sports and sport organizations themselves, and this is *not* easy.

Opportunities for African Americans Are Limited

The visibility of black athletes in certain spectator sports often has led to the conclusion that career opportunities for blacks are abundant in sports. For example, according to surveys done in the U.S., over half of all adults, both blacks and whites, agreed with these statements: "There are more opportunities in sports than in any other field for the social advancement of blacks and other minorities" and "Athletics is

tions will continue to privilege those perceived as tough, strong, and aggressive—and those doing most of the hiring tend to perceive women less often than men in these terms.

Many women who do work in sport organizations face the burden of dealing with an organizational culture that they have had little or no role in shaping. This burden can contribute to higher rates of turnover among women than among men. For example, in the early 1980s, when the male-controlled NCAA took over women's sports from the female-controlled Association for Intercollegiate Athletics for Women one of the best ways for blacks to advance their social status" (*Miller Lite Report*, 1983). Such beliefs have been supported by testimonials from successful black athletes who attribute all their fame and wealth to sports.

These beliefs are as strong as ever today. However, the extent to which job opportunities for blacks exist in sports has been greatly overstated. Very little publicity is given to the actual number and proportion of blacks who play professional sports and work in sports in the United States. Instead, there are numerous references to *individual* success stories about black athletes. Of course, these stories are real, but they draw attention away from two very crucial facts. *First*, sports provide almost no career opportunities for black women. *Second*, the number and proportion of black males making their living as athletes in professional sports is so small it is an almost insignificant percentage of the 34 million African Americans and over four billion people of color around the world.

A review of the professional sport scene shows few blacks in hockey, golf, tennis, and auto racing—four of the most lucrative sports for athletes. Professional track and field offers a few opportunities to black athletes, but the rewards are generally small, and careers seldom last more than a few years. The same goes for soccer. Even in professional boxing, there are few black fighters making a comfortable living. History shows that only a handful of even the most successful black boxers have retired in comfort or used their athletic careers as stepping stones into other careers (Hare, 1971; Weinberg and Arond, 1952; Wacquant, 1992, 1995a, c).

My best guess is that less than 3,500 African Americans, or about 1 in 10,000, are making their livings as professional athletes. At the same time (in 1996), there are about 30,015 black physicians and about 30,800 black lawyers currently employed in the U.S. Therefore, there are twenty times more blacks working in these two professions than playing top-level professional sports. And physicians and lawyers usually have lifetime earnings far in excess of the earnings of professional athletes, whose playing careers, on average, last less than five years. This means that it is very misleading to suggest that playing sports is the primary way for young African Americans to achieve economic success in the form of upward social mobility. In fact, if some other business organization tried to encourage all young blacks, especially black males, in the United States and Canada to dedicate their childhood and adolescence to developing highly specialized skills useful in only 3,500 jobs, it would be accused of fraud. Yet this is the message that has been delivered for many years in connection with professional sports. But instead of being seen as fraudulent, it has been eagerly endorsed by many people (Smith, 1993, 1995).

Unfortunately, most of the skills required in sports are worthless in the general job market. What jobs exist for a twenty-two-year-old who has spent the last fifteen years learning how to shoot a 30-foot jump shot or run 100 meters in 10.5 seconds? Young African American men and women would be much better off putting away basketballs and track shoes and trying to become president of the United States. While their chances of getting elected would be slim to nonexistent, the skills they learned and the educational credentials they earned while pursuing the presidency would enable them to be successful in many other careers.

Despite the dismal odds, young blacks often set their sights on making it as professional athletes, and they often are encouraged by teachers, coaches, friends, and occasionally, parents (Braddock, 1980a; Harris, 1994; Joravsky, 1995; Oliver, 1980; Lapchick, 1991). Research shows that in elementary and junior high school, the proportions of black boys and white boys who aspire to be professional athletes are about equal. During senior high school, however, white males tend to develop other occupational goals, while black males often maintain their focus on sports, especially basketball and football. In fact, over 50 percent of all black high school athletes, compared with 18 percent of white high school athletes, believe they can make the pros in their sports (Lapchick, 1996a: 174). Of course, this does not mean that young blacks are ignoring their educations as they pursue their sport dreams, but it does suggest a need to provide them with regular reminders that academic goals should be primary goals (Sellers, 1993; Fudzie and Hayes, 1995).

Without these reminders, it is likely that young African Americans, especially males, will focus too much attention on making it to the pros in the two or three sports in which fewer than 1,500 black men are making big money (those in the minor leagues don't make much). With the powerful sport images that come into the lives of young people every day, sport dreams can be very seductive, especially when other dreams are absent. As one commentator has observed, "The eyes of youth . . . , left without hope for harmonious tomorrows and social justice, have been focused on mainly images of success on television, exemplifying strength and [physical] beauty" (Higgs 1995: 304). Unfortunately, many young black males in particular see so little hope and justice in the world around them that they focus on televised coverage of black athletes in the NFL and NBA, who offer such images of success, strength, and beauty. And those images are awfully powerful!

EMPLOYMENT BARRIERS FOR BLACK ATHLETES When sports were first desegregated in the United States, African Americans faced **entry barriers:** they had to be outstanding athletes with exemplary personal characteristics before they were given professional contracts (see Kooistra et al., 1993). Prejudices were strong, so those hiring assumed that blacks would not be accepted by teammates, coaches, or spectators unless they could make immediate, significant contributions to a team. Black athletes with average skills were passed by. At the same time, white athletes received contracts even when they were not expected to be standout players. The result was that black athletes had

performance statistics surpassing those of whites. Ironically, this contributed to myths about black athletic superiority that led to increased efforts to locate and sign exceptional black players in certain sports and in certain positions on teams (as I explained in chap. 9).

As entry barriers declined between 1960 and the late 1970s, new barriers related to retention took their place. **Retention barriers** were identified by Richard Lapchick (1984) in an analysis of data from the National Basketball Association (NBA). In the early 1980s, Lapchick found that black NBA players had to maintain higher scoring averages than white players to be re-signed to contracts after five years in the league. In other words, marginal white players had a much better chance than marginal black players to be retained and paid by NBA teams.

This pattern was also found in the NFL as recently as the early 1990s. Using information on the players designated as "protected" and "marginal" by NFL teams during "free agency drafts," sociologist Paul Kooistra and his colleagues found that a disproportionate number of white players were assigned to the marginal category. Their analysis concluded with this statement:

> [Our] findings . . . support the belief that there is unequal opportunity for equal ability in the National Football League. It appears that marginal players, as judged by management, are far more likely to be white. From this we might infer that marginal nonwhite players are discriminated against in the NFL. To remain in the pool of players comprising the league, nonwhites must in general be better than whites (Kooistra et al., 1993: 253).

The extent to which race-based retention barriers still exist in different sports is not clear; for example, a recent study of major-league baseball did *not* find evidence of such barriers (Leonard, 1995). Also unclear is the reason these barriers have existed in the past. It may have been that team management staff, all of whom were white, made player personnel decisions that prevented their teams from becoming "too black"; they may have thought this was important in cities where racism existed and whites purchased nearly all game tickets. Or it may have been that older white players in many cities developed a base of fan support that management wanted to maintain because it boosted public relations and ticket sales. Or it may have been that experienced white players were regarded by management as more dependable than experienced black players, or more willing to sit on the bench and play supporting roles on the team. But whatever the reason, management seems to have considered the skin color of players, consciously or unconsciously, when assessing the worth of marginal players in certain sports; physical skills were not the only things that mattered. If this still happens today, it occurs on a very subtle level, and selectively, on a team here or there.

On a positive note, there is little evidence of race-based salary discrimination among players in any of the major team sports. Players from all racial and ethnic backgrounds seem to be paid equally for their abilities (Leonard, 1995; Purdy et al., 1994). The reason for this is probably that it is now relatively easy to measure abilities, because objective statistics are kept on nearly every conceivable dimension of an athlete's performance. Furthermore, salaries now are negotiated by experienced agents who use these performance statistics while representing players. Because agents receive a percentage of players' salaries, they have a built-in incentive to make sure that discrimination does not affect the contracts signed by the players, black, brown, or white.

EMPLOYMENT BARRIERS IN COACHING AND OFF-THE-FIELD JOBS IN SPORTS
In 1987 the longtime director of player personnel for the Los Angeles Dodgers said that blacks were excluded from coaching and administrative jobs in baseball because they "lacked the necessities" to handle such jobs. Even though he later apologized for his remark, he caused people to wonder if his beliefs about blacks explained why, during the nearly thirty years he helped shape

the coaching and management staff on the Dodgers, the team never had a black general manager, a black field manager, a black pitching coach at any level, or a black third-base coach (the most influential coach below the head coach on a baseball team).

Of course, the Los Angeles Dodgers were not the only team with such a record. For example, when the Dallas Cowboys won the Super Bowl in 1994, a press release issued by a national black organization (the NAACP) accused the team of having plantation-like hiring practices. Seventy-five percent of the players on the team were African American, while all eleven of the top administrators were white men (Shropshire, 1996). This led Jesse Jackson to form the Rainbow Coalition for Fairness in Athletes, which began to work with the Center for the Study of Sport in Society (CSSS) to put pressure on professional and college sport teams to increase the representation of ethnic minorities and women in administrative and staff positions. In fact, since 1990 the CSSS, located at Northeastern University in Boston, has published an annual "Racial Report Card" in which the hiring practices of the NBA, the NFL, and MLB are rated for their racial, ethnic, and gender fairness (see Lapchick, 1996b).

Fairness has improved since 1990, but lawyer Kenneth Shropshire recently presented a convincing case that race remains "a determining factor for the absence of blacks in the positions of power in sports" (1996). Former NFL standout player Kellen Winslow notes that his personal off-the-field job-hunting experiences in sports support Shropshire's case. Winslow explains it this way:

> What my experiences have taught me time and time again is that race is still, and will be for some time to come, a major factor in the decision-making process for off-the-field positions in professional and college sports (in Shropshire, 1996).

Winslow's personal observations are supported by data showing a disproportionately low

At top levels of sport, where coaches and administrators are paid well, African Americans and other ethnic minorities are usually underrepresented. At the youth level, where coaches volunteer for unpaid positions, African American and Latino men are strongly represented in certain sports. Research on this topic is needed.

number of blacks in head coaching and administrative positions in both professional and major college sports (Lapchick, 1996b).

Why has desegregation been so slow in off-the-field jobs in sports? Answers to this question vary (see Brooks and Althouse, 1993), but it is clear that when people in positions of power recruit candidates for top management positions, they look for people who think like they do so they can work closely together. This is the reason they often hire old fraternity brothers or fellow alumni from college. Those who share similar backgrounds are "known quantities"; they are people with whom personal connections can be made or already exist. So if those doing the hiring are white males, they may raise more questions about the job qualifications of those who come from different racial or ethnic backgrounds—backgrounds they may know little about. When candidates have different histories and experiences, those hiring may ask: Can they be trusted? Are they dependable? Will they think

like others in top management? If there are *any* doubts, conscious or unconscious, those doing the hiring will usually stick with candidates like themselves. This process long has been operating in sports, and as long as it continues, minority men and all women will be underrepresented in the power positions in sports.

Affirmative action programs have produced results in certain mid- and lower-level job categories in sport organizations, but they have not produced significant changes in the racial and gender compositions of top-management job categories (Lapchick, 1996b; see also figure 9–2). Significant changes at the level of top management will occur only when the white males who currently hold positions of power in sport organizations become more aware of the skills of minority and women candidates and the advantages of ethnic and gender diversity in sport organizations. If this does not occur fast enough, then maybe lawsuits and political pressure will force those in control to open their doors to others who aren't "just like" them. Certainly, affirmative action is still needed to push the doors open farther (Brooks and Althouse, 1993; Shropshire, 1996).

SPORT PARTICIPATION AND OCCUPATIONAL CAREERS AMONG FORMER ATHLETES

What happens in the occupational lives of former athletes? Are their career patterns different from those of their counterparts who never played competitive sports? Is sport participation a stepping-stone to upward social mobility in society? Does playing sports have economic payoffs after active participation is over? These are difficult questions, and there are only a few studies that have compared former athletes with others on issues related to social class and social mobility. Those studies suggest that as a group, the young people who have played sports on high school and college teams experienced no more or less occupational success than others from comparable backgrounds. This does not mean that playing sports has never helped anyone in special ways; it only means that there have been no consistent research findings indicating that former athletes have some systematic advantage over comparable peers when it comes to future occupational careers and social class position. Of course, research done more than a few years ago may not be indicative of what is happening today, because the meaning and cultural significance of sport participation changes over time, and may be related to career processes in some way.

At this point we don't know much about the precise ways in which sport participation in different contexts may be connected to processes of career development. Here are four possibilities: (1) It may be that under certain circumstances, sport participation teaches young people interpersonal skills that carry over into various jobs and enable them to be successful. (2) Former athletes may be defined or labeled by others as good job prospects and given opportunities enabling them to develop and demonstrate work-related abilities that serve as the basis for career success. (3) Those young people who were very high-profile athletes may be able to use their reputations to obtain and succeed at certain types of jobs. (4) Playing sports may put young people in touch with others, especially adults with connections and power, who can help them get good jobs after they retire from sports.

After reviewing many studies of former athletes,* I would argue that playing sports is most likely to work in favor of occupational success

and upward mobility when sport participation is defined or organized to do the following things:

1. increase opportunities to complete academic degrees, develop job-related skills, and/or extend knowledge about the organization and operation of the world outside of sports
2. lead close friends and family members to provide consistent social, emotional, and material support for *overall* growth and development
3. provide opportunities to make friends and develop social contacts with people connected to activities and organizations apart from sports and sport organizations
4. provide material resources along with the management abilities needed to use those resources to create or nurture career opportunities
5. expand personal and social experiences fostering the development of non-sport-related identities and awareness of abilities with implications apart from sports
6. minimize the risk of serious injuries restricting physical movement or requiring extensive and expensive medical treatment

This is not an earthshaking list of conclusions. It contains no surprises. It simply emphasizes that sports have the potential to either constrict or expand a person's overall development (see chap. 4). When expansion occurs, participation is likely to be associated with the development of work-related abilities and increased access to career opportunities. When constriction occurs, the development of work-related abilities and access to career opportunities are likely to be subverted.

Julius Erving (Dr. J.), a legendary pro basketball player in the 1970s now in a successful second career, has noted that former professional athletes sometimes have problems making transitions into occupational careers after they retire from sports. He says,

> I see so many athletes not feeling they have a purpose once their [playing] careers are over. That's

---

*See especially Allison and Meyer, 1988; Braddock, 1981; Coakley, 1983b; Curtis and Ennis, 1988; DuBois, 1978, 1979; Eisen and Turner, 1992; Greendorfer and Blinde, 1985; Hanks, 1979; Hanks and Eckland, 1976; Hare, 1971; Howell and Picou, 1983; Howell et al., 1984; Koukouris, 1994; Loy, 1969; McPherson, 1980; Melnick and Sabo, 1992; Melnick, Sabo, and Vanfossen, 1992; Miracle and Rees, 1994; Nixon, 1984; Otto and Alwin, 1977; Picou et al., 1985; Reynolds, 1981; Sabo, Melnick, and Vanfossen, 1993; Sack and Thiel, 1979; Semyonov, 1984; Snyder and Baber, 1979; Spady, 1979; Spreitzer, 1992; Stevenson, 1976; and Swain, 1991.

why so many of them make "comebacks." . . . It's a lot easier if you begin your business career before your sports career is over (in Hunter-Hodge, 1995).

Of course, Erving realizes that when athletes anticipate what they will face in their lives after sports, they are more likely to use their sport experiences to expand their experiences, contacts, and knowledge. When athletes don't do this, they run the risk of being unprepared to face the challenges of life off the field.

Sport Participation, Class Relations, and Career Success

Because sport participation and class relations are linked, the chances for career success following sport participation vary from sport to sport. Some sports, such as tennis and golf, offer experiences that often enhance career opportunities. Other sports, such as boxing, rodeo, and motocross, do not usually involve career-enhancing experiences.

Although it is an extreme case, boxing provides a good illustration of this point. Schools do not sponsor boxing. This forces young people to develop their skills apart from formal education. In fact, trainers may encourage promising boxers to drop out of school to concentrate on training; seldom do young men earn college degrees while training to be boxers. Boxers come from the racial and ethnic groups most likely to face occupational discrimination and from families that have few material resources to promote overall growth and development. Boxing seldom increases social contacts with people outside the tightly bounded social world of boxing; it seldom leads to financial payoffs or learning of financial management skills; it does not offer opportunities for identity development apart from the ring and the gym; and it often leaves participants with millions of dead brain cells—not an advantage when starting an occupational career!

The result of this combination of factors is that boxing seldom serves as a springboard into good occupational careers; in fact, it sometimes

does the exact opposite. Nathan Hare vividly described this in a study of retired professional boxers. None of the forty-eight boxers in Hare's study had been able to save much of the money they earned during their careers. Hare described the reality of life after boxing this way:

> In the gyms, I watched the active fighters working and waiting for the lucky break which, they believed, would take them to the wealth and glory of a championship. In the taverns and poolrooms, I listened to the former fighters reliving their own fighting careers, boasting to sustain their pride, dissatisfied now with their present lot and trying to call back in conversation the youth and skills that had once been theirs (Hare, 1971).

Of course, there are a small number of exceptions to this pattern. We know that since the advent of pay-per-view television, a few heavyweight boxers have made many millions of dollars in connection with bouts marketed around the world.

A very different picture emerges when we shift our attention to a sport like golf. Opportunities after retirement from either intercollegiate or professional competition in golf are likely to be much more abundant and attractive than such opportunities for boxers. Golf is played in settings where athletes meet many people who have wide-ranging contacts that will be useful when they are looking for jobs. The club settings in which golf occurs provide the athletes with opportunities to develop general social skills, in addition to meeting people. The people they meet while golfing generally value education, and can serve as educational advocates, since they themselves have gone to college and professional schools. And playing golf does not lead to debilitating injuries that would interfere with occupational success.

Although these are two extreme examples, I give them to illustrate a number of factors that may or may not link sport participation to occupational success. Sport participation can put people in touch with or cut them off from experiences and social contacts that might help them prepare for, gain access to, and take advantage of occupational opportunities. In this way, the social worlds that form around sports can interfere with or promote transitions into careers that offer possibilities for upward social mobility.

Highly Paid Professional Athletes and Occupational Success

Conclusions about the connection between sport participation, career success, and social mobility must be qualified in light of the dramatic jump in the annual incomes of some professional athletes over the past fifteen to twenty-five years. Before the late 1970s, few athletes made enough money in sports to pave their ways into other careers after they retired. However, some athletes today make enough money in a few years to finance any one of a range of career alternatives after they retire from sports—if they do not throw their money away or do irreparable damage to their reputations! For example, Pete Sampras, even without a college degree, will have no trouble supporting himself after he quits the tennis tour. His financial status will not depend on the support of family or friends, although other aspects of his adjustment to life after competitive tennis will require support from those close to him. He will have millions in the bank to fund whatever he wants to do. Sampras, along with an increasing number of athletes in the NBA, the NFL, the NHL, major-league baseball, tennis, golf, autoracing, and a few other sports now have salaries and endorsements that guarantee they will retire from playing careers with all the resources they need to comfortably explore what they would like to do and develop the skills to do it.

Of course, not all professional athletes earn enough to retire under these conditions. Many sport careers are short-lived, and many athletes do not earn anything close to the extremely high salaries publicized in the media coverage of superstars. Those who are not stars frequently enter occupations in which they receive lower salaries than they received in sports. This can

present problems if they developed lifestyles and tastes dependent on large salaries (Gruneau and Whitson, 1993). But if this is not the case, they are likely to experience patterns of success and failure similar to the patterns experienced by comparable others who did not play sports. Their post-sport careers may not enable them to drive new cars, travel to exciting places, or read their names in newspapers every week, but this does not mean they should be seen as failures or victims of sports.

WHEN DOES RETIREMENT FROM SPORTS PRESENT PROBLEMS? When people think of retirement as a life-changing event that happens at a particular point in time, without warning or preparation, they usually assume that retiring from sport careers is traumatic and disruptive. But research shows that retirement from sports is best described as a process rather than a single event (Swain, 1991). In fact, retirement from sports often occurs in connection with other changes or transitions in a person's life, such as high school or college graduation, marriage, the birth of a child, the availability of a career opportunity, a desire to return to school, or the sense that it is time to move on to other things. Therefore, making the transition out of competitive sports is often part of an anticipated process corresponding with developments in a person's overall life course.

Most athletes don't retire from sports on a moment's notice; instead, they gradually disengage from sports and shift their personal priorities in the process (Blinde and Greendorfer, 1985; Curtis and Ennis, 1988; Greendorfer and Blinde, 1985; Koukouis, 1994; Swain, 1991). Many continue sport participation at a less intense level in community sport programs or other settings that offer challenging competition. Others may continue working out in their sports for their own enjoyment, health, and fitness. A few even seek new competitive challenges at later points in their lives by participating in Masters or Seniors events (Hastings et al., 1989).

SIDELINES

Only a small proportion of former athletes are able to cash in on their athletic reputations. The rest must seek opportunities and work just like the rest of us. Those opportunities vary, depending on qualifications, experience, contacts and connections, and a bit of luck.

....

Although most athletes smoothly disengage from sports, develop other interests, and move into relatively satisfying occupational careers, some do encounter varying degrees of adjustment problems that interfere with occupational success and overall life satisfaction (Ogilvie and Taylor, 1993). For example, when sociologist Mike Messner interviewed former elite athletes, he found that many men who had been heavily involved in sports since childhood encountered serious adjustment problems as they tried to make the transition out of sports. A former NFL player highlighted these problems with the following explanation:

> [When you retire] you find yourself scrambled. You don't know which way to go. Your light . . . has been turned out. . . . Of course you miss the financial deal, but you miss the camaraderie of the other ballplayers. You miss that—to be an elite, to be one of a kind. . . . [T]he game itself . . . the beating and all that . . . you don't really miss. You miss the camaraderie of the fellas. There's an empty feeling . . . the one thing that has been the major part of your life is gone. . . . [Y]ou don't know how people are

going to react to you . . . you wonder and question (1992: 120–21).

Messner's research led him to suggest that retiring athletes, especially those who had dedicated themselves to playing sports ever since they were children, face two major challenges:

1. reconstructing their identities in terms of activities, abilities, and relationships unrelated to sport participation
2. renegotiating relationships with family members and close friends so they receive feedback and support for identities having little or nothing to do with playing sports

Messner also noted that young men from low-income families were more likely to have problems when retiring from sports because they had fewer material resources to aid them in the transition process, and because they were more likely to have identities deeply rooted in playing sports. Men from middle-class backgrounds, on the other hand, seemed more likely to benefit from the doors opened by sports and the social connections related to sport participation; they also had greater access to material support and were less likely to have identities exclusively rooted in playing sports.

Studies also have shown that adjustment problems are more likely when an injury forces retirement from sports. Injuries often complicate retirement and tie it to other problems related to self-esteem or health; injuries disrupt "life plans" by throwing off the timing of retirement and forcing a person into life decisions before they are expected (Kleiber et al., 1987; Kleiber and Brock, 1992). This is not surprising, and athletes often need career-related assistance when this occurs.

When athletes have problems making the transition out of sports into careers and other activities, it seems that sport organizations have some responsibility to offer assistance. Some sport organizations, including universities and national governing bodies, are beginning to do this through various forms of career transition programs. These programs often involve workshops dealing with career self-assessments, life skills training, career planning, resume writing, job search strategies, interviewing skills, career placement contacts, and psychological counseling.

Of course, some organizations do not see the issue of career transition as a high priority, or do not have the resources to initiate and conduct transition programs or hire others to do so. But there is a growing belief that after young men and women are asked to dedicate full-time energy and attention to playing sports, the organizations that benefit from their dedication have an obligation to help them make a successful transition into life after sports. I agree.

Athletic Grants and Occupational Success

Whenever sport participation is discussed in connection with career success and upward social mobility, people raise the topic of athletic scholarships. It is widely believed that these scholarships are valuable mobility vehicles for many young people. This belief raises a number of questions: How many athletic scholarships are actually given? How much are they worth to the students receiving them? Who receives them? How many scholarship recipients could not afford to attend college without their athletic awards?

Surprisingly, the information needed to answer these questions is difficult to obtain. Colleges and universities are not currently required to report the total number of athletic scholarships they give to students or the amount of athletic aid that goes to particular student-athletes. So we cannot say who receives scholarships, how much the scholarships are worth, or how important they are in the educational lives of recipients. We do know that the actual number of *full* athletic scholarships is often exaggerated. For example, high school students who simply receive standard recruiting letters from one or more university coaches often tell people they are anticipating *full* scholarships; in fact, they

may receive only partial aid or no aid at all. College students receiving tuition waivers or other forms of partial athletic aid often lead people to believe they have full scholarships. Athletic scholarships are awarded one year at a time and may not be renewed for certain athletes, who may continue their education and even their sport participation without athletic aid. Finally, many people simply assume that college athletes, especially those who play at big universities, all have scholarships. Of course, such exaggerations are misleading, causing people to think that sport participation has more significance in students' lives than it really does.

We can begin to understand the educational significance of athletic scholarships by looking at data from the 305 U.S. universities that have big-time, Division I sport programs (NCAA divisions are explained in chap. 14). According to 1996 data, there were over 2.7 million undergraduates enrolled in those 305 universities. Just over 64,000 of those undergrads, or 2.3 percent, received athletic aid (NCAA, 1996). According to researchers at the NCAA office, less than 25 percent of those receiving aid had scholarships that paid for full tuition, room, and food. The other 75 percent were receiving aid covering some portion of total expenses. This means that in the 305 universities with the largest sport programs, only about 15,000 student-athletes were receiving full scholarships; this amounts to about one-half of 1 percent of all students enrolled in those universities. Clearly, far fewer students receive full athletic scholarships than is commonly believed. In fact, academic scholarships are many times more plentiful than athletic scholarships, even though most high school students think otherwise.

Of course, when athletic aid goes to financially needy young people who focus on educational attainment and graduation while they attend a university, sport participation is very likely to increase their chances for career success. But how many of those athletic scholarships, full and partial, go to young people who could not or

The vast majority of intercollegiate athletes in the U.S. play without any form of athletic aid. Even at the 305 U.S. universities with the largest and most successful athletic programs, only 2.3 percent of the undergraduate student body receives any form of athletic aid, and most of them receive only partial scholarships. (College Relations, The Colorado College)

would not attend college without them? Unfortunately, we don't know the answer to this question. But we do know that a portion of those who receive athletic scholarships can and would attend college without that form of financial support. This does not mean that the legitimacy of athletic grants should be questioned; it merely means that the various links between playing sports, receiving athletic scholarships, achieving career success, and experiencing upward social mobility must be carefully qualified.

SUMMARY

ARE SPORTS RELATED TO ECONOMIC INEQUALITY AND SOCIAL MOBILITY IN SOCIETY?

The study of sports as social phenomena is important, because sports are connected to issues of social class and class relations in society. Organized sports depend on those who have the money, facilities, and organizational experience to sponsor them. Therefore the economic inequalities that exist in society spill over into sports in a variety of ways.

In the process of sponsoring the sports that provide entertainment and participation opportunities, those with money and power fund and promote sport forms that fit their own interests and foster ideas supportive of economic arrangements that work to their advantage. This is the reason dominant sport forms in North America promote an ideology of competition and achievement that stresses two explanations of success and failure in society: (1) "You get what you deserve through competition," and (2) "You always get what you deserve, and you always deserve what you get." This ideology constitutes a type of class logic that drives a combination of individual achievement and consumption in society. The use of this logic leads to favorable conclusions about the character and qualifications of those who are wealthy and powerful in society, while it disadvantages those who are poor and powerless. Furthermore, it leads to the conclusion that economic inequality in society is not only good but also natural.

Class relations also are manifested in connection with the ways wealthy and powerful people around the world have become involved in sport team ownership, event sponsorship and organization, and the media coverage of sports. In fact, sport events seem to be one of the vehicles these people can use to transfer public money into the private sector under their control. As the public seeks to support major forms of sport entertainment in their cities and regions, those with wealth and power receive subsidies and income they can use to maintain their privilege.

Sport participation patterns in society and around the world reflect the impact of material resources and social class on how people live their lives. Organized sports are a luxury that many people around the world cannot afford. Even in wealthy societies like those of the U.S., Canada, the countries of Western Europe, sport participation is most common among those in the middle and upper classes. Patterns of sport participation throughout a society reflect class-based lifestyles that emerge as people make decisions about how they will use the resources they do have.

Sport participation patterns also reflect the combination of class and gender relations. We see this in the case of lower-income girls and women who have low participation rates, and in the case of lower-income men who see sports in terms that have unique identity implications in their lives. Boxing provides an example in which class, gender, and race relations come together in a powerful combination in sports. The boxing gym provides a safe space that takes minority men in poor neighborhoods away from the poverty, racism, and despair that spawn violence and desperate behaviors among their peers. The same social forces that lead minority men to choose boxing also give rise to variations of *hoop dreams* that captivate the attention of young ethnic minorities, especially black males. But even these dreams are now being subverted as public schools in low-income areas are dropping their sport programs.

Sport spectatorship patterns also reflect the impact of social class. This is demonstrated by the increased segregation of fans in stadiums and arenas. Luxury boxes, club seating, and patterns of season ticket allocations separate people by a combination of wealth and power, so that social class often is reaffirmed when people attend sport events.

Opportunities for careers that hold the hope of upward social mobility for some people do exist in sports. In the case of athletes, these opportunities are scarce and short-lived, and they reflect patterns of gender and ethnic relations. These patterns take different forms in the case of careers in off-the-field jobs. Although opportunities in these jobs have become increasingly open over the past decade, white men still widely hold the top positions in sport organizations. This will change only when the organizational cultures of sport teams and athletic departments become more inclusive and provide new ways for women and ethnic minorities to fully participate in shaping policies and norms used to determine qualifications in sports.

Research on the connection between sport participation and the process of career development generally indicates that when young people are able to use sport participation to expand their social worlds and personal experiences, they have an advantage when seeking occupational careers. However, when sport participation constricts social worlds and personal experiences, it is likely to have a negative effect on occupational success. The existence of these patterns varies by sport. Of course, the extremely high incomes of some athletes today almost guarantee their future career success and economic security.

Retirement from athletic careers often creates stress and personal challenges, but most athletes move through the retirement process without experiencing *excessive* trauma or difficulty. Those who do experience difficulties are usually those whose identities and relationships have been built exclusively on sports. These people may need outside assistance as they move into the rest of their lives and face the challenge of seeking jobs, maintaining satisfying occupational careers, and nurturing mutually supportive and intimate social relationships.

Athletic scholarships help some young people further their educations and possibly achieve career success, but the number of so-called full scholarships is very limited. Furthermore, athletic aid awards do not always change the future career patterns of young people, because many grant recipients have the motivation and resources to attend college without sport-related financial assistance.

In conclusion, sports clearly are tied to patterns of social inequality in society. And we should accept the idea that sports are paths to success only with reservations. It applies to a limited number of people, and it depends on much more than the display of physical skills on the playing field.

SUGGESTED READINGS

Coakley, J. 1983. Leaving competitive sport: retirement or rebirth? *Quest* 35:1–11 (*a review of the literature on what happens to top-level athletes when they stop participating in competitive sports*).

Eitzen, D. S. 1995. Classism in sport: The powerless bear the burden. *Journal of Sport and Social Issues* 20 (1): 95–105. (*a brief overview of how class relations operate in sports; focuses on issues of publicly subsidized stadiums, the rising costs of spectatorship, exploitation of intercollegiate athletes from low-income family backgrounds, and the unequal funding of public school sport programs*).

Foley, D. E. 1990. *Learning capitalist culture deep in the heart of Tejas.* Philadelphia: University of Pennsylvania Press (*an ethnography that shows class, ethnic, and gender relations in connection with high school sports; as Foley notes, "Sports, and football in particular, may have many virtues, but one of its more undesirable and unintended consequences is to promote or reproduce various forms of social inequality"*).

Frey, D. 1994. *The last shot: City streets, basketball dreams.* Boston: Houghton Mifflin (*deals with the same issues as Joravsky's* Hoop Dreams *and Telander's* Heaven is a Playground *[see below]; shows how sport participation among low-income minority males cannot be understood apart from issues of class and class relations*).

Hargreaves, J. 1986. *Sport, culture and power.* New York: St. Martin's Press (*an analysis of ties between sport and power in Britain; the first seven chapters focus on class relations as a context for the social construction of sports*).

Joravsky, B. 1995. *Hoop dreams: A true story of hardship and triumph.* New York: Harper Perennial (*written in connection with the film of the same name, this book also illustrates the power of dreams to succeed in sports among young African American males whose life chances are depressingly low. Although the hoop dreams project had a major impact on the lives of the two young men followed in the story, it is easy to see how "hoop dreams" are often empty fantasies that can subvert attempts to seek other avenues of upward social mobility*).

Miracle, A. W., and C. R. Rees. 1994. *Lessons of the locker room: The myth of school sports.* Amherst, NY: Prometheus Books (*Chap. 6 provides a concise overview of research findings related to social mobility issues and participation in high school sports in the U.S.*).

Sabo, D., M. J. Melnick, and B. E. Vanfossen. 1993. High school athletic participation and postsecondary educational and occupational mobility: A focus on race and gender. *Sociology of Sport Journal* 10 (1): 44–56. (*uses data from a national study to examine mobility patterns among young people who have played varsity sports in high school; race and gender are considered in the analysis; good references listing past research on this topic*).

Shropshire, K. 1996. *In black and white: Race and sports in America.* New York: New York University Press (*written by a lawyer, focuses on legal processes and issues related to decision-making processes that determine off-the-field positions in professional and college sports; discusses why affirmative action is needed to eliminate historically based, current barriers limiting access of blacks to management and ownership positions in sports*).

Sugden, J., and A. Tomlinson. Forthcoming. Sport, social class and status. In J. Coakley and E. Dunning, eds. *Handbook of sport and society.* London: (*a thoughtful, readable overview of the theoretical perspectives sociologists have used to understand socioeconomic inequality and class-based lifestyles in society, and the ways class and status inequality is related to the organization of sports and to patterns of sport participation*).

Swain, D. A. 1991. Withdrawal from sport and Schlossberg's model of transitions. *Sociology of Sport Journal* 8(2):152–60 (*an excellent source of information on retirement from sports; the study has a very small sample, but Swain's analysis is insightful*).

Telander, R. 1995. *Heaven is a playground.* Lincoln NE: University of Nebraska Press (*a reprint of a book that refuses to go out of date because we in the U.S. have done little over the past twenty years to deal with the oppressive poverty in inner-city areas; author becomes a basketball coach to gain access to and describe the lives of young African American boys in a poor Brooklyn neighborhood*).

11

(Jay Coakley)

Do we have enough money to finance stadiums for owners worth $500 million and players who make $1 million a year at the same time we are cutting Head Start programs? That's a logical public policy question.

Byron Dorgan, member, U.S. Congress (1996)

Sports and the Economy
What are the characteristics of commercial sports?

Sports is not simply another big business. It is one of the fastest-growing industries in the U.S., and it is intertwined with virtually every aspect of the economy. . . . [S]ports is everywhere, accompanied by the sound of a cash register ringing incessantly.

Michael Ozanian, assistant managing editor, *Financial World* (1995)

Sports is an elite business, its dealings conducted by powerful individuals behind closed doors. . . . Business is the inner game of sports, the game of the really big players—the owners.

Jerry Gorman and Kirk Calhoun, Ernst & Young Business Consultants (1994)

What corrupts an athletic performance . . . is . . . the presence of an unappreciative, ignorant audience and the need to divert it with sensations extrinsic to the performance. It is at this point that . . . sports . . . degenerate into spectacle.

Christopher Lasch, social critic (1977)

It's an epidemic. Cities have two choices. Forget about major league sports. Or feed the monster.

Charles Euchner, urban politics professor, Holy Cross College (1996)

Throughout history, sports have been used as forms of public entertainment. However, sports never have been so heavily packaged, promoted, presented, and played as commercial products as they are today. Never before have decisions about sports and the social relationships connected with them been so clearly influenced by economic factors. Never before have economic organizations and large corporate interests had so much power and control over how sports are defined and organized. Never before have the economic stakes been so high for athletes and sponsors. The bottom line has replaced the goal line for many people, and sports no longer exist simply for the interests of the athletes themselves.

Today sports are evaluated in terms of gate receipts and revenues from the sale of concessions, licensing fees, merchandise, and media rights. Games and events are evaluated in terms of market shares, ratings points, and advertising potential. Athletes are evaluated in terms of endorsement potential and on-camera image; their very popularity may depend on their ties to corporate names and logos. Stadiums, teams, and athletic events now are named after large corporations rather than historical figures and places with local meaning. Corporate interests influence everything from the choice of team colors to the times events are scheduled and the ways they will be covered by the media. In fact, media companies own a growing number of sport teams and sponsor more and more events. Sports are now corporate enterprises, integrally tied to marketing concerns and processes of global capitalist expansion. The names of transnational corporations have become synonymous with the athletes, events, and sports that provide pleasure in people's lives.

Because of the importance of economic factors in sports, this chapter will focus on the following questions:

1. Under what conditions do commercial sports emerge and prosper?
2. How does commercialization influence the way sports are played and organized?
3. Who are the people that own, sponsor, and promote sports, and what are their interests?
4. How much money do athletes make, and what is their legal status in different sports?

THE EMERGENCE AND GROWTH OF COMMERCIAL SPORTS

General Conditions

Commercial sports are organized and played for the purpose of generating revenues as entertainment events. The existence of these sports depends on a combination of gate receipts, sponsorship support, and the sale of media broadcasting rights. This means that commercial sports grow and prosper best under certain social and economic conditions. *First*, they are most prevalent in market economies, where material rewards are highly valued by those connected with sports, including athletes, team owners, event sponsors, and spectators.

Second, because they require large concentrations of potential spectators, commercial sports usually exist in societies with large, densely populated cities. Although it would be possible to maintain some forms of commercial sports in rural, agricultural societies, revenues would support neither full-time professional athletes nor full-time sport promoters.

Third, commercial sports require that people in a society have time, money, and freedom of movement to attend sport events regularly. In this sense, commercial sports are a luxury. They prosper only in societies where the standard of living is high enough that people can afford to spend time and resources playing and watching events that produce no tangible products. They require relatively sophisticated transportation and communication systems: the easier it is to get to sport events and the more widely they can be publicized or presented, the more profitable they will be. Therefore, commercial sports are most commonly found in relatively wealthy, urban, industrial or postindustrial societies; they are found less often in labor-intensive, poor societies where people focus their energy and resources on staying alive rather than paying to be entertained by athletes.

Fourth, commercial sports rely on the availability of *large amounts of capital* to build and maintain stadiums and arenas in which events can be played and watched. Capital funds can be accumulated in either the public or the private sector, but in either case, the willingness to invest in sport depends on anticipated payoffs in the form of publicity, profits, or power. Private investment in sports is motivated primarily by expected financial profits; public investment is motivated primarily by a belief by those in power that commercial sports will serve their own interests, the interests of "the public," or a combination of both.

Fifth, commercial sports are most likely to flourish in cultures where lifestyles are based on high rates of consumption and emphasize material status symbols. This enables everything associated with sports to be marketed and sold: athletes (including their names, autographs, and images), merchandise, even team names and logos. When people express their identities through possessions such as clothing or equipment, and through associations with visible representatives of the community, they are likely to buy sport tickets and other possessions that associate them with sports, teams, and athletes.

Class Relations and Commercial Sports

Which sports become commercialized in a society? As we noted in the previous chapter, priority is usually given to the sports that are followed and watched by people who possess or control economic resources in society. For example, golf has become a major commercial sport, even though it does not lend itself to commercial presentation. It is inconvenient to stage a golf event for a live audience, and it is difficult to cover golf on television. Camera placement and media commentary are difficult to arrange, and live spectators see only a small proportion of the action. Golf does not involve vigorous action or head-to-head competition, except in rare cases of match play. Basically, if you don't play golf, you have little or no reason to watch it.

Commercial sports prosper in urban areas where large amounts of capital are available, where people have resources to devote to leisure activities, and where consumption and material status symbols are emphasized. (Dennis Coakley)

But a high proportion of those who *do* play golf are relatively wealthy and powerful people. These people are important to advertisers because they make consumption decisions not only for themselves and their families, but also for businesses and thousands of employees. They don't just buy luxury cars or computers for themselves; they buy thousands of company cars and PCs for their employees. Furthermore, they make investment decisions involving money from a variety of sources, and they buy high-ticket items that other people can't afford. Golfers as a group have economic clout!

This makes golf an attractive sport for advertisers who want to pitch images or products to consumers with money and influence. This is the reason auto companies with high-priced cars sponsor and advertise on the PGA and Senior PGA tours. This is also the reason major television companies cover golf tournaments: they can sell commercial time at a high rate per minute, because those watching golf have money to spend—their money and the money of the companies, large and small, that they control. The converse of this is also true: sports attracting low- and middle-income audiences often are ignored by television or covered only under special circumstances.

Market economies always privilege the interests of those who have the power and resources to influence which sports will be selected for promotion and coverage. Unless people with power and resources are interested in playing, sponsoring, or watching a sport, it is not likely to be commercialized on a large scale. When wealthy and powerful people are interested in a sport, it will be covered, promoted, and presented as if it had cultural significance in society. The sport even may be described as a "national pastime" and come to be associated with the development of ideal personal character, community spirit, civic unity, and political loyalty. And it may be supported with public money allocated for the construction of stadiums and arenas, even if this directly subsidizes and benefits wealthy team owners, sponsors, and promoters.

This portrait of popular commercial sports is not the one painted by those who claim that sports promote the overall democratization of a society. To the contrary, it is only when sports promote the interests of powerful and wealthy people that they are likely to be commercialized. This is one reason football has become "America's game." Football celebrates and privileges the values and experiences of the men who control and benefit from corporate wealth and power in North America. This explains why men get in line to pay hundreds of dollars to buy ex-pensive season tickets to college and professional football games, male executives spend thousands of dollars to buy "company tickets" to football games, and male corporation presidents write checks to pay for luxury boxes and club seats for themselves, their friends, and their clients. Not only is football entertaining for these spectators; it also reproduces a way of viewing the world that fits their interests. (Of course, women who want to be a part of the power structure often discover it is wise to do what the men do.)

The Creation of Spectator Interest in Sports

How do so many people become sport spectators in certain societies? Why do they look to sports for entertainment? Although these are complex questions with many answers, we can say that in many societies, spectator interest is related to a cultural emphasis on material success, personal experiences in sports, and easy access to sports through the media. We explain each of these factors below.

SUCCESS IDEOLOGY AND SPECTATOR INTEREST Many people watch games or read about them now and then, but spectator involvement is highest among people committed to the twin ideas that success in any aspect of life is based on hard work, and that hard work always leads to success. These people often use sports as a model of the way, in their opinion, the occupational world *should* operate. When sports are organized to emphasize the idea that success is achieved only through hard work and dedication to efficiency, these people have their beliefs and expectations reaffirmed, and they are willing to pay for that reaffirmation. This is the reason sport commentators on radio and television often emphasize that athletes and teams make their own breaks and that luck comes to those who work hard. This is also the reason large corporations have used the bodies of elite athletes to represent their public relations and marketing images emphasizing efficiency, power, the use of technology, and the achievement of success (Hoberman, 1994).

YOUTH SPORT PROGRAMS AND SPECTATOR INTEREST Spectator interest often is created and nurtured during childhood sport participation. When organized youth sport programs are publicized and made available to many young people in a society, commercial sports have a better chance to grow and prosper. With some exceptions, sport participation during childhood leads to spectator interest during adulthood. Children who learn to value sport skills and emphasize competitive success in their personal sport experiences generally will grow up wanting to watch the "experts" compete with one another. For those who continue to participate actively in sports, watching the experts provides models for improving skills and maintaining interest in participation. For those who have discontinued their own active participation, watching the experts provides opportunities to maintain connections with sport and vicariously experience success through the achievements of the athletes with whom they identify. These patterns of spectator interest usually continue long after people have stopped participating in youth programs.

MEDIA COVERAGE AND SPECTATOR INTEREST The media are closely associated with the commercialization of sports (see chap. 12). They provide needed publicity and create and sustain spectator interest among large numbers of people. In the past, newspapers and radio did this job, but today television has the greatest effect on spectator involvement.

Along with increasing spectator access to events and athletes all over the world, television provides a unique "re-presentation" of sports. It lets viewers see close-up camera shots of the action on the field and the athletes and coaches on the sidelines. It replays crucial plays and shows them in slow motion, helping viewers to imagine that even they could do what elite athletes do. It even brings viewers into the locker rooms of championship teams. On-air commentators serve as "fellow spectators" for a viewing or listening audience; they are the links through which iden-

tification with athletes can be heightened. Commentators dramatize and embellish the action in the event; they supply "inside stories," analyze strategies, describe athletes as personalities, and glorify the event, magnifying its importance.

Television is especially effective in recruiting new spectators, because people who have not played a sport themselves need opportunities to learn a sport's rules and strategies before they will become committed fans. This learning occurs easily through television. No tickets need be purchased, and questions that may sound stupid in front of strangers can be asked without embarrassment in the family living room. In other words, television provides a painless way to become a spectator, and it increases the number of people who will buy tickets, regularly watch televised games, and even become pay-per-view customers in the future.

Economic Motives and the Globalization of Commercial Sports

Commercial sports now have gone global in a big way, for two reasons. *First*, those who control, sponsor, and promote sports are looking constantly for new ways to expand their markets and make more money. *Second*, transnational corporations with production and distribution operations in many different countries can use sports as vehicles for introducing their products and services all around the world. Recent examples illustrate each of these reasons.

SPORT ORGANIZATIONS LOOK FOR GLOBAL MARKETS Sport organizations, like other businesses, are interested in expanding their operations into as many markets as possible around the world. For example, team and league profits would increase significantly if the U.S.–based NFL and the North American–based NBA, NHL, and major-league baseball (MLB) could sell broadcasting rights to television companies in countries around the world and if they could sell licensed merchandise (hats, shirts, jackets, etc.) to people around the world. This is already occurring, but the continued success of many major sport organizations in countries around the world depends on their creating spectator interest outside the boundaries of their host nations. It also depends on effective use of the media to export a combination of game knowledge and identification with the athletes who play the games. In this way, sport organizations become exporters of culture as well as products to be consumed. The complex export-import processes that occur in connection with sports have been studied by sociologists in the past, and are attracting more attention today (Donnelly, 1996; Guttmann, 1994; Houlihan, 1994; Maguire, 1993, 1994a, c; Maguire and Stead, 1996; Wilcox, 1994).

The desire for global expansion was the main reason the NBA was happy to let the so-called "Dream Team" play in the Olympics starting in 1992, even though the players risked injury and fatigue that could have jeopardized their participation in the following NBA season (and did in a few cases!). The worldwide coverage of Olympic basketball provided the NBA with publicity worth many millions of dollars. This publicity has helped to market NBA broadcasting rights and "official NBA products" all over the world. High-profile NBA players have been introduced to hundreds of millions of people, and many of these people have become more interested in seeing these players in action. Therefore, the NBA finals and the NBA All-Star games are now televised in over one hundred countries every year. Baseball and hockey are now following the NBA's lead, with hopes of their own "dream teams" in future Olympics.

The spirit of global expansion has led NFL, NBA, NHL, and MLB teams to play games in Mexico, Japan, England, France, Germany, and a number of other countries. The NHL always has been a Canadian–U.S. league; MLB and the NBA now have franchises in large Canadian cities; the NFL has assisted in the formation of the World Football League and even subsidized the formation of a football league in England (Maguire, 1990). Other investors have formed sport organizations to compete for international

markets in a range of other sports, the latest being roller hockey. The Global Basketball Association and the World Basketball League represented attempts to capture international sport markets during the early 1990s.

This spirit of global capitalist expansion is not new; nor is it limited to North American sport organizations. The International Olympic Committee (IOC) gradually has incorporated national Olympic committees from over two hundred nations, and has turned the Olympic games into the most successful and lucrative media sports events in human history. Roone Arledge, the president of ABC News in the U.S., emphasized this after two decades of work in televising the Olympics:

> I don't think the essence of the [Olympic] Games has very much to do with the heroic words that we use to describe them. It's basically a commercial enterprise that tries every four years to make as much money as it possibly can (in Reid, 1996).

John Horan, the publisher of *Sporting Goods Intelligence*, made the same point in a more wistful manner:

> It's not the Free World versus Communism anymore. Now you take sides with sneaker companies. Now everybody looks at the Olympics as Nike versus Reebok (in Reid, 1996).

Tennis and golf long have been international sports, with tournaments around the world. Soccer's FIFA (Fédération Internationale de Football Association) has a long history of global expansion that now includes playing the World Cup in the United States (Sugden and Tomlinson, 1996; Tomlinson, 1986). When the 1994 Soccer World Cup was scheduled in North America, the people in charge of FIFA clearly realized they had much to gain if they could create spectator interest in soccer among Americans. Even though the growth of professional soccer in the U.S. has been relatively slow since 1994, the media rights fees for televising future World Cup tournaments will increase, because of emerging spectator interests in North America.

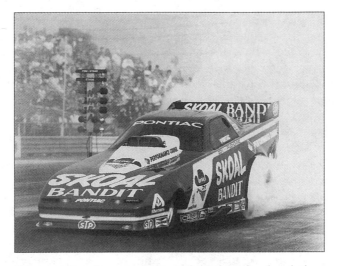

Corporations whose profits come from the sale of acohol, tobacco, fast food, and candy are eager to sponsor sports. They want their products associated with activities defined as healthy or deeply connected with important cultural values, such as those related to the automobile and individualism, power, and speed. (*Colorado Springs Gazette*)

Furthermore, media companies in the U.S. have discovered that traditional and new ethnic populations in many U.S. cities are eager to see soccer teams representing their nations of origin or the nations of their parents or grandparents.

CORPORATIONS USE SPORTS AS VEHICLES FOR GLOBAL EXPANSION The fact that sports, sporting events, sport teams, and athletes can be used to capture the attention and the emotions of millions of people has not gone unnoticed in the world of business. Since the 1980s, we have seen corporate names and logos become synonymous with athletes, teams, events, and sport facilities. People around the world now associate Michael Jordan with the "Air Jordan" trademark copyrighted by Nike. They frequently associate the Olympics with Coca-Cola. In the U.S., the crowning Olympic achievement is to have your image on a cereal box. Children now wear expensive shoes and clothing with official logos and other sport images on them. Companies whose profits depend on the sales of alcohol, tobacco, fast food, and candy are eager to have their products associated with the healthy image of athletes and sports; this enables them to respond to those who would challenge the wholesomeness of their products. After all, if beer, cigarettes, beef burgers, and candy bars bring us the sports we love, how can they be so bad for our health?

As we enter the twenty-first century, we are in an era of the transnational corporation. Of the one hundred largest economies in the world, one-half are corporations, not nations (Anderson and Cavanagh, 1996). Mitsubishi, Mitsui, General Motors, and Ford Motor Company each have economies greater than those of over 80 percent of the nations around the world. The two hundred largest corporations in the world control nearly 30 percent of the economic activity around the globe. The decisions made by executives in these corporations influence the economies of entire nations and even regions of the world: they affect which people have jobs, what they do in those jobs, how much they make, what the working conditions are, what products will be available for purchase, and how much they will cost.

When these corporations enter the world of sports, they are able to negotiate deals that promote their interests and increase their power in the realm of transnational relations. At this point, their power is largely unchecked, because they operate outside the laws of any single nation. In the past, capitalist expansion was at least partly regulated, and its negative consequences were partly softened by nation-states. But now that corporate capitalism operates on a transnational basis, somewhat outside the control of nation-states, there are few formal mechanisms through which it can be regulated. As these corporations and the multibillionaires who own or control them continue to do business, they need to create global images of themselves as positive cultural, political, and economic forces.

This is the reason corporations pay billions of dollars every year to sponsor sports. Why did Coca-Cola spend nearly $500 million in connection with the 1996 Olympic Games in Atlanta, and why does the company plan to do the same in Sydney in 2000? Like other transnational corporations, Coca-Cola has an interest in creating the widespread belief that enjoyment and pleasure in people's everyday lives depends on the corporation and its products. When this belief is internalized, it becomes what we might call an *ideological outpost* in the minds of people around the world.* Corporate executives realize that they can use such outposts to defuse opposition or resistance to corporate policies, and as points through which they can deliver a wide range of ideological messages about what is and should be happening in the world. And sport seems to be an avenue through which corporations can establish these outposts in people's minds. For example, when a Coca-Cola executive gave a presentation to IOC officials before the opening of the 1996

Games, he assumed that after nearly eighty years of sponsoring the Olympics, Coca-Cola had established outposts in the minds of these officials, and that he could use these outposts to deliver messages about Coca-Cola effectively. So he told the officials the following:

> Just as sponsors have the responsibility to preserve the integrity of the sport, enhance its image, help grow its prestige and its attendance, so too, do you [in sports] have responsibility and accountability to the sponsor (in Reid, 1996).

Of course, in the face of millions of sponsorship dollars, these officials were not likely to oppose the interests of Coca-Cola, or to resist the notion that they were responsible for promoting Coke's interests around the world and would be held accountable for doing so.

Outposts in action: Beer and football. In an analysis of the growth of American football in England, British sociologist Joe Maguire (1990) has provided a classic example of the way transnational corporations and sport organizations often team up to promote their mutual interests in global capitalist expansion. During the 1980s, the executives at Anheuser Busch, the company that makes Budweiser beer, worked with the NFL to introduce American football to England, because they thought the association between Budweiser and football would improve the beer's image with British men. The link between beer drinking and masculinity is strong in England, and many British men learn to define a dark, heavy, barrel beer ("bitter") as more consistent with a strong, masculine image than a light, carbonated, foamy beer ("lager"). Because lager beers such as Budweiser were perceived as weak—similar to soft drinks—they were not the beers of choice among British men. Of course, their choices also were influenced by the relative quality of the beers and taste preferences among British beer drinkers.

At any rate, company executives knew they had to shed their product's image as a weak beer if they were to capture any of the beer market in England, or in most of Europe for that matter.

---

*This metaphor is taken from Sally Kempton (1995), who said, "It is difficult to fight an enemy with outposts in your head."

And what better way to shake the image of a weak, "unmanly" beer than to connect Budweiser with a sport emphasizing toughness, the use of force, physical domination, playing with pain, throwing "bombs," "punishing the opposition," and carrying "injured warriors off the field"? The executives hoped that when British men saw a high-profile football warrior in full gear praising Budweiser in commercials, at least some of them would begin to believe that they could drink Budweiser without compromising their masculine identities.

The combined financial interests of Anheuser Busch, the NFL, and a major private television company in England spurred the introduction of American football in England during the early 1980s. In the decade that followed, American football, sponsored by Budweiser, was televised weekly in England, and Budweiser helped fund the formation of the "Budweiser League," initially consisting of 105 football teams, all trying to reach the postseason "Budweiser Bowl." In 1986 Anheuser Busch teamed up with TWA and American Express to sponsor the first "American Bowl," in which two NFL teams played an exhibition game in England; these games continued in the 1990s. Since the mid-1980s, the sponsorship of American football in England has become increasingly complicated (Maguire, 1990), but in the late 1990s, Budweiser remained a central sponsor of football television coverage and of a league of American football teams across England. Young men from middle-class backgrounds, especially those in colleges and universities, have become more interested in the American game. As football has become more trendy, more Budweiser has been sold in England, and young men are more likely to see lager as an appropriate beer for men to drink, especially when they watch football.

The Budweiser experience is not unique. Various sporting goods companies long have used similar strategies to promote products around the world. Internationally known golfers endorsed golf clubs long before golf became a commercialized television sport. Nike was very

aware that if Michael Jordan played in the 1992 Summer Olympic Games and caught the world's attention, its market for sport shoes and clothing could expand dramatically. After all, there are over 2.4 billion feet in China, and those running Nike would like to see Air Jordans or one of its other shoe brands on every one of them.

We might be tempted to predict that in the future we could see sport events in which Nike athletes, playing in Nike shoes and clothing, using Nike equipment in a Nike facility, competing with one another in events covered by Nike announcers working for the Nike sport television network. But one of the things that keeps this from happening on a regular basis is corporate executives' knowledge that they can make more money if cities build stadiums and provide other public subsidies for teams and events; why pay for it yourself when you can convince the taxpayers to pay for it? We will discuss this later in the chapter.

In summary, commercial sports grow and prosper best in urban, industrial societies with relatively efficient transportation and communications systems combined with a standard of living that allows people the time and money to play and watch sports. Class relations usually are involved in the process through which sports become commercialized. Spectator interest in sports is connected with ideologies emphasizing efficiency and hard work, heavily promoted and popular youth sport programs, and media coverage that introduces people to the rules of sports and the athletes who play them. Sport organizations and powerful transnational corporations have fostered the global expansion of certain commercial sports with economic payoffs. This expansion will continue into the foreseeable future, and it will be carefully discussed and analyzed in the sociology of sport as it occurs.

COMMERCIALIZATION AND CHANGES IN SPORTS

What happens to sports when they become commercialized and dependent on revenues? Do they change, and if so, in what ways?

We know that whenever a sport is converted into commercial entertainment, its success depends on spectator appeal. Although spectators have a variety of motives underlying their attachment to sports, their interest in sport events usually is related to a combination of three factors:

- the uncertainty of an event's outcome ("Is it going to be a close contest?")
- the risk or financial rewards associated with participating in an event ("How much is at stake in the contest?"; "How much money is involved, or pride, ego, and physical well-being?")
- the anticipated display of excellence, heroics, or dramatic display by the athletes ("Who is playing, and can I expect to be entertained by their competence or their dramatic personal displays?"; "Are the Bulls playing Seattle, how many points will Jordan get, and what color is Rodman's hair?")

In other words, when spectators say they have seen a "good game" or an "exciting contest," they usually are talking about one in which (a) the outcome was in doubt until the last minutes or seconds, (b) the stakes were so high that athletes were totally committed to and engrossed in the action, or (c) there were a number of excellent, heroic, or dramatic performances. Games or matches that contain all three of these factors are remembered and discussed for a long time.

If spectators are attracted by uncertainty, high stakes, and excellent/heroic/dramatic performances, commercial sports are likely to emphasize these things to attract large audiences. To understand the changes associated with commercialization, we must look at three aspects of sports:

1. the structure and goals of sports
2. the orientations of athletes, coaches, and sponsors
3. the organizations through which sports are controlled

Structure and Goals

Commercialization has had an impact on the structures and goals of most newly developed sports, but it has not produced dramatic changes in most long-time, established sports. In the case of new sports developed for commercial purposes, it is clear that rules have been designed to promote on-the-field action that a targeted audience will see as entertaining. Entertainment is *not* the only issue considered in connection with the structure and goals of these sports, but it is a primary issue. This is apparent in the case of sports such as indoor soccer, arena football, beach volleyball, roller hockey, and certain forms of "extreme games" as presented by ESPN2 on recent "X Games" telecasts. For example, the rules in the X Games were designed to attract the attention of younger viewers who had less interest in football and tennis than in skateboarding, in-line skating, and bicycle jumping; rules emphasized dangerous and spectacular moves as well as the use of technical equipment manufactured by program sponsors.

Established sports have undergone rule changes to make action more exciting and understandable for spectators, but the changes have not altered the basic designs and rule structures of the games themselves. For example, the commercialization of the Olympic Games has led to minor rule changes in certain events, but the basic structure of the typical event has remained much as it was before the days of corporate endorsements and the sale of television rights. Of course, we also must note that some events with little spectator appeal have been dropped from the Olympics, and new sports have been added to attract new viewers, especially viewers from wealthy countries where people have money to spend on sponsors' products. Another example is American football, in which rules have been changed to protect quarterbacks, encourage the use of passes in offensive strategy, discourage strategies that emphasize field goals over touchdowns, and give teams an extra time out in connection with a two-minute warning at the end of each half of play.

These changes have increased entertaining action and provided more time for commercial breaks in the games; however, the basic structure and goals of football have changed little.

Rule development and rule changes associated with commercialization usually are intended to do a combination of five things: (1) speed up the action in an event so that fans won't get bored, (2) increase scoring to generate more excitement, (3) balance competition so that events will have uncertain outcomes, (4) maximize the dramatic moments in the competition, and (5) provide commercial breaks in the action so that sponsors can advertise products (this is most common in North America, where commercial sponsorship on television is more prevalent than it is in other countries).

A review of rule changes in many sports shows the importance of these five factors. For example, the designated hitter position in the American League was added to increase scoring opportunities and heighten the dramatic action in major-league baseball. Soccer rules have been changed to prevent matches from ending in ties. Tennis scoring has been changed to meet the time requirements of television schedules. Golf tournaments now involve total stroke counts rather than match play, so that big-name players will not be eliminated in the early rounds of televised events. Free throws have been minimized in basketball to speed up action. Sudden-death overtime periods have been added to many sports so that spectators can determine the winner easily, without having to assess the overall quality of play in an event.

Even though many of these changes have been prompted by concerns for generating revenues, they have not altered the basic structures and goals of most established sports. Furthermore, the ways in which new sports are developed and established sports are changed also reflect the concerns and interests of the players themselves. After all, players often have more fun when there is more action, more scoring, and a closer contest, and many players become accustomed to

commercial breaks and TV time outs—in fact, coaches and players anticipate TV time outs and use them in their overall game strategies!

Because sports are social constructions, they change in connection with social relationships and with shifts in social conditions and power relations in the society as a whole. Some people regard the structures and goals of sports as sacred and unchangeable, but they overlook the fact that *people* established the rules for all sports, and the orientations of those people were tied to their social relationships and the cultural conditions prevalent at the time the rules were made. Of course, it is important to acknowledge that the changes that are being made at this point in history are heavily influenced by economic relations and conditions.

People may voice complaints about changes in the structure and goals of sports when they attend events that have been organized intentionally as *total entertainment experiences*, complete with loud rock and rap music, video displays designed to provide entertainment having little to do with sports, paid cheerleaders and mascots who direct crowd behavior, fireworks displays, and on-site announcers who manage spectator emotions with their own excited verbal descriptions of and responses to the action. As dedicated, long-time sports fans sit through this "total entertainment experience" in which others do the wave, watch cartoon characters on the video display, and respond to the antics of paid mascots dressed in Disney-type costumes, they complain that the game has changed. But on the field of play, the game probably has stayed much the same as it always was; the big changes are in the context surrounding the game.

Orientations of Players, Coaches, and Sponsors

When sports are commercialized, they usually come to be characterized by a "promotional culture" (Gruneau and Whitson, 1993). Like other entertainment industries, that of commercial sports is geared to selling public performances

Commercial sports are organized increasingly to be total entertainment experiences. At Sky Sox Stadium in Colorado Springs, minor-league baseball fans can even watch the game from hot tubs in right field. Fans in the U.S. have learned to expect more than just a game when they attend sport events. (Casey B. Gibson, Colorado Springs Sky Sox)

and products associated with those performances. Sports are promoted through marketing hype based on myths and images created around players and team identities. In addition to being highly skilled players of their sports, athletes become entertainers; some even become celebrities. In connection with the promotional culture of commercial sports, the orientations of sport participants tend to emphasize heroic actions in addition to aesthetic actions. This occurs in the following way:

When sports become entertainment, it's necessary to attract a mass audience to buy tickets or watch events on television. Attracting and entertaining a *mass* audience is not easy, because this audience is made up of many people who don't have technical knowledge about the complex athletic skills and strategies used by players and coaches. Without this technical knowledge, people are easily impressed by things extrinsic to the game or match itself; they are easily taken in by hype. During the event itself, they often focus on things they can easily understand. They enjoy situations in which players take risks and face clear physical danger; they are attracted to players who are masters of dramatic expression or willing to go beyond their normal physical limits to the point of endangering their own safety and well-being; and they like to see players dedicated to teams and committed to victory regardless of personal cost.

For example, when people lack technical knowledge about football, they are more likely to be entertained by a running back's end-zone dance after a touchdown than by the lineman's block that enabled the running back to score the touchdown. Those who lack technical knowledge about basketball are more likely to talk about a single slam dunk than about the well-coordinated defense that enabled a team to win a game. Those who know little about the technical aspects of ice skating are more entertained by triple and quadruple jumps than by routines carefully choreographed and practiced until they are smooth and flawless. Without dangerous jumps, naive spectators get bored.

Spectators without technical knowledge about the sports they watch like athletes who project exciting or controversial personas, and they often rate performances in terms of dramatic expression leading to dramatic results. They are impressed by style as well as skills. They are thrilled by long touchdown passes, not 9-minute touchdown drives made up of 3- to 4-yard runs. They call for home runs, not sacrifice flies. They are more impressed by athletes who collapse as they surpass physical limits than by athletes who know their limits so well they can play for years without going beyond them.

Sports are not the only activities affected by commercialization in this way. For example, rock music has been developed as a form of mass entertainment so that *style* (that is, the ability to project a distinct and dramatic persona) often supersedes musical ability as a basis for popularity and commercial success. Some popular rock stars are great musicians, others are average, and some are lousy. When audiences lack technical knowledge about music, significant differences in musical ability can be buried under large amounts of style. It is style that sells; musical ability may be important, but it will not take a person to the top of the promotional culture of the rock music world.

Basketball player Dennis Rodman, has recognized the importance of style in commercial sports. In fact, he has worked hard to develop a style and display an image that entertains people apart from his ability to play basketball. Rodman refers to his style, including his demeanor, his tattoos, and his hair color, as part of his persona as an entertainer. He explains in the following words:

> I'm not finished crafting this art form, either. . . . It's not just the statistics that are important, it's *the flair* and *the style*. The next step for me is to expand the style. . . . That's why I relate to *Pearl Jam* so much. . . . The connection between me as a basketball player and them as a band comes from the *emotion* we both show when we perform. It's easy to show emotion, but the key is to get other people to feel it. . . . I might play the same game every night, but it's always a different performance (Rodman, 1996).

After observing many athletes in all the major sports in the U.S., commentator Bob Costas has noted that Rodman is not alone in his approach:

> The players have all caught on to what the cameras want. They know what postures and noises will get them on air. [NBA players] know that cameras are under the basket. So a guy dunks the ball, looks right at the camera and screams. . . . There is too much emphasis on the power and the assertion of power for its own sake. I'm tired of this "In Your Face" thing (in Pluto, 1995).

Costas knows that the players look at things differently when they are entertainers; in fact, after they do something entertaining, they even look at the replay screens from the field of play to view their actions as spectators.

Thus, when a sport comes to depend on the entertainment of mass audiences, those who play and coach often revise their ideas about what is important in athletic performances. The danger of movement becomes important in addition to the beauty of movement; style and dramatic expression become important in addition to fundamental skills; pushing beyond limits becomes important in addition to exploring limits; and being committed to victory for the team and sponsor becomes important in addition to remaining an active participant. Not everyone goes as far as Dennis Rodman in the emphasis on heroic actions, but clearly, when sports become

NEED TO ENTERTAIN PEOPLE WHO DON'T HAVE TECHNICAL KNOWLEDGE ABOUT A SPORT

Low   High

⟶   ⟶   ⟶   ⟶   ⟶   ⟶   ⟶   ⟶   ⟶   ⟶

Emphasis is on "aesthetic orientations"	⟶	Emphasis is on "heroic orientations"
• Beauty and pleasure of movement	⟶	• Danger and excitement of movement
• Ability and mastery of technical skills	⟶	• "Style" and mastery of dramatic expression
• Willingness to explore limits	⟶	• Willingness to go beyond limits
• Commitment to staying active and involved as a participant	⟶	• Commitment to victory and the success of the team/sponsor

FIGURE 11-1   How orientations change when sports become a form of mass entertainment.

commercialized, most people associated with them develop *heroic orientations* in addition to *aesthetic orientations*.

Figure 11-1 explains these terms and outlines how athletes, coaches, and others associated with a sport might change the way they assess on-the-field performances as a sport becomes increasingly commercialized. It shows that when there is a need to entertain people who don't have technical knowledge about a sport, orientations change. In fact, games or matches even may be referred to as "showtime," and athletes may describe themselves as entertainers. This does *not* mean that aesthetic orientations cease to be important or that people are no longer impressed by beauty and skills in sports, but it does mean that heroic orientations enter into the mix of what constitutes a sport performance. The heroic is what attracts those spectators who may not know enough to appreciate the strategic and technical aspects of a game or match.

As the need or desire to please naive audiences becomes greater, so does the emphasis on heroic orientations. This is the reason television commentators for U.S. football games continually talk about danger, injuries, playing with pain, and courage. During the 1996–97 season, the NFL marketed its games with visual images of bone-crunching hits followed by the slogan, "Feel the Power"; the advertisers knew that risky displays of power were easier to under-

stand than the technical complexities of a well-executed play.

Some athletes, however, realize the dangers associated with heroic orientations and try to limit the emphasis on heroic actions in their sports. For example, some former figure skaters have called for restrictions on the number of triple jumps that can be included in skating programs. These skaters are worried that the commercial success of their sport is coming to rely on the danger of movement rather than the beauty of movement. Other skaters, however, seem to be willing to adopt heroic orientations in an effort to please audiences and meet the expectations of many athlete-peers in skating. The dynamics of this process are complex. We noted this in chapter 6, in our discussion of the way athletes come to use the norms of the sport ethic to evaluate themselves and others in their sports.

Another indicator of the emphasis on heroic orientations and actions in commercialized sports appeared during the 1996 Olympics. As the games drew to a close, a number of corporate sponsors, agents, and advertising executives were asked by *USA Today* reporters to rate highly visible Olympic athletes on the *USA Today's* Olympic Advertising Index (7 August 1996: 3B). Athletes were rated on four 10-point scales: (1) Pizazz Factor (flair, warmth, and charm), (2) On-Camera Appeal (poise, ability to project a positive and intelligent image), (3) Athletic

Ability (medals won, records set), and (4) Rodman Potential (a negative scale related to marketing risk factors, unpredictability).

Scores on the four scales provided new ways of assessing athletes within the promotional culture of sports. These scores are used for endorsement purposes, but might they not also be used to evaluate the revenue-generating potential of athletes as they are recruited and signed to contracts? Use of the scores in this way would be a logical extension of the commercial logic of today's spectator sports.

Sport Organizations

Commercialization also leads to changes in the organizations that control sports. When sports begin to depend on the revenues they can generate, the control of sport organizations usually shifts farther and farther away from the players. In fact, the players often lose effective control over the conditions of their own sport participation. These conditions come under the control of general managers, team owners, corporate sponsors, advertisers, media personnel, marketing and publicity staff, professional management staff, accountants, and agents (Gaterson, 1994).

The organizations that control commercial sports are usually complex, since they are intended to coordinate the interests of all these people, but their primary goal is to maximize revenues. This means that organizational decisions generally reflect the combined economic interests of many people having no direct personal connection with a sport or the athletes involved. The power to affect these decisions is grounded in a variety of resources, many of which are not even connected with sports. Therefore, athletes in many commercial sports find themselves cut out of decision-making processes, even when the decisions affect their health and well-being, as well as the rewards they receive for playing.

As decision making in sport organizations moves farther away from athletes, there is a tendency to hire employees, develop policies, and negotiate deals that give a low priority to the interests of athletes. These organizational changes

have important implications for what happens in sports. They also make it necessary for athletes to seek new tactics for promoting their own interests, financial and otherwise.

As corporate interests come to dominate sports, athletes often defer to the policy recommendations of team owners, agents, advertising executives, media people, and corporate sponsors. This was vividly illustrated by Chicago Bulls player Scottie Pippen, who was asked why he was playing in the Olympics despite a bad ankle that would interfere with his ability to play for the Chicago Bulls if he didn't give it rest. Pippen said, "I made a commitment to a lot of companies, and I'm sticking with it." After he realized he had spoken too truthfully, he added, "But endorsements aren't the focal point. To play in an Olympics in my own country is something I've always wanted to do" (*The Denver Post*, 1996). But despite his quick cover-up, it was clear that Pippen's interests as an athlete took a back seat to the interests of his corporate sponsors. He knew he was dependent on corporations, and he answered to them more than to anyone or anything else.

Commercialization brings rewards to athletes lucky enough to sign contracts, but it further removes the control of the conditions of sport participation from the athletes. Corporations now are defining what sports are all about. This is not especially new in the U.S., where people gradually have come to associate their enjoyment of sports as much with corporate names as with the names of athletes. But this shift is occurring more and more in other countries, where corporate interests promote the use of the U.S. commercial model for their sports, or where transnational corporations take the corporate model wherever they think money or publicity is to be gained through the ownership and sponsoring of sports.

OWNERS, SPONSORS, AND PROMOTERS IN COMMERCIAL SPORTS

Professional Sports in North America

Professional sports in North America are privately owned. The owners of most teams and franchises at all levels of professional sports, from the smallest minor-league teams to the top franchises in the NFL, the NBA, the NHL, and MLB, are individuals or small partnerships. A growing number of the top franchises are owned by large corporations. Similarly, sponsors and event promoters range from individuals and small businesses to large transnational corporations.

Most people who own the hundreds of minor-league teams around North America do not make much money. In fact, most are happy to break even and avoid the losses that are commonplace at this level of professional sports ownership. Also, many teams, leagues, and events have been financial disasters over the past thirty-five years. Four football leagues, a hockey league, a soccer league, a volleyball league, two men's and three women's basketball leagues, a team tennis league, and a number of basketball and soccer teams have all gone out of business, leaving many owners, sponsors, and promoters in debt. This list covers only the United States, and doesn't include all those who have lost money on tournaments and special events.

Ownership of the top professional franchises in North America is different from ownership at other levels of professional sports. Franchise values range from $34 million to $272 million (Atre et al., 1996). Owners are large corporations, partnerships of wealthy individuals, or very wealthy individuals who have millions and even billions of dollars in personal assets. Leagues are organized as monopolies, teams usually play in publicly subsidized facilities, owners make good to excellent returns on their investments, and support from media companies and corporate sponsors almost guarantees continued financial success at this level of ownership.

Similarly, those large corporations that sponsor particular events, from major golf and tennis tournaments to NASCAR and Grand Prix races, know the costs and benefits associated with the events. Their association with top events not only provides them advertising platforms, but also connects them with clearly identified categories of consumers. The sponsorship of events enables large television companies to control their own programming. It enables entertainment companies to control multiple aspects of the entertainment marketplace and link them together in mutually supporting ways—from Disneyland to TV networks to cable channels to the Anaheim Mighty Ducks to nationwide promotions at fast-food restaurants selling figures of sport celebrities with kids' meals. Sport sponsorship enables companies that sell tobacco, alcohol, and various forms of food with questionable nutritional value to link their products and logos to popular activities. Because people associate sports with physical performance and strong bodies instead of cancer, heart disease, obesity, and other forms of poor health, these companies are eager to be sponsors.

Investments in sports and sport events are motivated by many factors. In many cases, investors are sport fans with money; they invest to satisfy lifelong fantasies, build their egos, or vicariously experience the achievements of athletes. Sport ownership and sponsorship gains them more prestige than other business ventures. Sometimes it makes them instant celebrities in their cities; they are famous all over town, from the mayor's office and the Chamber of Commerce to neighborhood bars and local elementary schools. Commercial sports enable these wealthy people to combine business and power seeking with fun.

However, those who invest in sports seldom get so carried away with fun and fantasy that they forget business or what it takes to promote capitalist expansion. They do not enjoy losing money or sharing power. They may look at their athletes as heroes and may even treat them as their children, but they want to control their athletes for the purpose of securing returns on their investments. They may be civic boosters and supporters of public projects, but they see the public good in terms that emphasize capitalist expansion as it furthers their business interests

(Schimmel et al., 1993). When it comes to the business of sports, those who own sport teams and sponsor sport events focus primarily on generating revenues and establishing a firm basis for continued financial success. They may not agree with fellow owners and sponsors on all issues, but they do agree on the need to protect their investments and maximize profits.

TEAM OWNERS AND SPORT LEAGUES AS MONOPOLIES The tendency to think alike has been especially strong among the team owners in the major North American sport leagues: the NBA, the NFL, the NHL, and MLB. In fact, unity among these owners has led to the formation of some of the most effective monopolies in the history of North American business. Even though each sport franchise in these leagues is a separate business, the franchise owners in each sport have come together to form organizations representing their collective interests. They traditionally have used these organizations to limit the extent to which teams compete against each other for players, fans, media revenues, and sales of licensed merchandise; they also have used them to eliminate competition from those who might try to form other teams and leagues in their sports.

For example, each league (the NBA, the NFL, the NHL, and MLB) has developed a system to force new players entering the sport to negotiate contracts only with the specific teams that have drafted them; this enables owners to sign new players to contracts without bidding against other teams that might be willing to pay the players more money. Owners also have agreed to prevent new teams from being added to their leagues without their collective permission; when permission is given, the new team (franchise) owner is charged a heavy entry fee to become a part of the league. Table 11–1 lists franchise fees new teams have paid to become a part of these leagues since the early 1960s. Joining the NFL costs new owners $140 million; joining MLB most recently cost the new Phoenix and Tampa Bay teams an estimated $130 million

each. These are just entry fees; they do not include any other start-up expenses, player salaries, or operating costs, which in baseball amounted to approximately $60 million per year as of 1996; nor do these fees include "infringement payments" to existing teams sharing the same TV markets, or the forfeiture of TV revenues during the first year of operation (about a $10 million loss). A new owner can locate only in a city approved by current owners, and existing owners cannot move their teams to other cities unless all owners collectively approve of the moves.

These policies do two things: (1) they prevent new teams from competing with established teams for players, spectator interest, gate receipts, and local broadcasting rights, and (2) they regulate the competition between existing owners. Team owners in each league never allow changes that could threaten their collective interest, their control over the sport, or their ability to generate revenues.

The owners in each sport league also have agreed to sell the broadcasting rights to their games as a group, and then equally share the revenues from national media contracts. This limits the number of games available to the viewing public, and it even prevents some people from seeing their home teams play in the stadiums built by public money! But it enables team owners to make huge sums of money in their media contracts while they force people to buy tickets to games at the same time. Amazingly, the U.S. Congress has approved this monopolistic method of doing business. In fact, it even passed an amendment to the U.S. Code stating that "antitrust laws . . . shall not apply to . . . [the] organized professional team sports of football, baseball, basketball, or hockey." This rule not only has guaranteed revenues for team owners in these professional sports, but also has given them the power to influence television companies and the commentators working for those companies; in fact, television commentators provide uncritical cheerleading for the sports their companies pay to broadcast.

Table 11–1   Increasing franchise fees for selected new teams in the NFL, the NBA, NHL, and MLB, 1960s through 1990s

League	Year	Team	Franchise Fee in millions	Franchise Value in millions, 1996
NFL	1960	Dallas Cowboys	$0.60	$320
	1961	Minnesota Vikings	$1.00	$186
	1966	Miami Dolphins	$7.50	$242
	1968	Cincinnati Bengals	$7.50	$188
	1976	Tampa Bay Buccaneers	$16.00	$187
	1976	Seattle Seahawks	$16.00	$171
	1995	Carolina Panthers	$140.00	$240*
	1995	Jacksonville Jaguars	$140.00	$239*
NBA	1966	Chicago Bulls	$1.25	$214
	1967	Seattle Supersonics	$1.75	$137
	1968	Phoenix Suns	$2.00	$220
	1970	Cleveland Cavaliers	$3.70	$180
	1974	New Orleans Jazz	$6.15	$163[†]
	1980	Dallas Mavericks	$12.00	$104
	1988	Miami Heat	$32.50	$118
	1988	Orlando Magic	$32.50	$156
	1995	Toronto Raptors	$125.00	$138
	1995	Vancouver Grizzlies	$125.00	$127*
NHL	1967	Los Angeles Kings	$2.00	$83
	1967	Pittsburgh Penguins	$2.00	$96
	1970	Vancouver Canucks	$6.00	$91
	1972	New York Islanders	$6.00	$74
	1979	Edmonton Oilers	$6.00	$52
		Hartford Whalers	$6.00	$48
	1991	San Jose Sharks	$50.00	$104
	1992	Ottawa Senators	$50.00	$67
	1993	Anaheim Mighty Ducks	$50.00	$104
	1993	Florida Panthers	$50.00	$67
MLB	1961	Los Angeles Dodgers	$2.10	$178
	1962	New York Mets	$1.80	$144
	1969	Kansas City Royals	$5.50	$88
	1969	Montreal Expos	$12.50	$77
	1977	Toronto Blue Jays	$7.00	$155
	1977	Seattle Mariners	$6.25	$107
	1993	Florida Marlins	$95.00	$123
	1993	Colorado Rockies	$95.00	$184
	1998	Phoenix	$133.00[§]	[‡]
	1998	Tampa Bay	$130.00[§]	[‡]

Sources: USA Today, 21 October 1994; *Financial World*, 17 June 1997.
*Based on revenues for only one year.
[†]Now the Utah Jazz.
[‡]Not available in 1997.
[§]Estimated.

Furthermore, team owners have combined their monopolistic media tactics with exclusive-use clauses in their contracts with the stadiums or arenas they use. This has been an effective tool for preventing other leagues from forming and competing for spectator interest. Other leagues in each sport have been driven out of business because existing owners have been allowed to operate as cartels. In fact, we can expect owners in each league to devise strategies for extending their monopolies to other countries. Global sport league monopolies will exist in the future.

Exempting existing professional sport leagues from antitrust laws in the United States has done much to drive up the value of franchises. Being a part of a legal monopoly has enabled many team owners to make massive sums of money when they have sold their teams. In the mid-1960s, NFL teams were bought and sold for about $10 million; in the mid-1990s, the average sale price was about $175 million. That's a $165 million capital gain over thirty years on an original investment of $10 million. This rate of return is far greater than the return in the stock market on the same investment (Quirk and Fort, 1992). But this is what a monopoly does: it limits the supply of franchises and drives up the value of existing franchises. Of course, it has not eliminated complaints from team owners, who regularly say they must raise ticket prices because they are not making enough money. Monopolies also foster greed.

Even though I have grouped the NBA, the NFL, the NHL, and MLB together in this section, I must point out that these leagues differ from one another in many important respects. These differences are complicated, and they regularly change, as each league encounters new and unique challenges and opportunities. For example, contracts with networks and major cable television companies vary from one league to another. The NHL has been the least successful in negotiating big-money contracts, whereas the NBA and the NFL have been the most successful in recent years. Each league also has unique internal agreements regulating how teams can

negotiate the sale of *local* broadcasting rights to their games. The NFL does not allow teams to sign independent television contracts for local broadcasts of their games, but MLB does allow teams to negotiate the sale of local broadcast rights—although a labor agreement signed in 1996 (after four years of conflict and negotiation!) set up a system by which small-market teams could share the revenues earned by big-market teams.

The biggest differences between the NBA, the NFL, the NHL, and MLB are related to their contractual agreements with players' associations in each league. Although each league traditionally has tried to give athletes as few rights as possible, athletes have fought for over thirty years to gain control over important parts of their careers and increase their salaries in the process. We will discuss this later in the chapter.

TEAM OWNERS AND FORMS OF PUBLIC ASSISTANCE The belief that cities must have professional sport teams and must provide big sport events in order to be "world class" has led to many forms of public support for sport owners and sport organizations (Gruneau and Whitson, 1993). The most common form of support is the use of public funds to construct and maintain arenas and stadiums. As we noted in chapter 10, this type of "stadium socialism" has enabled a few wealthy individuals to use public money for their personal gain.

Owners have justified stadium subsidies and other forms of public support for professional sport teams using five major arguments (Lavoie, forthcoming):

1. A stadium and a pro team create jobs; those who hold the jobs spend money in the city and pay taxes in the process.
2. Stadium construction infuses money into the local economy; this money is spent over and over again as it circulates through the city; and the sales of construction materials generate tax revenues.
3. The team will attract other businesses to the city, and also bring visitors from outside the area who will spend money in the city.

What defines a "world-class city"? Powerful local businesspeople and their political allies often believe that sports and sports facilities are necessary to stimulate the economy and attract people to their cities. On what basis do they make such claims? Who is privileged by the policies based on these claims? These questions should be asked in all cities. (Jay Coakley)

4. The team will attract regional and national media attention that will boost the tourist industry, enable local firms to sell their products outside the city, and contribute to overall regional economic development.
5. The team will create positive psychic and social benefits, making people feel better about themselves as individuals and better about the city as a whole; pride and social solidarity will be increased in connection with the team's identity.

These arguments sound good, and they often are supported by studies commissioned by team owners and others who want public money to be used to subsidize teams. But dozens of studies done by *independent* economists, both liberal and conservative, do *not* support these

arguments.* These studies highlight the following issues:

1. Teams and stadiums do create jobs—but apart from the high-paying jobs held by players, stadium jobs are low paying and seasonal. Football stadiums are used for fewer than fifteen game days per year, and the ushers, parking lot attendants, ticket agents, and concessions workers don't make full-time living wages. The vast majority of players' salaries are not spent in the cities where they play; in fact, players may not even live in those cities.
2. Construction materials often are brought in from other locations, as are specialized construction workers. The companies that design and build stadiums are seldom local, and they spend their consulting dollars in other cities.
3. Stadiums do attract other businesses, but these are often restaurant and entertainment franchises with headquarters in other cities. To make matters worse, these franchised businesses often drive longtime local operations out of business. Spectators do come from out of town, but the vast majority of these people live close enough that they do not spend the night in connection with attendance at a game, and they spend a limited amount of money on food and other forms of entertainment outside the stadium.
4. Stadiums and the teams that use them do generate public relations for the city and for tourism, but tourists who visit the city for other reasons may stay away when big sport events are in town or when games are scheduled. Regional economic development is limited, because local people who spend money

---

*A selection of these studies and overviews includes the following: Baade and Dye, 1988, 1990; Brady and Howlett, 1996; Coclough et al., 1994; Euchner, 1993; Gouguet and Nys, 1993; Johnson, 1993; Lavoie, forthcoming; Osterland, 1995; Passmore et al., 1996; Quirk and Fort, 1992; Sage, 1993b, 1996b; Schimmel et al., 1993; Scully, 1989, 1995; Whitson and Macintosh, 1993, 1996.

at and around the stadium have fewer dollars to spend in their own areas in the city. An inner-city stadium does great things for the area around the stadium, but it often hurts other businesses, because discretionary money is limited in any population: spending over $3,000 on a pair of season tickets to NBA games often means that one will spend less money on going out to dinner and to shows.

5. A pro sport teams may make some people feel better, but the macho orientations that accompany the games of most men's pro teams actually may make some people feel uncomfortable. Also, when teams have losing records or lose big games, there is evidence that fans do not feel better about their lives.

Despite these counterarguments, most economists can show that there are positive benefits whenever a city spends $100 million to $200 million on a public project. But the question is whether the public good might be better served if the money were spent on something other than a stadium used by wealthy owners and players to further increase their already sizable assets. For example, many people in Baltimore, Maryland complained in the mid-1990s when over $270 million of public money was spent to subsidize the wealthy owners of two NFL teams (the Ravens and the Redskins); they said these expenditures made no public policy sense when schools in Baltimore were rationing toilet paper and chalk and students were wearing coats to class because schools could not pay their heating bills. Art Modell, who had moved his NFL franchise from Cleveland to Baltimore because Maryland gave him the use of a $200 million stadium (and all its revenue-generating potential), responded to the critics by saying the following:

> I feel for the schools. I feel for welfare. But look at the positive effects of pro football on a community, the emotional investment of people at large. You can't equate that with fixing up the schools (in Brady, 1996).

"I hope the city council takes pity on me. I just can't afford the rent on the new stadium built with taxpayers' money. Don't they realize I'm doing them a favor by keeping my team here?"

Opposition to building stadiums with public money is often difficult to mount because social activists who might lead the opposition must deal full-time with current problems related to drugs, education, homelessness, and the overall shortage of social services. They cannot take leave from these urgent tasks to lobby full-time against the use of public money to benefit millionaire team owners (Euchner, 1993).

Meanwhile, the team owners enlist the services of large architectural firms that provide them with lobbyists, political advisors, and public relations people who make sure the local media cover the campaign for a new stadium from a positive angle. The lobbyists focus on gaining support from politicians and members of committees formed to study the feasibility of building a stadium. The advisors work with owners to make sure votes on bond issues are held in political off-years so that voter turnout will be light. And the public relations people devise ads that subtly threaten that teams will move unless public money is used in their interest. This tactic of threatening to move teams unless subsidies are increased is becoming so common that it has a name. It is called **sportmail**—a form of blackmail used by sport team owners to coerce public support from cities (Purdy, 1988).

Once a stadium is built, franchises increase in value about 25 percent and team owners are in a powerful negotiating position to get what they want when it comes to using the stadium for their own benefit. Their success has been so complete that *Financial World* magazine noted that "virtually every stadium is a money pit for taxpayers by any normal measure of return on investment"(Osterland, 1995: 107). Of course, the final irony is that many taxpayers cannot afford to buy tickets to see games in the stadiums their money has built.

In addition to facility subsidies, team owners receive other forms of public support. For example, through 1993, the federal government allowed businesses to deduct 80 percent of the cost of game tickets as business expenses on their federal tax returns; since 1994, this has been a 50 percent deduction. This is the reason businesses buy about 75 percent of all season tickets sold by top sport teams, and even a higher percentage of luxury boxes and club seats. Companies not only save on taxes while their executives and clients use company tickets to attend games, but they also help teams sell out their seats. This in turn drives up ticket prices, even for those who are not deducting them as business expenses. Meanwhile, other wealthy people sit in luxury skyboxes sometimes built with public money. Of course, the skyboxes are rented, but the rent payments usually are deducted from corporate taxes as business expenses. This lowers tax revenues that could be used for needed public programs.

SOURCES OF INCOME FOR TEAM OWN-ERS The owners of top pro franchises make money from the following sources: (1) gate receipts, including club seats; (2) media revenues, including radio and national, local, cable, and pay-per-view TV; (3) stadium revenue, including leases on luxury suites and boxes, concessions,

the sale of stadium advertising and naming rights, and parking; and (4) licensing fees and merchandise sales. The amounts and proportions of each of these sources of revenue for the four major men's sport leagues are shown in table 11–2.

The main reason so many new stadiums have been built since the late 1980s is that owners now see venue revenues as an income category that they can increase without going into debt themselves. This is the reason a new stadium looks like a combination shopping mall and food court, with a playing field in the middle. Owners sell luxury suites to large corporations wanting to entertain executives and clients by watching competitive sports in prestigious, private-club settings; they cater high-priced food and drinks into the suites; they operate or lease in-stadium luxury restaurants, bars, and fast-food outlets; their stadium shops sell merchandise that may not be available at other shops in the city; and they may even attach hotels or night clubs to the stadium. Most new football stadiums contain from 100 to 250 luxury suites that lease for $60,000 to $125,000 per year. If each suite contains 16 seats, the average cost per seat for each game is about $700, not including catering costs.

The goal of owners is to capture as much of the entertainment dollar as they can inside the stadium itself, and to do it with taxpayer money so that they can avoid debt payments. They also want to sell as many surfaces as possible inside and around the stadium to corporations wanting to advertise; in fact, it is now possible to make $3 million or more per year by selling even the name of the stadium to a large corporation. Most of these new stadium revenues are not yet reflected in the 1996 data used in table 11–2.

The stadium now is considered to have so much revenue-generating potential that the value of a franchise enjoying a new stadium increases about 25 percent. This means that if a city builds a $200 million stadium for a sport team, and the franchise is worth $140 million, the franchise value will increase about $35 million when the stadium is completed. Of course,

TANK MᶜNAMARA®

by Jeff Millar & Bill Hinds

Vast amounts of public money are now being spent to build new stadiums that contain exclusive luxury seating areas. This is one way that public resources are being used to reproduce social class inequalities rather than maximizing the common good. Team owners have convinced people that their profits and the comforts of those who can afford luxury boxes are part of the common good.

Table 11–2   Revenue sources for franchises in the NFL, the NBA, the NHL, and MLB, 1996*

League	GATE RECEIPTS		MEDIA REVENUES		VENUE REVENUES		LICENSING AND MERCHANDISE SALES		Average Team Revenues, 1996	Average Franchise Value, 1996
	Amount	%	Amount	%	Amount	%	Amount	%		
NFL	22.6	38	43.0	55	7.6	10	4.5	5	$77.7	$205
NBA	23.3	41	21.2	37	7.5	13	5.4	6	$57.4	$148
NHL	25.6	60	6.3	15	8.0	19	2.4	15	$42.3	$90
MLB	25.7	39	25.2	38	12.6	19	2.5	3	$66.0	$134

*Source: Based on data from *Financial World* 166(6), 17 June 1997.

this increase will go directly into the pocket of the owners when they sell the franchise. In the meantime, the owners can borrow money against the new franchise value to expand their other business investments.

Of course, owners realize that many people may not feel comfortable with the idea of putting public money into the pockets of the wealthy, so they make sure that when their teams take the field or court or ice, announcers describe them as

"your" Buffalo Bills or Chicago Bulls or Detroit Red Wings or Seattle Mariners (Sage, 1996b). The owners are happy to have people feel as if the teams belong to them, as long as these people let the owners collect all the revenues.

Amateur Sports in North America

Amateur sports don't have owners, but they do have commercial sponsors and governing bodies that promote and sanction events and control athletes. Generally, the sponsors are large corporations that support amateur sports for advertising purposes. The governing bodies of amateur sports operate on a nonprofit basis, although they do use revenues from events to maintain their organizations and their power over amateur sports.

In most countries around the world, amateur sports are administered by centralized sport authorities working with the governing bodies of individual sports. Together, these groups attempt to exercise consistent control over events, athletes, and revenues. Sport Canada and the Canadian Olympic Association are examples of such centralized authorities; they develop policies that govern the various national sports organizations in Canada (Whitson and Macintosh, 1990). In the U.S., however, the organization and control of amateur sports is much less centralized. Policies, rules, fund-raising strategies, and methods of operating all vary from one organization to the next. For example, the major governing body in intercollegiate sport is the National Collegiate Athletic Association (NCAA). However, rules for intercollegiate sports and for athletes vary in each of the five major membership divisions in the NCAA (see chap. 14 for an explanation of NCAA divisions). Each member school in the NCAA is also free to develop its own policies to supplement NCAA policies. Schools must finance sport programs on their own; they receive little direct aid from the NCAA.

Amateur sports in colleges and universities also are controlled by the National Association for Intercollegiate Athletics (NAIA) and the College Football Association (CFA); until 1983, the Association of Intercollegiate Athletics for Women (AIAW) also had authority over them. The rules in these organizations usually have differed from the rules in the NCAA.

For many amateur sports not directly connected with universities, the major controlling organization is the United States Olympic Committee (USOC). However, within the USOC, each of over fifty separate national governing bodies (NGBs) regulates and controls a particular amateur sport. NGBs raise most of their own funds through corporate and individual sponsors, and each one sets its own policies to supplement the rules and policies of the USOC. The USOC has tried for many years to develop continuity in American amateur sports, but the NGBs and other sport organizations are very protective of their own turf, and they seldom give up power to regulate their sports; instead, they fight to maintain control over their rules, revenues, and athletes. This has been the basis of many political battles between organizations.

As the USOC has been more effective in raising money, it also has been able to use a system of monetary grants to increase its control over various NGBs. This will continue, although most NGBs will strive to maintain their autonomy, independence, and control over athletes and events in their sports. As one strategy for doing this, they have maximized the commercial appeal and potential of their sports. However, the USOC consistently has maintained control over the negotiation of television rights for all amateur sports and over the sale of merchandise associated with various ones.

Despite variation and confusion in amateur sports, all amateur sport organizations share an interest in two things: *power*, and the *money* generated through sponsorships and revenue-producing sports events. For example, when the popularity of women's sports reached new heights in the early 1980s, the NCAA's interest in maintaining power over all college sports led it to abandon its longtime policy of ignoring women's teams; it started to sponsor championship events for women and quickly forced the Association for Intercollegiate Athletics for Women (AIAW) out of existence, even though the AIAW had controlled women's intercollegiate sports for many years. The NCAA's interest in money has led it to operate as a monopoly in its control of intercollegiate sports. This is especially true in the case of revenue-producing sports, through which the NCAA has been able to make considerable money by selling broadcasting rights. However, this monopolistic control was partially eroded in 1984, when a series of court decisions made it possible for individual universities to break away from the NCAA in order to sell broadcasting rights on their own and then keep the money from the sales. But despite this change, the NCAA remains a powerful organization in amateur sports.

Sponsorship patterns in amateur sports also take many forms. Football bowl games now are funded and partially controlled by large corporations. Intercollegiate sport programs now seek various forms of corporate support. Some universities have in effect sold their athletic departments, consisting of all athletic teams and the bodies of athletes, to corporate sponsors, in exchange for money, scholarships, and equipment. If Reebok, for example, were the sponsor of a university's teams, athletes probably would be required to wear Reebok shoes and display the Reebok logo on their uniforms; in addition, Reebok probably would have exclusive rights to market all clothing bearing the university's logo or athletic team names (see Naughton, 1996a). At this time a growing number of university athletic departments have contracts with either Nike or Reebok. In the future, others will sign contracts with Adidas and Converse, or maybe even with Pepsi, Coke, or MARS. Contracts in the future may require athletes and even other students to drink only certain soft drinks or eat certain candy bars on campus or in the locker room at halftime. Of course, this form of sponsorship is a clever way for privately owned corporations to use tax-supported institutions as vehicles for their own profit making, while being hailed on campus as the saviors of sport teams. Corporations and universities enter these agreements outside of any democratic processes that might involve votes on the part of students, athletes, or the taxpayers whose money funds the universities. This may become an issue in the future; at present, few people have considered the long-term implications of these agreements.

In 1981 this cartoon was funny because it was an exaggeration. Now it is an understatement. We have entered the era of the corporation in sports; corporate names and logos are now an expected part of the sports scene. In fact, they are an expected part of the clothing of many people who don't object to paying for the privilege of becoming walking billboards for corporations. This is how corporate hegemony operates.

....

The NGBs of amateur sports long have depended on corporate sponsorship money, and they continue to seek those sponsorships to pay for athlete training, operating expenses, and the staging of events. Designated corporate logos now appear on most of the clothing worn and equipment used by amateur athletes in certain sports. In some cases, individual athletes seek corporate sponsorships on their own, hoping to remain free to train and compete without having their lives completely controlled by NGBs. As this model of corporate sponsorship of both NGBs and athletes continues to be used more and more around the world, the economics of sports increasingly will become tied to the fortunes and fluctuations of market economies and large corporations. Just one potential consequence is that economic recessions could mean the end of sponsorships. And will athletes and NGB employees be required by the terms of sponsorships to become spokespersons and cheerleaders for the interests of international corporate capitalism in the world? I think this is already the situation, and it will become even more pervasive in the future.

LEGAL STATUS AND INCOMES OF ATHLETES IN COMMERCIAL SPORTS

Whenever sports are organized to generate revenues, athletes become entertainers. This is obvious at the professional level, but it is also true in other commercial sports, such as big-time college football and basketball and other elite amateur sports. Professional athletes get paid for their efforts, whereas amateur athletes receive rewards within limits set by the organizations that govern their sport participation.

Two of the most important questions related to athletes in commercial sports are these: (1) What is the legal status of the athlete-entertainers who work in these sports? (2) How are athlete-entertainers rewarded or paid for their work?

Many people have a difficult time thinking of athletes in commercial sports as workers, and they hesitate to consider owner-player relations in professional sports as employer-employee relations (Gruneau and Whitson, 1993). This is the case because people usually associate sports with play in their own lives: they see sports as fun rather than work. However, when sports are organized for the purpose of generating revenues and making profits, players are workers, even though they may have fun on the job. Of course, this is not unique: many workers enjoy their jobs and have fun doing them. I have fun teaching. But regardless of how much people enjoy their work, issues of legal status and rewards for work are important. Like playing basketball, singing is a fun activity—but when a person or group sings in front of twenty thousand people who have paid $25 each for their tickets, singing becomes work, and singer-entertainers become workers concerned with concert contracts, their fair share of ticket and merchandise sales, and who controls the audio tracks and videotapes recorded at the events. So it is with athlete-entertainers.

In this section of the chapter, I will provide information on the legal status and incomes of professional athletes and athletes in other forms of revenue-producing sports. My primary focus will be on commercial sports in the United States. I will not consider those sports that may collect a few gate receipts but never make enough money to pay for anything beyond basic expenses for the events; therefore, I will not deal with high school sports, non-revenue-producing college sports, or other nonprofit local sports in which teams may sell tickets to events.

Professional Athletes

LEGAL STATUS: TEAM SPORTS For many years, the legal status of athletes has been the most controversial issue in professional team sports in the United States. Until the mid-1970s, professional athletes in the major sport leagues had little or no legal power to control their own careers. They could play only for the team drafting them. They could neither pick the team for which they wanted to play nor control when and to whom they might be traded during their careers, even when their contracts expired. To make matters worse, they were obliged to sign standard contracts forcing them to agree to forfeit all rights over their careers to team owners. Basically, they were bought and sold like property, and seldom consulted about their own wishes. They were mercenaries at the mercy of team owners and officials hired by team owners.

In all sports, this set of employee restrictions has been referred to as the **reserve system**. Although the precise nature of this system has varied from one league to another, it enabled team owners to restrict the movement of athlete-employees from one team to another. As long as owners were allowed to limit the extent to which athletes could seek the best contract they could find, salaries remained low and athletes had no power to control the conditions under which they played their sports.

In any other business, this system would have violated antitrust laws. For example, it would be illegal for the owners of all computer software firms to form relationships and decide among themselves which people with degrees in information systems each wanted to hire next year. It also would be illegal for them to agree not to hire graduates who had been "reserved" by another company. This type of "reserve system" would destroy the freedom of professionals in information systems to choose where and with whom they wanted to work. Furthermore, if these workers could not take jobs with other companies without permission from their current employers, even after their employment contracts had expired, their salaries would be kept low, because companies would not have to compete with each other to hire the people with the best skills. And if these workers could be sold or traded to other companies without being consulted, they would have no real control over their own careers.

But this type of reserve system has been defined as legal in sports, and owners have used it for many years with minimal interference from any government agency. Team owners have justified this form of control over the careers of athletes by saying it was needed to maintain competitive balance between the teams in their leagues. They argued that if players were free to work for anyone they wanted to, the wealthiest owners in the biggest cities and TV markets would buy up all the good athletes and prevent teams in smaller cities and TV markets from maintaining competitive teams. The irony of this argument was that team owners were all wealthy capitalists who praised free market economics in other settings. But in the business of sports, they said that the free market would destroy competition and the entire basis for economic success among sport teams. In other words, these capitalists became "sport socialists" to protect their power and wealth under the umbrella of a monopoly inconsistent with principles of free enterprise.

Professional athletes regularly objected to the reserve system, but they could not mount an effective legal challenge of the system until the 1970s. Then, in 1976, the courts ruled that under certain conditions professional athletes had the right to become *free agents*. This right was important, because it allowed players whose contracts had expired to seek contracts with other teams who might bid for their services. This legal change had a dramatic effect on the salaries of NBA and MLB players beginning in the late 1970s (see fig. 11-2 on p. 356). Team owners in the NFL and the NHL avoided much of the effect of this legal change by negotiating restrictions on free agency with players' associations. But in 1992, after players in both leagues had mounted challenges, these restrictions were partially lifted. The hockey players went on a ten-day strike during the Stanley Cup playoffs and forced owners to sign a short-term contract in which they obtained slightly more control over their careers. The football players, after challenging the NFL for about five years in a series of court cases, won an antitrust suit that forced team owners to agree to let NFL players become free agents after being in the league for five years.

It would take many pages to explain the full implications of recent court decisions and labor negotiations on the legal status and rights of players in each professional team sport. Furthermore, explanations change every time a new case is resolved or a new labor agreement is made in a particular league. In part, it was this complexity that kept most players from challenging the restrictions of the reserve system over the years. It was not until the formation of players' associations and unions in the 1970s that they had the support and organization they needed to push for changes. Each players' association used the collective strength of all the players in its league to bargain against the collective strength of all the owners in that league.

Although the players' associations often have been unpopular with many sport fans and detested by team owners and league officials, they have enabled players to gain more and more control over their salaries and working conditions since the late 1970s. Labor negotiations and players' strikes in all professional team sports always have focused on issues of freedom and control over careers, even though money issues have attracted most of the attention in the media coverage. Players always have known that when they had the freedom to sell their skills to the highest bidder, salaries would increase to the highest level that the owners could afford to pay.

Free agency now exists for veteran players in all leagues. The drafting of rookies still occurs, but the number of rookies reserved through the draft gradually has been cut back, allowing more players to try out with teams that they think offer them the best chances of getting contracts. Definitions of who qualifies as a veteran and the amount of freedom enjoyed by free agents vary from league to league. Generally, players don't qualify as veterans until they have spent three to seven years under contract in a league, and player movement from one team to another is subject to certain restrictions in each league.

Although players' organizations and unions have done much to change the legal status of athletes in various professional sports, it has not been easy to keep players organized (Beamish, 1988; 1993). Owners have not looked kindly on players who have served as representatives in unions or players' associations. Athletes are often hesitant to join any organization that may ask them to strike for an entire season, especially since their careers seldom last more than four to seven years in team sports. Therefore, a season-long strike for the average player means sacrificing 15 to 25 percent of lifetime income as a professional athlete. Strikes are also risky, as team owners may hire nonunion players waiting for a chance to be professional athletes. Finally, the highest-paid players in certain leagues are now so wealthy and in such good positions to negotiate contracts on their own that they do not identify with other players, about 20 to 35 percent of whom make the minimum salaries in the leagues. Although the unions and players' associations

created the conditions for the current good fortune of these superstars, some of them no longer see these organizations as useful to them. The superstars depend on their agents, not on athlete-worker organizations. All these factors make it very difficult to keep players organized.

Finally, professional athletes in most minor leagues have few rights and little control over their careers. As one former coach in the Continental Basketball League noted, "In this league, [trades are] so easy that teams trade every day. It's like bubble gum cards. I swear, if Michael Jordan were in the CBA, he'd have been traded at least three times" (in Pluto, 1995). In the CBA, when a player is injured, he can be cut on the spot, no questions asked. For the pros at this level—who are more numerous than those working at the top levels of professional sports—the pay is low, careers are uncertain, rights are few, and owners have the last word. In fact, the average high school teacher in the U.S. has a higher salary and more rights as a worker than nearly all the pro athletes in the minor leagues. It's too bad more young people don't know this.

LEGAL STATUS: INDIVIDUAL SPORTS
The legal status of professional athletes in individual sports varies greatly from sport to sport and even from one athlete to another. Although the situations in boxing, bowling, golf, tennis, auto racing, rodeo, horse racing, track and field, skiing, and other sports are all different, a few generalizations are possible.

The legal status of athletes in individual sports largely depends on what athletes must do to train and qualify for competition in their sports. For example, few athletes can afford to pay for all the training needed to develop professional-level skills in a sport. Few athletes are in positions to meet the other requirements associated with official participation in sport competitions, which may include having a recognized agent or manager (as in boxing), being formally recognized by other participants (as in most auto racing), obtaining membership in a professional organization (as in most bowling, golf, and tennis tournaments), or gaining a special invitation through an official selection group (as in pro track and field meets).

Whenever athletes need sponsors to pay for their training and whenever contractual arrangements with other persons or groups are required for their participation, the legal status of athletes is shaped by their agreements with sponsors and sanctioning groups. This is the reason the legal status of athletes in individual sports varies so much from one athlete to the next. Let's use boxing as an example of one particular case. Because boxers frequently come from low-income backgrounds, they cannot develop on their own the skills they need to become recognized competitors. They need trainers, managers, and sponsors of their training. After their skills are developed, it takes money and carefully nurtured business connections to arrange and promote bouts.

Relationships with trainers, managers, and sponsors all come with conditions attached for the boxers. These conditions may be written in formal contracts or based in informal agreements. But in either case, they require the boxers to give up control of their lives and a portion of the rewards they may earn in bouts in return for the help they need to become professionals. Unless boxers have good legal experience or win a few big-money fights, they are likely to have almost no control over their careers. In a sense, they are forced to trade control over their bodies and careers for the opportunity to continue boxing. This is a classic example of how class relations operate in sports: when people lack resources, they are unable to negotiate the conditions under which their sport careers develop.

The legal status of athletes in individual sports is defined in the bylaws of some professional organizations, such as the Professional Golf Association (PGA), the Ladies Professional Golf Association (LPGA), the Association of Tennis Professionals (ATP), and the Professional Rodeo Cowboys Association (PRCA), among many others. Because these organizations are heavily controlled by the athletes themselves, their official policies are supportive of athletes' rights. Also, the organizations serve as mechanisms through which athletes can control the conditions under which they compete. Without these organizations, athletes in these sports would have few guaranteed rights.

INCOME: TEAM SPORTS Despite the publicity given to the supercontracts of some athletes in the NBA, the NFL, the NHL, MLB, and premier soccer leagues in Europe, salaries vary widely across the different levels and divisions in professional team sports. For example, many players at the minor-league level in baseball, hockey, and other team sports make less than social workers, teachers, and other nonsport workers. Salaries for over three thousand players on 158 minor-league baseball teams range from about $1,500 to $3,500 per month (in 1996 dollars), depending on the level at which teams play. The players do not always get paid twelve months a year; their jobs are seasonal. This pattern is also characteristic in other professional sports, including men's and women's basketball, football, hockey, soccer, and volleyball. Furthermore, there are many more pro athletes playing at minor-league levels than at the top level we hear so much about.

To understand this disparity in incomes, consider that superstar Michael Jordan made more in the first 16 games of the Chicago Bulls' 1996–97 season than all 80 women playing in the ABL made over their entire 40-game season. He made more in 33 games than the combined salaries of all the men playing in the 10-team Major Soccer League during their 1996 season. He made twice as much as the next-highest-paid player in the NBA and nearly three times as much as the highest-paid player in baseball. The hockey players on over 100 minor-league teams across North America have the goal of reaching $20,000 per year so that they can avoid taking minimum-wage jobs in the off season; the salaries paid to the top NHL players are completely out of their league.

Calvin and Hobbes

by Bill Watterson

....

As national and international media celebrities, some athletes make obscene amounts of money compared to the incomes of those who watch them. This fact seems to impress Calvin.

....

It's also important to remember that mega-salaries are quite new in professional team sports; they did not exist before 1980. For example, when I graduated from college in 1966 with a degree in sociology, I had a job offer from a public agency that would have paid me nearly 60 percent of the average salary of NBA players that year. Today a new graduate with a bachelor's degree would be lucky to find a job paying more than 1.5 percent of the average NBA salary!

According to economist Marc Lavoie, major-league baseball players in the 1950s made about $14,000 per year, which was about $77,000 in 1996 inflation-adjusted dollars (Lavoie, forthcoming). So even after adjustments for inflation, the 1996 average baseball salary of over $1.1 million was 15 times more than what players made in the 1950s! NHL players made about $8,000 in the 1950s, or about $45,000 in 1996 inflation-adjusted dollars; but in 1996 they averaged $760,000, which was 17 times more than their counterparts made in the 50s! Lavoie further notes that the average U.S. worker in 1957 made $4,300, or $23,500 in 1996 inflation-adjusted dollars. So while the top pro player-to-worker

salary ratio in the 1950s was no more than 4:1, it is now 44:1 in MLB, 28:1 in the NHL, 88:1 in the NBA, and about 30:1 in the NFL! This is surely the reason many fans today object to player strikes and contract holdouts; they have a difficult time seeing why athletes want so much more than the average worker has (Lavoie, forthcoming).

The dramatic increase in average salaries at the top level of professional team sports is primarily due to two factors: (1) changes in the legal status and rights of players, which have led to free agency and the use of salary arbitration processes, and (2) increased revenues generated by new forms of media coverage of sports and the increased popularity of pro sports. The pattern of salary increases is illustrated in figure 11-2. Salaries for every year in each major team sport since 1970 show that large increases in salary levels have corresponded closely to court decisions and other events changing the legal status of athletes and giving them bargaining power in their contract negotiations with team owners.

Baseball is a good case in point. Salary increases prior to the 1976 season were gradual.

Income disparities between the top moneymakers and others in individual sports has increased in recent years. Part of that disparity is caused by the high appearance fees that some athletes receive just to play in tournaments, apart from what they might win. Endorsements also contribute to the disparities; only a handful of athletes get big endorsement contracts. (Lennox Mc-Clendon, AP/Wide World Photos)

Then there was a series of dramatic jumps. These jumps were associated with the growing revenues from gate receipts and the sale of television rights, but they were primarily *caused by* the changes in the legal status of the players themselves. Because of a favorable court decision prompted by the efforts of their union, baseball players received the right under certain conditions to become free agents and sell their abilities to the highest bidders after the 1976 season. This allowed a number of top players to negotiate lucrative long-term contracts. For example, during the twenty years before free agency (1956 to 1976), salaries increased about 350 percent, from $14,500 to $51,500. In the twenty years since the existence of free agency (1976 to 1996), average salaries have increased by 2,000 percent. In terms of absolute dollars, salaries went up $36,000 between 1956 and 1976, while they went up over $950,000 between 1976 and 1996!

However, not all baseball players have shared equally in the increases since free agency. The *average* or *mean* salary listed for a sport is always pulled up and distorted by players who have large contracts. This is the reason we should compute the *median* and *modal* salaries to obtain a more realistic idea of the salaries of all players in a sport. For example, in baseball, the median salary in 1996 was under $500,000, and the modal salary was $109,000. That means that

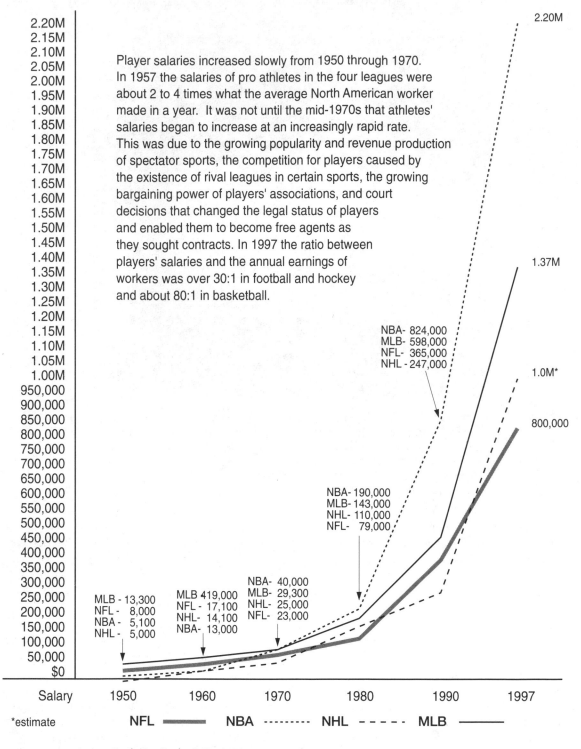

Player salaries increased slowly from 1950 through 1970. In 1957 the salaries of pro athletes in the four leagues were about 2 to 4 times what the average North American worker made in a year. It was not until the mid-1970s that athletes' salaries began to increase at an increasingly rapid rate. This was due to the growing popularity and revenue production of spectator sports, the competition for players caused by the existence of rival leagues in certain sports, the growing bargaining power of players' associations, and court decisions that changed the legal status of players and enabled them to become free agents as they sought contracts. In 1997 the ratio between players' salaries and the annual earnings of workers was over 30:1 in football and hockey and about 80:1 in basketball.

NBA- 824,000
MLB- 598,000
NFL- 365,000
NHL - 247,000

NBA- 190,000
MLB- 143,000
NHL- 110,000
NFL- 79,000

NBA- 40,000
MLB- 29,300
NHL- 25,000
NFL- 23,000

MLB 419,000
NFL - 17,100
NHL- 14,100
NBA- 13,000

MLB - 13,300
NFL - 8,000
NBA - 5,100
NHL - 5,000

Salary 1950 1960 1970 1980 1990 1997

*estimate

NFL ▬▬▬ NBA ·········· NHL ‑ ‑ ‑ ‑ MLB ▬▬▬

FIGURE 11-2 Average salaries in the NFL, NBA, NHL, and MLB.

Note: The data on which this graph is based come from a variety of sources, including USA Today Research, league players' associations, and research done by Marc Lavoie (Lavoie, forthcoming) at the University of Ottawa. Average salaries before the mid-1970s are estimates, because there were no players' associations keeping accurate records of salaries, and the records used

even though the mean salary was over $1.1 million, half the players in MLB made less than $500,000, and more players were paid the league minimum salary of $109,000 than were paid any other amount.

Finally, professional athletes seldom remain under contract at the top level of competition for more than three to seven years. As former baseball legend Willie Mays once said, "The financial careers of most professional athletes can be summed up in these words: short and sweet—but mostly short."

INCOME: INDIVIDUAL SPORTS As with team sports, publicity is given to the highest-paid athletes in individual sports. However, not all players of these sports make enough money from tournament winnings to support themselves comfortably. In fact, many golfers, tennis players, bowlers, track and field athletes, auto and motorcycle racers, rodeo riders, figure skaters, and others must carefully manage their money so they do not spend more than they win as they travel from event to event. When tournament winnings are listed in the newspaper, nothing is said about the expenses for airfares, hotels, food, and transportation, or about competition expenses for coaches, agents, managers, and other support people. The top money winners don't worry too much about these expenses, but most athletes in individual sports are not big money winners.

In recent years the disparity between the top money winners and others has increased considerably on the men's and women's golf and tennis tours (Scully, 1995). This means that even in these high-profile sports, the majority of athletes do not win enough prize money to support themselves without another source of income. In some cases, athletes in individual sports have to share their winnings with investors who sponsor them. The investors cover expenses during the lean years, but then take a percentage of winnings when the athletes win matches or tournaments. For example, boxers traditionally have received very little of the prize money from their bouts; even today, much goes to promoters, managers, trainers, and sponsors. Only a few boxers avoid this situation or make so much that it is not important; many others face bankruptcy or a working-class lifestyle soon after their careers are over. But these boxers are ignored as attention is focused on the multi-million-dollar purses in highly publicized heavyweight bouts covered on pay-per-view television. People read that Mike Tyson made $75 million for just over fifty minutes of prize fighting in 1996, and they talk about that instead of about all those whose fighting did not cover their expenses.

Sponsorship agreements sometimes have caused problems for professional athletes in individual sports. Being contractually tied, for example, to an equipment manufacturer or another sponsor often puts athletes in a state of dependency. They may not have the freedom to choose when or how often they will compete, and they may be required by sponsors to attend social functions at which they talk with fan-consumers, sign autographs, and promote products.

The money is very good for some athletes in individual sports, while others may struggle to cover expenses. Only when sport events are broadcast on television can athletes expect to

---

by team and league management were inconsistent. For example, figures for any given year within leagues often varied because computations were based on different rosters at the beginnings or ends of seasons. Estimates also varied because some figures included signing bonuses or prorated portions of signing bonuses.

Salary figures since the late 1970s often vary because they may or may not include prorated salary deferrals and signing bonuses, performance incentives, and postseason playoff income. Furthermore, salary deferrals without interest may be discounted at varying rates, and signing bonuses may be increased by varying rates of interest. None of the salary amounts in this graph includes endorsement income.

The average salaries of the women playing in the ABL during the 1996–97 season was about $70,000. Gender issues related to salaries in professional sports are highlighted by the fact that, according to *Forbes* magazine (Vol. 158, No. 14) there was not one woman athlete from any sport among the "40 Highest Paid [U.S.] Athletes in 1996."

compete for major prize money and earn large incomes.

COMMONLY ASKED QUESTIONS ABOUT PROFESSIONAL ATHLETES

Are pro athletes overpaid? The answer to this question is no, but it needs to be qualified. As previously noted, the majority of pro athletes make less than $30,000 per year and enjoy little or no job security. They play on teams, in leagues, and in events that make little money. Only about 30 percent of the male athletes in the top professional team sports and a handful of men and women in golf and tennis make at least $1 million per year; a few players in North American team sports and European soccer make over $5 million per year; and a handful of athletes in team sports and boxing make $10 million or more. At the top in 1996 was Mike Tyson at $75 million, although in 1997 Michael Jordan earned a salary of $30 million per year, about $40 million in endorsements, and about $30 million in movie-related and other income. But these are unique cases.

Certain commercial sports, along with a few other forms of entertainment, generate vast amounts of money today. For example, a 1996 heavyweight boxing title bout between Mike Tyson and Evander Holyfield generated about $80 million in pay-per-view access fees and over $14 million in gate receipts; a rematch scheduled for 1997 was expected to generate more than $125 million, with about $50 million to $60 million allocated to the two boxers.* Athletes and other entertainers are part of a media-based, global celebrity culture. When celebrity exists on a national or global level, its income-generating potential is huge.

An interesting point is that few players in the NBA, for which the average salary was $2.2 million during the 1996–97 season, could match the salaries of other entertainers in television, film,

and music (La Franco, 1996). Oprah Winfrey made three times Michael Jordan's $30 million salary in 1996, and Jordan makes over twice as much as any other salaried athlete. Arnold Schwarzenegger made $52 million in 1996; Michael Jackson, $45 million; Jim Carrey, $34 million; Garth Brooks, $29 million; Jerry Seinfield, $28 million; and Tom Cruise, Clint Eastwood, Harrison Ford, and Robin Williams, over $25 million. Roseanne and Mariah Carey each made over $20 million, as did John Travolta, Kevin Costner, Bruce Willis, Denzel Washington, Michael Douglas, and opera star Luciano Pavarotti. Actors and actresses with global popularity make between $10 million and $25 million per film, because anticipated revenues are so high.

Athlete-entertainers also have incomes that reflect revenues generated. This is the reason players' associations have made sure that salary caps are set so that athletes' salaries make up between 40 and 67 percent of the gross revenues collected by team owners. Generally, athletes make big money when owners and promoters think they are worth it in terms of gate receipts and other revenues. Economic research clearly shows that athletes are not overpaid, and that superstars, with a couple of exceptions, "pay for" their own salaries by attracting new revenues for team owners (Lavoie, forthcoming; Morrison, 1996). This is the reason the owners pay them as they do. The money is there. The question is who gets it: the owners or the players people pay to watch?

Team owners know that spectators are attracted by star performers, and the best way to create *stars* in sports is by signing athletes to big-money contracts. The contracts generate massive media coverage, which serves as wonderful publicity for the team. Additionally, spectators often see money as an indicator of excellence, so they will pay to see a game played by highly paid athletes. Using big money to attract audiences also occurs in individual sports such as tennis, golf, and boxing. Sponsors and promoters know

---

*Apparently, people are willing to pay dearly to see two men reaffirm traditional notions of masculinity by beating each other senseless in a boxing ring.

SIDELINES

©1982 M.T.F.-T.W.S.-Lakewood, CO

"I make $6 million a year . . . and I don't feel guilty!"

....

Most athletes generate revenues that match their salaries and prize moneys. Like other entertainers, a few of them have benefited from national and international media exposure. Sport events are now marketed in connection with the celebrity status and lifestyles of athlete-entertainers.

....

that big prize money attracts big-name athletes, and big-name athletes create spectator interest and television coverage. Interest and coverage mean profits for sponsors and promoters.*

The unbelievable amount of money made by some athletes is warranted in economic terms, but it also raises interesting questions about values and priorities in our culture. With at least 20 percent of the world's population facing poverty and hunger on a daily basis, with 1.3 billion people making less than one dollar for a full day of work, do 100-million-dollar contracts for athletes seem obscene? Should a special tax be developed to limit what might be seen as "windfall profits" associated with new forms of media-generated celebrity made possible by global communications technology? Should a portion of the revenues generated by mega-entertainment sports be used to fund projects for lower-income people in the cities where teams play and where tax monies have been used to build stadiums as personal stages for athletes? Should teams be assessed a value-added tax on all revenues they collect, so that youth sports and high school sports can be saved or expanded? Are there any good reasons not to do these things? Building 300-million-dollar stadiums for wealthy owners and athletes in cities where children don't have sports programs seems incongruous to me.

I think it is time to add these questions to public discourse about the salaries of celebrities who now ride the wave of new forms of global technology; as global celebrity culture expands and generates increasing amounts of money, these questions will become even more important.

How much do athletes make on endorsements? Data on all forms of endorsements across different sports are hard to collect. Athletes can make great amounts of money on endorsements if they have the exposure, personalities, and images that lead people, especially people who have money to spend, to recognize, identify with, and trust them.

Of course, gender relations and race/ethnic relations clearly come into play in endorsements. For example, the "advertising value" of women athletes is thought to be low, except when they can endorse products purchased by other women. The endorsement record of Martina Navratilova shows also that being a lesbian dramatically decreases one's advertising value. While heterosexual male tennis players were making $10 million or more every year on endorsements, she made only a fraction of that, even though she was clearly the top player in women's tennis for many years.

The advertising value of African American athletes usually depends on whether they can transcend color in the eyes of white consumers. If African American athletes present themselves in ways that create fear or anxiety in white consumers, or remind them of the racial divisions

---

*This is the reason appearance fees, both legal and illegal, sometimes are paid to athletes in individual sports, especially tennis. These fees range from a few thousand dollars to over $250,000 for a single event. The athletes collect the fees whether they win or lose.

that still exist in the culture, their endorsement potential is low. Most black athletes who have endorsement contracts clearly know that disarming smiles are important, that sullen or sulky looks are out of bounds, that racial issues are to be avoided in public statements, and that certain behaviors or mistakes can lead them to be "racialized" very quickly (Andrews, 1996).*

Of course, the complexity of gender and race/ethnic relations makes it difficult to make generalizations about endorsement potential. For example, Dennis Rodman has turned his "gender-bending" behavior, which includes wearing dresses and makeup, into an endorsement selling point. Golfer Tiger Woods has been used in Nike ads that remind consumers that racism *does* exist in golf, while at the same time other golf equipment and apparel companies have presented Woods to promote the belief that golf *is no longer* an exclusive sport for wealthy white men.

Athletes who are connected with specialized groups of consumers also may receive endorsement contracts. For example, Nike used Andre Agassi to promote its shoes and clothing among young people from seventeen to twenty-three years old—the age group that accounts for half of all dollars spent on sports apparel in the U.S. Nike used Agassi's rebel image to market new styles of sports apparel that did not fit with the traditional "white shorts" image of tennis.

Overall, endorsement income can be significant—up to tens of millions of dollars per year—but it is limited to those *few* athletes advertisers think will be influential spokespersons for their products. The fact that golfers Jack Nicklaus and Arnold Palmer have been among the top ten sports endorsers from the early 1970s until the late 1990s shows that establishing a connection with white consumers with money is a central factor in the endorsement potential of athletes.

*When one is "racialized," one is identified in terms of racial identity and one's behavior is associated with race-related concerns.

Do athletes' salaries affect ticket prices to sports events? "There is no relationship whatsoever between ticket prices and owners' costs." This is the conclusion of Gerald Scully, a highly respected economist who has studied the business of sports for three decades (in Brown, 1993a). He and other economists explain that ticket prices and athlete salaries are both primarily a function of the public demand for sports. Each goes up or down as the entertainment value of a sport goes up or down. When this occurs, it looks as if salaries are causing ticket prices to go up, but this is not the case.

For example, the basketball fan in 1996 was not paying $43 for a Chicago Bulls ticket because Michael Jordan was paid $30 million. The ticket price was $43 because so many people were willing to pay that much to see Jordan and the Bulls play basketball. The ticket price would have been the same even if no player on the Bulls were making over $100,000—*as long as the consumer would pay that much to see a game.* The people who control ticket prices are in the business of making money, and they will charge whatever they can get from spectators. This is the reason tickets to see football games played by the University of Colorado are about the same price as tickets to see the Denver Broncos, even though the university "pays" (in scholarship dollars) its players less than 2 percent of what the Broncos pay their players. Universities charge whatever the market will bear; ticket prices for big-time college football games have increased many times during the past forty years, even though player costs have been tightly controlled and stayed much the same over that time. Pro teams operate in the same way.

The economic reality of sports is that team owners and event promoters gladly would pay athletes less money if they could get away with it, but they will set ticket prices at whatever spectators are willing to pay. Athletes' salaries increase *only* when they have the power to force owners and promoters to give them a greater share of the expected gross revenues in sports. In fact, part of the reason the price of game tickets has gone up so much is that many tickets are bought in blocks by corporations for "business purposes." Because they can afford higher prices, the cost of tickets for everyone else is driven up. So the CEO and his five business associates using "company tickets" affect ticket prices; player salaries are the result of these increased prices, not the cause.

Do big salaries influence the motivation of athletes? In 1996, these four statements were made by four different athletes:

- "I'd do this for free!" (Olympic medal-winning swimmer Amy Van Dyken)
- "Offering me $5 million was an insult. And $6 million obviously isn't much better. I'd rather quit than play for $6 million" (Chicago Bulls basketball player Dennis Rodman)
- "I make so much money to fight; how can I not come back [and fight again?]" (boxer Mike Tyson)
- "I made a commitment to a lot of companies, and I'm sticking with it" (an injured Scottie Pippen before playing basketball in the Olympics and risking further injury)

The motivation of athletes is grounded in many different factors. But a central motive for most of them is a dedication to their sport and pride in their abilities and their dedication. Money is also a motivator, but it is doubtful that Michael Jordan was more or less motivated in 1996, with a salary of $30 million, than in 1995, with a salary of $4 million. The same is true for most other professional athletes.

Motivation is difficult to measure, but if we had motivation scores over the past fifty years in different sports, I doubt we would see much variation with salary amounts. In fact, back in 1925 baseball player Ty Cobb complained that "most of the players are in the game for the money that's in it—not for the love of the game" (in Brown, 1993b). Since 1925 some things have changed—playing styles are different, and today's athletes generally train year-round—but

motivation probably has not varied much from one generation of athletes to the next. However, is it possible for athletes to lose their motivation when they think they should be making more money than they are? Similarly, would athletes whose salaries were only a fraction of the salaries paid to superstars lose their motivation over time? Does NBA player Dominique Wilkins play less hard than Michael Jordan because he makes $3,018 per game, compared to Jordan's $367,561 per game? These are interesting questions that await future research. The latter question is especially important to ask, because salary disparities in some sports are becoming exceptionally wide (Scully, 1995).

Amateur Athletes in Commercial Sports

LEGAL STATUS OF AMATEUR ATHLETES The primary goal of amateur athletes always has been simple: to train and compete. However, the achievement of that goal has not always been easy, because amateur athletes have not had significant control over the conditions of their sport participation. Instead, in the U.S., control has rested in the hands of amateur sports organizations, such as the Amateur Athletic Union (AAU), the NCAA, the IOC, the USOC, forty-plus international sport federations, and more than fifty NGBs within the USOC (for each of the amateur sports in the United States).

Each of these organizations sets rules restricting the training and competition of amateur athletes. Although these rules usually are intended to insure fairness in competition, they sometimes have been used to protect the power and interests of the organizations, rather than the athletes they are supposed to serve. When this has happened, amateur athletes have not been able to participate when and where they would prefer to.

The total powerlessness of amateur athletes led to the formation of a U.S. President's Commission on Olympic Sports in 1975. The report of the commission was instrumental in the passage of the Amateur Sports Act of 1978. The Amateur Sports Act did not guarantee amateur

SIDELINES

"The one thing that helps me win so many tournaments? That's easy—greed!"

"If we're going into overtime, does that mean we get time and a half?"

The greedy golfer implies that cash rewards do indeed motivate him. However, as the bored basketball players suggest, one possible danger of commercial sports is that athletes might become so focused on external rewards that they lose their intrinsic motivation. When this happens, they become cynical about their own participation.

....

athletes any rights, but it did clarify the relationships between various sport organizations, so that disagreements and bickering over control issues among organization executives would interfere less than they had with participation opportunities for athletes. However, disagreements and bickering continue in the 1990s.

The continued powerlessness of amateur athletes is especially evident in U.S. intercollegiate sports. Even in the revenue-producing intercollegiate sports, athletes have few rights and no formal means to file complaints when they have been treated unfairly or denied the right to play their sports. The athletes have no rights enabling them to share in the revenues they generate, and no control over how their skills and their names and images can be used by the university or the NCAA (Marrs, 1996). For example, when college athletes become local or national celebrities, they have no "right of publicity" enabling them to benefit from their celebrity status. They cannot endorse products or be paid when their iden-

tities and images are used by universities to promote ticket sales or market sport merchandise for profit.

Although many athletes recognize the problems associated with their lack of rights, it has been difficult for them to lobby for changes. Challenging the university and the NCAA in court is expensive, and would take years of a young person's life. Forming an athletes' organization would make it possible to bargain for rights, but bringing athletes from different campuses together would require many resources; and convincing athletes, many of whom have adjusted to their dependency and powerlessness, to take assertive and progressive action would be a major challenge. Furthermore, the prospect of college athletes engaging in collective bargaining to gain rights and benefits would be seen as a serious threat to the whole structure of big-time college sports. Athletes may be treated as employees by coaches and athletic departments, but there is a fear that if they were legally defined as employees, they would be eligible for the same considerations granted to other workers in the United States. This makes everyone from coaches to university presidents nervous.

At this point, changes in the legal status of college athletes in revenue-producing sports are most likely to come in connection with a combination of three things: (1) the appointment of student-athletes as voting representatives to NCAA committees, (2) the service of university representatives to the NCAA as assertive advocates for the rights of athletes, and (3) the establishment on campuses and in the NCAA of ombudspersons through whom athletes may appeal decisions that affect their lives unfairly. The likelihood of a real change in athletes' rights is not great. The NCAA has called for the formation of athlete advisory committees at the NCAA, conference, and campus levels, but there has been no formal structure established through which athletes will have any real power. In the meantime, I think that athlete advocacy groups outside the university are needed; athletes need support in gaining at least some control over their sport lives and the revenues created by their skills.

INCOME OF AMATEUR ATHLETES Amateur athletes in revenue-producing sports are in a paradoxical position: they generate money through their performances, but they are restricted from sharing that money with sponsors and sport organizations. Although American college athletes may receive limited athletic aid and U.S. and Canadian national team athletes may receive stipends for living expenses while they train, most amateur athletes receive no compensation at all for their involvement in events generating gate receipts and media rights payments.

Intercollegiate athletes playing big-time college football and basketball may generate hundreds of thousands of dollars for their universities, but the rules of the NCAA prohibit them from receiving anything more than renewable one-year scholarships, and those scholarships can cover nothing more than tuition, room, meals, and books. This means that a basketball player from a low-income family can bring fame and fortune to a school for three or four years and never legally receive a penny for college expenses outside the classroom—no money for laundry, dates, transportation around town, or travel home for vacations; no money for non-sport-related medical or dental bills, phone calls home, clothes, a personal computer, academic photocopying, school supplies, and so on.

It is the unfairness of this situation that has led to many of the under-the-table cash payments to college athletes. These payments and other illegal gifts have become so commonplace that many leaders in college sports have suggested that the NCAA revise its policies on compensation for athletes. Developing a fair method of arranging such payments presents a major challenge. In the meantime, top-level college athletes will aspire to play professional sports before they have completed their eligibility or their degrees. This trend will be heightened in basketball if a new professional league is established for male players under twenty-one (or possibly twenty-three) years old. The intent of such a league would be to provide young men with opportunities to be paid for playing basketball before they tried to make the NBA. According to those organizing this league, players would be required to attend college or take courses related to the business of sports. But their salaries would be much higher than their tuition and living expenses, so they could directly benefit from the revenues they helped generate.

Outside of intercollegiate sports, athletes competing at the amateur level traditionally have been unable to capitalize on their commercial value. However, new rules governing eligibility allow participation by athletes who have made money in connection with their sport skills. In other words, amateur restrictions no longer apply to athletes outside of intercollegiate sports. However, once athletes take money *beyond* an approved basic cost-of-living stipend and travel expenses related to training and competition in any sport, they are not eligible to participate in

NCAA events in that sport. Therefore, if a six-teen-year-old gymnast on the U.S. national team takes money to be a part of an exhibition tour after the Olympics, she is not eligible to participate in NCAA college gymnastics. This also means she may not receive an athletic grant to attend college.

Even though the restrictions of amateurism have been lifted in Olympic-type sports, many athletes do not share in the revenues generated by the events in which they participate. For example, the Olympic Games generate hundreds of millions of dollars in gate receipts and sponsorships, but the athletes who make the games possible receive none of that money, apart from training support through the sport organizations that they are affiliated with and the cash awards medal winners *sometimes* receive from those organizations. Questions about the fairness of this situation have been raised by an increasing number of athletes. And University of Ottawa economist Mark Lavoie has noted that "the day cannot be too far off when the so-called amateur athletes will threaten to go on strike in order to get their share of the huge revenues generated by worldwide mega-events such as the Olympic Games" (forthcoming).

SUMMARY

THE CHARACTERISTICS OF COMMERCIAL SPORTS

Commercial sports have become visible parts of many contemporary societies. This development is associated with urbanization, industrialization, improvements in transportation and communications technology, the availability of capital resources, and class relations. People's interest in paying to watch sports is encouraged by a cultural emphasis on individual success, widely available youth sport programs, and extensive media coverage of sports. The recent expansion of commercial sports also has been fueled by sport organizations seeking global markets and

transnational corporations using sports as vehicles for global expansion. The global character of commercial sports will continue to develop as long as it meets the advertising needs of transnational corporations.

Commercialization has influenced changes in the structure and goals of certain sports, as well as the orientations of people involved in sports and the organizations through which sports are controlled. Those connected with commercial sports tend to emphasize heroic orientations over aesthetic orientations. It seems that style and dramatic expression impress mass audiences, whereas fine distinctions in ability often are overlooked, except by those who have an in-depth knowledge about a particular sport. Overall, commercial sports have been packaged as total entertainment experiences for spectators, even spectators who know little about the games they are watching.

Commercial sports are unique businesses. Many of them at the minor-league level do not generate substantial revenues for owners and sponsors; in fact, they are risky businesses. However, team owners at the top levels of professional sports are successful businesspeople or large corporations that have worked together to make their leagues into effective monopolies with nearly absolute control over their sports. Along with event sponsors and promoters, these owners are involved with commercial sports in the hope of making money while having fun and establishing good public images for themselves or for their nonsport products. In the major team sports, they have been able to use monopolistic business practices to keep costs down and revenues up. Profits also have been enhanced by public support and subsidies. It is ironic that North American professional sports often are used as models of competition, when, in fact, they have been built through a system of autocratic control and monopolistic organization. As Art Modell, past owner of the Cleveland Browns, once said about himself and his fellow team owners in the NFL, "We're twenty-eight Republicans who vote socialist." What he meant was that the NFL owners were all wealthy conservative businessmen who had eliminated competition in their sport businesses and used public money and facilities to increase their wealth and power.

The administration and control of amateur commercial sports rests in the hands of numerous sports organizations. Although these organizations exist to provide support and guidance for amateur athletes, many of the people who run them have become concerned primarily with power, control, and revenue generation. Power struggles in amateur sports usually have been won by those with the most money; athletes seldom have the resources needed to promote their own interests in these struggles. At this point, corporate sponsors have become a major force in amateur sports, and it is their interests that influence what happens in these sports.

Commercialization also has turned athletes into entertainers; athletes generate revenues through their performances. With this change, issues related to rights and income have become very important. In professional sports, the issue of players' rights always has been a major concern. As rights have increased, so have salaries. Salaries also have gone up with the increased gate receipts and television money in certain sports.

Not all athletes in professional sports make vast sums of money; many outside the NBA, the NFL, the NHL, and MLB have incomes that are surprisingly low. Income among amateur athletes is limited by the rules set by sport organizations. Intercollegiate athletes in the United States have what amounts to a maximum wage in the form of athletic scholarships. This has led to illegal under-the-table payments to some college athletes, especially those from low-income backgrounds. In other amateur sports, athletes may receive direct cash payments for performances and endorsements, and some receive support from the organizations to which they belong, but few make large amounts of money.

When we discuss commercial sports, we must remember that the structure and dynamics of those sports vary from country to country. Commercial sports in most of the world have not generated the massive amounts of revenues associated with a few high-profile, heavily televised sports in North America, Japan, and western Europe. Profits for owners and sponsors in the United States and Canada have depended on working out supportive arrangements with the media and government. These arrangements have done much to shape the character of all sports in North America, professional and amateur (Wilson, 1994).

We should note that the commercial model of sport is not the only one that might provide athletes and spectators with enjoyable and satisfying experiences. However, because most people are unaware of alternative models, they simply continue to express a desire for what they get, and their desires are based on limited information manipulated by commercial and corporate interests (Sewart, 1987). Therefore, changes will occur only when people connected with sports are able to develop visions for what sports could and should look like if they were not shaped so overwhelmingly by economic factors.

SUGGESTED READINGS

Beal, B. 1995. Disqualifying the official: An exploration of social resistance through the subculture of skateboarding. *Sociology of Sport Journal* 12 (3): 252–67 (*a close-up look at how some young skateboarders resist the promotional culture and emphasis on heroic actions that are encouraged by commercialization*).

Beamish, R. 1993. Labor relations in sport: Central issues in their emergence and structure in high-performance sport. Pp. 187–210 In A. G. Ingham and J. W. Loy, eds., *Sport in social development.* (Pp.187–210). Champaign, IL: Human Kinetics (*discussion of labor issues in the lives of elite national athletes in Canada; excellent analysis of issues related to athletes' legal status and rights within state controlled bureaucracies*).

Euchner, C. C. 1993. *Playing the field: Why sports teams move and cities fight to keep them.* Baltimore, MD: The Johns Hopkins University Press (*a political analysis focusing on why sport teams, even though they are not major economic forces within cities, have* attracted such attention and public support; argues that an absence of standards for understanding team-city relationships enables team owners to exploit cities).

Financial World Magazine, 1995. Sports: Following the money—a special report. Vol. 164(4) (*this February 14 issue includes nineteen articles on economic/business topics; it contains valuable information on everything from labor issues and the media to stadium construction and money-making strategies used in different sports in North America and around the world*).

Financial World Magazine, 1996. Sports: The high-stakes game of team ownership. Vol. 165(8): 52–70 (*this May 20 issue provides information on "why owning a pro team can be more lucrative than owning stocks and bonds"; also outlines the risks of ownership from a business perspective*).

Gorman, J., and K. Calhoun. 1994. *The name of the game: The business of sports*. New York: John Wiley (*book based on information gathered by the firm, Ernst & Young, hired by professional sports teams and leagues to do consulting, accounting, tax advising, and audits; provides history and current descriptions of pro sports as businesses from a business perspective*).

Gruneau, R., and D. Whitson. 1993. *Hockey night in Canada: Sport, identities, and cultural politics.* Toronto: Garamond Press (*Parts I and III explore the history of professional hockey and the connection between hockey and community in Canada; good information on how economic issues related to sports cannot be understood apart from historical and cultural issues*).

Lavoie, M. Forthcoming. Economics and sport. In J. Coakley and E. Dunning, eds. *Handbook of sport and society*. London: Sage. (*an overview of research on labor economics and the economics of professional sports; issues receiving special attention are salary determination, free agency, salary caps, profit maximization, and franchise location*).

Sage, G. H. 1990. *Power and ideology in American sport.* Champaign, IL: Human Kinetics (*Chapters 5–8 provide a good overview of commercialization and sports*).

Schimmel, K., A. G. Ingham, and J. W. Howell. Professional team sport and the American city. Pp. 211–24 In A. G. Ingham and J. W. Loy, eds., *Sport in social development* (pp. 211–44). Champaign, IL: Human Kinetics (*an in-depth analysis of how the relationship between selected U.S. cities and professional sport team franchises have emerged in a cultural and economic context*).

USA Today, 1996. Ballpark construction's booming. September 6: 13C–21C (*a special section outlining economic issues related to stadium construction; provides a profile of each of the eighty-nine stadiums used by top-level men's pro franchises in North America*).

Wilson, J. 1994. *Playing by the rules: Sport, society, and the state.* Detroit: Wayne State University Press (*insightful social political analysis of how the relationship between sport and the state in the U.S. has developed to enable the commercialization of sports to occur; deals with economic issues as they are connected with public policy and law through recent history, and with emerging global issues*).

12

(Jay Coakley)

Sports and the Media
Could they survive without each other?

At the start, the marriage of sport and the media was a love match. It later became a marriage of convenience and today, with the advent of [global] television, it has become, in addition, a marriage based on money.

Jacques Marchand, French Journalism Official (1994)

The lure of money is already altering sport and will change it more. Increasingly, games will be reorganised to turn them into better television.

Editor, *The Economist* (20 July 1996)

It used to be we presented games as competitions. Now we sometimes show these things as confrontations. Intensity is something you want to sell . . . [b]ut too often, we presented some of these things as mean-spirited turf war, and that bothers me.

Bob Costas, TV sports commentator, NBC (1995)

The media loved me because I would give them whatever they wanted. I would say wild shit, whatever came to mind, and they started hanging out by my locker after games—even if I didn't do anything in the game.

Dennis Rodman, NBA player, 1996

If a man watches three football games in a row, he should be declared legally dead.

Erma Bombeck (1986)

367

The media, including newspapers, magazines, books, movies, radio, television, video games, and the Internet, pervade human culture. Although we all incorporate the media into our lives in different ways, the things we read, hear, and see in the media constitute important parts of our experience. They frame and influence how we think about the world; we use media images and messages as we evaluate social events and envision the future. We also use them as we form ideas about everything from personal relationships and consumer products to political candidates and international affairs. This does not mean that we are slaves to the media or that we are passive dupes of those who control the media. As one sociologist explains, "the media [don't] tell people what to think, [although] they are adept at telling them what to think about" (Whannel, 1992). Our lives and our social worlds are clearly informed by media content, and if the media didn't exist, our lives would be different.

Sports and the media are interconnected parts of our lives. Sports programming is an important segment of media content, and many sports depend on the media for publicity and revenues. In light of these interconnections, this chapter will consider four general questions:

1. What are the characteristics of the media in today's societies?
2. In what ways have sports and the media become interconnected?
3. What images and messages are emphasized in the media coverage of sports in North America?
4. What are the characteristics of the profession of sports journalism in both print and broadcast media?

UNIQUE FEATURES OF THE MEDIA

The media provide three things: (1) information about events and people, (2) interpretations of what is going on in the world, and (3) numerous forms of entertainment. Sometimes they do all three of these things simultaneously, in "interpretive infotainment"! The media are bridges between us and the rest of the world: they connect us with information, experiences, people, images, and ideas that would not otherwise be part of our everyday lives. However, they direct our attention to *selected* items of information, to *selected* experiences, people, images, and ideas. In general, the media expose us to only a part of the reality that surrounds us.

The part of reality brought to us through the media—what we read, hear, and see—is always edited and "re-presented" by those who control them: the producers, editors, program directors, technicians, programmers, camerapersons, writers, commentators, and sponsors. These people try to provide information, interpretation, and entertainment, but their decisions on how to do this are based on their interest in five things: (1) making profits, (2) shaping values, (3) providing a public service, (4) building their own reputations, and (5) expressing themselves in technical or artistic forms.

In countries where most of the media are privately owned and operated, the dominant interest is profit making. This is not the only interest, but it is usually the most influential. In countries where the media are controlled and operated by state officials, dominant interests are shaping values and providing a public service.

Although decisions about media content are influenced by one or more of these interests, they also are influenced by power relations in society as a whole. Those who make media content decisions act as "filters" as they select and create the images and messages to be re-presented through the media. In the filtering process, they tend to give preference to images and messages consistent with dominant ideologies in the society as a whole. Thus, the media are tied to power relations, and often serve the interests of those who have power and wealth in society. Of course, there are exceptions to this, but whenever media content challenges dominant ideologies, those responsible for that content may have their credibility and trustworthiness scrutinized. This is a problem when it banishes someone from a media career, subverts particular types of programming, or leads to self-censorship that defers to the interests of those with power and money. Even when there is freedom of the press, as in the U.S., those who work in the media often think carefully before presenting images and messages that challenge the interests of those who have power and influence in society.

This means neither that we in media audiences are forced to read, hear, and see things we are not interested in, nor that those who control the media ignore what we think. But it does mean that we seldom have direct control over the content of what we read, listen to, and see in the media. The media "re-present" to us edited versions of information, interpretation, and entertainment—versions that media people think we want to consume. For example, in the case of sport, those controlling the media not only select which sports and events will be covered, but also decide what kinds of images and commentary will be emphasized in the coverage. When they do this, they play an important role in constructing the overall frameworks that we in media audiences use to define and explain sports in our lives (Whannel, 1992).

Those of us who have grown up with radio, television, video games, and computers seldom think about media content in this way. For example, when we watch sports on television, we don't often notice that the images and messages we see and hear have been carefully designed to heighten the dramatic content of the event and emphasize dominant ideologies in the society as a whole.* The pregame analysis, the camera coverage, the camera angles, the close-ups, the slow-motion shots, the attention given to particular athletes, the announcer's play-by-play descriptions, the color commentary, the quotes from athletes, and the postgame summary and analysis are all presented to entertain the media audience and keep the broadcast sponsors happy.

---

*See Barnett, 1990; Blain et al., 1993; Bryant et al., 1977; Creedon, 1994; Gruneau, 1989a, b; Hargreaves, 1986; Hesling, 1986; Hilliard, 1994; MacNeill, 1996; Real, 1989; Weiss, 1996; Wenner, 1989, 1994, 1997; Whannel, 1992.

In the United States, the emphasis in media coverage of sports is on action, competition, aggression, individual heroism, individual achievement, playing with pain, teamwork, and the importance of final scores as the measure of success (Kinkema and Harris, 1992). But this emphasis comes in a form that makes it seem as if the "real" game is the one on television, not the one seen in the stadium. Magazine editor Kerry Temple explains:

> It's not just games you're watching. It's soap operas, complete with story lines and plots and plot twists. And good guys and villains, heroes and underdogs. And all this gets scripted into cliffhanger morality plays. . . . And you get all caught up in this until you begin to believe it really matters (1992).

Even though the media coverage of sports is carefully edited and "re-presented" in an entertainment package, most of us believe that when we see a sport event on television we are seeing it "the way it is." We also think that when we hear the commentary, the commentators are "telling it like it is." We don't usually think that what we are seeing and hearing is a series of images and messages selected for particular reasons and grounded in the social worlds of those producing the event, controlling the images, and making the commentary. Of course, television coverage gives us only *one* of *many* possible sets of images and messages related to a sport event; there are a wide array of images and messages that we do *not* get. For example, if we went to the event in person, we would see something quite different from the images "re-presented" on television, and we would come up with our own descriptions and interpretations, which might be completely unrelated to those provided by media commentators.

This point was clearly illustrated in the NBC coverage of the 1996 Olympics in Atlanta. NBC strategically created entertaining drama by re-presenting what media analysts have described as "plausible reality" in their broadcasts; to do this, they deliberately withheld information so they could frame events in their terms, even though they knew those terms to be contrary to what was

During the 1996 Olympics broadcast in the U.S., the NBC-TV commentators purposely led millions of viewers to believe that a team gold medal depended on injured gymnast Kerri Strug's vault. The event was presented as if it were "live," and commentators "told it like it wasn't" in order to entertain. Should we expect accurate news or entertainment in the media coverage of sports? (Susan Ragan, AP/Wide World Photo)

expressed by the athletes and others involved. They gave priority to entertainment over news and information. Former Olympic swimmer Diana Nyad, who was in Atlanta for the event, observed, "Compared to the TV audience, the people in Atlanta have seen a completely different Olympics" (National Public Radio, 1996). She also noted that television and other media coverage revolves around a focus on gold medals, which is a distortion of what the live events involve for most of the athletes and spectators. According to *New York Times* writer Robert Lipsyte (1996), televised sports have become a form of "sportainment" that is the equivalent of a TV movie that purports to be 'based on a true story'." In other words, television constructs sports and viewer experiences in important ways. And it happens so smoothly that most people think that when they watch a game on television they are experiencing sports in a "natural" form!

Too often we watch sports on television without thinking about *why* we are seeing what is on our screens or *why* we are hearing the commentators say certain things. But whether we are aware of it or not, our experiences as television spectators are heavily influenced by the decisions of those who control the media, and their decisions are influenced by social, political, and economic factors—including dominant ideologies related to gender, race, and class (see chaps. 8 to 10). I will discuss this later in the chapter, but first I will examine the relationship between sports and the media, and outline how each has influenced the other. My major frame of reference in the next section will be the United States, although I will use examples from other countries whenever possible.

SPORTS AND THE MEDIA: A TWO-WAY RELATIONSHIP

The media and the commercialization of sports are closely related topics in the sociology of sport. In fact, the media intensify and extend the process and consequences of commercialization. For this reason, much attention has been given to how sports have been influenced by the media, while little attention has been given to how the media have been influenced by sports. But there is actually a reciprocal relationship between these two important spheres of life: each has influenced the other, and each has grown to depend on the other for its popularity and commercial success.

Do Sports Depend on the Media?

Many sport forms do not depend on the media. However, the existence and success of commercial sports and sport organizations do depend on the media. People played sports long before the newspaper sports section, television, and the Internet were around to cover and "re-present" the events. Even now, people participate in a variety of sports receiving no media coverage. When sports exist just for the participants, there is no urgent need to advertise games, publicize results, and interpret what happened. The players already know these things, and they are the only ones who matter. These sports exist for the players, not to entertain ticket-buying spectators. It is only when sports become commercial entertainment that they depend on the media.

Sportswriter Leonard Koppett (1994) describes sports as unique forms of entertainment. Unlike other forms, sports require the media to provide a combination of coverage *and* news. People attend plays, concerts, and movies and engage in many other leisure activities without needing regular up-to-the-minute media coverage to enjoy these activities. However, with sports, this coverage is very important. When a stage play is over, it's over—except for a review after opening night and the personal conversations of those who attended the play. But when a sports event is over, many people are interested in discussing statistics, important plays, records, standings, the overall performances of players and teams, upcoming games or matches, the importance of the game or match in terms of the season as a whole, the postseason, the next season, and so on. The media are important vehicles for these discussions.

Without media coverage, the popularity and revenue-generating potential of commercial spectator sports would be seriously limited. Information about events generates interest, and interest generates revenues from the sale of tickets, luxury boxes, club seats, concessions, parking, team logo merchandise, and licensing rights. After games or matches have been played, the scores become news items, and the interpretations of action become entertainment for fans, regardless of whether they attended the event in person or not. This seems to be the case from one culture to another—for bullfights in Mexico, hockey games in Canada, soccer matches in Brazil, and sumo wrestling in Japan.

Sports promoters and team owners, especially those in countries with market economies, are well aware of the need for media coverage for sports. Therefore, they often go out of their way to accommodate reporters, commentators, and photographers (Koppett, 1994). Media personnel often are given comfortable seats in press boxes, special access to the fields of play and the players' locker rooms, special summaries of statistics and player information, and special play-by-play information on what is happening during events. Providing these services costs money, but it guarantees media coverage, and it encourages those covering the events to be supportive and sympathetic in what they write and say.

Although all commercial spectator sports depend on the media, some of them have a special dependence on television. For example, in many countries, television is different from the other media in that it actually provides a direct source of revenues for certain sports. Unlike other media organizations, the television companies pay considerable amounts of money for broadcasting rights. These "rights fees" paid by television companies provide sports with relatively predictable sources of income. Once contracts are signed, television money can be counted on regardless of bad weather, injuries to key players, and other factors that often interfere with ticket sales and other on-site revenue streams.

Television revenues also have much greater growth potential than revenues from gate receipts. Only so many tickets can be sold to an event, and tickets can cost only so much without turning people off. But television audiences can include literally billions of viewers, now that satellite technology transmits signals to most locations around the globe. For example, the 1994 Soccer World Cup final game was televised in 190 countries and was watched by nearly 1.3 billion people.

The size of the potential TV audience and the deregulation of the television industry are the two main reasons television rights have increased in value at phenomenal rates since the early 1970s. Television rights fees not only have made commercial sports more profitable for promoters and team owners, but also have in-

creased the attractiveness of sports as vehicles for advertising products nationally and internationally (Williams, 1994, 1995). They also have increased the potential incomes of athletes and turned some athletes into national and international celebrities, who then can use their celebrity status to make money endorsing products sold around the world. For example, Michael Jordan's global popularity is due as much to the invention of the satellite dish as to his basketball skills or the shoes he wears!

HAVE COMMERCIAL SPORTS SOLD OUT TO THE MEDIA? There is no question that some sports have become very dependent on television for revenues and publicity. The NFL, for example, brings in nearly 60 percent of its revenues from television contracts. But the benefits of television seldom come without strings attached. Accommodating the interests of commercial television has required numerous changes in the ways sports are packaged, scheduled, and presented. Some of these changes include the following:

- The schedules and starting times for many sports events have been altered to fit the programming needs of television.
- Halftime periods in certain sports have been shortened so that television audiences will be more likely to stay tuned to events.
- Prearranged schedules of time outs have been added to football, basketball, and hockey games to make time for commercials.

Many other changes that have been associated with television coverage are not entirely due to the influence of television. For example, college football teams added an eleventh game to their schedules, and professional teams extended their seasons and the number of games played. But these changes would have occurred even without television. Commercial sports would have added extra games simply to increase gate receipts. Extra games do make television contracts more lucrative, but the economic reasons for adding games include more than just the

"The TV people said the public would never watch professional swimming unless we made it more exciting."

sale of television rights. The same thing is true for the additions of sudden-death overtime periods in some sports, the tiebreaker scoring method in tennis, the addition of medal play in golf, and the three-point shot in basketball. Each of these changes is grounded in general commercial interests that are independent from television coverage. But *television adds to the urgency and importance of these changes.*

Television *expands* the commercial interests that are already an important part of spectator sports in many societies (*The Economist*, 1996b). Although some changes in sports result from the requirements of television coverage, the real reason for most changes over the past three decades has been the desire to produce more marketable entertainment for all spectators and a more attractive commercial package for sponsors and advertisers. Furthermore, these changes have been made willingly in most cases. The trade-offs usually have been attractive for both players and sponsors. In fact, many of the sports and athletes not currently receiving television coverage gladly would make changes in the way their events are packaged, scheduled, and presented if

they could reap the attention and money associated with television contracts. Are there limits to what they would change for television coverage? In many cases, yes; in a few cases, no. Selling out is not so much a matter of making changes; it is a matter of giving up control and autonomy as you participate in sports.

HAVE THE MEDIA CORRUPTED SPORTS?
When people discuss sports and the media, many of them voice the concern that dependence on the media, especially dependence on television, might corrupt sports. Some people argue that this already has happened, and that television is the root of all evil in sports (Rader, 1984). However, this argument fails to take into account two factors:

1. *Sports are not shaped primarily by the media in general, or by television in particular.* The idea that television by itself has somehow transformed sports does not hold up under careful examination (Gruneau, 1989a). Sports are social constructions; as such, they have been created gradually through interactions between athletes, facility directors, sport team

owners, event promoters, media representatives, sponsors, advertisers, agents, and spectators—all of whom have diverse interests and backgrounds. The dynamics of these interactions have been grounded in power relations and shaped by the resources held by different people at different times. Although admittedly, not everyone has equal influence over changes occurring in sports, media interests are not the only factors producing changes in sports or in the relationship between sports and the media. It is unrealistic to think that media people have been able to shape sports to fit their interests alone.

2. *The media, including television, do not operate in a political and economic vacuum.* The concerns of those connected with sports and the relationships they have with one another are heavily influenced by the social, political, and economic contexts in which they live. For example, the media in both the United States and Canada have been and continue to be regulated by various government agencies and policies. Although these regulations have been loosened in recent years, the media must negotiate contracts with teams and leagues under legal constraints. Economic factors also constrain the media by setting limits on the value of sponsorships and advertising time, and by shaping the climate in which types of programming, such as pay-per-view sports, might be profitable. Finally, the media also are constrained by social factors that inform people's decisions on whether they will read about, listen to, or watch sports.

These two factors raise serious questions about whether the media corrupts sports. There are certainly important connections between these two spheres of life, but those connections are grounded in complex sets of social, economic, and political relationships. It is these relationships that we must understand if we are to understand the media's impact on sports. In other words, the conclusion that the media corrupt sports is based on an incomplete understanding of how the social world works and how sports are connected with social relations in society (Stoddart, 1994).

In summary, *noncommercial sports* neither depend on the media nor are likely to be changed or "corrupted" by the media. *Commercial sports*, on the other hand, depend on the media for their success as entertainment. For some commercial sports, the dependence on television is especially strong, but media people alone have not determined how sports are planned, packaged, presented, and played. The coverage of media sports emerges from relationships between media people and many others connected with sports, especially those with commercial interests, such as sponsors and advertisers. Those relationships, however, are formed within a social, political, and economic context influencing the interest and the power of everyone involved. As national governments deregulate the media and allow the media companies to operate exclusively in connection with market forces, people increasingly will evaluate and change sports to "turn them into better television" (*The Economist*, 1996b).

According to editors of *The Sporting News* (December, 1995; published in the U.S.), six of the ten most powerful people in sports around the world are CEOs and/or owners of major, global television companies; each of these six is a white male from an English-speaking country, and each is interested in turning certain sports into what he thinks is more salable television. Each wants to offer programming that people around the globe will watch and that transnational corporations will sponsor and use as advertising vehicles. The sports selected for national and global coverage have been and will continue to be dependent on the media for their commercial success, and the salaries and endorsements of athletes in those sports also will depend on the media. But in this process, the organizations and the people who control and even play in those sports will gain power. This brings us to the next issue.

Do the Media Depend on Sports?

As we all know, there is much more to the media than sports coverage. This is certainly true for magazines, books, radio, movies, and the Internet, although it is less true for newspapers and television. The Internet does not depend on sports, but certain on-line services may make money on sports fans who use the Internet to get up-to-the-minute scores, to obtain special information about particular events, and to enter on-line discussions about athletes, teams, and events.

Neither the book publishing nor the movie industry depends on sports. Until recently, there have been very few successful books or movies about sports. The urgency and uncertainty that is so compelling in live sports is difficult to capture in these media. But since the late 1980s, both publishers and movie studios have given more serious attention to sports figures and stories.

Most radio stations give coverage to sports only in their news segments, although football, baseball, and men's basketball games often are broadcast on local radio stations when local teams are playing. However, some communities have "talk radio" stations that feature sports talk programs that attract large audiences. These audiences have clearcut demographics: they are mostly young and male, and this helps radio stations sell advertising.

Most magazines devote little or no attention to sports coverage, although the number of general and special-interest sport magazines in the U.S. and other countries is increasing. People who are interested in skiing, biking, motocross, car racing, and dozens of other sports now have magazines devoted to their interests.

The media most dependent on sports are newspapers and television. The companies that control these media are at least partially dependent on sports for their commercial success.

Table 12–1 The increasing importance of the sports section in [*The*] *Chicago Tribune*, 1990–1975

Year	Percentage of newsprint given to sport*	Ratio of sport news to other news[†]
1900	9	.14 (about 1 : 7)
1925	12	.28 (about 2 : 7)
1950	15	.32 (about 1 : 3)
1975	17	.52 (about 1 : 2)

Source: Data from Lever and Wheeler (1984).
*Excludes advertising space.
[†]Includes local, national, and international news items; does not include society pages, arts and leisure, photo pages, comics, or business sections.

This is especially true in the United States. Let's look at some examples.

NEWSPAPERS Newspaper coverage of sports began around the turn of the century in the United States. In a typical big-city newspaper at that time, the sports "page" consisted of only a few notices about upcoming activities, a short story or two about races or college games, and possibly some scores involving local teams. By the late 1920s, the sports page had grown into the sports "section," which resembled the sports sections of today's newspapers (Lever and Wheeler, 1993). As sports have become a highly visible part of popular culture in many post industrial societies, special daily and weekly "sports newspapers" have emerged, that are completely dependent on sports.

In a detailed study of *The Chicago Tribune* between 1900 and 1975, Janet Lever and Stan Wheeler (1984) found that sports coverage became an increasingly significant part of this newspaper during those years (table 12–1). Sports coverage made up 9 percent of the total newsprint (minus advertisements) in 1900, and 17 percent in 1975. But even more significant was the ratio of sports coverage to general news coverage (excluding special features, comics, and so on): it grew from 14 percent in 1900 to slightly over 50 percent in 1975! Similar patterns have existed in other North American newspapers. In *USA Today*, the only national daily newspaper in the United States (apart from *The Wall Street Journal*), sports coverage accounts for 25 percent of the entire paper, and about 50 percent of daily news items.

In most major North American newspapers, more daily coverage is given to sports than to any other single topic of interest, including business or politics. The sports section is the most widely read section of the paper, and according to some estimates, accounts for about 30 percent of the total circulation for big-city newspapers (Greendorfer, 1983; Smith and Blackman, 1978). In other words, if the sports section were eliminated, newspaper sales would go down 30 percent—along with the advertising revenues tied to circulation figures. Many newspapers depend on sports for advertising revenues, as well as for general subscriptions and sales.

Additionally, the sports section attracts advertisers who might not put ads in other sections of the paper. Advertisers know that if they want to reach young to middle-aged males with average or above-average incomes, they should place their ads in the sports section. This is an attractive prospect for businesses that sell tires, automobile supplies, new cars, car leases, airline tickets for business travelers, alcoholic beverages, power tools, building supplies, sporting goods, hair growth products, and even steroids. Other advertisers may be clinics and doctors specializing in treating impotence or providing testosterone and other hormone therapies, bars or clubs providing naked or near-naked female models and dancers, and organizations offering gambling opportunities (see a sample of major-city newspapers to confirm this). Ads for all these products and services generate considerable income for newspapers.

TELEVISION COMPANIES Some television companies in North America also have developed a dependence on sports for programming content and advertising revenues. For example, sports events are a major part of the programming schedules of national network stations in the U.S. and a growing number of cable and satellite-based stations; some television companies even sponsor events that they then promote and televise. Sports account for a growing proportion of income made on the sales of commercial time by television companies. Many cable stations, including ESPN, ESPN2, PSN (Prime Sports Network), Fox Sports Net, TBS (Atlanta), WGN (Chicago), TNN (The Nashville Network), CSN (Classic Sports Network, playing reruns of past events/games), BSkyB (based in England), Star TV (in Asia), and a growing number of other cable companies, have used sports programming to attract subscribers from particular segments of the viewing public; many also use sports to attract advertisers. In the mid-1990s, ESPN transmitted sports coverage to 150 countries in 14 different languages, and it was continuing to expand. In fact, people in the U.S. and some other parts of the world can watch over 7,500 hours of sport programs every year, if they have the time, interest, and cable hook-ups; this is about 20 hours per day, 365 days a year!

An attractive feature of sports programming for the major networks (ABC, CBS, NBC, and Fox), is that it can be scheduled on Saturday and Sunday afternoons—the slowest time periods of the week for television viewing. This is one of the reasons many of the new corporate owners of professional sport teams in the United States also own television broadcasting companies; they see the interests of both as interconnected. Of course, television executives recognize that regular-season games do not usually receive high ratings compared to most prime-time weeknight shows. But they also know that the games are the most popular weekend television programs, especially among viewers who may not watch much television at other times during the week. This means the networks are able to sell advertising time at relatively high rates during what normally would be "dead time" for programming.

The networks also use sports programming to attract particular commercial sponsors that might take their advertising dollars elsewhere if television stations did not cover certain sports. For example, games in the major men's team sports are ideal for promoting the sales of beer, life insurance, trucks and cars, computers, investment services, credit cards, and air travel. The people in the advertising departments of major corporations realize that these games attract male viewers. They also realize that most business travelers are men and that many men make family decisions on the purchases of beer, cars, computers, investments, and life insurance. Finally, they also may be interested in associating their product or service with the culturally positive image of sport. This is especially important for a product such as beer, which has a dubious image in the U.S., where some people have strong prohibitionist sentiments.

Golf and tennis are special cases for television programming. These sports attract few viewers and the ratings are exceptionally low. However, the audience for these sports is attractive to certain advertisers. It is made up of people from the highest income groups in the U.S., including many professionals and business executives. This is the reason television coverage of golf and tennis is sponsored by companies selling luxury cars and high-priced sports cars, business and personal computers, imported beers, investment opportunities with brokers and consultants, and trips to exclusive vacation areas. This is also the major reason the networks continue to carry these programs: although few people watch them, they generate revenues from sponsors with special products to sell to high-income consumers.

In the mid-1990s, television executives "discovered" women viewers of sports and women's sports. Data since the late 1980s had indicated that women made up more than half the viewing audiences for both winter and summer Olympic Games. This led NBC to focus on women's sports and on women viewers in the 1996 telecasts of the games. The success of this approach will inform future media coverage and serve as a basis for attracting new sponsors with products to sell to women. Additionally, in 1996 the new eight-team Women's National Basketball Association was the first women's sport league to sign a national broadcast contract (with NBC, through the year 2000). And the American Basketball League signed a contract with SportsChannel Regional Network to have games telecast on a regional basis through 1998. Television companies have seen that women's sports are likely to be a growing source of revenues.

Cable and satellite television companies also have found they can attract advertising money by televising sports that appeal to other clearly identified segments of consumers. For example, the "X Games" (Extreme Sports) which consist of sports appealing to young people, especially young males between twelve and twenty-five years old, attract advertisers selling soft drinks, beer, telecommunications products, and specialized sports equipment like helmets, shoes, skateboards, etc.

Over the past two decades, television companies have paid rapidly increasing amounts of money for the rights to televise certain sports. The contracts for these rights are negotiated every few years; some may be negotiated annually. In the case of the major men's spectator sports in the U.S., contracts may involve hundreds of millions of dollars—even more than a billion dollars, in the cases of the NFL, the NBA, and the NCAA Men's College Basketball Tournament. To give you an idea of the trends, figure 12-1 provides the television rights fees paid for the Olympic Games and major men's professional team sports by U.S. companies.

The escalation of rights fees clearly shows that television companies want to include sports in their programming lineups, and they think sports will make them money. They realize that the Olympics have become the biggest world television event in human history, that fifteen of

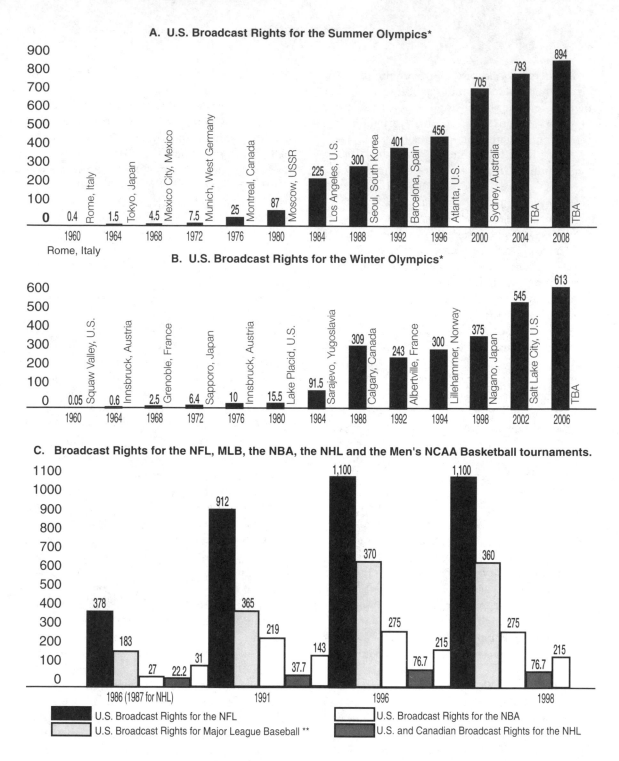

FIG. 12-1 Media money in sports (in millions).

---

*The IOC also receives rights fees from other television companies around the world. Europe, Japan, and continental Asia are paying increasingly high fees.

Continued

Table 12–2 The Top 20 U.S. Telecasts Ranked by Household Projections (1961–1997)

Program	Year	Ave. U.S. Audience (in millions)
1. M*A*S*H* (special)	02/28/83	60.2
2. Winter Olympics	02/23/94*	45.7
3. Super Bowl XXX	01/28/96	44.2
4. Super Bowl XXVIII	01/30/94	42.9
5. Cheers	01/20/93	42.4
6. Super Bowl XXXI	01/26/97	42.0
7. Super Bowl XXVII	01/31/93	42.0
8. Winter Olympics	02/25/94*	41.5
9. Super Bowl XX	01/26/86	41.5
10. Dallas	11/21/80	41.5
11. Super Bowl XXVII	01/30/83	40.5
12. Super Bowl XXI	01/25/87	40.0
13. Super Bowl XVI	01/24/84	40.0
14. Super Bowl XXIX	01/29/95	39.4
15. Super Bowl XIX	01/20/85	39.4
16. Super Bowl XXIII	01/22/89	39.4
17. Super Bowl XXV	01/27/91	39.0
18. Super Bowl XXVIII	01/22/84	38.8
19. Film, *The Day AFter*	11/20/83	38.6
20. (tie) Super Bowl XXII	01/31/88	37.1
20. (tie) Super Bowl XXVI	01/26/92	37.1

Source: Based on data from A.C. Nielson.
*Telecasts on these days featured women's figure skating specifically the programs skated by Nancy Kerrigan and Tonya Harding.

the top twenty television programs in history have been Super Bowls (see table 12–2), that the cost of advertising on the *top* sport events is generally much higher than it is for other types of programs ($1.2 million for each of fifty-eight 30-second slots during the 1997 Super Bowl), that sports involve minimal production costs, and that sports have relatively predictable ratings. Even though there have been cases in which television companies have lost money on sports, profits are generally good, and sports programs can be used as a basis for promoting other programs with hard-to-reach viewers.

Another trend is that as televised sport events have increased, the ratings for many particular events have gone down. As people have more choices, the viewing audience becomes fragmented. More people are watching television sports, but there are more choices than ever before. This means that rights fees for the very large events will continue to increase, but fees for other events, including some "special interest" events (like bowling, in-line skating championships, international skiing races, etc.) will be limited. When interest among particular viewers is especially strong, as for championship boxing and certain other sport events, pay-per-view (PPV) sports programming will push rights fees to high levels. Television companies know that PPV sports have the potential to be big moneymakers, but they also know that pay-per-view coverage must be introduced cautiously and selectively. Many viewers are not willing to pay up front to see an event on television; nor are they accustomed to doing so. But changes are gradually occurring, and we can expect more sports events to be available only through PPV in the future.

The fragmentation of the television sports audience will continue into the twenty-first century. Fiber-optic television technology may bring as many as five hundred channels into people's homes. Some of these channels will provide sports coverage, and in fact, come to depend on sports for their income. As new digital television technology is sold to consumers around the world, it is certain that television companies will use sport events strategically to encourage consumers to invest in the switch from their old analog televisions to digital sets.

Regular sports programming is an established part of the television industry. Even though it occasionally loses money, it provides opportunities for major television companies to promote their

Continued

**To be prorated in late 1997. Estimates for what the NFL will receive each year are as high as $2 billion. This will affect players' salaries, because the salary cap is tied to league income.
†Figures for baseball do not include local broadcast rights fees negotiated by individual teams.

other programs and boost ratings during the rest of the week. It also serves a public relations function, by enhancing the image of television among people who may watch very few programs other than sports.

In 1994, Rupert Murdoch, owner of the Fox Television Network in the U.S., paid the NFL $1.58 billion in an attempt to use pro football and hockey coverage between 1995 and 1999 as the centerpiece of a global corporate expansion strategy. As a writer from *The Sporting News* explained, Murdoch's "idea [was] to use Fox-televised athletes as a sort of human growth hormone for the network's other programming" (Knisley, 1996). He knew that people in North America were dedicated to watching NFL football and NHL hockey, so he used that to leverage his attempt to acquire local television affiliates and thereby compete with the major television networks. He also planned to use the NFL and other sports coverage as part of global expansion through his other companies around the world (including the three-channel BSkyB in England and Star TV in Asia). This reminds us that television dependence on sports is now a global phenomenon, not just something that exists in North America.

Sports and the Media: A Symbiotic Relationship Fueled by Economic Forces

When people discuss the relationship between sports and the media, they focus much attention on the impact of the media on sports. There is no question that this impact has been significant in the case of commercial spectator sports, although noncommercial sports continue to exist and often thrive without media coverage. But relatively little attention has been given to the impact of sports on the media. Although the media cover much more than sports, some newspapers and television companies have come to depend on sports nearly as much as sports depend on them.

Newspapers devote considerable space to the coverage of sports, and television uses sport events to fill its programming needs on week-

ends and holidays. People who read newspapers and watch television have come to expect this coverage. Furthermore, it attracts many people who normally may not buy newspapers or watch much television. Finally, the coverage of sports links both newspapers and television to an increasingly popular sphere of life in contemporary society. This link is a crucial part of their commercial success.

In countries with market economies and privatized media, the interdependence of sports and the media is grounded in concerns about money and profits. Sports can sell newspapers and attract television viewers; this helps newspapers sell advertising space and television companies sell advertising time. In turn, the media can generate revenues for sport organizations and create sport-related images that can be sold in connection with everything from coffee mugs and jackets to shoes and baseball gloves. Sports and the media clearly have a *symbiotic* relationship.* In this case, each depends on the other for its commercial success and its prominent place in popular culture in many societies around the world.

Since the 1970s, the symbiotic relationship between sports and the media has been dramatically intensified by global economic factors. Major transnational corporations need vehicles through which they can develop worldwide name recognition and product familiarity; they also need images through which they can promote a way of life based on consumption, competition, and individual achievement and status (Williams, 1994). Media sports clearly meet these needs of global corporations: certain sport events attract worldwide attention, satellite technology takes television signals around the world, sport images are associated with recognizable symbols and pleasurable experiences by billions of people, and sports and athletes usually can be presented in politically neutral ways so that they can be linked to local identities and then used to

---

Symbiosis is an intimate relationship between two dissimilar organisms for their mutual benefit.

market products, values, and lifestyles (Wenner, 1994). Therefore, powerful global corporations have underwritten or sponsored the media coverage of sports, especially on television (see the box on pp. 382–383 for a discussion of this in the context of the Olympics).

Another source of corporate sponsorship money comes from the alcohol and tobacco industries. For them, sports media are a key vehicle for presenting and promoting their products in connection with activities defined by most people as healthy. This enables them to present product images that they hope will counteract other negative images in the culture (Crompton, 1993). We find these product images most frequently in such print media as sport magazines, in prime advertising space such as back or inside covers; ads on TV have been outlawed in many countries. And research clearly indicates that the magazines receiving large amounts of advertising money from these companies do not publish articles that are antismoking or antidrinking (Crompton, 1993).

It is clear that the marriage of sports and the media has been held together and strengthened by the vast amounts of money coming from corporations whose executives see sports as tools for promoting their interests. And this marriage held together by money is true symbiosis.

IMAGES AND MESSAGES IN MEDIA SPORTS

To say that sports are "mediated" is to say that they are "re-presented" to readers, listeners, and viewers through selected images and/or messages. A growing number of sociologists are interested in digging into these selected images and messages to identify the ideas or themes upon which they are based. As they do their digging, sociologists assume that media sports are symbolic constructions, much like Hollywood-produced action films, television soap operas, and Walt Disney cartoons (Duncan, 1989). In other words, a telecast of a football game is a representation of certain people's ideas about football, social life, human beings, what is important in the world, and what the viewing au-

dience wants to see and hear. Although sociologists realize that different people interpret media images and messages in different ways (Oriard, 1993), they also realize that many people use mediated sports as reference points as they form, revise, and extend their ideas about sports, social life, and social relations.

Because media sports have become a part of everyday experience in today's societies, it is important to consider the following questions:

1. How are sports constructed in and through the media?
2. What general ideas or themes underlie the images and messages "re-presented" in media sports?
3. Does reading about, listening to, and viewing sports have an effect on other types of behavior, such as active sport participation, attendance at sport events, and gambling on sports?

How the Media Construct Sports

The media provide selected versions of sports. In societies where media are privately owned and depend on financial profits, sports are selected for coverage on the basis of their entertainment value. The images and messages are presented to provide as much of the event as possible (Stoddart, 1994), and to fit the perceived interests of both audience and sponsors. Research suggests that mediated sports in the U.S. emphasize action, competition, final scores, performance statistics, records, elite athletes and events, aggression, heroic action, and athletes' emotions and personalities (Kinkema and Harris, 1992).

The sports pages of American newspapers give scores, statistics, accounts of "big plays" and individual heroics, and behind-the-scenes stories; newspaper photos generally capture action or drama. American television coverage focuses on the ball (puck, etc.) and/or the athlete who currently is winning the game, match, meet, or race. Commentators interpret the event, discuss heroic actions and heroic athletes, and emphasize toughness, sacrifice, aggression, and achieve-

REFLECT ON SPORT

Television and the Olympic Games
A Marriage of Mutual Interest?

The Olympics are a good example of the marriage between sports and television. When the Olympics (as represented by the International Olympic Committee) and television companies first came together, the relationship was a true love match; each partner was concerned about the other. Then, as both partners "did their own thing" and grew in separate ways, the relationship became a marriage of convenience. Finally, after both partners became passionately involved with transnational corporations, the relationship turned into a marriage based on money.

During their marriage of nearly forty years, both the Olympics and television companies have changed, partly on their own, and partly due to each other's influence. As in all marriages, it is a constant struggle to maintain a true balance of interests over the long run. Many people think that television has been the dominant partner in the marriage, and that the Olympics have done more giving than receiving. But a look at the record shows that the Olympics, as represented by the IOC, may not be a powerless partner.

First, *history shows that money from the sale of television rights has established the legitimacy and power of the IOC, fueled the organization and growth of the Olympic movement around the world, and turned the Olympic Games into the largest single television event in the world.* The IOC receives one-third of the total amount paid for television rights to the games. The remaining two-thirds go to the Olympic Organizing Committee (OOC), which, as host of the games, is expected to cover all expenses. The amount received by the IOC is divided into thirds, with one share going to the international federations for each of the Olympic sports, a second share going to promote unity between the national Olympic committees (NOCs), and a third share kept by the IOC for its own administration. In 1964 (Tokyo), the IOC split about $500,000 into thirds; but in Atlanta there was $300 million to divide! Nagano, Sydney, Salt Lake City, and future games will provide continually escalating amounts of money for the IOC and the games themselves (see fig. 12-1 on p. 378). These figures clearly indicate that the IOC has used television to gain power and legitimacy, and that television has made the Olympics an increasingly visible and significant world event.

Second, *television networks in the United States have benefited from their coverage of the Olympic Games.* Benefits have come in the form of advertising revenues and programming content. The Summer Olympic Games occur at a time of year when TV viewing rates are low in the U.S. This means that televising the games can boost a network's ratings and give it a stage for promoting its new fall lineup of shows. The Winter Games are also valuable to a network, because they usually occur during the "February sweeps," when crucial viewer ratings are compiled and used to compute advertising rates. Therefore, even if a network breaks even or loses money on Olympic coverage, there are considerable carryover benefits of presenting either the Summer or the Winter Games. This is the major reason the bidding levels have escalated to such high amounts through the games in 2008. In fact, in

· ·

ment in the form of records, scores, and wins. Of course, there are important differences in the coverage provided by print and broadcast media. Table 12–3 summarizes these differences.

The media also have been known to "hype" sports by exaggerating the spectacular, inventing rivalries that don't exist, and manufacturing reasons that events are important and should be read about, listened to, or viewed. The media also emphasize *elite* sport competition. For example, Lever and Wheeler's study (1984, 1993) showed that over the years, the *Chicago Tribune* has increased its coverage of professional sports and decreased its coverage of amateur sports, including high school and college sports. This is also the case with other big-city newspapers, and this pattern has continued through the last quarter of the twentieth century. Over the same pe-

1995 NBC paid nearly $3.6 billion for the rights to televise the games in the years 2000, 2002, 2004, 2006, and 2008. NBC executives know that covering the Olympics can boost annual profits and build corporate status and power in the U.S. and around the world.

Third, *while the IOC has made changes in the Olympic Games to meet the needs of television, those changes have been made voluntarily through negotiations, not dictated by television.* Over the years, the IOC has made the Summer Games a seventeen-day rather than a fifteen-day event, so that there would be two extra prime-time weekend days of competition to generate advertising revenues. The dates for some Winter Games have been shifted so that the host U.S. network could benefit from the February ratings period. The IOC, however, did not approve these changes without receiving something in return; in fact, they partly explain why rights fees paid to the IOC and organizing committees have increased so dramatically.

Game locations are very important to U.S. television networks. When locations permit live telecasts during prime-time viewing hours in the United States, the potential for advertising revenues goes up. This drives up bids from the networks, and it probably has influenced IOC members to choose locations such as Mexico City, Montreal, Lake Placid, Los Angeles, Calgary, Atlanta, and Salt Lake City for nine Olympiads since 1968. Before television was a source of big money for the Olympics, only two out of fifteen summer games were held in the Western Hemisphere (1904 in St. Louis and 1932 in Los Angeles).

The scheduling of events during the games also has been influenced by television interests. In most cases the changes have been minor. Also, there have been only minor changes in the rules for events; for example, athletes are required to wear visibly displayed numerals on their uniforms so that television commentators can identify them.

Finally, the Olympic Charter has undergone one change to accommodate television: it now states that the IOC can award exclusive broadcast rights to a single television company, and that no other companies can show any film coverage of an event until after the end of the broadcast day in which the event occurred.

Overall, it seems that the IOC and the Olympic Games have had enough power to resist *major* changes based on the interests of television. Changes have occurred, but all marriages involve compromises by one or both partners. And the compromises made on the part of the Olympics have gained the games power, resources, and status. Some people argue that the IOC and the Olympics have sold their collective soul to television for money. But I would say that both the Olympics and television have joined together more closely to sell themselves to transnational corporations that are using them both for their own purposes. Those corporations have been interested primarily in delivering their messages to people in the U.S. and other wealthy countries around the world. Therefore, the real losers may be the residents of those countries of the world that don't have high per capita incomes. What do you think?

riod, television consistently has focused attention on professional sports, with some coverage given to selected big-time intercollegiate sports for men. This exaggerated coverage of professional sports ultimately emphasizes the importance of winning and heroic actions over other factors associated with sport participation. The result is that media audiences get "slanted" versions of sports, versions matching what media

people think they want to see and matching the interests of sponsors buying advertising time.

Even though mediated sports are slanted, most people do not give much thought to how and why sports are re-presented as they are. In fact, most people just enjoy what they read, listen to, and view. They are not inclined to ask critical questions, and media re-presentations do not encourage audiences to be critical. For example,

Table 12–3   Differences between the print and broadcast media: the case of sports coverage*

Print media	Broadcast media
• Emphasize news, analysis, and special features.	• Emphasize entertainment in the form of action and drama
• Offer summaries of events that already have occurred	• Offer play-by-play descriptions and interpretations.
• Provide broad scope of tangible information	• Provide immediacy in coverage of on-the-spot action.
• Success depends on maintaining credibility.	• Success depends on generating hype.
• Coverage is diversified and aimed at a set of separate and distinctive sudiences	• Coverage is focused and aimed at a large single audience at a particular point in time.
• Content is more likely to provide criticism of sports and sport personalities.	• Content is more likely to provide support for sports and sport personalities.

*This comparison is based on material in Leonard Koppett: *Sports illusion, sports reality* (1994).

sociologist Dan Hilliard (1994) explains that televised sports deal with controversy and conflict as they are connected with individuals and personality issues, *not* as they are connected with social and cultural issues. Thus, television coverage may mention controversy and conflict in terms of the actions of particular sport team owners, but *not* in terms of an ownership system where leagues are organized as cartels and operate in monopolistic ways. Coverage may focus on an individual who tests positive for drugs, but it will *not* focus on the politics of drug testing or on the way the organization of sports and sport cultures may encourage or even reward drug usage. Coverage may emphasize the character defects of the drug user, but *not* the defects in the system in which drugs are used or the social and cultural issues raised by drug usage.

According to Hilliard, the only time social, cultural, or ideological issues get raised in the television coverage of the Olympics, for example, is when Cuban athletes defect to the U.S., when Chinese athletes take drugs because of *their* "system," or when communist countries experience contentious political problems that might be indirectly related to sports or sports training. It seems that television "uncovers the sport-ideology connection in its coverage of the communist states, just as it obscures that same connection in coverage of American athletes"

(Hilliard, 1994). But overall, the coverage discourages any form of critical social analysis. This leads Hilliard to conclude the following:

> Because television is so much a part of the way most people experience sport, recognition of the antisociological bias in televised sport may be a first step in developing greater public awareness of the ideological work embedded in sports programming (1994: 98).

Many sociologists agree with Hilliard, questioning the way media re-presentations of sports are incorporated into people's ideas about sports: their definitions of what sports are, what they should be, how sports should be included in their lives, and how they should evaluate themselves when they participate in sports. For example, does the almost exclusive focus on gold medals in the Olympics encourage people to set unrealistic expectations for themselves when they play sports? Do young people who watch sports on television as they grow up learn to define sports as activities that resemble media sports? Research is needed to answer these and other questions, but at this time there are good reasons to believe that people's ideas about sports are heavily informed by the images and messages represented in mediated sports. Furthermore, the themes underlying these images and messages also can inform our ideas about social relations and social life in general. In other words, cultural ideology is embedded in media coverage. We discuss this in the following sections.

Themes Underlying Images and Messages

SUCCESS THEMES The images and messages re-presented in mediated sports emphasize selected themes that identify important issues and particular ways of looking at and interpreting the world. When people read about, listen to, and view sports, these themes may inform their own ideas about the world. For example, television broadcasts of sports in the United States emphasize success through competition, hard work, assertiveness, domination over others, obedience to authority, and coming up with "big plays" like home runs, long touchdown passes, single-handed goals, and so on. The idea that success also can be based on empathy, supporting others, autonomy, intrinsic satisfaction, personal growth, cooperation, compromise, incremental changes, or the achievement of equality gets little or no attention.

The "success theme" underlying images and messages in U.S. media sports is less apparent in other cultures. For example, in a comparison of the media commentary in the coverage of sports in the United States and England, Chandler (1983) found that commentaries in the U.S. emphasized competition, dominance, and final scores; commentaries in England downplayed these things and focused more on strategies and the flow of the game. In her analysis, Chandler explains these differences in this way:

> [In Britain] where mobility is usually achieved by sponsorship, the importance of competition in all facets of public and private life is played down. . . . TV executives working in Britain and the United States thus have to deal with quite different public attitudes towards the importance of competition. I am not suggesting that the British do not want "their side" to win; but winning is by no means "the only thing." I do not know of the British equivalent of the American term "loser"; the nearest is probably "also-ran." Nor does one speak of "winners";

the equivalent term varies according to the context, but in educational activity it would be "high-flyers."

> In both soccer and cricket, it is honorable to draw; indeed, to gamble on winning rather than to play for a draw, may be regarded as simple-minded and rash, whatever the outcome (p. 21).

Things have changed in England over the past twenty years, as conservative governments have emphasized deregulation, privatization, and competition, and I suspect that sports commentaries in media broadcasts also have changed. But televised sports in the U.S. now emphasize winners, losers, and final scores more than ever. Even silver medals are defined as consolation prizes at best; bronze medals seldom are discussed; and games for third place no longer are even played. Commentators talk of "shoot-outs" and sudden-death playoffs instead of ties; success is defined as dominating others; and praise goes to those who make "big hits" and sacrifice their bodies for the sake of a win. Talk of learning, enjoyment, and competing *with* others is rare, even if players see their participation in these terms. Commentaries don't "tell it like it is"; rather, they tell it in a way that fits the interests of those with power and influence in society.

MASCULINITY AND FEMININITY THEMES The media coverage of sports generally emphasizes that sport participation is more appropriate for boys and men than for girls and women, that males are naturally superior to women when it comes to sports, that women's sports are less important than men's sports, and that women's ideas about sports are neither as important nor as interesting as men's ideas about sports.

The evidence supporting these themes is overwhelming. Some of that evidence is summarized in the following list:

- Men's sports still receive well over 85 percent of the coverage in all media, including newspapers, sport magazines, radio, and television (Creedon, 1994; Duncan et al., 1990; Kane and Parks, 1992, 1992; Lumpkin and

Williams, 1991; Messner et al., 1996; Shif-flett and Revelle, 1994a, b). Women's sports are televised more than they were, especially on certain cable stations, but the air time given to women's sports is not much more than 15 percent of total sports air time. Apart from the Olympics, major tennis and golf tournaments, and a growing number of volleyball and basketball games, the coverage of women's sports is not a priority in the media. The coverage of women's sports in big-city newspapers has not increased over the past twenty years (although I expect this to change as we enter the twenty-first century). Nor has there been an increase in coverage in certain sport magazines (Salwen and Wood, 1994). This pattern of underrepresentation of women's sports in the media exists around the world (For Canada, see Crossman et al., 1994; for England see Mathesen and Flatten, 1997; for Australia, see Menzies, 1989, and Stoddart, 1992; for Japan, see Kimura and Saeki, 1990; for Germany, see Pfister, 1989). In fact, in England, between 1984 and 1994 the number of articles on women in sport, the space given to coverage of women, and the number of photographs of women athletes actually decreased (Mathesen and Flatten, 1996)!

- The women's sports that have been given priority in the media are those emphasizing grace, balance, and aesthetics—attributes consistent with traditional images of femininity. Partly for this reason, Olympic coverage focuses on women gymnasts in the summer games and women figure skaters in the winter games (Deford, 1996; MacNeill, 1996). The men's sports most likely to attract media coverage are those emphasizing bulk, height, physical strength, and the use of force and intimidation to physically dominate opponents—all qualities consistent with traditional images of masculinity. For example, football is the most popular televised men's sport in the U.S., and television coverage emphasizes traditional notions of masculinity (Trujillo, 1995).

- Commentaries on women's sports sometimes undervalue the achievements of women athletes by emphasizing their appearance, male partners or husbands, children, mothers, domestic interests and skills, and vulnerabilities and weaknesses (Daddario, 1994; Lumpkin and Williams, 1991; Heinz, 1991). In general, the media "paint a very confused picture of female athletes—strong, but weak; courageous, but vulnerable; powerful, but cute" (Heinz, 1991). Images of strength and weakness often are mixed together in ways that signal ambivalence about women in sports (Blinde et al., 1991; Creedon, 1994; Duncan and Hasbrook, 1988; Halbert and Latimer, 1994; Higgs and Weiler, 1994). The photos (including one I have included in this text, p. 235) of an injured Kerri Strug grimacing while executing a near-perfect landing off the vault during the 1996 Olympics and then being carried to the award podium by her big, strong male coach were a classic representation of this ambivalence.

- Television commentators for women's sports still may refer to women athletes by their first names and as "girls" or "ladies," although this pattern has been changing since sociologists and others have begun pointing it out. Commentators for men's sports seldom refer to men athletes by their first names and almost never call them "boys" or "gentlemen" (Duncan et al., 1990). It is assumed that playing sports turns boys into men.

- References to physical strength have been much more common in commentaries about men athletes, and references to weaknesses are much more common in commentaries about women athletes (Duncan et al., 1990). References to the character flaws of men athletes have emphasized that men are too aggressive, too independent, and too determined to succeed, whereas references to the character flaws of women athletes have em-

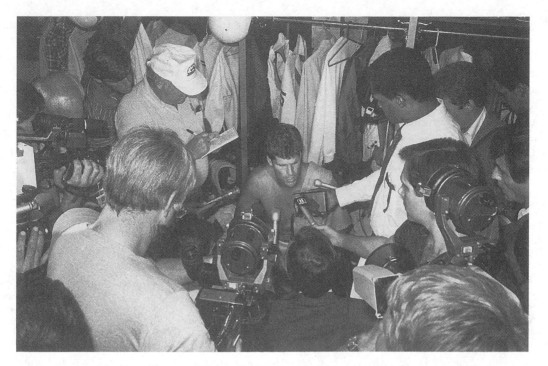

When women journalists first entered the all-male world of men's team locker rooms, they disrupted accepted boundaries and a social world in which male power and privilege were celebrated, often at the expense of women.

phasized that women are too emotional, too dependent, or too unfulfilled in their overall lives (Daddario, 1994; Hilliard, 1984).

• Men's sports events often are promoted or described as if they had some special historical importance, whereas women's sports events usually are promoted in a lighter, less serious manner (Duncan et al., 1990; Messner et al., 1996). Men's events are referred to as *the* ("real") events (for example, *the* NCAA Basketball Championship Tournament), whereas women's events almost always are referred to as *women's* events (for example, the NCAA *Women's* Basketball Championship Tournament—[Blinde et al, 1991]).

• Women's sports events and women athletes receive few major headlines in newspaper sports sections. Over the years, men have been featured on about 90 percent of the covers of *Sports Illustrated*, and half of the women featured on *SI* covers have not even been athletes (Reid and Soley, 1979; Women's Sports Foundation, 1987); data suggests that the greatest amount of coverage given to women occurred during the 1950s (Salwen and Wood, 1994). Even in *Sports Illustrated for Kids*, there have been subtle but powerful photographic images suggesting that most sports are *mainly* for boys and men, and some sports are *only* for boys and men (Duncan and Sayaovong, 1990). *Women's Sports and Fitness* magazine has over the years moved away from sports coverage to focus on physical activities more consistent with traditional notions of femininity (Creedon, 1994; Leath and Lumpkin, 1994). Coverage patterns in the new women's sports magazines scheduled for publication in the late 1990s may break this pattern; future research will analyze the coverage in these new magazines.

- The entire system of sports information in the United States, Canada, and most other countries is set up to make it easy to cover men's sports. Even the work schedules of sports reporters have been established so that men's sports get regular coverage, and women's events are covered only when they are identified as special features (Creedon, 1994; Theberge and Cronk, 1986).

- The *vast* majority of sports media personnel are men (Creedon, 1994). Although women in the print media now regularly cover men's sports, few women ever have done regular commentary for a men's sport (although this has occurred in tennis). When women reporters cover men's sports, they often are regarded as outsiders "invading" men's turf. This occurs because locker-room talk about women generally treats women as nonpersons, sex objects, butts of sexist and homophobic jokes, and victims of male athletes' bedroom conquests (Curry, 1991; Disch and Kane, 1996; Kane and Disch, 1993; Messner, 1991, 1992; Nelson, 1994). When women reporters enter the locker room, they threaten male power and privilege. In the past men were so threatened that they sexually harassed the reporters. A few highly publicized cases of such harassment have led to changes in the locker-room behavior of male athletes. The threat of fines, along with increased understanding that women reporters are no more interested in seeing men's bodies than are men reporters, has made the locker room a safer place for women reporters.

Some of these patterns have begun to change, partly as a result of the critical analyses of sociologists and scholars in media studies. But in the past, they have been so strong that they have supported cultural ideas that sports are "naturally" suited to men rather than women, that men are better athletes than women, that women's sports are much less important than men's sports, and that women were never meant to be sports reporters or commentators because they just don't have the same "feel" for sports that men do (Creedon, 1994; Ordman and Zillman, 1994). Past changes have resulted from the asking of critical questions and the performance of critical analyses of gender ideology and sports; future changes will require more critical questions and analyses.

RACE THEMES Just as the media coverage of sports can influence ideas about gender and gender relations, it can influence ideas about race and race relations. However, patterns related to race have not been so clear as those for gender. Studies done in the 1970s and 1980s (Braddock, 1978a, b; Condor and Anderson, 1984; Pearman, 1978; Rainville and McCormick, 1977) identified the ways that media coverage used and perpetuated stereotypes through descriptions of black athletes and white athletes. For example, coverage in the past tended to criticize black players more and praise them less than white players in the same positions with similar abilities. Announcers emphasized the physical and cognitive skills of whites and described them as aggressive and in control of their own actions; blacks were described more often as the targets of aggression and as players whose actions were determined by factors other than their own choices and decisions.

A study done by Derek Jackson at the *Boston Globe* (22 January 1989) analyzed commentary in seven NFL playoff games and five NCAA men's basketball games during the 1988–89 season. Jackson found that commentators were more likely to describe or refer to white athletes' character and intelligence, but to black athletes' physical assets and abilities. White athletes were criticized more often for lacking physical talent, and black athletes for mental errors. Of course, the commentators did not use these descriptions and references with any conscious racist intent;

nor were they meant to perpetuate destructive and dangerous ideas about race. But racial ideology is so deeply rooted in Western societies that racism sometimes exists without awareness or intent. Manifestations of racial ideology have not disappeared (Murrell and Curtis, 1994), even though people, especially those in the media, have made serious attempts to avoid stereotypes in their coverage. Past research has had a major impact on this change (Sabo and Jansen, 1994; Sabo et al., 1996; Thomas, 1996).

Interviews with black sports journalists and announcers indicate that they are still wary of what they think are a disproportionate number of "poor boy makes good" stories written about black athletes, and about coverage highlighting the material possessions of black athletes who have large pro contracts (Thomas, 1996). It seems that successful black athletes have lifestyles that don't fit white stereotypes, and this lack of fit may be defined by some whites in the media as "news."

One way to reduce covert racial bias in the media is to hire more reporters, editors, photographers, writers, producers, directors, camerapersons, and commentators from ethnic minority groups (Sabo and Jansen, 1994). Lip service has been paid to this goal, and some progress has been made in certain media. But members of racial and ethnic minorities are still underrepresented in sports newsrooms, press boxes, broadcast booths, and media executive offices. For example, during the mid-1990s, there were only six African American sports editors at the 1,600 daily newspapers in the U.S., and only one of these was in a major media market; there were less than a dozen African American sports columnists; and 90 percent of the 1,600 newspapers did not have one full-time African American sportswriter on staff (Lapchick, 1995; Thomas, 1996). Another way to increase racial awareness is to provide personnel with good training workshops on racial ideology and racial relations. Where this has been done, it has been effective (Thomas, 1996).

Finally, there is a chance that race themes underlying the images and messages of mediated sports also will influence the aspirations and choices of African American children, especially boys. If black children watch television and see black athletes excelling in various sports, and if they think their personal and cultural destiny is to achieve great things in sports, these children may dedicate themselves to becoming athletes and give lower priority to pursuing educational and other occupational goals (Bierman, 1990; Gaston, 1986; Murrell and Curtis, 1994). The award-winning documentary *Hoop Dreams* (1995) illustrated this very clearly. Recognizing this, some black urban radio stations have sponsored community service promotional events that emphasize the importance of education (Johnson, 1995); if blacks were in power positions in other media, this might occur more widely.

OTHER IDEOLOGICAL THEMES IN MEDIATED SPORTS It is not easy to identify themes underlying the images and messages in mediated sports. Analyses using critical theory have focused on the extent to which images and messages in mediated sports represent dominant ideas about social life and social relations in society as a whole. Studies using critical theory have identified the three themes I have already discussed (success, gender, race), as well as themes related to nationalism, competitive individualism, teamwork, aggression, and consumerism (Blain et al., 1993; Hargreaves, 1986; Kinkema and Harris, 1992; Sabo et al., 1996).

These themes should not surprise anyone who has read about, listened to, and viewed sports in the United States. The images and messages in mediated sports clearly emphasize *nationalism and national unity* grounded in traditional American loyalty and patriotism. In fact, the sports "invented" in the United States—football, basketball, and baseball—are the most widely televised sports in the country. Other sports may get covered, but if they don't fit with traditional ideas about what it means to be an American, they will not receive priority coverage. When teams or ath-

Calvin and Hobbes   by Bill Watterson

....
Commercial images and messages clearly promote consumerism. Hobbes understands, but Calvin has not yet raised any critical questions about the promotional messages. Hopefully, his sociology of sport course will encourage him to do so in the future.

....

letes from the United States are competing against teams or athletes from other countries, the sport events are usually framed in an "us versus them" format. When American teams or athletes win, media commentary emphasizes that "we won." We will discuss this topic further in chap. 13.

Even in team sports, media images and messages emphasize *individual efforts* to achieve competitive victories. Games often are promoted with announcements like this: "Brett Favre and his Packers are looking for blood against Troy Aikman and his Dallas Cowboys"; or "It is Michael Jordan versus Shaquille O'Neil as the Bulls face the Lakers." This emphasizes the idea that individuals must take responsibility for what happens in their lives, and that team failures can be traced to individual character flaws. This idea is central to the ideology of American individualism, which influences everything from the structure of our welfare system to the way employees are evaluated and rewarded in the economy.

Apart from emphasizing individualism, media images and messages also stress *teamwork*, in the form of obedience to authority, group loyalty, and willingness to sacrifice for the good of the group (Kinkema and Harris, 1992). Media coverage

clearly identifies coaches as the organizers and controllers of teams; commentators praise athletes for being team players, and praise coaches for their ability to fit players into team roles that lead to victories. This teamwork theme clearly fits with ideology underlying the American market economy and most American business organizations: teamwork means loyalty and productivity under the direction of a leader-coach.

The importance of *mental and physical aggression* is another theme underlying the images and messages in mediated sports. Rough, aggressive play is described as a sign of commitment and skill. Tackles in football are described as bone-crushing hits, hard fouls in basketball are described as warnings to the opposition, brushback pitches in baseball are said to keep batters on their heels. Even the scores on the late-night news are full of violent images: the Bulls *annihilated* the Knicks, the Jets *destroyed* the Dolphins, the Blackhawks *scalped* the Bruins, Seles *blew away* Sabatini, and on and on. The scores start to sound like the results of military operations in a war!

In fact, the language of media sports in the United States is a language of violence and warfare (Jansen and Sabo, 1992; Segrave, 1994; Trujillo, 1994). Aggression is celebrated, while kindness and sensitivity are dismissed as indications of weakness. This clearly fits with the ideology many Americans use to determine strategies in interpersonal and international relations; "kicking ass" is a celebrated goal, and failing to punish the opposition is a sign of weakness.

Finally, we must remember that over 15 percent of the air time of televised sports is commercial time; newspapers are full of ads placed around sports stories. "TV time outs" are a standard feature of televised football and basketball games, and announcers remind media audiences that "this game is being brought to you by. . . ." Super Bowl commercials are even the subject of special analyses, and media audiences are polled to see which Super Bowl commercials they liked and did not like. Commercial images and messages promote *consumerism*. The audiences in mediated sports are encouraged to express their connections to teams and athletes by purchasing shirts, shoes, jackets, official NFL hats, official NBA sweatpants, and Notre Dame coffee cups. This is clearly consistent with consumer ideology in American society. "You are what you buy" is one of the tenets of a market economy.

Overall, the images and messages in the media coverage of sports in the United States stress themes representing conventional ideology and widespread ideas about how the world does and should work: order, control, and tough discipline are essential; gender differences are grounded in nature, not culture; the primacy of the nation must be preserved; individuals must be accountable, work in teams, and outproduce others; and consumption is essential to happiness as well as the basis for identity. These themes run through mediated sports. This is the reason media coverage of sports is heavily sponsored by people and corporations with power and influence in society: they like these themes, and promote images and messages that keep them part of the public consciousness in American society. Of course, similar patterns also exist in other societies.

SIDELINES

"Why can't you guys stay in better condition?"

....

Televised sports inspire some people to active participation; others may watch sports rather than participate.

....

Media Impact on Sport-Related Behaviors

ACTIVE PARTICIPATION IN SPORTS Does reading about, listening to, and watching sports cause people to be more active sport participants, or does it turn them into couch potatoes? This question has generated considerable debate; in the United States, for example, the media often are blamed for everything from obesity to a perceived shortage of gold medals in the Olympics.

We do know that when children watch sports in highly promoted television broadcasts, some of them will develop participation interest in those sports. Children are great imitators and they have great imaginations, so when they identify with popular and successful Olympic athletes in gymnastics or swimming, they may join youth sport programs to pursue their dreams. However, media-created interest does not last long, especially after the young people and their parents discover that noteworthy accomplishments require years of dedication and expense. But in the process, some people develop healthy participation patterns. For example, the editors at *The Economist* have argued that global television is a marvelous machine for promoting sports. Far more people run or swim or kick a ball for sheer pleasure than ever before. Thanks to television, many have discovered sports they might never have known existed: rock-climbing, perhaps, or archery or synchronized swimming (*The Economist*, 20 July 1996: 13).

We also know that many adults—both men and women—who watch football, basketball, baseball, and ice hockey on television play none of these sports. In fact, as the television coverage of sports has increased in the U.S., so too have obesity and inactivity. However, we do not know if those who watch sports are less physically active than others with similar characteristics (age, gender, occupation, etc.). At this point, the safest conclusion is that the media probably have no major *net* effect one way or the other on active participation in sports and other physical activities (Irlinger, 1994).

ATTENDANCE AT SPORT EVENTS Game attendance is related to many factors (Wakefield, 1995), and its relationship to the media is complex. On the one hand, the owners of many professional teams enforce a television blackout rule based on the belief that television coverage hurts game attendance and ticket sales. In support of this belief, many people do say that they would rather watch certain sport events on television than attend them in person. On the other hand, it is clear that the media publicize sports, promote interest in them, and provide the information people need to identify with athletes and teams and to become committed fans—and, therefore, game attenders (Weiss, 1996; Zhang et al., 1997).

The most logical conclusion to make at this point is that the media and game attendance are positively related: people who watch more games on TV also attend more games (Zhang et al., 1996a). However, we must qualify this conclusion. *First*, as ticket prices increase, and as the numbers of local elite games increase across different sports, more people may limit attendance when there is the option of watching a local

game on television (Wakefield, 1995; Zhang et al., 1996b). *Second*, because the media focus attention on elite sports, they may undermine attendance at less elite events: people may watch and attend NBA games rather than attend games at the local high school. Thus, the media may be positively related to attendance at the top levels of competition, but negatively related to attendance at lower levels of competition (Zhang et al., 1996b). Research is needed to explore this issue in more depth.

GAMBLING ON SPORTS Some have argued that people who listen to and watch mediated sports don't experience the excitement that goes with attending an event in person, so they place bets on sports to regain some of that excitement. Is this why there are so many "betting pools" at offices and among friends? We know that gambling on sports is widespread (Frey, 1992; Layden, 1995a, b, c; McGraw, 1997; Savage, 1997). But the only certain link between gambling and the media is an indirect one. The media, especially newspapers and television, make people aware of *point spreads* and *betting odds* for different events. Point spreads and betting odds are determined by bookies who want to make sure they don't go broke by taking too many bets on a particular outcome in a sport event. When the media publicize point spreads and odds, they make it easier for many forms of gambling to occur. But it cannot be said that they *cause* gambling.

At this point in time, relatively few people define gambling on sports as an important legal or moral issue within society as a whole. Occasional articles on sports gambling have shown that it can have destructive consequences for those who become dependent on the "rush" associated with having money on a game (Layden, 1995a, b, c), but it has not become a social or political issue in the minds of most people, even though people in the U.S. bet an estimated $90 billion illegally each year (McGraw, 1997). After all, many people are now accustomed to buying lottery tickets and participating in other state-sponsored gambling activities.

Audience Experiences with Media Sports

People use sports coverage in the media for a variety of social purposes, including the following: (1) developing and maintaining personal and social identities connected with athletes and teams, (2) feeling a personal sense of significance and control in their lives, (3) engaging in social interaction, and (4) maintaining social relationships. People usually read about sports alone, but use that information in conversations with both strangers and friends. They may watch sports on television alone, but often do so in social situations varying from intimate to impersonal. For example, someone may watch a game with a spouse or partner, and/or other family members or close friends. Or, the person may watch it in a sports bar, with acquaintances and fellow fans. Or, he or she may watch it in an airport lounge or similar place that contains dozens of strangers. Each of these experiences is different; they now are being studied by a number of scholars with media interests (Duncan and Brummett, 1993; Eastman and Riggs, 1994; Gantz et al., 1995a, b; Weiss, 1996; Wenner, 1997).

Walter Gantz and his colleagues conducted an interesting series of studies on television sports and relationships. They used telephone interviews to collect information on the role of televised sports in married life. They found that watching television sports was not a major activity in the lives of most couples, but when it did occur, it was usually a nondisruptive and positive activity in the relationships. In other words, they found few "football widows" in their sample. The men did watch sports more than the women did, and the men were more likely to be committed fans. But among those who were committed fans, both men and women reacted and responded to televised sports in nearly identical ways; fanship was more important than gender when it came to the viewing experiences. Scheduling and viewing conflicts did occur for some couples, but they were usually resolved without negative effects on the relationships. Partners usually learned to accommodate each other's viewing habits over time as they lived together. In those cases in which there was resentment associated with differences in viewing habits and fanship, relational satisfaction was low. But relational satisfaction was the result of much more than sports-watching habits.

Future studies along these lines will tell us more about how media sport experiences are integrated into our lives and how they become activities around which social life occurs.

THE PROFESSION OF SPORTS JOURNALISM

Leonard Koppett, a well-known and respected sportswriter, has said that one of the goals of sports journalism is "the generation of more and more entertaining material about something that doesn't *really* matter too much." However, sports do matter—not because they produce a tangible product or make an essential contribution to our survival, but because they are constructed and "mediated" to re-present ideas about how the world works and what is important in life. Therefore, sports journalists do things that matter very much when it comes to ideas and ideology in the public consciousness.

In addition to constructing the meanings that underlie people's experience of sports, journalists also help people enjoy and understand sports. Furthermore, the words of sports journalists often affect the sports they cover and the athletes they write and talk about.

In this section we will look at how sports journalists do their jobs and how they are connected to the sports and the athletes they cover. Our definition of *journalists* will include newspaper and magazine writers as well as announcers for radio and television.

Before Television: When Sports*writers* Created the Images and Messages

It is 1928, and the baseball writers covering the New York Yankees on this rail trip are sitting in the train's club car, playing nickel-ante poker. Suddenly, the door to the club car bursts open and Babe Ruth sprints down the aisle, followed closely by an attractive young woman wielding a knife. "I'll kill you, you son of a bitch!" the woman screams as she disappears after Ruth into the next car. The writers observe the action, then turn and look at one another. "That'd make a helluva story," one of them says. The others chuckle and nod, and the poker game resumes. Of course, no one reports the incident. . . .

This true story was used by Rick Telander (1984), staff writer for *Sports Illustrated*, to show how the press covered sports before World War II. He explains that sportswriters in the pretelevision era did things much differently than journalists do them now:

> Those were the days. . . . [Sportswriters] dealt in mythology. They felt that if they told the truth about athletes, readers would revolt and there would be no need for sports sections or sports reporters. The Babe was not real. Few people could see him; almost nobody could hear him; his prowess on the field was all that counted. Thus his bout with gonorrhea in 1926 was passed off as "stomach cramps." A 1919 home run of his rose "into some floating white clouds" while opponents stood "transfixed with the splendor of it."

Radio simply reinforced the images and messages re-presented in the press. Media audiences were influenced by those images and messages as they formed ideas about sports and the connection between sports and the rest of their lives. Since people could not actually see what happened at games, writers and radio broadcasters could make athletes bigger than life; they could make them into heroes. And so they did. Their words constructed images of heroic deeds and dramatic action. These words did much to contribute to what is now called the *"golden age of sports"* in the United States. And that "golden age" was one during which women received no media coverage, and blacks were excluded from participating with whites in elite sports covered by the media (who would refer to this as "golden"?).

This process of hero building and the creation of drama was clearly tied to dominant definitions of sports at that time in history. (White, male) athletes were painted as superhuman characters shaped by sport participation; sports were de-

fined as exciting and challenging forms of competition. This did much to intensify the traditional turn-of-the-century idea that sport participation and competition built character in boys and young men.

After Television: A New Age for Sports Journalists

In the 1950s, things changed. Television created a new situation. Newspapers and magazines had to cover more than scores and descriptions of the action. Since people now could *see* sports at home, sportswriters had to have stories that went beyond the action. They "had to tell readers more about the players as personalities, delve more thoroughly into the reasons for strategies, be more critical of managers and coaches, and report more thoroughly the behind-scenes maneuvering and conflicts" (Ray Sons, quoted in Telander, 1984). This type of coverage created serious tension in player-press relationships in North American sports, and some of that tension still exists today (Bourgeois, 1995).

When the sportswriters needed to come up with stories going beyond the action in sports, players discovered they had no privacy. No matter what they said or where they said it, their words could end up in print if there were a sportswriter around. This kept most athletes from saying the spontaneous things that made good material for reporters (Koppett, 1994). The reporters, on the other hand, were under constant pressure to get good stories—to dig into the lives of the athletes their readers were watching on television.

The tension between players and sportswriters escalated in the 1960s, when journalism increased its emphasis on the personal and the spectacular. Newspapers and magazines published sports stories written in the same style as paperback novels. The stories were full of intrigue, but they often offended athletes and invaded their personal lives. In 1970, baseball player Jim Bouton published the book *Ball Four*; and players realized once and for all that even their private conversations with other players could end up in print! This was new, and it made

SIDELINES

LIVE.

"The losing team has made it clear to me that they are in no mood to be interviewed. Back to you, Ron."

Tension between athletes and media personnel increases when the search for dramatic stories infringes on the privacy of athletes and coaches. Tensions also are grounded in the fact that many athletes don't believe that reporters understand what it means to be an athlete.

athletes wary of what journalists might write about them. At the same time, journalists were more likely to be on the lookout for big stories that revealed the underside of sports.

Tensions were intensified by the growing differences in the salaries and backgrounds of players and sportswriters. When players did not earn much more than sportswriters, the writers and players could identify with one another. But when players' salaries increased at dramatic rates in the 1980s, the basis for this mutual identification disappeared. Athletes became national superstars instead of local heroes, and their incomes far surpassed the incomes of the reporters who wrote about them. The fact that many of the athletes were blacks without college degrees, while the reporters were whites with degrees, also interfered with mutual identification. In the face of these differences, reporters no longer felt compelled to protect or glorify athletes in their stories, and athletes became more protective of their newfound wealth and status. In fact, some professional athletes had personal policies of not talking with sportswrit-

ers. The athletes believed they could use television and television commentators to keep their names in front of the public, so they no longer felt obligated to respond to sportswriters.

As players became less willing to talk, sports management people became worried. Promoters and team owners realized the importance of the written media in marketing their games, matches, and other products. Some sport team owners even offered players seminars on the importance of newspaper coverage, and others provided training sessions to teach players how to handle interviews without saying things that would sound bad. In some cases, teams even fined players who refused to talk to the press. This awareness of the importance of press coverage continues in commercial sports today. However, tension between sportswriters and athletes also still exists. In some cases, it has been so strong that players have threatened writers and writers have quit their jobs in search of less stressful occupations.

Ethics and Sports Journalism

Questions about ethics apply to all forms of sports journalism, but they are especially important for the print media. The foundation of the written media is its reputation as a dependable source of facts. Before television, sportswriters were mere extensions of the teams and players they covered. In some cases, they were even on team payrolls; and if they weren't, they often depended on teams and team owners for travel funds, hotel rooms, transportation to games, meals, and other favors. As radio and television coverage became increasingly popular, announcers and commentators replaced sportswriters as the voices of public relations for sports. In fact, some radio and television commentators now are hired by teams and given guidelines on what to say and what not to say during broadcasts. Most audiences realize this, and simply expect the commentators to be personable entertainers. However, with sportswriters, it's different. Writers are expected to dig into sports and report things that cannot simply be shown on television. A detailed illustration of

Table 12–4   Sportwriters and sports announcers: a comparison of roles

Role characteristics	Sportswriters*	Sports announcers[†]
• **Job security**	High	Low
• **Salary**	Low	High
• **Popularity/public recognition**	Low	High
• **Freedom of expression in job**	Moderate to high	Low; heavily restricted
• **Purpose of role**	To give information about sport events	To "sell" sport events
• **Role expectations**	To be objective investigators	To be personable entertainers
• **Opportunities to do investigative reporting**	Sometimes	Very rare
• **On-the-job contacts**	Copy desk editors and sub-editors	Broadcast executives, team management, sponsors, advertising people
• **Relationships with players**	Often tense and antagonistic	Friendly and supportive
• **Level of response evoked from public**	Low	High

Source: Data from Koppett, 1994.

*The primary focus here is on newspaper reporters, Magazine writers have similar jobs, but they are different in some important respects.

[†]The primary focus here is on television announcers. Radio broadcasters have similar jobs, but they are different in some important respects.

the differences between the role of sportswriter and the role of television commentator is in table 12–4.

Sportswriters no longer depend on teams for money or favors. They seldom are bought off as they were in the past. But there are still factors that discourage tough, investigative reporting. According to Koppett (1994), the judgment of many reporters is distorted by very subtle aspects of their jobs. He points out that to get more information for their stories, reporters must get well acquainted with the people they are assigned to cover. The better acquainted they get, the more likely they are to take on the attitudes of those people (players and sponsors). When this happens, they find it difficult to do critical, investigative reporting. In fact, the easy way out is simply to "report" what the teams tell them in press releases and other materials, and do little or no independent investigations of what is occurring in sports.

In discussing this issue, Koppett has noted that writers must strive to be fair and thorough in their reporting. But this does not mean writing without personal opinion. In fact, personal opinions will always influence what a person writes. Fairness simply depends on not letting opinions "distort the accuracy of your account, to whatever extent you can be aware of distortion." In other words, being a sportswriter is similar in some respects to being a sport sociologist: both must be aware of the perspectives they use to look at sports, and both must try to use systematic methods and critical thinking to explore the questions they raise.

Another important ethics issue is related to the impact of the media on the people they cover. Journalists, especially those in the print media, must be especially sensitive to this issue. They are called on to be fair, but they must also take care not to jeopardize people's reputations simply for the sake of entertainment. This does not

Radio and television commentators are entertainers. Most are paid by the organizations that own or control the teams they cover. The people who pay them expect that they will be "cheerleaders," not critics. People generally do not expect them to do investigative reporting or cover games objectively. (University of Colorado Media Relations)

mean that a journalist should avoid criticism that might hurt someone. But according to Koppett (1994), a journalist should never hurt someone unintentionally; the writer should do so only intentionally and with good reason. Otherwise, the sportswriter is simply engaging in a destructive, self-serving form of sensationalism that raises ethical concerns about the invasion of privacy.

Sportswriters and Sports Announcers: A Comparison

Not everyone who covers sports for the media emphasizes the same things. In the print media the focus is on information and analysis, and in the broadcast media it is on entertainment. This difference has important implications for writers and commentators, which Leonard Koppett has discussed in detail in his book *Sports Illusion,*

Sports Reality. I have summarized his discussion in table 12–3.

According to Koppett, the main difference between the print and the broadcast media is this:

A newspaper woos the readership with reliability and thoroughness and hires people who strive in that direction. A broadcast tries to dazzle and fascinate the audience enough to keep it glued to the set and hires people who can create that effect (1994).

This is the reason why the best investigative reporting is done by newspaper and magazine writers (especially the latter), and the reason why the most popular media personalities sit in television broadcasting booths.

However, while looking at table 12–3, remember that there are exceptions to these role descriptions. Some writers—especially certain syndicated columnists—write to entertain. The successful ones have relatively high salaries and a reasonable amount of job security. On the other hand, some television announcers do investigative reporting in which information and analysis take priority over entertainment. However, the major patterns for the roles of sportswriter and sports announcer are accurately represented by the information in the table.

The efforts of television companies to provide a combination of expert analysis and entertainment are evident in the fact that they hire popular retired athletes and coaches to do commentaries for games. Some people complain that ex-athletes have few skills to make them successful broadcasters, but most television executives realize that media spectators identify with athletes and coaches. So they put former athletes or coaches in the broadcast booth for entertainment purposes, even when former athletes and coaches know little about broadcasting.

In summary, sports journalism is important because people use the images and messages writers and commentators provide to make sense out of their mediated sports experiences. In the first half of this century, sportswriters and radio commentators created heroes and heroic deeds: the illusions and images on which much of the attractiveness of sport always has rested. Television destroyed much of the mystique of the written media and forced sportswriters to take a different approach to their coverage. The growth of televised sports also changed the relationship between players and the press. With sportswriters searching for good stories and athletes trying to protect their privacy, tension has grown between the two groups.

The media coverage of sports also involves ethical issues. The task of writers and commentators is to describe and analyze what happens in sport while avoiding coverage that needlessly hurts the people they write and talk about. Responsible journalists generally regard hurting others for the purpose of entertainment as unethical, although this seems to be happening with increased frequency.

SUMMARY

COULD SPORTS AND THE MEDIA LIVE WITHOUT EACH OTHER?

> Media today saturate our daily lives. . . . [They serve] as the central nervous system of modern society. . . . Popular media today operate on a scale of inclusiveness unimaginable in earlier generations. . . . [They create] the environment where identities are formed.

This statement by media studies professor Michael Real (1989) indicates that it is difficult to understand social life today without giving serious attention to the media and media experiences. This is the major reason we must try to understand the relationship between sports and the media.

In this chapter we have noted that the media, like other parts of culture, are social constructions. This means they are created, organized, and controlled by human beings whose ideas are grounded in their experiences and perspectives on the world. Therefore, the media don't *reflect* reality as much as they provide *"re-presentations"* of selected versions of reality. These selected "re-presentations" are grounded in the power relations of society as a whole. This means that the images and messages contained in the media are likely to represent dominant ideas and ideologies in the society, and to promote the interests of those who benefit the most from those ideas and ideologies.

Sports and the media have grown to depend on each other as both have become more important parts of culture in many societies. They could survive without each other, but they would both be different than they are now. Commercial forms of sports would not be so widespread, and there would be less emphasis on elitist forms of sports, although active participation in sports would not automatically increase. Without exposure to sports through the media, people would probably give lower priority to sports in their everyday lives.

The media also could survive without sports. But they too, especially newspapers and television, would be different. Newspaper circulation probably would decrease, and television programming on weekends and holidays would be different and less profitable for television companies.

More important than trying to determine whether sports and the media are interdependent is understanding the ways in which mediated sports are incorporated into the lives of human beings. The strong symbiotic relationship between them guarantees that none of us will live to see organized sports without media coverage or the media without sports programming. However, history suggests that the relationship between sports and television has developed within a larger cultural context, one in which commercial profits and the creation of media events often are given high priority. This relationship did not take shape on its own; it has been and continues to be created through the ever-changing interactions between athletes, agents, coaches, administrators, sport team owners, sponsors, advertisers, media representatives, and a diversified collection of spectators. Each group has tried to exert influence on the relationship between sports and television, and they have had differing amounts of resources to use in the process.

What exists today are what we might call **"videated" sports**—that is, sports that are "represented" to viewing audiences through video technology used to create dramatic, exciting, and stylized images and messages for the purpose of entertaining viewers and maintaining sponsors. The influence of these "videated" sports in our lives depends on how much information about sports we get through the media and how much we get through direct experiences. Direct experiences with sports influence how we interpret and use what we read, listen to, and view in the media. But when we have little direct experience in and with sports, we depend more exclusively on media images and messages to construct our sport experiences and connect those experiences to other parts of our lives.

Research suggests that dominant ideologies related to success, gender, race, nationalism, competition, individualism, teamwork, violence, and consumerism are perpetuated through the images and messages contained in the media coverage of sports in the U.S. Future research in the sociology of sport will tell us more about how people use media images and messages in the construction of ideas about sports, about the world, and about their relationships to one another. In fact, we also will need research on how people "create" their own video images on the Internet and through computer technology. I know thirteen-year-olds who would much rather play video sport games in which they can choose teams and designate player characteristics than watch a game on television. And I know twenty-five-year-olds who enjoy the sport-related interactive experiences they have on the Internet more than the games themselves. Media sports and the experiences associated with them are rapidly changing; they will be interesting to study.

SUGGESTED READINGS

Barnett, S. 1990. *Games and sets: The changing face of sport on television.* London: BFI (*an excellent introduction to how sports are covered on television in England and the policies that influence that coverage; useful points of comparison to sports and television in the U.S.; written by an expert on broadcasting policy in England*).

Blain, N., R. Boyle, and H. O'Donnell. 1993. *Sport and national identity in the European media.* Leicester, England: Leicester University Press (*insightful analysis of sports and media in Europe; focuses on how media coverage of international sports influences the formation of national identities, ideas about the "national character" of people from other countries, and international political processes*).

Cantelon, H., and R. Gruneau. 1988. The production of sport for television. In J. Harvey and H. Cantelon, eds. *Not just a game.* Ottawa, Ontario: University of Ottawa Press (*critical analysis of the production and consumption of images and meanings as-*

sociated with sport on television; focuses on the unique characteristics of television as a medium for the production of culture).

Chandler, J. 1988. *Television and national sport: The United States and Britain.* Urbana, IL: University of Illinois Press (*good cross-cultural information on differences in the ways sport is defined and perceived and differences in the economics of television in the two countries; focuses on network coverage of live events*).

Creedon, P. J., ed. 1994. *Women, media and sport.* Thousand Oaks, CA: [Sage] (*thirteen papers on the history and experiences of women in sports journalism, the media coverage of women's sports, connections between sports and gender ideology; a major source for material on women and the media*).

Duncan, M., M. A. Messner, L. Williams, and K. Jensen. 1990. *Gender stereotyping in televised sports.* Los Angeles: Amateur Athletic Foundation (*this report of two studies funded by the Amateur Athletic Foundation in Los Angeles received widespread national publicity because it so clearly documented the extent to which gender ideology permeates television sports*).

Kinkema, K., and J. Harris. 1992. Sport and the mass media. *Exercise and Sport Science Reviews* 20:127–159 (*this excellent review article provides 152 references, along with information on the production, content, and audiences of mediated sports*).

Koppett, L. 1994. *Sports illusion, sports reality: A reporter's view of sports, journalism, and society.* Urbana, IL University of Illinois Press (*a reporter's analysis of issues related to how the media cover sports; a thoughtful insider's perspective*).

Lever, J., and S. Wheeler. 1993. Mass media and the experience of sport. *Communication Research* 20(1):125–143 (*a brief but informative overview of the history of the media-sport relationship*).

Wenner, L., ed. 1989. *Media, sports, and society.* Newbury Park, CA: Sage (*thirteen articles on mediated sport; focus on production of media sports, content, and audience experiences; very good source*).

Wenner, L., ed. In press. *Mediasport: Cultural sensibilities and sport in the media age.* London: Routledge (*the twenty-two papers in this anthology review theory and research on media and sport, describe the media sport production complex, and examine cultural issues raised by representations in mediated sports; an essential source for the serious sport and media student*).

Whannel, G. 1992. *Fields in vision: Television sport and cultural transformation.* London: Routledge (*based on a cultural studies approach, this is an insightful investigation of sport, television, and culture; good material on global issues and the attractiveness of televised sports for the viewer; the primary focus is the coverage of sports on British television*).

Whannel, G. Forthcoming. Sports and the media. In Dunning and Coakley, eds. *Handbook of sport and society.* London: Sage (*a readable overview of the sport-media relationship and its implications for global social processes*).

(Kimberly Gunn)

I know why we're here. We're here to spread basket-ball internationally and make more money for some-body. . . . We're going to win the gold medal, but there won't be any life changing decisions made be-cause of it. . . . [P]oor people will still be poor and racism and sexism will still exist. . . .

Charles Barkley, USA Olympic basketball team (1992)

[The Olympics and the Olympic Movement] are more important than the Catholic Church.

Juan Antonio Samaranch, president, International Olympic Committee (1996)

Sports, Politics, and the State
What makes sports political?

No person shall roller-skate, skateboard or operate a bicy-cle in violation of the limita-tions set forth on regulatory signs posted pursuant to this section.

Los Angeles Municipal Code, sec. 85.07 (1997)

The [Catholic] Church ap-proves and encourages sports seeing in it . . . a training for social relations based on respect for others . . . and an element of social cohesion which also fosters friendly re-lations on the international level.

Pope John Paul II (1979)

While people of all nations cheered their own athletes [during the 1996 Olympics], Europeans judged that Americans carried things to the point of showing disre-spect for other athletes and the Olympic ideals.

Ray Moseley, political re-porter, *The Chicago Tribune* (1996)

We now have to face the re-ality that the Olympics con-stitute not only an athletic event but a political event.

Peter Ueberroth, former president of the Los Ange-les Olympic Organizing Committee (1984)

401

Organized competitive sports long have been connected with politics, government, and the nation-state. The term **politics** used in a sociological sense, refers to the processes through which power is gained and used in social life; **government** refers to all those formal organizations and agencies that have the authority to make rules regulating what people do as members of a society; and **nation-state** refers to a legally defined set of organizations and agencies that make and enforce rules governing people within official geographical boundaries.

For many years, the sociological study of politics focused primarily on how the policies and regulations of the state at all levels of government influenced the distribution of rewards in society; sociologists studied *who got what* under the conditions set by government policies and regulations. But today the study of politics has been extended to cover many forms of power, even those that exist in connection with the ability to influence ideas and values. It is this expanded approach to power that I will take in this chapter.

In light of this broader definition of politics, the goal of this chapter is threefold. First, I will describe the relationship between sports and government. Second, I will discuss how individuals and organizations use sports as they attempt to influence ideas, values, and the distribution of material rewards on local, national, and global levels. And third, I will focus on the political processes that occur *in* sports and sport organizations, because the issue of who has power in sports is crucial in the lives of those who play sports and use them for their livelihoods.

The questions asked in this chapter include the following:

1. Why do governments become involved in sponsoring and controlling sports?
2. How are sports connected with important political processes on local, national, and global levels?
3. Do the Olympic Games and other international sports have an impact on global poli-

tics by fostering peace and friendship among nation-states?
4. What political processes occur within sports and sport organizations?

When reading this chapter, remember that *power* is the key concept in politics. As I use it in this chapter, the term **power** refers to an ability to influence others and achieve goals even in the face of opposition from others (Weber, 1968/1922). **Authority** refers to a form of power that comes with a recognized and legitimate status or office in an organization or set of relationships. For example, a large corporation has *power* if it can influence how people think about and play sports, and if it can use sports to meet its corporate goals. Sport organizations such as the IOC, FIFA, the NCAA, or a local parks department have *authority* over the sports they administer, as long as people associated with those sports accept the organizations as legitimate sources of control. This example alerts us to the fact that in this chapter, *politics* refers to more than issues concerning formal sport governing bodies; instead, it refers to all forms of power relations in sports.

THE SPORTS-GOVERNMENT CONNECTION

As sports grow in popularity in a community or society, government involvement often increases. Sport events and activities require sponsorship, organization, and facilities—all of which depend on resources that few individuals possess on their own. For example, sport facilities are often so expensive that regional and national governments may be the only community entities with the power and the capital to build and maintain them. For this reason, many people see government involvement in sports as a necessity. Government involvement also is tied to the belief that sport participation, sport organizations, and the people associated with sports often need to be regulated and controlled by an "outside" agency that represents the interests of all people in a community or society.

The nature and extent of government involvement in sports varies from one community and society to the next, but the reasons for involvement generally fall into the following six categories (Allison, 1993; Houlihan, 1994; Wilson, 1994):

1. to safeguard the public order
2. to maintain and develop fitness and physical abilities among citizens
3. to promote the prestige of a community or nation in wider realms of political relations
4. to promote a sense of identity, belonging, and unity among citizens
5. to emphasize values and orientations consistent with dominant political ideology in a community or society
6. to increase citizen support of political leaders and the political structures they represent
7. to promote general economic development in the community or society

We will give explanations and examples of each of these reasons in the following sections.

Safeguarding the Public Order

To protect individuals and groups with different interests, governments often make rules about what types of sports are legal or illegal, how sports are organized, who should have opportunities to play sports, where certain sports may be played, and who can use public sports facilities at certain times. For example, to protect individuals, a local or national government may officially outlaw sports such as bullfighting, barefisted boxing, or even bungee jumping. In the case of commercial sports, government agencies may regulate the rights and duties of owners, sponsors, promoters, and athletes; government rules even may set official limits on the extent to which sports organizations legally can control the lives of athletes.

Local governments may try to eliminate conflicts between citizens by regulating the use of public facilities and playing fields through reservation or permit systems. Government agencies may pass rules prohibiting certain sports activities in public places so that the general public can use those places freely and safely. For example, skateboarding, in-line skating, and bicycling may be banned on city sidewalks or in certain public parks, or confined to certain areas, so that pedestrians will feel safe. Likewise, local law enforcement officials may close streets or parks to the general public temporarily so that sports events can be held under controlled and safe conditions. For example, marathons in such places as New York City and London require the involvement of the government and government agencies such as the city police.

Because *fairness* often is defined as a matter of public order, governments may pass laws or establish policies to make sure that participation in publicly funded sports is open to a range of citizens. Title IX is a classic example of a federal government regulation that defines what is fair when it comes to who should have opportunities to participate in sports programs sponsored by U.S. schools receiving federal funds. Sport Canada, the national organization that oversees high-performance sports in Canada, has gone a step further than the United States by establishing a nationwide policy on women in sport. This policy, developed in response to federal antidiscrimination legislation, outlines equity strategies to be used in government-sponsored sport programs throughout the country. Government agencies in Canada now are drafting policies mandating or regulating access to sport participation for persons with disabilities.

Government interests in safeguarding the public order also may lead to the policing of sports events. Local police or even military forces may be called on to control crowds and individuals that threaten the safety and well-being of others. For example, Russian army units often are used to patrol Moscow's Lenin Stadium during major events such as soccer games. After the games, hundreds of soldiers form lines to channel the flow of spectators leaving the stadium. The police in England are conspicuously present

Local governments often regulate where and when certain sports may be played. These boys feel their interests have not been fairly represented by governmental decisions about where they can skateboard. For that reason, they regularly challenge the regulations. (Danielle Hicks)

at most soccer games, and they may even ride the trains that carry spectators from one city to another. The Atlanta Olympic Organizing Committee utilized nearly seventeen thousand military and law enforcement officials from federal, state, and local governments to assemble a security force to safeguard the public order during the 1996 Summer Games; similar government involvement will occur in Sydney in 2000 and in Salt Lake City in 2002.

Some governments have attempted to safeguard the public order by sponsoring sports events and programs for special groups of people that have been labeled as potentially disruptive

within communities and societies. Sports, it is argued, can be used to keep certain people off the streets. For example, The Sports Council, an official policy-making agency in the British government, has sponsored sports programs in the hope of providing constructive activities for young people, unassimilated ethnic minorities, and the unemployed. The ultimate goal of these programs is to use sports to control crime rates, vandalism, loneliness, and alienation in British society by bringing certain people into organized, state-funded programs. However, the failure of these programs to achieve their goals has led critics to argue that sport participation, by itself, cannot eliminate the deprivation, racism, poverty, dislocation, community disintegration, and political powerlessness that often cause social problems in communities and societies.

Finally, sports often have been used in military and police training. It is a common assumption that playing sports prepares law enforcement personnel to safeguard the public order. For example, military academies in the United States and other countries traditionally have sponsored numerous sports for their cadets. In fact, national sport programs in some countries are administered through government defense departments. Even the founding of the modern Olympic Games was grounded partially in Baron Pierre de Coubertin's belief that sports could be used to motivate young Frenchmen to safeguard French society by developing the skills they needed to be effective leaders and soldiers (Tomlinson, 1984). And the World Police and Fire Games have been held every two years for some time because of a widespread belief that sport participation keeps law enforcement officials and firefighters prepared to safeguard the public order.

Maintaining and Developing Fitness and Physical Abilities

Governments also have become involved in sports to promote fitness among citizens. For example, nations with government-funded health insurance programs often promote and sponsor sports to improve physical well-being in the general population and thereby reduce the cost of health services. This was one of the major reasons the Canadian government promoted and funded fitness and sport programs during the mid-1970s. The government was facing serious financial crises and officials believed that sports participation among Canadians ultimately would increase fitness and cut health-care costs (Harvey and Proulx, 1988).

Similar motives have led to government sponsorship and organization of fitness and sports programs in other nations, including England, Sweden, Norway, and China. Many people believe that sport participation improves fitness, fitness improves health, and good health reduces medical costs. I should point out that this set of beliefs persists in the face of the following factors (Wagner, 1987; Waddington, forthcoming):

- Many of the illnesses that increase health-care costs are caused by environmental factors and living conditions, and cannot be changed through any sports or fitness program.
- Certain forms of sport participation do not lead to overall physical fitness or identifiable health benefits.
- The win-at-all-costs orientation that sometimes develops in connection with sports may actually contribute to injuries and increased health-care costs (for example, forty thousand knee injuries in American football every year require costly care, surgery, and rehabilitation).
- The demand for health care sometimes increases when people become more concerned with fitness and the physical condition and appearance of their bodies; in other words, under certain conditions, people who participate in sports can become so concerned with their abilities to perform that they become obsessed with physical and health issues, and demand more health care.

When they consider these factors in the formulation of official policies, governments become cautious and selective in their sponsorship of sports for health purposes. Today, governments are more likely to emphasize noncompetitive physical activities with clear aerobic benefits, and less likely to sponsor highly competitive sports involving physical contact and norms promoting the physical domination of opponents.

In the past, government involvement in sports also was grounded in the belief that fitness and physical abilities were related to economic productivity. For example, the former Soviet government and other governments in nations with socialist or planned economies often promoted and sponsored sport participation in the hope that their workers would become more fit, more skilled, and more productive. The words of Russian sociologist Nikolai Ponomaryov (1981) illustrate this approach:

> The main way to train people for work activity is to strengthen their health and improve their physical development. . . . Physical culture . . . encourages a more rational use of work resources, since it extends the bounds of actual work capacity beyond [the normal retirement] age, i.e., it prolongs the active life of workers. . . . "Athletic" employees [also] are less prone to sickness and therefore take less time off.

Ponomaryov also argued that when workers had highly developed physical skills, they could handle on-the-job stress and respond more quickly to the physical demands of changing production processes. However, the government of the Soviet Union discovered that trying to use sports to control workers was not effective in the long run. Other governments have learned the same lesson.

Although many people may question this emphasis on the work-related consequences of sport participation, I should point out that many private corporations in the United States, Canada, and other countries with market economies fund their own fitness centers and sport programs for some of the same reasons underlying the former Soviet government's intervention in sports and physical culture. But these companies usually are discovering the same things the Soviet Union

REFLECT ON SPORT

Unity for What?
The Political Consequences of Cheering for the Home Team

Sports differ from other cultural forms in society. Art, literature, drama, and music also have the power to bring people together, but sports are unique. In spite of the complex rules in some games, most sports are simple and easy to understand. Events have definite beginnings and endings; game boundaries are usually clear-cut. Opponents in most sports are identifiable, and they often compete directly with one another. Scores are objective and outcomes are clear. These characteristics make many sports easy to understand. Sports also provide a combination of action, drama, and uncertainty that often brings people together to cheer for the same athletes or teams, despite differences related to social class, gender, race, ethnicity, religion, language, education, and cultural heritage.

After an extended analysis of soccer in Brazil, sociologist Janet Lever (1983) concluded that soccer brought people together from all over the country and gave them "a set of common symbols and a basis for identity and interaction"—even when they cheered for opposing teams in interregional games. In other words, soccer games showed Brazilians it was possible to forget their differences and join together with others from diverse backgrounds.

What Lever found in Brazil was accurate. In fact, her findings still describe how sports operate in many areas around the world. For example, community-based sport teams, such as high school teams in small towns across the United States, often have been sources of this type of togetherness among townspeople. However, an analysis of sports and social solidarity must do more than simply show that games and teams bring people together. It must also explore and document the *consequences of togetherness.*

Alan Klein, a social anthropologist from Northeastern University in Boston, has emphasized the need to study carefully the consequences of the unity and togetherness created by sports. In a review of Lever's research, Klein (1984) raised doubts about whether the unity created by soccer has had any effect on the political and economic realities of Brazilian life. He agreed that soccer created a temporary form of emotional unity among people from a wide array of backgrounds, but he questioned whether this unity actually helped people deal with their differences in a manner that would improve their quality of life.

· ·

found: productivity and worker satisfaction are related to the overall quality of working conditions and the autonomy of workers, not to employee fitness or opportunities to participate in sports. In fact, even though physical fitness has health benefits, overall health in a society is related more to environmental and working conditions than to individual physical activities or sport participation rates.

Promoting the Prestige of a Group, Community, or Nation

Government intervention in sports frequently is motivated by a quest for recognition and prestige. This quest can occur on a local, national, or global level. For example, a spokesperson for the South Korean government said that its sponsor-ship of the 1988 Summer Olympic Games was an announcement to the world of its emergence as a developed nation with a strong economy. The 1996 Summer Games provided an occasion for local boosters to present Atlanta as a "world-class city" symbolizing the "new South," now open to all people regardless of race or national background. Sydney, the host of the 2000 Summer Games, will be presented to the world as a city with clean air in a country with a pleasant climate and vital business connections with emerging nations in Asia.

This quest for recognition and prestige also underlies government subsidies for national teams across a wide range of sports, usually those designated as Olympic sports. Government officials use international sports to establish their

Klein's review implied that any discussion of the unity and togetherness created by sports must address the following questions:

- How large a territory does the unity cover? Does it go beyond the community or regional level? When does this happen? Can it bring groups of countries together?

- What form does the unity take? How long does it last? Does it go beyond the emotional level?

- Does the unity affect everyone equally? Are some groups able to benefit from it more than others?

- Most important, does the emotional unity that accompanies sports affect interaction patterns apart from sports? If so, how are they affected?

In connection with these questions, Klein made the following observations. In spite of a regular schedule of soccer games that consistently has brought Brazilians together, social life in Brazil remains plagued with political tension and economic problems. For those who lack economic and political power in Brazil, soccer has provided nothing more than momentary relief from the pressures of making a living and supporting a family.

The unity created by soccer has not changed the realities of important political and economic relations; it has not addressed issues of poverty or the need for democratic political involvement, both of which have been (and still are) crucial issues in Brazil.

Today, the forms of unity that exist in connection with sports are more symbolic than concrete, and they are based primarily on media spectatorship and consumption patterns. Togetherness is expressed through commonly worn clothes emblazoned with a nation's name or flag. But emotionally sharing the fate of a national team and wearing similar sweatshirts does not alter the social, political, and economic realities of life in any way. In fact, after games end, social distinctions quickly are reaffirmed as people go about their everyday lives (Arbena, 1988).

Of course, the emotional unity that sports sometimes create feels good, and it even may be associated with a spirit of possibility. But it usually distracts people's attention from the need for social transformation, rather than inspiring collective action that might transform society and make it more democratic and economically fair. What do you think?

· ·

nation's legitimacy in the international sphere, and they believe that when athletes from their nation win medals, their national image is enhanced around the world. This belief is so strong that many governments now offer their athletes financial rewards for winning medals in the Olympics. The importance of national success in sports is not new. Even in 1958, when Brazil won its first World Cup in soccer, there was a strong feeling among most Brazilians that they could now stand tall in the international arena and that their way of life was equal to or perhaps even better than those of the nations of Europe. They felt that Brazil now had to be recognized and dealt with as an equal in international relations (Humphrey, 1986). Similar feelings have been expressed more recently in connection with

World Cup performances by soccer teams from such African nations as Cameroon and Nigeria.

In a similar manner, many people believe that a nation's failures in international sport events cause a loss of prestige in the global cultural arena. For example, when national teams from England lost in major international competitions to teams from countries that had learned to play sports invented in England, some people in England worried that the losses were symptoms of their nation's general decline in world affairs (Maguire, 1994a).

Attempts to gain recognition and prestige also underlie local government involvement in sports. For example, cities may fund sport clubs and teams, and then use those teams to promote themselves as good places to live, work, locate a business, or spend a vacation. In fact, some people in the North America feel that if their city does not have one or more major professional sport team franchises, it cannot claim "world-class" status (see Whitson and Macintosh, 1996). Even small towns will use road signs to announce the success of local high school teams to everyone driving into the town: "You are now entering the home of the state champions" in this or that sport. State governments in the United States traditionally have subsidized sport programs at their colleges and universities for similar reasons: competitive success is believed to bring prestige to the entire state, as well as to the school represented by the athletes and teams; prestige attracts students, and students pay tuition.

Promoting a Sense of Identity, Belonging, and Unity

Sports long have been used by groups, organizations, towns, cities, and nations to express collective sentiments about themselves.* Any team or athlete representing a specific group has the potential to bring people together and create emotional unity among group members. For example, when a nation's soccer team plays in the World Cup, people across the nation are united, regardless of differences in race, religion, language, education, occupation, and income. This unity may be connected with their feelings of attachment to the nation as a whole and their convictions about the nation's history and traditions, and even about its destiny in the world order.

But it is important to ask critical sociological questions about the long-term consequences of this emotional unity, to ask whose interests are served by the images, traditions, and memories around which identities are expressed (see the box on pp. 406–407). When government involvement and sponsorship of a sport is designed to promote a sense of identity and unity among a

collection of people, it is important to understand how that identity and unity is connected with patterns of power and social relations. For example, when men's sports are sponsored and women's sports are ignored, what does that say about a group's identity and the values around which the identity is created? What if the sport involves participants from only one ethnic group, or from a particular social class? These questions show that identity itself is political, in the sense that it can be constructed around different ideas of what is important in a group.

Local government involvement in sports is also motivated by concerns to promote and express particular forms of identity. Club soccer teams in Europe often receive support from local governments, because the teams are major focal points for community attention and involvement. The teams not only reaffirm community identity among local citizens, but also bring large numbers of community people together when games are played. In fact, the games often become important social occasions within towns or regions and provide opportunities for meeting new people, renewing old acquaintances, and maintaining a personal sense of belonging to a group. In this context, we can consider sports to be *invented traditions* used to remind people of what they share and how they are connected with one another.

When the population of a community or society is very diverse, or when social change is rapid and widespread, governments are even more likely to intervene in sports for the purpose of promoting a sense of identity and unity (Maguire and Stead, 1996). For example, in the 1970s, the Canadian government developed sport policies designed to highlight the participation and achievements of groups that did not feel they were a part of Canadian culture (Harvey and Proulx, 1988). The hope was that sports could be used to create a feeling of unity in the midst of diversity and political alienation. As national boundaries become less and less visible and relevant in people's lives, many national governments around the world are using sports to promote internal unity around a national identity (Houli-

---

*Allison, forthcoming; Bairner, 1996; Blain et al., 1993; Gruneau and Whitson, 1993; Houlihan, forthcoming; Jackson, 1994; Jarvie, 1993; Maguire, 1994a, c; Maguire and Stead, 1996; Nauright, 1996a, b.

Sports have been used to promote a sense of identity among citizens and to emphasize values and orientations consistent with dominant political orientations in particular societies. This photo shows how clearly these identities differed in the years before World War II. (USOC Archives)

han, 1994). Even though the long-term effectiveness of this strategy is difficult to assess, many government officials are convinced that sports create more than temporary good feelings of togetherness. Of course, it is important to remember that nearly all of these officials are men, and the sports they support often are tied to traditions that have privileged men in the past. As always, there are several layers to the politics associated with sports.

Emphasizing Values and Orientations Consistent with Dominant Political Ideology

Governments also become involved in sports to promote certain values and ideas among citizens. Governments generally have strong vested interests in maintaining the idea that success is based

on discipline, loyalty, determination, and the ability to keep working in the face of hardship and bad times. Sports, especially world-class and elite competitive sports, have been used in many nations to promote these values and foster particular interpretations of how social life does and should work. For example, this was a major motive underlying the sponsorship of elite sports in the former Soviet Union, as articulated by Soviet sociologist Ponomaryov:

Physical culture is an important means to educate . . . an active fighter for communism, and it is an effective social factor in the ideological education of the public. . . . When people engage in physical exercise their ideology and moral consciousness are shaped through acquiring information on sports ethics and its manifestation in the activities of

Soviet athletes; this is assimilated through the practical mastery of communist standards of behavior during training and competition (Ponomaryov, 1981).

The Soviet government also used sports to emphasize the importance of "teamwork, common aims and interests, . . . collectivism, comradeship, [and] hard work and responsibility for the common cause." These were the values that the government connected with Soviet sport, and the hope was that people would adopt them in their lives as Soviet citizens. However, because most people in the Soviet Union did not accept government-sponsored ideas, they attached their own meanings to Soviet sports. Instead of associating them with collectivism and comradeship, they saw them as symbols of government coercion, exploitation, and distorted national priorities (Riordan, 1993).

In nations with market economies, such as the U.S. and Canada, among others, sports often are associated with success and hard work so instead of references to collectivism and the common good, there are references to competition and individual achievement. Instead of an emphasis on comradeship, there are stories showing how individuals have reached personal goals and experienced self-fulfillment through sports. An emphasis on competition, personal achievement, and individual fulfillment pervades the media coverage of sports in nations with market economies. Although we do not know whether such an emphasis actually strengthens a popular commitment to dominant cultural ideology, it clearly provides people with a vocabulary and real-life examples that are consistent with that dominant ideology. In a sense, the vocabulary and stories that accompany sports in market economies tend to emphasize that using competition to achieve personal success and to allocate rewards to people is natural and normal, while alternative approaches to success and allocating rewards are inappropriate. And in all nations, the vocabulary and the stories usually are associated with flags, emblems, anthems, and national colors.

A classic example of a government's use of sport to promote its own political ideology occurred in Nazi Germany in 1936. Most countries hosting the Olympic Games have used the occasion to present themselves favorably to their own citizens and the rest of the world. However, Adolph Hitler was especially interested in using the games to promote the Nazi ideology of "Nordic supremacy" through the Berlin Games that preceded World War II. The Nazi government devoted considerable resources to the training of German athletes, and those athletes won 89 medals: 23 more than U.S. athletes won, and over four times as many as any other country won during the Berlin Games. This is the reason the performance of Jesse Owens, an African American, was so important to countries not aligned with Germany at that point in history. Owens's four gold medals and world records challenged Hitler's ideology of Nordic supremacy, although it did not deter Nazi commitment to a destructive political and cultural ideology.

The Cold War era following World War II was also full of incidents in which countries, especially the U.S., the USSR, and East Germany, used the Olympics and other international sport competitions to claim the superiority of their political and economic systems. Today, such claims are less apt to be associated with international sports; instead, there is a growing emphasis on the logos and products of corporate capitalism.

Increasing Citizen Support for Individual Political Leaders and Government Itself

"All governments, regardless of . . . type, use sport to generate political support." This is the conclusion made by political scientist Art Johnson (1982) in his analysis of the connection between government and sport. Johnson also indicates that even in political systems that promote a

> . . . belief in the separation of sport and government, it is likely that intervention . . . will be needed to ensure that sport serves the purposes of

government rather than its opponents. Sport, therefore, will become too important to be left alone to excite the fans; it will be needed to service the state (1982).

These comments suggest that governments use sports not only to increase the legitimacy of their political systems, but also to generate support for the ruling parties within those systems.

Johnson also points out that if government officials do not use sports in this way, those who oppose the political system or the ruling party will use sports to generate support for themselves. When governments sponsor or promote activities and events that people value and enjoy, they increase their perceived *legitimacy* in the eyes of citizens. Without legitimacy, governments and government officials risk losing their power. This is the reason many political figures present themselves as friends of sport, even as faithful fans. They may make it a point to attend highly publicized sports events and associate themselves with high-profile athletes or teams that win major competitions. For example, the prime ministers of Canada often are photographed when attending the CFL's Grey Cup championship games, and U.S. presidents also traditionally have connected themselves with successful athletes and teams. In fact, Olympic teams and championships teams from college and professional sports are invited to the White House regularly for photo opportunities with the president.

Former President Ronald Reagan was especially adept at using sports to his political advantage. Before the 1984 election, his campaign staff hinted at a connection between Reagan's first four years in the White House and the United States' success at the 1984 Olympic Games in Los Angeles. The claim was that Reagan had restored American pride and America's place in the international political arena. Even though U.S. athletes were not subsidized directly by the federal government, Reagan tried to enhance the legitimacy of his political ideology and the American political system by implying a connection between his presidency and all the gold medals won by U.S. athletes. Following in the footsteps of other recent presidents, Reagan also invited national championship teams in the country's most popular sports to the White House for press conferences and photographs, attracting extensive national media coverage. In 1985 he even shortened his inauguration ceremony so that it would not interfere with the telecast of the Super Bowl, and then he scheduled an appearance during the game in front of the largest television audience of the year (Shaikin, 1988).

President Clinton used the 1996 Olympics, held in July and early August, to complement his reelection campaign, which would culminate in November. Of course, U.S. politicians are not the only ones to do this; there are similar examples from other countries. When taken together, these examples provide strong support for the idea that governments and government officials use sports to promote themselves.

Promoting General Economic Development in the Community or Society

Since the early 1980s, governments increasingly have become involved in sports for the purpose of promoting economic development. Cities may spend large amounts of money to assemble and submit bids to host the Olympic Games, World Cup tournaments, world or national championships, Super Bowls, and All-Star Games, or high-profile auto races, golf tournaments, and track and field meets. Although most of these sport events have not been moneymakers in the past, some have been turned into moneymakers in recent years. And even when the events themselves do not show a profit, segments of the local community do make money.

Governments are also interested in the long-term economic benefits of hosting events. Officials even may use the events as occasions for making contacts with corporations looking for new sites to locate their operations. Or they may use them to highlight and promote products made by local businesses. Japan (1964, 1998), Mexico (1968), and South Korea (1988) invested

President Clinton, like other U.S. presidents, uses sports for political advantage. He seldom misses opportunities to be seen or connected with highly visible championship teams and successful athletes. Politicians in other societies have done the same thing, although few have used sports as much as politicians in the U.S. have. (Doug Mills, AP/Wide World Photos)

in hosting the Olympics and in their own national Olympic teams for clear economic development purposes. For Salt Lake City and other hosts of Winter Games, sport events are occasions for promoting tourism and recreational opportunities. In many cases, the hosting of a sport event now combines the interests of civic boosters and government officials in a general effort to enhance the local economy (Huey, 1996).

In summary, it is important to raise questions about government involvement in sports and the "public good." Of course, it would be ideal if government promoted equally the interests of all citizens, but differences between individuals and

groups make this impossible. This means that government involvement in sports usually reflects the interests of some people more than those of others. The individuals and groups that benefit most tend to be those capable of influencing policy makers and those who think and act as policy makers think and act. This does not mean that government policies always reflect the interests of wealthy and powerful people, but it does mean that they reflect political power struggles between various groups within a society.

History shows that when government intervention occurs, priority is often given to elite sport programs rather than to general sport participation. Of course, there are exceptions to this, but seldom are elite programs ignored or given a low priority. Those who represent elite sports often are organized, generally have strong backing from other organized groups, and can base their requests for support on visible accomplishments achieved in the name of the entire country, community, or school. Those who would benefit from mass participation programs are less likely to be politically organized or backed by other organized groups, and less able to give precise statements of their goals and the political significance of their programs. This does not mean that mass participation is ignored by government decision makers, but it does mean that it usually has lower priority for funding and support.

Opposition to the priorities that guide government involvement often is defused by the myth that there is no connection between sports and politics. Those who believe this myth seldom have their interests reflected when government involvement occurs. Those who realize that sports have political implications and that governments are not politically neutral arbitrators of differences within societies are likely to benefit the most when government intervention occurs. Sports are connected with power relations in society as a whole; therefore, sports and politics cannot be separated.

SPORTS AND GLOBAL POLITICAL PROCESSES

International Sports: Ideals Versus Realities

Achieving peace and friendship between nations has been a longstanding ideal underlying international sports. The hope that sports could bring nations of the world together has been emphasized ever since Baron Pierre de Coubertin founded the modern Olympic Games in 1896. There have been many expressions of this ideal over the past century, but it has never been described more clearly than in the following statement by Alan Reich (1974), a former U.S. State Department official:

- Sports open doors to societies and key leaders. They pave the way for expanded contact—cultural, economic, and political. . . .
- Sports provide an example of friendly competition and two-way interchange which, hopefully, will characterize and lead to other types of friendly relationships between nations. . . .
- Sports convey on a person-to-person basis and through the media to the broader public a sense of commonness of interest shared with other peoples across political boundaries. . . .
- Sports enhance understanding of another nation's values and culture, so important but often absent in many forms of international communication.
- Sports thus can help to improve perceptions of other peoples and to close the gap between myth and reality [in how people from different cultures see one another]. . . .
- Sports organizations, in administering international sports activities, develop the bases for ongoing communication and cooperation. In this work, [they] travel and communicate across national boundaries . . . further the ideals of freedom . . . [and] also develop leadership, which is needed especially by the developing nations as they struggle to reduce the gap between the "have" and "have not" peoples of the world.

This statement summarizes the political ideals underlying a century of efforts by representatives of nation-states to organize and promote international sports.

In the twentieth century, these ideals have been achieved in varying degrees on some occasions. Even though sports have had little impact in the realm of **serious diplomacy,** they have been used in connection with **public diplomacy.** In other words, when it comes to issues of vital national interest, sports are politically irrelevant; government officials do not use sports in connection with their negotiations about crucial national and international policies. But when it comes to providing a vehicle for cultural exchanges and general communication between officials from different nations, sports have been useful at times (Frey, 1984; Whitson and

Macintosh, 1994). Sports can provide opportunities for these officials to meet and talk, even though they don't influence what is discussed or the outcomes of the discussions.

Apart from these occasions when sports have been used to foster public diplomacy, history shows that most nations have used sports and sport events, especially the Olympic Games, to pursue their own interests rather than the collective goals of international communication, friendship, and peace. Nationalist themes have been clearly evident in many events. Most nations have used sport events regularly to foster explicitly their own military, economic, political, and cultural goals. This was particularly apparent during the Cold War era following World War II and extending to 1991 (Heinila, 1985; Hoberman, 1986; Macintosh and Hawes, 1992, 1994; Tomlinson and Whannel, 1984; Vinokur, 1988). Statements substantiating this pursuit of national interests over and above the international common good are not difficult to find. The following quotations from the past illustrate this point:

> [It is] in our national interest that we regain our Olympic superiority—that we once again give the world visible proof of our inner strength and vitality. (Bobby Kennedy, U.S. attorney general, 1964)
>
> Do we realize how important it is to compete successfully with other nations? Not just the Russians, but many nations are growing and challenging. Being a leader, the United States has an obligation to set high standards. . . . A sports triumph can be [as] uplifting to a nation's spirit as . . . a battlefield victory. (U.S. President Gerald Ford, 1974)
>
> Sport [in East Germany] did its part in obtaining recognition internationally for the German Democratic Republic. Sport led the way in increasing the international prestige of our socialist republic and led to its diplomatic recognition by a majority of states of the world. (Guenther Heinze, vice president of the German Sport and Gymnastic Federation, 1973)
>
> The increasing number of successes achieved by Soviet sportsmen in sport has particular signifi-

cance today. Each new victory is a victory for the Soviet form of society and the socialist sports system; it provides irrefutable proof of the superiority of socialist culture over the decaying culture of the capitalist states. (Yuri Kotov and Ivan Yudovich, USSR political writers, 1978)

These statements do not represent all the motives underlying the participation of all nations in international sports, but they do illustrate one dominant motive underlying the participation of major nation-states during the Cold War era. To an extent, they also illustrate the way the media covered international sports throughout much of the world. In fact, many international sport events, especially the Olympics, were presented as extensions of so-called "superpower politics."

The connection between international sports and politics was so widely recognized in the early 1980s that Peter Ueberroth, president of the Los Angeles Olympic Organizing Committee, concluded in 1984 that "we now have to face the reality that the Olympics constitute not only an athletic event but a political event." Ueberroth was not being prophetic when he made this statement; he was simply summarizing his observations of Olympic history. From his perspective in 1984, it was clear that nations seldom put international friendship and world peace ahead of their own interests in connection with the Olympics. The demonstration of national superiority through sports was the major priority of most nations.

Powerful industrial countries have not been the only ones to use international sports to promote national interests. For example, many nations lacking international political and economic power have used sports in their overall quest for international recognition and legitimacy. For them, the Olympics and other international sports have been stages for showing that their athletes and teams can stand up to and sometimes defeat athletes and teams from wealthy and powerful nations. For example, the ability of athletes and teams from the West Indies to do well in important cricket competitions

A twenty-seven-year ban on South Africa's participation in the Olympics was lifted after racial apartheid was declared illegal. Racial divisions still exist in South Africa, but in 1996 the nation sent its first desegregated team to the Olympics. When Josiah Thugwane won the marathon, he became the first black South African to win a gold medal. This photo of Thugwane carrying his country's flag had special political meaning for many people around the world. Instead of symbolizing nationalism, it was seen as a symbol of black self-determination and racial justice. (Doug Mills, AP/Wide World Photos)

against teams from England has been seen by West Indian people as a symbol of their emerging independence and autonomy in relation to one of the countries that colonized their islands centuries ago.

Some emerging industrial nations also have realized that hosting the Olympics is a special opportunity to announce to the world their readiness and ability to participate fully in international politics and trade relations. This is the reason Tokyo spent hundreds of millions of dollars to host the 1964 Summer Games, the reason Seoul spent even more to host the 1988 Summer Games, and the reason China continues to submit bids to host a future Olympics. Hosting the games provides opportunities to generate international recognition, display national power and resources to a global audience, and invite investments into a nation's economy.

The political goals of nations hosting major international events have been highlighted when other nations have boycotted those events. For example, the 1980 Moscow Games were boycotted by the U.S., Canada, and their political allies to protest the presence of Soviet troops in Afghanistan. The USSR and its allies then boycotted the 1984 Los Angeles Games to protest the commercialization of the games and to avoid potentially threatening behavior by what they expected to be flag-waving nationalistic U.S. spectators. However, each of these Olympic games were held despite the boycotts, and each host nation took care to display its power and resources to other participant nations. Furthermore, the boycotts had no major effect on national policies in any of the countries involved.

Global media coverage since the 1970s has intensified and added new dimensions to the connection between sports and politics (Blain et al., 1993; Real, 1989; Whannel, 1992; Whitson and Macintosh, 1996). For example, television companies, especially the American networks, traditionally have attracted viewers to their Olympic coverage by stressing political controversies along with national interests and symbols. The theme of their coverage in the past has been less one of international friendship than one of "us versus them," highlighted by competitions presented in terms of "this nation versus that nation." The networks have justified this coverage by claiming that U.S. viewers preferred nationalistic themes extolling U.S. values and claiming U.S. political superiority.

Although past media coverage of the Olympics and other international sports encouraged ethnocentrism and a military approach to international relations, more recent coverage has reflected the end of the Cold War and the dissolution of the USSR and the German Democratic Republic. No longer are events presented in "capitalist versus communist" terms. Nationalist themes still exist (Sabo et al., 1996; Whannel, 1992), but they have been less evident in recent events.

NATION-STATES, SPORTS, AND CULTURAL IDEOLOGY Sports have been and still are used to promote ideas and orientations that fit the interests of the most powerful and wealthy nations in the world. For example, participation in major international sports events often has meant that less powerful nations must look to their "big brothers," the so-called superpowers, for guidance and resources. This not only has encouraged people in relatively poor nations to deemphasize their traditional folk games, but also has focused their attention on sports that are largely unrelated to their own values and experiences. Furthermore, it has led them to be involved in events over which they have little control. Generally, if they want to play, they must go along with what more powerful nations decide.

When this occurs, the people in poorer nations sometimes approach those in wealthy nations to buy, beg, or borrow everything from technical assistance to new equipment. In the process of doing this, poorer nations risk becoming increasingly dependent on economically powerful nations, and sports become vehicles through which powerful nations can extend their control over important forms of popular culture around the world. When people in poorer nations are committed to maintaining traditional cultural practices, including their native games, they will resist the ideological influence associated with this type of "cultural imperialism," but resistance can be difficult when the rules and organization of popular international sports are so closely tied to the ideologies of powerful nations. For example, when an American sport such as football is introduced to another country, it comes with an emphasis on ideas about individual achievement, competition, winning, hierarchical authority structures, and the use of technology to shape bodies into efficient machines. These ideas may not be completely accepted by those learning to play and understand football, but they do tend to encourage orientations that work to the advantage of the United States, and to the long-term disadvantage of the less powerful nations.

Ideally, sports can be vehicles for real cultural exchanges through which people from different nations *share* information and develop *mutual* cultural understanding. But true fifty-fifty sharing and mutual understanding is rare when two nations have unequal power and resources. This means that sports often become cultural exports shipped from wealthy nations and incorporated into the everyday lives of people in other nations. Of course, these imported sports may be revised and reshaped by people to fit their traditional values and lifestyles. But even when that occurs, it is likely that the people in the traditional cultures will become increasingly open to the possibility of importing and consuming other goods, services, and ideas from the wealthy nations. Unless political power and economic resources are developed in connection with this process, poorer nations are likely to become increasingly dependent on wealthy nations. Of course, this is a complex process, involving many issues in addition to those related to sports.

New Political Realities in an Era of Transnational Corporations

Today, international sports are less likely to be scenes for nationalistic displays than to be scenes for commercial displays by large transnational corporations. This was clearly evident in Atlanta, and will probably be the case in Nagano (1998), Sydney (2000), Salt Lake City (2002), and future locations. Global politics have changed dramatically over the past decade. Nation-states have been joined by powerful transnational organizations in global power relations. As we noted in chapter 11, 51 of the 100 largest economies in the world are corporations, *not* nation-states. As nation-states have lifted trade restrictions, decreased tariffs, and loosened their internal regulations in the bid against other nations to have large corporations locate within their bound-

aries, the corporations themselves have become increasingly powerful. Many of them are now more powerful in economic terms than the nations in which they have production facilities.

This means that instead of focusing just on international relations when we study sports and political processes, we must broaden our focus to consider *transnational relations.* This enables us to acknowledge that nation-states are now joined by major corporations and other powerful transnational organizations as global political players.

Nationalism still exists in connection with international sports, especially those played in regions where political and economic issues call attention to national differences and interests. But in the case of most global sport events, national identity is becoming increasingly blurred. This trend was highlighted in a statement by Phil Knight, the CEO of the U.S.–based Nike Corporation, as he explained his team loyalty during the 1994 World Cup:

> We see a natural evolution . . . dividing the world into their athletes and ours. And we glory ours. When the U.S. played Brazil in the World Cup, I rooted for Brazil because it was a Nike team. America was Adidas (in *The New York Times,* February 7, 1996).

Knight's point is that teams and athletes are now identified in terms of logos, not nationalities. Nike's markets do not end at the U.S. borders. They are worldwide, and this is the reason Nike gave Brazil's national sport teams $200 million for the right to use the Brazilian soccer team to market Nike products around the world through the year 2005. Knight sees logo loyalty as more important than national loyalty when it comes to international sports; he sees consumerism replacing patriotism when it comes to identifying athletes and teams; he sees international sport events as settings through which Nike and other corporate sponsors can deliver advertising messages promoting their companies' interests along with the general interests of global capitalist

TANK McNAMARA®   by Jeff Millar & Bill Hinds

Nationalist images and messages in sports have been replaced rapidly by the images and messages of international corporate capitalism. What we see and hear in the media coverage of sports today and in the future will be consistent with corporate interests. Will spectators object to this and challenge this type of coverage?

expansion. And—an important point—he and other corporate executives see this as good for the people of the world.

To the extent that media coverage is influenced by corporate sponsors, international sports televised around the world become vehicles for presenting to massive audiences a range of messages promoting the interests of corporate capitalism (Donnelly, 1996b). These messages are directed to spectator-consumers, not spectator-citizens. Instead of keying in on patriotism or nationalism, the messages that come with international sports now key in on status consciousness and individual consumption. Sports that don't enable corporations to deliver their messages to consumers with purchasing power are not sponsored. If spectators and media audiences are not potential consumers, corporations see little reason to sponsor events. So unless the media are publicly owned, they are not likely to cover events viewed by those who have little purchasing power.

As corporations join or replace nation-states as sponsors of athletes and teams around the world, sports become framed in new political terms. According to John Horan, the publisher of *Sporting Goods Intelligence*, "It's not the Free World versus Communism anymore. Now you take sides with sneaker companies. Now everybody looks at the Olympics as Nike versus Reebok" (in Reid, 1996). Horan's conclusion is probably distorted by his own interest in seeing global sport events in this manner, but it certainly demonstrates the intent of transnational corporations as they become major players in international sports.

The speed at which this intent is becoming a reality in connection with sport events such as the Olympics was illustrated in a 1996 statement by Roone Arledge, currently the president of ABC News, and formerly the director of ABC Sports:

> I don't think the essence of the [Olympic] Games has very much to do with the heroic words that we use to describe them. It's basically a commercial enterprise that tries every four years to make as much money as it possibly can (in Jennings, 1996b).

In another statement, Dick Ebersol, president of NBC Sports, explained why NBC became a part of this commercial enterprise by paying over $3.5 billion for the U.S. rights to televise all Olympic Games from 2000 to 2008:

The Olympics . . . has this amazing ability to put the whole family in front of the television together, which is what advertisers are grabbing at (in Steinbreder, 1996).

These statements, made only twelve years after the president of the Los Angeles Olympic Organizing Committee described the Olympics as an athletic-political event, illustrate the power of corporate capitalism. In just over a decade, the characterization of the largest sport event in the world has changed from athletic-political to athletic-economic. Ironically, some of the seeds for that change were planted by Ueberroth as he shaped the focus of the Summer Olympics in 1984; he took a political event and used it to turn a financial profit.

Of course, Ueberroth was not the first or only person to see and use sports in this way. Over the past few decades, representatives from many major corporations around the world have seen the potential of sports to establish new commercial markets and promote the ideology of consumerism that drives those markets. Although the sponsorship money coming from these corporations is a welcome help to those who benefit from it, the primary goal of those who own and control the corporations is to make profits. For example, Coca-Cola may sponsor the Olympics because it wants to bring people together and quench their thirst, but it is primarily interested in selling as many Cokes as possible to the six billion people around the world (Farhi, 1992). This is also the reason the MARS candy company pays millions to be the official snack food of the Olympics, and McDonald's uses the Olympics to market hamburgers and fries around the world.

According to Sut Jhally, a communications professor from the University of Massachusetts, transnational corporations pay billions of dollars to sponsor global sports in an effort to become "global cultural commissars." Jhally says that if you listen closely and critically to the advertisements of these sponsors, you'll discover that in addition to their products, they are selling a way of life based on consumption. They use sports to present images and messages emphasizing individual success through competition, productivity, and consumption. They know that elite competitive sports are good vehicles for presenting these images and messages, because such sports have become primary sources of entertainment around the world. When people are being entertained while watching these sports in person or on television, they are emotionally primed to hear what the sponsors have to say.

Of course, many people ignore the images and messages emphasized by sponsors, or redefine them to fit local and personal circumstances. But this does not prevent large corporations from spending billions to deliver them! Advertisers understand that sooner or later the images and messages associated with sources of pleasure and entertainment in people's lives will in some form enter the imaginations and conversations of a proportion of those who see and hear them. The images and messages do not dictate what people think, but they certainly influence what people think about, and, in this way, they become a part of the overall discourse that occurs in a culture.

We should not interpret this description of the new politics of sports to mean that sports around the world somehow have fallen victim to a global conspiracy hatched by transnational corporations. It means only that transnational organizations have joined nation-states in the global political context in which sports are defined, organized, planned, promoted, played, and presented to the world. (We discuss the implications of this for the Olympic Games in the box on pp. 422–424.)

Other Global Political Issues

As teams and leagues have become increasingly commercialized, and as national boundaries have become less relevant in sports, an increasing number of athletes have become global migrant workers. They go where their sports are played, where they can be supported or earn money while they play. This global migration of athletes has raised new political issues in connection with sports.

Professional wrestling, like most entertainment sports, uses images that enable spectators to identify with athletes. The British Bulldog wears a costume expressing a national identity that attracts attention and gives spectators a reason for supporting or opposing him when he has a match. Other athletes, teams, and leagues have used national colors and flags for the same purposes. (Tom Buchanan, Titansports, Inc.)

Another global political issue is related to the production of sporting goods. As the demand for sport equipment and clothing has increased in wealthy nations, transnational corporations have cut costs for those products by having them manufactured in labor-intensive poor countries where production costs are extremely low. The result has been a clear split between the world's haves and have-nots when it comes to sports: those born into privilege in wealthy nations consume the products made by those born into disadvantaged circumstances in poor nations. This is not a new issue, but it ties sports to global politics in yet another way.

These issues receive further attention in the next two sections.

ATHLETES AS GLOBAL MIGRANT WORKERS Human history is full of examples of labor migration, both forced and voluntary. Industrial societies in particular have depended on mobile labor forces responsive to the needs of production. Now that economies have become more global, the pervasiveness and diversity of labor migration patterns have increased (Bale, 1990; Maguire, 1994b, 1996; Maguire and Bale, 1994; Maguire and Stead, 1996). This is true in sports as well as in other occupational categories. Athletes frequently move from their hometowns when they are recruited to play elite sports, and then they may move many times after that, as they are traded from team to team or seek opportunities to play their sports.

As sociologist Joe Maguire and geographer John Bale have noted in a book on athletic talent migration (1994), athletes move from state to state and region to region within nations, and from nation to nation within and between continents. They have noted also that each of these types of move raises issues related to the following: (1) the personal adjustment of migrating athletes, (2) the rights of athletes as workers in different nations, (3) the impact of talent migration on the nations from and to which athletes migrate, and (4) the impact of athlete migration on patterns of personal, cultural, and national identity formation.

Some migration patterns are seasonal, involving temporary moves as athletes travel from one climate area to another to play their sports. Some patterns follow annual tour schedules, as athletes travel from tournament to tournament around a region or the world. And some migration patterns involve semipermanent or permanent moves from one region or nation to another.

The range of personal experiences among migrating athletes is great. They vary from major forms of culture shock to chronic loneliness to minor homesickness. Some athletes are exploited by teams or clubs, while others make great amounts of money that enable them to return home when they are not playing games or practicing. Some encounter prejudice against foreigners or various forms of racial and ethnic bigotry, while others are socially accepted and make good friends. Some cling to their national identities and socialize with fellow athletes from their homelands, while others develop more global identities unrelated to one national or cultural background. In some cases, teams or clubs expect foreign athletes to adjust on their own, while others provide support for those who need to learn a new language or become familiar with new cultural settings (Klein, 1991).

Athletic talent migration also has an impact on the nations involved (Maguire and Bale, 1994). For example, many Latin American nations have their best baseball players recruited by major-league teams in the U.S. This not only depletes the talent they need to maintain professional baseball in their local economies, but also forces them to depend on U.S.–based satellite television companies even to watch the players from their nations. During the television coverage, they often are exposed to images and messages consistent with the advertising needs of corporations headquartered in the U.S. Similar patterns exist in connection with European soccer teams that recruit players from around the world. In fact, soccer has higher rates of talent migration than other sports, although hockey, track and field, and basketball have high rates as well. The impact of this migration on national talent pools and on the ability of local clubs and teams to maintain economically viable sport programs is complex. Talent migration usually benefits the nation to which athletes move more than it benefits the nation from which athletes move, but this is not always the case.

The impact of global migration by athletes on how people think about and identify themselves in connection with nation-states is something we know little about. On the one hand, there seems to be a tendency among many people to appreciate athletic talent regardless of the nationality of the athletes. On the other hand, there is also a tendency among many people to have special affections for athletes and teams representing their nations of citizenship or their nations of origin. Leagues such as the NHL are open to athletes of all nations. In fact, even though most of the teams are located in U.S. cities, less than 20 percent of the players are U.S.–born; about 60 percent are from Canada, and nearly 30 percent are from European nations. Other leagues impose quotas limiting the number of foreign-born or foreign-nationality players they may sign to contracts (Greenberg and Gray, 1996). For example, in the early 1990s, Japan banned U.S. women basketball

The Olympic Games
What Makes Them Special?

Are the Olympics just another international sport event, or are they special in what they do and what they mean? According to the ideals of Olympism, the Olympic Games provide opportunities for people to learn about and connect with others from different societies and cultural backgrounds. These ideals are important, because our collective future on this planet depends on the ability of human beings to work together as global citizens. The goal of this togetherness is not to inspire everyone to think alike or believe that all human beings are basically the same. Instead, it is to establish global processes through which human beings learn to understand and appreciate their differences, and work together to sustain healthy and safe lifestyles for people around the world. If the Olympic Games can be organized and played to promote these goals, they are indeed special.

At this point in history, the Olympic Games clearly fall short of meeting their promise of promoting this type of understanding and togetherness. The themes of nationalism and commercialism exert so much influence on how the Olympic Games are planned, promoted, presented, and played that the goal of global understanding and togetherness receives only token attention. Of course, some people use the Olympic Games as occasions for intercultural learning and connecting in positive ways with people from different cultural backgrounds, but this would occur more often if the games were organized and presented differently.

According to Michael Real (1996), a professor of communication who has studied the Olympics as a media spectacle, the current method of selling media broadcasting rights tends to subvert Olympic ideals. Television companies buy the rights to take whatever video images they want from the Olympics and combine them with their own commentaries as they present their coverage to audiences in their countries. So instead of bringing the world together around a single experience, the coverage presents its two billion TV consumers with the Olympic Games shown in "nationalized" terms heavily influenced by the commercial interests of the sponsors and producers. It is, of course, possible for these consumers to impose their

own meanings on this coverage, but the coverage itself serves as the starting point for their thinking about and making sense of the Olympics.

Viewers who wish to use the Olympics as a basis for visualizing forms of global community constructed around cultural differences and mutual understanding can do so, but current TV coverage provides little assistance in this quest. In the U.S., for example, those watching the 1996 games in Atlanta found it much easier to focus on U.S. athletes, the U.S. flag, the U.S. national anthem, and spectators chanting "USA! USA!" than to focus on athletes as part of a global community where people come together to learn about each other and form positive relationships. It was also easy to accept the association between large corporate sponsors and human achievement and to believe that corporations really do make the Olympics possible. During the 174 hours of TV coverage, consumers saw nearly 40 hours of messages from those corporations, the companies that in the words of the announcers "brought you the Olympics." People don't accept these messages in literal terms, but corporate sponsors bet hundreds of millions of dollars every two years that the association between their logos and the Olympic rings not only discourages criticism of their products, but encourages people to consume these products regularly.

The overt commercialism in the Olympics has led many people, including officials and athletes, to raise questions about the meaning of the Olympics. Shirley Babashoff, a U.S. swimmer who won two gold and six silver Olympic medals in 1972 and 1976, watched the 1996 games and said this:

> The Olympics is not about sports any more. It's about who can win the most money. It's like going to Disneyland (in Reid, 1996).

A high-ranking Olympic official agreed, and came to his own conclusion:

> I'm on the verge of joining those who think it's time for the Olympics, in their present context, to die. And they need to die for the same reason the ancient Olympic Games died—greed and corruption. And they're just about at the point now (in Reid, 1996).

Charles Barkley, an outspoken member of the U.S. men's basketball "Dream Team," noted in 1992 that the purpose of the games had little to do with Olympic ideals. He said,

> I know why we're here. We're here to spread basketball internationally and make more money for somebody. . . . We're going to win the gold medal, but there won't be any life changing decisions made because of it. . . . [P]oor people will still be poor and racism and sexism will still exist. . . .

These quotations indicate there is a need to make changes in how the Olympic Games are planned, played, and presented to the world. The IOC issues regular press releases full of rhetoric about friendship and peace, but it has made no concerted effort to take that rhetoric seriously. It has not constructed programs and processes through which it becomes clear to athletes and spectators that the games are about cultural understanding and working together in socially responsible ways. This point has been made by Bruce Kidd, a former Olympian who is now a physical and health educator at the University of Toronto. Kidd (1996) argues that the time is right to make the Olympic Games special by using them to highlight cultural and social issues and to promote social responsibility around the globe.

Kidd suggests that athletes should be selected to participate in the Olympics on the basis of their actions as global citizens as well as their athletic accomplishments. There also should be a curriculum through which athletes learn about fellow competitors and their cultures. The games should involve formal, televised opportunities for intercultural exchanges, and athletes should be ready to discuss their ideas about world peace and social responsibility during media interviews. Special projects should be sponsored by the IOC so that participants have opportunities to build on their Olympic experiences through service to others around the world. A proportion of TV rights fees should be used to make this happen. IOC members then could talk about real examples of social responsibility connected with sports. The personal stories that NBC and other television companies present during coverage of the games could then highlight the ways that athletes are socially responsible, rather than soap-opera-like personal tragedies and experiences. TV viewers may find stories about how the Olympics make the world a better place as entertaining and inspiring as tabloid-like coverage of heartbreaking stories about how selected individuals beat the odds to win medals.

Additionally, the IOC should control both nationalism and commercialism more carefully as it organizes the games and sells broadcasting rights. I offer the following suggestions:

- Do away with national uniforms for athletes. Let athletes choose from uniforms designed by artists from different countries to express various cultural themes from around the world. This would minimize symbols that promote nationalism and even would inspire forms of commercialism that promote cultural understanding.
- Revise the opening ceremonies so that athletes enter the arena with other athletes in their events. The emphasis would be on unity and fellowship among athletes, not on the political and economic systems in which the athletes were born through no choice of their own. Artists from around the world would be commissioned to design the flags for different sports. National flags could be displayed in the middle of the field during the ceremonies, but they would not be associated with any particular group of athletes.
- Eliminate national anthems and the display of national flags during the award ceremonies. Present medals in the stadium at the end of each day of competition in such a way that the emphasis during awards ceremonies would be on athletes as representatives of all humanity, rather than of particular nations.
- Eliminate medal counts associated with countries. National medal counts always have been contrary to the spirit of the Olympic Movement. They do nothing but foster chauvinism and fan the fires of existing political differences between countries. Furthermore, they distract attention from the

Continued

achievements of athletes and focus attention on nationalist sympathies and animosities.

- Eliminate or revise team sports. Team sports, as they are now structured, automatically focus attention on national affiliations. They encourage players and spectators to define games in terms of national honor and pride. If team sports are not eliminated, then develop a method of choosing teams so that athletes from different countries play on the same teams, and athletes from any one nation play on different teams. Then "dream teams" would emphasize international unity, rather than a nationalist and commercial approach to sports.
- Eliminate sports associated with the commercially driven, consumption-oriented lifestyles in wealthy countries, and add to each games "demonstration sports" native to the cultural regions in which the games are being held. Because television plays a central role in the way sports are imagined, created, and played around the world, encourage TV coverage of these native games so that people have expanded notions of physical activities that may influence and inspire their own sport participation.
- Use multiple sites for each Olympic Games. This would make it possible for additional countries, especially those without massive economic resources, to submit bids to be hosts. Poorer nations that hosted only a portion of the events could benefit economically from hosting the Olympics. Multiple sites would enable media spectators to see a wider range of cultural settings, while still seeing all the events traditionally included in the games.
- Include in television contracts guidelines for integrating themes emphasizing global responsibility into coverage and commercials. These themes could be developed by athlete committees working with committees from the Olympic Academy, some members of which are scholars committed to the spirit of Olympism. This would link corporate sponsors to the special meaning of the Olympics and provide support for athletes as global citizens.

Because the Olympic Games capture the attention of one-third of the world's population, they should be used as something other than global marketing opportunities for transnational corporations and medal harvests for wealthy nations that can produce world-class athletes. The present is a good time for the Olympics to put into practice the ideals of the Olympic Charter. As this is done, the Olympics should formulate a new motto, one that goes beyond "Citius, Altius, Fortius" ("faster, higher, stronger"), one that takes the Olympics beyond nationalism and commercialism. What about "Excellence For Humanity"? What do you think?

• •

players from its professional league. At the same time, professional leagues in Italy, Spain, and France allowed their teams to have up to two foreign players, many of whom were from the U.S. In 1996, England lifted all quotas for both men's and women's pro basketball teams; during the same year, the new MLS (Major League Soccer) in the U.S. limited the number of non–U.S. players to four per team. Currently, some people in the U.S. are calling for limits on the number of foreign student-athletes who can play on intercollegiate teams, while at the same time many athletic departments are recruiting more student-athletes from outside the U.S.

As commercial sport organizations expand their franchise locations across national borders, and as they recruit athletes regardless of nationality, talent migration will increase in the future. The social implications of this trend will be important to study and understand.

GLOBAL POLITICS AND THE PRODUCTION OF SPORT EQUIPMENT AND CLOTHING The free trade agreements (for example, GATT and NAFTA) signed by many nations in the mid-1990s have created a new global economic environment. In this environment, it is cost effective for large corporations selling vast amounts of goods to people in wealthy nations to locate their production facilities in labor-intensive poor nations. These corporations now are taxed at much lower rates when they move products from nation to nation, so they can make products in nations where labor is cheap and regulations are scarce and then sell them in wealthy nations where people have money to buy them.

These political-economic changes meant that during the mid-1990s, many athletic shoes costing well over $100 a pair in the U.S. were cut and sewn by workers making less than 25 cents per hour in China and Indonesia, less than 75 cents per hour in Thailand, and less than $2.25 per hour in South Korea (Enloe, 1995). Similar patterns existed in connection with the production of clothes bearing patriotic-looking red, white, and blue NFL and NBA logos and sold in the U.S. (Sage, 1996). Soccer balls sanctioned by FIFA, the international soccer federation, often were hand-sewn by child laborers making far less than poverty-level wages in poor nations where people were desperate for any kind of work. And while Nike athletes were making millions of dollars on their shoe endorsements, Nike shoes were being made by Indonesian and Vietnamese people living in poverty and working under conditions the U.S. State Department described as oppressive.

Even though these and other examples attracted some attention during the mid-1990s, they received little coverage in the mainstream media, where a portion of the advertising income depends on the very corporations that produce the sporting goods and clothing. Of course, these global economic issues are complex; the social, political, economic, and cultural conditions in China and Indonesia are different from those in wealthy nations, and they cannot be assessed using the same standards. However, it is possible to make judgments about safety issues and whether full-time workers are paid wages enabling them to live above the poverty line in their communities. To make these judgments, we must become familiar with global political issues.

Making Sense of New Political Realities

It's not easy to explain all the changes outlined in the previous sections. Are sports simply a part of general globalization processes through which various sport forms come together in many different combinations? Are we witnessing the modernization of sports? Are sports being Americanized? Europeanized? Asianized? Are we seeing sports simply being diffused throughout the world, with people in some countries emulating the sports played in other countries, or are sports being used in connection with new forms of cultural imperialism and colonization? Are sports tools for making poorer nations dependent on wealthy ones, or are they tools for establishing cultural independence and autonomy in emerging nations? Is it accurate to say that sports are becoming commercialized, or should we say that sports are becoming corporatized in ways that promote global capitalist expansion? Are sports becoming more democratic, or have new forms of sponsorship actually restricted people's choices about when and how they will play sports?

Those who study sports as social phenomena now are devoting more of their attention to these and related questions. The best work on these issues involves data on global *and* local levels (Donnelly, 1996b; Guttmann, 1994; Harvey et al., 1996). This work calls attention to the fact that powerful people do not simply impose certain sport forms on less powerful people around the world. Even when sports from powerful nations are played in other parts of the world, the meanings associated with them are grounded in the local cultures in which they are played. It is important to understand global trends, but it is also important to understand the local expressions of and responses to those trends. Power is a process, not a thing; it is always exercised through social relations. So the study of power must focus on how people agree and disagree with one another as they attempt to live their lives on terms enabling them to achieve some sense of personal significance. This is true in connection with sports, as it is in other dimensions of social life.

POLITICS IN SPORTS

The term *politics* usually is associated with affairs of the state. However, politics includes all processes of governing people and administering policies, at all levels of organization. Therefore, politics is an integral part of sports, and many local, national, and international sport organizations are referred to as "governing bodies."

Sport organizations do many things, but most are concerned with providing and regulating sport participation opportunities, establishing and enforcing policies, controlling and standardizing competitions, and acknowledging the accomplishments of athletes. This sounds like a straightforward set of tasks. However, they seldom are accomplished without some form of opposition, debate, and compromise. Members of sport organizations may agree on many things, but they also have different interests or orientations. In fact, conflicts of interest often arise as people deal with the following questions surrounding sports and sport participation:

1. What qualifies as a sport?
2. What are the rules of a sport?
3. Who makes and enforces rules in sports?
4. Who organizes and controls games, meets, matches, and tournaments?
5. Where will sport events take place?
6. Who is eligible to participate in a sport?
7. How are rewards distributed to athletes and other organization members?

Because many people mistakenly assume that sports make up a special part of life, separate from politics and other real-world processes, they are sometimes surprised and shocked when they hear that sports involve politics. But just as sports are connected with the larger politics of the state, sport events and organizations have politics of their own. These politics affect everyone involved, from athletes, coaches, and administrators in sport organizations to promoters, sponsors, and spectators. Let's look at a few examples.

What Qualifies as a Sport?

As we noted in chapter 1, there is no universal agreement on the definition of *sports*. What is considered a sport in a society or in a particular event such as the Olympics is determined through political processes (Donnelly, 1996a).

The criteria used to identify sports reflect the ideas and interests of some people more than others. In the Olympics, for example, a competitive activity or game for men will not be considered for recognition as a sport unless it is played in at least seventy countries; an activity or game for women must be played in at least forty countries. It also must have an officially designated international governing body, a requisite number of national governing bodies, and a history of international championships before the IOC even will consider recognizing it as an Olympic sport. Additionally, in these days of multi-billion-dollar media contracts, the activity or game is more likely to be recognized as a sport if it is attractive to television and if it attracts the interest of younger viewers, who in turn attract new advertisers and corporate sponsors to the Olympics. It also helps if the activity is played by women, because more women than men watch the Olympics, and because men's sports still outnumber women's sports in the Olympics.

Of course, this way of defining sport favors those nations that historically have had the resources to export their games around the world. Former colonial powers are especially favored, because they used their national games as a way of introducing their cultural values and traditions to colonized peoples around the world. Wealthy nations today not only have their national sports broadcast on satellite channels around the world, but also have the resources to subsidize the development of these sports so that they are played in many countries. So when it comes time for IOC recognition, the sports from wealthy nations are at the top of the list. When they are recognized, the cultural values and traditions of these nations are reaffirmed. In this way, their games become the sports of the world.

This is also the reason native games in traditional cultures are not a part of the Olympic Games. Games played in limited regions of the globe don't qualify for recognition as sports. So if people from nations with traditional cultures want to participate in the Olympics, they must learn to play activities and games popular in wealthy nations. Since these people seldom have access to the equipment and facilities needed to train in their homelands, where resources are scarce, they must depend on support from people and organizations in wealthy nations to become international athletes in recognized sports. In this way, sports become vehicles through which people and organizations in wealthy nations can gain a foothold in traditional cultures and influence social change processes to their own advantage.

This type of political process also occurs in other contexts. For example, for well over one hundred years, the men who have controlled athletic departments in North American high schools and colleges have used a power and performance model to designate certain activities as varsity sports. Then they have organized these sports to emphasize competition and dominance, so that the sports fit with their notions of character and excellence. Over the years, this way of defining and organizing sports seldom has been questioned. But as athletic programs are beginning to deal with the issue of gender inequity, some people now are arguing that full equity never will be achieved unless such questions are raised. If power and performance sports attract far fewer girls and women than boys and men, it may be time to ask questions about what gets to

count as a varsity sport, and why. When we ask these questions, we immediately notice the existence of politics in sports.

The development of criteria underlying the meaning and organization of sports also occurs on a global scale. Sociologist Peter Donnelly (1996a) illustrates this in his analysis of the way the ideologies of Olympism and professionalism are being combined to form a global sport monoculture that he calls "prolympism." Prolympism is quickly becoming the model for determining what activities count and get funded as sports in nations around the world, even in nations where traditional games are clearly inconsistent with professionalism in any form. So the politics of defining sports are both local and global in impact.

What Are the Rules of a Sport?

Sports are social constructions. This means that people formulate them as they interact with one another and create physical challenges within the constraints of environment and culture. The rules that govern sports are also social constructions, and as such, are determined through political processes. Why should first base be 90 feet from home plate in major-league baseball? Why should a basketball rim be 10 feet above the ground? Why should a women's basketball be slightly smaller and lighter than the ball men use? Why should six-year-olds hit a baseball off a tee instead of hitting a pitched ball? Why should the top of a volleyball net be $88\frac{1}{8}$ inches off the ground in international women's volleyball? Why can't pole vaulters use any type of pole they want? Why can't tournament golfers use any type of golf club or golf ball they want? Why can't a 145-pound high school wrestler compete voluntarily in the 185-pound weight category? This list of questions could go on and on. But the point is that the rules of sports can be based on many different concerns and this makes them political.

Many people fail to realize that whenever there are formal rules governing what people

In the process of becoming identified as "official" sports, physical activities come to be controlled by governing organizations. These organizations determine and enforce rules for their sports, organize and control competitive events, and identify who is eligible to participate and who will receive rewards for participating. These processes often lead to conflict and require mediation and negotiated decisions. This means that politics is an inherent part of sports. (Jay Coakley)

can and can't do, there always will be political processes. Because sports have more rules than most human activities, they are more political than most things we participate in during our lives.

Who Makes and Enforces Rules in Sports?

The rules of a sport are determined by a governing body of people who over time come to be recognized as official sources of information and regulation for those who play the sport. The process of becoming recognized as the *sole* governing body of a sport clearly involves politics. Governing bodies have power, status, and control over resources, so it is common for more than one group to claim it is the rightful rule-making body. The simultaneous existence of different governing bodies can create confusion for athletes and spectators in a sport. Professional boxing, for example, currently has five governing

bodies (the WBO, the WBU, the WBF, and the IBC), each with its own weight categories and championships, and each claiming to be the official rule-making body for boxing. Such new sports as skateboarding and in-line skating each have at least two different organizations vying to be official governing bodies. As these organizations seek to establish power over these sports and the athletes who participate in them, they battle each other to recruit dues-paying members and sponsor competitive events. In the process, however, their policies confuse athletes and limit participation opportunities. When this occurs, people clearly see the politics in sports.

When rules exist, there is also a need for rule enforcement. This adds another political dimension to sports. Anyone who has ever refereed or officiated a game or match will tell you that rule violations are seldom clear-cut, that identifying violations is difficult, and that few people see violations the same way. Rule violations occur on a regular basis in many sports, but the best referees have learned when to call fouls or penalties in connection with these violations. In fact, referees and officials discuss when they should or should not call fouls during games and matches. Making sports appear to be fair to both athletes and spectators is a political challenge.

Enforcement in the case of alleged off-the-field rule violations is also a political challenge. The process of investigating rule violations, determining innocence or guilt, and punishing rule violators involves determinations of what is good and bad for sports, sport organizations, and various people connected with sports. These determinations may be grounded in ideas about fairness, moral principles, economic interests, personal reputations, organizational prestige, or other factors. How these factors are defined and which ones prevail in the rule enforcement process is a matter for discussion, debate, and compromise. The belief that "justice is blind" may be necessary to keep order in a group, but a close examination of the process of justice in sports shows that it seldom is truly blind.

We also see the politics of rule enforcement when we examine the policies of sport organizations. For example, the NCAA, the primary governing body for intercollegiate sports in the U.S., is made up of representatives from member universities located all around the U.S. Because college sports mean different things from one region of the country to another, these representatives have different and often contradictory ideas about what is legitimate conduct and what is not (Baxter et al., 1996). Developing a set of rules and enforcement procedures under these conditions involves intensely political processes. Rule enforcement inevitably creates dissent among those members whose ideas about legitimate conduct are not consistent with what the NCAA has determined to be "right and official." When this occurs, political processes become heated; and it occurs often.

Who Organizes and Controls Games, Meets, Matches, and Tournaments?

The organization and control of sport events is often in the hands of representatives from official governing bodies. Standards emerge when the governing body is stable, but standards never are established once and for all time. For example, even though officials from governing bodies have tried to devise organized standards for evaluating and judging performances in sports such as figure skating, diving, and gymnastics, "statistical evidence suggests that political loyalties have played a role in judges' voting preferences." This was the conclusion Seltzer and Glass (1991) reached after a twenty-year study (from 1968 to 1988) of figure and dance skating events in the Winter Olympics. They found that judges gave higher scores to athletes from their own countries, and scoring patterns often were linked to Cold War political blocs. Of course, this is disheartening to athletes, but it should be no more disheartening than the knowledge that "cuteness," "hairstyles," "body build," or "eye color" can influence judges when it comes to women athletes in certain events. This is the reason some athletes spend thousands of dollars on everything from braces for their teeth to plastic surgery for their jaws and noses. Politics comes in many forms!

Now that sports have become increasingly commercialized, the organization and control of events may be shared by official governing bodies and a combination of corporate sponsors and media production people. The location and timing of events, event schedules, which people will be given press passes to cover events, which television company will have the rights to broadcast the events, which corporate logos will be associated with the events, how much tickets will cost, and other issues are resolved through political processes. The participants in those processes and their interests change from one event to the next; this means that the politics in sports never ends.

Where Will Sport Events Take Place?

The politics of place are an integral part of sports. Site selection decisions become increasingly contentious, as sports, teams, and events use and are used by towns, cities, and nations for economic purposes (Lenskyj, 1996; Whitson and Macintosh, 1996).

Certainly, the selection of Olympic sites is a political process, as anyone who ever has helped to organize an Olympic site bid will agree. For example, the selection of Atlanta for the 1996 Summer Games was part of an overall political process during which IOC officials were wined, dined, bribed, and pressured to choose between Atlanta, Athens, Toronto, Melbourne, Manchester, and Belgrade (Simson and Jennings, 1992). Officials considered everything from television rights fees coming from American television companies to the location of a major corporate Olympic sponsor in Atlanta. In fact, evidence suggests that Atlanta was chosen to host the games because it was the home of the international headquarters of Coca-Cola, the largest corporate sponsor of the Olympics in the world (Jennings, 1996). After seeing the red-and-white Coke logo all around Atlanta and the Olympic venues, some observers, in fact, described the games as the "Coca-Colympics." The involvement of media companies and corporate sponsors in the site selection process is now a key dimension of the politics of place in sports.

The 2000 World Cup site selection was so political that Japan and South Korea were chosen as cohosts in an effort to avoid alienating any segment of the emerging Pacific Rim economies needed to drive the expansion of soccer in Asia. Japan and South Korea together spent over $100 million on their bids! Site bids for events such as Super Bowls, All-Star games, and the NCAA men's and women's basketball tournaments may not cost as much as bids to host global events, but they are just as political. In fact, the major men's professional sport leagues in North America often use site host awards for big events as incentives for cities to commit millions of public dollars to building new stadiums that will benefit the league as well as local franchise owners: "If you build it, the All-Star game will come to your city."

Sports and the politics of place in many parts of the world also reflect environmental issues. For example, the use of open space or agricultural land for golf courses now is being contested in Europe, Japan, and even North America. The Global AntiGolf Movement has developed in connection with widespread objections to the use of chemical fertilizers and massive water resources to keep grass soft and green for golfers representing the economic elites in societies. This organization has 250 member lobbying groups in fifteen countries, and has coordinated protests and other antigolf campaigns around the world. Ski resort expansion in North America, Europe, and Japan also has been resisted for environmental reasons. Such examples highlight the fact that the politics of place in sports often involves local opposition to the hosting of events and the building of facilities.

Who Is Eligible to Participate in a Sport?

Who plays and who doesn't play is often a hotly contested issue in sports. Even when children play informal games, they discuss and occasionally argue over who will play and who will sit out. In sport organizations, these discussions and arguments are more formal. People with authority in these organizations—volunteers, elected representatives, or appointees—make determinations about participation eligibility. They may use factors such as gender, age, weight, height, ability (and disability), place of residence, citizenship, educational affiliation, grade in school, social status, income, or even race and ethnicity to determine participation eligibility. Although eligibility policies often are presented as if they somehow are based on unchanging truths about human beings and sports, they are grounded in standards debated and agreed upon by groups of officials; the agreements are forged through political processes.

People often have contested the arbitrariness of eligibility rules. For example, NCAA eligibility rules are so complex that the organization publishes a monthly paper in which pages of eligibility appeals are listed and explained. Lawsuits sometimes have followed unsuccessful appeals, because people feel they have been excluded unfairly from participation. High school students have made similar challenges when their families have moved from one school district to another and they have found they are ineligible to play varsity sports. Even in youth sports, there are frequent debates about age and weight rules often used to determine eligibility. Athletes with disabilities regularly have challenged rules prohibiting their participation in certain sports. Within events such as the Paralympics, the international event held immediately following the Summer Games in recent Olympics, there are frequent debates about disability classifications and eligibility.

These eligibility debates become particularly heated when there is much at stake for the athletes and officials involved. This was the case when the IOC banned South African athletes from participating in the Olympics (from 1964 to 1991) because of their nation's formal policy of racial apartheid. Because the South Africa National Olympic Committee (SANOC) formally used race to determine eligibility on its national teams, the IOC decided that South African athletes no longer were eligible to participate in the Olympics. However, we should note that the IOC ban on South Africa was hotly contested, both within the IOC itself and around the world, among people associated with national sport organizations. The IOC decision was influenced partly by antiapartheid activists who threatened massive boycotts of the Olympic Games in the early 1960s if the IOC did not withdraw its recognition of South Africa.

Similar pressures and threats were associated with the "eligibility politics" associated with women's participation in the marathon and other distance events, which the men in the IOC thought were too strenuous for what they defined as "the weaker sex." During the 1996 Summer Games, a Paris-based group called *Atlanta Plus* lobbied the IOC to exclude from the games all countries with policies that precluded or made unlikely the participation of women on their national teams. Because Islam was the dominant religion in many of those countries, the politics in sports became tied to issues of morality and cultural traditions. Similar issues of morality occasionally have entered debates about the eligibility of women in wrestling, boxing, and a few other sports in North America, where sports are more open to girls and women.

An Olympic eligibility standard that changed in the 1980s was the one calling for amateur participants. The definition of *amateur* long had been debated in sport organizations. Most definitions served to exclude those who could not afford to train in and play sports without making money in connection with their sport skills. Only economically privileged people could train full-time and not worry about money. Then, as grassroots concerns about fairness and democracy were coupled with economic concerns related to the fielding of "dream teams" and the hyping of high-profile professional athletes in the Olympics, there were changes in eligibility rules. Now the Olympics involve professional as well as so-called amateur athletes.

As sports become more globalized, issues arise about citizenship and eligibility. When concerns about citizenship are combined with issues of sponsorship, the political issues become very interesting. In fact, Jose Cuervo, the largest Tequila producer in the world, recently has considered buying an island, naming it Cuervo, and requesting sovereignty as a nation so it can have its own volleyball team in the Olympics. This would enable Cuervo to have its name and logo in the Olympics and use the Olympic rings without paying the IOC millions of dollars to be one of the top sponsors. Although this sounds like a bizarre political strategy, there are indeed a number of wealthy and powerful transnational corporations that can afford to buy countries if they want to. Who knows what the sport eligibility politics of the future will involve?

There are literally hundreds of other noteworthy cases of eligibility politics in amateur and professional sports. The "no pass, no play" rules in U.S. high school sports have been the subject of political debates in many states. Similar debates occur around the issue of academic eligibility in college sports. Amateur sports have been the scene of longstanding debates over the meaning of *amateur* and qualifications for "amateur status." Because these meanings are socially determined, they change over time. This always will be the case; and this is one of the many reasons politics always will be a part of sports.

How Are Rewards Distributed to Athletes and Other Organization Members?

The distribution of rewards is an issue at all levels of sport participation, even at the lowest levels of youth sports. Coaches, league administrators, and parents often must decide who will receive special commendations, certificates of accomplishment, or trophies. "Who gets what?" is a political question, and the answers are not always clearcut. People discuss, debate, and sometimes argue heatedly over the issue of rewards. As the level of competition increases, so do the stakes associated with participation. At the highest levels of competition, the politics of rewards can involve massive amounts of money and status.

With the increased commercialization of sports, there have been longstanding, heated debates about how revenues should be distributed. These revenues could be allocated in various proportions to sport organizations, organization officials, owners and promoters, athletes, and others connected with sports. As we noted in chapter 11, the political processes associated with the distribution of revenues in commercial sports are complex and never-ending. Of course, these processes take different forms and come to

different resolutions in different countries and in different sports. The debates even involve different decision-making bodies, depending on whether they occur in countries with market (capitalist) economies or planned (socialist) economies.

Why should a talented intercollegiate football player who risks health and personal well-being while generating millions of dollars for his university over a four-year period be limited to receiving an athletic grant-in-aid that is only a fraction of what NFL players are paid? Why is this player not allowed to make a penny selling his own image on shirts or coffee mugs, while the university uses his image to market everything from the school itself to merchandise with the university logo on it? Why should professional sport team owners make more money than the best players on their teams? What percentage should agents receive when they negotiate player contracts? Why should Olympic athletes not be paid for their participation when they collectively generate over a billion dollars during a Summer Olympics? Why should the IOC receive 33 percent of the revenues for the Olympic Games, when it does little other than award the games to a particular city and get wined and dined in lavish style in the process? Why should the USOC receive 12.75 percent of the money paid by U.S. television companies for the rights to broadcast the Olympics? Why should professional athletes who receive medals not be allowed during the medal ceremonies to wear warm-up suits made by the companies who pay them endorsement fees? Should athletes receive compensation when companies use their images and uniform numbers in expensive video games that sell million of copies? Who should receive profits on a shirt that displays Dennis Rodman's tattoos? Who owns the surfaces of athletes' bodies, and who may use them for commercial purposes? These and hundreds of similar questions show that the "politics of rewards" is an integral part of sports.

Sometimes rewards involve status or prestige rather than money. For example, in 1992 there was considerable debate in Japan over whether Akebono (formerly named Chad Rowan), an American sumo wrestler from Hawaii, would be voted into the rank of *yokozuna*, or grand champion, by the Yokozuna Promotion Council. Many Japanese people warned the council that if such a prized honor were not reserved for native Japanese, Japan might lose control of a celebrated part of its own culture. And when the council voted to name Akebono as the sixty-fourth *yokozuna* in over three hundred years of sumo wrestling, many people voiced objections.

Similar political debates over status occur in connection with the selection of American professional athletes for Halls of Fame and All-Star games. Even Little League teams have a "politics of status" connected with "the most improved player of the year," "the most valuable player," "the most dedicated player," and so on. When people agree on the players who should receive such awards and special status, they tend to forget that the selection process is political. It is only when they don't agree with the selection that they talk about politics in sports.

SUMMARY

WHAT MAKES SPORTS POLITICAL?

The idea that sports and politics can be kept separate is naive. Sports do not exist in cultural vacuums. They are integral parts of the social world. As parts of that world, they are influenced by social, political, and economic forces. Sports do not exist apart from the people who create, organize, and play them. The lives of these people and their relationships with one another are connected at least partially to issues of power and control. Therefore, politics becomes a part of sports just because politics is a part of people's lives. It is unavoidable.

Actual government intervention in sports is related to the need for sponsorship, organization, and facilities. The fact that sports are important parts of people's lives and that sports can be the scene for problems often leads to government regulations and controls. The form of government involvement in sports varies by society, but when it occurs its purposes are (1) to protect people and maintain order, (2) to develop physical abilities and fitness, (3) to promote the prestige of a group, (4) to establish a sense of social solidarity among group members, (5) to reaffirm political ideology within a group, (6) to increase the legitimacy of the political system and the people in power, and (7) to promote economic development.

Government involvement that occurs in state-controlled societies with planned economies is especially clear. Sponsorship of sports is direct; facilities are owned and operated by the state; and the state determines rules and policies about sports and the conditions under which they are played. Government involvement in countries with market economies is less direct, but usually quite extensive. Sport programs and facilities often are supported by city, state, provincial, or federal funds. Various government officials and agencies regulate who may participate in what sport activities under what circumstances, and they often regulate the circumstances under which commercial sports are sponsored and played.

The rules, policies, and funding priorities set by government officials and agencies reflect the political struggles between groups within any society. This does not mean that the same people always will benefit when government involvement occurs, but it does mean that involvement seldom will result in equal benefits for everyone. For example, when funds are given to elite sport programs and the development and training of elite athletes, fewer funds are available for general-participation programs. Of course, funding priorities could favor mass participation instead of elite sports, but the point is that the priorities themselves are subject to debate and negotiation. This political process is an inevitable part of sports.

History shows that groups with the greatest resources, organization, and outside support and with goals that fit most closely with the political positions of public officials are most likely to be favored when government involvement in sports occurs. The groups least likely to be favored are those that fail to understand the connection between sports and politics or that lack the resources to influence political processes effectively. As long as people believe the myth that sports and politics are unrelated, they remain at a disadvantage when rules and policies are made and funds are allocated.

People often discuss the connection between sports and global political processes in terms of sports' impact on international relations. Ideally, sports are used to bring nations together in contexts supportive of peace and friendship. Although this has occurred, the reality is that most nations have used sports to foster their own interests. In fact, displays of nationalism have been and continue to be common at international events. The Olympic Games are a good case in point. The major emphasis among many of those who promote and watch the Olympics is on national medal counts and expressions of national superiority.

As powerful transnational corporations have joined nation-states as major parties in global politics, sports have been used increasingly for economic as well as political purposes. Nationalism and the promotion of national interests remain a part of global sports, but consumerism and the promotion of capitalist expansion have become more important since the end of the Cold War. Within the context of transnational relations, athletes and teams now are associated with corporate logos as well as with nation-states. Global sport events are now political *and* economic in character. They serve as settings for presenting numerous images and messages asso-

ciated with the interests of nation-states and corporate sponsors. The dominant images and messages are consistent with the interests of the major corporate sponsors, and tend to promote an ideology infused with capitalist themes related to work, individualism, productivity, and consumption.

Global political processes also are associated with other aspects of sports, such as the migration patterns of elite athletes and the production of sporting goods. Political issues are raised when athletes cross national borders to play their sports, and when transnational corporations produce sports equipment and clothing in labor-intensive poor nations, and then sell those items in wealthy nations. We best can understand these and other issues associated with global political processes when we study sports on both global and local levels. This enables us to determine when sports involve reciprocal cultural exchanges leading to mutual understanding among people from different parts of the world, and when sports involve processes through which powerful nations and corporations exercise subtle influence over social life and political events in less powerful nations around the world. Research on this topic suggests that the role of sports in global political processes is very complex.

Politics is also part of the very structure and organization of sports. Political processes exist because people in sport organizations must answer questions about what qualifies as a sport, what the rules of a sport should be and how they should be enforced, who should organize and control sport events, where sport events should occur, who is eligible to participate, and how rewards will be distributed. This is the reason many sport organizations are described as "governing bodies": they are the context for political decision making that affects everyone connected with sports.

A look at sports from the inside and a look at their connections with social relations in local, national, and international contexts clearly show that they are inseparable from politics and political processes.

SUGGESTED READINGS

Allison, L., ed. 1993. *The changing politics of sport.* Manchester, England: Manchester University Press (*ten papers focusing on various aspects of sports and world politics; articles deal with issues of nationalism, commercialism, and the performance principle in an international context*).

Bale, J., and J. Maguire, eds. 1994. *The global sports arena: Athletic talent migration in an interdependent world.* London: Frank Cass (*sixteen papers dealing with the patterns and processes of the migration of athletic labor around the world; papers focus on the experiences of the athletes themselves as well as issues of political economy and nationhood*).

Blain, N., R. Boyle, and H. O'Donnell. 1993. *Sport and national identity in the European media.* Leicester, England: Leicester University Press (*an insightful study of how print and electronic media coverage of sports in European countries is framed to portray the nationalities of people and athletes; examples show how sports are turned into politics as national stereotypes are used to explain everything from tactics and techniques on the playing field to the character of fans and athletes from different countries*).

Brownell, S. 1995. *Training the body for China: Sports in the moral order of the People's Republic.* Chicago: University of Chicago Press (*based on ethnographic data collected in China, written by an anthropologist, this book provides detailed analyses of how sports become a part of political processes on many different levels—the public, the personal, the national, and the local; the author looks at how ideas about morality, work, citizenship, and the body are produced, reproduced, and contested in connection with sports*).

Donnelly, P., ed. 1994. *Sociology of Sport Journal* 11 (4) (*this issue contains five articles focusing on sports and global culture, globalization, satellite television, and national identity*).

Eichberg, H. 1984. Olympic sport—Neocolonialization and alternatives. *International Review for the Sociology of Sport* 19(1): 97–106 (*a discussion of how powerful nations have used international sport to make less powerful nations dependent on them*).

Hoberman, J. 1986. *The Olympic crisis: Sport, politics and the moral order.* New Rochelle, NY: Aristide D. Caratzas (*an in-depth and still timely critique of the modern games and why they have failed to promote internationalism*).

Houlihan, B. 1994. *Sport and international politics.* Hemel Hempstead, England: Harvester-Wheatsheaf (*analysis of the relationship between sports and international politics since World War II; the analysis draws insights from traditional theories of international relations, with special attention given to globalization theory*).

James, C. L. R. 1984. *Beyond a boundary.* New York: Pantheon Books (*a classic analysis of cricket and British colonialism in the West Indies; first published in 1963*).

Jarvie, G. 1991. *Highland Games: The making of the myth.* Edinburgh: Edinburgh University Press (*a critical historical and sociological analysis of the emergence of contemporary forms of Highland Games in Scotland; focuses on the role of sports in shaping cultural identity*).

Kruger, A., and J. Riordan, eds. 1996. *The story of worker sport.* Champaign, IL: Human Kinetics (*a unique collection of papers highlighting the ways in which sports have been used for explicitly political purposes by workers in Europe, the former USSR, and Canada; papers show how sports can be used to inspire a collective consciousness among people at various levels of social organization*).

Lucas, J. A. 1992. *The future of the Olympic Games.* Champaign, IL: Human Kinetics (*an "insider's look" into Olympism and the Olympic movement; uncritical but informative description and analysis of recent IOC policies, programs, and prospects for the future*).

Macintosh, D., and D. Whitson. 1990. *The game planners: Transforming Canada's sport system.* Montreal, Quebec, and Kingston, Ontario: McGill-Queen's University Press (*an informative study of national sport organizations and how their policy-making processes are influenced by government funding and philosophy; lists recommendations for limiting and directing government involvement in sports*).

Segrave, J.O., ed. 1996. Perspectives on the modern Olympic Games. *Quest* 48: 1 (*a special issue containing eight articles on the Olympics as they exist at the end of the twentieth century; authors generally focus on what makes the Olympics unique as a world event*).

Wenner, L., ed. 1996. Focus: On theorizing global sport. *Journal of Sport & Social Issues* 20: 3 (*six excellent articles pulled together under the supervision of Peter Donnelly; the articles illustrate the range of topics and conceptual issues discussed in the sociology of sport through 1996*).

Wilcox, R. C., ed. 1993. *Sport in the global village.* Morgantown, WV: Fitness Information Technology, Inc. (*thirty-eight papers dealing with globalization, identity issues, international sports, and cross-cultural issues; authors come from a range of backgrounds and sixteen different countries*).

Wilson, J. 1994. *Playing by the rules: Sport, society, and the state.* Detroit, MI: Wayne State University Press (*an analysis of how the relationship between sport and the state in the U.S. has developed to enable the commercialization of sports to occur on the professional and amateur levels; deals with sports, sport participation, sport facilities, public policy, and law through recent history*).

14

(H. Armstrong Roberts)

*[As an African American if]
you make 20 points, you get
10 rebounds, [universities
will] find you. But you make
straight A's in the same
school, they don't even know
you're there. And that's sad.
That's very sad about this
country.*

**Charles Barkley, NBA
player (1995)**

Sports in
High School and College
*Do varsity sports programs
contribute to education?*

*The overall message being
drilled into our kids is clear
and dangerous. . . . Superstars sign 5-year contracts
for $20 million. Teachers
sign 1-year contracts for
$20,000. In those circum-
stances, to whom will you listen, your teacher or your
coach? Where will you spend
your time, in the library or
the gym?*

**Tom McMillen,
former NBA player and
member of U.S. Congress,
Out of Bounds (1996)**

*Sports [in U.S. public
schools] is one of the last bas-
tions of male privilege underwritten by the taxpayers.*

**Martha Burk, president,
Center for Advancement of
Public Policy (1995)**

*In 1970, only one out of 27
high school girls played varsity sports. Today [thanks to
Title IX] that figure is now
one of three!*

**Wendy Hilliard, president,
Women's Sports Founda-
tion (1996)**

*While university sports pro-
grams generate millions of
dollars, the NCAA's anti-
quated rules have created a
class of athletes, made up
largely of those from poorer
families, who don't have
enough walking-around
money to buy an off-campus
hamburger.*

***Sports Illustrated,* 24 June
1996.**

The emergence of modern organized sports is closely tied to education in both England and North America. But competitive interscholastic sports do not exist in many countries. In fact, few schools outside North America and Japan sponsor and fund interschool varsity sport programs. Organized sports for adolescents and young adults in most countries are tied to community-based athletic clubs funded by the state or a combination of public and private sources. However, interscholastic sports have become an accepted and important part of U.S. high schools and colleges, and they are becoming increasingly important in Canadian and Japanese schools.

This chapter focuses on whether interscholastic sports have an effect on the achievement of the overall educational mission of high schools and colleges. In exploring this issue, I will consider four questions:

1. What are the arguments for and against varsity sports?
2. How are interscholastic sports programs related to the experience of student-athletes and other students in high schools and colleges?

3. Do high schools and colleges experience organizational benefits from interscholastic programs?
4. What are the major problems associated with high school and college sport programs, and how might they be solved?

ARGUMENTS FOR AND AGAINST INTERSCHOLASTIC SPORTS

Most people in the U.S. take interscholastic sport programs for granted; they have been an expected part of life at school. However, recent budget cutbacks and highly publicized problems in certain high school and college sports programs have raised questions about how sports are related to educational goals and to the overall development of young people. Similar questions are being raised about interscholastic sports in Canadian schools. Responses to these questions are varied. Program supporters claim that interscholastic sports support the educational mission of schools; critics claim that they interfere with that mission. I have summarized the main points made on both sides of this debate in table 14–1.

Table 14–1   Popular arguments for and against interscholastic sports

Arguments for	Arguments against
1. involve students in school activities and increase interest in academic activities	1. distract the attention of students from academic activities
2. build the responsibility, achievement orientation, and teamwork skills required for occupational success	2. perpetuate dependence and conformity and focus the attention of students on a power and performance orientation no longer appropriate in postindustrial society
3. provide fitness training and stimulate interest in physical activities among all students in the school	3. relegate most students to the role of spectator and cause too many serious injuries to active participants
4. generate the spirit and unity necessary to maintain the school as a viable organization	4. create a superficial, transitory spirit subverting the educational goals of the school
5. promote parental, alumni, and community support for all school programs	5. deprive educational programs of resources, facilities, staff, and community support
6. give students opportunities to develop and display skills in activities valued in the society at large	6. apply excessive pressure on student-athletes, who often develop unidimensional identities around their athletic skills

Although interscholastic sport programs have been studied frequently, the debate about their educational relevance continues today. When people enter this debate they often exaggerate the benefits or the problems associated with varsity sport programs. Supporters emphasize glowing success stories, and critics emphasize shocking cases of excess and abuse, but the most accurate descriptions probably lie somewhere in between. Nonetheless, both the supporters and the critics call attention to many of the important issues in the relationship between sports and education. This chapter will focus on some of those issues.

INTERSCHOLASTIC SPORTS AND THE EXPERIENCES OF HIGH SCHOOL STUDENTS

Do varsity sport programs affect the educational and developmental experiences of high school students? This question is difficult to answer. Education and development occur in connection with many activities and relationships. Even though varsity sport programs are very important in some schools and for some students, they constitute only one of many sources of potentially influential experiences. Research on this issue has focused primarily on the characteristics of student-athletes, although some social scientists have tried to study how sports are connected with the overall school-based culture that exists among high school students.

High School Student-Athletes

Studies have shown consistently that when compared with students who do not play varsity sports, high school athletes, *as a group*, generally have better grade point averages, more positive attitudes towards school, more interest in continuing their education after graduation, and a slightly better educational achievement rate (see Miracle and Rees, 1994). These differences usually have been modest, and it has been difficult for researchers to separate the effects of sport participation from the effects of family backgrounds, support from friends, and other factors related to educational attitudes and perfor-

mance. However, membership on a varsity team is a valued source of status in most U.S. schools, and it seems to go hand in hand with positive educational experiences for some students (Marsh, 1993). But research has not told us what it is about sport participation that might cause those positive experiences.

Of course, the most logical explanation for differences between varsity athletes and other students is that interscholastic sports, like other extracurricular activities, attract students who already have characteristics associated with academic and social success in high school. Most studies have not been able to test this explanation, because they don't actually follow students throughout their high school careers to keep track of how and why changes occur in their lives. Usually, the studies simply report information collected from students at one point in time and then compare those on sport teams with those who are not on teams. This makes it impossible for researchers to say whether playing varsity sports really changes people, or whether students who try out for varsity teams, get selected for teams, and continue as team members are simply different from other students *before* they become varsity athletes.

Even when researchers think that young people do change while playing varsity sports, they are unable to say anything about specific aspects of sport participation that account for the changes. The mere fact that young people grow and develop during the same years they play on varsity teams does not mean that sport participation *causes* the growth and development. After all, fourteen to eighteen-year-olds grow and develop in many ways, whether they play varsity sports or do other things. Most studies do not distinguish among all the different factors that might explain growth and development.

Fortunately, there are a few studies that follow students over time and measure changes that occur in their lives. For example, Elmer Spreitzer, a sociologist from Bowling Green State University, did a study in which he analyzed data from a national probability sample of 12,000 young men and women from 1,100 public and private schools around the United States. Spreitzer collected information from high school sophomores and seniors in 1980, and then gathered follow-up information from the same students in 1982, 1984, and 1986. This enabled him to track students who played on varsity sport teams, and to compare them with other students as they got older. Spreitzer found that compared with other students, young people who played on varsity sport teams were more likely to come from *economically privileged* backgrounds, and have *above-average* cognitive abilities, self-esteem, and academic performance records (grades and test scores). In other words, students who tried out for teams, made teams, and stayed on them were different in certain ways from other students *before* they became high school athletes.

Spreitzer found that this type of "selection" pattern was common to nearly all extracurricular activities, not just varsity sports. In other words, students who choose to participate in official, school-sponsored activities tend to be slightly different from other students. These differences are greatest in those activities in which student self-selection is combined with formal tryouts in which teachers or coaches choose students for participation. In the case of varsity sports, this self-selection and choice process is especially powerful, because it begins in youth sports and continues through junior high school.

Spreitzer also found that young men and women who started playing varsity sports as sophomores and continued through their senior years were different from those who were cut from teams or who voluntarily quit teams. Students who discontinued varsity sport participation were more likely to come from *less advantaged* economic backgrounds; they were more likely to have *lower* cognitive abilities, lower self-esteem, and lower grade point averages; and they were less likely to take college preparation courses. Furthermore, young women were twice as likely as young men to discontinue

participation. These findings suggest that in addition to a selection process, there is a complex but nonrandom *filtering-out* process that occurs in varsity sports.

One of the difficulties Spreitzer faced when he analyzed the data was that many young people who played varsity sports also participated in other extracurricular activities. Therefore, he could not say whether changes in the lives of these young people were due to their playing sports or to their participation in other activities, such as working on the yearbook, being involved in a student club or student government, or doing community service.

Spreitzer also tracked changes during the six-year period after students left high school. He found that those who played varsity sports as seniors were no different on a number of traits from those who did not play. The traits included psychological adjustment, patterns of alcohol use, level of self-esteem, age at marriage, and age at birth of first child. There was a slight difference in educational achievement, but playing varsity

Sport participation often gives girls and young women opportunities to establish personal and social identities based on skills respected by peers and the community at large. (Tini Campbell)

sports was not nearly as important as other factors affecting college attendance and degree completion. Furthermore, playing varsity sports seemed to be important only for white males, not for females or African Americans.

Other studies that track students over time have reported findings very similar to Spreitzer's (Fejgin, 1994; Melnick, Vanfossen, and Sabo, 1988; Rees, Howell, and Miracle, 1990). Both selection and filtering do occur, although sport participation does seem to reduce dropout rates (McNeal, 1995) and increase identification with the school (Marsh, 1993). So what does this research tell us about interscholastic sports?

- *First*, it tells us that we should be very careful when generalizing about the educational value of interscholastic sports. Playing varsity sports does not produce negative effects, but neither does it automatically change high school students in positive ways—indeed, in any ways that make them significantly different from other high school students. Usually those who try out for teams, get selected by coaches, and stay on teams for more than one year are somewhat different from other students to begin with. Therefore, simple statistical comparisons between the two types of students don't prove anything about the value of sport participation itself.
- *Second*, the research suggests that if we want to learn more about the effect of interscholastic sports in the lives of high school students, we must do long-term studies enabling us to look at the overall lives of students, not just their sport lives. Growth and development occur in connection with many different experiences—some outside the school and some inside the school. Unless we know something about young people's lives in general, we can't claim that varsity sport participation is more influential than working at a part-time job, joining the debate team, writing for the school newspaper, or caring for younger brothers and sisters.

- *Third*, the research suggests that we should examine how the educational lives of student-athletes might be different from those of other students. Do those who play sports take courses in which high grades are characteristic? Do they receive more academic help? Do teachers evaluate them differently.? Do they make different academic decisions than other students do, and if so, how does the issue of eligibility affect those decisions?
- *Fourth*, the research also suggests that we should study the effect of varsity sports on the larger student culture that exists in high schools. It may be that the social importance of sports rests in how they are connected with gender, class, and race and ethnic relations in an entire school. It would seem to be a higher priority to study this possibility than to focus only on the students who try out for and make teams. This brings us to the next topic.

Student Culture in High Schools

Sociologists long have recognized that varsity sports are among the most important social activities sponsored by high schools (Miracle and Rees, 1994). Being a varsity athlete brings a student prestige among peers, formal rewards in the school, and recognition from teachers, administrators, and even people in the local community. Athletes, especially males in high-profile sports, usually are accorded recognition that guarantees them popularity in the student culture. Pep rallies, homecomings, and other special sport events traditionally have been scheduled and promoted as major social occasions on school calendars. These social occasions often are important for students because they provide opportunities for social interaction—especially male-female interaction—outside the classroom. Furthermore, high school sport events usually are defined by parents (even strict, controlling parents) as approved social activities for their sons and daughters; parents often will permit their children to attend while forbidding them to go other places.

From a sociological perspective, it is important to ask what varsity sports contribute to student culture in a high school. Because these sports and sport events are socially significant activities in the lives of many students, they have the potential to influence values and behaviors among students. For example, do they influence how students evaluate one another or how they think about social life and social relations?

SPORTS AND POPULARITY For many years, sociologists studied student culture simply by studying the factors that high school students have used to determine popularity (Coleman, 1961a, b; Eitzen, 1975; Thirer and Wright, 1985). Usually they found that when male students were given the choice of how they wished they could be remembered after graduation, they chose "athletic star" over "brilliant student" or "most popular." Female students, on the other hand, were more likely to choose "brilliant student" and "most popular" over "athletic star" (Thirer and Wright, 1985). More recent research indicates that many young men in high school prefer to be known as "scholar-athletes," whereas young women generally prefer to be known as "scholars" and "members of the leading social group" (Chandler and Goldberg, 1990). Therefore, the link between being popular and being an athlete is stronger for male students than for female students. When it comes to popularity for high school women, being in the "in-group" is crucial, and being an athlete does not by itself put a female student in the in-group (Chandler and Goldberg, 1990).

What do these research findings mean? Are young men more concerned with being athletes than with being scholars? Are young women unconcerned about sports? The answer to both these questions is *no*. In fact, most high school students *are* concerned with academic achievement. They are aware of the importance of finishing high school and going on to college or a trade school, and their parents usually remind

them regularly of how important school should be in their lives. However, *outside* the classroom, high school students are concerned with four things: (1) social acceptance, (2) personal autonomy, (3) sexual identity, and (4) "growing up" into adults. They want to be popular enough to fit in with their peers and have friends they can depend on; they want to have opportunities to control their own lives; they strive to feel secure about their own sexual identity; and they want to show others they are "mature" enough to be taken seriously.

This means that a wide range of factors are important in the *social* lives of adolescents. Because males and females in North America are still treated and evaluated in different ways, adolescents use different strategies for seeking acceptance, autonomy, sexual development, and recognition as young adults. As things are now, sport participation is an important basis for popularity for young men, as long as they don't completely neglect their academic lives. According to Donna Eder (1995), who has studied adolescent culture in the U.S., young men who don't act tough are often marginalized in student culture, so they put a premium on playing sports, especially contact sports.

Sport participation is also important for young women, but being an athlete usually must be combined with other things for a young woman to be popular within the student cultures of most high schools. Young women don't have to conform to traditional definitions of femininity, but to be popular they usually need to show they are something other than just tough and competitive in sports; physical attractiveness is more often a basis for a young women's popularity in student culture than playing sports (Eder, 1995).

So it seems that the "physical capital" gained by high school athletes has a greater "cash-in" value for men than for women in the social economy of student culture (Rees and Miracle, 1997).

SPORTS AND IDEOLOGY Interscholastic sport programs do more than simply affect the

TANK McNAMARA®

by Jeff Millar & Bill Hinds

Playing sports long has been a basis for the popularity of boys and young men in U.S. schools. Now it also has become a basis for the popularity of girls and young women. But the "physical capital" earned through sport participation seems to have a slightly greater "cash-in" value for males than for females in the status systems existing in most schools.

status structures of high school students. H. G. Bissinger clearly illustrated this in his book *Friday Night Lights* (1990). Bissinger, a noted Pulitzer Prize–winning author, wrote about a football team in a Texas high school known for its emphasis on football. His account was deliberately dramatic, and he made the case that in Odessa, Texas, as in many other American towns,

> football stood at the very core of what the town was about. . . . It had nothing to do with entertainment and everything to do with how people felt about themselves (p. 237).

As Bissinger described events through the football season, he noted that football was important because it celebrated a male cult of toughness and sacrifice and a female cult of nurturance and servitude. When the team lost, people accused the coaches of not being tough enough and the players of being undisciplined. Women stayed on the sidelines and faithfully tried to support and please the men who battled on behalf of the school and town. Students and townspeople could go to football games and have their ideas about "natural differences" between men and

women reaffirmed. Young men who couldn't hit hard, physically intimidate opponents, or play with pain were described as "pussies." "Gay bashing" was considered an approved weekend social activity by many of the athletes. And a player's willingness to sacrifice his body for the team was taken as a sign of commitment and character.

Bissinger also noted that high school sports were closely tied to a long history of racism in the town, and football itself was organized and played in ways that reaffirmed traditional racial ideology among whites and produced racial resentment among African Americans. Many Anglo townspeople in 1988 still referred to blacks as "niggers," and they blamed blacks and Mexicans for most of the town's problems. They had accepted racial desegregation in 1980 because they thought it could be used to strengthen their school's football team. The irony associated with a situation in which young black males worked hard to benefit whites who wanted a successful team was noted by a local black minister when he observed that "Today, instead of the cotton field, it's the sports arena" (p. 109). When a white coach was asked what the star halfback would be without football, he quickly answered, "a big ol' dumb nigger" (p. 67). Meanwhile, white people generally used physical explanations based on traditional racist ideology to explain the abilities or lack of abilities among black players: when these players succeeded, it was due to their "natural physical abilities," and when they failed, it was due to a lack of character or intelligence.

Unfortunately, Bissinger did not write about the students who didn't participate in sports or those who didn't agree with the values and experiences celebrated through football. His account provides only a partial picture of sports and student culture. But another study, done by anthropologist Doug Foley (1991), provides a much more complete picture of student culture. Foley studied a small Texas town and focused much of his attention on students in the local high school. He paid special attention to the school's football team and the way the team and its games were incorporated into the overall social life of the school and the local community. He also studied social and academic activities among a wide range of different students, including those who ignored or deliberately avoided sports.

Foley's findings revealed that student culture in a high school cannot be summarized simply by studying the football team. In fact, Foley emphasized that student culture "was varied, changing, and inherently full of contradictions" (p. 100). Football and other sports provided important social occasions for getting together with friends, flirting, and defusing the anxiety associated with tests and overcontrolling teachers, but sports were only one small part of the lives of adolescents at the school. Students used their status as athletes in their "identity performances" with other students and with adults, but for most students, identity was grounded more in gender, class, and ethnicity than in sport participation.

Foley concluded that sports were important to the extent that they presented students with a language or vocabulary they could use to identify

important values and experiences. For example, most sports came with a vocabulary that extolled and treated as "natural" individualism, competition, and differences related to gender, race, ethnicity, and social class. As students adopted this vocabulary, they became instrumental in perpetuating the status quo in the school and the town as a whole. In this way, traditional forms of gender logic, race logic, and class logic continued to influence social relations in the town's culture.

At this point, we need more qualitative research on student culture, but existing research suggests that the most important social consequences of interscholastic sports may be their effects on ideas about social relations rather than their effects on grade point averages, attitudes toward school, or student popularity (see also Rees and Miracle, 1997).

Additional Consequences of High School Sports

A main theme running through this book is that sports are social constructions. That is, sports can be organized and played in many different ways, and people can creatively influence the meanings associated with sports to meet specific goals. However, most people associated with interscholastic sports simply have assumed that sports and sport participation *automatically* produce positive results, so they have not taken the time to critically examine sports in student culture as a whole.

GETTING NOTICED AND REWARDED
Research on interscholastic sports has led me to conclude that in and of themselves, sports are not educational. However, if sports are organized and played in certain ways, they can be used to meet educational goals. For example, when varsity sports are organized so that young people are taken seriously as human beings and valued by those who are important in their lives, sport participation can contribute to their educational development. But if varsity sports are organized in ways that lead young people to think that adults are controlling them for their

Some high school and college students have raised serious questions about who has the right to use Native American names and images as a basis for school nicknames, logos, and mascots. However, research suggests that sports are seldom contexts for the raising of critical questions about gender, ethnicity, or social class relations. Sports tend to introduce students to a vocabulary and images that reaffirm dominant traditional ideologies, as happens in this high school gym, where a stereotypical image of a menacing-looking Indian looks down on opponents. (*Colorado Springs Gazette*)

own purposes, interscholastic programs become developmental dead ends and students become cynical about school and society.

Adolescents need to be an integral part of their schools, they need opportunities to develop and display their competence in settings where they are noticed and rewarded, and they need chances to prove they are on their way to becoming valued adults in their communities. If interscholastic sports are organized to do these things, they can make valuable contributions to education and development. And students who play sports then will be more likely to identify with the school and its educational mission (Marsh, 1993).

ATTRACTING ADULT ADVOCATES Interscholastic sports also can be valuable if they are intentionally organized to provide young people opportunities to connect with adults who can serve as advocates in their lives. This is especially important in schools located in low-income and impoverished areas, where young people are most in need of advocates. Sports can give these young people chances to be noticed for something good, rather than for how "bad" they are in the school hallways or on the streets. And when adult advocates are scarce in the local neighborhood, sports can provide these young people with the adult "hook-ups" they need to guide them into the world of adulthood.

PROVIDING OCCASIONS FOR LEARNING Finally, sports also can be valuable educationally if teachers and coaches take them seriously as learning experiences. For example, Jomills Braddock and his colleagues (1991) have studied the importance of sports to young African American males and argued that sports in middle schools could be used to rekindle a commitment to education among young people who are ready to give up on classroom learning by the time they are seventh- or eighth-graders. They suggest the following:

> Both players and nonplayers . . . could write or contribute to sport columns in school or local newspapers, thereby enhancing student writing and language skills. Students could collect and generate team and player statistics for a variety of school and local sport activities, utilizing . . . crucial . . . mathematical skills. . . . [Students] could organize the sport sections of school yearbooks,

REFLECT ON SPORT

Intercollegiate Sports Are Not All the Same

The amount of money spent every year on intercollegiate sports varies from less than $100,000 at some small colleges to over $30 million at a few large universities. Large universities may sponsor ten to eighteen different varsity sports for men and a similar number for women. In small colleges, coaches are often members of the teaching faculty and one person may coach two or more teams. Larger universities have multiple coaches for all sports, and these coaches are not likely to have faculty appointments.

Because intercollegiate sports are so diverse, it is difficult to discuss them without grouping them into categories. One way to group them is simply to identify the athletic associations with which schools are affiliated. Schools with intercollegiate sports can be affiliated with either of two major national associations: the National Collegiate Athletic Association (NCAA), or the National Association of Intercollegiate Athletics (NAIA). A third group, the College Football Association (CFA), was formed by NCAA schools with big-time football programs.

The NCAA, with 995 member institutions and 208 affiliated conferences and professional organizations, is the largest and most powerful association;[†] its power rests partly in the TV revenues it receives and then allocates to members. Member institutions are divided into five major divisions reflecting program size, level of competition, and the types of rules that govern programs. *Division I* includes schools that have what we might describe as big-time programs; 307 institutions are classified in this category. Division I is broken down into three subgroups: schools with big-time football teams (I-A, involving 110 schools), schools with smaller football programs based on stadium size and average paid attendance (I-AA, involving 118 schools), and schools without football teams (I-AAA, involving 79 schools). *Division II* and *Division III*, both

of which have grown considerably through the 1990s, contain 289 and 399 schools, respectively; these schools have smaller programs and compete at less than a big-time level.

So-called *big-time programs* usually emphasize either football or men's basketball, because most people consider these sports to be the best potential money-makers.

Football has the greatest potential to make money, although large losses are also possible and very common. Men's basketball seldom generates as much money as football, but it costs less and the risk of large losses is lower. Although hockey and women's basketball make money in a handful of schools, no other sports make enough money to pay their own expenses, except in unique individual situations.

The general level of athletic talent is higher in NCAA Division I schools than it is in Divisions II or III or the NAIA. Athletes in Division I schools are more likely to have scholarships and access to academic support programs sponsored by athletic departments. In addition, the amount of team travel in Division I schools is greater, the national and regional media coverage is more extensive, and the consequences of winning and losing are usually greater.

Not all schools maintain membership in the NCAA. Some choose to affiliate with the NAIA. NAIA schools also have teams in a range of sports; scholarships may or may not be given, and most of their teams are not considered big-time. The NAIA listed 376 colleges and universities as members in 1996, fifty fewer members than in 1993. The NAIA currently has a difficult time maintaining its membership in the face of the growing power and influence of the NCAA, which has nearly complete monopoly control over intercollegiate sports. The budget of the NCAA is at least fifty times greater than the budget of the NAIA.

Even though the majority of intercollegiate programs are not considered big-time, people often assume that the universities whose teams play in televised games have typical programs. The University of Notre Dame, the University of Michigan, the University of Florida, UCLA, the University of Kentucky, and similar schools are exceptions rather than the rule in intercollegiate sports.

Some smaller colleges and universities maintain one or two big-time sports, and this supports the mistaken idea that all colleges and universities have big-time programs. The NCAA does not allow Division II or III schools to have big-time football teams, but it does allow them to compete at a big-time level in one or two other sports. Because some Division II and III schools choose to do this, many people assume that all their sports are played at a big-time level. *But this is not true.* Big-time teams capture 90 percent of the media attention and spectator interest, but most sports at most schools are not played at a big-time level. When our attention is restricted to big-time sports, we get a distorted picture of intercollegiate programs.

LOWER-PROFILE PROGRAMS

Many intercollegiate programs operate much as larger high school programs do. The major difference is that because college athletes are free to choose their schools, college coaches actively recruit for their teams. Depending on their skills, athletes may receive some form of financial assistance. The most valued form of direct assistance is a scholarship covering all expenses for room, board, tuition, fees, and books. However, most schools with lower-profile programs cannot afford to give many full scholarships. They often limit their direct financial assistance to tuition waivers, free meal tickets, or similar benefits. Indirect forms of financial assistance include helping student-athletes find jobs or inexpensive housing.

Unfortunately, we know little about student-athletes in schools with lower-profile intercollegiate programs. No data exist on how these programs influence on-campus social life, the way students view the world around them, and the educational achievements of the athletes themselves. Researchers, like the media, generally have focused their attention on big-time programs.

BIG-TIME PROGRAMS

Big-time programs are unique. Athletic departments in large universities often operate as separate organizations, and much of their funding may come from outside sources such as gate receipts, contributions from boosters, media rights, and corporate sponsors. Athletes in big-time programs often receive grants or scholarships, and some enjoy the adulation of people on campus and in the surrounding community; a few have regional or national reputations.

Most research on intercollegiate sports and most data on athletes focus on Division I programs and on the revenue-generating sports in those programs. We discuss some of this research in this chapter. It is important to know about these programs because they receive so much attention in U.S. culture, but it is also important to remember that few sports and sport teams on college campuses resemble big-time football and men's basketball teams. Most intercollegiate sports, even in large universities, do not get much publicity, and athletes in these sports are not as likely as football and men's basketball players to receive special attention or adulation. What do you know about *these* student-athletes?

---

†All data in this paragraph are for 1996.

participate on a sports debate team, or perhaps start a sports enthusiast club (p. 129).

The point of these suggestions is to use sports as part of a larger process of giving students responsibility, including them in activities that will help them develop skills, rewarding them for their competence, and connecting them with adults who can exert positive influence in their lives.

This notion of deliberately designing sports to give students responsibility has been emphasized in applied research on moral development (see Shields and Bredemeier, 1995) and prosocial behavior (Hellison, 1985, 1990, 1993). This research also suggests that unless adult leaders take care, sport participation actually can subvert moral development and responsibility among young people. But it does not have to be that way if teachers, coaches, and others work together to make sports into learning experiences (Alexander et al., 1996).

INTERCOLLEGIATE SPORTS AND THE EXPERIENCES OF COLLEGE STUDENTS*

Does varsity sport participation affect the educational and developmental experiences of college athletes? This has been a hot question for the last two decades. Stories about the academic failures of college athletes and the failures of colleges and universities to take the education of student-athletes seriously have appeared regularly in newspapers, magazines, books, and television specials. Some research on this issue also has been done, but it seems that sociologists are more likely to study sports in high schools than those on their own campuses.

It is difficult to assess media and research reports without an overall picture of intercollegiate sports. I provide part of this picture in the box titled Intercollegiate Sports Are Not All

the Same, on pp. 446–447. It is important to recognize the variety in intercollegiate programs. However, most people focus attention on *big-time, entertainment-oriented* intercollegiate sports; these are the ones that get heavy media publicity, and have most of the problems.

Unfortunately, most people forget that many college athletes participate in programs somewhat similar to high school programs. Most athletes in these *lower-profile* programs do not have scholarships; they participate on a voluntary basis, just as they would in any extracurricular activity. Playing varsity sports may be a source of prestige in some schools with lower-profile programs, but it is not likely to have much effect on how students evaluate one another. In many of these programs, coaches even may go out of their way to set up practices and game schedules that don't interfere with students' coursework. Studies of lower-profile programs show that the academic performance of their athletes is very similar to that of other college students (Eitzen, 1987b; McTeer, 1987; Meyer, 1990; Sack, 1987). Teams that fit into this lower-profile category generally include many women's teams, most teams in NCAA Division III and Canadian university programs, and teams in many non-revenue-producing sports.

Student-Athletes in *Big-Time* Programs

Being an athlete in a *big-time* intercollegiate program is not always compatible with being a good student. This is especially true for those who play on *entertainment-oriented* sport teams—the teams that attempt to attract significant revenues. Athletes in big-time programs often have some form of scholarship aid, and are expected to commit much time and energy to their sports. When commitments to sports interfere with academic work and social activities, these student-athletes must make choices.

There isn't much information on how student-athletes handle these choices on a daily basis. However, there is reason to believe that male athletes in big-time, entertainment-oriented sports often rank their athletic and social lives ahead of

---

*Throughout the discussion in this chapter, we will focus on four-year institutions. Junior colleges and two-year community colleges will not be discussed separately. Research is needed that will describe the similarities and differences of sport programs in four-year and two-year institutions, and discuss their sociological implications.

their academic lives (Adler and Adler, 1991). For example, Shareef Abdur-Rahim, who left the University of California after his first year to play in the NBA, described his college experience this way:

> I don't think there's too much the NCAA can do to change things. The reality is, you're going to miss classes, you're going to be behind in your schoolwork. You get caught up in taking finals on the road, taking them late, getting to class late (*USA Today*, 20 September 1996: 20C).

Not all student-athletes have the same experience, but putting academic work ahead of sports and social life is not an easy choice, and even after it's made, the task of taking a full load of courses while playing sports is very challenging (Wiley, 1993). Those with poor academic preparation usually have to limit their course loads so they can handle coursework and still honor their commitments to sports. Many others have to arrange course schedules around their sports, and then catch up on coursework during summers and the off-season. The dynamics underlying these choices are explained in the box on pp. 450–452.

An interesting fact is that women intercollegiate athletes, even many women in big-time programs, are much more likely than their male counterparts to sacrifice their social lives to make the most of educational opportunities. It seems that the atmosphere on most women's teams is quite supportive of educational achievement and intellectual development, whereas the atmosphere on many men's teams is clearly antiintellectual (Meyer, 1988, 1990). But this will change in the future, as certain women's sports become entertainment oriented in the same way certain men's sports are.

Because many highly visible student-athletes in big-time, entertainment-oriented sports give priority to their athletic lives rather than their academic lives, serious questions have been raised about the educational relevance of intercollegiate sports. This has caused embarrassment for many colleges and universities, because their

Student-athletes in high-profile, big-time college sports face difficult choices when it comes to allocating their time and energy to academic work, sport participation, and social activities. When academic work is given a low priority, there is good reason to raise questions about the educational relevance of intercollegiate sports. (Brian Lewis, University of Colorado Media Relations)

athletic departments were organized so that student-athletes were encouraged and even required to give low priority to their academic lives. Also embarrassing is the fact that university presidents, academic administrators, and faculty allowed this to occur and did not make serious attempts to change it until recently.

During the 1980s and early 1990s, much publicity was given to evidence that many big-time, entertainment-oriented athletic departments

REFLECT ON SPORT

Making Choices:
The Experiences of Athletes in Big-Time Programs

Intercollegiate athletes often are described using statistical profiles, but we know little about what goes on in their everyday lives and how they make choices related to sports, school, and social life. Fortunately, two studies provide a glimpse of this choice-making process. One was done by Peter and Patricia Adler (1991), who observed and interviewed members of a major college men's basketball program over a nine-year period. The other, by Barbara Meyer (1988, 1990), involved a series of in-depth interviews with members of women's volleyball and basketball teams at a major university.

The Adlers' study led them to conclude that playing in a big-time basketball program and being seriously involved in academics seldom went hand in hand. The young men they studied usually began their first year of coursework in college with optimism and idealism; they expected their academic experiences to contribute to their future occupational success. However, after one or two semesters, they discovered that the demands of playing basketball, the social isolation that went along with being an athlete, and the powerful influence of the athletic subculture of which they were a part drew them farther and farther away from academic life.

Even though coaches often told them to focus on their coursework, the athletes discovered it was necessary to select easy courses and the least challenging majors if they were to meet the coaches' expectations on the basketball court. Fatigue, the pressures of games, and limited time kept the players from becoming seriously involved in academic life. Furthermore, nobody ever asked these athletes about their studies. Attention always was focused on basketball, and few people really expected the athletes to identify themselves as students or to give priority to their academic lives.

When these young men received positive feedback, it was for athletic, not academic, performances. Difficulties in their courses often led the athletes to view academic life with pragmatic detachment; in other words,

they became very "practical" in the way they chose classes and arranged their course schedules. They knew what they had to do to stay eligible, and coaches would make sure their course schedules were arranged so they could devote their time and energy to basketball. After taking a series of easy but uninteresting courses, and having a tough time in other courses, the student-athletes gradually detached themselves from academic life on their campus.

This entire process of academic detachment was encouraged by the peer subculture that developed among the athletes. These young men were with one another constantly—in the dorms, at meals, during practices, on trips to away games, in the weight room, and on nights when there were no games. During these times they seldom talked about academic or intellectual topics. If they did talk about the courses they were taking, it was in negative terms. They encouraged cutting classes rather than regular attendance, and they joked about each other's bad tests and failing papers. They provided each other with needed social support, but it was support for their athletic identities rather than academic identities. Therefore, many came to see themselves as athletes, not as *student-*athletes.

Not all the athletes studied by the Adlers underwent this change in their academic lives. Some managed to strike a balance between their athletic and academic lives. This was most common among those who had entered college with realistic ideas about academic demands and those who had family members actively supporting their academic achievements. But striking this balance was never easy. It required solid high school preparation combined with ability or luck in developing relationships with faculty and other students.

These relationships with people outside of sports were important, because they emphasized academic achievement and provided day-to-day support for academic identities. Therefore, even though all the basketball players faced pressures to give first priority to their athletic lives, there were some who were able to balance athletics and academics.

The most important thing the Adlers found was that much of the structure of big-time intercollegiate sports works against maintaining a balance between athletics and academics. For example, when the basketball players in their study did have time away from sport, they often chose to ignore schoolwork and catch up on their social lives instead. As high-profile people on campus, they had many social opportunities, and it was difficult for them to pass up those opportunities to focus on coursework.

The Adlers suggested that this structure would not change unless athletes in big-time programs were protected from the seductive attention and publicity that comes with a high-profile status. As part of this protection process, they suggested that freshman eligibility be banned, so that student-athletes could be more fully integrated into the social and academic life of the university when they first arrive on campus. Other suggestions were that athletic dorms should be abolished and that academic advisors, not coaches, should assist student-athletes in scheduling their courses and choosing their majors. Finally, athletes also should have faculty sponsors who encourage them to view their academic experiences from a different perspective than that of the athletic department.

WOMEN'S EXPERIENCES

Barbara Meyer's study was much less involved than the Adlers' study, but it remains important because it focused on the experiences of women athletes. As in the Adlers' study, Meyer found that the basketball and volleyball players she studied entered college with positive attitudes about school and the value of a college education. They wanted to earn degrees, and they weren't too concerned about issues of athletic eligibility. They said that their sports were time consuming and much more work-like than sports had been in high school. Their roommates often were athletes, and they generally spent much of their time with other

athletes, who usually became their best friends. All this was similar to the experiences of the men.

But Meyer also found a big difference between the women in her study and the men in the Adlers' study. Unlike the men, the women gradually became *more* interested in and concerned with their courses and academic lives. Unlike the men, they did not expect special treatment in their classes; rather than depending on coaches for academic advice, they talked with academic advisers and friends about their course selections and majors. They also received support for academic achievement from their parents and their teammates; they thought their classes were interesting and useful; and they saw participation in their sport as having an overall positive effect on academic achievement. Furthermore, the atmosphere on their teams was clearly supportive of academic and intellectual development.

The women athletes wanted to have good seasons, but they were less concerned with winning games than they had been in high school. Even though they were good athletes, other people treated them as students and reaffirmed their academic identities instead of their athletic identities. And none of the women had dedicated their lives to the goal of playing professional sports, as some of the men had done. When the women had time away from their sports to catch up on either coursework or their social lives, they often sacrificed their social lives in favor of academic work.

In summary, both men and women student-athletes began college with similar attitudes and orientations. However, the social world created around the big-time men's program and the subculture created by the men emphasized priorities different from those of the social world and subculture associated with the women's sports. The men gradually withdrew from academic life, whereas the women gradually became more involved in it. The reasons for this difference probably include one or more of the following:

- The women may have come from different social and educational backgrounds, which encouraged them to give priority to academic choices.

Continued

- The women's programs probably did not receive the attention the men's program received, making it easier for the women to develop and maintain academic identities and make different choices in their everyday lives.
- The women may not have received the same kind of encouragement as the men to focus on sport, because their friends and parents did not see sport as a possible career option after college graduation.
- The women may not have received the same kind of encouragement to reaffirm their athletic image in social relationships and social activities on campus. Because women's sports are not publicized or defined by most students in the same way high-profile men's sports are, women may not be seen by other students as heroes or sought out to lend prestige to campus social activities and events.

Regardless of the reasons for the differences in the experiences of men and women athletes in these two studies, both studies emphasize that student-athletes face choices during their college lives, and that the decisions they make depend on the context in which they play, study, and interact with others. Will differences disappear as women's sports receive more emphasis and as women athletes have new opportunities to play their sports at the professional level after college? What do you think?

• •

were systematically ignoring the educational experiences of student-athletes. Information about how some athletic departments recruited, used, and abandoned young men in their quest to win games and make money became so widespread that the integrity of the universities themselves was questioned. Many people started to think that big-time sports were subverting education rather than promoting it, and that young people simply were being used to make money and generate publicity, not taken seriously as students or as human beings. During the 1990s universities began to confront their academic oversights and made serious attempts to encourage and assist student-athletes in the pursuit of educational goals. At many schools, student-athlete support services were developed or expanded, university presidents took more interest in the educational relevance of athletic department policies and procedures, and faculty oversight committees were put into place.

It is important to understand the connection between intercollegiate sport participation and academic performance when we discuss sports and education. The next section outlines some of the things we know about the academic lives of student-athletes.

Grades and Graduation Rates: How Do Big-Time College Athletes Compare with Other College Students?

Unlike student-athletes in high schools and small colleges, student-athletes in big-time university programs often differ from other students on campuses. Although their characteristics vary from one sport to another, they tend to come from more diversified socioeconomic backgrounds than other students, and they often choose different courses and majors. This makes it difficult to compare their academic achievements with the achievements of other students. Comparisons are also difficult because grade point averages (GPAs) have different meanings from one university to another and from department to department within a single university; it is even difficult to use graduation rates as indicators of academic experiences across schools.

Research findings on grades and graduation rates are confusing. Some studies show athletes earning higher grades than students who do not play on varsity teams; other studies show the exact opposite. Some studies show athletes attending graduate school more often than non-athletes, and others show athletes taking an abundance of courses requiring little or no intellectual effort (Case et al., 1987). Any interpretation of information on grades must take into account the following possibilities:

1. Athletes in certain sports sometimes are overrepresented in specific courses and majors. This phenomenon is known as *clustering* (Case et al., 1987), and it seems to happen most often on teams emphasizing eligibility over academic achievement and intellectual development. Therefore, we should not lump together all intercollegiate athletes when we discuss grades and graduation rates. Clustering does not occur among athletes in all sports, and when it does occur, it may be due partly to the need to schedule courses around the time demands of sports. Experiences from sport to sport vary according to many factors.

2. Athletes in entertainment-oriented sports often come to college with lower high school GPAs and lower ACT and SAT scores than other students, including other athletes, at their universities. Sometimes their academic goals are quite different from the goals of other students; their academic choices and their grades are affected strongly by their goals.

Studies of graduation rates are also confusing, partly because rates can be computed in many different ways. Some computations are based on the proportion of seniors on a particular team who graduate in a given year; others are based on the proportion of graduates among those who have used all their years of athletic eligibility at the school. Some computations give the proportions of student-athletes in a particular class who

graduate four years after they started as freshmen, and others are based on those who graduate after five or six years. Still others take into account those who transfer to other schools and graduate, or who leave school in good standing. And most computations do not take into account the players who enter professional sports before they complete four years of college. For example, during one year in the mid-1980s, the graduation rate for the University of Nebraska football team was reported to be 48 percent, 60 percent, 69 percent, 70 percent, and 92 percent, depending on the computation method used (see Eitzen, 1987b). Each of these different rates was "true," but none of them gave a complete picture of what really went on in the football program.

It is not surprising that reported graduation rates for athletes vary by conference, school, and sport. In the past, the rates in big-time sports programs at many universities were shameful. This was especially the case in entertainment-oriented sports such as football and men's basketball, where the pressure to win and make money led many coaches and athletes to focus on eligibility rather than on learning and graduation. This pressure is as strong as ever, but student-athletes now receive better academic support than ever before.

According to data on graduation rates at NCAA Division I universities, we can draw the following conclusions (see Brady, 1991; Siegel, 1994; Weiberg, 1996):

• College athletes with scholarships graduate at about the same rate and in the same length of time as other students do (about 58 percent in six years after entering college).
• The graduation rate for female athletes is higher than that for male athletes (67 percent vs. 53 percent), and higher than the rates for other women students and the general student body; graduation rates at schools where women's teams have become more entertainment oriented have declined slightly through the 1990s.

- Graduation rates are lowest in the revenue-producing sports, especially men's basketball and football; these rates are below the rates for other student-athletes and for the general student body.
- Schools ranked in the top 20 in football and basketball (men's and women's) have lower graduation rates among student-athletes in those sports than other less highly ranked schools have; basketball teams that go to NCAA post-season tournaments have lower graduation rates than teams at other schools.
- The graduation rates for minority male athletes are lower than those for other athletes (under 40 percent), but they are higher than the rates for black males and Hispanic males in the general student body (under 33 percent). Also, rates for black males increased after the minimum academic standards for scholarship athletes were increased, but rates among black males in basketball and football decreased slightly in the mid-1990s; rates for white males in basketball decreased considerably in the mid-1990s.
- Black student-athletes are more likely than their white counterparts to leave school with GPAs lower than 2.0. Approximately one-third of black scholarship athletes leave school not in good academic standing; over one-fourth of schools have graduation rates of less than 25 percent for minority males, most of whom are black.

What do these patterns mean? To whom should we compare athletes when we attempt to determine the academic integrity of big-time sports? On the one hand, student-athletes might be compared best to regular full-time students who work thirty or more hours per week, because athletes often devote at least that many hours to their sports. On the other hand, student-athletes might be compared best to other students with full scholarships, or to those who enter college with similar ACT or SAT test

SIDELINES

"Your lecture on the importance of a strong bench really inspired me, coach!"

Despite what this cartoon implies, the "dumb athlete" stereotype is not supported by most of the data on grades and graduation rates among student-athletes.

scores and high school grades, or to those who enter college with similar academic goals.

My conclusion is that there is no single ideal comparison; we must make many comparisons to get a comprehensive and fair idea of whether sport teams, athletic departments, and universities are living up to the spirit of higher education.

Finally, even though graduation is an important educational goal, it should not be the only criterion used to judge academic success. Degrees are important, but they may not mean much unless those who receive them have learned something while in college. Unfortunately, it is difficult to measure "learning" or "increased intelligence" in a survey of student-athletes. However, it is possible to go into universities to examine whether their athletic departments are being run in academically responsible ways. Until this is done, we must depend on grades and graduation rates to indicate what is going on. However, statistics don't tell the whole story. They alert us to possible problems and the need for action, but they don't tell us what all the problems are or what we need to do to correct them.

Recent Changes in
Big-Time Intercollegiate Sports

Big-time sport programs—especially entertainment-oriented programs—are *very* difficult to change. Teams in those programs are tied to many interests having nothing to do with education. Some athletes on those teams may be in school only to get the coaching they need to stay competitive in amateur Olympic sports (such as swimming, track and field, volleyball, wrestling, and rowing), or only to become draft prospects in professional sports (such as baseball, basketball, football, and hockey). Coaches for those teams may view sports as businesses, and they may be hired and fired on the basis of how much revenue they can attract to the athletic program. Even academic administrators, including college presidents, may use the programs for public relations or fund-raising tools instead of focusing on them as programs that should be educational in themselves.

Today, major corporations sponsor media coverage of intercollegiate sports and support teams for advertising purposes. These corporations have little or no interest in the academic development of athletes. When a shoe company pays a coach or school to put athletes' feet in its shoes, or when a soft drink company buys an expensive gym scoreboard with its logo on it, company executives don't care if student-athletes are learning in their classes, as long as they are attracting attention to the company's products. Similarly, the local businesses that make money when the home team attracts fans are not concerned about whether the athletes scoring touchdowns and doing slam dunks have 1.6 grade point averages or are on the honor roll; they just want them to be eligible to pack spectators into the stadium or arena.

In the face of these noneducational interests, athletic departments have needed "outside encouragement" to make changes and to take seriously the idea of academic reform. Today's programs have been shaped by a number of factors since the mid-1980s. Here's a time-line of the factors having the most influence:

- 1983—*NCAA passes Proposition 48* setting minimum standards for a first-year athlete to be eligible to play on Division I college teams.
- 1986—*Proposition 48 takes effect.* First-year students are eligible to participate in sports at a Division I school *only* if they have a 2.0 GPA in 11 core subjects in high school *and* a score of 700 on the Scholastic Aptitude Test (SAT) or 15 on the American College Test (ACT). Proposition 48 permits students who meet only one of the requirements (SAT/ACT score *or* a 2.0 GPA in core courses) to be accepted at college and given athletic aid *if* they graduated from high school with a 2.0 GPA in *all* their courses. But these partial qualifiers are not permitted to work out with their teams during their first year, and they have to forfeit one year of athletic eligibility, which means they can play for only three years instead of the normal four years.
- 1990—*U.S. Congress passes a law* requiring all colleges to make public their athlete graduation rates starting in 1991.
- 1991—USA Today *and major media companies publish data* on athlete graduation rates; this creates an embarrassing situation for many universities with low rates.
- 1991—*The Knight Foundation Commission on Intercollegiate Athletics publishes its report,* "A New Model For Intercollegiate Athletics." The report emphasizes that university presidents must control big-time sports, and that intercollegiate programs must have academic and financial integrity.
- 1993—*NCAA boosts Proposition 48* initial-eligibility requirements to a 2.5 (not 2.0) high school GPA in 13 (not 11) core courses and a minimum score of 68 (not 60) on the

new ACT scale, or 820 (not 700) on the new SAT scale.

- 1996—*New initial-eligibility requirements take effect.* All high school students wishing to play sports at Division I or II schools must register and be certified by an NCAA Initial-Eligibility Clearinghouse. An index of GPA and test scores is used to determine "qualifiers" and partial qualifiers." The lower the GPA is, the higher the test scores must be. For example, a student with a 2.0 high school GPA must score an 86 on the ACT or a 1010 on the SAT to be fully eligible; a student with a 2.75 GPA needs a 59 on the ACT and a 720 on the SAT. Students failing to meet the standards cannot play in games, practice with a team, or receive athletic grants during their first year, although they can get need-based financial aid.

- *Other NCAA changes in the 1990s:* Athletic dormitories were eliminated; training table was limited to one meal a day; new limits were placed on the hours teams can practice during a week and on the length of seasons; new definitions were formulated of "academic progress" that must be used to determine student-athlete eligibility on a year-to-year basis; new degree completion grants were established for selected students who have completed athletic eligibility and remain 30 or fewer hours away from graduation; all athletic departments must conduct annual exit interviews with student-athletes as part of a team-by-team self-assessment process; and junior college transfers must have 48 credits and a two-year degree to be eligible.

The purpose of all these changes was three-fold: (1) to send messages to high schools and high school student-athletes that a commitment to academic achievement was required to play big-time college sports, (2) to set new guidelines for colleges and universities that had ignored their academic mission in connection with their

sport programs, and (3) to give college student-athletes the support they needed to meet academic requirements and achieve academic goals.

Generally, these changes have been effective. Things have changed, although problems still remain. For example, there have been cases in which people have used junior colleges and certain private schools to create academic records for student-athletes that enable them to meet qualifying rules without academic benefit (Bagnato, 1995; Wolff and Yaeger, 1995). Also, attempts to contain spiraling costs in intercollegiate programs generally have failed. Big-time programs that make large amounts of money in their revenue-producing sports and have successful fund-raising programs do not want to forfeit this competitive advantage; they can outspend their competitors and win games in the process. But this approach tends to obscure the educational foundations of intercollegiate sports.

In light of past progress, some people want to raise academic standards further; others argue that this strategy ultimately will exclude many young people from attending major universities on athletic scholarships. For example, the Black Coaches Association has argued that those most likely to be excluded are low-income and minority students who have not had the benefit of high-quality high school educations or personal tutoring to score well on the ACT or SAT test. Proposition 48 did temporarily reduce the number of blacks receiving athletic scholarships, although the actual number of black athletes who graduated increased at the same time. More recently, black high school students have worked to meet the new standards, so that it is now difficult to argue that the standards are detrimental.

The new rules governing athletic departments have forced coaches, athletes, and others associated with sport teams to acknowledge educational goals. But more progress is needed. And big-time intercollegiate sport programs still must come to terms with the fact that they are now part of the world of entertainment. Is the provision of entertainment a proper goal of a university program? When does the entertainment side of sports conflict with the educational side, and what can be done to control the economic forces that drive concerns with entertainment? If certain sports are a form of revenue-producing entertainment, should not the workers (athlete/entertainers) be paid a fair portion of the revenues? These questions, along with others, will be hotly debated in the future.

DO SCHOOLS BENEFIT FROM VARSITY SPORTS PROGRAMS?

The influence of high school and college varsity sport programs extends well beyond the athletes who play on teams. In this section we will look at the effect of these programs on school spirit, school budgets, and relations between a school and the larger community.

School Spirit

Anyone who has attended a well-staged student pep rally or watched the student cheering section at a well-attended high school or college game realizes that sports can generate impressive displays of energy and spirit. Of course, this does not happen with all sport teams in a school, nor does it happen in all schools. Teams in low-profile sports usually play games without student spectators, and teams with long histories of losing records seldom create a spirited response among more than a few students. However, in many cases, varsity sport events do provide the basis for spirited social occasions. And students frequently use those occasions to express their feelings about themselves, their teams, and their schools.

Proponents of varsity sports say that displays of school spirit at sport events strengthen student identification with their schools and create the feelings of togetherness needed to achieve educational goals. Critics say the spirit created by sports is temporary, superficial, and unrelated to the achievement of educational goals. What we know at this point is that being a part of any group or organization is more enjoyable when

There is no doubt that school sports often create loud and expressive displays of spirit among students, at least some students. The question is whether that spirit has any positive educational significance, or, in fact, subverts educational concerns. Research is needed to answer this question with confidence. (Brian Lewis, University of Colorado Media Relations)

there are feelings of togetherness that accompany the achievement of goals. In the United States—and to an increasing extent in Canada and Japan—sports are one of the ways these feelings of togetherness are created in schools (Miracle, 1980; Rees and Miracle, 1997). But there is nothing magical about sports. Schools in other countries have used other methods to bring students together and provide them with enjoyable, educational experiences revolving around recreation and community service.

People outside the U.S. often see varsity sports in U.S. schools as elitist activities that involve most students in the passive role of spectator, which produces little in the way of educational experiences. They note that the resources devoted to sports might be used to fund other integrative activities that would involve more than cheering for teams, while providing experiences making young people feel valued as contributing members of their communities. In response to the belief that sports "keep kids off the streets," they say that instead of varsity sports, there should be programs through which young people can make the streets better places to be.

In summary, we can acknowledge that varsity sports often create school spirit. However, for that spirit to take on educational significance, it must be part of an overall school program in which students are treated as valued participants and given a sense of ownership in the school and its programs. Unless students are actively involved in what happens every day at school, their cheering at weekly games is simply a superficial display of youthful energy having nothing much to do with education.

School Budgets

HIGH SCHOOLS What are the financial consequences of interscholastic sports programs? Nearly all high school programs are funded through school district appropriations. Seldom does the money spent directly on varsity teams exceed 3 percent of the budget for any school. In fact, in most cases, expenditures for interscholastic sports account for less than 1 percent of school budgets. When certain sports enjoy big budgets, much of the money comes from gate receipts and donations from booster clubs. This sometimes happens in towns in which people are focused on the high school team and in which there are large stadiums or arenas.

Usually, interscholastic sports do not cut into the resources used for basic educational programs. Nor do sports add to those resources. However, when classroom teachers try to do their jobs without adequate funds for educational supplies, varsity sports programs often are asked to make cuts, regardless of how little money they are using. In the face of recent budget problems, this continues to happen in many schools and districts. This has given rise to a search for funds through a combination of sport participation fees and corporate sponsor-

ships. Both these alternatives create problems. Participation fees make sport participation less accessible to students from low-income families and add to the elitist profile that high school sports already have. Corporate sponsorships connect the future of sport programs with the profit needs of private corporations. This can create problems, when profit needs do not match the educational goals associated with schools and school sports. For example, promotion of the consumption of candy, soft drinks, and fast foods through ads and logos on gym walls and team buses may not foster the health and nutrition principles being taught in school classes.

COLLEGES AND UNIVERSITIES The relationship between varsity sports and school budgets is much more complex on the college level. Intercollegiate sports at small colleges are usually low-budget activities funded through a combination of student fees and student support money. At larger schools with big-time programs, vast sums of money often are spent on intercollegiate sport programs. This money comes from student fees, boosters, gate receipts, the sale of media rights, concessions, logo license fees, corporate sponsors, and general university funds.

Big-time athletic departments are run as businesses. They try to be at least self-supporting, if not to turn a profit. However, in the mid-1990s the nearly 600 Division I and II athletic departments averaged about $1.3 million more in expenses than revenues per school; and they used money from the universities' general funds, student fees, and forms of government support to cover the losses (Basralian, 1995). Only the top 60 Division I athletic departments operate in the black, due primarily to recent television revenues generated by men's football and basketball teams. For example, top Division I-A football teams in the major conferences share over $100 million per year just from the payouts for football bowl games! These revenues are added to TV revenues for regular-season games and for regular-season and NCAA basketball tournament games. And Division I-A athletic departments also collect money from corporate sponsors that use teams and athletes to display their products and logos. But even with all these revenues, at least 30 of the 110 Division I-A schools show major losses in connection with their football and basketball teams; their total program losses range from $1 million to $4 million per year, and these losses occur despite the use of general fund and student fee money by the athletic departments (Wolff and O'Brien, 1995).

On a cash flow basis, men's sports do better than women's sports only in Division I-A and I-AAA. Women's sports in Divisions I-AA, II, and III have smaller deficits than men's sports (Basralian, 1995). This means that in over 80 percent of NCAA schools, women's teams do better financially than men's teams—that is, they have fewer losses!

When profits are made, they usually are kept in the athletic department and used to support other sports or to expand team budgets; sometimes profits made by a team are used to increase that team's budget. There have been only a few cases in which money made by sport teams has been used to support nonsport programs in the university. Most often, general fund money is used to support sport teams, not the reverse.

When big-time sports programs lose large amounts of money, why do universities continue to support them? There are two reasons: (1) many people believe the programs have *indirect* financial benefits, and (2) many people think the losses are justified in light of the values celebrated by sports, especially men's football.

"By indirect financial benefits," people mean tuition money from students who come to the school because of its sports teams, and other money somehow connected with the publicity created by sports. But data documenting these indirect benefits are hard to come by. Do students really choose a college to attend on the basis of the records of its sport teams? How many students do this? What kind of students are they? Do they leave school if the teams lose?

Are team records more important than such things as academic programs, tuition costs, housing arrangements, parents' wishes, the enrollment decisions of close friends, and the location of the school? These questions never have been answered systematically, even though schools spend millions of dollars on the untested assumption that sports do matter in student choices Doyle and Gaeth.

The idea that big-time sports inspire increased donations to the general educational funds of colleges and universities is also difficult to test. Winning teams do generate money for sports-related things—such as new artificial turf, a stadium addition, luxury boxes, or a new building to showcase sport trophies and house offices for coaches and athletic department staff. But studies suggest there is *no direct link between the success of a school's sport programs and the money given to support education and research programs* (Basralian, 1995; Frey, 1985; Lederman, 1988; Sheehan, 1996).

Even though there have been a few exceptions to this conclusion, most university development officers agree that successful fund-raising seldom is shaped by a school's sport teams or their win-loss records. For example, the assistant vice president for university relations at the University of Notre Dame claims, "There isn't any correlation between giving at Notre Dame and athletic success." The vice president for development at the University of Southern California says, "The bulk of our fund-raising would be intact with or without athletics" (both cited in Lederman, 1988). In fact, sometimes fund-raising improves after schools drop sport programs. The year after Tulane University dropped basketball, donations increased by $5 million, and Wichita State's donations doubled the year after its financially strapped football team was dropped (Lederman, 1988).

I do *not* give these examples to suggest that sport programs cannot be used in fund-raising efforts. University presidents and development officers often use sport events as social occasions

"I told you we sent our daughter to a top-notch school! Her basketball team just beat Duke University."
....

Do people equate a school's quality with the success of its athletic teams? Do students choose a school because of its athletic teams? Data on these questions are sometimes confusing, but most research indicates that winning athletic teams have little impact on fund-raising and no impact on educational quality.
....

to bring wealthy and influential people to their campuses. They know these people will not donate new buildings simply because the football team plays in a bowl game; they also know that pouring money into expensive sport teams is not the way to solve money problems at their schools. But this does not stop them from using the publicity created by varsity sport teams to call attention to the academic reputation and potential of their universities.

When sport is used in connection with fund-raising, university leaders must be careful not to create an image of the school as a "sports factory." This can cause prospective donors to question the quality of academic programs, and it can backfire if the athletic programs are perceived as lacking integrity and honesty, as occurs when, for example, they are found guilty of NCAA violations.

Finally, when sports long have been used to create a university's public relations image, varsity teams cannot be dropped suddenly without

causing problems. But if there are good reasons for dropping sports programs, most alumni and other donors respect the decision to do so. Furthermore, many schools have not used sports to create public relations images, and some of these schools have been very successful at fundraising. They highlight academic and research programs rather than coaches and quarterbacks. When their programs are good, their donations are as high as those to schools with publicized sport programs. Winning games and championships may receive good press coverage, but it will not consistently increase donations unless the school also has a good academic reputation.

School-Community Relations

Interscholastic sport programs always have done two things in the realm of school-community relations: they have attracted attention, and they have provided entertainment. In other words, interscholastic sports help make the school a part of community life, and they help bridge the gap between "town and gown" that exists in some communities. One of the only times people who do not have school-aged children hear about the local high school or college is when there is a news story about one of its sport teams. Even for some of the parents of students, the fates of varsity teams may be of more noticeable concern than the fates of academic programs. Sports are an easy connecting point for people in the community; they even may be "identity pegs" for significant numbers of people in a local community. Through sports, people can maintain an interest in their local high school or college without having to know about all the complex dimensions of academic life.

It is easy to see that sports can connect schools to communities, but we do not know if these connections benefit academic programs or the achievement of educational goals. Benefits are most likely in small towns, where local attachments to high schools are strongly reinforced by school teams. In the case of larger high schools in metropolitan areas, and universities with big-time sport programs, people may attend games and read team scores in the paper, but their attachments to the schools themselves seldom go beyond occasional attendance at games.

Do high schools and universities have an obligation to provide community entertainment through sports? It is difficult to argue this case, even though some communities seemingly have become dependent on school sports for weekend enjoyment. When varsity sports are defined as entertainment, the needs of student-athletes and students in general often become secondary to the need to put on a good show. This has happened in a few high schools and more than a few intercollegiate programs around the United States, and it usually subverts the achievement of educational goals.

VARSITY HIGH SCHOOL SPORTS: PROBLEMS AND RECOMMENDATIONS

Existing high school and college sport programs generally enjoy widespread support; many people have vested interests in keeping them the way they are. However, reforms are needed in many programs. Some high school programs are doing an excellent job; others have not only lost direct connections with education, but have subverted the educational process for some students. Problems vary from one high school program to the next. But the most serious problems include the following: (1) an overemphasis on "sports development" and "big-time" program models, (2) limited participation access for students, and (3) too many coaches who emphasize conformity and obedience rather than responsibility and autonomy.

Overemphasis on "Sports Development" and "Big-Time" Program Models

Some high school administrators, athletic directors, and coaches seem to think that the best way to organize high school sports is to model them after big-time intercollegiate programs. When this happens, people involved with varsity sports become overconcerned with winning records and presenting tightly organized, high-profile programs to the community at large; these programs often highlight football or men's basketball. In the process of trying to build high-profile sports programs, they often overlook the educational needs of all students in their schools. Their goal is to be "ranked" rather than to respond to the needs of students.

People who focus on "sports development" often give lip service to the idea that sports must be "kept in proper perspective," but many forget their own words when it comes to the programs at their schools. In fact, they may even encourage students to specialize in a single sport for twelve months a year, instead of encouraging them to develop a wide range of skills in different sports. They set up sport camps or identify camps that they strongly encourage "their athletes" to attend during summer break. They sometimes forbid their athletes to play other sports and then recommend that they join community clubs where they can continue playing through the off-season. And they continually tell students that they must sacrifice to achieve excellence in the future. This, of course, turns off many students who want to have fun with a sport right now, and who want to enjoy participation even if they do not plan on being all-American athletes in the future.

People who adhere to a "sports development" model hire and fire coaches on the basis of win-loss records rather than teaching abilities. They even may describe coaches as good teachers when teams have winning records, and as bad teachers when teams lose. Their goal is to build a "winning tradition" without ever critically examining how such a tradition is connected to the education of students; they just assume that "winning" is educational. This orientation has led an increasing number of high schools to recruit seventh- and eighth-grade athletes in certain sports to build big-time teams that will be highly ranked on the national or state level. They want to use the public relations generated by popular spectator sports to increase their visibility and status; private schools want to use the public relations to recruit more tuition-paying students.

These big-time sports programs have created an atmosphere in which many high school students mistakenly believe that athletics are a better route to rewards and college scholarships than academics. This is just one of the ways that some varsity sport programs can subvert the achievement of educational goals.

RECOMMENDATIONS Varsity sport programs ought to be subjected to regular educational assessments. Coaches should be provided with opportunities to learn more about the ways sports can be made into educationally relevant activities. Coaches also should be given access to coaching education programs and other professional development opportunities that emphasize "student development" rather than "sports development."

The educational value of state and national rankings should be assessed. Is there a need to crown national high school championship teams? State championship teams? Are there alternative ways to define and seek excellence other than through such a system? Why not give higher priority to sports involving active participation rather than just being a spectator? For example, there could be more combined male/female teams in sports such as long-distance running, doubles tennis and badminton, bowling, golf, cycling and tandem cycling, soccer, hacky sack, wall climbing, archery and shooting, volleyball, swimming, racquetball, and billiards. If high school is a time for social development, playing these sports would be more valuable than watching spectator sports based on entertainment models. Scoring and handicap systems could be designed to accommodate certain skill differences and promote human development and social development rather than sports development.

Limited Participation Access

The major advantage of interscholastic sports is that they provide students with opportunities to develop and test their skills, especially physical skills, outside the classroom. However, when high school programs emphasize power and performance sports, they discourage participation by some males and many females who prefer sports emphasizing pleasure and participation. In fact, this may be the major factor that prevents schools from meeting their gender equity goals, despite persistent attempts to make sure opportunities are available for females: females may not be as eager to play sports that are built around the idea of "proving who the better man is"!

Budget cuts also have interfered with the changing or expansion of programs in creative ways. And now one of the biggest threats to more open participation in varsity sports is the use of participation fees.

RECOMMENDATIONS Not everyone is physically able or motivated to participate in interscholastic sports based on a power and performance model. Those who do not measure up to their bigger, faster, taller, and stronger classmates need participation alternatives. There is no reason only one team should represent a school in varsity competition. Why not have two teams? Why not have a football league with players under 140 pounds, or a basketball league with all players under 5´8˝ tall, or track meets with height and weight breakdowns for certain events? In places where this has been tried, it has been successful.

There should be efforts to develop new interscholastic sports in which size and strength are not crucial for success. Too often the focus is on football and basketball rather than a variety of sports suited for a variety of participants. Why not have teams in frisbee, racquetball, flag football, softball, in-line skating, or any sport for which there is enough local interest to get people to try out? With a little guidance, the students themselves could administer and coach these teams and coordinate meets and games with opponents at other schools. If responsibility builds autonomy and decision-making skills, why not let students direct their own teams so that more of them would have opportunities to

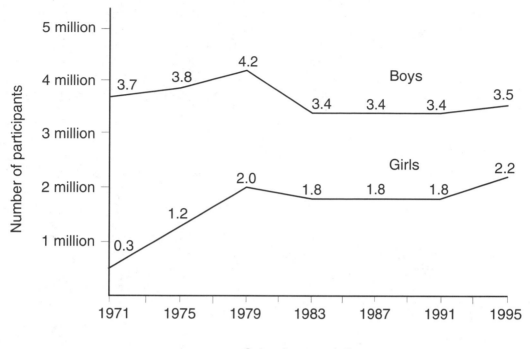

FIGURE 14-1 Number of boys and girls participating in interscholastic athletics, 1972 to 1995.
Source: National Federation of State High School Associations, 1996.

participate? This has been done with success in many countries.

Disabled students have been almost totally ignored by varsity sports programs. Schools need to develop sport participation opportunities for students with disabilities. This could occur in a combination of specially designed programs or by including disabled student-athletes on existing high school teams. This would not work in all sports, but there are certain sports in which disabled competitors could be included in games, meets, and matches.

Girls' sports still do not have the support that boys' sports enjoy. Of course, this problem has a history that goes far beyond the high school. But the result is that girls still participate at lower rates than boys (fig 14-1). In some areas there is still an emphasis on boys' teams as the most im-

portant teams in the school. Gender equity in varsity programs could be achieved in some schools through such gender-mixed sports as those we have just recommended, or by linking the boys' and girls' teams through the use of combined scoring methods in certain sports. For example, when the basketball teams of school A and school B played each other, the final outcome of the game would be determined by combining the score of the girls' team with the score of the boys' teams for each school. This would lead boys to take girls more seriously as basketball players, and even get them to recruit talented girls into sports and then attend the girls' games. After all, their place in league standings would depend on the girls' performance, and vice versa.

More schools are now using participation fees to save interscholastic sports. This strategy may work, but it may also limit participation among students from low-income families, even when fee waivers are available. If fees are necessary to save programs, there should be attempts to enable students to work for the money to pay fees, and there should be ways to get community organizations to establish scholarship funds to pay fees for students in need of assistance.

Emphasis on Conformity and Obedience Rather than Responsibility and Autonomy

Too many high school programs are organized to emphasize obedience rather than responsibility. But in fact, the educational benefits of sport involvement are greatest when athletes themselves make decisions affecting the nature of their sport participation. This does not mean that athletes do not need guidance; they do. But they also need chances to become independent, autonomous young adults. Autocratic coaches with rigid, externally imposed sets of rules reduce these chances and perpetuate immaturity and dependence—even though they may win games.

RECOMMENDATIONS Student-athletes in most high schools should be more involved in decision making for their teams. This can be accomplished in a variety of ways. In fact, sports are ideal settings for students to learn responsibility through decision making. For example, team members should be involved in the development of team rules and enforcement policies, they should be asked to play a role in developing team strategies, plays, and game plans, and they should have opportunities to voice their thoughts during games, meets, and matches at appropriate times. Why should adult coaches make all the decisions on student sport teams? How does that build responsibility?

Ideally, the coaches' goal should be to prepare teams to be self-coached. What would happen if coaches had to let players coach themselves for the last two games of the season? This would force coaches to build real leadership among players. Athletes also should be involved in the

evaluation of coaches and sports programs. Internships should be organized to enable senior athletes to serve as assistant coaches, or as coaches for junior varsity and junior high school teams. This would give them opportunities to handle many different tasks and get management experiences in the process.

Varsity sports should be based on the principle that responsibility grows out of making decisions and living with the consequences of those decisions. Responsibility is learned, not implanted in a young person's character by the commands and warnings of adults in positions of authority. Unfortunately, many varsity sports are organized to teach conformity and obedience instead of responsibility and independence. This should be changed carefully so that sports can become more clearly educational.

INTERCOLLEGIATE SPORTS: PROBLEMS AND RECOMMENDATIONS

Problems are not new to intercollegiate sports. Even in the late nineteenth century, college teams were accused of being too commercial and professional. In the mid-1920s the Carnegie Corporation commissioned a study that found intercollegiate programs to have problems related to commercialism, professionalization, and the neglect of educational issues (Savage, 1929). And these problems continued to grow along with the size, popularity, and scope of intercollegiate sports. Television created new sources of revenue, attracted new fans, and took sports farther away from educational concerns. Then, in the light of the women's movement, people realized that intercollegiate programs were sexist and unresponsive to the participation needs of women students. These and other issues, such as recruiting abuses and economic problems, led the American Council on Education to sponsor another investigation in 1973. It was not surprising that the study discovered the same kinds of problems found in the past (Hanford, 1974, 1979). In 1991, the Report of the Knight Foundation Commission on Intercollegiate

Athletics noted that big-time intercollegiate sports remained in need of drastic reforms.

The major problems now include the following: (1) commercialism and "corporatization," (2) lack of athletes' rights, (3) gender inequities, and (4) distorted priorities related to race relations and education.

Commercialism and "Corporatization"

According to one analysis, a significant segment of intercollegiate athletics has become "a huge commercial entertainment conglomerate, with operating methods and objectives totally separate from, and mainly opposed to, the educational aims of the schools that house its franchises" (Sperber, 1990). Evidence supports the notion that when sports programs become big businesses, financial concerns tend to take priority over educational concerns. When media rights to games are sold, the academic progress of the college players often becomes less important than television ratings and network profits. Corporate sponsors are not concerned with educational issues; their survival depends on profits, not the academic progress of student-athletes. Educational concerns may be not be given top priority when people having nothing to do with higher education are making many of the decisions affecting intercollegiate sports.

When experts in marketing, the media, and large corporations present intercollegiate sports under their logos for their interests, what happens? Even though this "corporatization" of intercollegiate sports has brought needed revenues to some sports in some programs, it has intensified the emphasis on entertainment over education, and it has marginalized certain sports that emphasize student-athletes, not spectators. The long-term implications of this need to be assessed carefully (Padilla and Baumer).

RECOMMENDATIONS Serious cost-containment measures should be implemented in big-time intercollegiate sports. Revenues from media contracts should be shared by all NCAA members, limits should be set on the amount of money spent by teams in different sports at different levels of NCAA membership, and rules should be made regulating corporate support and involvement in intercollegiate sports. Unless limits are set, student-athletes will be subjected to even more pressures to be entertainers rather than students. University presidents, together with committees of educators from the faculties and the athletic departments, should have ultimate control over athletic programs and their budgets. Schools with big-time programs in certain sports must find ways to control the "athletic arms race" that has pushed educational concerns to the margins of intercollegiate sports (Managan, 1996).

These cost-containment measures should be accompanied by evaluation of athletic departments in educational terms. In fact, the academic accreditation of universities should involve an assessment of the educational relevance of athletic programs (Yasser, 1993).

Corporate support should be tightly regulated so that programs do not depend ultimately on the advertising needs of private companies. Unless corporate support comes in the form of "community service" rather than marketing and advertising, perhaps it should not be accepted. Would we let an oil company hang its logo on an engineering building, pay faculty to wear lab coats with the logo on them, and get students to wear the logo in class? No, because that would interfere with education, student freedom, and the autonomy of the engineering program. This also should be an issue in the education programs we call "intercollegiate sports."

Controlling commercialism and corporatization within the current structure of big-time intercollegiate sports is difficult, if not impossible. This fact led James Loughran, the president of St. Peter's College in New Jersey, to tell university presidents on the NCAA committee charged with controlling intercollegiate sports that their efforts to make sport programs relevant to education were doomed to fail unless they separated winning and money, and unless they reduced the economic stakes associated with games. He told the presidents that they must face these facts: "Big-time college sports conflict not only with amateurism, but also with academic integrity and ideals of any good college; in the system that exists, this conflict is inescapable; and therefore, reform is impossible" (1996). He suggested that the presidents join with trustees, faculty, politicians, parents, and the public at large to discuss how to eliminate this conflict and determine where sports and competition belong in higher education. He suggested, further that if such an effort could not be mounted, "the NCAA be disbanded and . . . we institute a five-year moratorium on intercollegiate athletics so we can revive recreation and intramurals on campuses, and so the professional sports and entertainment industry could find some other outlet than the colleges." Loughran knew that his second suggestion would be defined as extreme, but he and many others are beginning to believe that extreme measures are needed to control the commercialism of intercollegiate sports. I agree.

Lack of Athletes' Rights

Student-athletes in big-time intercollegiate programs are rewarded with prestige and limited financial support, but their lives are pretty much under the control of others. According to sociologist Stan Eitzen this is a problem:

> Athletes do not have free speech or the right to a fair trial [within the context of athletic programs]. If they challenge the athletic power structure, they will lose their scholarship and eligibility. Athletes who have a grievance are on their own. They have no union, no arbitration board, and rarely do they have representation on campus athletic committees (Eitzen, 1992).

Eitzen also notes that some athletes generate millions for schools, but are limited in what they can receive from schools; athletes must make four-year commitments to schools, but schools often make only year-to-year scholarship commitments to athletes; athletes' privacy can be invaded routinely by coaches and representatives of the athletic department; athletes must accept all rules imposed by coaches and athletic departments, regardless of whether the rules would be considered fair by anyone but the coach; and athletes seldom have any means for formally objecting to cases of abusive and oppressive actions on the part of coaches.

RECOMMENDATIONS Student-athletes must be represented on university advisory committees to athletic departments and in the NCAA. Formal appeals systems should be put in place so that athletes can register complaints and have them investigated in ways that do not jeopardize their scholarships or status on teams. Athletes should be formally involved in the evaluation of coaches and team programs, and every team should be required to have a student-athlete advisory/disciplinary committee that handles team issues. Furthermore, every university should have an independent ombudsperson (an appointed official who investigates situations in which the rights of individuals may have been violated) to whom student-athletes can go when they need an advocate to help them deal with the athletic department, team, or coach about issues related to their rights.

Now that big-time sports have become highly visible forms of entertainment, student-athletes in those sports should receive a portion of the income they produce. Some athletic departments now resemble old southern plantations, where workers were used and given basic necessities, but did not share in the fruits of their labor.

Pay for student-athletes is the most contentious issue facing big-time sport programs today, and it highlights what happens when universities enter the entertainment business. Either universities should get out of the business, or they should treat their student-athletes as workers. They could do this in a variety of ways, including providing need-based financial aid packages enabling student-athletes to receive stipends for educational resources, vouchers for trips home to visit families on holidays, and insurance coverage

SIDELINES

"I like your new recruit, coach . . . an excellent example of higher education!"

In big-time intercollegiate sports, the meaning of higher education sometimes gets distorted by coaches and university presidents.

for all medical bills and treatments through college, and indefinitely for any condition indirectly related to their sport participation. Monthly stipends for living expenses also might be appropriate. And a variety of strategies could be developed so that student-athletes could combine learning with sharing revenues from their sports. It would seem that faculty members could work with student-athletes to involve them in individual and team-based business ventures. A student-athlete speakers' bureau could train athletes to do paid speeches for groups; part of the fee would go directly to the speakers, and part would allow the bureau to pay athletes to give speeches to those nonprofit groups that could not afford a fee, as a community service. There are many ways to combine learning with forms of just compensation to student-athletes. Most require creative leadership, but that's what universities have, or are supposed to have.

Gender Inequities

Men and women go to college in about equal numbers; they all pay student fees, and these fees often are used to support intercollegiate sports. This long has been the case, since the days before there were women's teams at many universities. For many years, women's fees subsidized athletic programs that offered opportunities to men only. Since the late 1970s, massive changes have occurred. However, in the mid-1990s, there were still over twice as many male athletes as female athletes, women received only one scholarship dollar for every two received by men, and women's teams spent only one dollar to recruit women athletes for every three spent to recruit men athletes. Figure 14-2 provides data for 303 NCAA Division I-A universities. The data highlight gender inequities common in most NCAA member schools. Beginning in 1997, all NCAA member institutions are required by the Equity in Athletics Disclosure Act to provide annual reports on gender and resource allocation. This new federal requirement will enable the government and other interested parties to monitor gender equity and enforce compliance.

Gender equity requires compliance with Title IX law. According to the U.S. Department of Education's Office of Civil Rights (OCR), a school must meet one of the following three tests to be within the law:

1. *Demonstrate that sports participation opportunities for each gender are substantially proportionate to its full-time undergraduate enrollment.* (According to court decisions, this means that if 49 percent of the students are female, no less than 44 percent and no more than 54 percent of the student athletes should be female; a 5-percentage-point deviation from exact equality generally is determined to be within the law.)
2. *Demonstrate a history and continuing practice of expansion in its women's athletics program.* (The OCR considers all actions and changes over the last three years as signs of expansion.)
3. *Demonstrate that the interests and abilities of members of the underrepresented sex have been fully accommodated.* (The OCR asks the school to prove that women don't have enough ability or interest to sustain additional

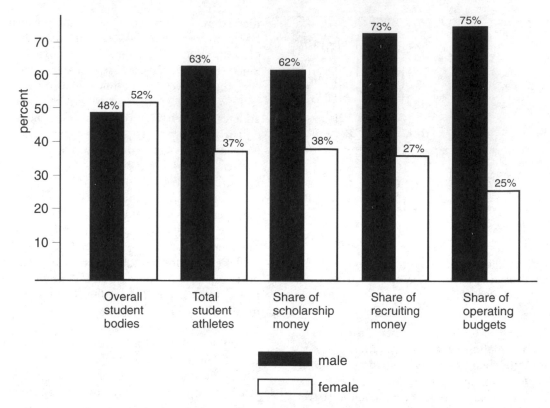

FIGURE 14-2 Gender Equity in NCAA Division I Universities: (1996)
Source: USA Today survey of 303 NCAA Division I schools (see *USA Today*, 3/3, 3/4, 3/5, 1997).
*From *1996 NCAA Division I Graduation-Rates Report.*

opportunities, or that new women's teams would not have reasonable opportunities to compete against other teams.)

There are three ways, then to comply with the law. Most colleges and universities that are within the law have met the second test: they have shown what are legally defined as good-faith efforts to make changes over the past three years. But those changes must continue until either of the other tests can be met. The ultimate goal is to meet the first test, the proportionality test.

Universities with large football programs have a difficult time meeting the proportionality test; in fact, as of late 1996, only 9 percent of Division I universities came within 5 percentage points of proportionality. Because of reluctance

to cut the resources allocated to football, some universities have cut other men's programs in an effort to approach proportionality. This has led men in the sports that have been eliminated to complain. But it is interesting that they complain about the resources going to women's teams, not the disproportionate resources going to football. Apparently, men in so-called minor sports have a difficult time siding with women and/or challenging the way football is organized and played. Some men even have gone so far as to suggest that football players be considered a "third sex" and not be included when Title IX compliance is assessed.

RECOMMENDATIONS Many equity recommendations have been made since 1972, when Title IX became law. Getting athletic departments to follow them has been the problem. Athletic departments claim that equity is not possible unless there are major changes in the way football is organized and played, and changes could jeopardize revenues. This is a serious dilemma, and I see no way around it. My recommendation would be that universities cut football expenses through cost-containment measures established at each NCAA division level, cut the size of football teams, and build some women's sports into revenue producers. After all, it took about one hundred years to build intercollegiate football into something that could make money for a few schools. Shouldn't women be given as much time to build their programs and make women's sports an important and visible part of the culture and life on university campuses? Or should universities get out of the spectator sport business altogether?

Distorted Priorities Related to Race Relations and Education

A 1996 survey by the National Collegiate Athletic Association (Benson, 1996) showed that while blacks made up only 9.8 percent of the full-time students at 305 NCAA Division I colleges and universities, they constituted about 25 percent of all students on some form of athletic aid, 63 percent of male basketball players receiving athletic aid, 52 percent of football players, and 36 percent of female basketball players. Overall, about 6 percent of all black students on the 305 campuses were student-athletes, whereas only 2 percent of white students were student-athletes. Over 10 percent of black males on these campuses were student-athletes, compared to 1 student-athlete in 50 black female students, 1 in 40 white male students, and 1 in 60 white female students. Also important was the fact that 92 percent of black male athletes were in only three sports (football, basketball, and track and field), and 80 percent of black women athletes were in only two sports (basketball and track and field). Overall, less than 16,000 African Americans received some form of athletic aid in Division I universities during 1996, and I estimate that less than 8,000 of these

student-athletes received what might be called *full* scholarships.* This constitutes about 1 in 350 African Americans between eighteen and twenty-two years old in the U.S. population. In other words 99.7 percent of college-age African Americans do not have full athletic aid (Hayes, 1993).

Figure 14-3 highlights some of these data. Note that other minority students do not have a profile that accentuates sport participation. It seems that African Americans disproportionately attend universities as athletes, especially in the high-profile revenue-producing sports.

Harry Edwards, a sociologist at the University of California at Berkeley, says that this situation not only reinforces dangerous racial stereotypes, but also demoralizes thousands of black students struggling to use education rather than sports in their pursuit of the American Dream. Before his death, Arthur Ashe responded to the data by saying, "The message is clear: The colleges are interested in us primarily as athletes" (cited in Lederman, 1992b).

Of course, many young black men and a growing number of black women benefit from athletic scholarships. This is not the problem. According to Andrew Hacker, a political scientist from Queens College in New York City, the problem is that universities cynically have capitalized on the fact that blacks historically have been led to believe that sports are their way to get ahead (in Lederman, 1992b). In other words, universities have used the results of racist history to their advantage: they have recruited blacks who have become good athletes because they have seen few other opportunities to be successful in material terms or to gain status in the society as a whole. At the same time, these universities have not tried hard enough to make changes

---

*Universities do not report the types and amount of athletic aid they award to students. According to researchers at the NCAA, only 15 to 20 percent of all students who receive athletic aid receive full scholarships; 80 to 85 percent of all student athletes at the 305 Division I NCAA universities receive no athletic aid or receive partial aid, such as tuition waivers, housing, or meal tickets.

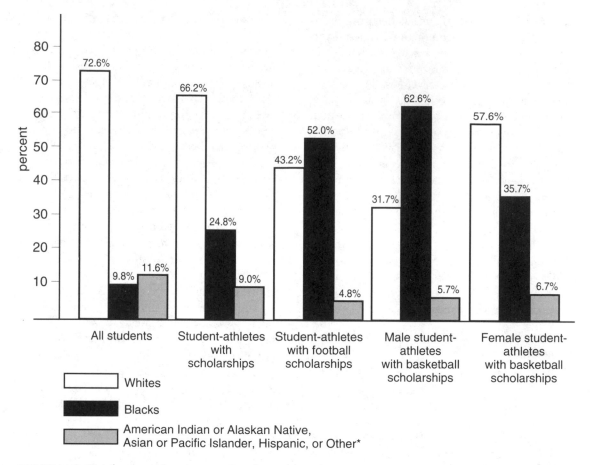

FIGURE 14-3 Distributions of students and student-athletes in NCAA Division I universities by skin color and ethnicity, 1996.

Source: 1996 NCAA Division I Graduation-Rates Report.

*Racial and ethnic classifications are based on student self-identifications.

in race relations in the student body or on the campus as a whole.

Meanwhile, many black athletes feel isolated on campuses where there are few African American students, faculty, or administrators. This isolation is intensified by (1) racial and athletic stereotypes used by some people on campus (Harrison, 1995; Sailes, 1993), (2) the amount of time student-athletes must devote to their sports, (3) barriers interfering with in-class, academic networking connecting black student-athletes to other students, (4) lack of campus

activities related to the interests and experiences of black students in general, (5) lack of social self-confidence among black student-athletes who find campus life unrelated to their experiences, (6) cultural differences between the black student-athletes and many other students, (7) feelings of jealousy among white students who mistakenly conclude that all black student-athletes have it made and don't have to work hard (see Davis, 1995; Eitzen, 1993; Fudzie and Hayes, 1995; Stratta, 1995, 1997). The isolation is especially intense if black student-athletes come from working-class or low-income backgrounds and the white students on campus come from upper-middle-income backgrounds. This provides a combination of ethnic and socioeconomic differences that may create problems unless the administration, faculty, and professional staff make a concerted effort to promote understanding and real connections between students from different backgrounds.

Ironically, many black male student-athletes play on teams that generate revenues to pay for athletic scholarships awarded to white student-athletes from wealthier backgrounds who play non-revenue-generating sports. Resentment among black athletes has been intensified by rules that have prohibited them from sharing in the revenues they generate, or even from holding part-time jobs enabling them to enjoy even a fraction of the privileges many other students enjoy. The athletes may express this resentment in ways that interfere with their educational achievement and intensify existing racial divisions on campus and in surrounding communities. NCAA awareness of this and related issues led the organization in 1997 to change its rules and allow athletes to hold part-time jobs. This may defuse some of the resentment, but many black athletes still will feel they are being used by the universities (Harrison, 1995).

African American women face similar situations in predominantly white institutions (Corbett & Johnson, 1993; Smith, 1992). However, they also deal with gender inequities, and so face the dual challenge of dealing with racism *and* sexism. They see not only a lack of African Americans in positions of power and authority within their schools and athletic departments, but also a lack of women, especially women of color.

Because black women face slightly different challenges than those faced by black men in U.S. society, and because women's athletics often are defined differently than men's athletics are in big-time universities, the experiences of black women student-athletes are often different from

The experiences of African American women student-athletes are influenced by a combination of social ideas about both gender and race. In 1996, about 80 percent of all African American women athletes in Division I universities played in two sports: basketball and track and field. (Brian Lewis, University of Colorado Media Relations)

black men's experience. These differences are poorly understood, and more research is needed.

RECOMMENDATIONS Universities must be more aggressive in recruiting and supporting minority students who are not athletes, and in recruiting minority coaches and faculty. It is not fair to bring black or other ethnic minority student-athletes to campuses where they have little social support and little they can identify with. Furthermore, white students and faculty must be made aware that not all blacks play sports or are even interested in sports. If universities would make more concerted efforts to incorporate racial and cultural diversity into all spheres of campus life, recruiting black athletes would not be defined as part of a distorted set of priorities.

We need more visible models of successfully created "campus cultures" in which students, staff, faculty, and administration appreciate cultural differences and use them as a basis for expanding their knowledge and understanding of the diverse world in which we all live. It seems to me that this should be one of the core organizing principles on all college campuses today. Unfortunately, it is not. When universities present to the world an image of physically talented black athletes and intellectually talented white scientists, racism is perpetuated. Universities somehow must present to young black males the message that they will be recruited primarily for their intellectual skills; the message to white students must be that the university offers a setting in which people from diverse backgrounds meet and use their differences to create a wide range of learning experiences. Sports can be a part of this process, but only when black students constitute about the same percentage of the student body as of the athletic department.

SUMMARY

ARE VARSITY SPORTS EDUCATIONAL?

It is difficult to generalize about varsity sports programs. They differ from one another in numerous ways. However, varsity sports have no place in high schools or colleges unless they are legitimate parts of educational programs and unless they receive their direction from educational purpose. In other words, if the programs do not benefit student-athletes educationally, they cannot be justified as school-sponsored activities.

At this time there is no consistent evidence that high school sports produce negative consequences for those who participate in them. Of course, some schools, coaches, parents, and student-athletes lose sight of educational goals in their pursuit of winning records and championships. Sports can be seductive, and people connected with high school teams sometimes require guidance to keep their programs in balance with what is going on in the rest of the school. It is up to school superintendents and principals to oversee what happens in their districts and schools. Parents also should be sensitive to the potential of sports to subvert educational goals. When sport participation interferes with educational achievement, steps must be taken to restore sports to their proper place.

The possibility that sport participation might interfere with the educational progress of student-athletes is greatest in big-time intercollegiate programs. The attractiveness of being an athlete in a big-time program is often enough to distract students from academic work. In fact, it can make coursework nearly irrelevant in the lives of impressionable young people, especially young men who see their destinies being shaped by sports, not academic achievement.

Interscholastic sport programs usually create school spirit. But we do not know if that spirit contributes to the achievement of educational goals. While it is certain that other school activities could be used to bring students together, sports do provide students with unique social activities that make schools more interesting places to be. Although they occupy the everyday attention of a considerable number of students, we do not know whether they systematically distract attention from academic matters.

It is doubtful that high school sport programs seriously cut into budgets for academic programs. The money they require is well spent if they provide students opportunities to explore their physical selves and meet challenges outside the classroom. On the intercollegiate level, the funding situation is complex and confusing. However, it is clear that most programs are not self-supporting, and that they do not generate revenues for their schools' general funds. What is not clear is the extent to which the athletic programs divert money from academic programs.

Interscholastic sport programs often bridge the gap between schools and surrounding communities. However, when those programs are controlled by people not connected with the schools, there is a tendency for educational goals to be overlooked. Some schools may be able to use their sport teams as vehicles to create community support for educational programs, but this goal is very rarely achieved.

When high school programs overemphasize "sports development," limit access to participation, and focus on controlling students rather than enabling them to become responsible, they subvert the achievement of educational goals. Similarly, when intercollegiate programs are characterized by commercialism, lack of rights for athletes, gender inequity, and distorted priorities related to racial issues and education, they are counterproductive to the reputation and mission of higher education. If the administrators of high schools and universities allow these problems to exist, there are no educationally sound reasons for their schools to continue sponsoring varsity sport programs.

Varsity sport programs never will be perfect. There always will be a need for critical evaluation and change, just as there is in any part of the curriculum. This means that the educational relevance of these programs depends on constant evaluation and assessment. A critical approach is the only approach that will enable sports to be meaningful activities in the everyday lives of students and in the social organization of the schools themselves.

SUGGESTED READINGS

Adler, P. A., and P. Adler. 1991. *Backboards & blackboards: College athletes and role engulfment.* New York: Columbia University Press, (*an excellent sociological study of college athletes; authors focus on male basketball players in a big-time program and deal with the sport experiences from the perspectives of the athletes themselves*).

Bale, J. 1991. *The brawn drain: Foreign student-athletes in American universities.* Urbana, IL: University of Illinois Press (*written by a geographer interested in the global competition for talented young athletes; focuses on the context and experiences of the over six thousand foreigners who play on U.S. intercollegiate sport teams*).

Bissinger, H. G. 1990. *Friday night lights.* Reading, MA: Addison-Wesley (*this dramatic journalistic account of a Texas high school football team during the 1988 season deals with issues of race and gender relations, education, and the connection between a varsity sport and the local community*).

Brooks, D. D., and R. C. Althouse, eds. 1993. *Racism in college athletics: The African-American athlete's experience.* Morgantown, WV: Fitness Information Technology, Inc. (*twelve papers deal with problems faced by African Americans in college sports, providing historical material; discussion of recruitment, retention, and mobility issues; analysis of the intersection of race and gender in sports; and prospects for change in the future*).

Chu, D., J. O. Segrave, and B. J. Becker, eds. 1985. *Sport and higher education.* Champaign, IL: Human Kinetics (*a comprehensive anthology on American intercollegiate sports; thirty-one articles by leading researchers; articles focus on history, athletes' rights, controversies, and recommendations for reform*).

Foley, D. E. 1990. *Learning capitalist culture.* Philadelphia, PA: University of Pennsylvania Press (*author pays special attention to high school sports in this excellent ethnography of a small Texas town; focuses on youth, community rituals, and the reproduction of class, ethnic, and gender inequalities*).

Fudzie, V., and A. Hayes. 1995. *The sport of learning: A comprehensive survival guide for African-American student-athletes.* North Hollywood, CA: Doubleplay Publishing Group (*written by former and current African-American student-athletes; deals frankly and practically with the issues and problems black men encounter as they strive to achieve academic and athletic success in predominantly white universities*).

Knight Foundation Commission Report on Intercollegiate Athletics. 1991. *Keeping faith with the student-athlete: A new model for Intercollegiate athletics.* Charlotte, NC: Knight Foundation (*this report and a follow-up published in 1992 inspired numerous discussions and national publicity focused on the need to reform intercollegiate sports; the report itself was not a critical document, but it incited much critical discussion*).

Miracle, A. W., and C. R. Rees. 1994. *Lessons of the locker room: The myth of school sports.* Amherst, NY: Prometheus Books (*a detailed examination of commonly held beliefs about sport in U.S. high schools; uses research as a basis for assessing those beliefs and showing most of them to be faulty*).

Rees, C. R., and A. W. Miracle. Forthcoming. Education and sport. In E. Dunning and J. Coakley, eds. *Handbook of sport and society.* London: Sage (*a concise overview; provides a brief history, identifies important issues, and reviews relevant research*).

Sperber, M. 1990. *College Sports, Inc.: The Athletic Department vs The University.* New York: Henry Holt and Company (*this book was published just before the Knight Foundation Commission Report was released; it was widely read because it dug into and criticized intercollegiate sports in a way that the commission did not. This book did much to inspire response to the commission report*).

15

(Jay Coakley)

In the rough and tumble-weed world of professional rodeo, the Cowboys for Christ are bulldoggin' the devil and lassoing lost souls.

Christopher Rose, Religion News Service (1996)

If somebody comes into my territory, my zone, I want to hit him hard. I don't ever want to take a cheap shot, but I'll hit him with all the love of Jesus I can muster.

Gill Byrd, NFL player (1991)

Sports and Religion
Is it a promising combination?

It is not just a parallel that is emerging between sports and religion, but rather a complete identity. Sport is religion for growing numbers of Americans.

Charles Prebish, professor of religious studies, Penn State University (1992)

I'm not playing for the fans or the money, but to honor God. I know my motivation. I know where I'm headed. Every night I try to go out there to honor Him and play great.

David Robinson, NBA player (in *Sports Illustrated*, 27 May 1996)

David Robinson believes that God wants him to be the best basketball player he can be. Nonsense. . . . He uses Jesus and God to rubber stamp ideas [contrary] to Christianity. . . . Jesus would be aghast at how we use his name to bless our sports contests.

Retired U.S. army chaplain (in *Sports Illustrated*, 27 May 1996)

God is truly interested in our physical well being. But you can't do it alone. You need to go to him and get his idea of what you can do. Then you'll succeed.

Cheryl Perkins, director, Colorado Springs Christian Aerobics Network (1996)

Through history, sports and religion have had a changing relationship. During some periods, sport activities have been either sponsored in connection with religious ceremonies and festivals or endorsed by church authorities as worthwhile pursuits. But during other periods, they have been either ignored or condemned as indulgent and sinful. Since the late nineteenth century, there has been a tendency in some Western societies for Christian churches to sponsor sport activities and for some individuals to combine religious beliefs (usually Christian beliefs) with their sport participation.

The purpose of this chapter is to explore how religion and religious systems of meaning inform the way sports are defined, organized, and played among different groups of people. As you read this chapter, remember that similar religious systems of meaning can be applied to sports and sport participation in different ways, depending on the experiences, relationships, and interests of individuals and groups. These are the questions we discuss in this chapter:

1. How is religion defined, and why do sociologists study it?
2. What are the similarities and differences between sports and religion?
3. Why have sports and Christian organizations and beliefs been combined?
4. What are the challenges associated with combining Christianity and sports?

In discussing this last question, we will give special attention to whether the combination of religion and sports offers any promise for eliminating racism, sexism, deviance, violence, or other problems in sports.

HOW DO SOCIOLOGISTS DEFINE AND STUDY RELIGION?

Sociological discussions of religion sometimes have created controversy in sociology of sport classrooms. This occurs because when people think about religion, they often use only their personal religious beliefs and practices as a point of reference; thus, they have strong feelings about and vested interests in how religion is discussed. Religion is powerful because it forms a foundation for general systems of meaning related to ultimate issues and questions. These systems of meaning affect the way people think about the world, about social life and social relationships, and even about sports.

A sociological discussion of religion and sports requires that we dismiss preconceived ideas about what religion should be and should do. Although there are many definitions of religion, most sociologists agree that *religion* is a socially shared set of beliefs and rituals focused on ultimate concerns of human existence: birth, life, suffering, illness, tragedy, injustice, and death. Religious beliefs and rituals consist of meanings and cultural practices that are special because people assume they are linked to a sacred and supernatural realm. And this assumption is based on faith.

Objects, symbols, and ceremonies are *sacred* when they are identified with the supernatural or with forces beyond the here-and-now world. Religious beliefs and rituals also make distinctions between the sacred and the *profane*. The profane consists of all things that are a part of common, everyday, worldly experience. Sacred things inspire awe, mystery, and reverence; profane things may be impressive, but they usually involve everyday issues and concerns among believers, rather than deeper matters.

We can illustrate the distinction between the sacred and the profane through examples from our experience. As you know, many Christians define certain types of crosses as sacred by connecting them with their God. Therefore, these special crosses (crucifixes) have been given symbolic meaning that can be understood only by their connection to the supernatural; they are part of the sacred. On the other hand, the letter jackets worn by some American high school student-athletes have no connection with the sacred or supernatural within a Christian religious belief system; letter jackets are understandable in terms of everyday meanings and experiences. These jackets and what they represent may be important to high school students, but they and their meanings belong to the world of the profane. Religion consists of objects, beliefs, and rituals that a group of people have agreed are associated with the sacred and supernatural.

It is important to remember that human beings have dealt with ultimate questions about life and death and coped with the inescapable problems of human existence in many different ways. In fact, they have developed literally thousands of rich and widely varied religions (Ferrante, 1995). Sociologists are not concerned with whether any particular religious belief system is true or false. Instead, they assume that all religions are true in their own way, because they enable believers to deal with ultimate questions and issues. This makes religion important sociologically, because it informs the way people think about who they are and how they are connected to the world and to one another.

Sociologists also study religion because it has unique social dynamics and social consequences. For example, religion and religious systems of meaning usually connect power, authority, and wisdom with a God, gods, or other supernatural forces. This connection can lead people to resist negotiation and compromise on any issue they see as tied to their religious beliefs. People avoid negotiating or compromising the word of their God or gods because they often fear that compromises would undermine the ultimate power, authority, and wisdom they use to make sense of their worlds and their lives.

This helps to explain why people responded the way they did in late 1992, when Irish rock singer Sinead O'Connor intentionally tore up a picture of Pope John Paul II on an American television program. O'Connor subsequently was booed off the stage at a multi-star rock concert, and a coalition of neighborhood groups outraged by her treatment of "the sacred" burned her recordings in protest on a New York street. Although many people who questioned O'Connor's action were neither Catholic nor very religious, they saw her as challenging authority connected with dominant conceptions of the sacred

and supernatural in the United States. Public responses would have been different and less dramatic if O'Connor had torn a photo of basketball player Michael Jordan. Even though Jordan is widely known and respected, he is associated with this world here and now, not with the eternal, not with what many people define as ultimate power, authority, and wisdom (even though Nike would like us to believe otherwise!).

Religious systems of meaning are also socially significant because they set believers apart from others and then explain that separation in other-worldly terms. This process of identification and separation can have important social consequences. For example, under certain conditions it might lead to any of the following:

- powerful forms of group unity and social integration, or devastating forms of group conflict and violent warfare
- a spirit of love and acceptance, or forms of moral judgment through which ideas and people are marginalized or condemned
- a commitment to prevailing social norms, or a rejection of those norms and calls for new norms
- an acceptance of the systems of power that influence social relations among men and women, racial and ethnic groups, social classes, homosexuals and heterosexuals, the able-bodied and the disabled, and other groups, or a rejection of those systems of power combined with visions for new forms of social relations

This is the reason religion is important in sociology: through its impact on individuals and groups, it influences definitions of morality and who is accorded moral power and authority in a society.

SIMILARITIES AND DIFFERENCES BETWEEN SPORTS AND RELIGION

Discussions about sports and religion are often confusing, because people see them as connected in different ways. Some people argue that sports are actually a new form of religion, or at least a "quasi-religion." Others argue that there are *essential* differences between what they define as the *nature of sport* and the *nature of religion*. Still others argue that sports and religions are simply two distinct forms of cultural practices that sometimes overlap as people devise ways to live with one another and attempt to make their lives satisfying and meaningful. The purpose of this section is to explain and clarify each of these three positions.

Sports as a Form of Religion

The most extreme position to take when discussing this issue is to say that sports are actually a form of religion. For example, Charles Prebish, a religious studies professor, has made the case that sport has become religion to such an extent that it is "a more appropriate expression of personal religiosity than Christianity, Judaism, or any of the traditional religions" (1992). He sees sport and religion as one and the same (see his words on the title page of this chapter).

Others stop short of this position. Theologian Michael Novak (1976) has argued that sports are a form of "natural" religion, because both sports and religion are shaped by "an impulse for freedom, respect for ritual limits, a zest for symbolic meaning, and a longing for perfection." Novak claims that sports are related to godliness because they emerge out of the same quest for perfection in body, mind, and spirit that leads people to form their conceptions of god—conceptions that always embody the ideals of a particular group or society.*

Sociologist Harry Edwards (1973) has described sport as a "secular, quasi-religious institution" because sports share with religion certain characteristics and social functions. James Mathisen (1992), also a sociologist, has described sports as forms of "folk religion," because they combine values, beliefs, myths, and cultic obser-

vances into a social form that has continuity and has become a part of tradition for masses of people in the United States.

These and other comparisons of religion and sports have highlighted the following similarities between sports and Judeo-Christian religious systems of meaning (see Hoffman, 1992 a, b, c, d, especially the introductions and articles in parts 1 and 2):

- Both have places and buildings for communal gatherings and special events; sports have stadiums and arenas decorated with pictures of athletes and championship trophies, while some religions have churches and temples decorated with statues of saints and/or stained-glass windows depicting great achievements.
- Both have procedures and dramas linked to personal betterment: sports have playbooks, practices, and time outs; religions have sacred books, prayers, and retreats.
- Both are controlled through structured organizations and hierarchical systems of authority made up of commissioners and bishops, athletic directors and pastors, coaches and priests.
- Both have events scheduled to celebrate values in the context of festival and festive occasions and both capture considerable attention on the sabbath.
- Both set aside certain times as special—Super Bowl Sunday and Easter Sunday, the NBA playoffs and Lent, Sunday morning worship and Monday night football.
- Both have rituals before, during, and after major events, such as initiations and baptisms, the national anthem and opening hymns, halftime pep talks and Sunday sermons, hand-slapping and the joining of hands, band parades and choir processions, shaking hands after games and greeting the minister after the services.
- Both have heroes and legends about their accomplishments; sport heroes are elected to

---

*The word *God* refers to *the* Supreme Being or *the* Creator in monotheistic religions. The words *god(s)* and *godliness* refer to deities across all religions, including polytheistic religions.

"halls of fame" and their stories are told repeatedly by sports journalists and fans; religious heroes are raised to sainthood, and their stories are told repeatedly by religious writers, ministers, and Sunday school teachers.

- Both are used to celebrate and reproduce the values of particular groups in society.
- Both can evoke intense excitement and emotional commitment from individuals and groups.
- Both can give deep personal meaning to people's lives and to activities that occur in a variety of circumstances.
- Both can be sources of existential experiences involving the temporary suspension of boundaries between self and the rest of the world; in other words, both can be sites for the transcendence of self and the experience of euphoric, emotional "highs."
- Both emphasize asceticism in that they stress discipline, self-denial, repetition, and the development of character; the notion of "no pain, no gain" is promoted by many coaches and ministers alike.

In summary, it is easy to see why many people talk about sports as quasi-religious. There are many similarities. Participation in sports, as a player or spectator, is characterized by many of the same trappings that characterize involvement in religion. In fact, the parallels are so apparent that it is often easy to get carried away with the similarities and ignore the differences between these two spheres of life.

"Essential" Differences Between Sport and Religion

Some people believe that both religion and sport have unique, separate "essences" that are grounded in divine inspiration and/or nature itself.*

---

* These people refer to "sport" in the singular because they assume that all sport forms express the same essence. I explain the problems associated with this approach in chapter 1, pp. 18–27.

They argue that religion and sport reveal different parts of a basic "human nature" that is unchanging, regardless of history, culture, or social circumstances. In other words, they assume that each system—religion or sport—has an essence that transcends time and space, and that human beings "live out" that essence when they participate in either religion or sport. In sociology, these people are referred to as "essentialists." These essentialists are concerned with discovering "nature" and then outlining the ways that human beings and human behavior are "natural." When they turn their attention to religion and sport, essentialists argue that the fundamental character of religion is different from the fundamental character of sport. For example, they would highlight the following differences:

- Religious beliefs, meanings, rituals, and events are grounded in the sacred and supernatural realm, whereas sport beliefs, meanings, rituals, and events are grounded in the profane and material realm.
- The purpose of religion is to transcend the circumstances and conditions of material life in the pursuit of spiritual goals, whereas the purpose of sport is to focus on material issues in the pursuit of pleasure, fame, or fortune here and now.
- Religion is fundamentally rooted in faith, whereas sport is fundamentally rooted in concrete rules and relationships.
- Religion is fundamentally noncompetitive, whereas sport is fundamentally competitive.
- Religion emphasizes a spirit of service and love of others, whereas sport emphasizes a spirit of personal achievement, self-promotion, and defeating others.
- Religious rituals are essentially expressive and process-oriented, whereas sport rituals are essentially instrumental and goal-oriented.
- Religion is fundamentally mystical and pure, whereas sport is fundamentally clear-cut and crude.

As you might guess, essentialists would say there are important differences in nature between the meanings attached to Super Bowl Sunday by sports fans and the meanings attached to Easter Sunday by Christians, despite the fact that both are defined as important days. Similarly, they would highlight fundamental differences between the meanings underlying a hockey team's initiation ceremony and a baptism, between a seventh-inning stretch and silent prayer during a religious service. They would see the meanings connected with St. Patrick's Cathedral as different from those connected with Yankee Stadium, even though both are important structures in New York City.

Some essentialists are religious people who claim that religion and sport are fundamentally different because religion is divinely inspired and sport is not. They believe that their religious dogma is sacred, whereas the rules of sports are secular. And they often worry that when religion and sport come together, the essential character of religion becomes secularized and corrupted by sport (Hoffman, 1992: 275–85).

In summary, essentialists would not say that sport is never religion-like, or that the social and psychological consequences of sport are always different from the consequences of religion. They would recognize overlap, but they would also stick to their position that sport and religion are fundamentally and essentially different.

Religions and Sports as Cultural Practices

A growing number of sociologists see both religions and sports as two forms of cultural practices created by groups of people as they devise ways to live with one another and struggle to make their lives satisfying and meaningful. These sociologists sometimes are called "social constructionists," because they do not assume that either religion or sport has an essential character. Instead, they see all religions and sports as "social constructions" or "social formations," with social dynamics and social consequences

that may overlap or differ, depending on social relations in particular social situations.

Social constructionists generally use some form of critical theory to guide their work. This leads them to focus on issues of power and social relations when they study religion or sports. For example, they would want to know why both sports and religions are male-dominated spheres of life, why men occupy nearly all the important positions of power in both religious and sport organizations, why beliefs and rituals in both sports and religions generally privilege men over women, and why events in both sports and religions focus on men as the major participants. They would be interested in patterns of class and racial and ethnic participation in both sports and religions, and in how those patterns are a part of general intergroup relations in the society as a whole.

This T-shirt design illustrates the themes around which some people connect religion and sports. History shows that both religions and sports are social constructions that represent and often reproduce the cultural contexts in which they exist. (Jay Coakley)

Social constructionists also assume that systems of meaning connected with both religions and sports *do* undergo change. They point out that religious beliefs and rituals vary from one social and cultural group to another, and that beliefs and rituals change with new revelations and visions, new prophets and prophecies, new interpretations of sacred writings, new teachers and teachings. They see these variations and changes as examples of the way the social acceptance of religious belief systems depends on the extent to which the belief systems are expressions of the cultural contexts in which they exist. They point out that when monotheistic people (those who believe in one God) describe their God, it is usually with characteristics that are highly valued and privileged in their culture (for example, as a white, male adult). They are interested in the fact that when religious beliefs contradict or conflict with dominant cultural ideologies and practices, believers often are persecuted or marginalized to such an extent that they may form religious sects or cults.*

Social constructionists are also interested in the many occasions in religious history when revelations, new teachings, and revisions in rules and beliefs have arisen in association with cultural changes. For example, Christian churches and denominations in some countries affected by women's movements now have approved the ordination of women as priests and ministers—a radical change for all of them. Other revisions of religious rules on everything from birth control to burial rituals also are associated with changes in social relations and cultural conditions.

Similarly, social constructionists would highlight changes in sports and differences in the way sports are defined, organized, and played from one society and culture to another. As noted in previous chapters, they would explore how changes in sports are connected to power relations in society as a whole, how sports celebrate particular definitions of masculinity and femininity, and how sports may encourage the marginalization of people who do not fit those definitions. Generally, they would be interested in sports as social spheres in which existing social relations are reaffirmed and reproduced or challenged and changed.

In summary, social constructionists emphasize that religions and sports are like any other cultural practices and cultural formations: that is, they come into being and they change as people struggle over how to live with one another and over what their lives mean.

Evaluation of Conceptual Approaches

Each of these conceptual approaches to religions and sports offers food for thought. I use a constructionist approach because it enables me to ask questions about religions and sports that deal directly with people's experiences and social relations. It also alerts me to the different meanings that religions and sports have for different people, meanings that affect how people see the world, themselves, and their connections to other people.

A major weakness of the research on religions and sports is that it focuses almost exclusively on the American experience and on the popular spectator sports played by men and promoted heavily by the media. Therefore, it does not help us understand the connection between sports and religious systems of meaning other than those grounded in Christianity (see the box on pp. 482–483). Those involved in the sociology of sport have much work to do to understand the connection between sports and religions. The rest of this chapter provides an overview of what has been done and what we know.

---

*A sect is a group organized around religious beliefs that differ in emphasis and priorities from dominant cultural beliefs in a community or society. A cult is generally a small, loosely organized group developed around a charismatic leader who promotes religious beliefs that are new, unconventional, and often in conflict with dominant cultural beliefs.

REFLECT ON SPORT

Sports and Religions Around the World

Most of what we know about sports and religion focuses on various forms of Christianity, especially Christian fundamentalism. Little has been written about sports and Buddhism, Confucianism, Hinduism, Islam, Judaism, Shinto, Taoism, or the hundreds of variations of these and other religions. The systems of meaning associated with each of these religions have implications for how people view physical activities, define their bodies, and relate to each other through human movement. However, apart from some African Americans who have combined Islamic beliefs with sport participation, these systems of meaning do not seem to be compatible with participation in formally organized competitive sports in the same way that various forms of Christianity have been made to be compatible.

Unfortunately, my knowledge of these issues is very limited. In fact, I know more about how some North American athletes have converted Zen Buddhist beliefs into strategies for improving golf scores and marathon times than I do about how Buddhism is related to sports and sport participation among the 350 million Buddhists around the world. (I am realizing more and more how my knowledge is grounded in a combination of Eurocentric science and limited personal experiences!) However, I am very interested in the fact that Buddhism and philosophical Hinduism, two systems of religious meaning that emphasize physical and spiritual discipline, do *not* seem to inspire believers with concerns for winning Olympic medals or physically outperforming or dominating other human beings in organized competitive sports. Instead,

In Sendai, Japan, youth baseball games are played on a field with a massive statue of Buddha in the background. Little is known about the ways in which religious beliefs may be connected with sport participation in countries outside of North America, and apart from some forms of Christianity. (Jay Coakley)

SPORTS AND CHRISTIAN ORGANIZATIONS AND BELIEFS

Sports and various Christian religions have had what we might describe as a symbiotic relationship since the middle of the nineteenth century. Despite important differences between the organization and goals of sports and those of religions, these two spheres of life have overlapped and been combined in mutually supportive ways over the past 150 years. People associated with certain religions and religious organizations have used sports as a means of achieving their personal and organizational goals, and people associated with sports have used various forms of

Buddhism and Hinduism seem to focus the attention of believers on transcending the self and all earthly matters. Their emphasis on transcendence does *not* seem to support a believer's interest in becoming an elite athlete. It is only elite athletes from Christian, capitalist countries who want to know how the practices and meditation rituals from these religions can be used to improve sport performances and give meaning to lives that revolve around competitive sports.

I am also interested in how Islam is used by African American and other black athletes around the world. Cassius Clay's conversion to Islam and changing of his name to Muhammad Ali in the 1960s created extensive publicity around the world, and especially in the United States, where many whites did not understand Islam or why some African Americans embraced it. Since then, many black male athletes have converted to Islam, and, in the process, changed their lives in ways that seem to be compatible with participation in sports, even power and performance sports.

We in the sociology of sport would greatly benefit from studies of how people holding various religious beliefs view the body, physical activity, human movement, and organized competitive sports. These studies would help us understand the lives of billions of people who *do not* grow up learning to compete in formally organized physical activities, who *do not* use physical and mental discipline to extend sport skills, who *do not* use competitive physical activities to give religious witness, and who *do not* use religious beliefs and organizations to promote and even glorify sports.

In-depth studies of the everyday experiences of people around the globe also would help us understand how various religions inform gender relations in ways that privilege some people and marginalize others when it comes to sport participation. For example, Muslim and Hindu beliefs have been used to legitimize extreme forms of patriarchy* and definitions of men's and women's bodies that discourage girls and women from sport participation or deny them access altogether. Physical activities among Muslims and Hindus are nearly always sex segregated; men are not allowed to look at women in certain settings, and women must cover their bodies in certain ways even as they exercise. Norms such as these are especially strong among fundamentalists in each religion. This is the reason the national Olympic teams from many Muslim and Hindu countries seldom have had women athletes or women's teams. And this also may be the reason that black female athletes outside of Islamic countries have not embraced Islamic beliefs as black males have.

Studies of religions and sports in diverse cultural settings would increase not only our understanding of other cultures, but also our abilities to reflect on our own experiences, to ask critical questions that would enable us to see more clearly the ways in which the cultural practices of religions and sports are integrated into our own lives.

---

*Patriarchy is a form of gender relations that privileges men over women, especially in regard to legal status and access to political power and economic resources.

religion to achieve their goals. This has occurred frequently enough in recent years to make the combination of sports and Christian organizations and beliefs very popular in some Western countries, especially the United States and Canada.

The growing popularity of these combinations raises interesting questions for the sociology of sport. Why have Christian organizations and beliefs been combined with sports? How have religious organizations used sports, and how have sports used religion and religious beliefs? What are the social consequences of these combinations? These are the topics covered in the remainder of the chapter.

The Protestant Ethic and the Spirit of Sports

In the late nineteenth century, German sociologist/economist Max Weber did a classic study, *The Protestant Ethic and the Spirit of Capitalism*, in which he outlined the connection between the reformist religious ideas of John Calvin and the growth of capitalist economic systems. His conclusion was that Protestant religious beliefs and the growth of capitalism went hand in hand, reinforcing and shaping each other in the process. Weber provided examples of how Protestantism promoted deep moral suspicions about erotic pleasure, physical desire, and all forms of idleness ("idle hands are the devil's workshop"). He also documented a connection between Protestantism and an emphasis on a rationally controlled lifestyle, in which emotions and moods were suppressed in a quest for worldly success and eternal salvation. This orientation involved defining work (that is, people's jobs in the economy) as a "calling" from God, through which a person's spiritual worth could be displayed and expressed.

Shaped over the last 250 years by the application of religious principles to economic and political life, the Protestant ethic traditionally has emphasized rationality, organization, discipline, hard work, success in one's occupational calling, and a willingness to sacrifice and endure pain in the process of honoring that calling. This emphasis has been socially significant because it has encouraged the public expression of spiritual beliefs through physical action, especially *work*.

What does the Protestant ethic have to do with sports? My explanation of the connection goes like this. Automation, the use of technology, and the loss of power among workers in many capitalist countries have so alienated many people from their jobs that work no longer serves as an important means of expressing personal worth or identity. Furthermore, the emphasis on rationality and efficiency that tradi-

tionally has driven the production of goods and services clearly does not fit with the narcissistic emphasis on the self that drives the consumption of goods and services. Organized, competitive sports, however, serve as a "cultural connecting point" for the social forces that drive both production and consumption. Their emphasis on rationality and efficiency *and* their emphasis on a narcissistic approach to the self come together in highly rationalized and work-like efforts to mold individual bodies into efficient performance machines. In other words, these sports serve as sites for merging production and consumption, for combining rationality and a focus on self to determine a person's worth and responsibility. This is the reason fat people, for example, are widely believed to have weak moral character: their bodies do not fit the current cultural image denoting moral worth and responsibility.

This way of defining the body in connection with sports seems to fit with how the body has been defined in Christian belief systems over the past century. Dominant Christian beliefs before the twentieth century emphasized that the body was the root of all evil, that pleasures of the flesh were to be avoided, or enjoyed only if they conformed with God's word. However, organized sports focused acceptable attention on the body, because organized sports could celebrate the body's productive potential, which could be achieved through discipline, sacrifice, denial, and even the endurance of pain. Because organized, competitive sports were about bodily performance rather than bodily pleasure, the athlete's body could be defined as a worthy spiritual tool, as a means of expressing spiritual worth in the very terms emphasized in the Protestant ethic. This may be one reason why competitive sports have been defined by many Christians during the twentieth century as sites for the building of character and the expression of moral worth.

In summary, sports increasingly have been incorporated into Christian organizations and beliefs because they emphasize a rationally controlled lifestyle characterized by discipline, hard work, sacrifice, and the endurance of pain in the pursuit of success. This, of course, fits with how character is defined in connection with the Protestant ethic. When sports are constructed in this way, Christian athletes can even define sport participation as their calling (from God). They can even say that God wants them to be the best they can be in sports. This is the way playing sports comes to be defined as a form of giving witness among some Christian athletes.

How Have Christians and Christian Organizations Used Sports?

TO PROMOTE SPIRITUAL GROWTH Around the middle of the nineteenth century, influential Christian men, described as "muscular Christians" in England and New England, promoted the idea that the physical condition of one's body had religious significance. They believed that the body was the instrument of good works and that meeting the physical demands of godly behavior required good health and physical conditioning. Although most religious people at the time did not agree with this approach, many began to consider the possibility that there might be a connection between the physical and spiritual dimensions of human beings, that there might be important links between body and spirit (Guttmann, 1988).

These new ideas that the body had moral significance and that moral character was associated with physical conditioning encouraged many religious organizations to use sports in their programs. For example, the YMCA and the YWCA grew rapidly between 1880 and 1920; they built athletic facilities in many communities, and they sponsored teams in numerous sports. In fact, Canadian James Naismith invented basketball in 1891 while he was a student at the Springfield, Massachusetts YMCA, and William Morgan invented volleyball in 1895 while he was the physical activities director at a YMCA in Holyoke, Massachusetts.

Sport programs also were sponsored by numerous Protestant churches and congregations, Catholic dioceses and parishes, Mormon wards, the B'nai B'rith, and a few Jewish synagogues.

The connections between sports and religion in general and Christian religious organizations in particular have changed throughout history. Today, for example, most religious schools sponsor sport teams and promote sports as an avenue through which students can express their *faith*. (Stuart Wong, Colorado Springs Gazette)

These organizations sponsored sports and sport programs because their leaders believed that sport participation developed moral character. For example, as World War II was ending, Pope Pius XII gave a worldwide address in which he talked about sports in religious terms:

> Those who accuse the Church of not caring for the body and physical culture . . . are far from the truth. . . . In the final analysis, what is sport if not a form of education for the body? This education is closely related to morality. How then could the Church not care about it? . . . [The words of St. Paul] illuminate the concept of sport with a mystical radiance. But what matters to the Apostle is the superior reality of which sport is the image and the

symbol. . . . [S]port must not be the supreme ideal, the ultimate goal, but must serve and tend towards that goal. If a sporting activity is for you a recreation and stimulus which aids you in better fulfilling your duties of work and study, then it can be said that it is being used in its true sense, and is attaining its true end (in Feeney, 1995).

Other religious leaders of the twentieth century have given similar messages about sports. For example, in 1971 evangelist Billy Graham, an outspoken promoter of sports as a builder of moral character, summarized the spirit in which many religious organizations have made use of sports over the past hundred years:

The Bible says leisure and lying around are morally dangerous for us. Sports keeps us busy; athletes, you notice, don't take drugs. There are probably more committed Christians in sports, both collegiate and professional, than in any other occupation in America.

In light of publicized cases of drug use by many athletes, Graham's statement may sound naive today. But it illustrates the commitment that people associated with Christianity have had for many years to using sports to symbolize and promote moral development—especially among boys and young men. This commitment is as strong today as it ever was.

TO RECRUIT NEW MEMBERS AND PRO-MOTE RELIGIOUS BELIEFS AND ORGANI-ZATIONS At the beginning of the twentieth century, American religious leaders were concerned that men did not participate in their congregations; the vast majority of active church members were girls and women (Rader, 1983). This encouraged many of these leaders to shift their emphasis from what they saw as "feminized" values (meekness, humility, and submissiveness) to a new set of "manly values." Their purpose was to attract young males and shape them into "manly youth." Sport teams and sport programs were used as recruiting tools because sports could be constructed to emphasize what the religious leaders defined as "Christian manliness."

According to historian Benjamin Rader (1983), a manly youth around 1900 was described in this way:

The manly youth . . . practiced sexual continence and resisted the "secret vice" [of masturbation—which was believed to deplete] the body of vital energy and [result] in a host of other dire consequences. . . . The manly youth cultivated self-command and absolute candor; he abhorred display, pretension, sentimentality, and capitulation to pain. He insisted on justice and was quick to defend honor with physical prowess; he was physically active, striving to develop the utmost robustness, animal energy, and personal courage. His spirit found its truest expression in the out-of-doors, in the refreshing vigor of the countryside, and on the athletic field.

This idea that a "manly man is a Godly man" has become popular again in recent years, especially among Christian fundamentalists. Today the incorporation of the image of the tough athlete into the character portrait of the "Christian man" has allowed men to rescue "the Bible from women and overly refined preachers" (Flake, 1992). For example, in 1991 Bill McCartney, the football coach at the University of Colorado at that time, formed a Christian fundamentalist men's movement called *The Promise Keepers*. The goal of the movement is to urge men to assume leadership of today's families and communities. McCartney says that "a Godly man is a manly man," and that society today is in a state of moral decline because men have not used the ultimate, unchanging truth found in the Bible to guide their lives. In 1996, *The Promise Keepers Men's Conferences* attracted over one million men to large sports arenas in twenty-two cities around North America. The success of this religious organization is at least partly due to its association with the image of a "manly man" as embodied in sports, especially sports involving the use of strength and power. According to many of these men, Jesus is "the Master Coach" with answers to all their questions; they have masculinized Christianity by connecting it with sports and using sport metaphors to articulate their religious beliefs.

Church-affiliated colleges and universities in the U.S. also have used sports as an organizational recruiting tool. For example, when Oral Roberts founded his university in Tulsa, Oklahoma in 1965, he emphasized the importance of its sports programs in the following statement:

> Athletics is part of our Christian witness. . . . Nearly every man in America reads the sports pages, and a Christian school cannot ignore these people. . . . Sports are becoming the No. 1 interest of people in America. For us to be relevant, we had to gain the attention of millions of people in a way that they could understand.

Jerry Falwell, the noted television evangelist, initiated the sports program at his Liberty University in the 1970s with a similar statement:

> To me, athletics are a way of making a statement. And I believe you have a better Christian witness to the youth of the world when you competitively, head-to-head, prove yourself their equal on the playing field (cited in Capouya, 1986).

Then in his opening prayer, Falwell declared, "Father, we don't want to be mediocre, we don't want to fail. We want to honor You by winning."

Other colleges and universities have used sports in similar but less overt ways to attract students. Catholic schools—including the University of Notre Dame, Boston College, and Georgetown University—traditionally have used their football and/or basketball programs to build their prestige as church-affiliated institutions. Brigham Young University, affiliated with the Mormons, also has done this. Smaller Christian colleges formed the National Christian Collegiate Athletic Association (NCCAA) in the mid-1960s to sponsor championships and recruit Christian student-athletes to their academic programs (Mathisen, 1990).

In some cases, religious organizations have developed solely around sports in an effort to attract more people to Christian beliefs and to provide support for athletes who already hold Christian beliefs. Examples of what some have called "Sportianity organizations" are the Fellowship of Christian Athletes (FCA), Athletes in Action (AIA), Pro Athletes Outreach (PAO), and a number of smaller groups (see the box on p. 448). These organizations often have a strong evangelical emphasis, and members are usually eager to share their beliefs in the hope that others will embrace Christian fundamentalism as they do.

Other Christian organizations and groups also have used sports as a context for evangelizing. For example, thousands of volunteers were in Barcelona at the 1992 Olympic Games to distribute *Winning for Life*, a 36-page booklet published by the International Bible Society. Over 18,000 booklets were given to athletes and Olympic officials, and an attempt was made to contact each of the 500,000 households in Barcelona. A spokesperson for the Bible Society explained:

> The Olympics serve as an opportunity to piggyback on the respect athletes have and communicate Christianity to those who would not normally be interested (quoted in Rabey, 1992).

For the 1996 Olympic Games, two organizations, Sports Outreach America and RBC Ministries, teamed up to produce a catalog so that churches, organizations and individuals could order materials for creating an "evangelistic ministry through sports." Materials included videos, casettes, CDs, magazines, special books and pamphlets, pins, sport ministry kits, and sport planning and clinic guides. Most of these featured athletes giving witness to the importance of bible-based religious beliefs in their lives. One of the books, *A Path to Victory*, published by the International Bible Society, contained 350 pages of Bible chapters and athlete testimonies. A 32-page book, *More Than Gold*, used Olympic terminology and images to promote religious beliefs. Hundreds of groups and thousands of volunteers used these materials in Atlanta and other places in the U.S. and around

REFLECT ON SPORT

Christian Sport Organizations that Have Sport Ministries*

COORDINATING UMBRELLA ORGANIZATIONS
International Sports Coalition (ISA)
Sports Outreach America

MAJOR ORGANIZATIONS
Athletes in Action (AIA)
Fellowship of Christian Athletes (FCA)
Pro Athletes Outreach (PAO)
Sports Ambassadors

OTHER ORGANIZATIONS
Athletes for Kids
Baseball Chapel
Beyond Victory Ministries
Champions for Christ

Christian Bowhunters Association
Christian Surfers Australia
Cowboys for Christ
Epistle Sport Ministries
Fellowship of Christian Anglers
Golf Fellowship
Hockey Ministries International
Motorsports Ministries
New Life in Sports
Pro Athletes for Christ
Professional Skiers Fellowship
Sports Association for Jesus
Team Jesus–Cycle Crusade
The Tennis Ministry

———
*This is a partial list; there are many dozens of similar organizations in North America.

the world to deliver their messages. Special attempts even were made to bring Christian messages to athletes and spectators from Islamic countries.

Such efforts are not new, but they are increasingly organized and coordinated today. Major sport ministries have been linked together through Sports Outreach America, whose goal is to "create a greater evangelistic ministry through sports." RBC Ministries, another fundamentalist Christian organization, publishes *Sports Spectrum*, a national magazine that uses a biblically informed perspective to report on sports and athletes. Articles in the magazine highlight Christian athletes and their religious testimonies. Most athlete profiles emphasize that life "without a commitment to Christ" is superficial and meaningless, even if one is successful in sports; accepting Christ gives life meaning and enables one to put sports into a "proper" perspective. The forms of Christian witness published in the magazine are clearly designed to promote religious beliefs among readers who look up to the athletes. This method of using elite athletes to "spread the gospel" has become very popular in most of these organizations.

TO PROMOTE CHRISTIAN FUNDAMENTALIST BELIEF SYSTEMS Most of the religious groups and organizations previously mentioned are nondenominational, but they usually promote a specific form of Christianity—one based on a conservative theology and a fundamentalist orientation toward life.

Religious fundamentalism is a complex social phenomenon (Ferrante, 1995). Even though it may not appeal to the majority of people in a particular society or religious group, it can capture the interest and involvement of a wide array of people from different social and economic backgrounds. This is true of both Islamic fundamentalism in Iran and Christian fundamentalism in the United States and Canada. Regardless of their religion, fundamentalists believe there is a need for people to return to what they define as their culture's religious roots, and that this return can occur only if individuals develop personal relationships with the supernatural source of truth (God, Allah, Christ, Mohammed, "the universe," the spirit world, etc.). Fundamentalists see the supernatural realm as the source of absolute, unchanging truths offering answers to personal and social problems. These answers are revealed through sacred writings or the verbal teachings of divinely inspired prophets.

Fundamentalist movements arise when people perceive moral threats or crises that involve what they see as corruption of an entire way of life that was once ideal because it was based on pure religious principles. Therefore, fundamentalists emphasize tradition. They usually desire a return to past ways of doing things, ways shaped by what they believe was a "one-and-only truth." And they often separate themselves from people who refuse to apply that truth to their lives.

It is largely within fundamentalist Christian movements in the United States, Canada, England, and Australia that people recently have been using sports to promote religious beliefs. Although individual athletes apply their Christian beliefs to their sport lives in many different ways, as we will discuss later in this chapter, the beliefs themselves tend to emphasize traditional and conservative values based strictly on a literal reading of the Bible.

How Have Athletes and Coaches Used Religion?

Religious beliefs and rituals are potentially powerful on both the personal and the social levels. People can use them to (1) cope with uncertainty, (2) stay out of trouble, (3) give meaning to sport participation, (4) put sport into perspective, (5) establish team solidarity, and (6) reaffirm the rules of coaches. For these reasons, particular types of religious beliefs have come to be used in many sport contexts. For example, athletes and coaches have used religion as a source of psycho-

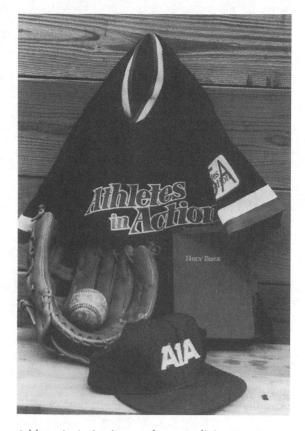

Athletes in Action is one of many religious sport organizations in the U.S. It sponsors teams that travel around the world so that athletes can serve as disciples spreading their religious beliefs. According to the AIA organizational philosophy, sports serve as an effective platform for delivering their message to others. (Jay Coakley)

logical support as they have coped with the challenge and uncertainty of competition in sports and as they have searched for meanings connected with their sport participation and with life in general. Religion also has served to produce team unity and provide a basis for social control among athletes and on teams. Each of these possibilities needs further explanation.

TO COPE WITH UNCERTAINTY Through history, people have used rituals based in religion, magic, and/or superstitions to cope with uncertainties in their lives. Because sport competition involves a high degree of uncertainty, it is not surprising that many athletes use rituals, some based in religion, to make them feel as if they have some control over what happens to them on the playing field. For example, Willye White, a former gold medalist in the women's long jump, explained her use of religion in the Olympics in this way:

> I was nervous, so I read the New Testament. I read the verse about have no fear, and I felt relaxed. Then I jumped farther than I ever jumped before in my life (quoted in *Life*, 1984).

Other athletes also have noted that religion has a calming effect on them as they face uncertainties in sports. NBA player Hakeem Olajuwon engages in a regular Islamic prayer ritual, and says, "My religion gives me direction, inner strength. I feel more comfortable. You can take life head on" (*USA Today*, 10 June, 1994).

Of course, not all religious athletes use their beliefs in this manner, but there is a tendency for many to call on their religion to help them successfully face challenges and uncertainty. This is the reason some athletes who pray before or during games seldom pray before or during practices, and the reason few athletes make the sign of the cross during batting practice or when they practice shooting free throws: it is the actual competition that produces the uncertainty that evokes the prayer or religious ritual.

Sometimes it is difficult to separate the use of religion from the use of magic and superstitions among athletes. Magic consists of recipe-like rituals designed to produce immediate and practical results in the material world. Superstitions consist of regularized, ritualistic actions performed to give a person or group a sense of control and predictability in the face of challenges. So when athletes pray that they might win games, avoid injuries, get a hit, make a free throw, or score a goal, it is difficult to say whether they are using religion or magic and superstition. But regardless of the basis of a ritual, its primary goal is to control uncertainty.

A good summary of the use of rituals of all types in sports is given in the box on p. 491.

TO STAY OUT OF TROUBLE Reggie White, an ordained minister and a defensive lineman in the NFL (he's called the "minister of defense"), explains how religion has kept him out of trouble with the following statement:

> Studying God's Word helped keep my life on track, even though there were bad influences like drugs and crime all around me. To continue to be the man God wants me to be, I have to stay in his word (IBSa, 1996).

Other athletes make similar statements with references to the need to avoid participating in the risky lifestyles common in the social worlds that develop around certain sports. Religious beliefs separate them from those lifestyles and keep them focused and in training. Religious beliefs also may influence them to become involved in church-related and community-based service programs—all of which keep them out of trouble.

TO GIVE SPECIAL MEANING TO SPORT PARTICIPATION Sport participation emphasizes personal achievement and self-promotion; it involves playing games that do not produce any essential goods or services in themselves, even though important social occasions may be created around sport events. In many ways, sport participation is a self-focused, self-indulgent activity; although training often involves personal sacrifices and pain, it is totally focused on the athlete's development and display of physical skills in meets, matches, and games. Realizing this can create a crisis of meaning for athletes who have dedicated their lives to sports. Ironically, this crisis of meaning is sometimes experienced by those who make millions of dollars and are looked up to by millions of people.

How do these athletes give meaning to this focus on self, to what they do as they train and play games, to their icon status as athletes? How do they justify the expenditure of so much time and energy on sports? How do they explain why their families have been disrupted or why so many family resources have been spent on their

REFLECT ON SPORT

Why Rituals Are Widely Used in Sports

According to anthropologist Mari Womack (1992), human beings frequently use rituals when they face uncertainty and challenges in sport competitions. The rituals, grounded in religion, magic, or superstitions, help them feel as if they have some control over what happens in the competitions.

After examining the use of rituals in sports, Womack concluded that athletes, coaches, spectators (and maybe even umpires and referees) turn to rituals for the following reasons:*

1. Ritual helps the player focus his (or her) attention on the task at hand. It can be used by the player to prevent anxiety or excessive environmental stimuli—such as the chanting of fans—from interrupting his (or her) concentration.
2. Ritual can signal intent to the other team. Specifically, ritual can be used to "threaten" the other team.
3. Ritual provides a means of coping with a high-risk, high-stress situation.
4. Ritual helps establish a rank order among team members and promotes intragroup communication.

5. Ritual helps in dealing with ambiguity in interpersonal relationships, with other team members, and with people on the periphery of the team, such as management and the public.
6. Ritual is a "harmless" means of self-expression. It can be used to reinforce a sense of individual worth under pressure for group conformity, without endangering the unity of the group.
7. Ritual directs individual motivations and needs toward achieving group goals.

The uncertainty in highly competitive sports is so great that many athletes use rituals. In fact, this practice has become so widespread that it has been described by journalists and noted by many spectators.

---

*From "Why athletes need ritual: a study of magic among professional athletes" by M. Womack. In *Sport and Religion* (p. 200) by S. J. Hoffman (ed.), 1992. Champaign, IL: Human Kinetics. Copyright 1992 by Shirl J. Hoffman. Reprinted by permission.

....

sport participation? How do they deal with the need to outperform and even dominate others if they want to continue playing or move to higher levels of competition? How do they rationalize their tendencies to overconform to the sport ethic to the point of jeopardizing the health and well-being of themselves and others?

One way people can justify, deal with, and explain all these things is to define sport participation and achievements in sports as acts of worship, avenues for giving witness, or manifestations of God's overall plan for their lives (Hoffman, 1992). This enables athletes to "sanctify" their commitment to sport. Through their religious beliefs, sport participation is converted into an activity done "for the glory of God," to bring God's word to others, or to follow God's

will. This, of course, gives sport participation ultimate meaning. In fact, it even makes it part of a person's spiritual destiny. At the same time, it keeps athletes motivated. As volleyball player Kim Oden says,

> Learning what Jesus knowingly went through for me gave me a lot of self-confidence. It also gave me a lot more reason to do what I do (IBSa, 1996).

An increasing number of athletes today have turned to religion for this reason: to give special meaning to their sport participation (Stevenson, 1997). For example, NFL player Glyn Milburn says that he keeps Jesus on his mind so much during games that "for me, it's almost a form of worship when I'm on the field" (in Briggs, 1994). NBA player David Robinson says that playing sports for him is "a great opportunity to model Christ in front of a lot of people by the way I play and the way I conduct myself" (in Bentz, 1996). Olympic swimmer Josh Davis, who won four gold medals in the 1995 World University Games, explains that swimming is part of God's plan for him:

> I've been given a gift to swim fast, and I think God expects me to use that gift to the best of my ability to reach my potential. . . . What Christ did on the cross supplies me with an everlasting motivation (in Robbins, 1996).

Many Christian athletes and coaches also refer to Colossians 3:23 in the Bible:

> Whatever you do, work at it with all your heart, but for the Lord, not for man (in Lee, 1996).

Of course, when athletes are following the advice in this Bible verse, playing sports is elevated for them from the realm of the profane to the realm of the sacred. In the process, it takes on what the athletes believe to be ultimate meaning. Their doubts about the worthiness of what they do as athletes disappear, and they come to view sport participation as integral to their spiritual life, as a vocation with ultimate meaning.

TO PUT SPORT IN PERSPECTIVE Related to the issue of meaning is the need for some athletes to feel that they will not be "swallowed up" by sports, or become overwhelmed by the drama, challenges, and regular failures that occur in sports. Some athletes feel that religious beliefs are vehicles for transcending their lives in sports. For example, Elana Meyer, an Olympic silver medalist in the 1992 10,000-meter run, explains this use of religion:

> Running is a way God can use me for His glory. Athletics is not my life. . . . Every competition is a challenge for me, but I don't make a separation between Elana the runner and Elana the Christian. God's love for me is unconditional—it doesn't depend on my winning a gold medal (IBSb, 1996).

With beliefs such as this, sport becomes a part of a divine plan in athletes' minds, and this makes it easier for them to face challenges and deal with the inevitable losses experienced in sports.

TO CREATE COHESION Religious beliefs and rituals can be powerful tools in creating strong bonds of attachment between people. When religious beliefs and rituals are combined with sport participation, they can link athletes together in ways that transcend the everyday lives of teammates. This, of course, can build team cohesion and team morale. This possibility has been noted by some coaches who have used their own Christian beliefs as rallying points for their teams. Because of their desire to promote their Christian beliefs and create a collective focus for team members, they bring religion into sports. For example, George Allen, a widely respected American former football coach, once said that he supported religious worship and team prayers among his athletes because they "foster togetherness and mutual respect like nothing I have found in 21 years of coaching" (cited in Hoffman, 1982).

Objections to this practice, especially when it involves the use of pregame prayers in public schools, has led some U.S. students and their parents to file lawsuits to ban religious expression in connection with sport events. But coaches and athletes continue to insist that prayers bring team members together in positive ways. Despite lawsuits, many people in the U.S. agree that "it's good for sporting events at public high schools to begin with a public prayer" (*USA Today*, 4 February 1988). However, these people usually assume that the prayer will *not* be a Jewish, Catholic, Islamic, Hindu, Baha'i, or Buddhist prayer. Their support is based on the assumption that the public prayer will support their own Christian beliefs about the sacred and supernatural. An Islamic prayer might not create the unity they desire.

TO MAINTAIN SOCIAL CONTROL Religion also can be used to sanctify norms and rules by connecting them with the sacred and supernatural. Similarly, it can be used to connect the moral worth of athletes with the quality of their play and their conformity to team rules and the commands of coaches. For example, Wes Neal, president of the Institute for Athletic Perfection, a Christian sport organization, explains that performance in sport is a means of revealing an athlete's love for God (Neal, 1981). This means that performances in sports are somehow connected to the moral worth of athletes. This connection encourages athletes not only to become committed to improvement and excellence, but also to become willing followers of their coaches and trainers.

In his *Handbook of Athletic Perfection*, Neal explains that the "complete Christian athlete" has a will "bound to the command of his coach." In discussing his own success in sports, Neal reveals that he always wants his actions "to be the instant and complete response" to his coach's desire for him. He believes that "by being obedient to my coach, I [am] also being obedient to God." He explains, "You may not agree with [your coach] on every point, but your role [as a Christian athlete] is to carry out his assignments. The attitude you have as you carry out each assignment will determine if you are a winner in God's sight" (1981: 193). This combination of religion and sport is very powerful: when the rules and assignments of coaches are tied to the religious beliefs of athletes, the athletes are much more likely to obey them without question. In this way, religion can be used by coaches, either intentionally or unintentionally, as a means of controlling the behavior of athletes.

Neal also explains that a Christian athlete's goal is to achieve what he calls a "Total Release Performance (T-R-P)." This goal can be achieved only when athletes accept the sacrifice and pain involved in training, give a total effort at all times, and dedicate their sport lives to Jesus Christ. This may sound like a worthy set of goals to Christians, but pursuit of them makes athletes easily controllable by coaches. According to Neal, this is desirable. In fact, he says that when an athlete becomes a true bond-servant of Christ, his "will is bound to the command of his coach, [so] if his coach yells

'jump!' the [true Christian athlete] doesn't waste time asking 'why?' He puts everything into the jump *immediately!*"(Neal, 1981: 194).

From a sociological perspective, it is not difficult to see why some coaches would see such an orientation as valuable and why they might encourage athletes to focus on "Total Release Performance." This connection between religion and social control is important, because many coaches are very concerned with issues of authority and control on their teams. They see obedience among players as necessary for team success; and religious beliefs can promote obedience. And if athletes also are using religious beliefs to stay out of trouble, coaches are even more pleased.

People may debate the merits of the religion-sport connection, but it is becoming increasingly prevalent in many societies, especially in the U.S. (Blum, 1996). For example, a U.S. journalist recently made the following observation:

> Christianity is sweeping the locker rooms of big-time professional and college teams. . . . [M]ore and more players are turning to God for direction, inspiration and the will to win. Never before, it seems, has the tie between religion and big-time sports been tighter (Briggs, 1994).

But as this occurs, it is necessary to outline the challenges faced when athletes and organizations combine sports and religious beliefs. This brings us to the next section.

THE CHALLENGES OF COMBINING SPORTS AND RELIGIOUS BELIEFS

Organized competitive sports and religions are cultural practices with different histories, traditions, and goals; they have been socially constructed in different ways, around different issues, and through different types of relationships. This means that combining religious beliefs with sport participation may require some adjustments in what a person believes or in the way the person plays sports.

Although a growing number of black athletes around the world, especially African Americans, have combined their Islamic beliefs with their sport lives, this section will focus specifically on the challenges faced by Christian athletes.

Challenges for Christian Athletes

According to Shirl Hoffman, editor of the book *Sport and Religion* (1992), Christian religious beliefs don't automatically fit with sport participation, because Christianity is based on an ethic emphasizing the importance of means over ends, process over product, quality over quantity, and caring for others over caring for self (pp. 122–23). Today's sports, however, especially those based on a power and performance model, tend to emphasize a contradictory ethic focused on winning, final scores, season records, personal performance statistics, and self-display.

This potential lack of fit between traditional Christian religious beliefs and the *dominant form* of sports in most societies today also involves these discrepancies:

- While Christianity emphasizes peace and turning the other cheek, sports emphasize the use of intimidation and other forms of aggression.
- While Christianity emphasizes that the body is to be treated with respect because it is made in the image of God, sports often encourage athletes to build their bodies into performance machines and to subject them willingly to the possibility of injury.
- While Christianity emphasizes a dedication to service and helping others in a spirit of humility, sports requires a focus on training the self and achieving personal success that is recognized and rewarded by others (unless personal success is recognized in sports, a person will be cut from the team, eliminated from competition, or demoted to a lower level of competition).

Do these differences present a challenge to Christian athletes? If so, how do athletes deal with it? For example, do Christian athletes raise questions about how their behaviors in highly competitive power and performance sports can be spiritual offerings and acts of worship? Does a Christian boxer have any doubts about using his performance in the ring as a spiritual offering, even though his goal is to punch another human being into senseless submission? Do Christian football players see any problems associated with using intimidation and "taking out" opponents with potentially injurious "hits"? Can athletes turn these actions into Christian acts simply by saying they are motivated by Christian love? Does this help heal the concussions and broken bones of those injured by the "loving hits"? What about Christian pitchers who throw high and inside as part of their pitching strategy? Does a strategy that deliberately risks hitting a batter's head with a ball thrown at 100 mph qualify as an act of worship? Is it part of God's plan for Christian base runners to slide into second base with spikes aimed at the opposing infielders in attempts to break up double plays? Do Christian athletes ask such questions, and, if so, how do they answer them?

Research suggests that Christian athletes combine their religious beliefs with sport participation in many different ways. For example, a study by Kelley et al. (1990) found that professed Christian students at small liberal arts colleges don't seem to view sports and sport participation any differently than other students do. Christian student-athletes who valued religion as a useful tool for achieving secular goals tended to emphasize the importance of winning in sports, whereas those who valued religion for its own sake tended to emphasize personal goals and the enjoyment of competition in sports. But overall, Christian athletes raised no serious questions about the "fit" between their religious beliefs and their behavior in sports. But these were athletes in small colleges, where there was little encouragement to emphasize a power and performance orientation in sports.

Research on elite athletes associated with the Christian organization Athletes in Action (AIA) indicated slightly different patterns (Stevenson,

1991a, b). Some of the athletes at this level avoided issues by compartmentalizing their religious beliefs and their sport participation. They simply ignored the possibility that there might be conflicts between these two dimensions of their lives. In other words, they raised no questions, and they had no problems playing sports like everyone else. Other elite athletes were aware of potential conflicts between their religious beliefs and what they were expected to do as athletes, but they avoided them by playing with what they called the "right attitude." This generally meant that they played by the rules and then used religion to deal with emotional or personal problems. While they played, they raised no questions about what they did on the playing field. Finally, a small number of Christian athletes clearly recognized a lack of "fit" between their religious beliefs and some of the things expected of them in sports. After considering different ways to deal with this, they gave priority to their religious beliefs and either altered their behavior in sports or dropped out of elite sports to do other things more consistent with their beliefs.

Anecdotal data often highlight Christian athletes who say that their religious beliefs actually make them more intense, if not more aggressive, on the playing field. For example, Danny Scheaffer, a major-league baseball player, says that his religious beliefs have made him more intense but not less aggressive during practices and games. He proudly notes,

> I'll be the first person to knock a Christian shortstop into left field on a play at second. I've been hit before by Christian pitchers. I've charged Christian pitchers [who have thrown pitches at me] (in Briggs, 1994).

Another Christian baseball player indicated that he expresses his Christian manliness to opposing pitchers by walking up to bat and looking "the pitcher right in the eye to let him know a Christian can still have aggression" (in Capouya, 1986). Rick Saul, a former NFL player, told his Christian opponents that when they faced each other on the field, he would hit them "with all the love I have in me" (in Hoffman, 1982).

When NFL player Reggie White was asked about the toughness of Christians on the football field, he responded with this statement:

> It's really an insult when people accuse Christians of being weak. If you think Christians are weak, put on some pads and line up across from me. We'll see (in Lee, 1996).

Boxer Evander Holyfield claimed in 1996 that it was God who actually beat Mike Tyson in an eleven-round fight in Las Vegas, and that he would fight Tyson again if it were God's will (*USA Today*, 11 November 1996).

Other statements from Christian athletes and stories about their lives (as described in Christian publications) suggest that some of them try to bring their religious beliefs and sport participation together by becoming especially dedicated to the ascetic aspects of sport. In other words, they emphasize discipline, self-denial, and avoiding bodily pleasures. This approach is used to enhance the moral worth of their own lives and of the sports they play; it also serves to focus their attention on sports and away from the reckless or indulgent lifestyles that sometimes exist among groups of male athletes.

Another way that Christian athletes assign moral significance to sports is by using them as platforms from which to evangelize and "spread the word" of their religious beliefs. This strategy is becoming increasingly widespread in the U.S., where Christian athletes publicly display their beliefs and use their visibility to witness to others (Stevenson, 1997). In fact, most Christian athletes feel they are obligated to do this. In their minds, this makes sport worthwhile as a spiritual offering, regardless of what happens on the playing field (short of breaking rules).

Finally, stories about Christian athletes are full of references to their working with children, being devoted spouses and parents, and being involved with service projects sponsored by community or church organizations. The point of

There are three aspects of power and performance sports that raise questions about whether certain forms of sport participation can be used as a spiritual offering or act of worship. Questions exist because sport often involves the following:

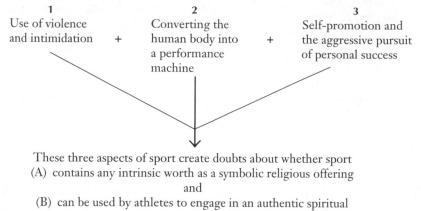

| 1 | | 2 | | 3 |
| Use of violence and intimidation | + | Converting the human body into a performance machine | + | Self-promotion and the aggressive pursuit of personal success |

These three aspects of sport create doubts about whether sport
(A) contains any intrinsic worth as a symbolic religious offering
and
(B) can be used by athletes to engage in an authentic spiritual encounter with the divine

These doubts can be eased or eliminated in three ways:

RESOLUTION A

Focus on the ascetic aspects of sports—the discipline, self-denial, and rejection of bodily pleasures. This often involves defining sacrifice and pain as the basis of self-worth and emphasizing the equivalent of a "Total Release Performance"

RESOLUTION B

Play sports as in the past, and do one or more of the following:

1. Ignore moral questions about what is done on the playing field and strive to be the best in the same ways that other athletes do.

2. Assign moral significance to traditional sport participation by using it as a platform to evangelize and give witness.

3. Focus on good works and service off the field.

RESOLUTION C

Give priority to religious beliefs and change sport behaviors, or seek out pleasure and participation sports, or withdraw from sports altogether.

FIGURE 15-1 Christian religious beliefs and sports participation: a model of conflict, doubt, and resolution (adapted from ideas in Hoffmann, 1992).

these stories is often to emphasize the many ways that highly visible athletes combine their commitment to sports with forms of good works and service off the field. Such stories not only are inspirational to many readers, but also may defuse doubts those readers might have about combining Christian religious beliefs with sports participation (see resolution B, no. 3 in fig. 15-1, p. 496).

Challenges for Christian Sport Organizations

One might think that on an organizational level, the combination of Christianity and sports would make people aware of issues and problems in sports, especially power and performance sports, and inspire them to call for reforms. However, this has not happened. Instead of calling for changes in sports, Christian sport organizations have focused on using sports to recruit new members and promote fundamentalist religious beliefs. They give primary emphasis to building faith, not changing sports. Consequently, they have not tried to identify problems or initiate reforms in how sports are defined, organized, and played.

According to Shirl Hoffman, this seems surprising, given the content of Christian beliefs. He says,

> The extent to which people are willing to overlook the moral crisis in sports to have a vehicle of mass evangelism is astounding. As soon as you apply the tenets of the [Christian] message to the medium [of sports, you would expect these organizations] to become staunch critics of sport (in Blum, 1996).

But this has not happened.

The policy position in many Christian sport organizations is that sports will be reformed only *after* all those associated with them accept Christ into their lives. Therefore, the racism, sexism, deviance, violence, recruiting violations, exploitation, and other problems that now exist will not disappear until all athletes, coaches, and spectators have developed a personal faith in Christ. When journalist Frank Deford (1993) did a special story on sports and Christianity a few years ago, he noted this acceptance of the status quo:

> No one in the movement—much less in any organization—speaks out against dirty play, no one attacks the evils of recruiting, racism or any of the many other well-known excesses and abuses. Sport owns Sunday now, and religion is content to lease a few minutes before the big games.

Deford's comments are strong, but they describe what has been a major policy thrust of most Christian organizations with sport ministries. This position is not very popular among those interested in immediate social reforms. We must acknowledge that some individuals in these Christian organizations *have* recognized the need for changes in sports, and are aware of the ways religious beliefs sometimes have been used to divert attention from dealing with problems. But the official policies in the organizations themselves, especially organizations in North America, seldom reflect the concerns of those calling for reforms in sports.

Today, Deford's conclusion would have to be qualified, because there seems to be a growing concern in some of these groups of the need for various forms of community service; although the service is not based on any critical analysis of how the world works, it is based partially on a commitment to performing good works for other human beings.

Adapting Religious Beliefs to Fit with Sports

History shows that both religions and sports undergo changes as people's values and interests change, and as power is gained or lost by various groups in communities and societies. In light of this, it is interesting that when Christian religious beliefs are combined with sports and sport participation, the cultural practices of sports change very little. Instead, it seems that religious beliefs and rituals are called into the service of sports or modified to fit how dominant sports are defined, organized, and played.

When religious beliefs are combined with participation in power and performance sports, some people try to construct religious images and beliefs to fit their ideas about sports. This image of a muscular Christ on a T-shirt, found in a Christian gift shop, clearly shows how some athletes conceptualize their religion. In fact, images of deities in any culture or subcultural group generally reflect idealized concepts of dominant values within that culture or group. (Jay Coakley)

This point has been made by Robert Higgs, author of *God in the Stadium: Sports and Religion in America* (1995). Higgs claims that the combination of sports and Christian beliefs has led religion to become "muscularized." A muscularized religion, he explains, emphasizes a gospel of discipline, duty, and self-righteousness, rather than a gospel of stewardship, social responsibility, and humility. Muscularized religion gives priority to the image of the knight and the sword over the image of the shepherd and the staff (Higgs, 1995: 306–33). This, of course, fits with the power and performance model in today's sports.

As Higgs points out, it seems that Christian religious beliefs have been used more often to transform winning, obedience to coaches, and commitment to improving sport skills into moral virtues than to call attention to problems in the social worlds created around sports. In other words, the use of Christian beliefs and rituals has reaffirmed and intensified current dominant characteristics of sports, sport experiences, and sport organizations in North America.

SUMMARY

IS IT A PROMISING COMBINATION?

Religion, unlike other social institutions, is focused on a connection with the sacred and supernatural. This makes the systems of meaning associated with religion a unique part of cultural life. Because these systems of meaning affect how believers think about the world, themselves, and their connections to others, religions can have a powerful effect on social life in groups, communities, and society as a whole. This makes religion an important phenomenon for sociologists to study.

Discussions about sports and religions often have focused on how these two spheres of cultural life are similar or different. Certainly they are socially similar, because they both create strong collective emotions and celebrate selected group values through rituals and public events. Furthermore, both have heroes, legends, special buildings for communal gatherings, and institutionalized organizational structures. On the other hand, those who assume that both sport and religion have unique fundamental essences fixed in nature argue that the inherent differences between these spheres of life are more important than any similarities. Most sociologists, however, recognize that sports and religions consist of socially constructed sets of cultural practices and meanings that sometimes overlap and sometimes differ, depending on social relations among fans and believers within communities and society as a whole. Therefore, sociologists see the beliefs and rituals of sports and religions as subject to change, as people struggle over how to live with one another and over what their lives mean.

Unfortunately, we in the sociology of sport know little about the relationship between sports and major world religions other than particular forms of Christianity. It seems that certain dimensions of Christian beliefs and meanings can be constructed in ways that fit well with the beliefs and meanings underlying participation and success in organized competitive sports. In fact, it may be that organized competitive sports offer a combination of experiences and meanings that are uniquely compatible with the rationality and asceticism that form at least part of what has been described as the Protestant Ethic.

Sports and certain forms of religion have been combined for a number of reasons. Some Christians have promoted sports because they believe that sport participation naturally fosters spiritual growth, along with the development of strong character. Christian groups and organizations have used sports to promote their belief systems and attract new members, especially young males who want to view themselves as possessing "manly virtues." Athletes, because of their visibility and popularity in society, often have been seen by religious groups as effective spokespersons for their messages.

People in sports, especially athletes and coaches, have used religious beliefs and rituals to cope with the uncertainty of competition, to sanctify athletic involvement and achievement, to foster cohesion on teams, and to reaffirm a commitment to norms in sports and the authority and control of coaches. The individuals and groups most likely to incorporate sports into their religious lives usually profess some form of Christian fundamentalism.

Although the differences between traditional Christian beliefs and the ethos of dominant sport forms would seem to create problems for Christian athletes and sport organizations, this has not occurred to any degree. In fact, data suggest that religion has been used to reaffirm and intensify orientations that lead to success in competitive sports. Neither Christian athletes nor Christian organizations have paid much attention to what might be identified as moral and ethical problems in sports. Instead, they have focused their resources on spreading beliefs—usually fundamentalist beliefs—in connection with sport events and sport involvement. Their emphasis has been on playing hard for the glory of God; using athletic performances as indicators of moral worth and as tools for giving Christian witness; uniting teammates into cohesive organizational units; and being obedient to the rules and recommendations of coaches.

In conclusion, the combination of sports and religious beliefs offers little promise for changing dominant forms of sport. In fact, in some cases, it may actually obscure an awareness of the need for reforms and social transformation. Of course, individual athletes may alter their sport-related behaviors when they combine sport and religion in their own lives, but at this time such changes have had no observable effect on what occurs in most sports.

SUGGESTED READINGS

British Journal of Sports History. 1984. Sport and religion. Special issue. Vol. 1(2) (*five papers on the historical dimensions of the combination of sports and religions; special reference to British experiences*).

Harvey, J. 1988. Sport and the Quebec clergy, 1930–1960. In J. Harvey and H. Cantelon, eds. *Not just a game: Essays in Canadian sport sociology.* Ottawa, Ontario: University of Ottawa Press (*an excellent critical analysis of how the Roman Catholic clergy in Quebec recognized the significance of sports in popular culture and used it as a tool in the French-Canadian resistance to the spread of Anglo-Saxon culture and Protestant religious beliefs*).

Higgs, R. J. 1995. *God in the stadium: Sports and religion in America.* Lexington, KY: The University of Kentucky Press (*a thoughtful historical analysis of the connections between sports and religions as cultural formations in the United States*).

Hoffman, S. J. 1992. *Sport and religion.* Champaign, IL: Human Kinetics (*this is the best available collection of work done on religions and sports in the United States. Twenty-five papers are organized into four sets devoted to sport as religion; sport as religious experience; religion in sport; and sport, religion, and ethics. Hoffman's introductions to the four sets of papers are very informative and thought provoking*).

Mathisen, J. 1990. Reviving "muscular Christianity": Gil Dodds and the institutionalization of sport evangelism. *Sociological Focus* 23(3):233–49 (*this article clearly outlines the historical roots of contemporary sport evangelism; it also shows how the meaning of "muscular Christianity" has changed from the use of sports as a tool for promoting religious beliefs to the use of religion to sanctify sports*).

Neal, W. 1981. *Handbook of athletic perfection.* Milford, MI: Mott Media (*written by director of the Institute for Athletic Perfection, a religious/sport organization; describes recommended applications of Christianity in sport*).

Stevenson, C. 1991. The Christian-athlete: an interactionist-developmental analysis. *Sociology of Sport Journal* 8(4):362–79 (*one of the few studies that looks at the way religion is combined with sport participation among athletes who profess Christian beliefs*).

(Jason Lee, Mountain Board Sports)

Sports in the Future
What can we expect?

Overall, athletes are loved by everybody until their consciousness is raised and they start to speak out on social issues.

Charles McNair, former student-athlete (1993)

Sports in the future? I think they'll be like Mountain Dew commercials. Hey, they already are—look at the "X Games"!

Sociology of sport student (1996)

By learning how to package sports we created a major American industry. But with the application of these new technologies . . . there will be no limits to what we can do [to provide fans with services and experiences].

Jerry Colangelo, owner, NBA Phoenix Suns (1995)

It is genetic engineering . . . that promises to bring about the most profound biological transformations of the human being, and it is likely that this technology will be used to develop athletes. . . .

John Hoberman, author of *Mortal Engines* (1992)

My Puritan soul burned with indignation at injustice in the sphere of sport. . . . Cricket had plunged me into politics long before I was aware of it. When I did turn to politics I did not have much to learn.

C. L. R. James, writer/activist from Trinidad, in *Beyond a Boundary* (1963)

501

Discussions of the future are often full of exaggerations. Predicting that tomorrow will bring dramatic changes is always more exciting than predicting that tomorrow will look much like today. Therefore people tend to describe the future in science-fiction terms and emphasize extreme hopes and fears. These types of predictions are fun. They spark our interest and sometimes leave us temporarily awestruck. But in most cases, they are neither accurate nor realistic accounts of what is likely to happen.

For better or worse, the future seldom unfolds as rapidly or dramatically as some forecasters would have us believe. Instead, changes usually are tied to a combination of existing social conditions and the efforts of people to shape those conditions to fit their visions of what life should be like. Of course, some people have more power and resources to promote their visions, and those people seldom want revolutionary changes, because their privileged positions depend on their keeping things under control and pretty much the same. This tends to slow the rate of deep structural change in societies, although it may speed up changes in technology and the availability of consumer products.

As you read this chapter, it is important to remember two things: (1) sports are contested activities (see the box on this topic in chap. 1), and (2) the future is not determined by fate, computer forecasts, supernatural forces, or sociologists. This means that the future of sports will not just unfold according to predictions in a sociology of sport book. Much more important than a sociologist's predictions are the visions people have for the future and the choices they make in connection with sports in their lives. Sports will take many forms in the future, and each form will be produced through the collective actions of human beings. Therefore, the primary goal of this chapter is to describe and evaluate different models of sports that people might use as they envision the future and make choices in their own lives.

MAJOR SPORT FORMS IN THE FUTURE

The major theme running through this book is that sports are social constructions: parts of culture invented and played by people as they interact with one another and shape social life to fit their ideas of what it should be. Therefore, dominant sports in any culture tend to reflect the interests and ideas of those who have power in that culture, and they usually celebrate the values and experiences of powerful people. However, dominant sports are not always accepted by everyone in a group or society. In fact, it is possible for people to modify dominant sports or develop alternative forms that challenge current systems of power relations and promote the interests and ideas of people who lack power and resources.

History shows that dominant sports in many societies traditionally have been grounded in the values and experiences of men concerned with military conquest, political control, and economic expansion. As I noted in previous chapters and explained in chapter 4, these sports are based on what I described as a **power and performance model.**

Although many people have used the power and performance model as the "standard" for determining what sports are about, not everyone has accepted it. In fact, some people have maintained or developed other sports grounded in values and experiences related to their connections with one another and their desire to express those connections through playful and enjoyable physical activities. As I noted in chapter 4, these sports are based on what we described as a **pleasure and participation model.**

These two models do *not* encompass all the different ways that sports might be defined and played. However, they are consistent with two important sets of values in many postindustrial societies, and for that reason, we can use them as a starting point for thinking about what sports might be like in the future.

Power and Performance Sports

As far as I can tell, power and performance sports will continue to be the most visible and publicized

My descriptions of power and performance sports and pleasure and participation sports are intended as starting points for an examination of sports in our everyday experiences. Many sport experiences include elements from both these types. Ultimate (frisbee) is a good example of this. (Bob Byrne, Ultimate Players Association)

sport forms in the near future. These sports, based on the "sport ethic" (as Bob Hughes and I described it in chap. 6), emphasize the use of strength, speed, and power to push human limits and aggressively dominate opponents in the quest of victories and championships.

Although power and performance sports take many forms, they usually are based on the idea that excellence is proved through competitive success and achieved through intense dedication and hard work, combined with making sacrifices and risking one's personal well-being. They also encourage people to stress the importance of setting records, to push human lim-

its, to use the body as a machine, and to view technology as a performance aid. According to many athletes in power and performance sports, the body is to be trained, controlled, and constantly monitored so that it will respond to the challenges and demands of sports efficiently and forcefully; sports are defined as battles in which the opposition is to be intimidated, punished, and defeated.

Power and performance sports also tend to be exclusive. Participants are selected for their physical skills and abilities to dominate others; those who lack these skills and abilities are cut or put in "developmental" programs. Organizations and teams in power and performance sports feature hierarchical authority structures in which athletes are subordinate to coaches and coaches are subordinate to owners or administrators. In coach-athlete relationships, it is generally accepted that coaches can humiliate, shame, and derogate athletes to push them to be the best they can be. Athletes are expected to respond to humiliation by being tougher competitors willing to give even more of themselves in their quest for excellence.

The sponsorship of power and performance sports generally is motivated by the idea that it is important to be associated with activities that stress efficiency, organization, competition, hard work, and the endurance of pain for the sake of progress (Hoberman, 1994); being associated with teams and athletes popularly identified as "winners" is also important. Sponsors can use these associations to promote products while establishing favorable public relations profiles at the same time. Sponsors assume that winners are special and that their association with winning teams and athletes makes them special as well, in the eyes of consumers and in the lives of people throughout a culture. Of course, as long as the rewards of sponsorship go to those who are successful in power and performance sports, these sports will continue to thrive, and the athletes who play them will continue to be cultural celebrities who are paid to endorse the values of the sponsors.

Pleasure and Participation Sports

Even as power and performance sports have become increasingly visible forms of popular culture, many people have continued to realize two important things: (1) that there are many different ways to do sports, and (2) that dominant sport forms in society are not always consistent with their personal values and experiences. In the past, this dual realization has given rise to sport forms that differ from the dominant forms seen on television and written about in the sports sections of newspapers. This will continue to occur in the future.

A trend that will continue to grow in the future is the creation of alternative sports emphasizing a combination of *pleasure and participation*. These sports will involve physical activities in which participants are committed to a combination of challenge, freedom, and personal connections—connections between persons, between mind and body, and between physical activity and the environment.

Although pleasure and participation sports take many forms, they generally emphasize an ethic of personal expression, enjoyment, growth, good health, and mutual concern and support for teammates and opponents. They involve a focus on empowerment rather than domination, and on the notion that the body is to be experienced and enjoyed rather than trained and used as a tool. People who play pleasure and participation sports tend to see their bodies as gardens that must be cultivated to continue growing, rather than as machines to be used as tools and then repaired when they have broken.

Pleasure and participation sports generally are characterized by inclusiveness. Playing, not winning, is the most important thing. Differences in physical skills among participants are accommodated informally, or formally through the use of handicap systems, so that players can enjoy competition *with* each other even when they have unequal skills. Sport organizations and sport teams based on this model have democratic decision-making structures characterized by cooperation, the sharing of power, and give-and-take relationships between coaches and athletes. Humiliation, shame, and derogation are inconsistent with the spirit underlying these sports.

The sponsorship of pleasure and participation sports generally is grounded in the idea that it is socially useful to promote widespread participation in a wide range of physical activities and sports, and that overall participation, health, and enjoyment are more important than the achievement of performance excellence. Unfortunately, many people and corporations with power and money are more interested in sponsoring sports that emphasize power and performance than in sponsoring sports that emphasize pleasure and participation. But not everyone thinks that way, so there will continue to be support for the latter type of sports in the future. Sponsorship will grow as increasing numbers of people choose to include pleasure and participation sports in their lives.

FUTURE TRENDS IN SPORTS

The Growth of Power and Performance Sports

Power and performance sports will continue to be the most visible and publicized sport forms in the foreseeable future. This does not mean that everyone will automatically accept these sports without question, or that alternative sports won't become increasingly popular. But vested interests in these sports are very strong, and those who benefit from them have considerable power and influence. For example, the popularity of power and performance sports is tied to dominant forms of gender relations. When attention is focused on the pushing of physical limits, men often will be the center of that attention, especially when limits are related to strength, power, and speed. Women may outperform men in ultraendurance events and a few other sports in the future, but efforts to push human limits will usually celebrate not only the differences between men and women but the superiority of men over women. This in itself will preserve the dominance of sports based on the power and performance model for many years to come; but it will also give rise to questions about the place of these sports in many societies.

Power and performance sports will remain dominant for another reason: they attract corporate sponsors. American football, the classic embodiment of these sports, continues to attract billions of dollars in television rights fees and other revenues, and games are televised in an increasing number of countries around the world. In the U.S., the NFL proudly markets its games under the slogan "Feel the Power." Athletes in the NFL and in other power and performance sports are portrayed in the media as heroic figures and exemplars of values supportive of corporate interests in productivity, efficiency, and dedication to performance despite pain and injury. Spectators are encouraged to identify with these athletes and their teams, and to express their identification through the consumption of licensed merchandise and other products. As long as people continue to identify with teams and athletes in power and performance sports, and as long as that identification can be used to stimulate production and consumption in market economies, these sports will continue to receive the sponsorships and media coverage they need to maintain their dominant position in the future.

Because power and performance sports often involve the pushing of human limits, they are especially alluring to many people. Attempts to break barriers or do what no one else has done before can be seductive. Sports emphasizing these things are relatively easy to market and sell. Throughout this century, we have seen the development of what some people have called "technosports," that is, forms of power and performance sports in which technology and human beings are combined to push limits and dominate opponents (Johnson, 1974). Widespread fascination with technosports is clearly illustrated through examples such as the following:

- parents willing to have synthetic human Growth Hormone given to their children in the hope of "creating" world-class athletes (Hoberman, 1992)
- athletes constantly searching for technological aids to help them become bigger, stronger, and faster

- people of all ages seeking sports equipment made with new, lightweight, strong materials such as kevlar, titanium, and carbon fibre, so that they can develop new challenges and experiences

After examining how athletes and sport scientists have used technology in connection with sports based on the power and performance model, social scientist John Hoberman predicted that we might see some form of genetic engineering in the sports of the twenty-first century. He noted that the Human Genome Project already has developed information that could in the future guide "gene grafting techniques that would permit the crossing of men and beasts" and other efforts that would lead to the creation of genetically engineered "designer athletes" (Hoberman, 1992).

In addition to genetic engineering, there also may be attempts to push human limits by regulating human brains. For example, a noted German sport physician told fellow sport scientists in the late 1980s, "Every adaptation to training occurs in the brain, in the nervous system." He went on to declare, "It is [in the brain], through the hormonal regulation of the body, that we must do our regulating" to boost athletic performance (cited in Hoberman, 1992: 285).

Although these changes will raise many bioethical issues, they will be accepted by many people who use power and performance sports to form their standards for judging what sports should be in the future. For example, many young people today have grown up with rapidly changing mediated images that blur the boundaries between human and nonhuman. And the notion of bionic parts long has been a dream of people who needed artificial organs or who could benefit from the use of synthetic bones, tendons, and ligaments. Therefore, it won't be shocking when superstrong synthetic ligaments, bones, and joints are used to repair bodies injured in power and performance sports. It may not even be shocking when mechanical body parts are used to replace injured limbs and to improve performance in sports. According to

Technology often is used to push limits and create new experiences. Do some forms of technology enable human beings to push their limits too far? On what basis can we answer such a question? (Jay Coakley)

Hoberman (1994), those who watch athletes in power and performance sports will increasingly accept the injuries and the abuse of athletes' bodies as the medical and physical costs of pushing limits.

However, this acceptance will not come without resistance. Questions *will* be raised about the use of technology in sports. Dominant sports will not simply be the result of what is technologically possible. In their extreme forms, technosports eliminate the "human" element in contests and games—the errors, the oversights, the mistakes, the letdowns—in order to perfect athletic performances and achieve competitive success. These sport forms are based on the idea that humans reach their potential only when they become machinelike. This approach to sports ultimately subverts creativity, freedom, spontaneity, and expression among athletes, and it turns sports into programmed spectacles involving dramatically presented physical actions.

Both athletes and spectators will have problems with this set of possibilities. Some athletes will resist becoming pawns in such activities, and some spectators will not watch them regularly, because it will be difficult to identify with robotlike athletes playing games lacking human spontaneity and expression. Unless athletes *feel pressure*, *emotionally respond* to victory and defeat, *make mistakes*, *work hard* for success, and *have their good and bad days*, spectators may have trouble identifying with them. If this happens, dominant sports will lose much of their commercial value. Because the success of power and performance sports depends on fan identification with athletes, that success may be jeopardized if technology is used to make athletes too unlike the spectators who pay to watch them.

There are also questions of fairness associated with the use of technology in power and performance sports. When the cost of technology is so high that only wealthy individuals, corporations, or countries can use it to their benefit, people will come to question the meaning of athletic success. Will new definitions of success emerge? And who will benefit from these definitions? These and many other questions will beg for answers as new forms of technology enter the realm of power and performance sports.

The Growth of Pleasure and Participation Sports

The future certainly will bring a diversity of sport forms, and many of these forms will embody at least some characteristics from the pleasure and participation model. Reasons for this include growing concerns about health and fitness, participation preferences among older people, new values and experiences brought to sports by women, and groups seeking alternative sports. We discuss each of these reasons in more detail in the following sections.

GROWING CONCERNS ABOUT HEALTH AND FITNESS As health-care policies and programs around the world increasingly emphasize the prevention of illness and injury, people will become more sensitive to health and fitness issues. In North America, for example, health-care programs may give a higher priority in the future to patients' staying well as a strategy for cutting costs and maximizing their profits. In connection with this, people may be encouraged to avoid participation in certain power and performance sports and to increase their participation in pleasure and participation sports for which health benefits are much higher. Health and fitness concerns also will be promoted through changes in physical education curricula. Physical educators will continue to move away from teaching students to play power and performance sports, and toward teaching them a range of alternative sports involving lifetime skills, noncompetitive challenges, inclusive participation philosophies, respect and support for other participants, and concerns for health—all characteristics of pleasure and participation sports.

If people begin to see that healthy exercise can promote personal, family, and community interests, they will have built-in incentives for individual and group involvement in a wide array of pleasure and participation sports in the future.

PARTICIPATION PREFERENCES AMONG OLDER PEOPLE As the median age of the population in many societies gets older, as people live longer, and as older people represent an increasingly larger segment of the world's population, there will be a growing interest in sports that do not involve intimidation, the use of physical force, domination of opponents, and the risk of serious injuries. As people age, they are less likely to risk their physical well-being to establish a reputation in sports. Older people are more likely to see sports as social activities, and more interested in making sports inclusive rather than exclusive. Older people also realize that they have but one body, and it can be enjoyed only if it is cultivated as though it were a garden, rather than driven as if it were a machine. I figured this out at around forty years old!

Older people generally are not attracted to power and performance sports. Instead, they prefer noncompetitive physical activities and altered versions of competitive activities. So the future will see more "senior" sport leagues in which rules are changed to emphasize the pleasure of movement, connections between people, and the challenge of controlled competition. But there also will be an increased emphasis on walking, hiking, weight lifting, and other activities that will be taken seriously but done in settings in which the focus is on health, fitness, and social connections, rather than on setting records or using the body to dominate opponents.

The rising popularity of golf is indicative of general trends we will see in the twenty-first century. Golf involves healthy exercise, it's nonviolent, it doesn't involve "punishing" the opposition, and it has a handicap system so that people with different skills can play as equals in competitive events. An important feature is that men and women, and parents and children, can play golf together. Although golf has traditions of exclusiveness and is too expensive for many people to play, older people will develop similar but less expensive pleasure and participation sports as they seek healthy physical activities with aerobic and anaerobic benefits.

Pleasure and participation sports also could be sites for the challenging of dominant ideas about aging. In the past, aging has been seen as a process involving increasing dependency and incapacity, but the achievements of older athletes support the notion that getting old doesn't automatically mean becoming weak and incapacitated.

NEW VALUES AND EXPERIENCES BROUGHT TO SPORTS BY WOMEN As women continue to gain more power and resources, some of them will seek more assertively to develop sports based on their full or partial rejection of the ideology underlying power and performance sports. Although many women will seek equity in these sports without raising questions, others will try to change sports to correspond with ideologies more consistent with pleasure and participation sports. The "feminist softball" described in chapter 2 provides a good illustration of how sports might be transformed by women interested in playing a sport, but not interested in playing it the way most men do (Birrell and Richter, 1994).

Today there are a growing number of situations in which women have transformed both the rules and the spirit of a sport to moderate the emphasis on power and performance and increase the emphasis on pleasure and participation (Fasting, 1996; Hargreaves, 1994; Theberge, 1996; Zipter, 1988). Even when women play sports such as rugby, soccer, and hockey, there are indications that they often emphasize inclusiveness and support for teammates and opponents in explicit ways that are seldom present in the men's versions of these sports. The "in your face" power and performance orientation is replaced by an orientation that is less confrontive and more expressive of the joy of participation.

Women sometimes encounter difficulties when trying to enlist sponsors for sports that differ from men's power and performance sports; because they don't emphasize physical domination, the women's versions of the sports often are seen as second rate or not serious enough to attract the attention sponsors seek. But as women are choosing such sports in greater numbers, sponsors are beginning to respond. As they continue to do so, various versions of pleasure and participation sports will receive increased support.

GROUPS SEEKING ALTERNATIVE SPORTS Groups of sport participants who reject some or all of the ideology underlying power and performance sports also will fuel the formation of alternative sports. For example, high school students will continue to form their own sport groups and play games on their own, rather than put up with the constraints of playing on varsity teams where coaches often try to control their lives, and where the emphasis on competition and win-loss records is given priority over enjoyment and the experience of participation. Whether more students will look outside the school for alternatives to dominant sports largely depends on how schools organize their sport programs in the future.

Unique sport subcultures often have developed around alternative sports. For example, sport sociologist Becky Beal (1995) studied skateboarders in Colorado and found that many of them resisted attempts to turn their sport into a commercialized, competitive form. Even when the Colorado Skateboard Association sponsored contests, Beal found that many skaters deliberately tried to subvert the formality and the power and performance dimensions of the event. Nonregistered skaters crashed the event; registered skaters pinned competition numbers on their shirts so that they were upside down or difficult to read; they focused on expressing themselves rather than outdoing opponents; and they didn't follow the prearranged patterns for warming up and competing. When they were disqualified, their mass protest stopped the event.

There are segments of many sport subcultures that resist attempts to dilute the pleasure and participation emphasis in their activities. They don't want competition and the domination of opponents to replace expression and support of fellow participants. For example, when a twelve-year-old snowboarder was asked in 1996 what he thought about the possibility of adding his sport to the Olympics, he said, "Don't kill the ride, dude. Let us be free." Even at age twelve, he knew that the ideology of power and performance would subvert the elements of pleasure and participation in his sport.

Disabled and physically challenged people have sought to develop alternative sports as well as to adapt dominant sports to fit their needs and physical characteristics. Although some programs for athletes with disabilities clearly have emphasized power and performance sports, others have emphasized a range of sport forms in which pleasure and participation are central. Concern and support for teammates and opponents, as well as inclusiveness related to physical abilities, characterizes these sports.

Young people who resist the organization and adult control found in many organized sports seek physical challenges through activities they invent for themselves. Mountain boarding is one of those alternative sports. (Jason Lee, Mountain Board Sports)

In the future, people with disabilities will not only participate in sports in greater numbers but also affect how sports are played and what new sports are developed. Creatively designed equipment now permits new forms of sports involvement for both the able-bodied and the disabled, as shown in this photo of trail riders. (Rob Schoenbaum)

The Gay Games also represent an example of an alternative sport form emphasizing participation, support, inclusiveness, and the enjoyment of physical movement (Messner, 1992; Pronger, 1990). The 1992 games held in Vancouver, Canada involved over 7,000 athletes from 27 countries, and the 1994 games in New York City drew nearly 10,000 athletes from 35 countries. Although the Gay Games resemble dominant sports in some ways, they explicitly challenge the notions of heterosexual masculinity and femininity and the homophobia that underlie those sports. Gay and lesbian athletes will continue to form sport groups and teams to provide enjoy-

able experiences in their social lives. One lesbian explains:

> I use sports . . . to meet people—I rarely go to bars for that purpose. . . . Team sports are the main social outlets in my life. I depend on them for emotional support, physical activity, a sense of belonging, a comfortable atmosphere, and an outlet for my competitive nature (quoted in Zipter, 1988: 82).

Similar feelings were expressed by a gay man in Brian Pronger's study of sports and homosexuality:

> The nice thing about playing gay sports is . . . to interact with gay people in other than a bar environment. And it's also really nice to do sports . . . [where you] don't have to be on guard. You can joke around, you can play. That's a good feeling. It's also the sense of community that comes from it. . . . It's not that I didn't fit in [when I played

REFLECT ON SPORT   What Will Happen If More People Play Sports?

Most research shows that less than 20 percent of the population in the United States accounts for over 80 percent of the sports participation. Even the fitness boom that began in the 1970s has not involved 60 percent of adult Americans. So what would happen if the 60 to 80 percent of "inactive" adults in the country began to participate regularly in physical activities and sports? Would this lead to changes in the way sports are organized and defined by most people? Would pleasure and participation sports become more popular than power and performance sports in society as a whole? These questions are difficult to answer, but we can get an idea of what increased sports participation might bring by extending current trends into the future. Here's a step-by-step description of what we might expect:

1. Higher participation rates will increase demands on existing spaces and facilities where people do sports. And it is likely that demands will be especially high on specialized physical settings that are expensive to construct and maintain. In many communities, the participants in tennis, racquetball, bowling, softball, soccer, golf, volleyball, ice and roller hockey, and many other sport activities are already very aware of the shortage of spaces and facilities.

2. When existing spaces and facilities cannot handle increased demands for usage, conflict among groups of participants is very likely. Overt conflict already has occurred on softball and soccer/football fields, in gyms, and on tennis courts. Walkers, joggers, runners, bicyclists, and skaters (using skateboards, in-line skates, or four-wheel skates) in many cities have debated and fought over who should have priority access to precious sidewalk and street space; and young skateboarders have been banned from many public spaces and forced to use private facilities—an expensive alternative to sidewalks. Additional conflicts between surfers and swimmers, waterskiers and fishing enthusiasts, jet skiers and everybody else, snowmobile drivers and cross-

country skiers have created management crises in both urban and wilderness areas in North America. Future conflicts are most likely to occur in large cities, where the scarcity of spaces and facilities required for sport involvement is highest.

3. When scarcity leads to conflicts, most people call for more spaces and facilities, along with closer regulation of existing spaces and facilities. The continuing financial crises in most cities and communities will prevent new construction and may even interfere with the maintenance of existing spaces. In fact, as far back as the 1970s, parks and recreation officials in Los Angeles were instructed to "stop encouraging certain sports because competition for playing space between organized and unorganized factions [had] reached a point that [was] . . . sometimes too violent" (Stingley, 1972). This policy was extreme, but it illustrates that scarcity and conflict have led for some time to more comprehensive and tighter systems of administrative control over existing spaces and facilities. This pattern continues today.

4. When the use of spaces and facilities is regulated by public or private organizations, participation generally requires some combination of planned schedules, permits, memberships, user fees, reservations, and political influence. In meeting demands from different user groups, officials usually will give priority to *organized* groups of participants, especially those representing traditionally popular, highly structured programs. Beyond favoring individuals and teams in organized programs, officials also will tend to give highest access priority to the most skilled groups of users, to top-level athletes and teams, and to programs sponsoring power and performance sports. For example, interscholastic teams, especially those playing sports that attract spectators, will continue to receive priority in the use of school facilities. The best teams in community leagues will get priority use of public fields and gyms through

Increased participation in certain sports often leads to conflicts over who should have access to certain spaces and facilities. Conflicts often are resolved when official organizations regulate access. However, when this happens, priority usually is given to those with the most organized and elite programs, or those with the most money. If more children become involved in sports today, will we see more conflict over access issues tomorrow? What will be the consequences of such conflicts? (Karl Gehring, *The Denver Post*)

invitations to participate in preseason, midseason, and postseason tournaments, as well as in playoffs and championship games. All-star teams and other elite sport groups will be given priority for their practices so that they can be "respectable representatives" of their sponsors. Finally, there will be a tendency for officials to give high access priority to people with money for membership dues and user fees, especially in the private sector, where the expenses associated with certain forms of participation are and will continue to be extremely high.

The primary outcome of this four-stage process is that athletes and teams playing different versions of power and performance sports will continue to receive
Continued

priority. Since these sports are grounded in the values and experiences of men, sport participation will continue to celebrate traditional definitions of masculinity. A related outcome is that dominant sport forms will continue to emphasize competition, rationalization, bureaucratization, specialization, quantification, and record setting. In connection with these sport forms, girls and women will continue to be defined as "naturally" inferior because they are not as big, strong, and fast as men. Of course, many will oppose such definitions, but changing them and eliminating their impact on sports and sport organizations will not be easy.

Another outcome will be an intensification of the connection between money and sport participation. User fees associated with public spaces and the dependence on private clubs and facilities to play certain sports guarantee that class relations will remain central in the social organization of North American sports (Donnelly and Harvey, 1996). Low-income people will continue to be underrepresented in most sports, even if more people participate in sports.

In summary, more people may participate in sports at the turn of the century, but they will be playing, watching, and defining their experiences in much the same way people do today. An emphasis on pleasure and participation sports may grow in the future, but finding the spaces and facilities for playing many forms of these sports will not be easy, nor will it be cheap.

Of course, you should *not* take this set of comments as an infallible prediction of what will happen in connection with increased sport participation. Those interested in other types of outcomes will need to intervene in the process I have outlined. The challenge is finding strategies for accommodating sport participation increases without reproducing elitist sport forms. These strategies will vary from one community to another, and their effectiveness will vary with the creativity and political sensitivities of the people who put them into action.

· ·

volleyball at work, but it] is probably more relaxed in gay sports (Pronger, 1990: 238).

In summary, we will continue to see various alternatives to dominant sports in the future. They frequently will embody at least some of the characteristics associated with pleasure and participation sports. One of the challenges we will face in the future is how to maintain alternative sports as sport participation rates increase. We discuss this challenge in the box on pp. 510–512.

SPECIFIC FORECASTS

Professional Sports

In the future, professional sports will become increasingly global in a number of ways. Leagues will have more teams and more athletes from different countries; and more games will be tele-vised around the world. Sport organizations from wealthier nations will push for international expansion. The political implications of this expansion will be significant, because a North American model of professional and commercial sports will be taken all over the world and presented as the "right" way to organize, play, and sponsor sports. Soccer, basketball, and volleyball will be the most widely played team sports; baseball and hockey will grow in popularity, and football will attract spectator attention, but little on-the-field participation in countries outside North America. The number of pro teams and leagues will expand, and many will fail, especially in connection with those sports that are not already established in a society.

New stadiums for professional teams will be built as "sport malls," where the focus will be on shopping, eating, and drinking, as well as watching games. Pro teams will organize events as total entertainment experiences for spectators. For example, Ericcson Stadium, home of the NFL's Carolina Panthers, offers 416 separate shopping, eating, and drinking areas; it will be one of the models for future stadiums and arenas. The goal of team owners will be to induce spectators to spend as many of their entertainment dollars as possible inside the stadium.

If the academic requirements for participation in intercollegiate sports continue to increase, new professional "junior" or "rookie" leagues in basketball and football will be established in the U.S. These leagues will attract young athletes who are more interested in being professional athletes than in being college graduates. These leagues will have age limits (under twenty-one or under twenty-four) and athletes will earn salaries much lower than those of their NBA and NFL counterparts. As this happens, more communities will make bids for league franchises, and more voters will be asked to pass bond issues and tax increases to fund the building of arenas and stadiums. As new teams come into mid-sized cities, attendance at local high school games will be jeopardized, and revenues for high school sports and some college sports will decline. In addition, the talent pool for revenue-producing intercollegiate sports will decrease; this will jeopardize gate receipts and television rights contracts.

Professional athletes will gain more autonomy and power in the future, but they will not use their power to make any major changes in the structure of commercial sports or in society as a whole; their primary goal will be to increase control over their careers and guarantee their own financial security.

Intercollegiate Sports

Intercollegiate sports in the U.S. will continue to exist, despite all the investigations, exposes, and doomsday predictions. Gender equity will remain the central issue in many intercollegiate programs, and recent court decisions will put new pressures on athletic departments to achieve equity in terms of participation opportunities and resource allocation. The gender equity issue will cause discussions about the place of football in intercollegiate programs. However, most big-time football programs will continue to exist.

In the face of budget crises, colleges and universities will continue to cut the number of varsity sports they offer. Intercollegiate programs will become increasingly polarized in terms of size and emphasis. Those programs with revenue-producing teams will maintain a big-time emphasis; other programs will abandon the hope of becoming big-time and maintain fewer teams at lower levels of competition. Student-organized club teams will replace varsity teams in certain so-called minor sports. There also will be a continuation of efforts to make intercollegiate sport programs academically accountable. In some cases, athletic programs will be evaluated in connection with academic accreditation processes.

The NCAA will change its rules so that college athletes in revenue-producing sports can legally be paid money in addition to their athletic grants. However, student-athletes will continue to lack autonomy and power. This will lead to the development of advocacy groups, and some student-athletes will try to organize teammates to protest unfair or coercive tactics used by coaches. The success of these groups and organizational efforts will be mixed.

High School Sports

Playoffs, league championships, and state titles will continue to be important in high school sports, although funding shortages will force many schools to question the necessity of elitist sports programs in the schools. While these questions are being raised, some American high school teams will strive to be included in new national ranking systems, and cable television stations will begin to cover high-profile high school games in certain sports.

These developments will continue to encourage high schools to maintain sport programs along the lines of big-time college programs, if they can afford to do so. Standout athletes in elementary schools will be recruited heavily by high schools seeking national reputations; private high schools will recruit most heavily, because their student bodies are not restricted by geographic boundaries, as are those in public school systems. Private schools will use the reputations of their sport teams to market their academic programs and increase tuition revenues. This trend will lead to national tournaments and national championships in certain high school sports. High school game schedules will take the players all over the country.

Along with this trend toward sports elitism in some high schools, an increasing number of schools will continue to experience serious financial problems that will force them to cut back or eliminate varsity sports. As this happens, some schools and coaches will seek corporate sponsors for programs and teams, or will develop new alliances with local agencies and groups to maintain certain programs. Even if outside funding and support is acquired, some high schools will cut most of their varsity sports. The sports least likely to be cut will be boys' football and basketball, and girls' basketball and volleyball. Outside of these sports, high school students increasingly will play in programs sponsored by community clubs. In the varsity sports that continue to exist, the participation of girls will be encouraged, but their programs and teams will be modeled after boys' programs and teams. One of the major functions of varsity programs for both boys and girls will continue to be the development of players who have superior abilities, so that they can be "fed into" programs at higher levels of competition.

Youth Sports

Organized youth sports will become increasingly privatized in most American communities. Publicly funded programs will be cut back or eliminated, and parks and recreation departments increasingly will become brokers of public spaces

and facilities. Youth programs in middle-income and wealthy communities will be organized and funded through participation fees, and children in these communities will be encouraged by parents to join teams.

Coaching education programs, such as those that have been flourishing in Canada through the National Coaching Certification Program, will become more popular, because of an effort to certify youth coaches as experts. This change will occur to satisfy parents' demands for more professional approaches to youth sports and to minimize legal liability. Youth programs will emphasize "sports development" rather than recreation, and parents will become increasingly concerned about how their children's participation may pay off in the future—in scholarships and in social acceptance. In response to the structured character of youth programs, many young people will seek out alternative sports such as skateboarding, as well as various informal games in which they can make up their own rules and develop skills without being under the control of adults.

Spectators and Spectator Sports

In the immediate future, *spectator sports* will continue to be popular, despite some shifts in interest. For example, an increasing number of people may watch soccer and hockey in the future, while fewer may watch basketball and football—but people still will devote considerable time to watching sports. The media will encourage this trend with increased sport programming. At the same time, there will be more attempts to sell pay-per-view broadcasts of sport events.

Some spectators will form ad hoc organizations to represent their interests when it comes to setting prices for tickets and concessions, controlling the location of team franchises, and guaranteeing fan safety at events. Ad hoc spectator organizations will not become very influential because they will not attract many younger fans, who are more likely than older fans to accept commercialized sports, expensive ticket prices, and high salaries for athletes.

Spectator betting on sports will become more common, and across North America, states and provinces will continue to legalize sport gambling. Lotteries, which already have been used extensively in Canada to fund sport activities, will be used increasingly in some U.S. states to pay for sports and sport teams in their cities or schools.

Organization and Rationalization

At elite levels of competitive sports, athletes and teams will continue to enlist specialists to help them improve their performances. Therapists and sport psychologists, fitness advisers and drug advisers, aerobics instructors, nutritionists, cooks, biomechanists, and exercise physiologists will make up an expanding corps of "sports advisors" expected to help athletes hit their performance peaks when they compete in important events.

An expanding emphasis on the "constructive" use of leisure time will lead to an increasing number of highly organized leisure and sports programs. People will associate participation in the activities sponsored through these programs with achieving rationally chosen "participation goals" and with the consumption of clothing and equipment that will facilitate the achievement of these goals. There will continue to be many "sport experts" to whom eager new sport participants can go for lessons on how to play "correctly." Wealthier people will join athletic clubs in increasing numbers. Their social lives and friendships will be more heavily connected with their patterns of participation in sport activities; their children will learn how to swim, bowl, kick soccer balls, hit backhands, ski, sail, and do a variety of other things under trained sport tutors, who will also teach them that having fun depends on doing physical activities and playing sports the "right" way, by the "right" rules, with the "right" equipment, wearing the "right" clothes and shoes.

Like sport fans and athletes of today, people in the early twenty-first century will be interested in scores and records. They will continue to value rationality, hard work, the pursuit of excellence, and the achievement of goals through well-planned efforts and specialized skills. Corporate sponsors will promote these themes in connection with the coverage of sports. Sport participation will continue to be linked to character building, although its connection with nationalism will decline in importance.

Commercialism and Consumerism

As we enter the next century, sports will continue to be grounded in commercial interests and sponsored as a form of entertainment to generate profits or promote economic expansion. The ideology and organization of sports will continue to reflect the distribution of resources in society. The people with economic and political power will have the most influence on decisions about who will watch and participate in sports, and under what circumstances they will do so. As they have in the past, these people will play a major role in shaping the way sports are presented to and defined by the masses of people in their societies.

We will see large entertainment companies enter sports as team owners. Companies like Disney will buy teams in each of the major professional sport leagues and tie them to the rest of their entertainment enterprises. The images of athletes and teams will then be seen in everything from cartoons to films to toys, and they will be marketed in new forms all around the world.

If voters turn down proposals to publicly fund new stadiums, large corporations will build the stadiums themselves and turn them into monuments celebrating their corporate logos and products. A $300 million investment in a stadium is certainly not out of the question for a multi-billion-dollar corporation seeking legitimacy and acceptance in the culture.

Sports equipment manufacturers will continue to sell the idea that involvement in sports requires warm-up suits, numerous combinations of attire for different sports, the best equipment money can buy, and a spare set of everything in case of an emergency. Sports will offer wealthier people, a

The immediate future certainly will involve increased corporate control of sports. While Nike attempts to "swoosh-ize" sports, Reebok will use sports and a few athletes to try to claim the planet! This is just an ad slogan, but do advertising slogans ever tell us something about the culture in which we live? (Kimberly Gunn)

context in which they can announce their identities through appearance and visual display as much as through their physical abilities.

Finally, we will see sport science discourse increasingly incorporated into the marketing programs of large corporations. This tactic already has been used to sell everything from athletic shoes to candy products. In its first marketing programs in the late 1970s and early 1980s, Nike used scientific jargon, diagrams of foot physiology, and the endorsements of scientific experts to establish the legitimacy of its new running shoes. MARS, Incorporated now has a similar marketing strategy to sell its candy products; its ads use scientific discourse to make clever claims about how MARS products contribute to athletic performance and overall nutrition. Other corporations will follow these leads, and sport science will join sports as a marketing tool for corporations.

Technology and Media

Television will play a central role in the ways sports are imagined, created, and played in many societies around the world. People may not mimic what they see on television, but they will use the images from televised sports as a standard against which they will measure other physical activities. Those who control the world's media will have a great influence on discourse about sports and what they should be in the future.

Digital TV, the Internet, and video games all will be means through which sports enter people's lives. Interactive television technology also will be introduced on a limited basis. Fans with access to this technology will have opportunities to connect with players and coaches in new ways. Improved video games will enable people of all ages to create and coach their own simulated video teams made up of the players they select.

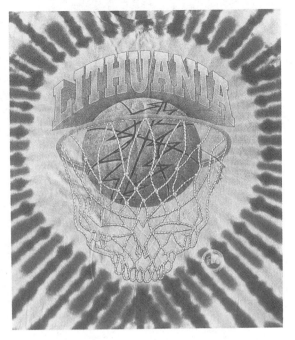 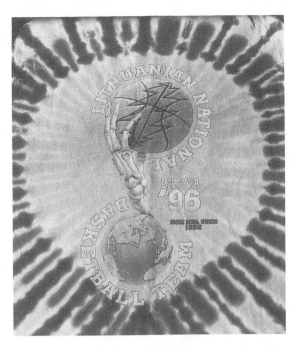

Both conservative and reformist approaches to change are shown in the images on this shirt. It was used to raise money to allow the Lithuanian men's basketball team to participate in international competitions. It was used also to call attention to political problems in Lithuania itself. (Jay Coakley)

SUMMARY

THE CHALLENGE OF MAKING THE FUTURE

For those interested in changes, the predictions in this chapter serve as a challenge: *changes will occur only if the people who want them actually make them.* We are not locked into what is written in this chapter, or any other set of predictions. It is possible for sports and the meanings of sport experiences to be altered on both the individual and societal levels. It is also possible to create new goals for sport involvement and new organizations to promote those goals, so that sports become more democratic and more compatible with a wider range of values and experiences.

The growing importance of sports in contemporary society will lead more people to take a closer and more critical look at how sports have been defined, organized, and played. As this occurs, some of these people will call for changes in dominant forms of sports, or reject those forms and call for the development of alternative sports. But we should not expect this process to lead to widespread, revolutionary changes in sports. The process of social transformation is always tedious and difficult; it requires long-term efforts and carefully planned strategies. Transformation does not occur overnight, and it does not occur without an organized effort.

Three Approaches to Change

Change means different things to different people. Efforts to make change generally fall into three categories: *conservative, reformist,* and *radical.*

A *conservative approach* is based on the assumption that changes in sports, like changes in the

REFLECT ON SPORT

Athletes as Change Agents:
Does It Ever Happen?

Athletes are among the most visible and popular people in many cultures today. Some athletes have the highest name and face recognition of any human beings in history. Such recognition puts them in good positions to act as change agents in society—or does it?

To explore this issue, we must understand that the visibility and popularity of athletes is tied to the public display of physical skills and media-generated images out of which their public personas are formed. Athletes control their sport skills, but the formation of their public personas is largely under the control of others, including team publicity departments, people in the media, agents, and corporate advertising executives who create and use the athletes' images and personas to promote and sell products and to hype sport events. This limits the extent to which athletes can be change agents, because if their words and actions don't fit with the interests of those who control their celebrated personas, they may lose the coverage and support they need to remain popular.

Most athletes are wary of becoming associated with any form of social change. Their acting as change agents instead of celebrities might jeopardize their popularity or alienate the powerful people who own sport teams and sponsor events. For example, when baseball player Eric Davis of the Los Angeles Dodgers was asked why he did not talk about racial problems and the need for changes in baseball, he explained in this way:

I'm a free agent at the end of the year. [If I go] around the country talking about racial slurs. . . . it looks like I'm a problem. No owner or management in their right mind is going to give a player an opportunity to play when they think he's a problem (in *USA Today*, 19 April 1993: 11C).

Davis knew that his celebrity status and his baseball contract depended on those with power in sports. If he raised issues that made them uncomfortable, his future in the game would be in jeopardy. This is even true for college student-athletes. For example, a recent graduate from the University of North Carolina at Chapel Hill explained why he avoided efforts to bring about social change while he played intercollegiate sports at UNC:

Overall, athletes are loved by everybody until their consciousness is raised and they start to speak out on social issues (quoted in Hayes, 1993).

When athletes *do* engage in efforts to make change, they usually take a conservative approach. In other words, they do things that reaffirm dominant societal values and strengthen the status quo. Therefore, successful professional athletes may form foundations to help disadvantaged children learn to read, but they are not likely to form organizations that work to reform or radically alter unfair methods of allocating the resources needed to teach reading in the schools. Athletes may make public service announcements supportive of charitable organizations, but they are not likely to identify poverty as a social issue and then call for changes related to employment, public

rest of society, should consist of raising more money, developing more effective marketing strategies, and generally strengthening traditional values, definitions, experiences, and organizational structures. Conservatives believe that people solve problems best by strengthening what already exists, rather than by making changes in social relations or social structures.

A *reformist approach* focuses primarily on eliminating problems and making sports more so-

cially useful and responsive. Reformists are concerned with issues such as discrimination against women and minorities, violence, the exploitation of athletes, cheating, unfair business practices, the use of drugs, extreme nationalism, and excessive concerns with winning and making money. In other words, they focus their attention on such issues as equity, safety, fairness, and the expansion of sports programs so that more people will have opportunities to play and enjoy sports.

transportation, and the availability of child care. Even when athletes enter politics, they generally represent conservative political positions aligned with preserving the status quo in society (at least, this has been the case in the U.S.).

Athletes identified as role models are usually those who strengthen the status quo. As spokespersons they generally represent those who have an interest in keeping things as they are or selling products to make profits. Nonconformist NBA player Dennis Rodman is very skeptical of his fellow athletes who take conservative approaches to change. He says,

> This role model business is mostly hypocritical bullshit. . . . When you make it you've got to go out there and do public service and make donations and start foundations. A lot of that stuff doesn't mean shit, though. Guys are setting up these nonprofit foundations or making appearances at soup kitchens because somebody's telling them it's good for their image and they might be able to make some money off it someday (1996).

Rodman's statement is extreme, but it calls attention to the fact that most athletes, even when they are sincerely involved in civic projects, take a conservative approach to change. For example, they donate money to charitable organizations and make public appearances to tell children to stay in school and stay off drugs. These actions are helpful in many communities, but they don't *reform* or *radically change* the community processes and structures that intensify poverty, despair, and other problems among some groups of people. Starting a foundation to help children from low-income neighborhoods is helpful, but it does not necessarily call attention to the need for reforms or radical changes in the social system that is failing the children from those neighborhoods.

When athletes become involved in reformist approaches to change, they usually do so in connection with established social organizations designed to promote reform. For example, the Center for the Study of Sport in Society (CSSS) at Northeastern University in Boston is a reformist organization that has developed programs through which current and former athletes work to control gender and ethnic discrimination, as well as violence in schools and communities. Athletes who want to go beyond conservative approaches to change often need an organization like the CSSS to provide the training and support they need to be effective in making reforms. Athletes may be able to influence others when it comes to minor issues such as what shoes or soft drinks to buy, but when they talk about major social issues such as racism, sexism, or economic exploitation, many people will not take them seriously unless they are connected with an organization that gives them credibility and support.

But the big problem faced by athletes, even when they are associated with organizations, is that their careers will be cut short if they say and do things that seriously challenge the interests of those who sponsor and control sports. What do you think?

· ·

A *radical approach* to change focuses primarily on changing how people think about sports, changing the way sports are defined, organized, and played, and using sports as sites for transforming the structure and dynamics of gender, race, and class relations so that power is more equally distributed in social life. Radicals want to create new models for sport experiences and build new sport organizations for the purpose of making changes in social life as a whole.

When people talk about changes in sports, they are most likely to take a conservative approach. They see change as expansion and growth, not transformation. They are interested in *management* issues, in strategies for keeping things organized and profitable; they are not interested in making real changes in the way sports are organized and played. In fact, when you listen closely to people using conservative approaches, you will detect an underlying concern with using sports as tools for social control, to teach other people lessons on how to behave in conformity with traditional values and expectations.

A reformist approach overlaps with a conservative approach to the extent that both emphasize expanding participation opportunities. However, the reformist is also interested in making sure that those opportunities are characterized by fairness and a lack of preferential treatment. Reformists are committed to democratic participation and deal with issues related to fairness and equality of opportunity in sports.

A radical approach to change overlaps with a reformist approach, in that both are concerned with inequities and democratic participation. But the radical believes that democracy ultimately depends on equality, empowerment, and the elimination of all forms of oppression and exploitation. Therefore, the radical is concerned with the redistribution of power in society and the reorganization of social relations so that people can pursue their interests equally, in connection with others. Radicals make many people nervous, because they take sides with socially marginalized groups and call for changes that challenge the structures and ideologies that have led certain groups to be ignored or pushed aside. This can be threatening to those who have learned to live their lives comfortably within the context of those structures and ideologies. Privileged people don't like radicals.

Each of these approaches to change can be found in connection with sports in society. However, conservative approaches are dominant in sports today. Those with power and resources in any society tend to be conservative in their own approaches to life. This is reflected in sports, because these people see sports, especially those forms emphasizing power and performance, as vehicles for promoting values consistent with their interests; for them, sports are a means for making money, increasing their influence, and promoting consumption and economic expansion. Radical approaches are rare in sports, because most radicals are more concerned with issues such as poverty, homelessness, universal

health care, quality education for children, the availability of public transportation, full employment, and guaranteed minimum standards of living (Marable, 1993). These issues are difficult to focus on in connection with sports. However, a few radicals concerned with ideological issues are starting to see sports as sites for challenging dominant definitions of masculinity and femininity, for raising questions about the meaning of race, and for getting people to think critically about the antidemocratic features of hierarchical relationships.

Four Vantage Points for Making Changes

Making the world a better place is a never-ending task. Participating in this process as a change agent is always challenging, regularly frustrating, and sometimes rewarding. For those interested in making changes related to sports and social life, there are four vantage points from which changes might be initiated (Hall et al., 1991). They are as follows:

- *Work within the system of sports.* People can become involved in sports and sport organizations and then use their position or power to influence or initiate changes in sports. Change agents with an "insider" vantage point can be very effective; sometimes, they even can use this vantage point to promote changes in society as a whole. However, becoming an insider often involves taking on the existing values of the organization in which you work. This means that even though people may become involved in sports with many ideas about needed changes, their commitment to making those changes may decrease as they move up through the organization into positions of increasing power. Once they are in positions to make changes, they themselves have a vested interest in keeping things as they are. This is not inevitable, but it does happen.

  Although an insider vantage point can be a good place from which to make changes, it is important to be realistic about what insiders

Athletes often are loved by everyone *until* they speak out on social issues. Tommy Smith and John Carlos discovered this when they used the victory stand during the 1968 Olympics in Mexico City to make a silent protest about race relations in the U.S. and around the world by using the black power salute. They were expelled from the Olympic village and sent back to the U.S. amid widespread criticism and condemnation. Meanwhile, the Civil Rights Commission continued to call attention to issues of racial oppression and discrimination across the U.S. (AP/Wide World Photos)

can do. This is important to remember when we think of athletes as possible change agents. We discuss this issue in the box on pp. 518–519.

- *Become involved in "opposition" groups.* People can become change agents by forming or joining political groups that challenge problematic sport policies and put pressure on sport organizations that have antidemocratic policies and programs. For example, such groups could lobby for the building of a community sport center in a low-income

Calvin and Hobbes

by Bill Watterson

.... Calvinball is an alternative to organized sports that provides Calvin with an experience full of spontaneity, expression, pleasure, and participation. But it is difficult to obtain resources to provide spaces and opportunities for creating alternative sports. Physical activities without explicit goals and standardized rules are seldom seen as worthy of support, except in certain physical education classes, where teachers give a higher priority to inspiring creativity in human movement than to teaching the rules of institutionalized games. ....

neighborhood, or they could lobby against building a stadium that primarily would serve the interests of already-privileged people in a community. Or they could apply pressure so that hosting a major sport event such as the Olympics would involve building low-cost housing for low-income community residents, in addition to using public money to enhance economic expansion for certain segments of the business community.

- *Create alternative sports.* People can reject or ignore dominant sports and the organizations that sponsor them, and develop new sports grounded in the values and experiences of a wide array of different groups of people. This is often difficult to do, because resources are seldom available to people who choose this vantage point for making change. This was discovered by those who developed New Games in the United States, Cooperative Games in Canada (see Orlick, 1978), and TROPS ("sport" spelled backwards) in Japan (see Kageyama, 1992). But this vantage point also can be effective even when it doesn't lead

to concrete institutionalized changes, because it provides clear-cut examples of new ways to look at and play sports, and new ways to look at and interact with other people. These examples then may inspire other people to envision how they can create alternative sports in their own lives and communities.

- *Focus on culture and social relations.* People could ignore sports and try to produce changes in social relations that indirectly would raise questions about the organization and structure of sports in society. For example, as people learn to question dominant ideas about masculinity and femininity and the cultural practices associated with these ideas, they also can be expected to push for changes in those sports that reproduce ideas and practices that are destructive in the lives of many women and men. This strategy has been used by some groups working to lower sexual assault rates in the U.S.: they have pressured the NFL, the NCAA, and other sport organizations to support policies that increase awareness of the problem and encourage behavioral changes in connection with male-female relationships.

Regardless of the vantage point used to make change, any significant social transformation requires some combination of the following three things:

1. a vision of what sports and social life *could* and *should* be like
2. a willingness to work hard to put visions into actions
3. the political ability to rally the resources needed to produce results

The future of sports will be created out of this combination of visions, hard work, and politically effective actions.

SUGGESTED READINGS

Note: There are few scholarly references on the future of sports. Most discussions of the future focus on how new forms of technology can or will be applied in sports. These discussions are useful, but an overall understanding of social change demands that we know about more than technological possibilities. The best way to understand what might occur in the future is to learn how to critically assess what exists in sports today and then promote changes that will make sports more democratic and more open to those who can benefit from participation. You could support those organizations working to change sports in these ways and those using sports as vehicles for making similar changes in society as a whole. Feel free to create your own versions of sports to fit the needs of people around you. Watch and talk to children as they play sports and develop their own versions of physical activities with their friends. This will give you ideas about what is possible in the future. And it is out of these possibilities that the future will emerge.

Bibliography

Acker, J. 1992. Gendered institutions. *Contemporary Sociology* 21, 5: 565–69.

Acosta, R. V. 1993. The minority experience in sport: Monochromatic or technicolor. Pp. 204–13 in G. L. Cohen, ed. *Women in sport: Issues and controversies.* Newbury Park, CA: Sage.

Acosta, R. V., and L. J. Carpenter. 1992. As the years go by—Coaching opportunities in the 1990s. *JOPERD* 63, 3: 36–41.

Acosta, R. V., and L. J. Carpenter. 1996. Women in intercollegiate sport: A longitudinal study—Nineteen year update, 1977–1996. Brooklyn, NY: Photocopied report.

Adams, S. 1994. Work ethic leads to tight end's success. *The Denver Post,* December 19: 5D.

Adang, O. 1993, Crowd, riots, and the police: An observational study of collective violence. *Aggressive Behavior* 19: 37–38.

Adler, P. A., and P. Adler. 1991. *Backboards & blackboards: College athletes and role engulfment.* New York: Columbia University Press.

Adler, P. A., and P. Adler. 1994. Social reproduction and the corporate other: The institutionalization of afterschool activities. *The Sociological Quarterly* 35, 2: 309–28.

Adler, P. A., and P. Adler. 1996. Preadolescent clique stratification and the hierarchy of identity. *Sociological Inquiry* 66, 2: 111–42.

Adler, P. A., S. J. Kless, and P. Adler. 1992. Socialization to gender roles: Popularity among elementary school boys and girls. *Sociology of Education* 65 (July): 169–87.

Albert, M. 1996. Science, post modernism, and the left. *Z. Magazine* 9 (July/August) 64–69.

Alexander, K., A. Taggart, and S. Thorpe. 1996. A spring in their steps? Possibilities for professional renewal through sport education in Australian schools. *Sport, Education, and Society* 1, 1: 23–46.

Allison, L. 1993. *The changing politics of sport.* Manchester: Manchester University Press.

Allison, L. Forthcoming. Sport and nationalism. In J. Coakley and E. Dunning, eds. *Handbook of sport and society.* London: Sage Publications, Ltd.

Allison, M. T., and C. Meyer. 1988. Career problems and retirement among elite athletes: The female tennis professional. *Sociology of Sport Journal* 5, 3: 212–222.

Anderson, D. 1993. Cultural diversity on campus: A look at collegiate football coaches. *Journal of Sport & Social Issues* 17, 1: 61–66.

Anderson, P. 1996. Racism in sports: A question of ethics. *Marquette Sports Law Journal* 6, 2: 357–408.

Anderson, S., and J. Cavanagh. 1996. *The top 200.* Washington, D.C.: Institute for Policy Studies.

Andrews, D. 1996a. The fact(s) of Michael Jordan's blackness: Excavating a floating racial signifier. *Sociology of Sport Journal* 13, 2: 125–58.

Andrews, D., ed. 1996b. Deconstructing Michael Jordan: Reconstructing postindustrial America. *Sociology of Sport Journal* 13, 4. Special issue.

Andrews, D., and C. Cole, eds. Forthcoming. *Nike nation: Technologies of an American sign.* Unpublished manuscript.

Ardrey, R. 1961. *African genesis.* New York: Dell.

Ardrey, R. 1966. *The territorial imperative.* New York: Atheneum.

Armstrong, G. 1994. False Leeds: The construction of hooligan confrontations. Pp. 299– 325 in R. Giulianotti and J. Williams, eds. *Game without frontiers: Football, identity and modernity.* Aldershot, England: Arena, Ashgate.

Armstrong, G., and R. Harris. 1991. Football hooligans: Theory and evidence. *Sociological Review* 39, 3: 427–58.

Arnold, P. J. 1996. Olympism, sport, and education. Quest 48, 1: 93–101.

Ashe, A. 1992. Can blacks beat the old-boy network? *Newsweek,* January 27: 40.

Ashe, A. 1993. A hard road to glory. 3 vols. New York: Amistad.

Atlanta Journal/Constitution. 1996. America's Olympic teams are increasingly marked by less diversity, more elitism. October 1: H7. Special report.

Atre, T., et al. 1996. Sports: The high-stakes game of team ownership. *Financial World* 165, 8 (May 20): 52–70.

Axthelm, P. 1970. *The city game.* New York: Harper & Row.

Baade, R. A., and R. F. Dye. 1988. An analysis of the economic rationale for public subsidization of sports stadiums. *The Annals of Regional Science* 22, 2: 37–47.

Baade, R. A., and R. F. Dye. 1990. The impact of stadiums and professional sports on metropolitan area development. *Growth and Change: A Journal of Urban and Regional Policy* 21, 2: 1–14.

Bagnato, A. 1995. The buck stops nowhere. *Chicago Tribune,* August 6: sec. 3, pp. 1, 5.

Bailey, N. 1993. Women's sport and the feminist movement: Building bridges. Pp. 297–304 in G. Cohen, ed. *Women in sport: Issues and controversies.* Newbury Park, CA: Sage.

Bairner, A. 1996. Sportive nationalism and nationalist politics: A comparative analysis of Scotland, the Republic of Ireland, and Sweden. *Journal of Sport & Social Issues* 20, 3: 314–34.

Baker, W. J. 1988. *Sports in the Western world.* Urbana, IL: University of Illinois Press.

Bale, J. 1991. *The brawn drain: Foreign student-athletes in American universities.* Urbana, IL: University of Illinois Press.

Bale, J., and J. Maguire, eds. 1994. *The global sports arena: Athletic talent migration in an interdependent world.* London: Frank Cass.

Bale, J., and J. Sang, eds. 1996. *Kenyan running: Movement culture, geography and global change.* London: Frank Cass.

Ballard, S. 1996. Broken back doesn't stall Indy winner. *USA Today,* May 28: A1.

Banks, D. 1993. Tribal names and sports mascots. *Journal of Sport & Social Issues* 17, 1: 5–8.

Barnett, S. 1990. *Games and sets: The changing face of sport on television.* London: British Film Institute (BFI Publishing).

Basralian, J. 1995. Amateurs . . . at best. *Financial World* 164, 4 (February 14): 117–22.

Baxter, V., A. V. Margavio, and C. Lambert. 1996. Competition, legitimation, and the regulation of intercollegiate athletics. *Sociology of Sport Journal* 13, 1: 51–64.

Beal, B. 1995. Disqualifying the official: An exploration of social resistance through the subculture of skateboarding. *Sociology of Sport Journal* 12, 3: 252–67.

Beal, C. R. 1994. *Boys and girls: The development of gender roles.* New York: McGraw-Hill.

Beamish, R. 1988. The political economy of professional sport. In J. Harvey and H. Cantelon, eds. *Not just a game.* Ottawa, Ontario: University of Ottawa Press.

Beamish, R. 1990. The persistence of inequality: An analysis of participation patterns among Canada's high performance athletes. *International Review for the Sociology of Sport* 25, 2: 143–53.

Beamish, R. 1993. Labor relations in sport: Central issues in their emergence and structure in high-performance sport. pp. 187–210 in A. G. Ingham and J. W. Loy, eds. *Sport in social development.* Champaign, IL: Human Kinetics.

Beaton, R. 1993. Mexicans best-suited to pitch, scouts say. *USA Today Baseball Weekly,* February 24–March 2: 11.

Becker, A. 1990. The role of the school in the maintenance of ethnic group affiliation. *Human Organization* 49: 48–55.

Becker, D., 1996. Nothstein: 'I enjoy the pain'. *USA Today,* July 24: 14E.

Becker, H., and M. M. McCall, eds. 1990. *Symbolic interaction and cultural studies.* Chicago, IL: University of Chicago Press.

Begg, D. J., J. D. Langley, T. Moffitt, and S. W. Marshall. 1996. Sport and delinquency: An examination of the deterrence hypothesis in a longitudinal study. *British Journal of Sport Medicine* 30, 4: 335–41.

Begley, S. 1995. Three is not enough. *Newsweek,* February 13: 67–69.

Beller, J. M., and S. K. Stoll. 1995. Moral reasoning of high school athletes and general students: An empirical study versus personal testimony. *Journal of Pediatric Exercise Science* 7: 352–363.

Bender, D. L., ed. 1988. *What should be done about the drug problem in sports?* St. Paul, MN: Greenhaven Press.

Benedict, J., and A. Klein. 1997. Arrest and conviction rates for athletes accused of sexual assault. *Sociology of Sport Journal* 14, 1: 86–94.

Benson, M., ed. 1996. 1996 NCAA Division I graduation-rates report. Overland Park, KS: NCAA.

Bentz, R. 1996. Robinson for three. *Sports Spectrum* (June): 14–15.

Berghorn, F. J., N. R. Yetman, and W. E. Hanna. 1988. Racial participation and integration in men's and women's intercollegiate basketball: Continuity and change, 1958–1985. *Sociology of Sport Journal* 5, 2: 107–24.

Berkowitz, L. 1969. Roots of aggression: A reexamination of the frustration-aggression hypothesis. New York: Atherton Press.

Berlant, A. R. 1996. Building character or characters? What the research says about sport participation and moral development. *Research Quarterly for Exercise and Sport* (Supplement): A-95.

Best, C. 1987. Experience and career length in professional football: The effect of positional segregation. *Sociology of Sport Journal* 4, 4: 410–20.

Bhasin, S., et al. The effects of supraphysiologic doses of testosterone on muscle size and strength in normal men. *The New England Journal of Medicine* 335, 1 (July 4): 1–7.

Bierman, J. A. 1990. The effects of television sports media on black male youth. *Sociological Inquiry* 60, 4: 413–27.

Birke, L. I. A., and G. Vines. 1987. A sporting chance: The anatomy of destiny? *Women's Studies International Forum* 10, 4: 337–47.

Birrell, S. 1989. Race relations theories and sport: Suggestions for a more critical analysis. *Sociology of Sport Journal* 6, 3: 212–27.

Birrell, S., and C. Cole. 1990. Double fault: Rene Richards and the construction and naturalization of difference. *Sociology of Sport Journal* 7, 1: 1–21.

Birrell, S., and C. Cole, eds. 1994. *Women, sport, and culture.* Champaign, IL: Human Kinetics.

Birrell, S., and D. M. Richter. 1994. Is a diamond forever? Feminist transformations of sport. Pp. 221–44 in S. Birrell and C. L. Cole, eds. *Women, sport, and culture.* Champaign, IL: Human Kinetics.

Birrell, S., and N. Theberge. 1994a. Ideological control of women in sport. Pp. 341–60 in D. M. Costa and S. R. Guthrie, eds. *Women and sport: Interdisciplinary perspectives.* Champaign, IL: Human Kinetics.

Birrell, S., and N. Theberge. 1994b. Feminist resistance and transformation in sport. Pp. 361–76 in D. M. Costa and S. R. Guthrie, eds. *Women and sport: Interdisciplinary perspectives.* Champaign, IL: Human Kinetics.

Bissinger, H. G. 1990. *Friday night lights.* Reading, MA: Addison-Wesley.

Black, T. 1996. Does the ban on drugs in sport improve societal welfare? *International Review for the Sociology of Sport* 31, 4: 367–84.

Blain, N., R. Boyle, and H. O'Donnell. 1993. *Sport and national identity in the European media.* Leicester, England: Leicester University Press.

Blauvelt, H. 1996. Women slowly crack athletic director ranks. *USA Today*, October 2: 1C–2C.

Blinde, E. M., and S. L. Greendorfer. 1985. A reconceptualization of the process of leaving the role of competitive athlete. *International Review for the Sociology of Sport* 20, 1–2: 87–94.

Blinde, E. M., and S. L. Greendorfer. 1992. Conflict and the college sport experience of women athletes. *Women in Sport & Physical Activity Journal* 1, 1: 97–114.

Blinde, E. M., S. L. Greendorfer, and R. J. Shanker. 1991. Differential media coverage of men's and women's intercollegiate basketball: Reflection of gender ideology. *Journal of Sport and Social Issues* 15, 2: 98–114.

Blinde, E. M., and D. E. Taub. 1992. Women athletes as falsely accused deviants: Managing the lesbian stigma. *The Sociological Quarterly* 33, 4: 521–33.

Blinde, E. M., D. E. Taub, and L. Han. 1992. Homophobia and women's sport: The disempowerment of athletes. Paper presented at the annual conference of the American Sociological Association, Pittsburgh (August).

Blinde, E. M., D. E. Taub, and L. Han. 1993. Sport participation and women's personal empowerment: Experiences of the college athlete. *Journal of Sport & Social Issues* 17, 1: 47–60.

Blinde, E. M., D. E. Taub, and L. Han. 1994. Sport as a site for women's group and societal empowerment: Perspectives from the college athlete. *Sociology of Sport Journal* 11, 1: 51–59.

Bloom, G. A., and M. D. Smith. 1996. Hockey violence: A test of the cultural spillover theory. *Sociology of Sport Journal* 13, 1: 65–77.

Blum, D. E. 1996. Devout athletes. *The Chronicle of Higher Education* 42, 22 February 9: A35–A36.

Bohmer, C., and A. Parrot. 1993. *Sexual assault on campus: The problem and the solution.* Lexington, MA: Lexington.

Bolin, A. 1992a. Vandalized vanity: Feminine physiques betrayed and portrayed. Pp. 79–99 in F. Mascia-Lees and P. Sharpe (eds.). *Tattoo, torture, mutilation, and adornment: The denaturalization of the body in culture and text.* Albany, NY: State University of New York Press.

Bolin, A. Forthcoming. Beauty or the beast: The subversive soma. In A. Bolin and J. Granskog (eds.). *Athletic intruders: Women, culture, and exercise.* Unpublished manuscript.

Bourdieu, P. 1978. Sport and social class. *Social Science Information* 17: 819–40.

Bourgeois, N. 1995. Sports journalists and their source of information: A conflict of interests and its resolution. *Sociology of Sport Journal* 12, 2: 195–203.

Boyd, R. S. 1996. Biologists reject the notion of race. *The Denver Post,* October 20.

Braddock, J. 1978a. The sports pages: In black and white. *ARENA Review* 2, 2: 17–25.

Braddock, J. 1978b. Television and college football: In black and white. *Journal of Black Studies* 8, 3: 369–80.

Braddock, J. 1981. Race and leadership in professional sports: A study of institutional discrimination in the National Football League. *ARENA Review* 5, 2: 16–25.

Braddock, J., et al. 1991. Bouncing back: Sports and academic resilience among African-American males. *Education and Urban Society* 24, 1: 113–31.

Brady, E. 1991. Players: 46% earn degrees in five years. *USA Today,* June 17. Cover story.

Brady, E. 1996. Some legislators say Baltimore's money misspent. *USA Today,* September 6: 19C.

Brady, E., and D. Howlett. 1996. Ballpark construction booming. *USA Today,* September 6: 13C–21C.

Bredemeier, B., and D. Shields. 1983. Body and balance: Developing moral structures through physical education. Paper presented at the meetings of the American Alliance for Health, Physical Education, Recreation and Dance, Minneapolis.

Bredemeier, B., and D. Shields. 1984. Divergence in moral reasoning about sport and everyday life. *Sociology of Sport Journal* 1, 4: 348–57.

Bredemeier, B., and D. Shields. 1985. Values and violence in sports today. *Psychology Today* 19, 10: 22–25, 28–32.

Bredemeier, B., and D. Shields. 1993. Moral psychology in the context of sport. Pp. 587–99 in R. N. Singer, M. Murphey, and L. K. Tennant (eds.). *Handbook of research on sport psychology.* New York: Macmillan.

Brennan, C. 1996. *Inside edge: A revealing journey into the secret world of figure skating.* New York. Scribner.

Briggs, B. 1994. God squads. *The Denver Post Magazine,* October 23: 12–15.

Brohm, J.-M. 1978. *Sport: A prison of measured time.* Translated by Ian Fraser. London: Ink Links.

Brooks, D. D., and R. C. Althouse, eds. 1993a. *Racism in college athletics: The African-American athlete's experience.* Morgantown, WV: Fitness Information Technology, Inc.

Brooks, D. D., and R. C. Althouse. 1993b. Racial imbalance in coaching and managerial positions. Pp. 101–42 in D. D. Brooks and R. C. Althouse, eds. *Racism in college athletics: The African-American athlete's experience.* Morgantown, WV: Fitness Information Technology Inc.

Brown, B. 1985. Factors influencing the process of withdrawal by female adolescents from the role of competitive age group swimmer. *Sociology of Sport Journal* 2, 2: 111–29.

Brown, B. 1993a. Supply and demand sets ticket prices. *USA Today,* May 11: 8C.

Brown, B. 1993b. Perceptions in a battle with economic reality. *USA Today,* May 11: 8C.

Brownell, S. 1995. *Training the body for China: Sports in the moral order of the People's Republic.* Chicago, IL: University of Chicago Press.

Bruce, T. 1993. Communique: Title IX: 21 years of progress. *Women in Sport & Physical Activity Journal* 2, 1: 73–80.

Bryant, J., P. Comisky, and D. Zillmann. 1977.

Drama in sports commentary. *Journal of Communication* 27, 3: 140–49.

Bryant, J., S. C. Rockwell, and J. W. Owens. 1994. "Buzzer Beaters" and "Barn Burners": The effects on enjoyment of watching the game to "down to the wire." *Journal of Sport & Social Issues* 18, 4: 326–39.

Bryant, J., D. Zillman, and A. A. Raney. In press. Violence and the enjoyment of media sports. In L. A. Wenner, ed. *MediaSport: Cultural sensibilities and sport in the media age.* London: Routledge.

Bryson, L. 1990. Challenges to male hegemony in sport. Pp. 173–84 in M. A. Messner and D. F. Sabo (eds.). *Sport, men, and the gender order.* Champaign, IL: Human Kinetics.

Bryson, L. 1994 (1987). Sport and the maintenance of masculine hegemony. Pp. 47–64 in S. Birrell and C. L. Cole, eds. *Women, sport, and culture.* Champaign, IL: Human Kinetics.

Buford, B., 1991. *Among the thugs.* London: Secker and Warburg.

Buhrmann, H. G. 1977. Athletics and deviancy: An examination of the relationship between athletic participation and deviant behavior of high school girls. *Review of Sport and Leisure* 2: 17–25.

Burroughs, A., L. Ashburn, and L. Seebohm. 1995. "Add sex and stir": Homophobic coverage of women's cricket in Australia. *Journal of Sport & Social Issues* 19, 3: 266–84.

Cahill, B. R., and A. J. Pearl, eds. 1993. *Intensive participation in children's sports.* Champaign, IL: Human Kinetics.

Cahn, S. K. 1994a. *Coming on strong: Gender and sexuality in twentieth-century women's sports.* New York: The Free Press.

Cahn, S. K. 1994b. Crushes, competition, and closets: The emergence of homophobia in women's physical education. Pp. 327–40 in S. Birrell and C. L. Cole, eds. *Women, sport, and culture.* Champaign, IL: Human Kinetics.

Caldwell, M. 1993. Eating disorders and related behavior among athletes. Pp. 158–67 in G. L. Cohen, ed. *Women in sport: Issues and controversies.* Newbury Park, CA: Sage.

Cantor, D. W., and T. Bernay (with J. Stoess). 1992. *Women in power: The secrets of leadership.* Boston: Houghton Mifflin.

Caplan, P. J. 1981. *Barriers between women.* Jamaica, NY: Spectrum.

Capouya, J. 1986. Jerry Falwell's team. *Sport* 77, 9: 72–81.

Carlston, D. 1986. An environmental explanation for race differences in basketball performance. In R. Lapchick, ed. *Fractured focus.* Lexington, MA: Lexington Books.

Carpenter, L. J. 1993. Letters home: My life with Title IX. Pp. 79–94 in G. L. Cohen, ed. *Women in sport: Issues and controversies.* Newbury Park, CA: Sage.

Carr, C. N., S. R. Kennedy, and K. M. Dimick. 1996. Alcohol use among high school athletes. *The Prevention Researcher* 3, 2: 1–3.

Carroll, J. 1986. Sport: Virtue and grace. *Theory and Society* 3, 1: 91–98.

Carter, D. 1996. Q & Amy. *Denver Post*, August 20: sec. D.

Case, B., H. S. Green, and J. Brown. 1987. Academic clustering in athletics: myth or reality? *ARENA Review* 11, 2: 48–56.

Cavallo, D. 1981. *Muscles and morals.* Philadelphia: University of Pennsylvania Press.

Centre for Sports Development Research. 1996. *Hit racism for six: Race and cricket in England today.* London: Department of Sport Studies, Roehampton Institute.

Chafetz, J. S. 1978. *Masculine, feminine or human?* Itasca, IL: F. E. Peacock.

Chafetz, J. S., and J. A. Kotarba. 1995. Son worshippers: The role of little league mothers in recreating gender. *Studies in Symbolic Interaction* 18: 219–243.

Chambers, M. 1995. *The unplayable lie: The untold story of women and discrimination in American golf.* New York: Pocket Books.

Chandler, J. 1983. Televised sport: Britain and the United States. *ARENA Review* 7, 2: 20–27.

Chandler, T. J. L., and A. D. Goldberg. 1990. The academic all-American as vaunted adolescent role-identity. *Sociology of Sport Journal* 7, 3: 287–93.

Chappell, R. 1996. Participation rates of Afro/Caribbeans in the 1st division of the English National Basketball League, 1977–1996. Paper presented at the annual meeting of the North

American Society of the Sociology of Sport, Birmingham, AL (November).

Chappell, R., R. L. Jones, and A. M. Burden. 1966. Racial participation and integration in English professional basketball, 1977–1994. *Sociology of Sport Journal* 13, 3: 300–10.

Charnofsky, H. 1968. The major league professional baseball player: Self-conception versus the popular image. *International Review for Sport Sociology* 3: 39–53.

Chu, D., and D. Griffey. 1982. Sport and racial integration: The relationship of personal contact, attitudes and behavior. In A. O. Dunleavy, A. Miracle, and R. Rees, eds. *Studies in the sociology of sport.* Fort Worth, TX: Texas Christian University Press.

Clark, N. 1993. Eating disorders among female athletes. Pp. 141–147 in A. J. Pearl, ed., *The athletic female.* Champaign, IL: Human Kinetics.

Clausen, C. L. 1996. Ethnic team names and logos— Is there a legal solution? *Marquette Sports Law Journal* 6, 2: 409–21.

Coakley, J. 1980. Play, games and sport: Developmental implications for young people. *Journal of Sport Behavior* 3, 3: 99–118.

Coakley, J. 1982. *Sport in society: Issues and controversies.* 2d ed. St. Louis, MO: Mosby.

Coakley, J. 1983a. Play, games and sports: Developmental implications for young people. In J. C. Harris and R. J. Park, eds. *Play, games and sports in cultural contexts.* Champaign, IL: Human Kinetics.

Coakley, J. 1983b. Leaving competitive sport: Retirement or rebirth? *Quest* 35, 1: 1–11.

Coakley, J. 1985. When should children begin competing? In D. Gould and M. R. Weiss, eds. *Sport for children and youths.* Champaign, IL: Human Kinetics.

Coakley, J. 1988–89. Media coverage of sports and violent behavior: an elusive connection. *Current Psychology: Research and Reviews* 7, 4: 322–30.

Coakley, J. 1992. Burnout among adolescent athletes: A personal failure or social problem? *Sociology of Sport Journal* 9, 3: 271–85.

Coakley, J. 1993a. Socialization and sport. In R. N. Singer, M. Murphey, and L. K Tennant (eds.). Pp. 571–86 in *Handbook of research on sport psychology.* New York: Macmillan.

Coakley, J. 1993b. Sport and socialization. *Exercise and Sport Science Reviews* 21: 169–200.

Coakley, J. 1994. Ethics in coaching: Child development or child abuse? *Coaching Volleyball*, December/January: 18–23.

Coakley, J. 1996. Socialization through sports. Pp. 353–63 in O. bar-Or, ed. *The child and adolescent athlete.* Vol. 6 of the *Encyclopaedia of Sports Medicine*, a publication of the IOC Medical Commission. London: Blackwell Science.

Coakley, J., and E. Dunning, eds. Forthcoming. *Handbook of sport and society.* London: Sage.

Coakley, J., and A. White. 1992. Making decisions: Gender and sport participation among British adolescents. *Sociology of Sport Journal* 9, 1: 20–35.

Coclough, W. G., L. A. Daellenbach, and K. R. Sherony. 1994. Estimating the economic impact of a minor league baseball stadium. *Managerial and Decision Economics* 15, 5 (September–October): 497–502.

Cohen, G. L. 1993. Media portrayal of the female athlete. Pp. 171–84 in G. L. Cohen, ed. *Women in sport: Issues and controversies.* Newbury Park, CA: Sage.

Cole, C. L. 1994. Resisting the canon: Feminist cultural studies, sport, and technologies of the body. Pp. 1–29 in S. Birrell and C. L. Cole, eds. *Women, sport, and culture.* Champaign, IL: Human Kinetics.

Cole, C. L., and D. Andrews. 1996. Look—It's NBA's *Showtime:* Visions of race in the popular imaginary. *Cultural Studies: A Research Volume* 1, 1: 141–81.

Cole, C. L., and H. Denny. 1995. Visualizing deviance in post-Reagan America: Magic Johnson, AIDS, and the promiscuous world of professional sport. *Critical Sociology* 20, 3: 123–47.

Cole, C. L., H. Denny, and J. Coakley. 1993. AIDS, surveillance, and sports. Paper presented at the meetings of the Society for the Interdisciplinary Study of Social Imagery, Denver (March).

Cole, C. L., and A. Hribar. 1995. Celebrity feminism: Nike style post-Fordism, transcendence, and consumer power. *Sociology of Sport Journal* 12, 4: 347–69.

Coleman, J. 1961a. *The adolescent society.* New York: The Free Press.

Coleman, J. 1961b. Athletics in high schools. *Annals of the American Academy of Political Science* 338 (November): 33–43.

Coleman, K. 1996. For many reasons, the sport packs a punch. *The Denver Post*, July 11: 5D.

Condor, R., and D. F. Anderson. 1984. Longitudinal analysis of coverage accorded black and white athletes in feature articles of *Sports Illustrated*, 1960–1980. *Journal of Sport Behavior* 7, 1: 39–43.

Connell, R. W. 1987a. *Gender and power.* Sydney, Australia: Allen & Unwin.

Connell, R. W. 1987b. *Gender and power: Society, the person and sexual politics.* Stanford, CA: Stanford University Press.

Connell, R. W. 1995. *Masculinities.* Berkeley, CA: University of California Press.

Conniff, R. 1996. New day for women's sports. *The Progressive* 60, 9 (September): 11.

Cooper-Chen, A. 1994. Global games, entertainment and leisure: Women as TV spectators. Pp. 257–72 in P. J. Creedon, ed. *Women, media and sport.* Thousand Oaks, CA: Sage.

Corbett, D., and W. Johnson. 1993. The African-American female in collegiate sport: Sexism and racism. Pp. 179–204 in D. D. Brooks and R. C. Althouse, eds. *Racism in college athletics: The African-American athlete's experience.* Morgantown, WV: Fitness Information Technology, Inc.

Coser, R. 1986. Cognitive structure and the use of social space. *Sociological Forum* 1, 1: 1–26.

Courson, S. 1988. Steroids: Another view. *Sports Illustrated* 69, 21: 106.

Cowley, G. 1996. Attention: Aging men. *Newsweek*, September 16: 68–75.

Creedon, P. J., ed. 1994. *Women, media and sport.* Thousand Oaks. CA: Sage.

Crompton, J. L. 1993. Sponsorship of sport by tobacco and alcohol companies: A review of the issues. *Journal of Sport & Social Issues* 17, 3: 148–67.

Crosset, T. 1995. *Outsiders in the clubhouse: The world of women's professional golf.* Albany, NY: State University of New York Press.

Crossman, J., P. Hyslop, and B. Guthrie. 1994. A content analysis of the sports section of Canada's national newspaper with respect to gender and professional/amateur status. *International Review for the Sociology of Sport* 29, 2: 123–34.

Csikszentmihalyi, M. 1990. *Flow: The psychology of optimal experience.* New York: Harper Perennial.

Curry, T. 1991. Fraternal bonding in the locker room: A profeminist analysis of talk about competition and women. *Sociology of Sport Journal* 8, 2: 119–35.

Curry, T. 1993. A little pain never hurt anyone: Athletic career socialization and the normalization of sports injury. *Symbolic Interaction* 16, 3: 273–90.

Curry, T., and R. H. Strauss. 1994. A little pain never hurt anybody: A photo-essay on the normalization of sport injuries. *Sociology of Sport Journal* 11, 2: 195–208.

Curtis, J., and J. Loy. 1978a. Positional segregation in professional baseball: Replications, trend data and critical observation. *International Review of Sport Sociology* 4, 13: 5–21.

Curtis, J., and J. Loy. 1978b. Race/ethnicity and relative centrality of playing positions in team sport. *Exercise and Sport Science Review* 6: 285–313.

Curtis, J., and R. Ennis. 1988. Negative consequences of leaving competitive sport? Comparative findings of former elite-level hockey players. *Sociology of Sport Journal* 5, 2: 87–196.

Daddario, G. 1994. Chilly scenes of the 1992 Winter Games: The mass media and the marginalization of female athletes. *Sociology of Sport Journal* 11, 3: 275–88.

Davenport, J. 1996. Breaking into the rings: Women on the IOC. *JOPERD* 67, 5: 27–30.

Davis, L. 1993. Protest against the use of Native American mascots: A challenge to traditional American identity. *Journal of Sport & Social Issues* 17, 1: 9–22.

Davis, L. 1994. A postmodern paradox? Cheerleaders at women's sporting events. Pp. 149–58 in S. Birrell and C. L. Cole, eds. *Women, sport, and culture.* Champaign, IL: Human Kinetics.

Davis, L., and L. Delano. 1992. Fixing the boundaries of physical gender: Side effects of anti-doping campaigns in athletics. *Sociology of Sport Journal* 1, 1: 1–19.

Davis, T. 1995. African-American student-athletes: Marginalizing the NCAA regulatory structure. *Marquette Sports Law Journal* 6, 2: 199–228.

Deford, F. 1996. The new women of Atlanta. *Newsweek*, June 10: 62–71.

DeKnop, P., B. Skirstad, L.-M. Engstrom, and M. Weiss, eds. 1996. *Worldwide trends in youth sport*. Champaign, IL: Human Kinetics.

DeNeui, D. L., and D. A. Sachau. 1996. Spectator enjoyment of aggression in intercollegiate hockey games. *Journal of Sport & Social Issues* 20, 1: 69–77.

DiPasquale, M. G. 1992a. Editorial: Why athletes use drugs. *Drugs in Sports* 1, 1: 2–3.

DiPasquale, M. G. 1992b. Publications by Mile High Publishing. *Drugs in Sports* 1, 3: 13–14.

DiPasquale, M. G. 1992c. Beating drug tests. *Drugs in Sports* 1, 2: 3–6.

DiPasquale, M. G. 1992d. Beating drug tests: Part II. *Drugs in Sports* 1, 3: 6–12.

Disch, L., and M. J. Kane. 1996. When a looker is really a bitch: Lisa Olson, sport, and the heterosexual matrix. *Signs: Journal of Women in Culture and Society* 21, 2: 278–308.

Dobie, M. 1987. Facing a brave new world. *Newsday*, November 8.

Domi, T. 1992. Tough tradition of hockey fights should be preserved. *USA Today*, October 27.

Donegan, L. 1994. Clubs winning fight against racism. *The Guardian*, Home News (May 11): 2.

Donnelly, P. 1988. Sport as a site for "popular" resistance. In R. Gruneau, ed. *Popular cultures and political practices*. Toronto: Garamond Press.

Donnelly, P. 1988–1989. On boxing: Notes on the past, present and future of a sport in transition. *Current Psychology* 7, 4: 331–46.

Donnelly, P. 1993. Problems associated with youth involvement in high-performance sports. Pp. 95–126 in B. R. Cahill and A. J. Pearl, eds. *Intensive participation in children's sports*. Champaign, IL: Human Kinetics.

Donnelly, P. 1996a. Prolympism: Sport monoculture as crisis and opportunity. *Quest* 48, 1: 25–42.

Donnelly, P. 1996b. The local and the global: Globalization in the sociology of sport. *Journal of Sport & Social Issues* 20, 3: 239–57.

Donnelly, P. Forthcoming. Interpretive approaches to the study of sports. In J. Coakley and E. Dunning, eds. *Handbook of sport and society*. London: Sage.

Donnelly, P., and J. Harvey. 1996. Overcoming systematic barriers to access in active living. Unpublished report submitted to Fitness Program, Health Canada, Ottawa.

Donnelly, P., and K. Young. 1985. Reproduction and transformation of cultural forms in sport: A contextual analysis of rugby. *International Review for the Sociology of Sport* 20, 1–2: 19–38.

Donnelly, P., and K. Young. 1988. The construction and confirmation of identity in sport subcultures. *Sociology of Sport Journal* 5, 3: 223–40.

Donohoe, T., and N. Johnson. 1986. *Foul play: Drug abuse in sports*. New York: Basil Blackwell.

Doyle, C. A., and G. J. Gaeth. 1990. Assessing the institutional choice process of student-athletes. *Research Quarterly for Exercise and Sport* 61, 1: 85–92.

Dubois, P. E. 1978. Participation in sports and occupational attainment: A comparative study. *Research Quarterly* 49, 1: 28–37.

Dubois, P. E. 1979. Participation in sport and occupational attainment: An investigation of selected athlete categories. *Journal of Sport Behavior* 2, 2: 103–14.

Dubois, P. E. 1995. Gender and the hiring of high school and small college coaches. Paper presented at the annual meeting of the North American Society for the Sociology of Sport, Sacramento (November).

Duncan, M. C. 1993. Beyond analyses of sport media texts: An argument for formal analyses of institutional structures. *Sociology of Sport Journal* 10, 4: 353–72.

Duncan, M. C. 1994. The politics of women's body images and practices: Foucault, the panopticon, and *Shape* magazine. *Journal of Sport & Social Issues* 18, 1: 48–65.

Duncan, M. C., and B. Brummett. 1993. Liberal and radical sources of female empowerment in sport media. *Sociology of Sport Journal* 10, 1: 57–72.

Duncan, M. C., M. A. Messner, L. Williams, and K. Jensen. 1990. *Gender stereotyping in televised sports*. Los Angeles: Amateur Athletic Foundation.

Dunn, Katherine. 1994. Just as fierce. *Mother Jones* (November/December): 35–39.

Dunning, E. 1993. Sport in the civilizing process: Aspects of the development of modern sport. Pp. 39–70 in Dunning, E., J. A. Maguire, and

R. E. Pearton, eds. *The sports process: A comparative and developmental approach*. Champaign, IL: Human Kinetics.

Dunning, E., J. A. Maguire, and R. E. Pearton, eds. 1993. *The sports process: A comparative and developmental approach*. Champaign, IL: Human Kinetics.

Dunning, E., and C. Rojek, eds. 1992. *Sport and leisure in the civilizing process: Critique and counter-critique*. Toronto, Ontario: University of Toronto Press.

Dunning, E., and K. Sheard. 1979. *Barbarians, gentlemen and players: A sociological study of the development of rugby football*. New York: University Press.

Eastman, S. T., and K. E. Riggs. 1994. Televised sports and ritual: Fan experiences. *Sociology of Sport Journal* 11, 3: 249–74.

Economist, The. 1996a. Sport and television: Swifter, higher, stronger, dearer. *The Economist* 340, 7975 (July 20): 17–19.

Economist, The. 1996b. The million dollar games. *The Economist* 340, 7975 (July 20): 13.

Eder, D. (with C. C. Evans and S. Parker). 1995. *School talk: Gender and adolescent culture*. New Brunswick, NJ: Rutgers University Press.

Edwards, H. 1973. *Sociology of sport*. Homewood, IL: Dorsey Press.

Edwards, H. 1993. Succeeding against the odds. *Black Issues in Higher Education* 10, 20: 136.

Eisen, G., and D. Turner. 1992. Myth and reality: Social mobility of American Olympic athletes. *International Review for the Sociology of Sport* 27, 2: 165–76.

Eisen, G., and D. K. Wiggins, eds. 1994. *Ethnicity and sport in North American history and culture*. Westport, CT: Greenwood Press.

Eitzen, D. S. 1975. Athletics in the status system of male adolescents: A replication of Coleman's *The Adolescent Society*. *Adolescence* 10, 38: 268–76.

Eitzen, D. S., 1987. The educational experiences of intercollegiate student-athletes. *Journal of Sport and Social Issues* 11, 1–2: 15–30.

Eitzen, D. S. 1988. The myth and reality of elite amateur sport. *The World & I* 3, 10: 549–59.

Eitzen, D. S. 1992. Treatment of athletes is the problem with college sports. *The Coloradoan*, Sunday, November 29: E3.

Eitzen, D. S. 1995. Classism in sport: The powerless bear the burden. *Journal of Sport and Social Issues* 20, 1: 95–105.

Eitzen, D. S. Forthcoming. Sport and social control. In J. Coakley and E. Dunning, eds. *Handbook of sport and society*. London: Sage.

Eitzen, D. S., and D. Furst. 1988. Racial bias in women's collegiate sports. Paper presented at the North American Society for the Sociology of Sport Conference, Cincinnati.

Eitzen, D. S., and M. B. Zinn. 1989. The deathleticization of women: The naming and gender marking of collegiate sport teams. *Sociology of Sport Journal* 6, 4: 362–70.

Elias, N. 1986. An essay on sport and violence. Pp. 150–74 in N. Elias and E. Dunning (eds.), *Quest for excitement*. New York: Basil Blackwell.

Elias, N., and E. Dunning. 1986. *Quest for excitement*. New York: Basil Blackwell.

Engelhardt, G. M. 1993. Educational psychology program challenges National Hockey League: Knockout fighting behavior. Paper presented at the annual conference of the American Psychological Association, Toronto (August).

Engelhardt, G. M. 1995. Fighting behavior and winning National Hockey League games: A paradox. *Perceptual and Motor Skills* 80: 416–18.

Enloe, C., 1995. The globetrotting sneaker. *Ms.* 5, 5: 10–15.

Euchner, G. C. 1993. *Playing the field: Why sports teams move and cities fight to keep them*. Baltimore, MD: The Johns Hopkins University Press.

Evans, J. R. 1988. Team selection in children's games. *The Social Sciences Journal* 25, 1: 93–104.

Ewald, K., and R. M. Jiobu. 1985. Explaining positive deviance: Becker's model and the case of runners and bodybuilders. *Sociology of Sport Journal* 2, 2: 144–56.

Ewing, M. E., and V. Seefelt. 1996. Patterns of participation and attrition in American agency-sponsored youth sports. Pp. 31–45 in F. L. Smoll and R. E. Smith, eds. *Children in sports: A biopsychosocial perspective*, Indianapolis: Brown & Benchmark.

Falk, B. 1995. Bringing home the violence. *Newsday* (January 8): 12–13.

Fallows, J. 1996. "Throwing like a girl." *The Atlantic*

Monthly (August): 84–87.

Faludi, S. 1991. *Backlash: The undeclared war against American women.* New York: Crown.

Fasting, K. 1996. 40,000 female runners: The Grete Waitz Run—Sport, culture, and counterculture. Paper presented at International Pre-Olympic Scientific Congress, Dallas (July).

Feeney, R. 1995. *A Catholic perspective: Physical exercise and sports.* N. p.: Aquinas Press.

Fejgin, N. 1994. Participation in high school competitive sports: A subversion of school mission or contribution to academic goals? *Sociology of Sport Journal* 11, 3: 211–30.

Ferrante, J. 1995. *Sociology: A global perspective.* Belmont, CA: Wadsworth.

Festle, M. J. 1996. *Playing nice: Politics and apologies in women's sports.* New York: Columbia University Press.

Fine, G. A. 1987. *With the boys: Little league baseball and preadolescent culture.* Chicago, IL: University of Chicago Press.

Fish, M. 1993. Steroids riskier than ever. *The Atlanta Journal-Constitution,* September 26: A1, A12–A13. Part I of four parts.

Fisher, A. C. 1976. *Psychology of sport.* Palo Alto, CA: Mayfield.

Flake, C. 1992. The spirit of winning: Sports and the total man. Pp. 161–76 in S. Hoffman, ed. *Sport and religion.* Champaign, IL: Human Kinetics.

Foley, D. 1990a. *Learning capitalist culture.* Philadelphia: University of Pennsylvania Press.

Foley, D. 1990b. The great American football ritual: Reproducing race, class, and gender inequality. *Sociology of Sport Journal* 7, 2: 111–35.

Franseen, L., and S. McCann. 1996. Causes of eating disorders in elite female athletes. *Olympic Coach* 6, 3 (Summer): 15–17.

Frey, D. 1994. *The last shot: City streets, basketball dreams.* Boston: Houghton Mifflin.

Frey, J. H. 1984. The U. S. vs. Great Britain responses to the 1980 boycott of the Olympic Games. *Comparative Physical Education and Sport* 6, 3: 4–13.

Frey, J. H. 1985. The winning team myth. *Currents: Journal of the Council for Advancement and Support of Education* 11, 1: 32–35.

Frey, J. H. 1992. Gambling on sport: Policy issues.

Journal of Gambling Studies 8, 4: 351–60.

Frey, J. H. 1994. Deviance of organizational subunits: The case of college athletic departments. *Journal of Sport & Social Issues* 18, 2: 110–22.

Frey, J. H., and D. S. Eitzen. 1991. Sport and society. *Annual Review of Sociology* 17: 503–22.

Fudzie, V., and A. Hayes. 1995. *The sport of learning: A comprehensive survival guide for African-American student-athletes.* North Hollywood, CA: Doubleplay Publishing Group.

Fuller, J. R., and E. A. Manning. 1987. Violence and sexism in college mascots and symbols: A typology. *Free Inquiry in Creative Sociology* 15, 1: 61–64.

Gantz, W., and L. A. Wenner. 1995. Fanship and the television sports viewing experience. *Sociology of Sport Journal* 12, 1: 56–74.

Gantz, W., et al. 1995a. Televised sports and marital relationships. *Sociology of Sport Journal* 12, 3: 306–23.

Gantz, W., et al. 1995b. Assessing the football widow hypothesis: A coorientation study of the role of televised sports in long-standing relationships. *Journal of Sport & Social Issues* 19, 4: 352–76.

Garrity, J. 1989. A clash of cultures on the Hopi reservation. *Sports Illustrated* 71, 21: 10–17.

Gaston, J. C. 1986. The destruction of the young black male: The impact of popular culture and organized sports. *Journal of Black Studies* 16: 369–384.

Gems, G. R. 1993. Working class women and sport. *Women in Sport & Physical Activity Journal* 2, 1: 17–30.

George, J. 1994. The virtual disappearance of the white male sprinter in the United States: A speculative essay. *Sociology of Sport Journal* 11, 1: 70–78.

George, N. 1992. *Elevating the game: Black men and basketball.* New York: Harper Collins.

Giulianotti, R. 1994. "Keep it in the family": An outline of Hibs' football hooligans' social ontology. Pp. 327–58 in R. Giulianotti and J. Williams, eds. *Game without frontiers: Football, identity and modernity.* Aldershot, England: Arena, Ashgate.

Giulianotti, R. 1995. Participant observation and research into football hooliganism: Reflections on the problems of entree and everyday risks. *Sociology of Sport Journal* 12, 1: 1–20.

Giulianotti, R., N. Bonny, and M. Hepworth, eds.

1994. *Football, violence and social identity.* London: Routledge.

Glassner, B. 1990. Fit for postmodern selfhood. Pp. 215–43 in H. Becker and M. M. McCall, eds. *Symbolic interaction and cultural studies.* Chicago, IL: University of Chicago Press.

Goffman, E. 1959. *The presentation of self in everyday life.* Garden City, NY: Anchor Books.

Goffman, E. 1961. *Asylums: Essays on the social situation of mental patients and other inmates.* Garden City, NY: Anchor Books.

Goldman, B. 1984. *Death in the locker room.* South Bend, IN: Icarus.

Goldman, B. (with P. Bush and R. Klatz). 1992. *Death in the locker room II.* Chicago, IL: Elite Sports Medicine Publications.

Goldstein, J., ed. 1988–1989. Violence in sports. *Current Psychology: Research and Reviews* 7, 4. Special issue.

Gonzalez, G. L. 1996. The stacking of Latinos in major league baseball: A forgotten minority? *Journal of Sport & Social Issues* 20, 2: 134–60.

Goode, E. 1992. *Drugs in American society.* New York: McGraw-Hill.

Gorman, J., and K. Calhoun (with Skip Rozin). 1994. *The name of the game: The business of sports.* New York: John Wiley & Sons.

Gouguet, J. J., and J. F. Nys. 1993. *Sport et developpement economique regional.* Paris: Dalloz. (Summarized in Lavoie, forthcoming).

Granjean, A. C., and K. J. Reimers. 1996. Creatine. *Olympic Coach* 6, 3 (Summer): 18–19.

Grant, C. H. B., and C. E. Darley. 1993. Equity: What price equality? Pp. 251–63 in G. L. Cohen, ed. *Women in sport: Issues and controversies.* Newbury Park, CA: Sage.

Green, T. S. 1993. The future of African-American female athletes. Pp. 205–24 in D. D. Brooks and R. C. Althouse, eds. *Racism in college athletics: The African-American athlete's experience.* Morgantown, WV: Fitness Information Technology, Inc.

Greenberg, M. J., and J. T. Gray. 1996. Citizenship based quota systems in athletics. *Marquette Sports Law Journal* 6, 2: 337–56.

Greendorfer, S. L. 1983. Sport and the mass media: General overview. *ARENA Review* 7, 2: 1–6.

Greendorfer, S. L. 1993. Gender role stereotypes and early childhood socialization. Pp. 3–14 in G. L. Cohen, ed. *Women in sport.* Newbury Park, CA: Sage.

Greendorfer, S. L., and E. M. Blinde. 1985. "Retirement" from intercollegiate sport: Theoretical and empirical considerations. *Sociology of Sport Journal* 2, 2: 101–10.

Greenfield, S., and G. Osborn. 1996. When the whites go marching in? Racism and resistance in English football. *Marquette Sports Law Journal* 6, 2: 315–36.

Grey, M. 1992. Sports and immigrant, minority and Anglo relations in Garden City (Kansas) high school. *Sociology of Sport Journal* 9, 3: 255–70.

Griffin, P. 1993. Homophobia in women's sports: The fear that divides us. Pp. 193–203 in G. L. Cohen, ed. *Women in sport: Issues and controversies.* Newbury Park, CA: Sage.

Gruneau, R. 1976. Class or mass: Notes on the democratization of Canadian amateur sport. Pp. 108– 40 in R. Gruneau and J. G. Albinson, eds. *Canadian sport: Sociological perspectives.* Don Mills, Ontario: Addison-Wesley.

Gruneau, R. 1988. Modernization or hegemony: Two views of sports and social development. Pp. 9–32 in J. Harvey and H. Cantelon, eds. *Not just a game.* Ottawa, Ontario: University of Ottawa Press.

Gruneau, R. 1989a. Television, the Olympics, and the question of ideology. Pp. 7/23–7/34 in R. Jackson, ed. *The Olympic movement and the mass media.* Calgary, Alberta: Hurford Enterprises.

Gruneau, R. 1989b. Making spectacle: A case study in television sports production. Pp. 134–54 in L. A. Wenner, ed. *Media, sports, and society.* Newbury Park, CA: Sage.

Gruneau, R., and D. Whitson. 1993: *Hockey Night in Canada: Sport, identities, and cultural politics.* Toronto: Garamond Press.

Gunther, M. 1996. Get ready for the Oprah olympics. *Fortune* 134, 2 (July 22): 62–63.

Gunzelman, K. 1996. The court gets tough with LSU over Title IX issues. *The Women's Sports Experience* (WSF Newsletter) 5, 3: 9–10.

Guterson, D. 1994. Moneyball! On the relentless promotion of pro sports. *Harper's Magazine* (September): 37– 46.

Guttmann, A. 1978. *From ritual to record: The nature of modern sports*. New York: Columbia University Press.

Guttmann, A. 1986. *Sport spectators*. New York: Columbia University Press.

Guttmann, A. 1988. *A whole new ball game: An interpretation of American sports*. Chapel Hill, NC: University of North Carolina Press.

Guttmann, A. 1991. *Women's sports: A history*. New York: Columbia University Press.

Guttmann, A. 1994. *Games and empires: Modern sports and cultural imperialism*. New York: Columbia University Press.

Halbert, C., and M. Latimer. 1994. "Battling" gendered language: An analysis of the language used by sports commentators in a televised co-ed tennis competition. *Sociology of Sport Journal* 11, 3: 298–308.

Hall, A., T. Slack, G. Smith, and D. Whitson. 1991. *Sport in Canadian society*. Toronto: McClelland & Stewart.

Hall, M. A. 1996. *Feminism and sporting bodies: Essays on theory and practice*. Champaign, IL: Human Kinetics.

Hallinan, C. J. 1991. Aborigines and positional segregation in Australian rugby league. *International Review for the Sociology of Sport* 26, 2: 69–78.

Hallinan, C. J. 1994. The presentation of human biological diversity in sport and exercise science textbooks: The example of "race." *Journal of Sport Behavior* 17: 3–15.

Hanford, G. 1974. *An inquiry into the need for and the feasibility of a national study of intercollegiate athletics*. Washington, DC: American Council on Education.

Hanford, G. 1979. Controversies in college sports. *Annals of the American Academy of Political Science* 445: 66–79.

Hanks, M., and B. K. Eckland. 1976. Athletics and social participation in the educational attainment process. *Sociology of Education* 49, 4: 271–94.

Hare, N. 1971. A study of the black fighter. *Black Scholar* 3, 3: 2–9.

Hargreaves, Jennifer, 1994. *Sporting females: Critical issues in the history and sociology of women's sport*. London: Routledge.

Hargreaves, Jennifer, and I. MacDonald. Forthcoming. Gramscian/cultural studies. In J. Coakley and E. Dunning, eds. *Handbook of sport and society*. London: Sage.

Hargreaves, John. 1986. Sport, power and culture. New York: St. Martin's Press.

Harris, J. 1994. *Athletes and the American hero dilemma*. Champaign, IL: Human Kinetics.

Harris, O. 1994. Race, sport, and social support. *Sociology of Sport Journal* 11, 1: 40–50.

Harrison, K. 1995. Perceptions of African American male student-athletes in higher education. Unpublished dissertation, School of Education, University of Southern California.

Harvey, J., and F. Houle. 1994. Sport, world economy, global culture, and new social movements. *Sociology of Sport Journal* 11, 4: 337–55.

Harvey, J., and R. Proulx. 1988. Sport and the state in Canada. In J. Harvey and H. Cantelon, eds. *Not just a game*. Ottawa, Ontario: University of Ottawa Press.

Harvey, J., G. Rail, and L. Thibault. 1996. Globalization and sport: Sketching a theoretical model for empirical analyses. *Journal of Sport & Social Issues* 20, 3: 258–77.

Hasbrook, C. A. 1993. The production and subordination of feminine bodies among first grade children. Paper presented at the annual meeting of the North American Society for the Sociology of Sport. Ottawa.

Hasbrook, C. A. 1995. Gendering practices and first graders' bodies: Physicality, sexuality, and bodily adornment in a minority inner-city school. Unpublished manuscript.

Hasbrook, C. A., and O. Harris. 1997. Physicality and the production of masculinities among first and second graders. *Masculinities* (in press).

Hayes, D. W. 1993. Sports images and realities. *Black Issues in Higher Education* 10, 20: 15–19.

Haynes, R. 1993. Every man(?) a football artist: Football writing and masculinity. Pp. 55–76 in S. Redhead, ed. *The passion and the fashion: Football fandom in the New Europe*. Aldershot, England: Avebury.

Heinila, K. 1985. Sport and international understanding: A contradiction in terms? *Sociology of Sport Journal* 2, 3: 240–48.

Heinz, M. 1991. Women's sports in the media. *Inside Track* (Spring). CBC radio program.

Heller, S. 1991. The human body and changing cultural conceptions of it draw attention of humanities and social-science scholars. *The Chronicle of Higher Education*, June 12: A4, A8.

Hellison, D. 1985. *Goals and strategies for teaching physical education*. Champaign, IL: Human Kinetics.

Hellison, D. 1990. Physical education for disadvantaged youth—A Chicago story. *JOPERD* 61, 6: 36–45. A five-article section.

Hellison, D. 1993. The coaching club: Teaching responsibility to inner-city students. *JOPERD* 64, 5: 66–71.

Hesling, W. 1986. The pictorial representation of sports on television. *International Review for the Sociology of Sport* 21, 2–3: 173–94.

Higgs, C. T., and K. H. Weiler. 1994. Gender bias and the 1992 Summer Olympic games: An analysis of television coverage. *Journal of Sport & Social Issues* 18, 3: 234–46.

Higgs, R. J. 1995. *God in the stadium: Sports and religion in America*. Lexington, KY: The University of Kentucky Press.

Hilliard, D. C. 1984. Media images of male and female professional athletes: An interpretive analysis of magazine articles. *Sociology of Sport Journal* 1, 3: 251–62.

Hilliard, D. C. 1994. Televised sport and the (anti)sociological imagination. *Journal of Sport & Social Issues* 18, 1: 88–99.

Hoberman, J. 1986. *The Olympic crisis: Sport, politics and the moral order*. New Rochelle, NY: Aristide D. Caratzas.

Hoberman, J. 1992. *Mortal engines: The science of performance and the dehumanization of sport*. New York: The Free Press.

Hoberman, J. 1995. Listening to steroids. *The Wilson Quarterly* 19, 1 (Winter): 35–44.

Hoberman, J. 1997. *Darwin's athletes: How sport has damaged black America and preserved the myth of race*. Boston: Houghton Mifflin.

Hoberman, J., and C. Yesalis. 1995. The history of synthetic testosterone. *Scientific American* (February): 60–65.

Hoffman, S. 1982. God, guts and glory: Evangelical-

ism in American sports. Paper presented at the meetings of the American Alliance for Health, Physical Education, Recreation and Dance, Detroit.

Hoffman, S. 1992a. *Sport and religion*. Champaign, IL: Human Kinetics (Note: 1992a references refer to Hoffman's section introductions in this book).

Hoffman, S. 1992b. Evangelicalism and the revitalization of religious ritual in sport. Pp. 111–25 in S. Hoffman, ed. *Sport and religion*. Champaign, IL: Human Kinetics.

Hoffman, S. 1992c. Recovering a sense of the sacred in sport. Pp. 153–60 in S. Hoffman, ed. *Sport and religion*. Champaign, IL: Human Kinetics.

Hoffman, S. 1992d. Nimrod, Nephilim, and the Athletae Dei. Pp. 275–86 in S. Hoffman, ed. *Sport and religion*. Champaign, IL: Human Kinetics.

Holman, M. J. 1995. Female and male athletes' accounts and meanings of sexual harassment in Canadian interuniversity athletics. Ph.D. dissertation, University of Michigan.

Holmlund, C. A. 1994. Visible difference and flex appeal: The body, sex, sexuality, and race in the *Pumping Iron* films. Pp. 299–314 in S. Birrell and C. L. Cole, eds. *Women, sport, and culture*. Champaign, IL: Human Kinetics.

Hood-Williams, J. 1995. Sexing the athletes. *Sociology of Sport Journal* 12, 3: 290–305.

hooks, bell. 1992. Theory as liberatory practice. *Yale Journal of Law and Feminism* 4, 1: 1–12.

Hornblower, M. 1996. Underdogs' day. *Time*, Augusts 5: 45–46.

Horne, J. 1996. Kicking racism out of soccer in England and Scotland. *Journal of Sport & Social Issues* 20, 1: 45–68.

Houlihan, B. 1994a. Sport and international politics. Hemel Hempstead, England: Harvester-Wheatsheaf.

Houlihan, B. 1994b. Homogenization, Americanization, and the Creolization of sport. *Sociology of Sport Journal* 11, 4: 356–75.

Howell, F., A. Miracle, and R. Rees. 1984. Do high school athletics pay? The effects of varsity participation on socioeconomic attainment. *Sociology of Sport Journal* 1, 1: 15–25.

Howell, F., and S. Picou. 1983. Athletics and income

achievements. Paper presented at the Southwestern Sociological Association, Houston.

Huey, J. 1996. The Atlanta game. *Fortune* 134, 2 (July 22): 43–56.

Hughes, R., and J. Coakley. 1991. Positive deviance among athletes: The implications of overconformity to the sport ethic. *Sociology of Sport Journal* 8, 4: 307–25.

Humphrey, J. 1986. No holding Brazil: Football, nationalism and politics. In A. Tomlinson and G. Whannel, eds. *Off the ball.* London: Pluto Press.

Hunter-Hodge, K. 1995. Athletes are finding second wind entering arena of big business. *Colorado Springs Gazette,* January 8: F4.

IBS. 1996a. *Path to victory: A sports New Testament with testimonies of athletes who are winning in life.* Colorado Springs, CO: International Bible Society.

IBS. 1996b. *More than gold.* Colorado Springs, CO: International Bible Society.

Irlinger, P. 1994. The contribution of televised sports to the spread of sport activities. *International Review for the Sociology of Sport* 29, 2: 201–10.

Jackson, S. J. 1994. Gretzky, crisis, and Canadian identity in 1988: Rearticulating the Americanization of culture debate. *Sociology of Sport Journal* 11, 4: 428–46.

James, C. L. R. 1984. *Beyond a boundary.* New York: Pantheon Books. American edition.

Jamieson, K. 1995. Latinas in sport and physical activity. *Journal of Physical Education, Recreation and Dance* 66, 7: 42–47.

Jennings, A. 1996. *The new lords of the rings.* London: Pocket Books.

Johns, D. 1992. Starving for gold: A case study in overconformity in high performance sport. Paper presented at the annual conference of the North American Society for the Sociology of Sport, Toledo (November).

Johns, D. 1996. Positive deviance and the sport ethic: Examining weight loss strategies in rhythmic gymnastics. *The Hong Kong Journal of Sports Medicine and Sport Science* 2 (May): xx.

Johns, D. Forthcoming. Fasting and feasting: Paradoxes in the sport ethic. *Sociology of Sport Journal.*

Johnson, A. 1982. Government, opposition and sport: The role of domestic sports policy in generating political support. *Journal of Sport and Social Issues* 6, 2: 22–34.

Johnson, A. T. 1993. *Minor league baseball and economic development.* Urbana, IL: University of Illinois Press.

Johnson, B. D., and N. R. Johnson. 1995. Stacking and "stoppers": A test of the outcome control hypothesis. *Sociology of Sport Journal* 12, 1: 105–12.

Johnson, P. 1995. Black radio's role in sports promotion: Sports, scholarships, and sponsorship. *Journal of Sport & Social Issues* 19, 4: 397–414.

Johnson, W. O. 1974. From here to 2000. *Sports Illustrated* 41, 26: 73–83.

Jones, G., et al. 1987. A log-linear analysis of stacking in college football. *Social Science Quarterly* 68: 70–83.

Jones, S. R. 1993. Race and baseball: Getting beyond business as usual. *Journal of Sport & Social Issues* 17, 1: 67–70.

Joravsky, B. 1995. *Hoop dreams: A true story of hardship and triumph.* New York: HarperCollins.

Kane, M. J. 1995. Resistance/transformation of the oppositional binary: Exposing sport as a continuum. *Journal of Sport & Social Issues* 19, 2: 191–218.

Kane, M. J., and L. J. Disch. 1993. Sexual violence and the reproduction of male power in the locker room: The "Lisa Olson Incident." *Sociology of Sport Journal* 10, 4: 331–52.

Kane, M. J., and J. B. Parks. 1992. The social construction of gender difference and hierarchy in sports journalism—few new twists on very old themes. *Women in Sport & Physical Activity Journal* 1, 1: 49–84.

Keefer, R., J. H. Goldstein, and D. Kasiarz. 1983. Olympic games participation and warfare. In J. H. Goldstein, ed. *Sports violence.* New York: Springer-Verlag.

Kelley, B. C., S. J. Hoffman, and D. L. Gill. 1990. The relationship between competitive orientation and religious orientation. *Journal of Sport Behavior* 13, 3: 145–56.

Kempton, S. 1995. *Progressive* 1995 calendar (March).

Kidd, B. 1984. The myth of the ancient games. Pp. 71–83 in A. Tomlinson and G. Whannel, eds. *Five-ring circus.* London: Pluto Press.

Kidd, B. 1987. Sports and masculinity. Pp. 250–65 in

M. Kaufman, ed., *Beyond patriarchy: Essays by men on pleasure, power, and change*. New York: Oxford University Press.

Kidd, B. 1995. Inequality in sport, the corporation, and the state: An agenda for social scientists. *Journal of Sport & Social Issues* 19, 3: 232–48.

Kidd, B. 1996a. Worker sport in the New World: The Canadian story. Pp. 143–56 in A. Kruger and J. Riordan, eds. *The story of worker sport*. Champaign, IL: Human Kinetics.

Kidd, B. 1996b. Taking the rhetoric seriously: Proposals for Olympic education. *Quest* 48, 1: 82–92.

Kimura, M., and T. Saeki. 1990. A study on the mechanism of the sexism strategies in the discourse of media reports on women's sports in Japan. Paper presented at the International Congress for the Sociology of Sport, Madrid (June).

King, 1994. Halt the head-hunting. *Sports Illustrated* 81, 25: 27–53.

King, A. 1996. The fining of Vinnie Jones. *International Review for the Sociology of Sport* 31, 2: 119–38.

King, P. 1995. Knock it off! *Sports Illustrated* 83, 17: 76–81.

King, P. 1996. Bitter pill. *Sports Illustrated* 84, 21: 25–30.

Kinkema, K. M., and J. C. Harris. 1992. Sport and the mass media. *Exercise and Sport Science Reviews* 20: 127–59.

Kjeldsen, E. 1980. Centrality and leadership recruitment: A study of their linkage. Paper presented at the meetings of the North American Society for the Sociology of Sport, Denver.

Kleiber, D. A., and S. C. Brock. 1992. The effect of career-ending injuries on the subsequent well-being of elite college athletes. *Sociology of Sport Journal* 9, 1: 70–75.

Kleiber, D. A., S. Greendorfer, E. Blinde, and S. Samdahl. 1987. Quality of exit from university sports and life satisfaction in early adulthood. *Sociology of Sport Journal* 4, 1: 28–36.

Klein, A. 1984. Review of *Soccer Madness* (Lever, 1983). *Sociology of Sport Journal* 1, 2: 195–97.

Klein, A. 1991. *Sugarball: The American game, the Dominican dream*. New Haven, CT: Yale University Press.

Klein, A. 1993. *Little big men: Bodybuilding subculture and gender construction*. Albany, NY: State University of New York Press.

Klein, A. 1995. Tender machos: Masculine contrasts in the Mexican baseball league. *Sociology of Sport Journal* 12, 4: 370–88.

Klein, A. 1996. Borderline treason: Nationalisms and baseball on the Texas-Mexico border. *Journal of Sport & Social Issues* 20, 3: 296–313.

Knight Foundation. 1991. Report of the Knight Foundation Commission on Intercollegiate Athletics. (Note: available through NCAA.)

Knisley, M. 1966. Rupeat. *The Sporting News*, January 1: S1–S28. Special section: The 100 most powerful people in sports.

Kolnes, L.-J. 1995. Heterosexuality as an organizing principle in women's sports. *International Review for the Sociology of Sport* 30, 1: 61–79.

Kooistra, P., J. S. Mahoney, and L. Bridges. 1993. The unequal opportunity for equal ability hypothesis: Racism in the National Football League. *Sociology of Sport Journal* 10, 3: 241–55.

Koppett, L. 1994. *Sports illusion, sports reality*. Urbana, IL: University of Illinois Press.

Koss, M., and J. Gaines. 1993. The prediction of sexual aggression by alcohol use, athletic participation and fraternity affiliation. *Journal of Interpersonal Violence* 8: 94–108.

Koukouris, K. 1994. Constructed case studies: Athletes' perspectives of disengaging from organized competitive sport. *Sociology of Sport Journal* 11, 2: 114–39.

Kozol, J. 1991. *Savage inequalities*. New York, NY: Crown Publishers.

Krane, V. 1996. Lesbians in sport: Toward acknowledgement, understanding, and theory. *Journal of Sport & Exercise Psychology* 18, 3: 237–46.

Kruger, A., and J. Riordan, eds. 1996. *The story of worker sport*. Champaign, IL: Human Kinetics.

Laberge, S., and D. Sankoff. 1988. Physical activities, body *habitus*, and lifestyles. Pp. 267–286 in J. Harvey and H. Cantelon, eds., *Not just a game*. Ottawa: University of Ottawa Press.

La Franco, R. 1996. The top 40. *Forbes* 158, 7 (September): 164–78.

Landers, D. M., and D. M. Landers. 1978. Socialization via interscholastic athletics: its effects on delinquency. *Sociology of Education* 51, 4: 299–303.

Landers, M. A., and G. A. Fine. 1996. Learning life's lessons in Tee Ball: The reinforcement of gender and status in kindergarten sport. *Sociology of Sport Journal* 13, 1: 87–93.

Langley, M. 1994. The cool pose: An Afrocentric analysis. Pp. 231–44 in R. G. Majors and J. U. Gordon, eds. *The American black male.* Chicago, IL: Nelson-Hall.

Lapchick, R. 1984. *Broken promises: Racism in American sports.* New York: St. Martin's/Marek.

Lapchick, R. 1988. Blacks and baseball. *The CSSS Digest* 1, 1: 4–12.

Lapchick, R. 1989. Blacks in the NBA and NFL. *The CSSS Digest* 1, 2: 1, 4–5.

Lapchick, R. 1991. *Five minutes to midnight: Race and sport in the 1990s.* Lanham, MD: Madison Books.

Lapchick, R. 1995. Front court. Preface. In V. Fudzie and A. Hayes. *The sport of learning: A comprehensive survival guide for African-American student-athletes.* North Hollywood, CA: Doubleplay Publishing Group.

Lapchick, R. 1996a. *Sport in society: Equal opportunity or business as usual?* Thousand Oaks, CA: Sage.

Lapchick, R. (with B. Fay and M. McLean). 1996b. *1996 racial report card.* Boston, MA: Center for the Study of Sport in Society, Northeastern University.

Laqueur, T. 1990. *Making sex.* Cambridge, MA: Harvard University Press.

Lavoie, M. 1989. Stacking, performance differentials, and salary discrimination in professional ice hockey: A survey of the evidence. *Sociology of Sport Journal* 6, 1: 17–35.

Lavoie, M. Forthcoming. Economics and sport. In J. Coakley and E. Dunning, eds. *Handbook of sport and society.* London: Sage.

Lavoie M., and W. M. Leonard, II. 1994. In search of an alternative explanation of stacking in baseball: The uncertainty hypothesis. *Sociology of Sport Journal* 11, 2: 140–54.

Layden, T. 1995a. Better education. *Sports Illustrated,* April 3: 68–90.

Layden, T. 1995b. Book smart. *Sports Illustrated,* April 10: 68–79.

Layden, T. 1995c. You bet your life. *Sports Illustrated,* April 17: 46–55.

Leath, V. M., and A. Lumpkin. 1992. An analysis of sportswomen on the covers and in the feature articles of *Women's Sports and Fitness Magazine,* 1975–1989. *Journal of Sport & Social Issues* 16, 2: 121–26.

Lederman, D. 1988. Do winning teams spur contributions? *The Chronicle of Higher Education* 34, 18: 1, 32–34.

Lederman, D. 1992. Blacks make up large proportion of scholarship athletes, yet their overall enrollment lags at Division I colleges. *The Chronicle for Higher Education* 38, 41: 1, A30–A34.

Lee, V. 1996. Wimps or warriors? *Sports Spectrum* (December) 22–25.

Lenskyj, H. 1986. *Out of bounds: Women, sport and sexuality.* Toronto: Women's Press.

Lenskyj, H. 1988. *Women, sport and physical activity: Research and bibliography.* Ottawa, Ontario: Ministry of State, Fitness and Amateur Sports.

Lenskyj, H. 1992a. Feminism, resistance and the remaking of sport: Theories, methodologies and practices. Paper presented at the annual conference of the North American Society for the Sociology of Sport, Toledo (November).

Lenskyj, H. 1992b. Unsafe at home base: Women's experiences of sexual harassment in university sport and physical education. *Women in Sport & Physical Activity Journal* 1, 1: 19–33.

Lenskyj, H. 1994a. *Women, sport and physical activity: Selected research themes.* Gloucester, Ontario: Sport Information Resource Centre (SIRC/CDS).

Lenskyj, H. 1994b. Girl friendly sport and female values. *Women in Sport & Physical Activity Journal* 3, 1: 35–46.

Lenskyj, H. 1994c. Sexuality and femininity in sport contexts: Issues and alternatives. *Journal of Sport & Social Issues* 18, 4: 356–76.

Lenskyj, H. 1996. When winners are losers: Toronto and Sydney bids for the summer games. *Journal of Sport & Social Issues* 20, 4: 392–410.

Leonard, W. M., II. 1977a. An extension of the black, Latin, white report. *International Review for Sport Sociology* 3, 12: 86–95.

Leonard, W. M., II. 1977b. Stacking and performance differentials of whites, blacks and Latins in professional baseball. *Review of Sport and*

Leisure 2: 77–106.

Leonard, W. M., II. 1987. Stacking in college basketball: a neglected analysis: *Sociology of Sport Journal* 4, 4: 403–9.

Leonard, W. M., II. 1988. Salaries and race in professional baseball: the Hispanic component. *Sociology of Sport Journal* 5, 3: 278–84.

Leonard, W. M., II. 1995. Economic discrimination in major league baseball: Marginal revenue products of majority and minority groups members. *Journal of Sport & Social Issues* 19, 2: 180–90.

Leonard, W. M., II. 1996. The odds of transiting from one level of sports participation to another. *Sociology of Sport Journal* 13, 3: 288–99.

Leray, C. 1994. Planet Dennis. *Inside Sports* (February): 28–33.

Lever, J. 1976. Sex differences in the games children play. *Social Problems* 23: 478–87.

Lever, J. 1978. Sex differences in the complexity of children's play. *American Sociological Review* 43, 4: 471–83.

Lever, J. 1980. Multiple methods of data collection: a note on divergence. *Urban Life* 10, 2: 199–214.

Lever, J. 1983. *Soccer madness.* Chicago, IL: University of Chicago Press.

Lever, J., and S. Wheeler, 1984. *The Chicago Tribune* sports page, 1900–1975. *Sociology of Sport Journal* 1, 4: 299–313.

Lever, J., and S. Wheeler. 1993. Mass media and the experience of sport. *Communication Research* 20, 1: 125–43.

Lewis, M. 1972a. Sex differences in play behavior of the very young. *JOPERD* 43, 6: 38–39.

Lewis, M. 1972b. Culture and gender roles: There is no unisex in the nursery. *Psychology Today* 5, 12: 54–57.

Ligutom-Kimura, D. A. 1995. The invisible women. *Journal of Physical Education, Recreation and Dance* 66, 7: 34–41.

Lipsyte, 1996. Little girls in a staged spectacle for big bucks? That's sportainment! *New York Times,* August 4: 28.

Lirgg, C., R. DiBrezzo, and A. Smith. 1994. Influence of gender of coach on perceptions of basketball and coaching self-efficacy and aspirations of high school female basketball players. *Women in*

Sport & Physical Activity Journal 3, 1: 1–14.

Longman, J. 1996. Slow down, speed up. *New York Times,* May 1: B11.

Longmore, A. 1994. Feminine touch marks sport's new age. *The Times* (London), February 19: 44.

Looney, D. S. 1996. Cash, check or charge? *The Sporting News,* July 1: 38–42.

Lopiano, D. 1991. Presentation at the Coaching America's Coaches Conference, United States Olympic Training Center, Colorado Springs, CO.

Lopiano, D. 1992. The stars are lining up in support of gender equity in sport. *GWS News* 19, 3: 3–4, 15–16.

Lopiano, D. A. 1993. Political analysis: Gender equity strategies for the future. Pp. 104–16 in G. L. Cohen, ed. *Women in sport: Issues and controversies.* Newbury Park, CA: Sage.

Lorenz, K. 1966. *On aggression.* New York: Harcourt Brace Jovanovich.

Loughran, J. N. 1996. Athletics reform is doomed to fail. *Trusteeship* (November/December): 35.

Loy, J. 1969. The study of sport and social mobility. In G. Kenyon, ed. *Sociology of sport.* North Palm Beach, FL: The Athletic Institute.

Loy, J. 1992. The dark side of agon: Men in tribal groups and the phenomenon of gang rape. Paper presented at the annual conference of the North American Society for the Sociology of Sport, Toledo (November).

Loy, J., D. L. Andrews, and R. Rinehart. 1993. The body in culture and sport. *Sport Science Review* 2, 1: 69–91.

Loy, J. W., J. E. Curtis, and G. H. Sage. 1978. Relative centrality of playing position and leadership recruitment in team sports. *Exercise and Sport Science Reviews* 6: 257–84.

Loy, J. W., and S. J. Jackson. 1990. A typology of group structures and a theory of their effects on patterns of leadership recruitment within sport organizations. Pp. 93–114 in. L. VanderVelden and J. H. Humprey, eds. *Psychology and sociology of sport: Current selected research.* Vol. 2. New York: AMS Press.

Luberto, D. K. 1994. The integration movement: Texas high school athletic and academic contests. *Journal of Sport & Social Issues* 18, 2: 151–68.

Lueschen, G. 1993. Doping in sport: The social structure of a deviant subculture. *Sport Science Review* 2, 1: 92–106.

Lumpkin, A., and L. D. Williams. 1991. An analysis of *Sports Illustrated* feature articles. 1954–1987. *Sociology of Sport Journal* 8, 1: 16–32.

Lyng, S. 1990. Edgework: A social pyschological analysis of voluntary risk taking. *American Journal of Sociology* 95, 4: 851–86.

Macintosh, D., and M. Hawes. 1992. The IOC and the world of interdependence. *Olympika* 1: 29–45.

Macintosh, D., and M. Hawes. 1994. *Sport and Canadian diplomacy.* Montreal, Quebec and Kingston, Ontario: McGill-Queen's University Press.

MacNeill, M. 1994. Active women, media representations, and ideology. Pp. 273–88 in S. Birrell and C. L. Cole, eds. *Women, sport, and culture.* Champaign, IL: Human Kinetics.

MacNeill, M. 1996. Networks: Producing Olympic ice hockey for a national television audience. *Sociology of Sport Journal* 13, 2: 103–24.

Maguire, J. 1986. The emergence of football spectating as a social problem, 1880–1985: A figurational and developmental perspective. *Sociology of Sport Journal* 3, 3: 217–44.

Maguire, J. 1988. Race and position assignment in English soccer: A preliminary analysis of ethnicity and sport in Britain. *Sociology of Sport Journal* 5, 3: 257–69.

Maguire, J. 1988–1989. Violence at soccer matches in Victorian England: Issues in the study of sports violence, popular culture and deviance. *Current Psychology* 7, 4: 285–97.

Maguire, J. 1990. More than a sporting touchdown: The making of American football in England, 1982–1990. *Sociology of Sport Journal* 7, 3: 213–37.

Maguire, J. 1991. Sport, racism and British society: A sociological study of England's elite male Afro/Caribbean soccer and Rugby Union players. Pp. 94–123 in G. Jarvie, ed. *Sport, racism and ethnicity.* London: The Falmer Press.

Maguire, J. 1993. Globalization, sport development, and the media/sport production complex. *Sport Science Review* 2: 29–47.

Maguire, J. 1994a. Globalisation, sport and national identities: "The Empires Strike Back?" *Society and Leisure* 16: 293–323.

Maguire, J. 1994b. Preliminary observations on globalization and the migration of sport labor. *Sociological Review* 3: 452–80.

Maguire, J. 1994c. Sport, identity politics, and globalization: Diminishing contrasts and increasing varieties. *Sociology of Sport Journal* 11, 4: 398–427.

Maguire, J. 1996. Blade runners, Canadian migrants, ice hockey, and the global sports process. *Journal of Sport & Social Issues* 20, 3: 335–60.

Maguire, J., and D. Stead. 1996. Far Pavilions? Cricket migrants, foreign sojourn and contested identities. *International Review for the Sociology of Sport* 31, 1: 1–24.

Majors, R. 1986. Cool pose: The proud signature of black survival. *Changing Men: Issues in Gender, Sex and Politics* 17 (Winter): 184–85.

Majors, R. 1991. Cool pose: Black masculinity and sports. Pp. 109–14 in M. A. Messner, and D. F. Sabo (eds.). *Sport, men, and the gender order.* Champaign IL: Human Kinetics.

Majors, R., et al. 1994. Cool pose: A symbolic mechanism for masculine role enactment and coping by black males. Pp. 245–59 in R. G. Majors and J. U. Gordon, eds. *The American black male.* Chicago: Nelson-Hall.

Malec, M. A. 1994. Gender (in)equity in the *NCAA News. Journal of Sport & Social Issues* 18, 4: 376–78.

Malec, M. A. 1995. Hoop shots and last dreams. *Journal of Sport and Social Issues* 19, 3: 307–11.

Mangan, K. S. 1996. U. of Houston considers the unthinkable for a Texas university: Ending its sports program. *The Chronicle of Higher Education* 43, 3(September 13): A47–A48.

Marable, M. 1993. A new American socialism. *The Progressive* 57, 2: 20–25.

Mark, M. M., et al. 1983. Perceived injustice and sports violence. In J. Goldstein, ed. *Sports violence.* New York: Springer-Verlag.

Marks, J. 1994. Black, white, other: Racial categories are cultural constructs masquerading as biology, *Natural History* 103, 12: 32–35.

Markula, P. 1995. Firm but shapely, fit but sexy, strong but thin: The postmodern aerobicizing female bodies. *Sociology of Sport Journal* 12, 4: 424–53.

Mars, J. M. 1996. The right of publicity: Untested marketing rights of college football celebrities. *Journal of Sport & Social Issues* 20, 2: 211–22.

Marsh, H. W. 1993. The effect of participation in sport during the last two years of high school. *Sociology of Sport Journal* 10, 1: 18–43.

Marsh, P. 1978. *Aggro: The illusion of violence*. London: Dent & Sons.

Marsh, P. 1982. Social order on the British soccer terraces. *International Social Science Journal* 34, 2: 247–56.

Mathisen, J. 1990. Reviving "Muscular Christianity": Gil Dodds and the institutionalization of sport evangelism. *Sociological Focus* 23, 3: 233–49.

Mathisen, J. 1992. From civil religion to folk religion: The case of American sport. Pp. 17–34 in S. Hoffman, ed. *Sport and religion*. Champaign IL: Human Kinetics.

Mathesen, H., and K. Flatten. 1996. Newspaper representation of women athletes in 1984 and 1994. *Women in Sport & Physical Activity Journal* 5, 2: 65–84.

May, R. 1972. *Power and innocence: A search for the sources of violence*. New York: W. W. Norton.

McCall, M. M., and H. S. Becker. 1990. Introduction. Pp. 1–15 in H. S. Becker and M. M. McCall, eds. *Symbolic interaction and cultural studies*. Chicago: University of Chicago Press.

McCormack, J. B., and L. Chalip. 1988. Sport as socialization: A critique of methodological premises. *The Social Science Journal* 25, 1: 83–92.

McDermott, L. 1996. Toward a feminist understanding of physicality within the context of women's physically active and sporting lives. *Sociology of Sport Journal* 13, 1: 12–30.

McGraw, D. 1997. The national bet. *U.S. News & World Report*, April 7: 50–55.

McKay, J. 1990. The "moral panic" of drugs in sport. Paper presented at the Australian Sociology Association Conference, Queensland (December).

McKay, J., G. Lawrence, T. Miller, and D. Rowe. 1993. Globalization and Australian sport. *Sport Science Review* 2, 1: 10–28.

McNeal, R. B., Jr. 1995. Extracurricular activities and high school dropouts. *Sociology of Education* 64: 62–81.

McPherson, B. 1980. Retirement from professional sport: the process and problems of occupational and psychological adjustment. *Sociological Symposium* 30: 126–43.

McTeer, W. 1987. Intercollegiate athletes and student life: two studies in the Canadian case. *ARENA Review* 11, 2: 94–100.

Mead, C. 1985. *Champion Joe Louis: Black hero in white America*. New York: Charles Scribner's Sons.

Melnick, M. J. 1988. Racial segregation by playing position in the English football league: Some preliminary observations. *Journal of Sport and Social Issues* 12, 2: 122–30.

Melnick, M. J. 1992. Male athletes and sexual assault. *JOPERD* 63, 5: 32–35.

Melnick, M. J. 1996. Maori women and positional segregation in New Zealand netball: Another test of the Anglocentric Hypothesis. *Sociology of Sport Journal* 13, 3: 259–73.

Melnick, M. J., and J. W. Loy. 1996. The effects of formal structure on leadership recruitment: An analysis of team captaincy among New Zealand provincial rugby teams. *International Review for the Sociology of Sport* 31, 1: 91–107.

Melnick, M. J., and D. Sabo. 1994. Sport and social mobility among African-American and Hispanic athletes. Pp. 221–41 in G. Eisen and D. K. Wiggins, eds. *Ethnicity and sport in North American history and culture*. Westport, CT: Greenwood Press.

Melnick, M. J., D. Sabo, and B. Vanfossen. 1992. Effects of interscholastic athletic participation on the social, educational, and career mobility of Hispanic girls and boys. *International Review for the Sociology of Sport* 27, 1: 57–75.

Melnick, M. J., B. Vanfossen, and D. Sabo. 1988. Developmental effects of athletic participation among high school girls. *Sociology of Sport Journal* 5, 1: 22–36.

Melnick, M. J., and R. Thompson. 1996. The Maori people and positional segregation in New Zealand rugby football: A test of the anglocentric hypothesis. *International Review for the Sociology of Sport* 31, 2: 139–54.

Menzies, H. 1989. Women's sport: Treatment by the media. Pp. 220–31 in K. Dyer, ed. *Sportswomen towards 2000: A celebration*. Richmond, South Australia: University of Adelaide.

Messner, M. A. 1984. Review of *Class, sports, and social development* (Gruneau, 1983) and *Sport, culture, and ideology* (Hargreaves, ed., 1982). *Journal of Sport and Social Issues* 8, 1: 49–51.

Messner, M. A. 1991. Women in the men's locker room. *Changing Men: Issues in Gender, Sex and Politics* 23 (Fall/Winter): 56–58.

Messner, M. A. 1992. *Power at play.* Boston: Beacon Press.

Messner, M. A. 1994. When bodies are weapons. Pp. 89–98 in M. Messner and D. Sabo, eds. 1994. *Sex, violence & power in sports.* Freedom, CA: The Crossing Press.

Messner, M. A. 1996. Studying up on sex. *Sociology of Sport Journal* 13, 3: 221–37.

Messner, M. A., M. C. Duncan, and F. L. Wachs. 1996. The gender of audience-building: Televised coverage of women's and men's NCAA basketball. *Sociological Inquiry* 66, 4: 422–39.

Messner, M. A., and D. F. Sabo, eds. 1992. *Sport, men, and the gender order: Critical feminist perspectives.* Champaign, IL: Human Kinetics Books.

Messner, M. A., and D. Sabo, eds. 1994. *Sex, violence & power in sports.* Freedom, CA: The Crossing Press.

Messner, M. A., and W. S. Solomon. 1993. Outside the frame: Newspaper coverage of the Sugar Ray Leonard wife abuse story. *Sociology of Sport Journal* 10, 2: 119–34.

Messner, M. A., and W. S. Solomon. 1994. Sin and redemption: The Sugar Ray Leonard wife abuse story. Pp. 53–65 in M. A. Messner and D. Sabo, eds. *Sex, violence & power in sports.* Freedom, CA: The Crossing Press.

Meyer, B. B. 1988. The college experience: Female athletes and nonathletes. Paper presented at the North American Society for the Sociology of Sport Conference, Cincinnati.

Meyer, B. B. 1990. From idealism to actualization: The academic performance of female collegiate athletes. *Sociology of Sport Journal* 7, 1: 44–57.

Miedzian, M. 1991. *Boys will be boys: Breaking the link between masculinity and violence.* New York: Anchor Books.

Mielke, R., and S. Bahlke. 1995. Structure and preferences of fundamental values of young athletes. Do they differ from non-athletes and from young people with alternative leisure activities? *International Review for the Sociology of Sport* 30, 3/4: 419–437.

Miller, L., and O. Penz 1991. Talking bodies: Female bodybuilders colonize a male preserve. *Quest* 43, 2: 148–63.

Miller Lite Report on American Attitudes Toward Sports. Milwaukee, WI: Miller Brewing Co.

Miller, S. 1991. *Arete: Greek sports from ancient sources.* Berkeley, CA: University of California Press.

Minton, L. 1995. The cheerleaders vs the girl players. *Parade,* July 23: 7.

Miracle, A. W., 1980. School spirit as a ritual by-product: Views from applied anthropology. Pp. 98–103 in H. B. Schwartzman, ed. *Play and culture.* West Point, NY: Leisure Press.

Miracle, A. W., 1981. Factors affecting interracial co-operation: A case study of a high school football team. *Human Organization* 40, 2: 150–54.

Miracle, A. W., and C. R. Rees. 1994. *Lessons of the locker room: The myth of school sports.* Amherst, NY: Prometheus Books.

Moore, D. L. 1991. Athletes and rape: Alarming link. *USA Today,* August 27: 1C–2C.

Morgan, W. J. 1994. *Leftist theories of sport: A critique and reconstruction.* Urbana, IL: University of Illinois Press.

Morgan, W. J. Forthcoming. Philosophy and sport. In J. Coakley and E. Dunning, eds. *Handbook of sport and society.* London: Sage.

Morgan, W. P. 1984. Physical activity and mental health. In H. M. Eckert and H. J. Montoye, eds. *Exercise and health* (The American Academy of Physical Education papers). Champaign, IL: Human Kinetics.

Morra, N., and M. D. Smith. 1996. Interpersonal sources of violence in hockey: The influence of the media, parents, coaches, and game officials. Pp. 142–155 in R. E. Smith and F. Smoll, eds. *Children and youth sport: A biopsychosocial perspective.* Madison, WI: Brown and Benchmark.

Morris, D. 1967. *The naked ape.* London: Jonathon Cape.

Morris, D. 1981. *The soccer tribe.* London: Chatto, Bodley Head & Jonathon Cape.

Morrison, R. 1996. Sports fans, athletes' salaries, and economic rent. *International Review for the Sociol-*

ogy of Sport 31, 3: 257–72.

Mosher, S. D. 1995. Whose dreams? Basketball and celluloid America. *Journal of Sport and Social Issues* 19, 3: 318–26.

Mrozek, D. J. 1983. *Sport and American mentality, 1880–1920.* Knoxville: University of Tennessee Press.

Murphy, P. K. Sheard, and I. Waddington. Forthcoming. Figurational/process sociology. In J. Coakley and E. Dunning, eds. *Handbook of sport and society.* London: Sage.

Murphy, P. J. Williams, and E. Dunning. 1990. *Football on trial: Spectator violence and development in the world of football.* London: Routledge.

Murrell, A. J., and E. M. Curtis. 1994. Causal attributions of performance for black and white quarterbacks in the NFL: A look at the sports pages. *Journal of Sport & Social Issues* 18, 3: 224–33.

Muscatine, A. 1991. The status of women's sports. *Women's Sports Pages* 3, 4: 12–13, 18.

Nash, H. L. 1987. Do compulsive runners and anorectic patients share common bonds? *The Physician and Sportsmedicine* 15, 12: 162–67.

National Coaching Foundation. 1996. *Guidance for National Governing Bodies on Child Protection Procedures.* Leeds, England: NCF.

Nativ, A. et al. 1994. The female triad: The interrelatedness of disordered eating, amenorrhea, and osteoporosis. *Clinics in sports medicine* 13, 2: 405–418.

Naughton, J. 1996a. Exclusive deal with Reebok brings U. of Wisconsin millions of dollars and unexpected criticism. *The Chronicle of Higher Education* 43, 2 (September 6): A65–A66.

Naughton, J. 1996b. Alcohol abuse by athletes poses big problems for colleges. *The Chronicle of Higher Education* 43, 4 (September 20): A47–A48.

Naughton, J. 1996c. Hundreds of students lose scholarships in widespread confusion over NCAA rules. *The Chronicle of Higher Education* 43, 3 (September 27): A49–A50.

Naughton, J. 1996d. A book on the economics of college sports says few programs are financially successful. *The Chronicle of Higher Education* 43, 7 (October 11): A57–A58.

Naughton, J., and R. Srisavasdi. 1996. Data on funds for men's and women's sports become available as new law takes effect. *The Chronicle of Higher Education* 43, 9 (October 25): A45–A46.

Nauright, J. 1996a. "A besieged tribe"?: Nostalgia, white cultural identity and the role of rugby in a changing South Africa. *International Review for the Sociology of Sport* 31, 1: 69–108.

Nauright, J. 1996b. "It's the world in union": Rugby tours, the Rugby World Cup, nostalgia and memory in maintaining the "Old (boys)" world order. Paper presented at the annual conference of the North American Society for the Sociology of Sport, Birmingham, AL (November).

NCAA. 1996. *1996 NCAA, Division I graduation-rates report.* Overland Park, KS: The National Collegiate Athletic Association.

Neal, W. 1981. *The handbook on athletic perfection.* Milford, MI: Mott Media.

Nelson, M. B. 1991. *Are we winning yet?* New York: Random House.

Nixon, H. 1984. *Sport and the American Dream.* New York: Leisure Press.

Nixon, H. L., II. 1993a. A social network analysis of influences on athletes to play with pain and injuries. *Journal of Sport and Social Issues.* 16, 2: 127–35.

Nixon, H. L., II. 1993b. Accepting the risks and pain of injury in sport: Mediated cultural influences on playing hurt. *Sociology of Sport Journal* 10, 2: 183–96.

Nixon, H. L., II. 1994a. Coaches' views of risk, pain, and injury in sport, with special reference to gender differences. *Sociology of Sport Journal* 11, 1: 79–87.

Nixon, H. L., II. 1994b. Social pressure, social support, and help seeking for pain and injuries in college sports networks. *Journal of Sport and Social Issues* 18, 4: 340–55.

Nixon, H. L., II. 1996a. The relationship of friendship networks, sports experiences, and gender to expressed pain thresholds. *Sociology of Sport Journal* 13, 1: 78–86.

Nixon, H. L., II. 1996b. Explaining pain and injury attitudes and experiences in sport in terms of gender, race, and sports status factors. *Journal of Sport and Social Issues* 20, 1: 33–44.

Noden, M. 1994. Dying to win. *Sports Illustrated,* August 8: 53–60.

Nosanchuk, T. A. 1981. The way of the warrior: the

effects of traditional martial arts training on aggressiveness. *Human Relations* 34, 6: 435–44.

Novak, M. 1976. *The joy of sports.* New York: Basic Books.

O'Brien, R., and A. Wolff. 1996. The wethead is dead. *Sports Illustrated* (Scorecard) (August 19): 32.

Ogilvie, B., and J. Taylor. 1993. Career termination issues among elite athletes. Pp. 761–75 in R. N. Singer, M. Murphey, and L. K. Tennant, eds. *Handbook of research on sport psychology.* New York: Macmillan.

Oglesby, C. 1993. Issues of sport and racism: Where is the white in the Rainbow Coalition? Pp. 251–68 in D. D. Brooks and R. C. Althouse, eds. *Racism in college athletics: The African-American athlete's experience.* Morgantown, WV: Fitness Information Technology, Inc.

Oliver, M. 1980. Race, class and the family's orientation to mobility through sport. *Sociological Symposium* 30: 62–86.

Ordman, V. L., and D. Zillman. 1994. Women sport reporters: Have they caught up? *Journal of Sport & Social Issues* 18, 1: 66–75.

Orlick, T. 1978. *The cooperative sports and games book.* London: Writers and Readers Publishing Cooperative.

O'Shea, M. 1995. What's your take on cheerleaders—Are they athletes? *Parade* (November 26).

Oriard, M. 1993. *Reading football. How the popular press created an American spectacle.* Chapel Hill, NC: The University of North Carolina Press.

Osterland, A. 1995. Field of nightmares. *Financial World* 164, 4 (February 14): 105–107.

O'Sullivan, C. 1991. Acquaintance gang rape on campus. Pp. 120–156 in A. Parrot and L. Bechhofer, eds., *Acquaintance rape: The hidden crime.* New York: Wiley.

Otto, L., and D. Alwin. 1977. Athletics, aspirations and attainments. *Sociology of Education* 42: 102–13.

Overdorf, V. G., and K. S. Gill. 1994. Body image, weight and eating concerns, and use of weight control methods among high school female athletes. *Women in Sport & Physical Activity Journal* 3, 2: 69–79.

Oxendine, J. B. 1988. *American Indian sports heritage.* Champaign, IL: Human Kinetics.

Ozanian, M. K. 1995. Following the money. *Financial World* 164, 4 (February 14): 27–31.

Padilla, A., and D. Baumer. 1994. Big-time college sports: Management and economic issues. *Journal of Sport & Social Issues* 18, 2: 123–43.

Papp, G., and G. Prisztoka. 1995. Sportsmanship as an ethical value. *International Review for the Sociology of Sport* 30, 3/4: 375–390.

Paraschak, V. 1995. The native sport and recreation program, 1972–1981: Patterns of resistance, patterns of reproduction. *Canadian Journal of History of Sport* (December): 1–18.

Paraschak, V. 1997. Variations in race relations: Sporting events for Native Peoples in Canada. *Sociology of Sport Journal* 14, 1: 1–21.

Parkhouse, B. L., and J. M. Williams. 1986. Differential effects of sex and status on evaluation of coaching ability. *Research Quarterly for Exercise and Sport* 57, 1: 53–59.

Passmore, D. L., C. Pellock, and G. Wang. 1996. Ballpark estimates: Impact of the 1994 baseball strike on the Pennsylvania economy. *Journal of Sport & Social Issues* 20, 2: 161–72.

Pastore, D. L. 1994. Strategies for retaining female high school head coaches: A survey of administrators and coaches. *Journal of Sport & Social Issues* 18, 2: 169–82.

Pastore, D. L., S. Inglis, and K. E. Danylchuk. 1996. Retention factors in coaching and athletic management: Differences by gender, position, and geographic location. *Journal of Sport & Social Issues* 20, 4: 427–41.

Patrick, D. 1991. Star decathlete defies easy labels. *USA Today,* December 16. Special issue: Race & Sports—Myth & Reality.

Pearman, W. A. 1978. Race on the sports page. *Review of Sport and Leisure* 3, 2: 54–68.

Pearton, R. 1990. A critical review of sociological explanations of football hooliganism and an empirical analysis of the phenomenon. Research report, Sport Science Department, Christ Church College, Canterbury, England.

Pfister, G. 1989. Women in the Olympics (1952–1980): An analysis of German newspapers (Beauty awards vs. gold medals). Pp. 11/27–11/34 in R. Jackson and T. McPhail, eds., *The Olympic movement and the mass media.* Calgary, Alberta:

Hurford Enterprises Ltd.

Phillip, M.-C. 1993. An uneven playing field. *Black Issues in Higher Education* 10, 20: 24–29.

Phillips, D. P. 1983. The impact of mass media violence on U.S. homicides. *American Sociological Review* 48, 4: 560–68.

Picou, S., V. McCarter, and F. Howell. 1985. Do high school athletics pay? Some further evidence. *Sociology of Sport Journal* 2, 1: 72–76.

Pilz, G. A. 1996. Social factors influencing sport and violence: On the "problem" of football hooliganism in Germany. *International Review for Sociology of Sport* 31, 1: 49–68.

Pluto, T. 1995. *Falling from grace: Can pro basketball be saved?* New York: Simon & Schuster.

Ponomaryov, N. I. 1981. *Sport and society.* Translated by J. Riordan. Moscow: Progress Publishers (and Chicago: Imported Publications, Inc.).

Prebish, C. S. 1992. "Heavenly Father, Divine Goalie": Sport and religion. Pp. 43–54 in S. Hoffman (ed.), *Sport and religion.* Champaign, IL: Human Kinetics.

Pronger, B. 1990. *The arena of masculinity: Sports, homosexuality, and the meaning of sex.* New York: St. Martin's Press.

Pronger, B. 1996. Sport and masculinity: The estrangement of gay men. Pp. 410–23 in D. S. Eitzen, ed. *Sport in contemporary society.* New York: St. Martin's Press.

Purdy, D. 1988. For whom sport tolls: Players, owners, and fans. *The World & I* 3, 10: 573–87.

Purdy, D., W. M. Leonard, II, and D. S. Eitzen. 1994. A reexamination of salary discrimination in major league baseball by race/ethnicity. *Sociology of Sport Journal* 11, 1: 60–69.

Pyros, J. 1987. Review of J. Feinstein (1986), *A season on the brink. Arete: A Journal of Sport Literature* 5, 1: 204–5.

Quirk, J., and R. D. Fort. 1992. *Pay dirt: The business of professional team sports.* Princeton, NJ: Princeton University Press.

Rabey, S. 1992. Competing for souls in Barcelona. *Colorado Springs Gazette,* August 8.

Rader, B. G. 1983. *American sports.* Englewood Cliffs, NJ: Prentice-Hall.

Rainville, R. E., and E. McCormick. 1977. Extent of covert racial prejudice in pro football announcers' speech. *Journalism Quarterly* 54, 1: 20–26.

Rankin, J. H. 1980. School factors and delinquency: interactions by age and sex. *Sociology and Social Research* 64, 3: 420–34.

Rayl, S. 1996. Dents in the color line: Professional basketball in the 1930's and 1940's. Paper presented at the annual meetings of the North American Society for the Sociology of Sport, Birmingham, AL (November).

Real, M. R. 1989. *Super media: A cultural studies approach.* Newbury Park, CA: Sage.

Real, M. R. 1996. The postmodern Olympics: Technology and the commodification of the Olympic movement. *Quest* 48, 1: 9–24.

Redhead, S., ed. 1993. *The passion and the fashion: Football fandom in the New Europe.* Aldershot, England: Avebury.

Rees, C. R. 1996. Race and sport in global perspective. *Journal of Sport & Social Issues* 20, 1: 22–32.

Rees, C. R., F. M. Howell, and A. W. Miracle. 1990. Do high school sports build character? *Journal of Social Science* 27, 3: 303–15.

Rees, C. R., and A. W. Miracle. Forthcoming. Sport and Education. In J. Coakley and E. Dunning, eds. *Handbook of sport and society.* London: Sage.

Reich, A. A. 1974. International understanding through sports. *U.S. Department of State Bulletin* 70: 460–65.

Reid, L. N., and L. C. Solely. 1979. Sports Illustrated's coverage of women in sports. *Journalism Quarterly* 56, 4: 861–863.

Reid, S. M. 1996. The selling of the Games. *The Denver Post,* July 21: 4BB.

Reilly, R. 1995. Order on the court. *Sports Illustrated* 83, 21: 136.

Retton, M. L. 1992. Family a big matter for every Olympian. *USA Today,* August 5: 6E.

Richmond, P. 1986. Weighing the odds. *Colorado Springs Gazette Telegraph,* January 19: F1–F4.

Rimer, E. 1996. Discrimination in major league baseball: Hiring standards for major league managers, 1975–1994. *Journal of Sport & Social Issues* 20, 2: 118–33.

Robbins, R. 1996. Josh Davis: Overcoming the trials. *Sports Spectrum* (June): 20–21.

Robinson, J. 1972. *I never had it made.* New York: G. P. Putnam's Sons.

Rodman, D. (with T. Keown). 1996. *Bad as I wanna be.* New York: Delacorte Press.

Rodriguez, R. 1993. Dispelling the myths of Latinos in sports. *Black Issues in Higher Education* 10, 20: 30–31.

Rose, C. 1996. Ropin', ridin', and religion. *Colorado Springs Gazette*, February 3: F1–F2.

Roversi, A. 1994. The birth of the "ultras": The rise of football hooliganism in Italy. Pp. 359–81 in R. Giulianotti and J. Williams, eds. *Game without frontiers: Football, identity and modernity.* Aldershot, England: Arena, Ashgate.

Rozin, S. 1994. Steroids and sports: What price glory? *Business Week*, October 17: 176.

Rozin, S. 1995. Steroids: A spreading peril. *Business Week*, June 19: 138–41.

Ruck, R. 1987. *Sandlot seasons: Sport in black Pittsburgh.* Urbana, IL: University of Illinois Press.

Russell, G. W., S. L. DiLullo, and D. DiLullo. 1988–1989. Effects of observing competitive and violent versions of a sport. *Current Psychology* 7, 4: 312–21.

Ryan, J. 1995. *Little girls in pretty boxes: The making and breaking of elite gymnasts and figure skaters.* New York: Doubleday.

Sabo, D. 1988. Title IX and athletics: Sex equity in schools. *Updating School Board Policies* 19, 10: 1–3.

Sabo, D. 1994. Pigskin, patriarchy, and pain. Pp. 82–88 in M. Messner and D. Sabo, eds. *Sex, violence & power in sports.* Freedom, CA: The Crossing Press.

Sabo, D., and S. C. Jansen. 1994. Seen but not heard: Black men in sports media. Pp. 150–60 in M. A. Messner and D. Sabo, eds. *Sex, violence & power in sports.* Freedom, CA: The Crossing Press.

Sabo, D., and M. J. Melnick. 1996. Research on sport and adolescent reproductive behavior: Some preliminary findings. *Women in sport & Physical Activity Journal* 5, 2: 99–104.

Sabo, D., M. J. Melnick, and B. E. Vanfossen. 1993. High school athletic participation and postsecondary educational and occupational mobility: A focus on race and gender. *Sociology of Sport Journal* 10, 1: 44–56.

Sabo, D., et al. 1996. Televising international sport: Race, ethnicity, and nationalistic bias. *Journal of Sport & Social Issues* 20, 1: 7–21.

Sack, A. 1987. College sport and the student-athlete. *Journal of Sport and Social Issues* 11, 1–2: 31–48.

Sack, A., and R. Thiel. 1979. College football and social mobility: A case study of Notre Dame football players. *Sociology of Education* 52, 1: 60–66.

Sage, G. H., ed. 1993a. Sociocultural aspects of sport and physical activity: A critical perspective. *Quest* 45, 2 (special issue).

Sage, G. H. 1993b. Stealing home: Political, economic, and media power and a publicly funded baseball stadium in Denver. *Journal of Sport & Social Issues* 17, 2: 110–24.

Sage, G. H. 1996a. Patriotic images and capitalist profit: Contradictions of professional team sports licensed merchandise. *Sociology of Sport Journal* 13, 1: 1–11.

Sage, G. H. 1996b. Public policy in the public interest: Pro franchises and sports facilities that are really "yours". Pp. 264–74 in D. S. Eitzen, ed. *Sport in contemporary society.* New York: St. Martin's Press.

Sailes, G. A. 1993. An investigation of campus stereotypes: The myth of black athletic superiority and the dumb jock stereotype. *Sociology of Sport Journal* 10, 1: 88–97.

Salwen, M. B., and N. Wood. 1994. Depictions of female athletes on *Sports Illustrated* covers, 1957–1989. *Journal of Sport Behavior* 17, 2: 98–107.

Sanday, P. 1990. *Fraternity gang rapes: Sex, brotherhood, and privilege on campus.* New York: New York University Press.

Sands, R. R. 1995. *Instant acceleration: Living in the fast lane—The cultural identity of speed.* Lanham, MD: University Press of America.

Savage, H., ed. 1929. *American college athletics.* Bulletin No. 23. New York: Carnegie Foundation.

Savage, J. 1997. *A sure thing? Sports and gambling.* Minneapolis, MN: Lerner Publications.

Schafer, W. E. 1969. Some social sources and consequences of interscholastic athletics: The case of participation and delinquency. In G. Kenyon, ed. *Aspects of contemporary sport sociology.* Chicago, IL: The Athletic Institute.

Scheinin, R. 1994. *Field of screams: The dark underside of America's national pastime.* New York: Norton.

Scher, J. 1993. Mr. Dirty. *Sports Illustrated* 78, 8: 40–42.

Schimmel, K., A. G. Ingham, and J. W. Howell. 1993. Professional team sport and the American city: Urban politics and franchise relocations. Pp. 211–44 in A. G. Ingham and J. W. Loy, eds. *Sport in social development.* Champaign, IL: Human Kinetics.

Schmitt, M. The state of women in sports media: Pp. 234–36 in R. Lapchick, ed. *Sport in society: Equal opportunity or business as usual?* Thousand Oaks, CA: Sage.

Schmitt, R. L., and W. M. Leonard, II. 1986. Immortalizing the self through sport. *American Journal of Sociology* 91 (March): 1088–111.

Schroeder, J. J. 1995. Developing self-esteem and leadership skills in Native American women: The role sports and games play. *Journal of Physical Education, Recreation and Dance* 66, 7: 48–51.

Scully, G. W. 1989. *The business of major league baseball.* Greenwich, CT: JAI Press.

Scully, G. W. 1995. *The market structure of sport.* Chicago: University of Chicago Press.

Segrave, J. 1986. Do organized sports programs deter delinquency? *JOPERD* 57, 1: 16–17.

Segrave, J. 1994. The Perfect 10: "Sportspeak" in the language of sexual relations. *Sociology of Sport Journal* 11, 2: 95–113.

Segrave, J., and D. Chu. 1978. Athletics and juvenile delinquency. *Review of Sport and Leisure* 3, 2: 1–24.

Segrave, J., and D. Chu. 1996. Introduction—The modern Olympic Games: A contemporary sociocultural analysis. *Quest* 48, 1: 2–8.

Segrave, J., and D. N. Hastad. 1982. Delinquent behavior and interscholastic athletic participation. *Journal of Sport Behavior* 5, 2: 96–111.

Segrave, J., C. Moreau, and D. N. Hastad. 1985. An investigation into the relationship between ice hockey participation and delinquency. *Sociology of Sport Journal* 2, 4: 281–98.

Sellers, R. M. 1993. Black student-athletes: Reaping the benefits of recovering from the exploitation. Pp. 143–76 in D. D. Brooks and R. C. Althouse, eds. *Racism in college athletics: The African-American athlete's experience.* Morgantown, WV: Fitness Information Technology, Inc.

Seltzer, R., and W. Glass. 1991. International politics and judging in Olympic skating events: 1968–1988. *Journal of Sport Behavior* 14, 3: 189–200.

Semyonov, M. 1984. Sport and beyond: Ethnic inequalities in attainment. *Sociology of Sport Journal* 1, 4: 358–65.

Sewart, J., 1987. The commodification of sport. *International Review for the Sociology of Sport* 22, 3: 171–192.

Shaw, P. 1995. Achieving Title IX gender equity in college athletics in an era of austerity. *Journal of Sport & Social Issues* 19, 1: 6–27.

Sheehan, R. G. 1996. *Keeping score: The economics of big-time sports.* South Bend, IN: Diamond Communications.

Shields, D. L. L., and B. J. L. Bredemeier. 1995. *Character development and physical activity.* Champaign, IL: Human Kinetics.

Shields, D. L. L., B. J. L. Bredemeier, D. E. Gardner, and A. Bostrom. 1995. Leadership, cohesion, and team norms regarding cheating and aggression. *Sociology of Sport Journal* 12, 3: 324–36.

Shifflett, B., and R. Revelle. 1994a. Gender equity in sports media coverage: A review of NCAA News. *Journal of Sport & Social Issues* 18, 2: 144–50.

Shifflett, B., and R. Revelle. 1994b. Equity revisited. *Journal of Sport & Social Issues* 18, 4: 379–83.

Shilling, C., 1994. *The body and social theory.* Thousand Oaks, CA: Sage.

Shropshire, K. 1996. *In black and white: Race and sports in America.* New York: New York University Press.

Siegal, D. 1994. Higher education and the plight of the black male athlete. *Journal of Sport & Social Issues* 18, 3: 207–23.

Silva, J. 1983. The perceived legitimacy of rule violating behavior in sport. *Journal of Sport Psychology* 5, 4: 438–48.

Simpson, K., 1996. Sporting dreams die on the "rez." Pp. 287–94 in D. S. Eitzen, ed. *Sport in contemporary society.* New York: St. Martin's Press.

Simson, V., and A. Jennings. 1992. *The lords of the rings: Power, money and drugs in the modern Olympics.* London: Simon and Schuster.

Sipes, R. G. 1975. War, combative sports, and

aggression: A preliminary causal model of cultural patterning. Pp. 749–62 in M. A. Nettleship, R. D. Givens, and A. Nettleship, eds. *War: Its cause and correlates.* The Hague: Mouton.

Sipes, R. 1996. Sports as a control for aggression. Pp. 154–60 in D. S. Eitzen, ed. *Sport in contemporary society.* New York: St Martin's Press.

Smith, E. 1993. Race, sport, and the American university. *Journal of Sport & Social Issues* 17, 3: 206–12.

Smith, E. 1995. Hope via basketball: The ticket out of the ghetto. *Journal of Sport and Social Issues* 19, 3: 312–17.

Smith, G. T., and C. Blackman. 1978. Sport in the mass media. Vanier City, Ontario: CAPHER.

Smith, M. 1983. *Violence and sport.* Toronto, Ontario: Butterworths.

Smith, R. E. 1986. Toward a cognitive-affective model of athletic burnout. *Journal of Sport Psychology* 8, 1: 36–50.

Smith, Y. 1992. Women of color in society and sport. *Quest* 44, 2: 228–50.

Snyder, E. E. 1994. Interpretations and explanations of deviance among college athletes: A case study. *Sociology of Sport Journal* 11, 3: 231–48.

Snyder, E. E., and L. Baber. 1979. A profile of former collegiate athletes and nonathletes: Leisure activities, attitudes toward work, and aspects of satisfaction with life. *Journal of Sport Behavior* 2, 4: 211–219.

Snyder, M. 1993. The new competition: Sports careers for women. Pp. 264–74 in G. L. Cohen, ed. *Women in sport: Issues and controversies.* Newbury Park, CA: Sage.

Spady, W. G. 1970. Lament for the letterman: effects of peer status and extracurricular activities on goals and achievement. *American Journal of Sociology* 75: 680–702.

Sperber, M. 1990. *College Sports, Inc.: The athletic department vs the university.* New York: Henry Holt and Company.

Spreitzer, E. 1992. Does participation in interscholastic athletics affect adult development: A longitudinal analysis of an 18–24 age cohort. Paper presented at the annual conference of the American Sociological Association, Pittsburgh (August).

Stark, R. 1987. Sports and delinquency. Pp. 115–24 in M. R. Gottfredson and T. Hirshi, eds. *Positive criminology.* Newbury Park, CA: Sage.

Staurowsky, E. J. 1995. Examining the roots of a gendered division of labor in intercollegiate athletics: Insights into the gender equity debate. *Journal of Sport & Social Issues* 19, 1: 28–44.

Staurowsky, E. J. 1996. Blaming the victim: Resistance in the battle over gender equity in intercollegiate athletics. *Journal of Sport & Social Issues* 20, 2: 194–210.

Steinbreder, J. 1993. The owners. *Sports Illustrated* 79, 11 (September 13): 64–86.

Steinbreder, J. 1996. Big spender. *Sky* (Delta Airlines magazine), July: 37–42.

Stephens, D., and B. J. L. Bredemeier. 1995. *Toward an understanding of moral behavior in sport: The relationships among motivational variables and judgements about unfair play in girls' soccer.* Unpublished manuscript.

Stevenson, C. 1976. Institutional socialization and college sport. *Research Quarterly* 47, 1: 1–8.

Stevenson, C. L. 1990. The early careers of international athletes. *Sociology of Sport Journal* 7, 3: 238–53.

Stevenson, C. 1991a. The Christian-athlete: An interactionist-developmental analysis. *Sociology of Sport Journal* 8, 4: 362–79.

Stevenson, C. 1991b. Christianity as a hegemonic and counter-hegemonic device in elite sport. Paper presented at Conference of the North American Society for the Sociology of Sport, Milwaukee (November).

Stevenson, C. 1997. Christian-athletes and the culture of elite sport: Dilemmas and solutions. *Sociology of Sport Journal* 14, 3 (in press).

Stingley, J. 1972. Recreation boom threatens to bust the city's seams. *Los Angeles Times,* Aug. 20.

Stoddart, B. 1994. Sport, television and practice reconsidered: Televised golf and analytical orthodoxies. *Journal of Sport & Social Issues* 18, 1: 76–88.

Stratta, T. 1993. Living in a bi-cultural reality: The African-American female athlete in a predominantly white institution. Paper presented at the annual conference of the North American Society for the Sociology of Sport, Ottawa (November).

Stratta, T. 1995. Cultural inclusiveness in sport—Recommendations from African-American women college athletes. *Journal of Physical Education, Recreation and Dance* 66, 7: 52–56.

Stratta, T. P. 1997. Contextual analysis of African-American women college athletes at a predominantly white university. *Research Quarterly for Exercise and Sport* 68, 1 (March Supplement): A115–A116.

Sugden, J., and A. Tomlinson. Forthcoming. Theorizing sport, social class and status. In J. Coakley and E. Dunning, eds. *Handbook of sport and society.* London: Sage.

Sundgot-Borgen, J. 1993a. Knowledge and practice of top level coaches about weight control and eating disorders. *Medicine and Science in Sports and Exercise* 5 (Supplement 25): 180.

Sundgot-Borgen, J. 1993b. Prevalence of eating disorders in elite female athletes. *International Journal of Sport Nutrition* 3, 1: 29–40.

Sundgot-Borgen, J. 1994a. Eating disorders in female athletes. *Sports Medicine* 17, 3: 176–88.

Sundgot-Borgen, J. 1994b. Risk and trigger factors for the development of eating disorders in female elite athletes. *Medicine and Science in Sports and Exercise.*

Swain, D. A. 1991. Withdrawal from sport and Schlossberg's model of transitions. *Sociology of Sport Journal* 8, 2: 152–60.

Swift, E. M. 1986. Hockey? Call it sockey. *Sports Illustrated* 64, 7: 12–17.

Telander, R. 1984. The written word: Player-press relationships in American sports. *Sociology of Sport Journal* 1, 1: 3–14.

Telander, R. 1988. *Heaven is a playground.* New York: A Fireside Book, Simon & Schuster.

Theberge, N. 1989. A feminist analysis of responses to sports violence: media coverage of the 1987 World Junior Hockey Championship. *Sociology of Sport Journal* 6, 3: 247–56.

Theberge, N. 1993a. The construction of gender in sport: Women, coaching, and the naturalization of difference. *Social Problems* 40, 3: 301–13.

Theberge, N. 1993b. Injury, pain and "playing rough" in women's ice hockey. Paper presented at the meetings of the North American Society for the Sociology of Sport, Ottawa.

Theberge, N. 1995. Gender, sport, and the construction of community: A case study from women's ice hockey. *Sociology of Sport Journal* 12, 4: 389–402.

Theberge, N. 1996. Playing with the boys. *Canadian Woman Studies/Les Cahiers de la Femme* 15, 4:37–41.

Theberge, N., and S. Birrell. 1994a. The sociological study of women in sport. Pp. 323–30 in D. M. Costa and S. R. Guthrie, eds. *Women and sport: Interdisciplinary perspectives.* Champaign, IL: Human Kinetics.

Theberge, N., and S. Birrell. 1994b. Structural constraints facing women in sport. Pp. 331–40 in D. M. Costa and S. R. Guthrie, eds. *Women and sport: Interdisciplinary perspectives.* Champaign, IL: Human Kinetics.

Theberge, N., and A. Cronk. 1994. Work routines in newspaper sports departments and the coverage of women's sports. Pp. 289–98 in S. Birrell and C. L. Cole, eds. *Women, sport, and culture.* Champaign, IL: Human Kinetics.

Thirer, J., and H. Ross. 1981. Examining the degree of on and off field social interaction between black and white male intercollegiate athletes. Paper presented at the meetings of the North American Society for the Sociology of Sport, Fort Worth, TX.

Thirer, J., and P. J. Wieczorek. 1984. On and off field social interaction patterns of black and white high school athletes. *Journal of Sport Behavior* 7, 3: 105–14.

Thirer, J., and S. D. Wright. 1985. Sport and social status for adolescent males and females. *Sociology of Sport Journal* 2, 2: 164–71.

Thomas, R. 1996. Black faces still rare in the press box. Pp. 212–33 in R. Lapchick, ed. *Sport in society: Equal opportunity or business as usual?* Thousand Oaks, CA: Sage.

Thorlindsson, T. 1989. Sport participation, smoking, and drug and alcohol abuse among Icelandic youth. *Sociology of Sport Journal* 6, 2: 136–43.

Todd, T. 1983. The steroid predicament. *Sports Illustrated* 59, 5: 62–78.

Todd, T. 1987. Anabolic steroids: The gremlins of sport. *Journal of Sport History* 14, 1: 87–107.

Tofler, I. R., et al. 1996. Physical and emotional problems of elite female gymnasts. *New England Journal of Medicine* 335, 4: 281–83.

Tomlinson, A. 1986. Going global: The FIFA story.

Pp. 83–98 in A. Tomlinson and G. Whannel, eds. *Off the ball.* London: Pluto Press.

Tomlinson, A., and G. Whannel, eds. 1984. *Five ring circus: Money, power and politics at the Olympic Games.* London: Pluto Press.

Toufexis, A. 1990. Sex in the sporting life: Do athletic teams unwittingly promote assaults and rapes? *Time,* August 6: 76.

Trujillo, N. 1995. Machines, missiles, and men: Images of the male body on ABC's *Monday Night Football. Sociology of Sport Journal* 12, 4: 403–23.

Trulson, M. E. 1986. Martial arts training: A novel "cure" for juvenile delinquency. *Human Relations* 39, 12: 1131–40.

Turner, B. S. 1984. *The body and society.* Oxford: Basil Blackwell.

U. S. General Accounting Office. 1996. Intercollegiate athletics: Status of efforts to promote gender equity. A report to the Honorable Cardiss Collins, House of Representatives. U.S. Government Printing Office, Document No. HEHS-97-10.

Vaz, E. W. 1982. *The professionalization of young hockey players.* Lincoln: University of Nebraska Press.

Veblen, T. 1899. *The theory of the leisure class.* New York: Macmillan. (See also 1953 paperback edition New York: A Mentor Book.)

Verma, G., and D. S. Darby. 1994. *Winners and losers: Ethnic minorities in sport and recreation.* London: The Falmer Press.

Vertinsky, P. A. 1987. Exercise, physical capability, and the eternally wounded woman in late nineteenth century North America. *Journal of Sport History* 14, 1: 7–27.

Vertinsky, P. A. 1992. Reclaiming space, revisioning the body: The quest for gender-sensitive physical education. *Quest* 44, 3: 373–96.

Vinokur, M. B. 1988. *More than a game: Sports and politics.* Westport, CT: Greenwood Press.

Voy, R. 1991. *Drugs, sport, and politics.* Champaign, IL: Leisure Press.

Wacquant, L. J. D. 1992. The social logic of boxing in Black Chicago: Toward a sociology of pugilism. *Sociology of Sport Journal* 9, 3: 221–54.

Wacquant, L. J. D. 1995a. The pugilistic point of view: How boxers think and feel about their trade. *Theory and Society* 24: 489–535.

Wacquant, L. J. D. 1995b. Why men desire muscles. *Body & Society* 1, 1: 163–79.

Wacquant, L. J. D. 1995c. Pugs at work: Bodily capital and bodily labour among professional boxers. *Body & Society* 1, 1: 65–93.

Waddington, I. Forthcoming. Sport and health. In E. Dunning and J. Coakley, eds. *Handbook of sport and society.* London: Sage.

Wagner, G. G. 1987. Sport as a means for reducing the cost of illness—Some theoretical, statistical, and empirical remarks. *International Review for the Sociology of Sport* 22, 3: 217–27.

Wakefield, K. L. 1995. The pervasive effects of social influence on sporting event attendance. *Journal of Sport & Social Issues* 19, 4: 335–51.

Wann, D. L. 1993. Aggression among highly identified spectators as a function of their need to maintain positive social identity. *Journal of Sport & Social Issues* 17, 2: 134–43.

Weber, M. 1968 (1922). Economy and society: An outline of interpretive sociology. Translated by G. Roth and G. Wittich. New York: Bedminster Press.

Wechsler, H., et al. 1995. Correlates of college student binge drinking. *American Journal of Public Health* 85, 7: 921–26.

Wee, E. L. 1995. Youth sports hit families in the wallet. *Washington Post,* October 15: A1.

Weinberg, S. K., and H. Arond. 1952. The occupational culture of the boxer. *American Journal of Sociology* 57: 460–69.

Weinstein, M. D., M. D. Smith, and D. L. Wiesenthal. 1995. Masculinity and hockey violence. *Sex Roles* 33, 11/12: 831–47.

Weiss, A. E. 1993. *Money games: The business of sports.* Boston, MA: Houghton Mifflin.

Weiss, O. 1996. Media sports as a social substitution pseudosocial relations with sports figures. *International Review for the Sociology of Sport* 31, 1: 109–18.

Weiss, O., and W. Schulz, eds. 1995. *Sport in space and time.* Vienna, Austria: Vienna University Press.

Welch, W. M. 1996. Federal taxpayers shut out of stadium payoff. *USA Today,* May 31: A1.

Wenner, L. A. 1989. The Super Bowl Pregame Show: Cultural fantasies and political subtext.

Pp. 157–79 in L. A. Wenner, ed. *Media, sports, and society*. Newbury Park, CA: Sage.

Wenner, L. A. 1994. The dream team, communicative dirt, and the marketing of synergy: USA basketball and cross-merchandising in television commercials. *Journal of Sport & Social Issues* 18, 1: 27–47.

Wenner, L., ed. 1997. *Mediasport: Cultural sensibilities and sport in the media age*. London: Routledge.

Whannel, G. 1992. *Fields in vision: Television sport and cultural transformation*. London: Routledge.

White, A., et al. 1992. *Women and sport: A consultation document*. London: The Sports Council.

White, P., and J. Gillett, 1994. Reading the muscular body: A critical decoding of advertisements in *Flex* magazine. *Sociology of Sport Journal* 11, 1: 18–39.

Whitson, D., and D. Macintosh. 1990. *The game planners: Transforming Canada's sport system*. Montreal, Quebec, and Kingston, Ontario: McGill-Queen's University Press.

Whitson, D., and D. Macintosh. 1993. Becoming a world-class city: Hallmark events and sport franchises in the growth strategies of western Canadian cities. *Sociology of Sport Journal* 10, 3: 221–40.

Whitson, D., and D. Macintosh. 1996. The global circus: International sport, tourism, and the marketing of cities. *Journal of Sport & Social Issues* 20, 3: 278–95.

Wieber, S., 1996. Athletes graduate near norm. *USA Today*, June 28: 12C.

Wiggins, D. K., ed. 1995. *Sport in America: From wicked amusement to national obsession*. Champaign, IL: Human Kinetics.

Wilcox, R. C. 1994. *Sport in the global village*. Morgantown, WV: Fitness Information Technology, Inc.

Wiley, E., III. 1993. Juggling is the toughest sport in college. *Black Issues in Higher Education* 10, 20: 10–14.

Wilkerson, M. 1996. Explaining the presence of men coaches in women's sports: The uncertainty hypothesis. *Journal of Sport & Social Issues* 20, 4: 411–26.

Williams, J. 1994. The local and the global in English soccer and the rise of satellite television. *Sociology of Sport Journal* 11, 4: 376–97.

Williams, J. 1995. Localism, globalisation and English football. Pp. 210–19 in O. Weiss and W. Schulz, eds. *Sport in space and time*. Vienna, Austria: Vienna University Press.

Williams, J., E. Dunning, and P. Murphy. 1984. *Hooligans abroad*. Boston, MA: Routledge & Kegan Paul.

Williams, K., K. M. Haywood, and M. Painter. 1996. Environmental versus biological influences on gender differences in the overarm throw for force: Dominant and nondominant arm throws. *Women in Sport & Physical Activity Journal* 5, 2: 29–50.

Williams, L. D. 1994. Sportswomen in black and white: Sports history from an African-American perspective. Pp. 45–66 in P. J. Creedon, ed. *Women, media and sport*. Thousand Oaks, CA: Sage.

Williams, R. L., and Z. I. Youssef. 1972. Consistency in football coaches in stereotyping the personality of each position's player. *International Journal of Sport Psychology* 3, 1: 3–11.

Williams, R. L., and Z. I. Youssef. 1975. Division of labor in college football along racial lines. *International Journal of Sport Psychology* 6, 1: 3–13.

Williams, R. L., and Z. I. Youssef. 1979. Race and position assignment in high school, college and professional football. *International Journal of Sport Psychology* 10, 4: 252–58.

Wilmore, J. 1996. Eating disorders in the young athlete. Pp. 287–303 in O. bar-Or, ed. *The child and adolescent athlete*. Vol. 6 of the *Encyclopaedia of Sports Medicine*—a publication of the IOC Medical Commission. London: Blackwell Science.

Wilson, J. 1994. *Playing by the rules: Sport, society and the state*. Detroit, MI: Wayne State University Press.

Wolf, N. 1991. *The beauty myth*. New York: Anchor Books.

Wolff, A., and D. Yaeger. 1995. Credit risk. *Sports Illustrated* 83, 6: 46–55.

Wolff, A., and R. O'Brien. 1995. The third sex (in Scorecard). *Sports Illustrated* 82, 5: 15.

Womack, M. 1992. Why athletes need ritual: A study of magic among professional athletes. Pp. 191–202 in S. Hoffman, ed. *Sport and religion* Champaign, IL: Human Kinetics.

Woodward, W. 1991. Zmeskal the 'lion' coach Karolyi never had. *USA Today*, September 9: C3.

Yasser, R. 1993. Athletic scholarship disarmament.

Journal of Sport & Social Issues 17, 1: 70–73.

Yetman, N. R., and F. J. Berghorn. 1993. Racial participation and integration in intercollegiate basketball: A longitudinal perspective. *Sociology of Sport Journal* 10, 3: 301–14.

Yetman, N. R., and D. S. Eitzen. 1984. Racial dynamics in American sport: Continuity and change. Pp. 324–44 in D. S. Eitzen, ed. *Sport in contemporary society.* 2d ed. New York: St. Martin's Press.

Young, I. 1990. *Throwing like a girl and other essays in philosophy and social theory.* Bloomington and Indianapolis, IN: Indiana University Press.

Young, K. Forthcoming. Sport and violence. In J. Coakley and E. Dunning, eds. *Handbook of sport and society.* London: Sage Publications, Ltd.

Young, K., and M. Smith. 1988–89. Mass media treatment of violence in sports and its effects. *Current Psychology* 7, 4: 298–311.

Young, K., and P. White. 1995. Sport, physical danger, and injury. The experiences of elite women athletes. *Journal of Sport & Social Issues* 19, 1: 45–61.

Young, K., P. White, and W. McTeer, 1994. Body talk: Male athletes reflect on sport, injury, and pain. *Sociology of Sport Journal* 11, 2: 175–94.

Zhang, J. J., et al. 1996a. Impact of TV broadcasting on the attendance of NBA games. *Research Quarterly for Exercise and Sport* 67 (March Supplement): A12.

Zhang, J. J., et al. 1996b. Negative influence of entertainment options on the attendance of professional sport games: The case of a minor league hockey team. *Research Quarterly for Exercise and Sport* 67 (March Supplement): A113.

Zhang, J. J., et al. 1997. Impact of broadcasting on minor league hockey attendance. *Research Quarterly for Exercise and Sport* 68, 1 (March Supplement): A117.

Zillman, D. 1996. The psychology of the appeal of portrayals of violence. In J. Goldstein, ed. *Attractions of violence.* New York: Oxford University Press.

Zipter, Y. 1988. *Diamonds are a dyke's best friend.* Ithaca, NY: Firebrand Books.

Name Index

Subject Index